BLACK SEA

Kura

Sevan

Karmir Blur

Araxes

Altıntepe

CASPIAN

URARTU

SEA

Van

Van

Gusçı

Three Great Early Tumuli

Urmia

Discount Price
$100

Hasanlu

Canadian Dollars

ASSYRIA

• Ziwiyeh

Carchemish

Nimrud

Assur

Tigris

LURISTAN

Euphrates

• Susa

0   100   200   300 KILOMETERS

THREE GREAT EARLY TUMULI

This volume was made possible by a grant from

THE GENERAL RESEARCH PROGRAM OF
THE NATIONAL ENDOWMENT FOR THE HUMANITIES

and by generous gifts from

THE DONORS TO THE RODNEY S. YOUNG FUND
The Archaeological Institute of America

THE DONORS TO THE GORDION PUBLICATION FUND
IN MEMORY OF RODNEY S. YOUNG
The University Museum, Philadelphia

The village of Yassıhüyük and Tumulus MM, from the west.

UNIVERSITY MUSEUM MONOGRAPH 43

THE GORDION EXCAVATIONS
FINAL REPORTS
VOLUME I

THREE GREAT EARLY TUMULI

Rodney S. Young

With contributions to the text by

K. DeVries   J. F. McClellan
E. L. Kohler   M. J. Mellink
G. K. Sams

E. L. Kohler, Editor

Published by
THE UNIVERSITY MUSEUM
University of Pennsylvania
1981

Production
   Publication Services Division, The University Museum

Book colophon
   Andy Seuffert

Typesetting
   Deputy Crown Inc., Camden, N.J.

Printing
Fisher-Harrison Durham
Durham, North Carolina U.S.A

Library of Congress Cataloging in Publication Data

Main entry under title:
The Gordion excavations.

   (University Museum monograph / University Museum,
University of Pennsylvania ; 43-   )
   Bibliography: v. 1, p.
   Includes index.
   Contents: v. 1. Three great early tumuli / Rodney S.
Young.
   1. Gordion (Turkey)   I. Series: University museum
monograph ; 43, etc.
DS156.G6G67   939′.26   81-13373
ISBN 0-934718-39-3 (set)   AACR2

CONTENTS

LIST OF PAGES WRITTEN BY PERSONS
OTHER THAN RODNEY S. YOUNG

TEXT

APPENDICES

LIST OF ILLUSTRATIONS IN THE TEXT

LIST OF PLATES

xv

ABBREVIATIONS

AA	*Archäologischer Anzeiger*
Aegean and Near East	Weinberg, S., ed. *The Aegean and the Near East: Studies Presented to Hetty Goldman on the Occasion of Her Seventy-fifth Birthday*. Locust Valley, N. Y.: J. J. Augustin, 1956.
AfO	*Archiv für Orientforschung*
AJA	*American Journal of Archaeology*
AJSL	*American Journal of Semitic Languages*
Akurgal, *Kunst Anat.*	Akurgal, E., *Die Kunst Anatoliens von Homer bis Alexander*. Berlin: W. de Gruyter, 1961.
Akurgal, *Kunst Heth.*	Akurgal, E. and M. Hirmer, *Die Kunst der Hethiter*. München: Hirmer, 1961.
Akurgal, *Phryg. Kunst*	Akurgal, E., *Phrygische Kunst*. Ankara: Türk Tarih Kurumu Basımevi, 1955.
Akurgal, *Spätheth. Bildk.*	Akurgal, E., *Späthethitische Bildkunst*. Ankara: Archäologisches Institut der Universität Ankara, 1949.
Akurgal, *Urart. altiran. K.*	Akurgal, E., *Urartäische und altiranische Kunstzentren*. Türk Tarih Kurumu Yayınlarından VI. Seri, No. 9. Ankara: Türk Tarih Kurumu Basımevi, 1968.
AnatSt	*Anatolian Studies*. London: British Institute of Archaeology, 1951–.
Art and Technology	Doehringer, S., D. G. Mitten and A. Steinberg, eds. *Art and Technology: A Symposium on Classical Bronzes*. Cambridge, Mass.: MIT Press, 1970.
AthMitt	*Mitteilungen des Deutschen Archäologischen Instituts: Athenische Abteilung*. Berlin: Gebr. Mann, 1876–.
Azarpay, *Urartian Art*	Azarpay, Guitty, *Urartian Art and Artifacts: A Chronological Study*. Berkeley and Los Angeles: Univ. of California Press, 1968.

Baker, *Furniture*

Baker, H. S., *Furniture in the Ancient World: Origins and Evolution, 3100–465* B.C. New York: Macmillan, 1965.

Barnett, *Assyrian Palace Reliefs*

Barnett, R. D., *Assyrian Palace Reliefs and Their Influence on the Sculptures of Babylonia and Persia.* London: Batchworth Press Ltd., n.d. [1958?].

Barnett, *Nimrud Ivories*

Barnett, R. D., *A Catalogue of the Nimrud Ivories with Other Examples of Ancient Near Eastern Ivories in the British Museum.* London: Trustees of the British Museum, 1957.

BASOR

Bulletin of the American Schools of Oriental Research.

Belleten

Belleten Türk Tarih Kurumu. Ankara: Türk Tarih Kurumu Basımevi (1937 +).

BibO

Bibliotheca Orientalis. Leiden: Nederlands Instituut voor het Nabije Oosten.

Bittel and Güterbock, *Boğazköy* I

Bittel, Kurt and H. Güterbock, *Boğazköy: Neue Untersuchungen in der hethitischen Hauptstadt.* Berlin: Preuss. Akademie der Wissenschaften, 1935. (*Abh.* 1935, pt. 1).

Bittel *et al., Boğazköy* IV

Bittel, Kurt *et al., Boğazköy* IV: *Funde aus den Grabungen 1967 und 1968.* Berlin: Gebr. Mann, 1969.

Bittel, *Grundzüge*

Bittel, Kurt, *Grundzüge der Vor- und Frühgeschichte Kleinasiens,* 2d ed. Tübingen: Wasmuth, n.d. [1950?].

Blinkenberg, *Fibules*

Blinkenberg, Chr., *Fibules grecques et orientales. Lindiaka* V. Copenhagen: A. F. Høst and Son, 1926.

Blinkenberg, *Lindos* I

Blinkenberg, Chr. *Lindos: Fouilles et recherches 1902–1914.* I: *Les petits objets.* Berlin: W. de Gruyter, 1931.

BMFEA

Bulletin of the Museum of Far Eastern Antiquities. Stockholm.

Boardman, *Greek Emporio*

Boardman, John, *Excavations in Chios 1952–1955: Greek Emporio.* London: Thames & Hudson, 1967.

Boehlau, *Nekropolen*

Boehlau, J., *Aus ionischen und italischen Nekropolen.* Leipzig: Teubner, 1898.

Boehmer, *Kleinfunde*

Boehmer, R., *Die Kleinfunde von Boğazköy* (*WVDOG* 87). Berlin: Gebr. Mann, 1972.

Botta and Flandin, *Mon. Nin.*

Botta, P. E. and E. N. Flandin, *Monument de Ninive.* 2 vols. Paris: Institut de France, 1848–1850.

BullNBC

Bulletin of the Needle and Bobbin Club. New York: Needle and Bobbin Club.

CVA	*Corpus Vasorum Antiquorum*
Dark Ages and Nomads	Mellink, M. J., ed. *Dark Ages and Nomads c. 1000* B.C.: *Studies in Iranian and Anatolian Archaeology.* Istanbul: Nederlands Historisch-Archaeologisch Instituut, 1964.
Deltion	*Archaiologikon Deltion*
Dergi	*Ankara Üniversitesi Dil ve Tarih-Coğrafya Fakültesi Dergisi.*
ESA	*Eurasia septentrionalis antiqua*
Expedition	*Expedition: Bulletin of the University Museum.* Philadelphia: University Museum.
Festschrift Matz	*Festschrift für Friedrich Matz.* Mainz: Von Zabern, 1962.
Forbes, *Technology*	Forbes, R. J., *Studies in Ancient Technology.* 8 vols. Leiden: E. J. Brill, 1955–1964.
Frankfort, *AAAO*	Frankfort, H., *The Art and Architecture of the Ancient Orient.* Baltimore: Penguin Books, 1954.
Furtwängler, *Olympia* IV	Furtwängler, A., *Die Bronzen und die übrigen kleineren Funde von Olympia* (= *Olympia Ergebnisse* IV). Berlin: Asher, 1890.
Ghirshman, *Sialk*	Ghirshman, Roman, *Fouilles de Sialk près de Kashan, 1933, 1934, 1937.* 2 vols. Paris: P. Geuthner. I, 1938; II, 1939.
Hogarth *et al., Carchemish*	Hogarth, D. G. *et al., Carchemish: Report on the Excavations at Djerabis on Behalf of the British Museum.* 3 vols. Oxford: Trustees of the British Museum. I, 1914; II, 1921; III, 1952.
Hogarth *et al., Ephesus*	Hogarth, D. G. *et al., Excavations at Ephesus: The Archaic Artemisia.* London: Trustees of the British Museum, 1908.
Hrouda, *KaF*	Hrouda, B., *Die Kulturgeschichte des assyrischen Flachbildes.* Bonn: Habelt, 1965.
IEJ	*Israel Exploration Journal*
ILN	*Illustrated London News*
In Memoriam Bossert	*In Memoriam Helmuth Theodor Bossert = Jahrbuch für kleinasiatische Forschung* 2, pts. 1–2 (1965). Istanbul: Universität Istanbul.
IstMitt	*Istanbuler Mitteilungen.* Istanbul: Archäologisches Institut des Deutschen Reiches.
Jacoby, *FGrHist*	Jacoby, F., *Fragmente der griechischen Historiker.* Berlin: Weidmann, 1923–1958.

Jantzen, *Samos* VIII

Jantzen, Ulf, *Samos* VIII: *Ägyptische und orientalische Bronzen aus dem Heraion von Samos.* Bonn: Habelt, 1972.

JdI

Jahrbuch des K. Deutschen Archäologischen Instituts.

JGS

Journal of Glass Studies

JHS

Journal of Hellenic Studies

JNES

Journal of Near Eastern Studies.

Johnston, *Pottery Practices*

Johnston, R. H., *Pottery Practices during the Sixth-Eighth Centuries* B.C. *at Gordion in Central Anatolia: An Analytical and Synthesizing Study.* Ph.D. dissertation, Pennsylvania State University, University Park, Pa., 1970. Ann Arbor: University Microfilms, 1971.

Karageorghis, *ENS* I

Karageorghis, Vassos, *Salamis* 3: *Excavations in the Necropolis of Salamis* I. Text, Nicosia: Government Printing Office, 1967. Plates, London: Harrison, 1967.

Karageorghis, *ENS* III

Karageorghis, Vassos, *Salamis* 5: *Excavations in the Necropolis of Salamis* III. Text, Nicosia: Zavallis, 1973. Plates, Haarlem: Enschedé, 1974.

Karageorghis, *SalRDC*

Karageorghis, Vassos, *Salamis: Recent Discoveries in Cyprus.* New York: McGraw-Hill, 1969.

Knudsen, *Phryg. Met. and Pot.*

Knudsen, A. K., *A Study of the Relationship between Phrygian Metalwork and Pottery in the 8th and 7th Centuries* B.C. Ph.D. dissertation, University of Pennsylvania, 1961. Ann Arbor: University Microfilms, 1961.

Kohler, *Wood and Ivory*

Kohler, Ellen L., *A Study of the Wood and Ivory Carvings at Gordion, Phrygia (ca. 750–500 B.C.).* Ph.D. dissertation, Bryn Mawr College, 1958. Ann Arbor: University Microfilms, 1959.

Körte, *Gordion*

Körte, Gustav and Alfred, *Gordion: Ergebnisse der Ausgrabung im Jahre 1900. Jahrbuch des Kaiserlich Deutschen Archäologischen Instituts, Ergänzungsheft* V. Berlin: Reimer, 1904.

Koşay, *Alaca, 1936*

Koşay, H. Z., *Ausgrabungen von Alaca Höyük: Vorbericht . . . 1936.* Ankara: Türkische Geschichtskommission (V, no. 2), 1944.

Koşay, *Alaca, 1937–1939*

Koşay, H. Z., *Les Fouilles d'Alaca Höyük . . . 1937–1939.* Ankara: Türk Tarih Kurumu (V, no. 5), 1951.

Kuniholm, *Dendrochronology*

Kuniholm, Peter I., *Dendrochronology at Gordion and on the Anatolian Plateau.* Ph.D. dissertation, University of Pennsylvania, 1977. Ann Arbor: University Microfilms, 1979.

LAAA	*Liverpool Annals of Art and Archaeology*
Luckenbill, *Anc. Records*	Luckenbill, D. D., *Ancient Records of Assyria and Babylonia*. 2 vols. Chicago: University of Chicago, 1926–1927.
Luschey, *Phiale*	Luschey, Heinz, *Die Phiale*. Bleicherode am Harz: Nieft, 1939.
MASCA	Museum Applied Science Center for Archaeology, University Museum, Philadelphia.
Material Culture	Lechtman, H. and R. S. Merrill, eds. *Material Culture: Styles, Organization and Dynamics of Technology*. 1975 Proceedings of the American Ethnological Society. St. Paul, Minn.: West Publishing Co., 1977.
McClellan, *Iron*	McClellan, Joanna F., *The Iron Objects from Gordion: A Typological and Functional Analysis*. Ph.D. dissertation, University of Pennsylvania, 1975. Ann Arbor: University Microfilms, 1976.
MDOG	*Mitteilungen der Deutschen Orient-Gesellschaft*
Mellink, *Hitt. Cem.*	Mellink, M. J., *A Hittite Cemetery at Gordion*. Philadelphia: The University Museum, 1956.
METU	Middle East Technical University, Ankara.
MIT	Massachusetts Institute of Technology, Cambridge, Massachusetts.
MMJ	*Metropolitan Museum Journal*
Muscarella, *Phryg. Fib. Gordion*	Muscarella, Oscar White, *Phrygian Fibulae from Gordion*. Colt Archaeological Institute Monograph 4. London: Quaritch, 1967.
NDA	*Neue deutsche Ausgrabungen im Mittelmeergebiet und im Vorderen Orient*. Berlin: Gebr. Mann, 1959.
Negahban, *Marlik*	Negahban, Ezat O., *A Preliminary Report on Marlik Excavation, Gohar Rud Expedition*. Tehran: Ministry of Education, 1964.
OIP	*Oriental Institute Publications*. Chicago: University of Chicago Press.
Ol. Forsch.	*Olympische Forschungen*. Berlin: W. de Gruyter.
Oppenheim, *Tell Halaf*	Oppenheim, Max Freiherr von, *Der Tell Halaf: Eine neue Kultur im ältesten Mesopotamien*. Leipzig: Brockhaus, 1931.
Oppenheim, *TellHalafNC*	Oppenheim, Max Freiherr von, ed. *Tell Halaf: A New Culture in Oldest Mesopotamia*. London and New York: G. P. Putnam's Sons, 1933.

Özgüç, *Altıntepe*	Özgüç, T., *Altıntepe.* 2 vols. Ankara: Türk Tarih Kurumu Basımevi, 1966, 1969.
Payne, *Perachora* I	Payne, Humfry *et al., Perachora: The Sanctuaries of Hera Akraia and Limenia.* Vol. I, *Architecture, Bronzes, Terracottas.* Oxford: Clarendon Press, 1940.
Perdrizet, *Delphes* V	Perdrizet, P., *Monuments figurés, petits bronzes, terres-cuites, antiquités diverses.* (= *Fouilles de Delphes* V). Paris: Fontemoing, 1908.
Piotrovskii, *Urartu*	Piotrovskii, B. B., *Urartu: The Kingdom of Van and Its Art.* Trans. and ed., Peter S. Gelling. New York: Praeger, 1967.
ProcAPS	*Proceedings of the American Philosophical Society.* Philadelphia: American Philosophical Society.
ProcBritAc	*Proceedings of the British Academy*
ProcSBA	*Proceedings of the Society of Biblical Archaeology*
Prop. Kunst.	*Propyläen Kunstgeschichte.* Berlin: Propyläen Verlag, 1966–.
Radiocarbon	*American Journal of Science Radiocarbon Supplement*
Rayonnement	*Rayonnement des civilisations grecques et romaines sur les cultures périphériques.* Huitième congrès international d'archéologie classique, Paris, 1963. Paris: E. de Boccard, 1965.
RDAC	*Reports of the Department of Antiquities, Cyprus.*
RE	Pauly-Wissowa (and Pauly-Wissowa-Kroll), *Realencyklopädie der klassischen Altertumswissenschaft.* Stuttgart: J. B. Metzlersche Verlag, 1893–.
REA	*Revue des études anciennes.*
Reinecke Festschrift	Behrens, G. and J. Werner, eds. *Reinecke Festschrift.* Mainz: E. Schneider, 1950.
Sams, *Painted Pottery*	Sams, G. Kenneth, *The Phrygian Painted Pottery of Early Iron Age Gordion and Its Anatolian Setting.* Ph.D. dissertation, University of Pennsylvania, 1971. Ann Arbor: University Microfilms, 1973.
SCE	Gjerstad, E. *et al., Swedish Cyprus Expedition.* Stockholm: Swedish Cyprus Expedition, 1934–.
Schaeffer, *Stratigraphie*	Schaeffer, C. F. A., *Stratigraphie comparée et chronologie de l'Asie Occidentale (IIIe et IIe millénaires).* London: Oxford University Press, 1948.

Schmidt, *Alishar 1928–29*	Schmidt, E. F., *The Alishar Hüyük, Seasons of 1928–29,* I and II. (*OIP* 19, 20). Chicago: University of Chicago, 1932–1933.
Schmidt, *Anatolia*	Schmidt, E. F., *Anatolia through the Ages: Discoveries at Alishar Mound 1927–29.* (*OIC* 11). Chicago: University of Chicago, 1931.
Singer *et al.*, eds. *Hist. Technol.*	Singer, C., E. J. Holmyard, and A. R. Hall, eds. *History of Technology,* I: *From Early Times to Fall of Ancient Empires.* Oxford: Clarendon Press, 1954.
SMEA	*Studi micenei ed egeo-anatolici.*
TAD	*Türk Arkeoloji Dergisi.* Ankara: Maarif Basımevi, 1933–.
TED	*Türk Etnografya Dergisi.* Ankara: Maarif Basımevi, 1956–.
TTAED	*Türk Tarih Arkeologya ve Etnografya Dergisi.* Istanbul: Maarif Matbaası, 1933–55.
TTK	Türk Tarih Kurumu (Turkish Historical Society).
UMB	*University Museum Bulletin.*
Van Loon, *Urartian Art*	Van Loon, Maurits N., *Urartian Art: Its Distinctive Traits in the Light of New Excavations.* Istanbul: Nederlands Historisch-Archaeologisch Instituut, 1966.
WVDOG	*Wissenschaftliche Veröffentlichungen der Deutschen Orient-Gesellschaft.*
Young, *City*	Young, R. S., *From the City of King Midas.* University Museum Exhibition Catalogue, 1958–1959.
Young, *Gordion Guide* (1968)	Young, R. S., *Gordion: A Guide to the Excavations and Museum.* Ankara: Archaeological Museum, 1968.
Young, *Gordion Guide* (1975)	Young, R. S., *Gordion: A Guide to the Excavations and Museum.* Ankara: Society for the Promotion of Tourism, Antiquities and Museums, 1975.

MINOR ABBREVIATIONS

app.	Appendix (in footnotes)	K-IV	Tumulus Körte IV
Ave.	Average	L.	Length
B	Bronze (in field/catalogue number)	*L*	left (e.g., pin to wearer's left, with reference to fibulae)
BI	Bone and Ivory (in field/catalogue number)	m.	meter
		Max. dim.	Maximum dimension
CC-1, 2, etc.	Clay-Cut Bldg. 1, 2, etc. on the city mound	Meg. 1, 2, etc.	Megaron 1, 2, etc., on the city mound
cm.	centimeter	mm.	millimeter
D.	Diameter	n.d.	not detected (in chemical analyses)
D. rim	Diameter of rim		
Est.	Estimated	no.	number
Fig.	Figure	OD.	Outside diameter
G	Glass (in field/catalogue number)	omph.	omphalos
GPH.	Greatest preserved height	p.	page
GPL.	Greatest preserved length	Pl.	Plate
GPTh.	Greatest preserved thickness	P	Pottery (in field/catalogue number)
GPW.	Greatest preserved width		
H.	Height	Rest.	Restored
H.-h.	Height to top of handle	*R*	right (e.g., pin to wearer's right, with reference to fibulae)
H.-rim	Height to rim		
I	Inscription (in field/catalogue number)	S	Sculpture (in field/catalogue number)
ID.	Inside diameter	T	Table
ILS	Iron, lead, silver when not jewelry (in field/catalogue number)	TB 1, 2, etc.	Terrace Bldg. 1, 2, etc., on the city mound
J	Jewelry (in field/catalogue number)	Th.	Thickness
		W	Wood (in field/catalogue number)
K-III	Tumulus Körte III	W.	Width

PREFACE

This volume is the first in a projected series of publications of the archaeological work sponsored at the site of Gordion by The University Museum of The University of Pennsylvania. Rodney S. Young was the field director from its initial year, 1950, until 1974, the year of his tragic death. Froelich G. Rainey, who was the director of the University Museum from 1947–1976, fostered and encouraged the Gordion project along with many other excavations of the museum through the years, and in 1975 appointed a publications committee to continue the preparation of publications from the point where Young had left off on volume I and to continue the planning of the entire Gordion Series, which is now in progress. The publication work was further encouraged by James B. Pritchard, director from 1976–1977, and has recently been greatly revitalized by the basic commitment to the publication of past University Museum excavations expressed by Martin Biddle, director from 1977-1981, and by Robert H. Dyson, Jr., the present acting director.

At the time of his death, Young left among his papers a manuscript that furnishes the major portion of volume I, including the chapters that comprise introductions to Tumuli P and MM and the three catalogues of finds from Tumuli P, MM, and W. However, Young had left gaps in the discussions accompanying the catalogues. The publications committee has filled in these gaps.

An effort has been made to change neither the style nor the content of any part that Young left to us. However, the major part of the footnoting and the updating of the notes left by the author have had to be supplied by the editor and others, and at a few points in the text a long editorial footnote, initialed by a member of the committee, has been appended. No illustrations had been selected; the editor takes full responsibility for them.

The original manuscript was gathered in scattered sections, unpaginated, but the committee believes that there is inner textual evidence that the author wished to keep the three tumuli in the order in which they were excavated. For this reason, discussions of the dating of the tumuli must remain out of chronological order until the results are gathered into the conclusions. It was fated that the committee members had to write many of the special comments upon which the final discussion must be based, and they are responsible for the conclusions reached in the last chapter. Young's own remarks throughout are clearly set off, and his other publications also stand as a record of his interpretations. Keith DeVries contributed the Introduction to Tumulus W, and Machteld Mellink wrote the Conclusions. The authors of small insertions in the text are noted in the footnotes and the list on page ix supplies the exact pagination of all contributions to the book by authors other than Young.

The Committee members are: Machteld J. Mellink, chairman; Ellen L. Kohler, executive editor; G. Roger Edwards and Keith DeVries. Other Gordion staff members who have written sections within the main text are G. Kenneth Sams of the University of North Carolina, and Joanna Fink McClellan of Laurel, Maryland. Editorial assistants have been Lynn Roller, Kathleen Ryan, Frances Bobbe, Mary E. Moser, and Karen A. Brown. Elizabeth Simpson prepared the plates and oversaw production of the volume.

ACKNOWLEDGMENTS

The excavations reported upon in this volume took place in 1956, 1957, and 1959, with a preliminary season of survey and drilling in 1955. Our first thanks go to the Ministry of Education and the Department of Antiquities and Museums (and, in recent years, the Ministry of Culture) of Turkey for their continuing sponsorship of the work at Gordion and for the generous and efficient aid and advice offered by individual directors, staff members, and representatives.

Raci Temizer, who is now director of the Museum of Anatolian Civilizations in Ankara, was the commissioner in 1956 (as he had been in 1950–1955); his immense contributions to the work at Gordion and Phrygian archaeology deserve our lasting appreciation. In 1957, the year of the Midas Mound excavations, Burhan Tezcan ably represented the Department of Antiquities, returning to the site after an initial assignment as trench supervisor in 1950. In 1959, epigraphist Lütfi Tuğrul, now of the Istanbul Museum, offered his friendly aid as the commissioner of the Department of Antiquities.

In the course of the years 1955–1959, many special appeals were made for help to the Department of Antiquities, to museum directors, to government officials, to engineers and technicians in various official and private capacities, to the kaymakam and citizens of Polatlı, and to the villagers of Yassıhüyük. Aid and advice were always forthcoming and are gratefully remembered here. The work could not have been completed without the resourcefulness of many individuals at all levels of participation.

The following staff members took part in the survey, drilling, excavation and recording of Tumuli P, MM, and W: R. S. Young (field director 1955–1959), G. Roger Edwards (1955), J. S. Last (surveyor and architect 1955, 1956, and 1959), Dorothy H. Cox (architect 1957), E. L. Kohler (conservator and recorder, 1955, 1957, and 1959), Ann K. Knudsen and Mabel L. Lang (conservators and recorders, 1956), and Donald F. Brown (in charge of drilling, 1955).

Samuel Eckert did many practical favors for the museum by selecting and sending the drilling machinery and pumping equipment to Gordion.

The following persons and institutions generously contributed to the excavation costs of the three tumuli discussed: R. S. Young, the Board of Managers of the University Museum, the Corning Glass Works (1957), two anonymous friends of the Gordion excavations, and one anonymous foundation.

Special donations for the preparation and printing of this volume were generously made by members of the family of R. S. Young, by Marian Welker, by two anonymous friends of the Gordion excavations, and by the numerous donors to the Rodney S. Young Memorial Publication Fund of the University Museum, established in November 1975.

A liberal subvention to the printing of volume I was received from the Archaeological Institute of America in honor of its former president, Rodney S. Young.

Finally, the sponsorship of the National Endowment for the Humanities* has allowed the proper organization of the Gordion excavation archives and the systematic preparation of the Gordion Publications Project under the editorship of Ellen L. Kohler. This essential aid is and will be gratefully acknowledged by all present and future members of the publications project, and by scholars consulting the Gordion archives.

---

*The findings and conclusions presented in this volume do not necessarily represent the views of the Endowment.

PHOTOGRAPHIC CREDITS

Bronson, Richard C.	Plates 13C,G,H, 14G, 16D, 17D, 18G, 20E, 25A, 50B,C, 58H, 67C, 81D,E, 88A, 89B,F, 95G
Eğecioğlu, Gürel	Plates 8D, 10I, 17C,E, 59A,C, 61I,N, 64E,F, 65C,F, 68A, 90G
Eiteljorg, Harrison	Plates 19C, 21B,D-G, 25C,D, 32I, 58F,K, 60D,E,G,M-P, 61A,G,J,P, 65A,D,E, 66E-G, 68D, 69A-C, F-J, 70A-D,F,L, 71A,C,G, 72B-K, 73A,C,K, 80A-E,G-M, 82C-E, 83B,P 87B, 88B,C, 89A, 90D,E, 91A-H,J,K,M-O, 92A,B,D,F, 93B,D,E,H, 94A-D,F
Ellis, Richard	Plates 99A-E, 100A-E, 101A-F
Goldberg, Reuben University Museum Philadelphia	Plates 8C, 16A,B,E,F, 17A,B, 55A,B, 57A-H, 58C,I, 59D, 60J-L, 62A-E, 64B,C, 66B,D, 67D,F, 68B, 71C, 73B
Öztartan, Selahattin Museum of Anatolian Civilizations, Ankara	Plates 15C, 18J, 19D,F-H, 20B, 36B, 37A,B, 38B, 39B, 53B, 58A,B,D,E,G 60A-C,F,I 61E,F,H,M 63A,D,E, 64D,E 65B, 68C, 80N,O, 92I, 93A, 98A, Color Plate IV
Steinberg, Arthur	Plate 99A
Whitmore, James Life © Time, Inc.	Plate 36A

Except for those specially listed above, all the photographs were taken by staff members at Gordion.

ART CREDITS

Boonin, Nicholas	Figure 29
Cox, Dorothy Hannah	Figures 51, 54, 64, 66, 105, 108-111
Ellis, Richard	Figures 135-148
Guerrero, Joseph (after J. S. Last)	Figure 50
Khalil, Ann Knudsen	Figures 117A, 120, 122
Last, J. S.	Figures 4, 9, 25, 27, 28, 30, 33, 35, 37, 39A-D,F,G, 40A-E, 41-44, 46, 114-116, 129
McClellan, Joanna	Figure 17
Muscarella, Grace Freed	Figures 72, 73, 76-78, 80, 81, 84, 85, 87, 92, 96, 98, 100, 134A-C; Plate 59B
Patch, Diana Craig	Map
Remsen, William	Figure 5
(after J. S. Last)	Figure 3
Sams, G. Kenneth	Figures 21, 103, 127
Seuffert, Andy	Figures 6-8, 10, 11, 19, 22, 24, 31, 32, 67, 68, 71, 74, 75, 79, 83, 86, 90, 91, 93, 107, 117B, 118, 119, 121, 123, 124, 133
Shaw, Maria C.	Figure 53
Simpson, Elizabeth	Figures 12-15, 23, 26, 34, 45, 49, 52, 82, 88, 89, 95, 99, 102, 104, 112, 113, 125, 128, 130-132
(after M. Akok)	Figure 1
(after D. H. Cox)	Figure 110
(after P. de Jong)	Figure 18, 94A,B
(after Ann K. Khalil)	Figures 69, 70
(after Ellen Kohler)	Figures 94C-G, 97, 131
(after J. S. Last)	Figures 36, 38, 39E, 40F, 47, 48, 126
(after Grace Muscarella)	Figure 20
(after Carol Ward)	Figure 16
(after R. S. Young)	Figure 2
(after unsigned artist)	Figure 106
Williams, II, Charles K.	Figures 55-63, 65, 134D,E

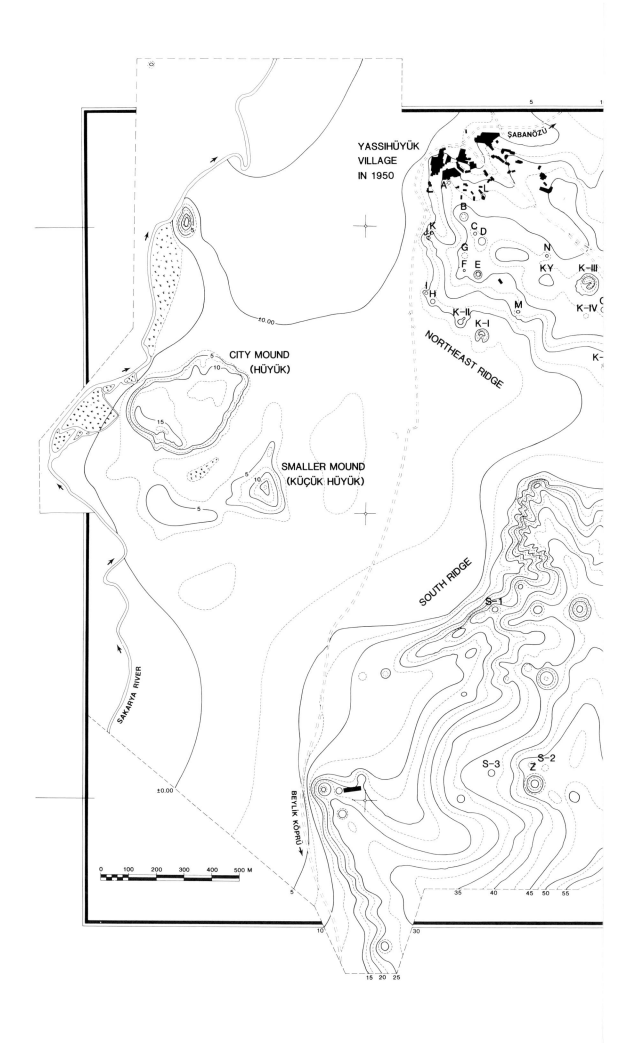

YASSIHÜYÜK
VILLAGE
IN 1950

ŞABANÖZÜ

A

L

B

K
J

C D

G

N

F E

KY

K-III

I
H

K-II

M

K-IV

K-I

NORTHEAST RIDGE

K-

±0.00

CITY MOUND
(HÜYÜK)

5
10

15

SMALLER MOUND
(KÜÇÜK HÜYÜK)

5
10

5

SOUTH RIDGE

S-1

SAKARYA RIVER

±0.00

S-3

S-2
Z

BEYLİK KÖPRÜ

0   100   200   300   400   500 M

5

35   40   45 50 55

10

30

5

15 20 25

INTRODUCTION

In 1948 Froelich G. Rainey, director of the University Museum, and John F. Daniel, curator of the Mediterranean Section of the museum, planned and put into its first phase an archaeological project in Turkey. In the fall a reconnaissance expedition was sent to Turkey for the purpose of selecting a site to be excavated in the ensuing years. J. F. Daniel was in charge, and he was joined by Rodney S. Young, then of the Agora Excavations in Athens. The Turkish government in the person of Hamit Zübeyr Koşay, director of the Antiquities Department, offered for consideration by the University Museum a large number of sites still available for excavation.

Daniel, who had worked in Turkey previously at the site of Tarsus, had been contemplating for several years the historical importance of Gordion, the capital of ancient Phrygia, and the possibility of its excavation. Daniel, a Bronze Age specialist, and Young, an Iron Age specialist, then went to inspect the site in great detail amid the discomforts of snow and floods of a particularly cold December. Daniel's report to Rainey remarked that "Young, never given to superlatives, thought it magnificent."

Other possibilities were, however, considered. Xanthos, the capital of Lycia, had already been awarded to the French; a Swedish expedition was beginning excavations in Caria at Labraunda. Daniel's feeling was that Ionia and Lydia were too well known (although in 1948 Sardis was available to the University Museum for excavation). One other area (besides Phrygia) still had fairly unfamiliar remains to offer: Pamphylia-Pisidia, where the plain of Korkuteli, northwest of Antalya, offered a number of attractive sites that might shed light on Late Bronze and Iron Age relations with Greece, and with Cyprus where the University Museum had conducted a long series of earlier campaigns. A trip to Korkuteli by the reconnaissance team,

now including G. Roger Edwards, was never finished or reported upon, due to the sudden death of John Daniel.

This tragedy, however, did not deter Rainey and the managers of the University Museum from deciding to initiate the new project at Gordion. Rodney S. Young was appointed field director and G. Roger Edwards, assistant field director. Work began on April 1, 1950, with the opening of Tumulus A, and continued in alternate unevenly numbered years (with a few supplementary campaigns in even years) through the campaign of 1973.

The following list gives the dates of the excavation campaigns, the field directors, and references to preliminary reports for each season:

1950	Young	Young, R. S., "Gordion—1950," *UMB* 16, pt. 1 (May 1951): 3–20.
1951 1952	Young Edwards	Young, R. S., "Progress at Gordion—1951-2," *UMB* 17, pt. 4 (December 1953): 3–39.
1953	Young	Young, R. S., "Gordion: Preliminary Report—1953," *AJA* 59 (1955): 1–18.
1955	Young Edwards	Young, R. S., "The Campaign of 1955 at Gordion," *AJA* 60 (1956): 249–266.
1956	Young	Young, R. S., "Gordion 1956: Preliminary Report," *AJA* 61 (1957): 319–331.
1957	Young	Young, R. S., "The Gordion Campaign of 1957," *AJA* 62 (1958): 139–154.
1958	Edwards	Edwards, G. R., "Gordion Campaign of 1958: Preliminary Report," *AJA* 63 (1959): 263–268.

1959	Young	Young, R. S., "Gordion Campaign of 1959: Preliminary Report," *AJA* 64 (1960): 227–244.
1961	Young	Young, R. S., "The 1961 Campaign at Gordion," *AJA* 66 (1962): 153–168.
1962	Edwards	Edwards, G. R. "Gordion: 1962," *Expedition* 5, pt. 3 (Spring 1963): 42–48.
1963	Young	Young, R. S., "The 1963 Campaign at Gordion," *AJA* 68 (1964): 279–292.
1965	Young	Young, R. S., "The Gordion Campaign of 1965," *AJA* 70 (1966): 267–278.
1967	Young	Young, R. S., "The Gordion Campaign of 1967," *AJA* 72 (1968): 231–242.
1969	Young	
1971	Young	
1973	Young	

Previous to the work by the University Museum expedition, Gordion had been the site of excavations by Gustav and Alfred Körte in 1900. They excavated five tumuli and made a trial trench on the south side of the city mound. Their report, *Gordion, Ergebnisse der Ausgrabung im Jahre 1900* (Berlin: Reimer, 1904), in addition to the results of the 1900 excavations, gives an account of the history of Phrygia and of Gordion in particular, with a collection of ancient sources referring to the topography and history of the site. The only additional reference that came to light after 1904 is *Hellenica Oxyrhynchia*.[1]

The site of Gordion has not yet yielded epigraphic testimony to its ancient name, but Alfred Körte's identification of Yassıhüyük as the center of the Phrygian capital of Gordion has been amply reinforced by the results of the University Museum excavations, especially by the excavation of the major royal tumulus reported upon in this volume (nicknamed "Midas Mound," MM, in what may be a correct anticipation of historical evidence; see the Conclusions of this volume).

The final series of excavation reports of the University Museum Gordion excavations begins with this volume on the three major burial mounds of the early period. The series will continue with a second volume on the lesser tumuli. Volumes III and IV and their subdivisions will deal with the excavations on the city mound. Volume V will be devoted to pottery, volumes VI and VII to wall paintings, sculpture, other carvings, and seals. The inscriptions and graffiti from Gordion will be published by Claude Brixhe in the framework of his corpus of paleo-Phrygian inscriptions; the individual epigraphic documents will also be listed in the volumes pertaining to their relevant stratigraphic or tumulus context (see appendix I-A in this volume).

Monographs will be prepared as detailed studies of special categories of finds, among which the following are planned:

Architectural terracottas
Terracotta figurines
Iron and bronze objects
Glass
Lamps
Stone objects
Human skeletal material
Animal bones
Botanical evidence
Textiles

The following monographs have appeared:

Cox., D. H., *A Third Century Hoard of Tetradrachms from Gordion* (Philadelphia: University Museum, 1953)

Mellink, M. J., *A Hittite Cemetery at Gordion* (Philadelphia: University Museum, 1956)

---

[1] Agesilaos, 396/395 B.C. See Jacoby, *FGrHist*, IIA *Zeitgeschichte* (1926), pp. 33–34, no. 66. ἀφικόμενος δὲ πάλιν πρὸς Γορδ(ί)ειον, χωρίον ἐπὶ χώματος ὠικοδομημένον καὶ κατεσκευασμένον καλῶς,* καὶ καταζεύξας τὸ στράτευμα περιέμενεν ἐξ ἡμέρας, πρὸς μὲν τοὺς πολεμίους προσβολὰς ποιούμενος, τοὺς δὲ στρατιώτας ἐ[πὶ π]ολλοῖς ἀγαθοῖς συνέχων. ἐπειδὴ δὲ βιάσασθαι τὸ χωρίον οὐκ ἠδύνατο διὰ τὴν Ῥαθάνου προθυμίαν, ὃς ἐπῆρχεν αὐτοῦ Πέρσης ὢν τὸ γένος, ἀναστήσας ἦγεν ἄνω τοὺς στρατιώτας, κελεύοντος τοῦ Σπιθριδάτου εἰς Παφλαγονίαν πορεύεσθαι.

*καλῶς Gr-H κακως P.

See also Vittorio Bartoletti, ed., *Hellenica Oxyrhynchia* (Leipzig: Teubner, 1959) XXI.6 and I. A. F. Bruce, *An Historical Commentary on the 'Hellenica Oxyrhynchia'* (Cambridge, 1967), 141–142.

Cf. Young, *AJA* 59 (1955): 6, n. 10.

Muscarella, O., *Phrygian Fibulae from Gordion* (London: Quaritch, 1967)

As interim studies, the following doctoral dissertations have presented special categories of finds:

G. E. Anderson, "The Common Cemetery at Gordion." Bryn Mawr College, 1980.

C. H. Greenewalt, "Lydian Pottery of the Sixth Century B.C.: The Lydion and Marbled Ware." University of Pennsylvania, 1966.

R. H. Johnston, "Pottery Practices during the 6th–8th Centuries B.C. at Gordion in Central Anatolia: An Analytical and Synthesizing Study." Pennsylvania State University, 1970.

A. K. Knudsen, "A Study of the Relation between Phrygian Metalware and Pottery in the Eighth and Seventh Centuries B.C." University of Pennsylvania, 1961.

E. L. Kohler, "A Study of the Wood and Ivory Carvings from Gordion, Phrygia (c. 750–500 B.C.)." Bryn Mawr College, 1958.

P. I. Kuniholm, "Dendrochronology at Gordion and on the Anatolian Plateau." University of Pennsylvania, 1977.

J. F. McClellan, "The Iron Objects from Gordion: A Typological and Functional Analysis." University of Pennsylvania, 1975.

G. K. Sams, "The Phrygian Painted Pottery of Early Iron Age Gordion and Its Anatolian Setting." University of Pennsylvania, 1971.

P. A. Sheftel, "The Ivory, Bone and Shell Objects from Gordion from the Campaigns of 1950 through 1973." University of Pennsylvania, 1974.

N. P. Zouck, "Turned and Hand-Carved Alabaster from Gordion." University of Pennsylvania, 1974.

The material from these and other shorter published studies will be incorporated and in part revised in the volumes of the final publications.

I

TUMULUS P

THE CHILD'S BURIAL

INTRODUCTION

Tumulus P[1] lies to the south-southeast of the Great Tumulus, about equidistant from it and from Tumulus K-III which lies to its west (fig. 1; pls. 1A, 2A). Its height was about 12 m., its lower diameter approximately 70 m.

THE DRILLING OF THE MOUND

The tumulus was drilled from October 10 to 26, 1955 (pl. 2B).[2] Sixty borings were made at regular intervals 2.50 m. apart on a grid running in approximately north-south and east-west lines, as may be seen from the sketch-plan (fig. 2). The results were entirely satisfactory.

The first bore, made just to the east of the peak of the mound, found rubble stone at a depth of 9.80 m. The second, 2.50 m. to the east of the first, found hardpan at a depth of 15.30 m.; evidently it lay outside the limits of the area covered by the rubble piled over the grave. Seemingly the burial was to be sought in the area to the west of the peak of the tumulus. Subsequent borings confirmed this; where rubble was found, it lay at a depth of 9.50 to 10.50 m. below peak-level, and

where rubble was not found, the drill went to hardpan and stopped at a depth of 14.50 to 16 m. From this it became possible to define roughly the limits and to a certain extent the shape of the rubble pile. The rubble occupied an irregularly oval area about 18.50 m. long (northeast to southwest) by 14 m. wide. At east, south, and west, near the limit of the rubble area, stone was found at a level about one meter deeper than at the center, suggesting a shallow domical stone pile thick at its center and thinning toward its perimeter. By far the greater part of its mass lay to the west and south of the peak of the mound. Four of the central borings nos. 45, 46, 47, and 48, seemed to pinpoint the grave itself. In all of these the drill bored through the clay filling of the mound, then dropped through empty space to a depth of about 1 m. before finding rubble. From this it seemed evident that in this area a cavity had been created by the collapse of the roof over the tomb, and with the collapse the fall of the overlying rubble into the cavity of the tomb itself. Evidently the clay filling of which the tumulus was made had become so compacted that it was strong enough to stand by itself as a shallow dome without the support of the rubble over which it had been laid down. In the case of the tumulus the drilling had not only delimited the area of the rubble pile over the burial but had also given

---

[1]A preliminary report appears in *AJA* 61 (1957): 325 ff.
[2]See note 8, p. 81.

strong indication of where the grave itself was to be found within that area.

THE EXCAVATION
OF THE TUMULUS

Following the evidence from the drilling, a trench was laid out in April 1956 just to the southwest of the peak of the mound, measuring 8 m. east-west by 10.50 m. north-south. This trench was centered around the four drillings that had shown empty space between the clay of the tumulus and the top of the stone pile under it. An access trench 4 m. wide and 20 m. long was made at the west side, prolonged at its outer end by a narrower cut 2 m. wide and 10 m. long to the edge of the mound. The wide inner part of the access trench was narrowed, when appropriate depth was reached, by leaving a meter-wide step at either side. Through this cut the Decauville railroad was eventually brought in, greatly facilitating the removal of the dug fill from the main trench over the grave.

The filling at the top of the mound was loose and gravelly, evidently disturbed to a depth of about 1.50 m.; in this were found a number of metal cartridge cases, no doubt left from the Battle of the Sakarya in 1921 when the peak of the tumulus would have served as an armed lookout point. Below this level the filling became harder, more compact, undisturbed clay. Between 1.50 and 2 m. below the top and about midway between borings nos. 46 and 47 but slightly to the north of their line, there appeared a small round hole in the clay, 0.10 m. in diameter; probing showed that this went down to a depth of more than 3 m. At a slightly lower level (at −2 m.) appeared a circular crack, *ca.* 5 m. in diameter, in the tumulus fill (pl. 3A); its center was the hole that had been noted the day before. Quite evidently the hole had once contained a wooden mast, which had been used as a center to guide the piling of the mound. The mast had been completely buried in the clay filling, and in the course of time the wood rotted away, leaving a hole, small bits of wood still

adhering to its sides. Striations still visible in the vertical clay faces around the hole, taken as from a mold, attested to the past presence of a wooden mast. The diameter of the hole increased with depth, suggesting a tapered mast or sapling. As this wooden guide mast lay about 8 m. to the southwest of the (present) peak of the tumulus, it seemed likely that the mast had been set up to mark the center of the grave rather than the intended peak of the mound over it. The crack in the tumulus filling encircling the central mast-hole had evidently been made by settling after the collapse of the tomb's roof; it was followed, with ever-increasing diameter, right down to the top of the stone packing over the grave.

At a depth of 5.70 m. below the top of the mound a second hole, 0.05 m. in diameter and 0.15 m. to the west of the first, appeared in the hard clay, evidently another mast-hole. Slightly below the level of its appearance the first hole came to an end; we had followed it to a depth of nearly four meters. Quite clearly when the first mast set up as a guide over the center of the grave had become buried in the rising filling of the tumulus, a second guide mast had been planted close beside its top to keep in view the same focal point during the piling of the upper levels of the mound.[3] In our excavation the hole left by the lower mast was followed as far as the cavity above the grave; the actual stump (D. 0.12 m.) of the mast itself (pl. 3B) was found in place below, embedded in rubble at the center of the fallen roof of the wooden burial chamber.

The filling of the tumulus was all of hard-packed clay, remarkably clean: only two potsherds and a few animal bones were found in it over the whole area that was dug. The clay must have been brought from elsewhere, probably the river plain of the Sangarios; the same clean clay was used for the piling of the other tumuli in this area—MM, K-III and W.[4] In the lower part of the mound, to a height of about 3.50 m. above the level of the tomb roof, the buff clay had indeed solidified to a homogeneous mass so compacted that the shallow dome-shaped roof left by the collapse of the tomb cover was strong enough to stand by itself, as we

---

[3] A similar guide mast over the tomb in his Tumulus III was noted by G. Körte (*Gordion,* 39–40). The presence of yet another was clear in Tumulus W (below, p. 196).

[4] G. Körte remarks on the hardness of the clay and its cleanness (*Gordion,* 38 f.). Fig. 5, p. 41, shows the grave as cleared; the rubble pile that overlay it runs under the clay scarp of his trench.

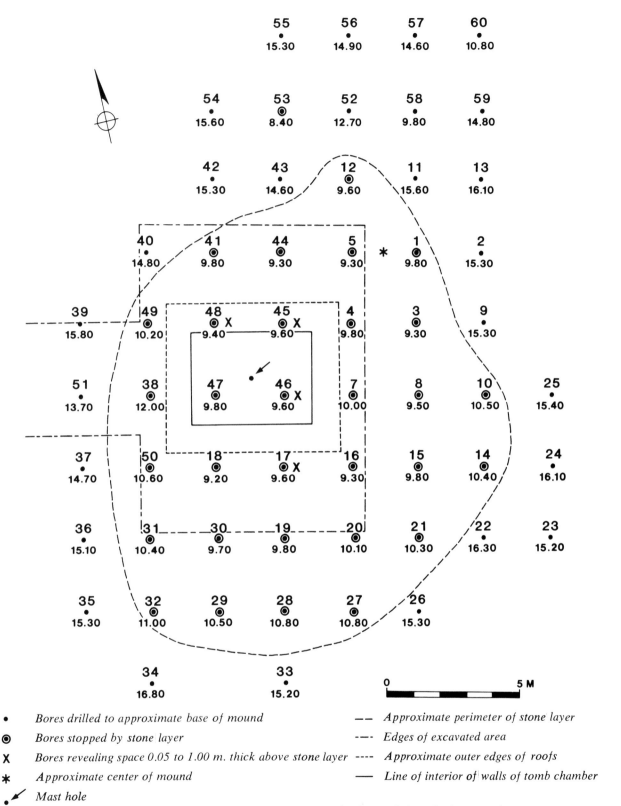

Figure 2. *Plot of the drill holes in Tumulus P. The figures below the bore-numbers give the maximum depth reached.*

3

had suspected at the time of drilling. The smoothness and solidity of this lower clay mass, as well as its strength, suggested that it had been piled in a damp state, perhaps even puddled before being put in place. In contrast, the upper clay filling was granular and lumpy, obviously laid down dry, and the line of demarcation between the two fillings was very clear all around the sides of our trench. Apparently, the Phrygian tumulus builders were aware of the potential of the material they used and laid it down with a view to waterproofing the tomb from above as well as reducing the pressure to be carried by its roof.

The circular crack in the clay noted near the top of the mound (pl. 3A) was followed right down to the level of the rubble over the grave; in fact at the lower levels only the roughly circular area within this crack was dug. This defined the position of the grave and the area affected by the collapse of its roof, for the outer periphery of the rubble pile underlay the clay outside the ring formed by the crack. Between the bottom of the unsupported clay and the top of the rubble beneath it there was empty space to a depth of about a meter at the center, less around the edges. The surface of the rubble lay at a depth of about 9.50 m. below the level of the peak of the mound. All of this had been forecast from the drilling.

The rubble was composed of smooth, rounded fist-size stones, interspersed with larger ones. These stones gave the impression that they had been much worn by water; they were evidently brought from a stream bed in the vicinity of Gordion. Among the stones a fair number of potsherds were found, some of them recognizable as Chalcolithic and Hittite, most of coarse Phrygian gray ware.[5] The rubble pile went to a depth of about 1.50 m.; at 10.70 m. below the peak the roof of the tomb was found (fig. 2).

THE WOODEN TOMB

The upper roof of the tomb measured up to 7.00 m. in length from east to west, by 5.20 in width. Somewhat to our surprise the orientation was east-west rather than north-south—the plan of attack projected after the drilling (figs. 2, 3) had anticipated a north-south orientation in conformity with the major axis of the overlying stone pile. The whole of the central part over the hollow of the grave was broken and had fallen in. The roof was made of eleven squared timbers of black pine[6] laid side by side over the length of the tomb and supported beneath by an inner roof of twelve timbers laid across its width. One more large timber lay lengthwise on the top of the outer roof down its center; beside it lay the stump of the guide mast embedded in rubble (pl. 3B) at about the center of the tomb roof, carried down with the collapse but evidently very little displaced from its original position by the fall. The two outermost timbers along the north and south edges of the roof were unbroken, since they rested to their full length on the side walls of the tomb and the rubble packing outside it. A third timber spanning the hollow of the grave at the north side was badly cracked but had not given way because it was supported beneath by some of the collapsed timbers of the inner roof (pl. 4A). The beams of the outer roof were sizable: thickness 0.35–0.40 m. and width 0.40–0.60 m. (the outermost beam at the south side, the largest, was 0.60 m. wide). In length they varied, so that the ends of the roof were not properly squared; the longest beam was just over 7 m. in length. Since the tomb beneath was 4.57 m. long on the interior, there was an overhang of the outer roof at either end of a meter or more.

The inner roof was made from twelve crossbeams *ca.* 0.40–0.50 m. wide and 0.25 thick, somewhat lighter than those of the outer roof. Again, the ends of these inner beams overhung the edges of the tomb, giving support to the edge-timbers of the upper roof. And again, the end beams of the inner roof rested above the end walls of the tomb and on the rubble packing outside it, so that only ten spanned the hollow of the grave.[7] These had snapped off close to the faces of the side

---

[5]Cf. sherds in rubble over G. Körte's Tumulus III, *Gordion*, 40, 42.

[6]See p. 290, app. III-A, Sample 1.

[7]These ten beams, as they were raised, one at a time, beginning at the east end, gave the positions of the objects

as recorded in the field. These beam-lines are used as very general aids in finding an object on W. Remsen's plan (fig. 5) and are printed in red. The approximate widths, from the east, are: (1) 0.43, (2) 0.40, (3) 0.48, (4) 0.48, (5) 0.43, (6) 0.43, (7) 0.50, (8) 0.51, (9) 0.45, (10) 0.48 m.

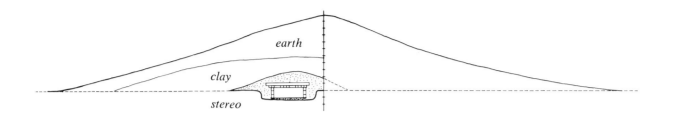

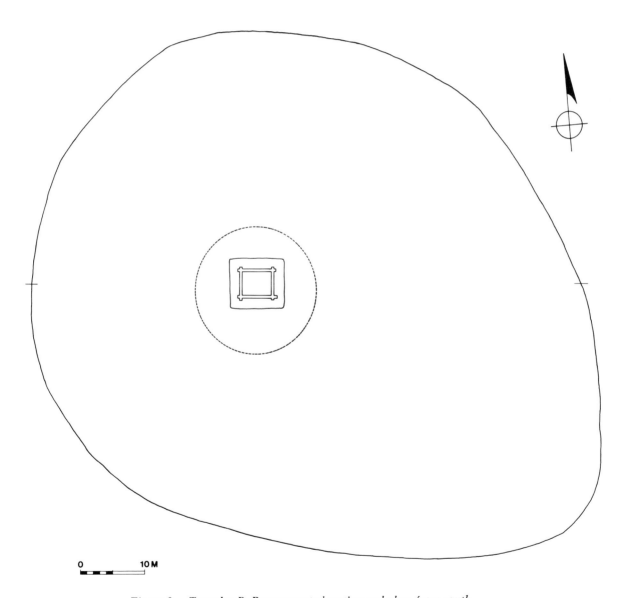

Figure 3.   Tumulus P. Reconstructed section and plan, from south.

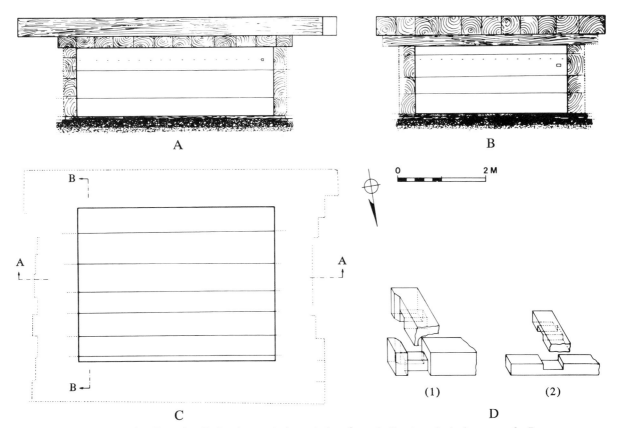

Figure 4. Tumulus P. Section and plan of chamber. A. Section A-A, from north. B. Section B-B, from west. C. Plan of floor, with indication of outer ends of upper roof beams. D. Mortising systems of (1) upper, and (2) lower, corner joints.

walls which supported them; the broken pieces lay slanted down, their upper ends leaning against the wall faces while the central parts lay flat over the contents of the grave (pl. 4A). In consequence some of the grave offerings, especially at the south side of the room, were to a certain extent protected from the inrush of stones from above by the broken pieces of crossbeams, while others were squashed flat.

The inside dimensions of the chamber were 4.57 m. long (east-west) by 3.48 wide (north-south) and 1.54 deep from floor to the under-face of the roof (fig. 4). It was floored by planks of varying width—the widest about 0.70 m.; there appeared to be two layers of these, each about 0.06 m. thick, the upper floor running east-west, the lower north-south and bedded on rubble. At the ends and sides these planks ran under the bottoms of the wall beams; we must conclude that the side and end walls were bedded on this floor. Each of the short ends of the tomb was constructed of

four superimposed horizontal timbers, the long sides of three. The largest of these beams was about 0.65 m. in height; their thickness was about 0.30 m. All four walls[8] were found to be bulged inward as a result of the pressure from the rubble outside; the end wall at the west had actually cracked down its center where there were large open cracks in the wood. The corners of the tomb, on the other hand, had held up well and remained practically vertical. This suggested a fastening together of the side and end wall timbers at the corners by mortising or other means. By careful probing with a penknife the architect J. S. Last found evidence for a system of corner mortises, and a reconstruction of this is included in his drawing of the tomb (fig. 4D). But it is difficult to comprehend how a corner mortise could have been made

8 A wood sample from an unspecified wall of Tumulus P was sent to the Centre Technique du Bois in Paris for identification; see app. III-B, p. 291.

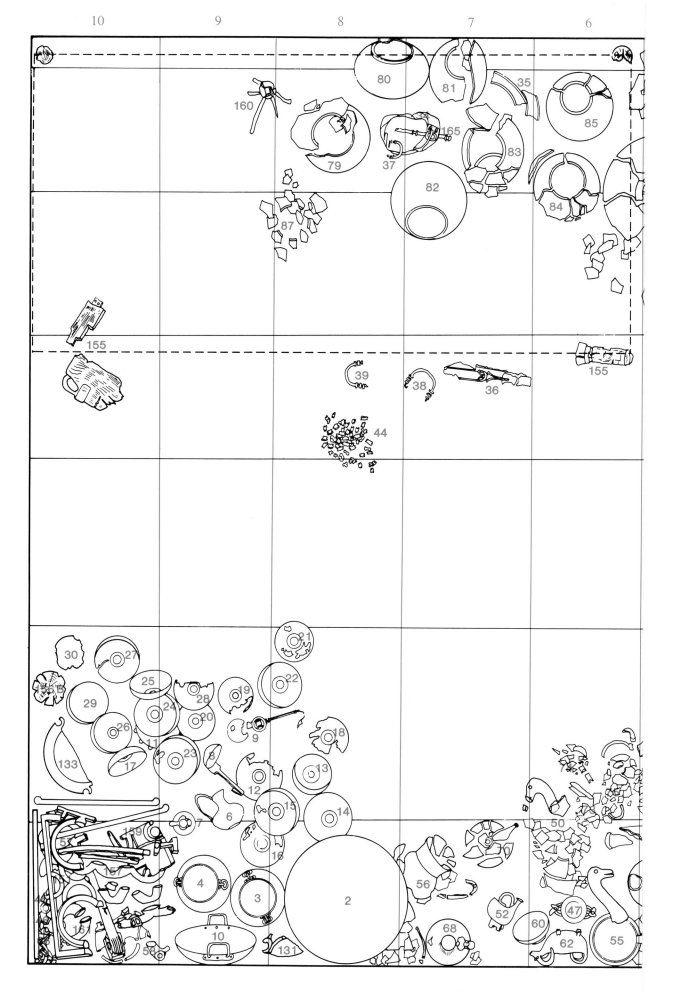

Figure 5. Reconstructed floor plan

unless the horizontal joints of side and end walls coincided in level, at least to a reasonable degree, and there were three horizontal joints in the end walls, but only two in the long sides. A thorough examination of the corners was precluded by the danger of an inrush of rubble from outside if the already badly weakened wood of the walls gave way. This detail, then, remains unclear, but it was evident that end and side walls were in some way fastened together at the corners, and there was some indication that mortises had been used.

There was a row of oblong peg holes all around the walls of the tomb at 0.25 m. below their top (pl. 4B). The holes were regularly spaced about 0.22 m. apart; each hole was 0.02 m. long and of like depth, by half a centimeter high. There were 17 in the face of each long side and 14 in each end. Near the west end of the north side one wooden peg remained in place in its socket, extending about 0.10 m. from the wall face horizontally into the tomb. In many other holes remained the ends of similar pegs, which had been snapped off at the wall face (fig. 4A, B) and in the debris inside the tomb were found many pegs complete or with one end broken off, just like the one still in place. These pegs were about 0.12 m. long and finished roughly to eight flat faces, with one end whittled down to fit the hole into which it was driven. Almost invariably the outer ends of these pegs showed traces of a fine, loosely woven, white linen cloth, with shreds or threads clinging to the wood.[9] It would seem that the pegs had served to carry hangings of cloth in front of the wooden walls of the tomb all around. No doubt these hangings were in imitation of cloth hangings in the room occupied by the child while it was living.

That the tomb was occupied by a young child is established by the teeth found in it[10] as well as by the nature and size of the grave offerings placed in it. Whether it was constructed specifically for the child is less sure; its very construction must have taken considerable time. If construction was started only after the death of the child, the body would have had to be kept somehow until the tomb was ready to receive it. On the other hand the death of a young child is not easy to predict much in advance of its occurrence, and a start of construction of a tomb for a child before its death is unlikely. It is thus possible that a tomb intended for somebody else was used for the child when it died. But in any case the body, the furniture, and the other grave offerings must have been placed from above into a tomb already completed except for the laying down of its roof.

CONTENTS OF THE TOMB AND CHRONOLOGY

The furniture in the tomb had been badly broken and crushed by the fall of the double roof and the consequent inrush of rubble from above. Many broken fragments were unrecognizable; many more had disintegrated completely. All the debris in the tomb—mostly disintegrated and flaked wood—was screened, and many fragments were recovered in the screening,[11] but the rest—the greater part— had disintegrated entirely or split and flaked into unrecognizable fragments. Only in the southwest corner was the furniture in a reasonable state of preservation.

The lifting of the broken beams of the outer roof revealed, just to the east of the center of the tomb, the large bronze cauldron (TumP 1) crushed down over its iron ring stand and packed inside with small wooden toys and utensils (pl. 5A).[12] The removal of this cauldron gave working space (see fig. 5) for the continued removal of fragments of both roofs. Close beside it at the north had stood a square table with inlaid top (TumP 154). The lifting of fallen beams 4 and 5 of the lower roof overlying it brought up a large part of the inlay which stuck to the under-faces of the cover beams. The lifting of the fallen roof fragments,

---

[9]See app. V, Fabric B, p. 302. There also appeared to be a slight change in color of the south wall at the level of the line of pegs (Gordion Notebook 43, 146–147). [Ed.]

[10]See below, p. 9.

[11]Items definitely mentioned (Gordion Notebook 43, 172–173) as being recovered in the screening were, of course, the child's teeth, discussed below, and various

---

small fragments of worked wood (pl. 28F–H), including many broken pegs from the wall.

[12]The fact that the cauldron was found lying between the upper and lower roofs seems to demonstrate that the lower roof gave way first but did not destroy the strong iron ring stand on which the cauldron stood. Only the fall of the second (upper) roof finally smashed cauldron and stand together. [Ed.]

moreover, seemed to disturb the equilibrium of the broken pieces leaning against the south wall of the tomb; in anticipation of their falling, these were removed, and the grave was cleared starting at the middle of the south side and working clockwise around the chamber. All along the south wall an enormous number of terra-cotta vases and vessels of bronze were found lying in no order, obviously having fallen. The position of finding was recorded by the order of crossbeams of the inner roof under which the objects lay; the beams were numbered 1–10 from east to west (the two outermost cross-beams overlay the end walls and did not span the hollow of the grave). Some of the offerings had been badly shattered and crushed by the fall of the roof; others, close to the wall face and protected by the slanting beam fragments from the inrush of rubble, were almost intact. Shreds of loosely woven white cloth clung to some of them. At the time of excavation it was assumed that they had been wrapped in cloth, but it now seems more probable that these shreds were remnants of the hangings of similar cloth in front of the face of the south wall of the tomb.

There was evidence for a long table with a painted top at the southeast corner of the tomb, its length extending along the south wall. Over the whole area beneath beams 1–4 at the south side were traces of color above the floor and separated from it by a thin layer of wood different from that of the floor itself—probably the table top. The colors noted were white, red, and yellow, but the whole was so mutilated and discontinuous that the painted design could not be made out except for what appeared to be part of a large ring or circle of red on a white ground. The limits of the area in which color was found suggested dimensions for the table top of about 1.50 by 0.80 m.[13]

Probably a second table, smaller than the first, had stood against the south wall of the tomb to the west of the first. Evidence for this was even less clear: one furniture leg was found in this area that seemed to have no relation to any of the pieces in the southeast corner, and fragments of legs to match were found during screening. A large number of bowls and other vessels of bronze found under cover beams 7–9 had obviously fallen to the positions they occupied. Two of the bronze bowls were found one within the other, and the glass bowl (TumP 48) lay broken inside a third. It seemed evident that these bowls had once been stacked one inside the other. Thus it would seem likely that the mass of objects found along the south side of the chamber had originally rested on top of one or other of two tables set against its south wall.

The southwest corner of the tomb was occupied by a mass of wooden furniture somewhat broken but with many of the fragments in a relatively good state of preservation, probably because the two westernmost cover timbers, 9 and 10, had merely cracked rather than snapped off at the wall face and fallen. They lay slanted down into the tomb, giving some protection to the objects in the corner underneath. The chief pieces here were the screen (TumP 151) and the stools or footstools (TumP 157 and 158). These to a great extent had fallen apart into their constituent pieces, and they required considerable study later on at the depot for their reconstruction. The screen at the time was called a "throne back" and the leg that supported it from behind, a "canopy holder."[14] The object itself was unprecedented and its reconstruction highly tentative; but the finding of two similar screens (MM 378 and 379 below) almost intact in the Great Tumulus the next year offered models

---

[13]The presence of a long, rectangular painted table in Tumulus P would appear to be still another "first" in Phrygian archaeology. At the time Tumulus P was dug, R. S. Young preferred the interpretation of the evidence as indicating a table, in spite of the fact that none of the wooden furniture legs scattered nearby could be assigned to it except for one possible example, TumP 156E (*q.v.*). This one leg would be sufficient and even suitable if one end and one side of the table were fastened firmly to the east and south walls of the tomb, if it were not for the fact that the GPH. of TumP 156E is only 0.23 m., whereas the H. of the boxlike object in the southeast corner (TumP 166) has been estimated at 0.34 m.

It appears that this interpretation of the evidence as a table causes a quandary. The reader's attention should, then, be brought to the evidence for paint on the wall of Tumulus W, found in 1959 (see p. 198) and one other Phrygian timber grave with painted wall decoration, as sources of an alternative solution to the problem. The latter was excavated in the Dinar district by H. Uçankuş; see *VIII. Türk Tarih Kongresi Ankara 11–15 Ekim 1976. Kongreye Sunulan Bildiriler I*, Ankara 1979 (Türk Tarih Kurumu Yayınları IX, 8), 305–334.

[14]R. S. Young, *AJA* 61 (1957): 326, 329–330 and pl. 95, fig. 35.

on which a less dubious reconstruction could be based. The seat slats of the stool, TumP 157, were found lying together but upside down—they had evidently turned over in falling—so that the remains of the purplish pink fabric (Fabric K, p. 309), which had covered the cushion on the seat, were underneath. For the details of the reconstruction of these wooden furnishings, see below in the catalogue.

Toward the south end of the west wall a brown-on-buff painted jug (TumP 57) stood on the floor. Large fragments of its body, which were not found, had evidently disappeared into the open gaps in the badly cracked timbers of the west wall.

The northwest corner of the room was occupied by a large bed (TumP 155), its head against the west wall. The dimensions, about 2.30 by 1.10 m., were roughly indicated by the positions at which the legs were found, one at each approximate corner, and by the somewhat warped and shrunken stretcher-rung that joined the legs at the head by the west wall. The lengthwise stretcher along the south side had disintegrated, but it had been of yellowish wood, and from this color its line could be traced over the floor nearly its entire length. The rest of the bed had also collapsed; its surface had evidently been of cloth or leather strips stretched between the frames. No certain traces of these strips were found, although there was a certain amount of cloth over the bed area. One small scrap still showed a checkerboard pattern in two colors—purplish and grayish blue—no doubt a fragment of the coverlet over the bed. Near the middle of the bed area (pl. 5B) lay a bronze fibula (TumP 37) with fragments of several more and a bronze belt (TumP 34). Those personal adornments had most probably been in wear on the body at the time of its entombment, and therefore, it is to be assumed that the body had been laid down near the center of the bed. Just beneath the belt was found a mass of dusty purplish stuff showing threads and evidently the remains of cloth, perhaps the dress in which the body was clothed. As no bones were found, it is impossible to surmise the posture of the body. In screening the debris from the immediate area, the hollow enamels of five human teeth were found; these were identified by Professor Muzaffer Şenyürek of the Ankara University as those of a child four to five years old—the sex of the child could not be determined from the teeth. But the pieced-together bronze belt

(TumP 34) confirmed the evidence of the teeth; it was 0.52 m. long when closed. Four- and five-year-old children of the modern village, caught and measured around the middle, closely fitted the circumference of the belt. One similar belt, TumP 35, was found on the bed to the northeast of the body and a second, TumP 36, was found on the floor beside the bed, probably having fallen from it when it collapsed. A pile of sheep astragals (TumP 44), found on the floor beside the bed, had probably once been contained in a bag or other holder; whether this had fallen from the bed or been placed on the floor beside it was not clear. One more object found within the circle of the belt (TumP 34) was called a "curtain rod" (TumP 165).[15] It is a polished rod of carved wood now much bent but probably straight originally. It is notched at regular intervals; in one notch a strap of leather remains in place around it, the ends fastened together by a triple row of stitching, evidently holding the edge of a cloth hanging between its ends. But this remains enigmatic; it is hard to imagine what hangings of cloth would have been over the bed, how and where their holder may have been fastened, and why it should have fallen precisely to the spot occupied by the child's body.[16]

The cloth or leather surface of the bed had disappeared entirely, and the objects that had been on the bed directly overlay those that had been underneath. Those were for the most part the black polished dinoi (TumP 79–87, pl. 5B), which were low enough to fit easily beneath the bed, for the legs of the bed were 0.38 m. high with the cuttings to hold the ends of the frame at the top. A substance thinly caked to the surface of the inside of the bowls presumably was food offered in the bowls at the time of burial.

To the east of the bed and the table (pl. 6A), by its foot, the end of the grave was occupied by a mass of closed and semiclosed pots, amphoras, and kraters of coarse and black polished ware. Presumably these had once contained offerings of liquid to wash down the solid food in the bowls under the bed. Among these pots, which stood upright on the floor, lay two large objects of iron (TumP 41, 42) of unknown use. A bifurcated ob-

---

[15] *Ibid.*, 327 and pl. 92, fig. 22.

[16] See below, p. 76, n. 146, where it is suggested that TumP 165 is a fan handle. [Ed.]

ject like TumP 41 was found in K-III and identified as "fire tongs,"[17] but as neither the iron "tongs" from Tumulus K-III nor TumP 41 is hinged at the junction of the two arms to the handle, it is difficult to see how they could have been used as tongs.

In the southern part of this area at the east end of the tomb (pl. 6B) were found the bronze quadriga (TumP 40) and some smaller pottery vessels of fine wares. These had probably fallen from the painted table at the southeast corner.

In addition to the major pieces of furniture mentioned above, the tomb must have contained more tables and stools of which fragments were recovered. There was a superfluity of furniture legs of assorted types and sizes (TumP 156 below), many of which could not be assigned. In many cases fragments of legs to match well-preserved ones could be recognized, but as it was not possible to tell how many legs were represented by these fragments, it was impossible to know whether they had belonged to two-, three-, or four-legged pieces of furniture.

We must assume that a young child sent to the other world accompanied by so many and such elaborate grave gifts was a child of some status— a young prince (or princess) of the royal family. Even if the tomb itself was not made for the child (a possibility mentioned above), the piling of the tumulus over the burial was done after the interment, and the piling of a mound 12 m. high was not a small undertaking. Again, the rich and varied offerings placed in the grave (fig. 5) must have been the possessions of the child during its life— the wooden toy animals, the tiny bronze quadriga, the painted and black polished vessels in the form of animals and birds, the bronze belts which could be adjusted in size by moving the end clasp— those, too, argue a child of outstanding wealth and status. Such a child, we take it, would have lived and died before the Kimmerian invasion of the be-

ginning seventh century. After the catastrophe, there would not have been the labor available to heap a tumulus of this size. Further, after the catastrophe there would have been no personal possessions left to bury with their owner; all would have been burned up in the destruction of the palace in the city.

Actually, close counterparts to objects found in the child's tomb were also found (burned) in the destruction levels of the palace in the Phrygian city, notably askoi painted overall with checkerboard pattern[18] like TumP 51–53. The child must have been buried at some time near the destruction, but before it, and if (with A. Körte)[19] we accept the earlier date (that of Eusebius, 696 B.C.) for the Kimmerian raid as the more probable approximation, we would date the burial around 700. This is the generally accepted approximate date for the burial in Tumulus K-III; and many close parallels between objects from P and K-III suggest that they should fall rather close to each other in time. The only object helpful for chronology found in the tomb itself is the glass bowl (TumP 48); this seems definitely to be of Sargonid times and is tentatively attributed by A. von Saldern to a "royal glass factory" at Nimrud.[20] In any case it was an import to Gordion, but not the only one: the vessels of blue paste or covered with blue glaze (TumP 45–47) came probably from the Levantine coast, and the black-on-red painted jug (TumP 59) from Cyprus. In the years before the burial trade routes to east and south were open and, one must assume, not yet disrupted by raiding Kimmerians.

Ionian bronze belts found at Emporio on Chios in levels dated to 690–660 B.C.,[21] imitations or adaptations of the Phrygian type of TumP 34–36, also suggest that the routes to the west, Lydia, and the coast remained open in the closing years of the eighth century and the first years of the seventh. Gordion, then, was still intact at the time this burial was made, and in touch with the outer world.

---

[17]G. Körte in *Gordion*, 81, no. 105 and fig. 70,*f*.

[18]E.g., P 2364, pl. 96G.

[19]*Gordion*, 20, 23.

[20]See p. 32 below, under TumP 48, and n. 65.

[21]J. Boardman, *Anatolia* 6 (1961): 179 ff.

CATALOGUE

BRONZE

LARGE CAULDRONS WITHOUT HANDLES
TumP 1, 2

The large cauldron, TumP 1, stood on an iron tripod ring stand near the center of the tomb (pl. 5A). Into it had been packed all the small wooden animals and utensils; there was no evidence that it had ever had a cover as did the cauldron in K-III,[22] which also was packed with small objects. The collapse of the tomb roof had crushed the cauldron down over its more rigid ring stand, so that the round area of its bottom within the ring was at a level only slightly lower than the rim, the wall forming a hollow circular cylinder around it. The wooden objects packed inside the cauldron were to some extent protected by it.

The smaller cauldron, TumP 2, lay bottom up against the south wall, beneath the eighth roof beam; it contained nothing. As the beams at the west end of the tomb (nos. 8–10) had not snapped off at the south wall face but had broken farther out, they lay slanted downward from the top of the south wall to the floor of the tomb, and the objects under them were not crushed, though they may have been somewhat displaced by the inrush of small stones from above. But it is possible that TumP 2 lay as it had been placed in the tomb.

TumP 1 **Large cauldron without handles**
B 701   Just east of center
GPH. 0.28 GPD. 0.715 m.
Pl. 5A

Condition crushed as noted above. Several holes and cracks and a large area of corrosion precluded cleaning, and therefore all details could not be seen. The fabric heavy and probably cast. The original shape must have been much like that of TumP 2 with rounded bottom and thickened rim flat on top and slightly everted. No trace of attachments for handles.

TumP 2 **Large cauldron without handles**
B 696   South wall, upside down
under beam 8.
H. 0.30 D. 0.495 m.
Pl. 7B

Intact, except for small holes made by corrosion and missing iron necking band. Squat profile, rounded bottom, thickened rim flat on top and slightly everted. The rim appears to have been a hoop of bronze added to a cast cauldron. A 0.02-m.-wide strip of iron rust all around the neck at the base of the rim suggests that the cauldron at one time had an iron collar. At least eight small round holes in the neck, a few of which are filled with bronze rivets, indicate the means by which the collar was attached.

The iron collar may have been intended merely to strengthen the rim, or it could have carried handles, presumably of iron. Although there is no concrete evidence, the iron band fragments, ILS 754 *A, B* and iron ring handle, ILS 753, may have been part of the cauldron's missing attachments.[23]

Possibly the iron collar was a later addition or repair. Four bronze cauldrons from Tumulus K-III (nos. 49–52) and a deep bowl (no. 58) had ring handles of iron, which G. Körte suggests were repairs, replacements of bronze originals.[24] An iron necking band completely encircling the rim of a large bronze bowl (no. 56) was also found in K-III. In addition, iron ring handles and collars partially encircling bronze vessels have been found on the city mound and in other tumuli at Gordion.[25]

RING-HANDLED SMALL CAULDRONS
WITH T-SHAPED ATTACHMENTS
TumP 3–5

The pair of small cauldrons, TumP 3 and 4, was found beside the south wall of the tomb, be-

---

[22]G. Körte in *Gordion*, 68–69, no. 49.

[23]See pp. 28–29.

[24]*Gordion*, 70 (no. 50) and 92 for further discussion.

[25]See p. 29, n. 49.

neath the ninth roof beam. The broken specimen, TumP 5, was also at the south side, crushed by the fourth roof beam which had fallen on it. The wooden carrying stick was found in three pieces but with one end still in place, passing through one of the upturned handles. The stick, of box-wood,[26] was roughly pared to a square section and was preserved to a length of 0.14 m.; one end was missing. Its position showed how these cauldrons were carried about when full and suggests that TumP 5 had contents of some sort when it was offered in the grave.

TumP 3 **Ring-handled small cauldron with T-shaped attachments**
  B 691 South wall, under beam 9
  H. 0.17 D. rim 0.145 D. 0.22
    W. rim 0.007 m.
  Pl. 8A–C

Intact. Fairly heavy fabric, probably cast. Deep rounded body with wall meeting shoulder at a sharpened curve above, and shallow convex bottom at a sharpened curve below. The rim, made in one with the body, thickened and flat on top. The handle attachments flat T-shaped plates cast together with the vertical carrying sockets at their crossings; the end of each arm fastened to the wall by a dowel with a round stud head outside, the other end flattened to a rivet head on the inside. The handles, bronze rods round in section, passed through the sockets, and then bent to circular rings, their ends opposed but not completely closed.

TumP 4 **Ring-handled small cauldron with T-shaped attachments**
  B 692 Along south wall
  H. 0.17 D. rim 0.145 D. 0.22
    W. rim. 0.007 m.

Intact. Exactly like TumP 3; the handle attachments slightly smaller. The two small cauldrons were evidently made and used as a pair.

TumP 5 **Ring-handled small cauldron with T-shaped attachments**
  B 702 South side
  H. 0.14 D. *ca.* 0.22 m.
  Pl. 8D

Once badly crushed; corroded; portions of the wall have been restored. Similar to TumP 3 and 4 but

---

[26]See p. 290, app. III-A, Sample 2.

shallower. Each arm of the T-shaped attachment ends in a disk, which leaves a margin around the edge of the rather large stud heads of the dowels; otherwise the attachments are like those of TumP 3 and 4. The position and nature of the carrying stick have been noted above.

SMALL JUGS WITH TREFOIL MOUTH
TumP 6, 7
(See also pp. 224–227.)

The two small jugs with trefoil mouth were found on the floor at the southwest corner of the tomb.

TumP 6 **Small jug with trefoil mouth**
  B 728 Southwest corner, under
    beam 9
  H-h. 0.18 D. 0.128 m.
  Fig. 6; Pl. 8E, F

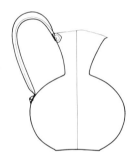

Figure 6. TumP 6. Small bronze jug with trefoil mouth. 1:5.

Intact; the surface pitted and discolored by corrosion. Flat bottom and squat globular body, meeting the funnel-shaped neck at a sharp angle above the slightly pointed shoulder. Plain trefoil mouth, not thickened at the lip. The fabric is apparently thin. Although there is no trace of a seam at the shoulder, it seems probable that the vessel was hammered in two pieces—neck and body—and joined. On the base, which is not an exact circle, hammer marks show at the edge and bottom; evidently the base was a flat, hammered disk attached by brazing or by solder. Folded handle of two plates; at its lower end the outer plate terminates in a rounded tab hammered up at the center to a stud-shaped knob. A pin, its flattened end showing in the knob, fastens it to the wall. At the top, two rounded tabs hammered up to round knobs like the one at the bottom, on the front above the rim; at the back added round studs. The ends of the fastening pins show in the faces of both of the knobs at the front and of the studs at the back.

TumP 7   Small jug with trefoil mouth
B 729   Southwest corner, under
beam 9
H-h. 0.125   D. 0.095 m.
Pl. 8G

Small holes eaten by corrosion; surface, however, in excellent condition, preserving final finish. Similar to TumP 6; smaller. A low raised base set off by a surrounding groove; probably a seam at this point. The handle of two plates folded together; both end at the bottom in round tabs pinned to the wall by a stud. At the top, double tabs also fastened by studs at the front, the flattened ends of their pins at the back.

<h2 style="text-align:center">LADLES
TumP 8, 9
(See also pp. 227–229.)</h2>

TumP 8   Ladle
B 730   Southwest corner
L. to top of h. 0.215   D. bowl 0.085 m.
Pl. 8H

Corrosion has caused holes in the back of the bowl and a nick in the side of the tang. Thin fabric; bowl, tang, and handle made in one piece, apparently by hammering. Shallow round bowl with nearly square tang rising above its rim at the back; the upper edge of the tang slightly convex, rising toward the center where the thin flat handle, recurved at the top, rises from it. The end of the handle slightly flared.

TumP 9   Ladle
B 731   South side, under beam 8
L. to top of h. 0.235   D. bowl 0.09 m.
Fig. 7; Pl. 8I

Broken into several pieces and mended; corrosion has eaten holes in the bowl. Shallow round bowl of rather heavy fabric, probably cast. Handle and tang cast in separate pieces and joined, probably by soldering.

The tang a disk, cast, with *à jour* decoration: at either side a lunette, around the center triangles (four above and five below) leaving rays around an inner disk. A flat raised border around the outer edge and the side lunettes; the rest thinner, and flat.

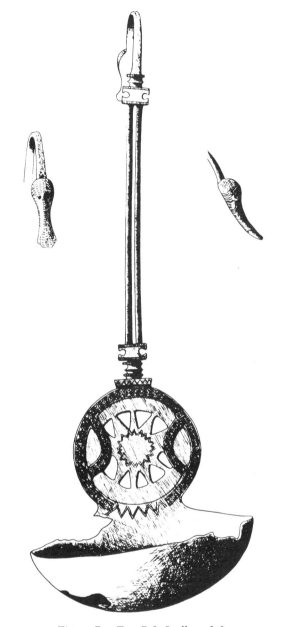

Figure 7. TumP 9. Ladle. 2:3.

The raised borders show stamped decoration: a triangular punch was used to make impressions in groups of four, all pointed toward a common center to make together a raised design like X's in squares. The uneven surface at the back reflects the punched decoration of the front face. The flat inner disk within the rays decorated by incised zigzag. Incised zigzag also decorates the neck where bowl and tang join, interrupting the border pattern of the tang, and also the oblong block which makes the transition from the circular tang to the handle above.

13

The handle consists of two long parallel rods of bronze, round in section, terminated above and below by groups of moldings into which the ends of the rods were probably socketed; at the bottom a block pierced at either edge by a round hole from front to back, and below it three reels—a sharp central one between blunt heavier ones, their edges milled; at the top a second block pierced by holes at the edges and above it a sharp reel and a heavier one with milled edge.

The elbow and upper end of the handle a thin flat strip of bronze, recurved and ending in a cast bird head. The deeply punched sockets suggest that the eyes were originally inlaid with some material now lost; the feathers of the head are represented by grooves made with a curved punch. The long, wide bill suggests that of a duck or a goose.

BASIN WITH LIFTING HANDLES
TumP 10

TumP 10

> B 895   Leaning against south
> wall, under beam 9
> H.-rim 0.082   H.-h. 0.125
> D. rim 0.315 m.
> Pl. 8J, K

Not cleaned. Much corrosion; part of the rim eaten away. Wide shallow bowl with convex bottom; the lip thickened to 0.0035 m. and flat on top. The handles, rods of bronze round in section bent upward near their ends, then across to form a nearly horizontal lifting bar. The handles seem to have been made separately from their flat attachment plates; there are traces of seams at the bases of the handles. The plates are flat, narrow strips of bronze rounded at the ends, each attached outside the rim by three bronze pins, one at the center, and one near each end. The outer ends of the pins were hammered to flat rivet heads; the inner ends were capped by round stud heads, of which only one remains in place, while the outlines of all the others are visible on the surface of the bronze inside the rim.

BOWLS
TumP 11–30

All the bronze bowls were found along the south wall of the tomb and in its western half, especially under the last three roof beams (8–10) at the southwest. They lay in all conceivable positions as they had fallen, probably from a wooden table against the south wall. It is likely that they had been stacked originally one inside the other; the glass bowl (TumP 48) was found inside one of the bronze bowls. They had also been wrapped in coarse, netlike linen cloth, either individually or by stacks; bits of the linen adhered to the rims of some, and on others the netlike pattern of the fabric left an imprint still visible even after cleaning. Of the eighteen omphalos bowls (TumP 11–28; see also pp. 233–236), one was knobbed (TumP 11), one ribbed on the inside (TumP 12), the rest plain with four or three raised ridges around the base of the omphalos. In addition, there were two plain bowls without omphalos (TumP 29, 30) found together with the omphalos bowls in the same part of the tomb.

OMPHALOS BOWLS
TumP 11–28

TumP 11   **Knobbed omphalos bowl**
> B 725   South side, under beam 10
> H. 0.055   D. 0.141   D. omph.
> 0.018 m.
> Fig. 8A–C; Pl. 9A–C

Eaten and discolored by corrosion; holes in one side. The shape basically hemispherical, with a vertical rim thickened to a flat lip 0.003 m. thick on top. The outer face of the rim shows five shallow parallel grooves running around it; the inner face plain. The small omphalos is less than hemispherical and flattened on top, with a compass prick at the center. It rests on a low, raised platform decorated by two ridges, triangular in profile, around the inner edge. High relief decoration in two zones on the wall: it appears as knobs on the outside, hollows inside. The flat bottom (outside) tongued around its perimeter by 12 radiating tongues; between these the lower points of 12 long diamond-shaped petals; over the tongues and between the upper parts of the petals 12 large drop-shaped knobs, their points downward. In the upper zone 12 much larger drop-shaped knobs in very high relief, their points downward. Between each pair of these a set of three small petals—a larger one with the point downward between the upward-pointed ends of the two others, set at a lower level. The fabric of the bowl is fairly heavy and the relief decoration quite regular, suggesting that the bowl was cast rather than hammered repoussé; and the grooving of the outside of the rim (not engraved) which does not appear on the inner face would seem to bear out this suggestion.

14

A

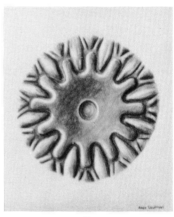

B

C

Figure 8. TumP 11. Knobbed omphalos bowl. A. From side. B. Base. C. Section through floor. 2:5.

TumP 12   **Ribbed omphalos bowl**
        B 724   South side, under beams
        8, 9
        H. 0.044   D. rim. 0.182   D. omph.
        0.027 m.
        Pl. 9D, E

About one-third of the wall and rim missing at one side through corrosion. Heavy fabric; the outside perfectly smooth. Wide, shallow bowl with wall curving continuously to the lip. The omphalos hemispherical, somewhat flared at its base. Three compass pricks on top, all off-center. Around its base three ridges triangular in profile, the outermost wider and shallower than the others. Beyond a narrow flat floor begins the fluted decoration of the wall: eight wide, shallow, concave horizontal flutes or grooves to the rim, evenly spaced, leaving between (and above) them eight low, rounded, horizontal ridges.

TumP 13   **Plain omphalos bowl**
        B 693   South side
        H. 0.046   D. rim 0.153   D. omph.
        0.029 m.

Small holes and cracks in wall. The outside plain; traces of a seam are visible on the bottom where omphalos and ridges were joined to the body of the bowl. Heavy fabric. Omphalos shallow, hemispherical, with a compass prick on top. Around its base four fine, sharp ridges, triangular in profile. Resembles TumP 14, pl. 9F, G.

TumP 14   **Plain omphalos bowl**
        B 694   South side
        H. 0.051   D. rim 0.185   D. omph.
        0.027 m.
        Pl. 9F, G

Small holes eaten by corrosion. Heavy fabric. Omphalos hemispherical, slightly flattened on top. Around its base four sharp ridges, triangular in profile.

TumP 15   **Plain omphalos bowl**
        B 710   South side, under beam 8
        H. 0.05   D. rim 0.173   D. omph.
        0.03 m.

Corrosion holes in wall at one side. Heavy fabric. Omphalos hemispherical, slightly flared at base; a compass prick at center on top. Around it four sharp ridges triangular in profile. Resembles TumP 14, pl. 9F, G.

TumP 16   **Plain omphalos bowl**
        B 711   South side, under beam 8
        H. 0.055   D. rim 0.178   D. omph.
        0.033 m.
        Pl. 10A

Several large corrosion holes in wall. Omphalos hemispherical, somewhat flared at its base; a central compass prick on top. Four ridges triangular in profile, the outermost larger than the others.

TumP 17   **Plain omphalos bowl**
        B 712   South side, under beams
        8–10
        H. 0.04   D. rim 0.16   D. omph.
        0.035 m.

A large hole in the wall at one side. Omphalos hemispherical. Four sharp triangular ridges as above. Resembles TumP 16, pl. 10A.

TumP 18   **Plain omphalos bowl**
B 713   South side, under beams
8–10
H. 0.04   D. rim 0.16   D. omph.
0.035 m.

About two thirds of the body eaten away by corrosion. Omphalos shallow hemispherical, a compass prick on top. Four sharp ridges as above. Resembles TumP 16, pl. 10A.

TumP 19   **Plain omphalos bowl**
B 714   South side, under beams
8–10
H. 0.045   D. rim 0.142   D. omph.
0.024 m.

A large piece of wall and rim at one side eaten away. Omphalos hemispherical, a compass prick on top. Four ridges as above. Resembles TumP 16, pl. 10A.

TumP 20   **Plain omphalos bowl**
B 715   South side, under beams
8–10
H. 0.054   D. rim 0.144   D. omph.
0.026 m.
Pl. 10B, C

Small corrosion holes. Bowl somewhat deeper than the others, and slightly inward-turned toward the rim. Shallow omphalos, flattened on top; a compass prick at the center. Four sharp ridges, triangular in profile. On the outside at the bottom traces of a seam where body is joined to omphalos and ridges.

TumP 21   **Plain omphalos bowl**
B 716   South side, under beams
8–10
H. 0.045   D. rim. 0.157   D. omph.
0.032 m.
Pl. 10D

Corrosion holes in wall. Omphalos shallow hemispherical, a compass prick on top. The innermost ridge larger than the others and somewhat rounded; the outermost pointed but wider and shallower than the central two.

TumP 22   **Plain omphalos bowl**
B 717   South side, under beams
8–10
H. 0.034   D. rim 0.171   D. omph.
0.033 m.
Pl. 10E, F

Small holes eaten by corrosion. The bowl very shallow and flat-bottomed. Omphalos shallow hemispherical, the top somewhat flattened; a compass prick on the under side. Around its base three ridges triangular in profile but blunted at the top.

TumP 23   **Plain omphalos bowl**
B 718   South side, under beams
8–10
H. 0.045   D. rim 0.173   D. omph.
0.032 m.

A large corrosion hole at one side. Bowl deeper than TumP 22, and not so much flattened at the bottom. Omphalos hemispherical. Three ridges triangular in profile, blunted at the top.

TumP 24   **Plain omphalos bowl**
B 719   South side, under beams
8–10
H. 0.043   D. rim 0.162   D. omph.
0.031 m.

The rim partly eaten away by corrosion. Traces visible of a seam at the bottom where omphalos and ridges were joined to the bowl. Omphalos shallow hemispherical, a compass prick on top. The three ridges triangular, the tops blunted.

TumP 25   **Plain omphalos bowl**
B 720   South side
H. 0.05   D. rim 0.161   D. omph.
0.029 m.
Pl. 10G, H

Intact; surface pitted by corrosion. Traces of a seam on the bottom, as on TumP 24; also marks left by cloth. Omphalos shallow hemispherical, a compass prick on top. Three ridges, the inner two triangular in profile and rather sharp, the outermost coarser and more rounded.

TumP 26   **Plain omphalos bowl**
B 721   South side, under beams
8–10
H. 0.043   D. rim 0.146   D. omph.
0.027 m.

Intact; surface pitted. Omphalos shallow hemispherical with compass prick on top. Three ridges as on TumP 25.

TumP 27   **Plain omphalos bowl**
B 722   South side, under beams
8–10
H. 0.045   D. rim 0.18   D. omph.
0.03 m.

Cracked; the surface badly pitted. Omphalos hemispherical, small. Ridges as on TumP 25 and 26.

16

TumP 28   **Plain omphalos bowl**
  B 723   South side, under beams
  8–10
  H. 0.045   D. rim 0.158   D. omph.
  0.023 m.

About half the bowl eaten away by corrosion. A seam visible on the bottom where omphalos and rings were joined to the bowl. Omphalos small, hemispherical flattened at top; a central compass prick. Three ridges triangular in profile, sharp at their tops.

PLAIN BOWLS
TumP 29, 30

TumP 29   **Plain bowl**
  B 726   South side, under beams
  8–10
  H. 0.045   D. rim. 0.145 m.
  Pl. 10I

A hole eaten by corrosion at one side; the surface pitted. Heavy fabric, probably made by casting. Shallow bowl with continuously curving walls and bottom. A compass prick at center of floor inside; a small round hole drilled just below the lip, probably for suspension by a string or wire.

TumP 30   **Plain bowl**
  B 727   South side, under beams
  8–10
  H. 0.044   D. rim 0.123 m.
  Pl. 10J

Most of the lip eaten away by corrosion, heavy fabric. Similar to TumP 29, but without a central compass prick and a suspension hole below the lip.

RING HANDLES FOR WOODEN BOWLS
TumP 31–33
(Compare also TumP 145–147,
and see pp. 229–233.)

Two bronze handles (TumP 31, 32) were found near the southeast corner of the tomb and the third (TumP 33) nearby. They had evidently been attached to bowls of wood, which had perished; compare TumP 145, 146 below, where similar bronze handles preserve bits of wooden bolsters which can be assigned to wooden bowls found with them. The handles, oval in contour and flattened at the top where there is a gap between the two ends,

were evidently intended to swivel freely around a half-bolster from which they were suspended at their ends. (Compare the bronze bowls MM 55–69).

TumP 31 and 32 are probably a pair from the same bowl (possibly TumP 147 to which handles could not definitely be assigned).

Compare also the pair of bronze handles, TumW 24.

TumP 31   **Ring handle for wooden bowl**
  B 735   Southeast quarter
  W. 0.095 m.
  Pl. 10K (*L*)

One end of handle slightly bent, pulled out. See TumP 32.

TumP 32   **Ring handle for wooden bowl**
  B 736   Southeast quarter
  W. 0.09 m.
  Pl. 10K (*R*)

Good condition. Bronze rod round in section, bent to oval ring. The ends opposed and straightened, with a gap between, for setting into sockets at either end of a bolster.

TumP 33   **Ring handle for wooden bowl**
  B 737   Southeast quarter
  W. 0.105 m.

Similar to TumP 31, 32; slightly larger. One end broken and mended. No mate was found; perhaps from a bowl with only one handle.

BELTS
TumP 34–36
(See also pp. 236–240.)

Three bronze belts were found in the area of the bed in the northwest part of the tomb. One (TumP 34) lay at the center of the bed; with it was a fibula (TumP 37), and presumably both had been worn on the body of the child at the time of its burial. The second, TumP 35, lay near the northeast corner of the bed; and the third, TumP 36, was on the floor just to the south of the bed.

All are narrow strips of very thin bronze once no doubt flexible but now become very brittle. They had been lined on the inner face with leather; pieces of this lining were found clinging to all

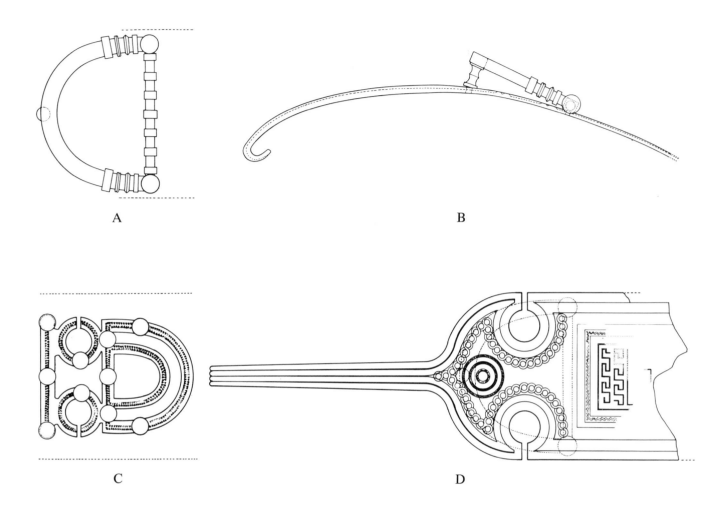

Figure 9. TumP 34. Fragmentary bronze belt. A. Handle. B. Profile of hook with handle in position. C. Catch-plate. D. Hook and belt end. E. Engraved decoration on a selected fragment from the central portion of belt. 2:3.

three. The leather had been secured in place by sewing it to the bronze along both edges; although only TumP 36 preserves the rows of holes for sewing at the edges, the other two showed traces of them when they were first found. The many perforations close together at the edges weakened the bronze, which was for the most part broken away at their line. At one end the thin bronze was rounded and thickened to provide the base for a long hook turned under at its end. Just above the base of the hook a fibula-like handle pinned to the surface of the belt offered a bar to pull for loosening or tightening the clasp. The handle, fastened at its ends flush to the face of the belt, was supported at its center by a short prop holding it away from the face so that the fingers might get a firm grip. Near the other end a plate of thin bronze, cut *à jour* and pinned to the face of the belt, served as a clasp into which to fasten the hook, with two or three alternative bars for tightening or loosening. The outer faces of all the belts were covered with decoration of various kinds of geometric pattern in finest engraving, which runs at one end as far as the base of the hook; it must have been done before the handles were pinned in place. At the other end the engraved decoration should stop at the inner edge of the catch-plates; the belt surface beyond these is not decorated, and the belts continue, with blank outer faces, for some distance (0.20–0.30 m.) beyond the outer edges of the catch-plates. In wear, these plain ends were evidently overlapped by the hook-ends of the belts. With the hook fastened in the "eye" of the clasp, the circuit of the belts was 0.52–0.54 m. when worn; their total length (including the overlapped ends and the hooks) from 0.75 to 0.95 m.

TumP 34   **Belt**

      B 739   Central group on bed
      W. 0.067   GPL. *ca.* 0.52 m.
      Fig. 9; Pls. 5B, 11A, 12A

Handle: flat fibula shape, an adaptation of Blinkenberg Group XII,7. Reels between blocks at both ends, above spherical knobs which are pinned underneath to the surface of the belt. Running between these a bar with squared blocks at regular intervals. The prop that supports the corner of the arc a double spool in profile.

Hook: a triple groove on its upper face.

Belt end: rounded below base of hook; at each side, where the curve begins, a round hole through

the bronze with an open slot running from it to the edge.

Decoration under handle: a running single-strand guilloche outlines the edge, and three concentric circles engraved with double zigzag decorate the center above the base of the hook.

Catch-plate: two arches, one within the other; below these two rings slotted at the sides, and a straight base. Ten pins with round stud heads fasten plate to belt: three across the bottom, two at the inner sides of the rings opposite the slots; three across the base of the double arch; and two at the sides of the outer arches. The faces of the bronze bars have punched decoration of two rows of tiny triangles, opposed. The inner arch, and the upper part of the outer, bent slightly upward so that the end of the hook can pass underneath.

Engraved decoration: a running guilloche sets off the edges at top and bottom. Between these a wide zone bordered by a double zigzag. Within this frame panels, alternating double oblong and square bordered by zigzag. Within the panels variations of meander and meander hook patterns set vertically or diagonally, multiple lozenges, swastika, etc.

TumP 35   **Belt**

      B 740   Northeast corner of bed
      W. 0.055   GPL. *ca.* 0.95 m.
      Fig. 10; Pls. 5B (upper *R*), 11B, 12B

The end of the undecorated part broken away. The catch is pinned over the end of the decoration; but a zigzag between lines across the width farther out on the undecorated surface suggests that this catch was intended to be set with reference to it, but was shifted back to fit the wearer.

Handle: flat fibula shape, again of Group XII,7 type with a reel between blocks at the ends, the faces of the blocks decorated with zigzag. Below these were flat round tangs for fastening to the belt by stud-headed pins.

Hook: two slightly raised flat bands down the center, with a groove between them.

Belt end: shallow concavities at either side, curving up to the base of the hook; below, open circles at each side with arcs cut off by the edges of the belt.

Decoration under handle: between side openings and base of hook, a six-pointed rosette, the petals compass-drawn in double outline, within a circle; the space between the petals filled by triangles alternately plain and with pricked decoration. Above the side openings small half circles decorated with zigzag; another, larger, at the base of the belt-end.

Catch-plate: at the end two arcs, one within the other; below, two oblongs, each divided by crossbars into narrow side panels and a wide central one. In each central opening a flat ring, free at its outer end. The whole fastened to the belt by three rivets across its inner end. This plate offers three, perhaps four, "eyes" for fastening the hook.

Engraved decoration: two bands of triple zigzag, separated by a hatched line, along each edge. At the hook end an oblong panel filled by a large quintuple zigzag, hatched. Below, square panels alternate with pairs of bars filled by multiple zigzag. The square panels filled by complicated meanders and meander-like patterns, usually set diagonally (see fig. 10).

TumP 36   Belt
B 741   Floor, south of bed
W. 0.042   L. *ca.* 0.75 m.
Fig. 11; Pl. 12C, D

The plain overlapped end rounded. The catch set to cover part of the last panel of engraved decoration; a break just below this leaves a gap, which forbids exact measurement of the length. Again the catch would seem to have been placed with reference to the circumference of the wearer.

Handle: fibula-like, with flat back and two flat planes meeting at a ridge at the center of the front. High cylindrical moldings at the ends, with flat round tangs below for fastening. The molding decorated with fine wavy engraved lines to represent hair, above a pair of eyes: animal heads are represented, apparently holding in their mouths the fastening tangs below—compare ladle TumW 8. Pins with round stud heads fasten the tangs to the belt.

Hook: semicircular cutouts at either side of the end of the belt leave points at their outer ends where they meet the curved sides of the inner part of the hook. The face of the hook divided by a narrow groove to two flat surfaces curving apart at the inner end; the depressed triangle between bordered by double zigzags.

Belt end: squared off by engraved meander decoration running between the studs which fasten the

handle. The section above this with the semicircular bites at the sides would seem to have been thought of as part of the hook.

Decoration under handle: double zigzag around the edge; half circle of checkerboard at end of belt; on lower part of hook a compass-drawn rosette with six petals within a circle; space between the petals filled by hatching.

Catch-plate: a double arc at the top, two single loops below; rounded projections at each side. Fastened at the base by two stud-headed pins.

Engraved decoration: the engraving much more careless and uneven than on the other two belts. A border of double zigzag between hatched lines all around; pairs of zigzag crossbars divide the belt into narrow and wide panels. In the narrow panels were rows of three round studs; the holes for their pins and the outline of their heads remain. In the wider panels hollow squares of hour glasses, lattice and single or double checkerboard; within these, meander pattern, swastikas, oblique checkerboard.

FIBULAE
TumP 37–39
(See also pp. 239–249.)

All the fibulae and fragments of fibulae were found in the area of the bed at the northwest corner of the tomb. Some of them may have been in wear on the body at the time of burial. Three fibulae of Blinkenberg's Group XII,3 survived in a condition fit for publication;[27] but in screening the fill from this area (broken wood from the roof and the bed) fragments (fig. 12) of eight more fibulae of the same subtype, but with double pins (compare TumW 27, 28 below, pl. 91B, C) were found, in every case the plate with the stubs of two pins, one above the other, and a fragment of the spring.[28] In addition, there were seven fragments

---

[27]The convention, following Blinkenberg, *Fibules* (1926) has been to illustrate fibulae with catch and spring at the bottom, whereas in actual wear, as on the İvriz Relief (Akurgal, *Phryg. Kunst,* text pl. C,1–2; *idem, Kunst Anat.,* 61, fig. 38), they appear with the bow hanging downward, catch and spring at the top. This is the position they would naturally take, the heavier part hanging down. Therefore, this modern convention of illustrating the fibulae upside down reverses the direction of their catches; and for this reason we have reversed the modern convention in illustrating the fibulae here.

For a general introduction to Blinkenberg's study of fibulae and his division into groups, types, and subtypes, please turn to pp. 239–242. Consult also Muscarella, *Phryg. Fib. Gordion,* 12–28.

[28]In fig. 12A, B, F, G there is evidence that, when the double pins point to the wearer's left, the spring is in the observer's sight between the inner end of the pin and the arc. This one might explain as an early aesthetic lack which was overcome in all pins (double and single) from Tumulus MM. [Ed.]

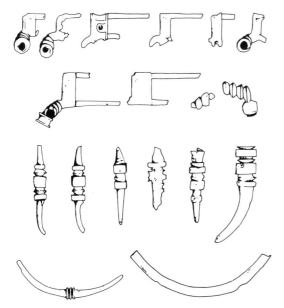

Figure 12. A selection from the uncatalogued fibula fragments.

preserving in part the opposite ends of the arcs with the catches, three ends of arcs with springs for single pins, four fragments of flat bows, and one of a bow round in section and with three moldings at the center of the arc—probably part of a Group XII,13 fibula. The fragments would seem to represent a minimum of fourteen fibulae in the tomb: eight springs with plates for double pins, six springs for single pins (including TumP 37–39). The catch and bow fragments could not be assigned; they may have belonged to the same fibulae as the spring fragments. The types represented in the burial were evidently XII,3 and XII,13.

GROUP XII,3
TumP 37–39

TumP 37 **Fibula**
B 732 Lying with belt on bed
H. 0.08 L. 0.09 m.
Pls. 5B, 12E

Mended from several fragments; spring and pin missing. Thin arc, oblong in section; at its ends squared blocks below triple-ridged tori which frame single reels. Catch at wearer's left.

TumP 38 **Fibula**
B 733 On floor beside bed
H. 0.08 L. 0.098 m.
Pl. 12F (back of fibula)

Corroded; pin and most of catch missing. Arc as on TumP 37; the end moldings three squared blocks, the central one cubical, separated by single reels. Catch at wearer's left.

TumP 39 **Fibula**
B 734 On floor beside bed
H. 0.065 L. 0.087 m.
Pl. 12G

Spring, pin, and part of the catch missing. End moldings like those of TumP 38, but smaller. Catch at left.

MINIATURE QUADRIGA*
TumP 40

TumP 40 **Miniature quadriga**
B 738 Southeast quarter, under
  beam 2
Horses: Ave. L. 0.05 H. 0.047 m.
Wheel: D. 0.045 m.
Strips *A* and *B*: L. 0.07 W. 0.01 m.
Strip *C*: PL. 0.099 W. 0.015 m.
Strip *D*: L. rectangular portion 0.088
  Max. dim. complete as bent 0.13
  W. 0.011 Th. at center 0.001
  Th. at other edges 0.002 m.
Figs. 13, 14A, B, 15A, B; Pls. 6B
  (center *R*), 13A–J

Preserved and found together were the four horses (the two at center yoked) standing with their feet riveted to two thin cross strips, *A* in front, *B* at rear, which are still attached to the slightly wider axial ground strip, *C* (fig. 13). Found loose, a third bronze strip, *D*, still preserving a long, thin hammered projection from each end. Also loose, two wheels, the left one, *E* and the right one, *F*. The horses and wheels are solid-cast of bronze; the strips are hammered. The draft pole, the undercarriage, and the box with its occupants, if any, were not found.

Detailed inspection showed that the crosspiece, *A,* is pierced by eight holes for rivets to secure the front feet of the horses. The second strip, *B*, has eight rivet holes for the hind feet; *A* and *B* are also fastened to the axial strip, *C*, by means of centrally located rivets

---

*Catalogue entry and discussion by Ellen L. Kohler.

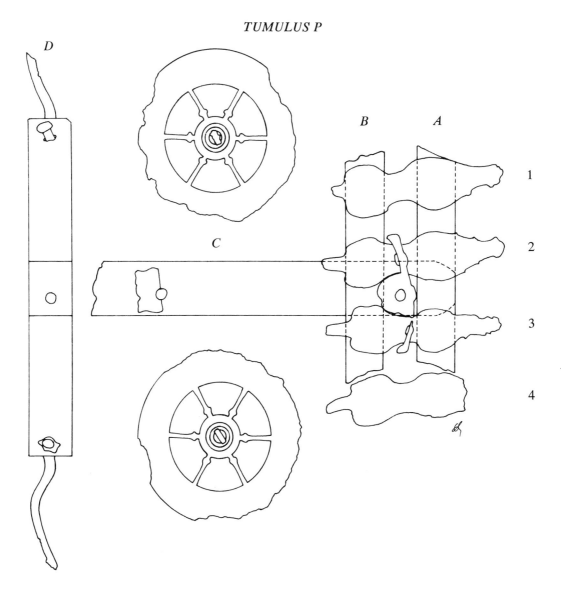

Figure 13. TumP 40. Miniature quadriga. The preserved pieces: horses 1 to 4 and strips A to D, top view, and the wheels, in the condition in which they were found. 1:1.

near the inner feet of the two center (yoked) horses. At the rear end on top of strip *C*, which is broken so that its original length is unknown, there is a remnant of another thinner, narrower, fragment of bronze sheet, with ends roughly broken away right near the rivet which fastens it down. The ends of the sheet were made to angle sharply up toward front and back (either originally, or at the time the chariot was torn from its base). If it is its original shape, then perhaps it had to do with supporting (from the ground) the underface of the quadriga box.

Strip *D* has a square sinking with a rivet hole at its center, and a rivet near each squarish end still holds a fragment of bronze sheet on the face where the sinking is, the sinking exactly fitting the width of Strip *C* and thus indicating that *D* may once have passed under it at the point where the rivet and sheet are located on strip *C*. An alternative crossing might be either under or over strip *C* farther back beyond the break in *C*. If such an alternative were considered and *D* were passed over *C*, the fragments of sheet on *D*, being turned downward, might indicate the material sheathing the plinth upon which the quadriga was fastened. However, the function of the hammered elongations on strip *C* remains essentially obscure.

The six-spoked wheels were cast in one with their naves, which were double-conical in profile with raised ridges around the inner and outer rims. The axle holes are still plugged by the remains of the

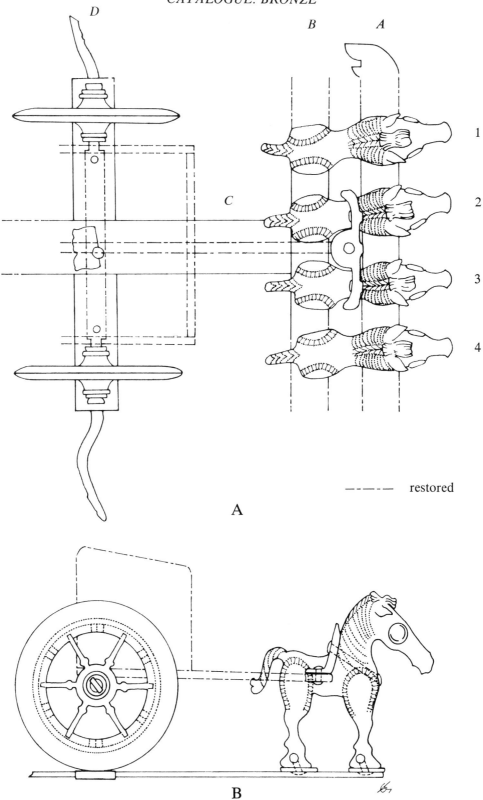

Figure 14. TumP 40. Miniature quadriga. A. Top view of group as restored with straight pole extending to axle. B. Side view of group in A with horses 3 and 4 removed to show pole-end, and yoke over horse 2.   1:1.

ends of the original axle, which was round where it went through the naves, but flat just at the inner end of each nave. Each flattened bit of axle shows where a rivet pierced next the nave, perhaps to make the axletree fast to the underside of the carriage assembly, with the result that the axle could not turn but the wheels could (freely in the air if the torn fragment on strip *C* is to be interpreted as the remains of a support mechanism). Perhaps the rivets continued through the carriage assembly into the floor of the box, if the box was not simply a removable piece. Both the inside and the outside faces of the wheel felloes have irregularly pricked decoration in the form of dotted lines to show the separation of spoke-piece from felloe, as well as tab-shaped incised indications of the clamps which fastened the inner spoke-rim to the felloe forming the outer rim. How the felloes are sectioned off is not shown.

The horses, standing four-square with no suggestion of motion, have short legs and bodies, and lifted short tails (or tails which were possibly knotted at the breaks). Their heads are large and very long with (where preserved) long pointed ears. Each horse has a knot of mane on top of its head and curving pendent lines to indicate the fall of the mane on the neck. Nostrils are hollowed; the eyes now represented by a hole running right through the width of the head, were each once filled by the ends of a bone peg, traces of which remain around the edges of several eyeholes. Bars of some contrasting material may have extended through the centers for the pupils. Various patterns of pricked surface decoration occur on the foreheads and all haunches and shoulders. The tails have pricked lines to show the hairs.

The tiny horses show no trace of harness except the yoke spanning the two at center; this yoke is a separately cut piece of hammered bronze sheet with a bent, tablike shelf extending outward toward the rear and is fastened across the two center horses by long rivets which extend through the breast of each. There is no trace of a draft pole to which the yoke may have been attached via the rivet-like bar which

runs downward from the center of the yoke's lower face, and which still has a fragment of thin sheet adhering to its lower end. Could this sheet be the remains of a metal cap probably once cylindrical and wrapped around the leading end of the pole?[29] The pole could have been straight, leading under the center of the lost box (fig. 111A), or it could have been a Y-pole, made of two bent poles leading to the two rivets on the axle just inside the wheel naves (fig. 15A, B).[30] Too much is lacking to allow any certain restoration of the draft pole or of the chariot box.

Contemporary examples of such a bronze miniature four-horse group do not seem to be extant. However, several separate aspects of the group are of interest in a comparative context.

The system of T-strips on the ground-line, providing a means of fastening the group down to something else, appears to have a very long tradition. One early example of such a T-strip arrangement is provided by the copper quadriga from Tel Agrab.[31] Here a one-man conveyance of the Early Dynastic III period (*ca.* 2500 B.C.) shows a very primitive sort of rig drawn by four asses. The driver stands on two treads over the axle and must clutch between his knees the heavy fleece-padded bar. In this case the T-strips occur under the front and hind feet of the four animals as in TumP 40, but there are two straps running back on the outside to support the wheels of the conveyance, and another across the rear between the wheels. The inner pair of asses was yoked, as on TumP 40, but all wore collars and an intricate harnessing system was preserved, whereby the driver carried reins to the inner pair of asses and the outer, trace, animals were fastened only to the outsides of the collars of the inner pair. The wheels were solid, made like those of the primitive country cart, with three parallel boards clamped together,[32] and had studded metal tires. The

---

[29]Actual pole caps, made of thin bronze sheet, were found in Tumulus E (B 115, 116) and Tumulus F (B 471).

[30]For a discussion of the triangular traction system, see J. Crouwel and M. A. Littauer in D. Collon *et al.,* "Bronze Chariot Group from the Levant in Paris," *Levant* 8 (1976): 75–78; for the possibility that some four-horse chariots of Assurnasirpal II employed the Y-pole system: Littauer and Crouwel, *AA* (1977): 3–6. Since TumP 40 shows no difference in height between the floor of the box and the pole rest on the yoke, the pole does not have to rise from box to yoke. A simple two-piece

Y-pole (fig. 15A) would have to be "steam-bent" in only one direction. A copy in bronze would follow this line. That the Phrygians at this period had knowledge of the steam-bending of wood is demonstrated by the curve of the "leg," TumP 151C (p. 64 and pl. 29E).

[31]H. Frankfort, *More Sculpture from the Diyala Region* (*OIP* 60) (Chicago, 1943), 12–13, 32, no. 310 and pls. 58–60. From the Shara Temple (Baghdad: Iraq Museum Ag. 36:150. Height 0.072 m.).

[32]S. Piggott, *Scientific American* 219 (July 1968): 82, 86; V. Gordon Childe in Singer *et al., Hist. Technol.,* 720.

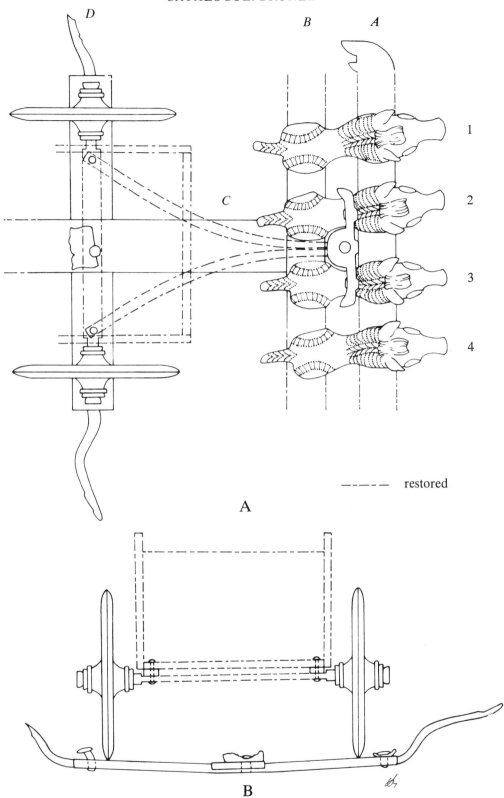

Figure 15. TumP 40. Miniature quadriga. A. Top view of group as restored with Y-pole extending to the axle under the box. B. Rear view of chariot if restored with Y-pole arrangement. 1:1.

wheels and the axle turned together in loops fastened to the center piece, whereas on TumP 40 the wheels were spoked, and turned while the axle, stationary, was secured, as we have seen, by at least two rivets to the undercarriage or perhaps even to the box.

Many details of TumP 40—the wheels with six-knobbed spokes, the large comparative size of the wheels, the spoke-rims indicated as being separate from the outer edge of the felloe, their clamping system, the knotted manes and tails—all lead back to the orthostates in the Northwest Palace at Nimrud in the time of Assurnasirpal II (884–860).[33] Citing the same sculpture and TumP 40 together, M. Littauer[34] discusses the possibilities (pro and con) that the Assyrian four-horse hitch involved a yoke for the central pair as in TumP 40, and that the outside horses were trace horses.

The four horses of the quadriga were treated very similarly although not identically in both form and decoration, and the general style shown appears related to that of TumP 106, the wooden horse whose similar cylindrical body elements have been molded by bulges. The face is long and has the same swollen and blunt muzzle. Hoofs have the same plain conical flare. The relationship to TumP 106, which is seen for the reasons enumerated on p. 56 to have been made at Gordion, speaks for the bronze group's also having been made locally. The pricked decoration occurring on the horses and on the wheels shows the same finely etched dots, strokes and lines that adorn

other finds from Tumulus P: the belts (TumP 34–36, figs. 9–11) and the pottery (TumP 55–57, pl. 17A–F). The stroke design on haunches and shoulders is found also on the ivory furniture inlays from Megaron 3 on the city mound.[35] Indeed, the fact that the clamps are not represented as effectually joining the spoke-rim to the felloes shows that the artist was not acquainted at first hand with such wheels.[36]

The small size of the horses may be accounted for by the breed,[37] or it may be merely the artist's whim.

The purpose of the quadriga group remains arguable: one might lean heavily toward the uses to which other miniature animals and groups in Tumulus P may have been put (p. 53 below). Tumulus K-III contained a miniature group in wood,[38] a lion holding a quadruped in its mouth, and standing on a plinth still clearly once attached to a cauldron lid.[39] From parallels abroad and at Gordion, no absolutely clear use has been found for strip *D*, so we use it in the reconstruction (figs. 14, 15) as passing under strip *C* on the ground in line with the axle.[40] The remains of sheet at the two rivets near its end and the pointed extensions remain an enigma.[41]

Also the nature of the relationships of pole to undercarriage and to yoke, and of undercarriage to box, remain unclear, but the Assyrian traits in general, discussed above, show a tradition going back to the ninth century B.C. for some important features.

---

[33]R. D. Barnett, *Assyrian Palace Reliefs,* pls. 14 ff. = H. Frankfort, *AAAO,* pls. 84, 87, 88. Cf. also Barnett, *op. cit.,* pls. 140–150 (the gates of Balawat) where the first campaign of Shalmaneser (860 B.C.) is represented, and some of the same details are visible.

[34]*Orientalia* 45 (1976): 222–225.

[35]E. L. Kohler in *Dark Ages and Nomads,* 61 and pls. XIX–XX, figs. 2–4. See also Young, *AJA* 64 (1960), pl. 60, fig. 25a–c.

[36]Cf. clamping systems in Hrouda, *KaF,* pl. 17.

[37]M. Littauer, *Iraq* 33 (1971): 26 and esp. note 14; 27 (ponies of the Oxus treasure); idem, *Antiquity* 45 (1972): 293–294 (kurgan of Pazyryk).

[38]G. Körte in *Gordion,* 68, no. 49, fig. 45 and pl. 5.

[39]See below, p. 53, n. 106. This purpose is not dissonant with the possible placement of strip *D* over strip *C* beyond its break. But a bronze handle would be a conduc-

tor of heat, whereas the wooden animals (TumP 106–114) would be more suitable as cauldron handles.

[40]As in the model from Agrab. See p. 24, n. 31 above. The off-center rivet hole fits well.

It is tempting to consider the turned-up points in the position of linch pins and the band placed under the box to serve as fixed axle. M. Littauer, *Levant* 5 (1973): 111, 113, provides many examples of such usage on wagon models. However, as mentioned above, the original axles are preserved in the naves of TumP 40.

[41]However, the points, still bent up, look suitable for insertion into two secondary wheels (wooden?). For the possible use of a model chariot upon a plinth for mounting upon four additional wheels, as a pull-toy, cf. the model from Marathus in the Louvre, L. Heuzey, *Cat. des figurines antiques de terre cuite du Musée du Louvre* (Paris, 1923), 53 and pl. V:1; Studniczka, *JdI* 22 (1907): 168, no. 17. Cf. also M. Littauer, *AA* (1977): 4 and figs. 3–6 (model from Ovgoros, Cyprus).

IRON

MISCELLANEOUS OBJECTS*
TumP 41–43; ILS 753–756

Two large iron tools were found on the floor at the east end of the tomb, lying nearly parallel to the east wall, TumP 41 near its midpoint, TumP 42 to the north. The first may have been used as a roasting spit, although a similar bifurcated iron object was found in Tumulus K-III (no. 105) and was interpreted as a pair of fire tongs.[42] There is no trace, however, of a hinge at its bifurcation. TumP 42, pointed at one end and hooked at the other, with small projecting ears or lugs on opposite faces above the point, may have been intended to stand upright or obliquely, with the point secured in the ground or in a wooden holder. At the center of the chamber, the ring stand TumP 43 supported bronze cauldron TumP 1.

Several smaller objects could be distinguished among the iron fragments collected from the debris on the chamber floor. An iron ring handle, ILS 753, may have belonged to the large handleless cauldron, TumP 2, or one of the wooden bowls of which the bronze handles, TumP 31, 32 (pl. 10K), and TumP 33, are considered to be the only remains. There is evidence that the smaller cauldron, TumP 2 (pl. 7B), originally had a band of iron attached by a series of rivets to the neck just below the rim. The two fragments, ILS 754A, B, may have been part of the missing band. (No trace of such a band, either in rust stains or rivet holes, was found on the larger cauldron, TumP 1.) The five fragments of iron rod, ILS 755, belonged to a socketed tool originally over 0.40 m. in length, perhaps a fire poker. Finally, a nail shaft, ILS 756, may have been part of the large iron spike found during the excavation under beam 1 along the south half of the east chamber wall, but not entered into the original catalogue.

TumP 41 **Fork**
        ILS 231   East half *ca.* center
        PL. *ca.* 0.92 W. *ca.* 0.09 D. prongs
        0.016 m.
        Fig. 16A, B; Pl. 6B (*L*)

Five fragments, all so corroded that they do not fit together exactly. At one end is a handle or tenon,

round in section, and about 0.16 m. long, which may have been socketed into a larger wooden handle. Below this the iron was bifurcated into two long prongs. The prongs are round in section and taper to points, and there are two flat sections 0.14 m. in length just below the bifurcation and 0.23 m. farther down the prongs. Two tiny ears project from each end of the flat sections.

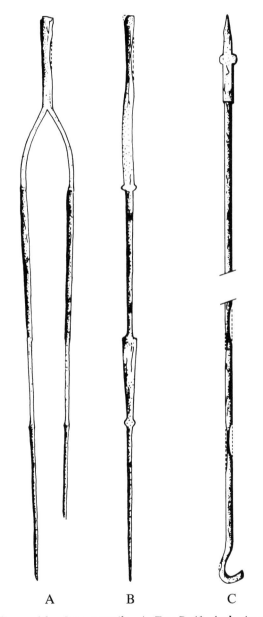

A   B   C

Figure 16. Iron utensils. A. TumP 41, fork, front.
B. TumP 41, fork, side. C. TumP 42, hooked rod.
Hook and tang. 1:6.

---

*Catalogue and discussion by Joanna F. McClellan.

[42]G. Körte in *Gordion*, 81, fig. 70,*f.*

TumP 42 **Hooked rod**
ILS 232   Northeast corner
L. 1.79   W. across hook 0.034
L. pointed section 0.095 m.
Fig. 16C

Unbroken but much eaten by corrosion. Traces of wood adhere in some areas. A very long iron rod which is mainly round in section. One end is sharply pointed with two small projecting lugs at opposite sides above the point. Above these the shaft is square in section for a distance of 0.065 m., and very clear traces of wood are preserved along its entire length. At the other end of the rod is a small, well-formed, shallow hook, its inner face rounded, not thinned to an edge.

TumP 43 **Tripod ring stand**
ILS 233   Under TumP 1
OD. ring 0.38   GPH 0.233 m.
Pl. 14A

Much corroded; the ends of two legs are broken off, the complete leg is mended. The ring is round in section, and the legs are flat and rectangular. Due to corrosion, it is not possible to determine how the ring and legs were joined.

See also pp. 250–251.

ILS 753[43] **Ring handle**
Not on plan
GD. 0.085   L. separation between
ends 0.021   H. 0.078 m.
Fig. 17A

Mended, badly corroded. Rod, round in section, tapering slightly at ends and bent into circle with ends close but not touching. Probably rode in sockets of a bolster handle, of which no trace remains.

ILS 754 A, B **Band fragments**
Not on plan
A. GPL. 0.165   GPH. 0.02
Th. 0.016 m.
B. GPL. 0.082   GPH. 0.025
Th. 0.008 m.
Fig. 17B

Mended, incomplete, badly distorted by rust and flaking. Two nonjoining bands which may have been flat-rectangular or low-hemispherical in section, bent

---

[43]The four iron objects (ILS 753 through 756) were added to the catalogue of Tumulus P in 1978, too late for the assigning of TumP numbers.

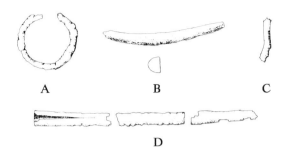

Figure 17. A. ILS 753, ring handle. B. ILS 754A, curved band with cross-section. C. ILS 756, nail fragment. D. ILS 755, fragments of socketed rod. 1:5.

in a slight curve. Concave side is flat and discolored, as if it had rested against something. A few spots of green bronze disease still adhere. The iron bands were possibly part of a collar under the rim of the bronze cauldron (TumP 2). There is no evidence of rivets or other attachment device on the iron fragments. It should be noted, however, that the rivet holes around the neck of TumP 2 are, on the average, from 0.165–0.21 m. apart, so that the largest band fragment, ILS 754*A*, which is 0.165 m. in length, if it belonged to the collar of TumP 2, would not necessarily have to preserve either rivet or rivet hole.

ILS 755 **Socketed rod**
Not on plan
GPLs. 0.105, 0.093, 0.093, 0.072,
0.033   L. socket 0.07   D. socket at
base 0.022   W. rod 0.017 m.
Fig. 17D

Five nonjoining fragments of solid rod, circular in section, whose end was flattened and formed into a hollow tubular socket. The laps of the socket do not meet but appear as a split in one side of the socket. Fragments of wood remain inside. There is no indication of a blade or tool at the end, nor any obvious taper to the rod above the socket. Possibly a skewer or fire poker.

ILS 756 **Nail shaft**
Not on plan
GPL. 0.06   GPW. 0.01 m.
Fig. 17C

Broken at both ends, bent into shallow S-curve. Short rod, round in section, to which fragments of wood adhere. Possibly the shaft of the spike mentioned in the original excavation records, which was found along the east wall in the southern half of the chamber.

Several iron objects from Tumulus P may have been cooking or fire-tending utensils: TumP 41 a roasting spit, TumP 42 a fire hook or pot support, and ILS 755 a skewer or fire poker. All three have either a tubular socket or a tang at the end to receive a wooden handle, an important addition if the instruments were used near the fire. The possibility of the tripod, TumP 43, having been a cooking utensil is discussed elsewhere (p. 250).

While TumP 41 and 42 are unique in size and design, objects of the same type have been found elsewhere. Besides the forked iron tool from Tumulus K-III already cited, a similar bifurcated iron tool was found in the nearly contemporary Tumulus II on the Anıttepe in Ankara.[44] In addition, bronze and iron double-tined forks have been found in tomb contexts at other sites, dating from the third to the first millennium.[45] Although these examples are generally smaller than TumP 41, they are often described as roasting forks or skewers. The size of TumP 41 suggests that, if it were used as a roasting fork, it could have accommodated a whole sheep or side of beef.

It is possible that TumP 42 and ILS 755 were firetending or cooking instruments. Pointed and hooked rods have been found in association with ovens and hearths on the city mound.[46] Alternatively, ILS 755 might have been a skewer for roasting meat. Socketed iron rods of similar length

found in eighth- and seventh-century contexts have been interpreted as *obeloi* (the Archaic Greek monetary unit), as spear points (the Cypriote "Sigynnae"), or as skewers. TumP 42 might also have been a cooking implement. With the pointed end stuck in the ground at an angle and the rod resting on a support approximately midway, a kettle could have been suspended over a fire from the hooked end. Three shorter hooked rods were found in Tumulus K-III.[47] G. Körte suggests these were stuck vertically into the ground in pairs and supported a kettle over the fire by its two handles.[48]

Iron necking bands, bolsters, and ring handles on bronze vessels are known at Gordion and elsewhere and are most commonly found on large cauldrons.[49] The possibility of iron ring handle ILS 753 and iron band fragments ILS 754*A, B* having originally been part of cauldron TumP 2, is discussed elsewhere (p. 11). Why the two metals were combined in this way is unknown, but one can imagine that the strength of iron determined its use for the neck bands and handles of the large cooking cauldrons found on the city mound. The iron parts could also have been later additions or repairs on TumP 2. The dowel holes in the neck of the cauldron were drilled on cold metal, and only one iron ring handle has been found in the tomb. It might have made a pair with one of the three bronze ring handles, TumP 31–33, thought to have belonged to wooden vessels.[50]

Finally, heavy nails or spikes, of which ILS 756 is an example, have been found in other tumuli at

---

[44]*Belleten* 11 (1947): 73 and pl. 19:38. Özgüç describes it as a "fork or tongs." Two unpublished bifurcated iron rods from Gordion, ILS 328 from Megaron 3 and ILS 484a,b from Tumulus F, seem to have been structural braces.

[45]Khurvin: L. Vanden Berghe, *La Nécropole de Khurvin* (Istanbul: Nederlands Historisch-Archaeologisch Instituut in het Nabije Oosten, 1964), 27 and pl. 39:272, with further references; Tel Halif: A. Biran and R. Gophna, *IEJ* 20 (1970), pl. 38B. In addition, Karageorghis, *RDAC* (1972): 171, n. 2, mentions a decorated metal bowl from Cyprus which shows a man tending a brazier and a companion holding in his hand a long double object with something at its lower end. It is possible that a forked skewer is represented.

[46]E.g., ILS 667b, one of four iron tools found on or near the hearth in the anteroom of TB-7 on the city mound. A red-figured kylix in Berlin, F 2294, illustrating scenes

of a metal foundry, pictures a very long hooked rod being used to stir the coals in the furnace, cf. *CVA* 12:21 (Berlin, *Bd.* 2), pl. 72:1.

[47]See Karageorghis, *op. cit.,* 171 (with n. 2)–172 for bibliography.

[48]*Gordion,* 81, no. 103, fig. 70,*d.*

[49]Gordion: ILS 384a, b; 400a, b; 419a, b from TB-1, and ILS 386 from TB-2 on the city mound; B 426 from Tumulus E; B 470 from Tumulus F; several from K-III, G. Körte in *Gordion,* 68–72, nos. 49–52, 56, 58. Chios: Boardman, *Greek Emporio,* 224, no. 383 and 225, fig. 146; Olympia: Furtwängler, *Olympia* IV, 133, no. 837, Inv. 6989.

[50]Several examples of a bronze object having been repaired with iron parts, or vice versa, have been found at Gordion, e.g., iron keyhole plate, ILS 138 with two iron nails and one of bronze (McClellan, *Iron,* 586–589). On the same subject, see also G. Körte in *Gordion,* 92.

Gordion, including MM.[51] They do not seem to have been used in the construction of the chamber or the furniture within it, but were used as wall hooks from which bronze vessels were suspended.

When found, the iron spike from Tumulus Z (B 1846) had the bronze ring handle of the vessel it held still adhering to its shaft.

BONE

KNUCKLEBONES
TumP 44

On the floor of the tomb to the south of the area of the bed and somewhat west of its center lay a large pile of sheep knucklebones. A count yielded 446 complete astragals plus fragments of at least 60 more, and a pile of unidentifiable white bone fragments represented probably many more that had disintegrated. Most (but not all) of the astragals preserved had a small hole drilled through one end. Six specimens preserved thin rings of bronze wire still in place, passed through the drilled holes, and two more rings were found, but greenish powder and granules of bronze throughout the pile suggested many more rings of bronze wire that had disintegrated. The use of these astragals in such large numbers is not clear. The bronze rings

and the drilled holes suggest suspension as pendants or stringing together. The bronze rings could hardly have been helpful in using the astragals as gaming pieces. The children of the modern village of Yassıhüyük value and collect astragals, which they use in a number of different games.[52] Two large collections were found in the Phrygian city at Gordion, one in a coarse pot in a storeroom behind Megaron 1, the other scattered over the mosaic floor of Megaron 2.

TumP 44 **Knucklebones**
 BI 289 West half, south of bed
 Ave. L. 0.03 Ave. W. 0.019 m.
 Pl. 14B

Six astragals with rings of bronze wire passed through drilled holes near one end; and two bronze rings evidently from disintegrated astragals.

BLUE GLAZE AND PASTE*

VESSELS
TumP 45–47

Two vessels, one of pottery covered by a thick turquoise-blue vitreous glaze and the other of fine matt, blue Egyptian paste, were found in the southwest corner of the tomb; the third, a two-handled dish also of Egyptian blue, lay at the south side under the sixth roof beam. These vessels are certainly not of local manufacture. As imports, probably from Syria or Phoenicia, they attest to a link between Phrygia and the East.

TumP 45 **Blue-glazed juglet**
 G 203 Southwest corner, under
  beam 10
 H. 0.104 D. 0.086 m.
 Pl. 14C

Mended from many pieces; some fragments missing. A small ring handle must have stood on the shoulder, probably high up, but it cannot be joined because the shoulder fragment with the stump of its attachment is missing. Ovoid body, with flat resting surface and slightly flared lip around a narrow hole mouth. Fabric light buff gritty clay; vitreous blue

---

[51]See below p. 100 and pl. 40B; for Tumulus Z, see McClellan, *Iron*, 515, no. 389 (ILS 597) and n. 88.

[52]For explanations of games with knucklebones, see P. G. Brewster, "A Sampling of Games from Turkey," *East and*

West 11 (1960): 16; Musa Baran, "Children's Games," *Expedition* 17, no. 1 (Fall 1974): 21–23.

*Catalogue and discussion of blue glaze and paste items by Machteld J. Mellink.

glaze crackled all over the surfaces (craquelé) on outside and partially on inside. A bump near the base is a flaw in the pottery or the glazing.

TumP 46   **Egyptian-blue juglet**
       G 204   Southwest corner, under
             beam 10
       H. 0.093   D. 0.057 m.
       Pl. 14D, E

Complete, the lip chipped. Ovoid body truncated below to a flat resting surface; narrow neck offset at an angle below a widely flaring rim. The handle from shoulder to mid-neck just below the bevel. Incised decoration: three sets of double concentric circles at sides and back below the handle; at the front, set on the upper body, a large X-pendant, topped by a chevron. All elements incised in parallel double lines. Fabric matt Egyptian blue paste throughout.

This juglet is made of Egyptian blue[53] in imitation of a popular Cypriote pottery shape. The ceramic counterpart in black-on-red ware occurs in this same tumulus as TumP 59 (pl. 17H); the shape is that of "Black-on-Red I (III)" ware.[54] Note that the decoration incised on the blue juglet from Gordion (two small concentric circles and intersecting chevrons) is similar to painted designs on Cypriote pottery jugs.

The place of manufacture of this blue juglet is unknown, although a Cypriote workshop may be conjectured. A related juglet was found in a tomb at Amathus.[55]

TumP 47   **Egyptian-blue lotus-handled dish**
       G 205   South side under beam 6
       H.-h. 0.063   D. rim 0.096 m.
       Pl. 14F–H

The tops of the handles chipped; stained on side, otherwise intact. Small dish of very thick fabric,

flattened at the bottom; thick plain rim flat on top. Heavy rolled horizontal handles, upward-tilted and supported at the top by struts run horizontally outward from just below the lip. On top of each handle a stylized lotus blossom with central calyx and a single petal at each side. Incised decoration: a double ring around the attachments of each handle, the space between the rings and the base of the handle divided into wedges by radiating straight lines; the space under the handles between these rings filled by four parallel horizontal lines with diagonal hatchins in the spaces between them. The hatching runs in opposite directions to form a double herringbone pattern. Fabric homogeneous matt Egyptian blue paste throughout.

This miniature vessel of Egyptian blue is a variant of a shape better known in bronze. Handles decorated with (lotus) flowers at their highest point appear on a bronze bowl found at Gordion in Tumulus K-III.[56] Similar bronze handles are known on bowls from Til Barsib and Tell Halaf;[57] on Cyprus, good examples were found in tombs at Amathus.[58] The type has been discussed by B. Hrouda, P. Jacobsthal,[59] and E. Akurgal.[60] An ivory handle from Nimrud[61] shows that there is a nonmetallic tradition of such handles. TumP 47 is a thick-walled bowl of a shape suitable to ivory or fine stone, with a strut to strengthen the handle and a small capacity. A parallel in stone(?) has recently been found among the foundation gifts in the eighth-century temple at Kition;[62] it also has a flat rim and handles with struts.

The ornaments incised at the base of the handles of TumP 47 are a decorative variant of the spectacle-shaped plaques appearing as strengtheners of the handle attachment on bronze bowls, as seen for example, on the bowl K-III, no. 57[63] and the Cypriote bowls from Amathus.[64]

---

[53]For technique of manufacture, see F. R. Matson, "Egyptian Blue," in Erich F. Schmidt, *Persepolis* II (*OIP* 69, 1957), 133–135.

[54]*SCE* II, pl. CXIII: A16.9 and A9.135.

[55]A. S. Murray, A. H. Smith, H. B. Walters, *The British Museum Excavations in Cyprus* (London: The British Museum, 1900), 115, fig. 166:3.

[56]G. Körte in *Gordion*, 72, fig. 51.

[57]B. Hrouda, ed. *Tell Halaf* IV (Berlin: W. de Gruyter, 1962), 65, pl. 48:7.

[58]*SCE* II, pl. 154.

[59]*Greek Pins* (Oxford: Clarendon Press, 1956), 47.

[60]*Orient und Okzident* (Baden-Baden: Holle, 1966), 120, 200–201.

[61]R. D. Barnett, *Nimrud Ivories*, pl. CXII: S 134–135.

[62]V. Karageorghis, *ProcBritAc* 59 (1973), pl. 17c.

[63]See above, n. 56.

[64]*SCE* II, 81, Amathus, Tomb 13:8, p. 118; Amathus, Tomb 21:42, p. 118; also *SCE* IV, pt. 2, p. 151.

GLASS

OMPHALOS BOWL
TumP 48

The glass bowl TumP 48 was found near the southwest corner of the tomb under roof beam 9, stacked inside one of the bronze bowls. It had been broken into many fragments; fortunately almost all were retained together inside the bowl.

TumP 48   Glass bowl
       G 206   Not on plan.
       H. 0.038   D. rim 0.154 m.
       Fig. 18; Pl. 15A, B

Broken and mended from many fragments; small bits and chips missing. Clear glass, practically colorless; a few small bubbles in the fabric. Shallow profile, slightly flaring at the rim. The bottom flat, with a central hollow beneath the omphalos. On the outside 32 petals radiating from the central hollow, their

Figure 18.   TumP 48. Glass omphalos bowl. Profile.
1:3.

relief increasing at the curve from bottom to wall, and decreasing toward the rim. Inside, a rounded central omphalos on a low circular platform stepped at the edge; from the step 32 radiating concave petals correspond to the 32 convex on the outside.

This bowl has been studied and published by A. von Saldern.[65] His conclusions are that the vessel was molded either by melting crushed glass in the mold, or by a lost-wax process. He believes the interior was ground and the design deepened by a cutting tool. He cites Sargonid parallels (one bearing the name of Sargon II in cuneiform) from Nimrud, of thick greenish glass, probably also molded, attributing them to a probable "royal factory" there. These pieces suggest a thriving glass-making industry in Assyria in the eighth and seventh centuries, to which our bowl (despite slight differences in quality and technique) is probably to be attributed. The shape, Luschey's "Zungenphiale,"[66] is at home in Assyria, and may have originated there. Our glass bowl, then, offers another link with Assyria and was very likely an import from there. It is thus important not only for the dating of our tomb but also as another indication of the outside relations of Phrygia in the eighth century.

POTTERY*

Of the 58 vessels discovered within the tomb, 13 were of fine painted wares (TumP 49–61), 17 of fine black polished fabric (TumP 62–78) and 28 of coarser black polished wares (TumP 79–105, including 87*bis*). Of the fine-ware pottery, two-thirds were concentrated in the south central part of the tomb, in the vicinity of roof beams 5 and 6 between the area of the southeast table and TumP 2 (TumP 49, 50, 52, 55, 56, 60, 62, 63, 67–78). The disposition of the pottery suggested

to R. S. Young the existence of a second table here whose collapse caused the vessels it held to scatter and many of them to break.[67] To the immediate east, within the area of the long southeast table, three more vessels of fine ware were found (TumP 53, 59, and 64), interpreted by Young as having once rested on the table.[68] In the southwest corner of the tomb, amidst the screen and fragments of other wooden furniture, four more fine-ware vessels rested (TumP 54, 57, 58,

[65]*JGS* 1 (1959): 25–34 (Group I), and 49 for the report of a spectrographic examination of TumP 48, courtesy of Corning Glass Works. Cf. also *idem* in A. L. Oppenheim *et al.,* eds., *Glass and Glassmaking,* 210.

[66]H. Luschey, *Phiale,* 76–95, 162.

*Introductory text by G. Kenneth Sams.

[67]R. S. Young, *AJA* 61 (1957): 327.

[68]*Ibid.*

TumP 56 under the seventh. Three are of the same brown-on-buff ware as the geese, the fourth (TumP 54) black-on-red. Another vessel of this shape but of black polished ware (TumP 66 below) was found in the tomb; the shape was a common one in Phrygia, and many examples have been found in the burned stratum of the city.

TumP 54   Black-on-red round-mouthed jug
    P 1402   Southwest corner
    H.-rim 0.164   H.-h. 0.194   D. 0.153
      D. rim 0.140 m.
      Pl. 16D

Broken and mended; small fragments and chips missing; the surface much pitted. Medium fine clay fired red; red surface slipped and burnished to a high luster; matt black paint over burnish. Flat bottom, ovoid body, and tall flaring neck with plain rim. Double rolled handle rising above the rim. The body reserved to the shoulder, which is bordered below by two straight bands above a wavy one. On the shoulder, a series of quadruple chevron triangles, their tops intersecting, their legs tangent at the base. Straight and wavy bands at the base of the neck, halfway up, and below the rim on the inside as well as the outside.

TumP 55   Brown-on-buff round-mouthed jug
    P 1408   South wall, under beams
      5–6
    H.-rim 0.23   H.-h. 0.30   D. 0.182
      D. rim 0.175 m.
      Pls. 16E, F, 17A–C

Intact except for chips; the surface scratched and pitted. Fabric same as TumP 49 and 50. Ring foot supporting a plump ovoid body which meets at an angle the high neck flaring to a plain rim. Strap handle rising above the rim, crossed at its top by a bolster.

Foot and lower body reserved and bordered above by a zone filled with evenly spaced double concentric circles, compass-drawn; another below the rim inside. A cross of similar circles, tangent, on the base of the handle and below it; single concentric circles used as filling ornament in all the panels. At the top of the shoulder and below the rim outside, zones of dotted crosshatching. On the handle, checkerboard above multiple bands across its base; the side faces solidly painted. The bolster is hatched; each of its flattened ends has a Maltese cross.

Above a multiple ground line, a zone spanning belly and lower shoulder is divided into four oblong panels by three columns of dotted lozenges with triangles at the edges; these alternate with latticed columns filled by dotted squares. In two of the panels a lion right, facing (in the adjacent panels) a bull, left. The neck is also divided into four panels by five columns of checkerboard pattern. Alternating in these panels are two ibexes or antelopes and two deer with many-branched antlers. All walk from left to right, but the heads of the deer are turned back to face the animals behind them. Apart from concentric circles, the only filling ornaments used are pendent triangles, crosshatched and dotted.

TumP 56   Brown-on-buff round-mouthed jug
    P 1455   South side, under beam 7
    H.-rim 0.185   H.-h. 0.24   D. 0.143
      D. rim 0.14 m.
      Fig. 19; Pl. 17D, E

Broken and mended but complete; the surface somewhat scratched and pitted; in places, particularly in the first panel at the left, detail is obscured by irregular stains, purplish in color. Fabric same as TumP 55. Similar to TumP 55 in shape, including a bolster on the handle; smaller.

The scheme of decoration also similar, with a zone of concentric circles above the reserved lower body and inside the lip, and in a cross at the base of the handle. On the handle, crosshatching at the back, checkerboard at the front; the rotelle at the top as on TumP 55. At the top of the shoulder and below the rim outside, zones filled by simple-line meander running from right to left. The decoration on the shoulder continues unbroken at the back under the handle. On the neck, two zones of dotted crosshatching with a checkerboard band between them, all terminated at the ends beside the handle by narrow latticed panels like those on the belly zone of TumP 55.

The belly and lower shoulder divided into four oblong panels (fig. 19) by five columns of checkerboard. Filling ornament in the panels as on TumP 55, with the addition of volute trees in front of the animals in the two central ones, a palm leaf tree in front of the animal in the right panel. In each panel an animal walking to the right: from the left, a sphinx; an ibex or antelope; a second ibex; and a deer with many-branched antlers, his head turned back. The drawing of the ibexes suggests that they are by the same hand as those of TumP 55. All details of the sphinx are not clear because of the surface stain; clear are a lion body, its tail ending in a bird head; a human head crowned by plumelike hair or headdress; and a complex of feathered wings of which the exact structure is obscured.

Figure 19. TumP 56. Brown-on-buff round-mouthed jug. Detail of panels.

TumP 57   **Brown-on-buff round-mouthed jug**
P 1456   Southwest corner
H.-rim 0.203   H.-h. 0.255   D. 0.178
D. rim 0.142 m.
Pl. 17F

Broken and mended; large fragments missing from the front and one side of the body; the paint in places much faded; the surface sprinkled with splotches of the same purplish stain noted on TumP 56. The last had evidently dropped onto the pot from above and spattered: perhaps resin from the pine wood of the tomb roof. Fabric same as that of TumP 55.

Shape the same as that of TumP 55 and 56; the same system of decoration. Two bands around the reserved part of the lower body; a zone of concentric circles below the level of the lower handle attachment. Handle laddered with thick bands; across its base, circles. A zone of dotted crosshatching at top of shoulder and below rim. On the neck, two zones of zigzag filled by dotted triangles above and below; between them a zone of tall checkerboard; all crossed at the ends beside the handle panel by columns of checkerboard. The belly and lower shoulder divided into four oblong panels by five columns of checkerboard. Filling ornament in panels as on TumP 55. In each panel an animal walking from left to right: a bull; probably a second bull, largely missing; a third bull; an ibex or antelope, its head turned back. The drawing of bulls and ibex suggests the same hand that painted TumP 55 and 56.

RAM JUG
TumP 58

TumP 58   **Black-on-red ram jug**
P 1403   Southwest corner
H. 0.191   L. 0.252 m.
Pl. 17G

Broken and mended; small fragment and chips missing. Fine red clay; red surface, well smoothed

but matt, with matt black paint. Elongated body on four feet round in section; at the center of the back a filling hole surrounded by a high collar. The tail arched over the back to the base of the neck, making a lifting handle trimmed to four flat faces. At the front, the roughly modeled neck and head of a ram, the snout pierced for pouring. Curly horns which make a complete loop so that the ends overlap their bases.

The body bordered near top and bottom all around by bands and a wavy line. Between these on one side three rows of latticed squares, their corners joined by small black checkers; on the other side, a large zone of plain checkerboard with small checks. At each side of the chest and neck a circular ladder, dotted at the center. Bands bordered by wavy lines at the top of the neck and around the top of the collar around the filling hole.

SMALL JUGLET
TumP 59

TumP 59   **Black-on-red juglet**
P 1404   South side, under beam 4
H. 0.092   D. 0.061 m.
Pl. 17H

Complete; neck and handle mended; pitted. Medium fine clay fired reddish yellow; red slipped and polished; black paint. Spherical body on a low base; tall narrow neck flared at the rim, with a raised ridge at half its height, where the small rolled handle joins. Simple linear decoration: a wide band at the level of greatest diameter; nine fine bands on the shoulder below the handle attachment; a thick band around the lower part of the neck and on the raised ring; finer bands around the upper neck; stripes across the outer face of the handle.

The small juglet differs in no way in its fabric from the other black-on-red vases of Tumulus P, except that its polished surface is less worn. Had it been found in Cyprus, it would have been called a "handle-ridge juglet" and classified "Black-on-Red I (III)," assigned to the Cypro-Geometric III period and dated *ca.* 850–700 B.C. Black-on-red ware appears in Cyprus in small quantity as imports from the Syro-Palestinian region during the Cypro-Geometric II period; with the beginning of Cypro-Geometric III it appears in great quantities, no longer imported but native. The type of handle-ridge juglet was not of Cypriote derivation;[71] the area of its provenance is to be looked for in the Syro-Palestinian region.[72] Nevertheless, it was common in Cyprus in the late ninth and throughout the eighth century. In shape, fabric and decoration TumP 59 closely resembles these Cypriote products; whether or not it is an import to Phrygia from Cyprus is for an expert on Cypriote pottery to say, but in any case even if it is an Anatolian imitation, it attests to relations between Phrygia and Cyprus in the eighth century. The reverse, importation from Phrygia to Cyprus, is suggested by the bronze, ring-handled Phrygian bowls found at Curium, now in the Metropolitan Museum: see pp. 229, 232. Unfortunately the juglet cannot pin down our chronology any more closely than to ninth–eighth century.[73] An import, TumP 46, close in shape, is made of Egyptian blue paste.

FOOTED BOWL
TumP 60

TumP 60 **Brown-on-buff footed bowl**
P 1409　　　South side, under beam 6
H. 0.054　D. rim 0.139 m.
Pl. 17I

Intact, but surface much stained and pitted. Fabric same as TumP 49 and 50. Shallow handleless bowl with plain rim, on a high flaring foot. Decorated inside and out with wide and narrow bands of paint.

FRUIT STAND
TumP 61

TumP 61　　**Bichrome fruit stand**
P 1699　　　Not on plan
H. 0.09　D. rim 0.207　D. foot
0.083 m.
Fig. 20; Pl. 17J

Original position in tomb uncertain. Put together from many fragments; many more missing. Chipped and pitted to the extent that little of the surface is preserved. Very fine clay, fired reddish yellow at core; surfaces well polished over black and red paint and fired buff where reserved; the fabric seems related to the fine brown-on-buff ware of TumP 49, 50, 55–57. Pedestal base, hollow; the foot set off by beveling and a sunken ledge. The plate section a flat disk with cutouts to leave lunettes around a saucer-like depression set off from the outer rim by a raised ridge. Painted designs occur only on the top of the broad, flangelike rim, although all or most of the remaining surface appears to have been coated with paint, perhaps intentionally mottled with the light clay ground. It is possible, given the decorative scheme, that there were originally only two lunettes in which triangles were painted in red and black. One type is clear, for either half or two-thirds of the

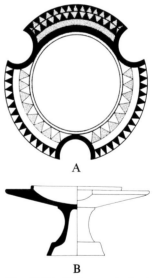

*Figure 20.　TumP 61. Bichrome fruit stand. A. Top.
B. Profile and side view. 1:5.*

---

[71]E. Gjerstad, *SCE* IV, pt. 2, p. 69; illustrated figs. XXV: 3a,b and XXXVIII: 3a,b.

[72]*Ibid.*, 253, 423 f., 435 f.

[73]It should be noted that, in *Gordion Guide* (1975), 46, R. S. Young clearly refers to TumP 59 as an import: "a lekythos of typical Cypriote ware." [GKS]

flange: a narrow row of solid black triangles at exterior, apices pointing outwards; a row of solid red triangles pointing inward; a reserved band between the two rows. The other scheme, for half or one-third, is less clear: apparently two rows of black triangles with resultant (that is, intermediate) triangles painted red (perhaps the flange was painted solid red first). The dividing band between the rows is also red.[74]

FINE REDUCED WARES
TumP 62–78

Seventeen vessels of fine monochrome ware were found, the majority along the south side of the tomb. They are of characteristic Phrygian black polished ware with lighter colored clay. Masses of pots of similar wares were found in the burned levels in the city; in color they ranged from black to gray to buff and to red. These variations in color were probably the result of secondary firing when the palace was burned: in fact there are many instances where fragments burned to different colors actually join. The vases from Tumulus P, which were not exposed to a second firing, are all black, suggesting that black was the norm for this Phrygian ware in the eighth century. Parallels in shape to the brown-on-buff vessels of Tumulus P and elsewhere would suggest that these painted vases were also of local fabrication.

ANIMAL-SHAPED VESSELS
TumP 62, 63

TumP 62   **Black polished goat jug**
P 1424   South side, under beam 6
H. 0.15   L. 0.21   W. 0.12 m.
Pl. 18A, B

Intact. Fine clay; well-polished black surface with a mica film.[75] Askoid body supported on four short peg feet. At the center of the back, a small filling hole surrounded by a low raised rim. At the rear the tail curves up and over to join the back beside the filling hole, forming a loop handle; and at the front the horns run back to join the shoulders at each side, forming another. Tiny ears, modeled, beside the

horns. The snout, squared off at the front, pierced by a small pouring hole. The eyes stamped rings; around the neck a collar of a double row of similar stamped rings.

In modeling the vessel the potter met the same technical problems that were presented by the brown-on-buff askoi (TumP 51, 52) and the black-on-red askos (TumP 53) and ram jug (TumP 58).

TumP 63   **Black polished deer or bull jug**
P 1425   South side, under beam 5
H.-h. 0.135   L. 0.155   D. 0.11 m.
Pl. 18C, D

Part of the handle, two feet and several chips missing. Medium fine, light brown clay; black surface polished to a high luster.

Ellipsoidal body, wheelmade, on four short square peg feet; small filling hole surrounded by low raised rim on top. The deer-head or bull's-head spout at one side surrounded by a low raised collar where it joins the shoulder and connected with the opposite shoulder by a squared basket handle which springs from behind the horns. The square-ended muzzle pierced by a round pouring hole; the eyes stamped rings.

TREFOIL JUGS
TumP 64, 65

TumP 64   **Black polished trefoil jug**
P 1418   South side, under beam 4
H.-h. 0.15   D. 0.145   D. base
0.048 m.
Pl. 18E

Complete; the handle mended; the surface much pitted and flaked. Medium fine, reddish brown clay; black surface slipped and polished to a medium luster with an overlay of lighter mica film. Piriform body with a rather long, high shoulder; flat resting surface. Neck narrow at the bottom, flaring to a trefoil mouth with rolled convex rim; a raised ridge at junction of shoulder and neck. Rolled handle from back of rim to level of greatest diameter.

In shape much like the bronze jug TumP 6. For an analogous jug from the destruction level within the city see pl. 96A.[76]

---

[74]According to R. S. Young, but not observed by me: "Some traces of burning on the floor of the central cupped area suggest use as an incense burner." [GKS]

[75]See p. 47, n. 85.

[76]Young, *AJA* 60 (1956): 262–263, pl. 94, fig. 46.

TumP 65   **Black polished trefoil jug**
P 1419   Northeast corner
H.-h. 0.15   D. 0.105   D. foot
0.047 m.
Pl. 18F

Mended complete; few small gaps; surface badly pitted. Medium fine, light brown clay; black surface slipped and well burnished and fired with blushes of brown. Low ring foot; piriform body with a slightly raised, wide flat band at the level of greatest diameter and a ledged ridge halfway up the shoulder; continuous curve into narrow neck, which has a raised ring at about midway. The rim of the trefoil mouth an outward-thickened band; pinched together so that the sides bridge over the space within the central spout. Rolled handle from back of rim to just above level of greatest diameter.

ROUND-MOUTHED JUG
TumP 66

TumP 66   **Black polished round-mouthed jug**
P 1422   Southwest corner, sherds
H.-rim 0.181   H.-h. 0.22   D. 0.188
D. rim 0.15 m.
Pl. 18G

Mended from many pieces; chips and small bits missing. Fine, heavily micaceous clay, fired reddish brown; equally micaceous slip or film, well burnished to a medium luster. Low ring foot, slightly flaring, below a plump ellipsoidal body; straight, wide neck ending in a slightly projecting rounded rim. Double oval handle rising above rim and joining body at level of greatest diameter.

HORN-SHAPED RHYTON
TumP 67

TumP 67   **Black polished horn-shaped rhyton**
P 1416   South side, under beam 5
L. 0.255   D. rim 0.07 m.
Pl. 18H

Broken and mended around the mouth; tip from lower end missing. Fine, micaceous clay, light brown; well-burnished black surface, coated with a mica film and fired with brown blushes. Horn-shaped drinking vessel, closed at the bottom. Outward-thickened band

rim; a raised flat collar around the bottom above the break.

RING VASE WITH TREFOIL MOUTH
TumP 68

TumP 68   **Black polished ring vase with trefoil mouth**
P 1417   South side, under beam 7
H.-h. 0.155   D. 0.175 m.
Pl. 18I, J

Intact except for a small bit at the base of the handle, which was broken off and mended; the surface much pitted and flaked. Heavily micaceous, medium fine clay, fired light brown; equally micaceous slip or film, well burnished originally and fired gray; luster due primarily to glitter of mica.

The body a closed tubular ring from which rises a straight cylindrical neck with a raised ring collar at half its height, and ending above in a trefoil mouth with rolled rim. Basket handle finished to five flat faces from back of mouth to top of ring opposite, forming a reverse curve.

TWIN JARS WITH LINKING
BASKET HANDLES
TumP 69

TumP 69   **Black polished twin jars**
P 1423   South side, under beam 5
H.-rim 0.105   D. each body 0.12
D. each rim 0.068 m.
Pl. 19A, B

The handles and connecting bars mended; most of one handle missing. Fine, reddish brown clay; burnished dark gray surface coated with a micaceous film. The jars ellipsoidal on low raised bases, with hole mouths surrounded by squared, slightly raised rims. The two jars, which do not touch each other, are joined at opposite sides by two horizontal bars of rolled clay, set at the level of greatest diameter; the bars are of unequal length. Two high basket handles of rolled clay; each links the outer shoulder of one jar to the inner shoulder of the other. Two additional handles (one missing) both at the same side, run up from close to the end of the connecting bar to the centers of the basket handles, meeting them at right angles.

BOWLS
TumP 70, 71

TumP 70   **Black polished socketed bowl with spout**
P 1420   South side, under beam 7
H. 0.057   D. 0.169 m.
Pl. 19C, D

Mended complete from many fragments. Fine, light brown clay; slipped and well burnished inside and out and fired black with a few blushes of brown. Shallow bowl with wall curving continuously from plain rim to base, where a hollow cylindrical socket rises to an outward turned rim at the level of the rim of the bowl. The vessel could have been set on a spiked stand. Rising above the rim at one side, a tubular spout; this is continued as a flattened tunnel against the inner wall of the bowl, to an inlet slit near the base of the socket. Spout and tunnel served as a suction straw for drinking.

TumP 71   **Black polished spouted bowl with two handles**
P 1421   South side, under beam 5
H. to top of spout 0.076   D. rim 0.165 m.
Pl. 19E–G

Mended complete from several fragments. Fine, light brown clay; polished black surface with thin, iridescent mica film. Shallow bowl with thickened rim, rolled slightly inward, and ring foot. Within the foot a shallow concavity, corresponding to the rounded omphalos at the center inside. But the omphalos must be double, since the inner part is pierced by two crossing double rows of pricked holes, forming a strainer connecting with a flattened tunnel up the inner face of the wall. From the level of the rim the tunnel is continued by a tubular spout, projecting at an angle, then flattening to the horizontal. A rounded knob at the angle of the spout suggests the head of a long-billed bird. Nearly opposite the spout a small arc-shaped handle at the rim, turned inward and slanted slightly upward; raised pellets at its center and two ends suggest metallic studs. A second handle, vertical and rolled, rises from the rim slightly to the right of the spout and curves down to join the wall above the foot. The spout again served as a drinking straw; the liquid was strained through the omphalos.

SIEVE-SPOUTED JUGS
TumP 72–78

TumP 72   **Black polished sieve-spouted jug with strainer top**
P 1429   South side, under beam 5
H.-rim 0.098   H.-h. 0.144   D. 0.123
D. rim 0.081   L. through spout 0.22 m.
Pl. 19H, I

Mended from many fragments; some missing, including sieve for spout. Fine, reddish brown micaceous clay; slipped and well burnished, coated with a mica film and fired with several brown blushes. Ellipsoidal body with a low disk base underneath; short, wide neck with tiny ridge at midway; small flaring rim. A long, upward-tilted spout from the shoulder; it is U-shaped, completely open at the top, and somewhat flared toward the end. The shoulder pierced by pricked holes in a pattern, forming a sieve, where the spout joins. At the top, the mouth is closed by another strainer slightly sunk below top of rim: a flat disc pierced by rows of pricked holes crossing at the center. Narrow vertical strap handle rising above the rim, set to the right of the spout.

TumP 73   **Black polished sieve-spouted jug**
P 1426   South side, under beam 6
H.-rim 0.071   H.-h. 0.115   D. 0.099
D. rim 0.063   L. 0.18 m.
Pl. 20A

Mended from many fragments; some missing. Fabric similar to TumP 72. Ellipsoidal body on a flat bottom; short, wide neck with fine ridge at base and plain flaring rim. Open trough spout attached at top flush with rim, the wall sieved where the spout joins. Rolled handle forming a very broad loop from greatest diameter to top of rim.

TumP 74   **Black polished sieve-spouted jug**
P 1427   South side, under beam 6
H. rim 0.066   H.-h. 0.115   D. 0.10
L. 0.188 m.
Pl. 20B

Mended from many fragments; many more, including most of the handle, missing; surface scratched in places. Medium fine clay, light brown; slipped and burnished to a high luster, and fired with a few blushes of brown. Similar in shape to TumP 73, but a little smaller and with a broader, more depressed body. On interior spout, near point of attachment, six deeply cut transverse notches.

TumP 75   **Black polished sieve-spouted jug**
P 1428   South side, under beam 6
H.-rim 0.07   H.-h. 0.10   D. 0.082
L. 0.17 m.
Pl. 20C, D

Mended with many small fragments missing; surface badly pitted and chipped. Fine light brown clay; surface slipped, well burnished, and fired a quite uniform black. Low ring foot; ellipsoidal body; a slightly raised ridge divides short neck from shoulder; plain flaring rim. The spout set horizontally, spanning mid-body; wall sieved at junction of spout; the spout shallow for most of its length and crossed inside by six wide, shallow grooves; inner end tubular, crossed at the top by a squared bar extending from edge of bridge to shoulder. Heavy rolled handle from top of rim to greatest diameter; crossed at top by a rotelle; a squared rod of clay extends from rotelle towards the rim, but is broken away in its lower length.[77]

TumP 76   **Black polished sieve-spouted jug with relief decoration**
P 1430   South side, under beam 5
H.-rim 0.073   H.-h. 0.13   D. 0.093
D. rim 0.061   L. 0.16 m.
Pl. 20E (*R*)

Mended from several fragments; part of handle missing. Fine, reddish brown clay, micaceous; slipped and burnished to a medium luster and fired with lighter blushing. Ring foot, slightly spreading and grooved at half its height. The ellipsoidal body decorated in relief pinched up from the clay and partially pushed out from inside: on the shoulder, pendent loops containing vertical tongues; on lower body, rising loops. Low rolled rim around a wide mouth. Spout set almost horizontally at level of greatest diameter; wall sieved at junction. The spout U-shaped and slightly flared at its end; the inner half bridged by a flat cover decorated on top with low relief ornament consisting of arcs and bars impressed with double rows of tiny punched squares. Narrow strap handle from top of rim to greatest diameter; across its top a rotelle, knobbed at center (representing a rivet head?). From rotelle to rim, the handle decorated with relief and stamped ornamentation of same type as that on the bridge: a pendent horseshoe, and two pairs of half-circles back to back, their surfaces decorated again with double rows of tiny punched squares.

---

[77]Pl. 20C as glued; pl. 20D after plastering.

TumP 77   **Black polished sieve-spouted jug with relief decoration**
P 1431   South side, under beam 5
H.-rim 0.076   H.-h. 0.130   D. 0.089
D. rim 0.059   L. 0.158 m.
Pl. 20E (*L*)

Small fragments missing; the surface badly pitted and flaked. Similar in fabric, shape, and decoration to TumP 76. The relief decoration on the handle substitutes a circle for the pendent horseshoe of TumP 76.

TumP 78   **Black polished sieve-spouted jug with relief decoration**
P 1432   South side, under beam 5
H.-rim 0.07   H.-h. 0.125   D. 0.105
D. rim 0.065   L. 0.18 m.
Pl. 20G, H

Complete; the spout mended. Fabric similar to TumP 75. Ring foot and low, rounded rim around mouth. The curved lower and upper bodies meet at a rather sharp curve. The upper body reeded, the ribbing running vertically and diagonally in both directions at haphazard; lower body less convex than upper, plain. Straight spout, U-shaped and flared toward its end; the inner part bridged, the upper face of the bridge ornamented with low relief patterns similar to those on the bridges of TumP 76 and 77. Rolled handle, crossed at the top by a bolster, ribbed across the upper face; the outer part of the handle plain, the inner spirally ribbed.

SEMI-COARSE AND COARSE WARES
TumP 79–105

With the sole exception of TumP 94, the large coarse vessels from the tomb are of black polished ware with a biscuit that is considerably lighter in color. In general, the dinoi are better refined in clay and surface treatment than the larger containers.

BLACK POLISHED DINOI
TumP 79–87 bis

Ten round-bodied storage vessels were put together from fragments found in the northwest corner of the tomb. These vessels must have been placed underneath the bed, the collapse of which crushed them; probably they contained offerings of food. Their shape suggests that they were the pottery counterparts of the bronze cauldrons and large deep bowls.

TumP 79   **Black polished dinos**
P 1433   North side, under beam 8
H. 0.207   D. 0.27   D. rim 0.151 m.
Pls. 5B (*L*), 20F

Mended; small gap in body and chips in rim; much of surface flaked away. Moderately coarse, reddish brown clay; surface slipped and burnished to a medium luster and fired black with blushes of light gray and brown; traces of a mica film. Ellipsoidal body with very low ring foot; wide hole mouth surrounded by a low, everted rim flattened on top.

TumP 80   **Black polished dinos**
P 1434   North side, *ca.* under beam 7
H. 0.241   D. 0.283   D. rim 0.171 m.
Pls. 5B (background), 20I

Intact but for large gap in rim; surface very badly flaked and deteriorated. Coarse micaceous clay fired reddish brown; slipped and polished surface has a patchy overlay of reddish brown mica film. Ellipsoidal body, not as broad as TumP 79, on a flattened base; everted rim, more pronounced than that of TumP 79, with a broad flat ledge on the interior.

TumP 81   **Black polished dinos**
P 1435   North side, *ca.* under beam 7
H. 0.215   D. 0.27   D. rim 0.128 m.
Pl. 20J
Mended with a few gaps and chips. Clay like TumP 79; surface slipped, burnished and fired with brown blushes. Broad ellipsoidal body, full and well formed, resting on a low ring foot; small everted rim with flattened top and narrow ledge on interior.

TumP 82   **Black polished dinos**
P 1436   North side, *ca.* under beam 7
H. 0.26   D. 0.295   D. rim 0.183 m.
Pl. 5B (foreground)

One piece; most of foot broken away; chips in body and rim. Coarse clay like TumP 80; surface like TumP 81 but poorly burnished. Plump spherical body on a ring foot; small everted rim, broad and flat on top.

TumP 83   **Black polished dinos**
P 1437   North side, *ca.* under beam 6
H. 0.24   D. 0.31 m.
Pl. 5B (*R*)

Mended; many fragments missing but profile complete. Clay like TumP 79; surface like TumP 80. Disk foot; broad, very depressed ovoid body; short neck below an everted rim flattened on top and trimmed to a sloping beveled face on the interior.

TumP 84   **Black polished dinos**
P 1438   North side, *ca.* under beam 6
H. 0.206   D. 0.261   D. rim 0.155 m.
Pl. 6A (*L* foreground)

Mended with many fragments missing but profile complete; surface very badly chipped, flaked, and pitted. Clay like TumP 80; surface similar to TumP 81, but uniformly burnished and with traces of a mica film. Rather high ring foot supporting a plump ellipsoidal body; low flat rim.

TumP 85   **Black polished dinos**
P 1439   North side, *ca.* under beam 6
H. 0.22   D. 0.26 m.
Pl. 6A (*L* background)

Mended with some gaps; surface badly deteriorated. Moderately coarse, heavily micaceous clay fired reddish brown; clay now laminated perhaps as a result of deterioration; surface polished over a mica film. Foot and body similar to TumP 79; low rim, rectangular in section, set atop the shoulder.

TumP 86   **Black polished dinos**
P 1440   *Ca.* under beam 6
H. 0.237   D. 0.287 m.

Fragmentary but profile complete; much of surface flaked away. Clay similar to TumP 85 but less micaceous; surface similar to TumP 80. Plump ovoid body on a flat base; low rim ledged on interior.

TumP 87   **Black polished dinos**
P 1441   North side, under beam 8
H. 0.229   D. 0.317   D. rim 0.193 m.

Mended with a few gaps. Fabric like TumP 81. Wide, flattened base; broad ellipsoidal body, well formed; wide, everted rim, ledged and close in profile to TumP 80.

TumP 87 bis   **Black polished dinos**
P 4778   Not on plan; position unknown, but probably from under bed
D. rim. 0.142   D. base 0.084 m.

Very fragmentary: base and upper shoulder with rim; much of surface deteriorated. Fabric similar to TumP 79. Low ring foot; low rim, rounded on edge and flattened on top. On bottom, a large, neat pattern-burnished **X**.

BLACK POLISHED KRATERS
TumP 88–90

Two of the kraters, TumP 88 and 90, were included in the mass of storage vessels which filled the east end of the tomb; the third stood near the center, just to the north of the cauldron TumP 1.

TumP 88   **Black polished krater**
P 1442   East end, *ca.* center
H. 0.422   D. 0.434   D. rim
0.352 m.
Fig. 21A; Pl. 21A

Mended with some fragments missing; pitted. Moderately coarse, light brown clay; burnished to a medium luster and fired with lighter blushes; overlay of mica film, light reddish yellow where heavily concentrated. Broad, depressed ovoid body with flattened resting surface; straight neck divided from the shoulder by a ledged ridge; two parallel raised ridges divide the neck into three approximately equal horizontal zones. Everted, overhanging rim, rounded at the edge; two stepped ledges on its interior. Strap handles, shoulder to neck; a raised ridge down the middle of each, and a finger hollow at the center of the lower attachment.

TumP 89   **Black polished krater**
P 1443   Northeast of cauldron
TumP 1
H. 0.435   D. 0.395   D. rim
0.355 m.
Fig. 21B; Pl. 21B

Mended with many fragments missing; much of surface deteriorated. Coarse, reddish brown clay; surface slipped, polished and fired with blushes in color of clay. Ovoid body, pointed toward the bottom, with a flattened resting surface. Continuous curve into short, wide neck; blunt ridges at base and midway. Everted, thickened rim, rounded at edge and broadly ledged on the interior. Double rolled handles, shoulder to middle of neck.

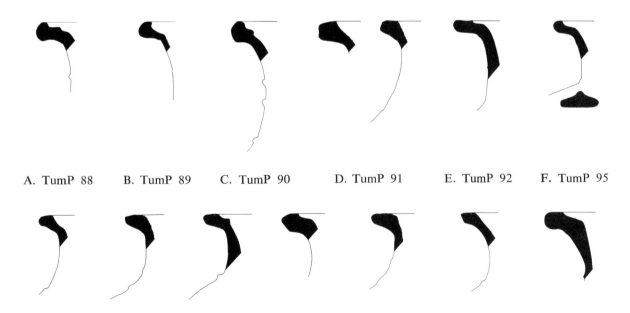

A. TumP 88   B. TumP 89   C. TumP 90   D. TumP 91   E. TumP 92   F. TumP 95

G. TumP 96   H. TumP 98   I. TumP 99   J. TumP 100   K. TumP 101   L. TumP 103   M. TumP 105

Figure 21. Profiles of rims and outlines of outer surface of necks of selected black polished storage kraters (TumP 88–90), amphoras (TumP 91–103 passim) and a jar (TumP 105). 1:4.

TumP 90   **Black polished krater**
P 1482   East wall, *ca.* center
Rest. H. 0.40   D. 0.47   D. rim
0. 41 m.
Fig. 21C; Pl. 21C

Mended; many fragments missing including most of base; badly pitted and flaked. Soft and powdery clay, fired yellowish red to pale brown; surface slipped and smoothed. Angular ovoid body, presumably flattened at the bottom. Wide straight neck, separated from the shoulder by a thick squared ridge at its base; two more thick ridges set close together just above the handle attachments. Everted, thickened rim, double-ledged like TumP 88. Strap handles from shoulder to neck; trimmed to a near-rectangular section; finger hollow at center of lower attachment.

AMPHORAS
TumP 91–104

Fourteen amphoras could be restored more or less completely; fragments remaining over suggest that there had been more. All of them were found in the eastern section of the tomb, where they had evidently been packed close together to support one another standing upright. No doubt they had all contained liquid offerings. Only TumP 94 is not of black polished ware.

TumP 91   **Black polished amphora**
P 1448   East wall, *ca.* center
H. 0.50   D. 0.408   D. rim 0.188 m.
Fig. 21D

Mended; many fragments missing, including one handle; much of surface flaked away. Coarse brown clay, crumbly and gritty; surface slipped and cursorily smoothed and fired black with some lighter blushes; traces of a reddish brown mica film. Ovoid body with flattened resting surface. The narrow neck curves continuously up from the shoulder, with a low, blunt ridge at the transition; on lower half, a pair of narrow raised bands. Thickened everted rim of irregular profile, flattened on top. Strap handles from shoulder to mid-neck; finger hollow at base of each.

TumP 92   **Black polished amphora**
P 1449   North wall, east half
H. 0.48   D. 0.388   D. rim 0.192 m.
Fig. 21E; Pls. 6A (foreground), 21D

Section of rim missing; otherwise intact; portions of surface crumbly and deteriorated. Moderately coarse, reddish brown clay with high concentration of fine mica; surface similar to TumP 91. Spherical body on a flattened resting surface; straight neck with a slight ledged ridge at base; broadly everted rim, flattened on top and with a shallow ledge on the interior. Strap handles from shoulder to mid-neck.

TumP 93   **Black polished amphora**
P 1735   Near east end, against
north wall
Pres. H. 0.265   Est. D. rim 0.195 m.

A fragment, preserved only from the lower shoulder up; surface almost entirely deteriorated. Very coarse, micaceous clay, fired reddish yellow; (now at least) clay soft and powdery; enough of surface preserved to show that it was black polished. Long, steep shoulder suggests an elongated body; straight, narrow neck with ridge at transition from body; everted rim, broad and flat on top. Double round handles, shoulder to mid-neck; knobs at the sides of the upper and lower handle attachments; two finger hollows at level of lower attachments.

TumP 94   **Fragmentary amphora of uncertain finish**
P 2189   Southeast corner, not on
plan
Pres. H. 0.39   D. 0.383   D. base
0.11–0.115 m.

The body put together from many fragments; neck and handles (except for lower stumps) missing; slip peeled away over much of surface. Coarse light brown clay; a lighter, reddish yellow slip, coated to an unknown extent with black paint and originally polished; the paint appears to have been mottled with the lighter colored ground. Ellipsoidal-biconical body with flattened bottom; narrow neck; strap handles rise from mid-shoulder, presumably to attach on the neck.

TumP 95   **Black polished amphora**
P 1454   North side, under beam 5
H. 0.394   D. 0.358   D. rim
0.150 m.
Fig. 21F; Pl. 21E

Mended with some gaps; surface pitted and largely deteriorated. Coarse reddish brown clay; surface polished and fired black with some blushes of brown. Spherical body, flattened at the bottom; short narrow neck; everted ledged rim. Strap handles ridged down the center of the outer face, arched from shoulder to lower neck.

TumP 96   **Black polished amphora**
P 1447   *Ca.* center of east half
H. 0.48   D. 0.452   D. rim 0.19 m.
Fig. 21G; Pl. 21F

Mended with gaps in body and rim; surface pitted and deteriorated to a lesser extent than is common among the Tumulus P amphoras. Moderately coarse, reddish brown clay, micaceous; slipped and well polished to a medium luster and fired black with a few blushes of brown. Plump ellipsoidal body, flattened at the bottom; short, straight neck separated from the shoulder by a low ridge, cabled; everted rim with a flattened top and a sloping ledge on the interior. Strap handles from shoulder to mid-neck, with pointed knobs at their tops.

TumP 97   **Black polished amphora**
P 1453   East side
H. 0.52   D. 0.445   Est. D. rim
0.20 m.

Mended with many fragments missing, including one handle; surface badly pitted. Light brown clay, soft and powdery like TumP 93; surface slipped and burnished and fired black with much lighter blushing; a patchy overlay of reddish brown mica film. Broad ellipsoidal body, flattened at the bottom; continuous curve into short, narrow neck; everted ledged rim. Strap handles with central ridge down outer face, mid- to upper shoulder; at their lower attachments, finger hollows.

TumP 98   **Black polished amphora**
P 1446   East of table, TumP 154
H. 0.46   D. 0.455   D. rim 0.172 m.
Fig. 21H; Pl. 21G

Intact but for one mended handle; chips in rim; badly deteriorated areas on surface. Coarse reddish brown clay; surface treatment similar to TumP 91. Broad ellipsoidal body on a flat resting surface; short, narrow neck with thick ridge at base; everted rim, broad and flattened on top. Strap handles from shoulder to base of neck; finger hollows at their lower attachments; one attached higher than the other.

TumP 99   **Black polished amphora**
P 1444   North wall, east of bed
H. 0.452   D. 0.427   D. rim
0.192 m.
Fig. 21I; Pl. 21H

Mended with fragments missing; much of surface deteriorated. Coarse reddish brown clay; surface

similar to TumP 97. Ellipsoidal-biconical body on a flat base; short, narrow neck set off from shoulder by a prominent ledged ridge; everted ledged rim. Strap handles set on the lower shoulder, their outer faces ridged down the center.

TumP 100   **Black polished amphora**
P 1445   East of bed
H. 0.47   D. 0.427   D. rim 0.21 m.
Fig. 21J; Pl. 6A (center foreground)

Intact; surface chipped and pitted; some surface separation on lower body. Clay similar to TumP 96; surface slipped and summarily polished and fired black with a few brown blushes. Body very similar to TumP 99; short, narrow neck set off from shoulder by a narrow ridge; everted rim, flattened on top and ledged on the interior. Strap handles set low on the shoulder; a low median rise along their faces.

TumP 101   **Black polished amphora**
P 1451   Southeast quarter
H. 0.443   D. 0.458   D. rim
0.185 m.
Fig. 21K

Mended; many fragments missing, including one handle. Much of surface deteriorated. In fabric and shape, practically identical to TumP 98.

TumP 102   **Black polished amphora**
P 1452   East of table, TumP 154
H. 0.404   D. 0.368 m.

Mended; many fragments missing, including entire rim. Clay similar to TumP 96; surface like TumP 91, but without mica film. Ellipsoidal body on a flat bottom; narrow neck with ledged ridge at base. Double rolled handles set on the shoulder; flattened pellet of clay in crevices near top; finger hollows at lower attachments.

TumP 103   **Black polished amphora**
P 1480   East wall, *ca.* center
H. 0.445   D. 0.37   D. rim 0.17 m.
Fig. 21L; Pl. 6B (*L* center)

Mended; many fragments missing, including the greater parts of both handles; surface pitted and flaked. Clay similar to TumP 97; surface similar to TumP 100, but with traces of mica film. Broad ellipsoidal body much like that of TumP 97; prominent ledged ridge at base of narrow neck; everted rim, flattened on outer face and top. Strap handles set on the shoulder.

TumP 104   **Black polished amphora**
P 1481   Northeast quarter
H. *ca.* 0.51   D. 0.455   D. rim
0.195 m.

Mended with many fragments missing; upper neck and rim practically floating above plaster; much of surface flaked away. Coarse, gritty clay fired light brown; surface similar to TumP 91, but with a greater range of lighter variegation. Broad ellipsoidal body, similar to TumP 97, tapering abruptly to a narrow flat base; narrow neck curves up continuously from shoulder and is set off by a low ridge; everted, ledged rim. Strap handles set on the shoulder, a high central ridge on the face of each; finger hollows at lower attachments.

STORAGE JAR
TumP 105

TumP 105   **Black polished storage jar**
P 1450   East half, southeast of
TumP 1
H. 0.495   D. 0.437   D. rim
0.26 m.
Fig. 21M; Pl. 21I

Mended with many fragments missing; most of surface deteriorated and flaked away. Reddish yellow clay, like TumP 93; surface similar to TumP 102. Spherical body, somewhat elongated, flattened at the bottom; thick ridge at transition to short, rather wide neck; everted rim, flattened on exterior and top and ledged on interior. Shoulder decorated by two low, raised bands, the lower one narrower; between the bands at opposite sides, two cylindrical lugs set horizontally, their ends crossed by raised vertical ribs.

SUMMARY OF POTTERY*

Of the four early tumuli of wealthy proportions, P provides the greatest quantity, and as well the richest and most varied array, of pottery furnish-ings. A total of 16 shapes are represented among the 58 examples of painted and monochrome wares. Tumulus K-III is the closest contender with its 46 vessels representing 12 shapes.[78] In comparison, Tumuli W and MM provide a much more limited variety of ceramic offerings, only three and two shapes respectively. The contrast is due primarily to the abundance and wide range of fine ware vessels in P and K-III, for all the tombs share more or less a similar variety of coarser pottery containers. Coupled with these varying degrees of ceramic representation is the fact that the pottery vessels of P and K-III outnumber the bronze, whereas the reverse is true in W and MM.[79]

Most of the fine ware vessels from P were found together in the south central area of the tomb. As noted elsewhere (pp. 8, 32), they may well have rested on a table which had collapsed.[80] Their grouping is analogous to the cache of 41 vessels deposited in the bronze cauldron no. 49 of K-III, and to the 20 vessels, only one being of pottery, placed in TumW 2. All suggest services, either for a funeral ceremony at the time of burial or for the afterlife of the deceased. The presence of sieve jugs in every group indicates the inclusion of beer (cf. p. 251) as do the two sipping bowls from P (TumP 70 and 71). Other vessels, with the possible exception of bowls, likewise suggest liquid as opposed to solid refreshment. It may be noted that the geese (TumP 49, 50) and other zoomorphs (TumP 58, 62, 63) would not have been suitable for the kind of beer suggested by the sieve jugs and sipping bowls unless the brew had already been strained. In the service of K-III's cauldron there is a repetition of sevens, beginning with two groups of seven sieve jugs, painted and black polished, and carrying through seven "Wasserkannen" and seven cups.[81] It is perhaps more than coincidence that Tumulus P's service also contained seven sieve jugs, all black polished like one of the groups of K-III, although there are no recurrences of the number. There may likewise be some significance

---

*Summary of pottery by G. Kenneth Sams.

[78]The four lids listed under no. 33 and the stand no. 45 are not included in the reckoning.

[79]In Tumulus P the number of pottery vessels is almost double that of the bronze, whereas in K-III there is a much narrower margin, only three less bronze vessels than pottery. In Tumulus W, on the other hand, there are almost twice as many bronze as ceramic containers; in

MM pottery represents only 10 percent of the tomb's total vessels.

[80]Whether the three vessels TumP 53, 59, and 64, together with the bronze cauldron TumP 5, can be associated with this group is not clear. R. S. Young (p. 8) assumed that they had rested on the southeast table.

[81]G. Körte in *Gordion*, 84.

in the several pairs of vessels that are included in the service from P: sipping bowls (TumP 70, 71),[82] geese (TumP 49, 50), painted round-mouthed jugs (TumP 55, 56), and black polished zoomorphs (TumP 62, 63). A pair of small bowls may also be added if the blue paste dish found in the group is coupled with a ceramic one (TumP 47 and 60). At the risk of pressing the point, one might also note the twin jars TumP 69.[83] If the three vessels in the area of the southeast table belong to the group too, a pair of askoi can also be included (TumP 52, 53).[84]

Of the various wares encountered in the tomb, reduced (dark) pottery predominates among the finer fabrics and, with the exception of TumP 94, is employed for the larger storage vessels as well. A similar emphasis upon reduced wares is seen also in Tumulus K-III. The technique encountered in Tumulus P is not a true bucchero, but rather a combination of oxidized and reduced firing, which produced vessels of light biscuit and dark surface. The reduction phase was seemingly of short duration, lasting long enough to darken the surface, yet not sufficiently prolonged to penetrate deeply into the fabric. The reduction firing was often uneven, leaving "blushes" of lighter color on the surface. Many such vases have an overlay termed here a "micaceous film," thereby causing the surface luster to be due in part at least to sparkle (cf. *inter alia* TumP 67 and 68).[85] These techniques are shared by the reduced vessels of W and MM and many pots from early levels of the city mound. The degree of surface finishing is normally in direct proportion to the fineness of the clay. Small vessels of well-refined and compacted clay are ordinarily well polished to a good luster, whereas large, coarse containers are more cursorily finished, wheel marks often being evident. Dinoi, intermediate in both size and the quality of their fabric, tend to be somewhat better finished than

larger vessels. The fragmentary amphora TumP 94 has been slipped and painted dark over a buff ground; the technique, insofar as it is observable on the badly deteriorated surface, is alien to Phrygian pottery as known at Gordion and in itself suggests importation.

The principal painted fabric is a distinctive brown-on-buff ware with fine quality clay and well-polished surface. It is the fabric of the tomb's finest painted pieces, the geese (TumP 49 and 50) and the three round-mouthed jugs with animal panels (TumP 55–57), as well as of two askoi (TumP 51 and 52) and the small bowl (TumP 60). The same ware is the prevailing painted fabric of K-III (nos. 3, 6–10, 12 and 13),[86] and is known from a single example placed in Tumulus W (TumW 61). The ware is rare in the early city settlement, the most notable exception being a sieve jug from the destruction level (pl. 96B). Stratigraphic evidence suggests that the ware continued in production for an as yet undetermined period of time after the destruction.[87] Similar in fabric, and perhaps a variant of this brown-on-buff ware, is the fruit stand (TumP 61). Yet, its use of bichrome painting under a high polish and the at least partial coating of the undecorated surface with paint, perhaps intentionally mottled, are features not otherwise encountered in the early city. In themselves they suggest importation, conceivably from another part of Phrygia. The remaining painted vessels are of black-on-red wares (TumP 53, 54, 58, and 59), a color scheme that is common in early Gordion. The juglet (TumP 59) betrays, more through shape than through fabric, its foreign origin (v. *infra*).

Of the 16 ceramic shapes found in P, half are standard items of Phrygian pottery, well attested in both the destruction level and earlier settlement contexts: round-mouthed jugs (TumP 54–57, 66), small trefoil jugs (TumP 64 and 65), a bowl

---

[82]Note in fig. 5, however, the somewhat removed position of TumP 70.

[83]The four sieve jugs of Tumulus W (if one includes the bronze example, TumW 5) were also placed in pairs within the two cauldrons TumW 1 and 2.

[84]See p. 46, n. 80.

[85]The term "film" is here used to describe a widespread phenomenon of early Phrygian monochrome wares. The overlay of mica appears in many cases to have been an additive (as a kind of micaceous wash, perhaps refined

from heavily micaceous clays), whereas in others (particularly where the clays themselves are high in mica content) it may be the result of inherent mica brought to the surface and deposited as a kind of film during the turning process. In most cases, however, the evidence is ambiguous.

[86]G. Körte in *Gordion*, 55–60.

[87]See G. K. Sams, *AnatSt* 24 (1974): 170–175 for further discussion of the ware and its distribution within Anatolia.

(TumP 60), side-spouted sieve jugs (TumP 72–78), dinoi (TumP 79–87 *bis*), kraters (TumP 88–90), amphoras (TumP 91–104), and a storage jar (TumP 105). All but the kraters and storage jar are seen again in K-III; the trefoil jugs of P are of a narrow-necked variety, whereas that of K-III is of a wide-mouthed type (no. 25) that was also popular in the early city. These parallelisms in kind, together with those of fabric noted above, imply that there was some consensus as to what a ceramically wealthy tomb like P or K-III ought to contain.[88] On the other hand, the varying emphases upon these basic shapes belie a rigorously maintained pattern or formula for the ceramic furnishings. Thus P contains only one pottery bowl as opposed to K-III's thirteen, while the ten dinoi and fourteen amphoras of P find only a pair of counterparts each in K-III. Both tombs contain as well their share of uncommon shapes. The range of each is very different from that of the other, due in part perhaps to the differing ages of the occupants.[89] The fact that P was a child's burial may well explain several of the bizarre shapes encountered there, particularly the five zoomorphs (TumP 49, 50, 58, 62, and 63) which, to a modern mind at least, seem quite appropriate. Neither these nor the fruit stand (TumP 61), juglet (TumP 59), rhyton (TumP 67), or twin jars (TumP 69) find parallels in other tumuli or in the early city. TumP 61 already seems a likely import by reason of its fabric; TumP 59, if not an import, would be the only known instance of an early Phrygian imitation in pottery of a typically Levantine shape.[90] The others, while unparalleled in form, are at least of fabrics and painting styles that are familiar to Gordion. The rhyton may be an innovative type; at any rate, it anticipates a local shape of the archaic period.[91] Other extraordinary vessels deposited in Tumulus P find correspondences in the

early city, either directly or obliquely. From the destruction level come close parallels in both shape and decoration for the askoi, TumP 51–53 (see, e.g., pl. 96G), while the same general context provides a doubled-over variation of the ring vase TumP 68 (see pl. 96I). The sipping bowls TumP 70–71 belong to a rare group of vessels that are related in function to the sieve jug.[92] The city has produced only two such bowls, neither from the destruction level,[93] while from the burned level a parallel in idea rather than form is provided by an elegant sipping chalice.[94] Such correspondences imply that these odd vessel types were not made exclusively for tombs.

Most extravagant among the tomb's ceramic offerings are its painted vessels, particularly those of the fine brown-on-buff ware described above. The linear animal style represented here by TumP 55–57 has been the subject of a separate study.[95] As free, painted renditions of North Syrian artistic forms in ivory, bronze, and presumably other portable media, the animals join with other categories of materials in reflecting the bonds that existed between Phrygia and neo-Hittite centers during the later eighth and early seventh centuries. Young has already noted that the uniform style of TumP 55–57 suggests the work of a single hand (p. 36 and pl. 17A–F). It is also possible that that same hand was responsible for the geese (TumP 49–50), since they are essentially ceramicized, three-dimensional versions of the animal style, as indicated by their decorative conventions, particularly the scale pattern of the breasts and the herringbone used for wings and tailfeathers, for these motives find similar usage among the two-dimensional painted forms.[96] The linear style is seen again on brown-on-buff vessels from K-III (nos. 3, 6, 10),[97] although here the animals invariably occur in a small-panel format as opposed to the large panels

---

[88]The tumulus standing on the Çiftlik Road in Ankara contained a similar range of standard Phrygian shapes; see M. J. Mellink, *AJA* 73 (1969): 214.

[89]In K-III, (*Gordion*, 55, 61, 65) the *Schnabelkannen* nos. 3, 14, and 15 and the cups nos. 26–32, together with their lids no. 33*a–d*, belong to this category.

[90]See commentary under TumP 59 in the catalogue.

[91]Cf. R. S. Young, *AJA* 59 (1955): 3 and pl. 1, fig. 5 (P 892).

[92]G. K. Sams, *Archaeology* 30 (1977): 114–115.

[93]*AJA* 68 (1964): 289 and pl. 89, fig. 25; *AJA* 72

(1968), pl. 76, fig. 14. The latter is from a much later deposit. The former, however, is from an ambiguous, pre-clay context which may have been deposited soon after the city's destruction; there is the possibility that the bowl itself dates earlier than the disaster.

[94]G. K. Sams, *Archaeology* 30 (1977): 114.

[95]G. K. Sams, *AnatSt* 24 (1974): 169–196.

[96]Cf. *ibid.*, 177, fig. 10, for an almost exact duplication of the scale pattern on a lion. For herringbone feathering, see *ibid.*, 174, fig. 8, and 179, fig. 15.

[97]G. Körte in *Gordion*, 55–58 and fig. 18.

of the three jugs from P. The only example of the style from a secure context of the early city is a brown-on-buff sieve jug from the destruction level (pl. 96B). In its use of small panels it is allied most closely with the vessels of K-III. Fragments of enormous painted kraters from various later contexts of the city display the large-paneled format, both single animals within frames, as seen in P, and groups.[98] The original associations of the kraters are ambiguous. Signs of secondary burning on several fragments, while not conclusive proof of an origin in the destruction level, allow this possibility, as do correspondences in scale and general form with huge monochrome kraters from destroyed buildings of the early city. Moreover, the style of both the animals and the ancillary geometric forms is so close to that of the jugs from P as to suggest an at least approximate contemporaneity.

The quasi-zoomorphic askoi (TumP 51 and 52) are of the same brown-on-buff fabric as the geese; yet their decoration, together with that of the black-on-red askos (TumP 53), assumes an entirely different nature. While the geese rely upon highly conventionalized patterns to transmit a sense of realism, the askoi reflect a much more traditional attitude to vase decoration through their use of a single geometric pattern. While a common Phrygian motif in itself, checkerboard used as a blanketing design is rare, and furthermore seems to be a device employed exclusively for askoi, perhaps in a surrealistic attempt to suggest feathers (or fur). Young has noted elsewhere the parallel of an askos from the destruction level whose form and decoration are practically identical to those of TumP 51 and 52 (p. 34). To this may be added another destruction-level example whose partial checkerboard covering parallels most closely the treatment of TumP 53.[99] Within the early city such askoi and their distinctive type of decoration are known only from the destruction level.

The ram jug TumP 58 is closest of all the painted zoomorphs to the idea of embellishing an animal as though it were a pot: the large, well-

defined zones on either side of its body would be perfectly at home on the belly or neck of a conventional Phrygian vessel. The contrast with the geese and the askoi is striking. Taken together, the vessels indicate that there were no fewer than three separate approaches to the decoration of zoomorphic forms, one the indirect result of eastern influence, the others most likely stemming from local Phrygian tradition.

Seemingly misplaced among the pretentious painted vessels of the tomb is the black-on-red round-mouthed jug TumP 54, yet it more than its companions represents the norm in Phrygian painting as known from the early city. The use of a simple chevron-triangle motif on the shoulder and the omission of a full-sized zone of decoration on the neck link this jug to a distinctive style of Phrygian painting that was not current in the early city until its final phase.[100] K-III possessed two examples of this simple painting style (nos. 4, 5), again an anomaly among otherwise elegantly painted vessels.[101]

The above synchronisms with the destruction level, combined with the absence of the principal links in pre-destruction settlement contexts, in themselves indicate a date for P that is no earlier than the early city's final phase. Aside from their occurrence in P, the askoi with their distinctive patterning are attested *only* in the destruction level. The linear animal style, however, continued for some time after the disaster, and the style employing chevron-triangles may have continued as well. At any rate, the tomb's earlier dating in relation to MM (p. 269) would appear to secure for it a date anterior to the destruction, if only by a little. The linear animal and chevron-triangle styles may also be called as evidence to indicate that K-III is not far removed from either P or the time of the destruction. Further synchronisms between the two burials are supplied by sieve jugs with relief decoration, particularly the shallow, impressed variety on spouts and handles (p. 253), and by the common use of ellipsoidal, shoulder-handled amphoras, a type not seen in the earlier Tumulus W (p. 256). Since analysis of the bronzes has yielded

---

[98] G. K. Sams, *AnatSt* 24 (1974): 175 and figs. 6–12.

[99] *AJA* 68 (1964), pl. 88, fig. 19 (P 3050).

[100] G. Kenneth Sams, "Schools of Geometric Painting in Early Iron Age Anatolia" in E. Akurgal, ed., *Proceedings*

of the Tenth International Congress of Classical Archaeology (Ankara, 1978), 230 and pl. 58, fig. 3.

[101] The tumulus on the Çiftlik Road in Ankara contained a dinos painted in a similar style.

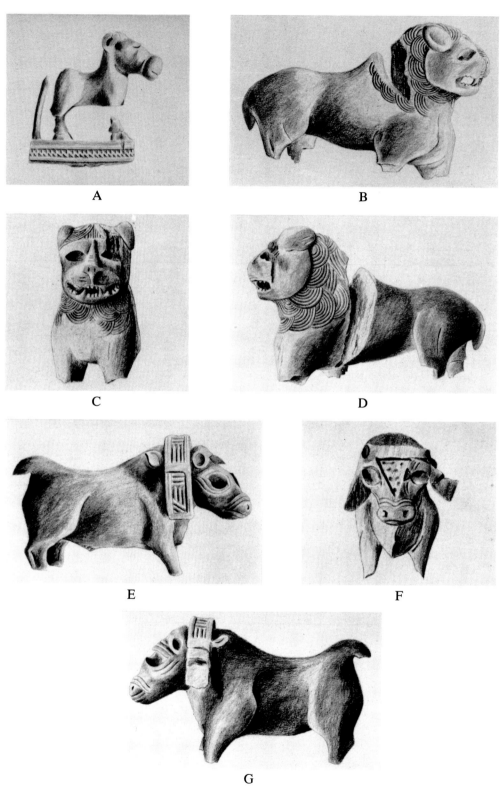

Figure 22. Miniature animals. A. TumP 106, horse. B. TumP 108, lion, side view.
C. TumP 108, lion, front view. D. TumP 108, lion, side view. E. TumP 110, ox, side
view. F. TumP 110, ox, front view. G. TumP 110, ox, side view.   3:4.

temporal priority to K-III, this tomb's regular employment of small animal panels may, as Young thought, be of chronological significance in representing a phase of development that preceded the large-panel format seen in P (TumP 55–57).[102] If the unusual relief decoration found on sieve jugs in the two tumuli is in fact the work of a single potter (p. 253), the gap between K-III and P can be narrowed to no more than an active lifetime; it was probably considerably less.

WOOD

MINIATURE ANIMALS*
TumP 106–114
(See also attachments TumP 148–150)

The following series of carved wooden animals was found inside the smashed cauldron TumP 1. Because it had stood on its iron tripod-ring near the center of the floor, it had unfortunately received the full impact of both sets of fallen roof beams and the stones. Since it was found standing, though crushed, between the upper and lower roofs, it must have in some way survived or deflected the fall of the inner beams, and have been finally flattened only by the fall of the upper beams. The animals had in general badly abraded surfaces, and extremities broken and/or rotted away. Also, upon exposure to the air, they cracked and warped somewhat further.

TumP 106	**Horse**
	W 5
	GPH. 0.048 GL. 0.044 L. plinth
	0.04 W. 0.018 m.
	Figs. 22A, 23; Pl. 22A, B

In two fragments; many parts missing, including top of tail, left ear, most of three of the legs, and inlay of the eyes. Placed on a flat oblong base to which the end of the long tail attaches. The vertical

Figure 23. TumP 106. Horse. Undersurface of plinth. 1:1.

---

[102]Young, *Gordion Guide* (1975), 47.

*Catalogue and discussion of miniature animals by Ellen L. Kohler.

edges of the base decorated with zigzag between ridges. At the center of its bottom face a large circular sinking set off by a rounded ridge, possibly for attachment to some other object (fig. 23). Since the ridge prevents its meeting any flat surface flush, perhaps it was meant as a finial of some sort to be attached to a pole.

The horse is very much like those of the bronze quadriga group, TumP 40 (p. 21) in its shape and proportions; the widely flaring hooves are clearly indicated as unsplit. Surfaces were originally polished, and fine incised details were added on head and ear.

TumP 107	**Lion**
	W 2
	H. 0.075 L. 0.097 W. 0.032 m.
	Pl. 22C–F

Much of the flat rectangular base and the right hind leg of the animal missing; many large cracks in the body. Striding lion, his tail curved down between his hind legs to join the base. Very large head, short body and legs. The mouth open in a snarl, displaying all the teeth and the end of the tongue lolling over the chin. The mouth edged by a ridge raised above the cheeks to either side. The eyes, very close together, appear as flat disks with tiny central sockets for inlay. Ears, laid back against the head, are ivy-leaf shaped with inward-turned volutes at the bottom, each bored at the center. On the ridge of the mane, crosshatched pattern; on the lower mane and breast, basket-weave pattern. The shoulder area defined by a border of dots between fine ridges. The claws sheathed and carefully articulated.

TumP 108	**Lion**
	W 4
	H. 0.050 L. 0.085 W. 0.03 m.
	Fig. 22B–D; Pl. 22G–I

The base missing, with the lower parts of all the legs and tail; the body much cracked and split. Striding animal, its head turned slightly toward the right. The proportions—longer body, smaller head, less prominent rump—are more natural than those of TumP 107; but its aspect is much less fierce. The mouth open, the ears closed down from the top. The inlay sockets for the eyes are oval with pointed ends, and deep. The mane an incised scale pattern of overlapping compounded half-circles, extending under the chin.

TumP 109   Group: Lion and bull
W 8
GPH. 0.068   L. 0.105
        W. 0.026 m.
        Pl. 23A–C

Marred on one face by its contact with TumP 122 in the cauldron; see pl. 5A. The base and the hind legs (except one, of the lion) and part of the tails of both animals missing. Cracking and warping in various places. On one face the impression of the rim of TumP 122 in the surface of the body of the bull. Lion attacking a bull; the figures grouped in chiastic arrangement with crossing bodies and heads turned backward, the lion to bite the back of the bull, the bull to defend himself with his horns. The mane of the lion shown by overlapping scale pattern (exactly like that of TumP 108); its eyes outlined by pointed oval incisions with central round borings. The legs are diminutive. The entire chest and neck of the bull faintly ridged; the eyes large round borings, probably to receive inlay, surrounded by double incised lines, pointed oval. Although the group is impressive, particularly for its composition and rendering of detail, it was obviously done by someone who took no interest in lions as fighters and the value of their claws as weapons.

TumP 110   Yoked ox
W 3
H. 0.047   L. 0.09   W. 0.035 m.
        Fig. 22E–G; Pl. 23D–G

The base missing together with the lower parts of the legs and tail. Probably the right one of a pair of oxen: the yoke where it turned inward toward the other (left) ox is broken off. The animal seems to have been represented as walking with its head turned considerably outward to its right. The large eyes were inlaid; inlays lost. On the forehead a triangular sinking with pricked holes at its bottom evidently once held inlay. Across the top of the neck a yoke, its upper face decorated with coarsely worked basket-weave pattern. Behind the yoke tiny ears, laid back; in front of it, sockets for the horns, to be

separately made and added. Details are worked for the most part on its right side: the outlining of the eyehole, the base of the horn, the ear.

TumP 111   Griffin eating fish
W 6
H. 0.066   L. 0.09   W. 0.03 m.
        Pls. 23H, 24A, B

The animal preserved in good condition except for the missing tail, left hind leg, and eye inlay; the thin rectangular base badly split and cracked; the fish's tail broken off. A hybrid creature standing foursquare on short legs ending in claws. Fairly long body, cylindrical, with plain wings attached at the shoulders. Long head, neck, and ears, with the end of the nose prolonged downward by a large bird beak, opened and eating. A protuberance on top of the nose at the end above the beak is pierced at the front by small twin borings—nostrils? The head bored through from side to side for the eyes which must have been the ends of a cylindrical rod of another material set through the hole. The left wing folded back along the flank; the right is extended forward and bent slightly inward, armlike, to steady the object that the grffiin is eating. This has a knoblike head with drilled round eyeholes, and a long tapering body. There is no doubt that a fish is intended.[103]

TumP 112   Deer (or bull?)
W 1
H. 0.064   L. 0.086   W. 0.037 m.
        Fig. 24A; Pl. 24C–E

Complete except for inlays (ears, forelock, horns, tail). Slight warping and cracking. Carved in one with its thin, flat, oblong base. Standing animal, its feet planted squarely, but with legs at an angle that brings the weight to the rear. Very large, long head, short neck, legs, and body, and wide, rounded rump. The mouth notched at the front; incised eyes are double rings with central dots. A slightly raised block across the top of the head, bored at either end with a round hole to receive separately made horns; there are separate holes for the ears to the rear of the horns. The missing tail was also separately made and added; its rounded socket, surrounded by a groove, remains. On the forehead a triangular sinking, roughened at the bottom, for inlay. Incised decoration of dotted concentric circles: two between

---

[103]An ivory plaque with a relief of a griffin eating an unmistakable fish (BI 332) was found in the city—in the burnt level of Megaron 3. See R. S. Young, *AJA* 64

(1960), pl. 60, fig. 25b; *Archaeology* 12 (1959): 286; *TAD* 10, pt. 1 (1960), pl. 6, fig. 12.

A   B

*Figure 24. Miniature animals. A. TumP 112, deer (or bull?). B. TumP 113, leaping
deer. 3:4.*

the horns, two on top of rump, three in a vertical row on the shoulder and neck at either side, and two on each haunch.

The precise identification is difficult because the nature of the added parts (horns and tail) is unknown. However, the feet show that it is a split-hoofed animal (deer, bull?). A forelock is seldom seen on a deer; however, a short raised flag-tail would seem right, as a long tail would have overhung the back of the plinth.[104] There is no indication of what the material of the inlays really was, but a lighter contrasting wood seems appropriate here for all the missing parts.

TumP 113 **Leaping deer**
               W 7
               GPH. 0.053   GPL. 0.067 m.
               Fig. 24B; Pl. 24F

Front legs are folded in. The hind legs broken off, but they were in leaping position. If there was a base, it was attached only to the hind feet. Head turned back, tongue protruding, short tail forward, up over back. No trace of horns or antlers. Mouth and nostrils shown by incision. Traces are still present of a contrasting wood used for inlay of the eyes.

_____

[104]See how the long tail has room for attachment to the plinth of TumP 106 (fig. 22A).

[105]R. S. Young left indications in his notes that he wished the wooden animals to be listed in the catalogue in groups by species: horse, lion, etc.; the styles of carving evidently were to be discussed at the end of the catalogue.

[106]If the animals are listed according to their methods of mounting, the following grouping results:

On plinth:
     TumP 111 (griffin and prey) probably handle to lid
     TumP 106 (horse) for attachment to pole

TumP 114 **Fragmentary reclining stag**
               W 65
               Rest. L. 0.09   GPH. *ca.* 0.03
                 GPW. 0.03 m.
               Pl. 24G

Restored from two fragments: the body, and part of the head with one antler. Legs and tail broken off except for stump of right rear leg; the right antler curved back to touch the shoulders, where stumps of attachments remain. The left side of the head preserved, with part of the left antler; stubs of four points above, two or perhaps more below.

The animals in the group TumP 106 to 114 (figs. 22 A–G, 23, 24A, B; pls. 22–24) form a fairly homogeneous group[105] on the grounds of size (Est. H. *ca.* 0.06–0.10 m.) even if one considers their various postures and actions. Their finding place in the cauldron is obviously a secondary one (that of toy storage for the child in this burial), furnishing no clue to their original purpose, which might have been as attachments to cauldrons, lids, or poles. Where plinths are preserved, they cannot be proven ever to have been attached to anything.[106] The whole group was made of the same

_____

TumP 107, 112 (lion, deer) purpose unknown
     K-III, no. 49 (lion eating quadruped). On good evidence found to be the handle of a cauldron lid. See G. Körte in *Gordion,* 68 and pl. V.

Perhaps on plinth:
     TumP 108 (lion)

No evidence for plinth:
     TumP 109 (lion and bull)
     TumP 110 (ox)
     TumP 113 (leaping deer)
     TumP 114 (reclining deer)

dark wood: yew. The inlays, though lost, were probably of light-colored wood: box.[107]

In style[108] the total must be broken apart according to the artistic traits represented. Beginning with the horse, TumP 106, we observe that its relationship with the horses of the bronze chariot group, TumP 40 (p. 26), is clear and, if we add TumP 112, the deer, we have a group of three objects from Tumulus P whose bodies and heads are built of cylinders with strategic bulges. Of these TumP 112 stands alone in the slanting position of an "Alişar animal" and wears the compass-drawn circles taken from the background of the pottery panels with which it is connected (see below, p. 55, n. 146). TumP 112 is the core figure of this group and the strongest.

TumP 107's short, compacted, barrel body, especially to the rear of the shoulders, resembles those of TumP 40 and 106, but in other ways 107 is in a class by himself—his spadelike muzzle profile, his open, voluted ears, his patterned, cross-hatched and basket-weave mane, as well as his tail curling under and touching the plinth, individualize him, and he has no partners. For large areas worked in basket-weave, one can compare the stone lions of Tell Halaf[109] in the pre-Kapara period.[110]

Two stone lions' heads found at Gordion, S 35 and S 43, show panels down the backs of their necks with the same linear pattern, running in the same direction as that on TumP 107.[111] The dotted line between lines employed to outline the shoulder zone of TumP 107 is to be seen on the two brown-on-buff jugs from Tumulus P: TumP 55 and 57. Akurgal has called TumP 107 Hittite, drawing attention to the cubic head, open mouth, and outstretched tongue.[112] One might also cite the open, voluted ear,[113] the tail brought forward between the legs and the presence of a plinth as on Hittite gate lions.[114] A remembered gate lion might cause the artist to work one side (here the left) in great detail and to render much less upon the side that was formerly invisible. However, if TumP 107 has Hittite traits, they are chosen from among many,[115] then lightened, smoothed, adapted and combined with localisms.

A third style is introduced by the lion, TumP 108. It walks, as did TumP 107, and *perhaps* the tail hung forward between the legs, but all the fierceness of lions is gone—the face and muzzle are smooth and relaxed. All that is left is the baring of teeth and the presence of a mane. On 108 the lines of the cheek, the ears, and the scallops of the mane employ the same gentle curves. Design seems most important.

To this group is to be added the lion and bull, TumP 109. The two lions must be by the same hand, and the bull expresses the same gracious curves and smoothed areas as the lion. The ridges of the heavier neck do not make the bull more fierce; they simply echo the curve to the point where the bodies form a cross-in-ellipse due to the adjusting of differences in lion and bull anatomy to allow no disturbing extrusion. Its thickness, which is less than "in-the-round," puts this in the class of double-faced plaques. The ferocity of a normal lion-and-bull fight is lacking. The subject is in general oriental but this chiastic-heraldic treatment within a round or elliptical area appears to be related to Iranian work, such as the roundels from

---

[107]R. S. Young in *AJA* 61 (1957): 326 referred to the lion, TumP 107, as being made of boxwood. The authority for his statement has not been identified among the analytical communications from botanists reporting. It seems to me more sensible if horns, eyes, deer's tails, etc., had been made from a wood lighter in color than the wood of the bodies into which they were set. If this be so, it should be noted that this method is opposite to that used in the inlaying of the screens. The dark wood is softer, easier to whittle, as was necessary in both cases, and the light wood harder, the better to retain the carved work in the case of the screen, but upon the animals the lighter inlays were lost due to the softness of the retaining medium.

[108]The discussion of style in this summary is based in part upon E. Kohler, *Wood and Ivory*, 20–75, 163–166.

[109]Oppenheim, *Tell Halaf* III, pl. 142; Frankfort, *AAAO*, pl. 158A.

[110]Oppenheim, *op. cit.*, 3–31; H. Kantor, *JNES* 15 (1956): 172.

[111]R. S. Young, *AJA* 60 (1956): 262 and pl. 92, figs. 42, 43.

[112]*Kunst Anat.*, 104 and fig. 66, citing his *Spätheth. Bildk.*, 46–47, figs. 35–40.

[113]*Ibid.*, pl. VIa (Zincirli); pl. IXa (Carchemish).

[114]The architectural socle in each case formed the base, which would become the plinth for the animal when carved in the round.

[115]E.g., the Hittite facial ruff and belly hair are left out.

Hamadan in the Chicago collection.[116] These are in gold, cut *à jour* and compounded to eights within eights. There is also from Hamadan a gold pendant in a modified elliptical form of lions, saltire rampant regardant. Two belt clasps of ram and lion from Kurgan II at Pazyryk[117] show the animals, couchant and regardant, worked out to an ellipse in a rectangular frame; these are found in nomadic territory, perhaps under pre-Achaemenid (Median) influence.

As we move from lion and bull to ox (perhaps bullock), TumP 110, we note as in the case of walking lion (TumP 108) and lion and bull (109), smoothly treated surface contours, soft facial planes, thickness through the neck area, curve of profile along spine, the same markings for leg tendons. The inferior carving of the near-basket-weave upon the yoke seems a disappointment and does not approach the finely scalloped manes of TumP 108 and 109 but approaches the primitive chevron patterning of the wings of TumP 148 and 149, *q.v.*, and the impression of coarse basket-weave given by the "Sarkophag" in Tumulus K-III,[118] and again by the stone lions' heads.[119] On TumP 110 there are a number of areas for a great amount of inlay: horn, large eyes, and forelock. Again a contrasting lighter wood (box?) pegged into position would seem appropriate.[120]

Next, the griffin TumP 111, marks a new departure—an elongated, cylindrical body with rounded rump, legs, and neck, with added wings and head delineated in rectangles and triangles, which are set off as raised and sunken planes marked off by ridges or carination. Such sharpened planes as well as the prey hanging from its mouth and the long sheathed beak are to be found in "nomadic art."[121]

Here as in some other instances, the Phrygians tend to simplify the more complicated pattern provided or remembered, and to adapt to their contemporary circumstances. TumP 111 is seen to be eating a large fish (a common type of food for those living on the banks of the Sakarya).

The sturdier form and the thick plinth of TumP 112 preserve in good repair the evidence of still another style of wood carving. Again the animal consists of cylinders with a series of fairly symmetrical bulges, so that the cross-sections of the separate cylinders remain circular. The decorative element added on the surface is also circles.

There is a long tradition of Anatolian preference for such a combination, going back to the Anatolian Copper Age. On the standards of Alaca, which are decorated with inlaid concentric circles on the rumps and haunches of bulls, the animals stand with their legs slanted, to confine them to their smaller bases.[122] Some part of this tradition must have continued into the Iron Age, since the pottery of the earlier periods at Alişar is decorated with deer, goats, and bulls—now in solid black, with the double concentric circles painted into the background as filling ornaments.[123] At Alişar the slant of the legs is freed to the parallel and developed to a "wind-blown" position.

TumP 112, then, appears to stand alone with regard to its Anatolian relationship, which may be with Alaca and Alişar, but there is still the tendency here, from nomadic art, to blur the identities of animals so far as the main body area is concerned and to depend upon attributes (type of horn, type of tail, etc.) for closer identification.

The oblique angle at which the leaping deer (doe?), TumP 113, ought to be placed, is difficult to determine. If one leg was on any ground line or plinth it had to be the right hind leg. The animal's tongue appears to be extended out (to reach the leaves of a tree?). Few parallels appear for a goat

[116]H. J. Kantor, *JNES* 16 (1957), pl. 3 top and pl. 9.

[117]S. I. Rudenko, *Kultura naseleniya gornogo Altaya v skifskoe vremya*, pl. 27:1,2 = K. Jettmar, *BMFEA* 23 (1951), pl. 29:1,2.

[118]G. Körte in *Gordion*, 43–45 and fig. 6.

[119]See p. 54, n. 111.

[120]It is to be noted that, if the tale of the tying of the Gordian knot was already circulating in the pre-Kimmerian age, the subject of a pair of oxen pulling a wagon would have been a popular one for representation at Gordion.

[121]E. H. Minns, *Art of the Northern Nomads, ProcBritAc* 28 (1942), pl. 1A,B; cf. pp. 3–4 for discussion of the wood-cutting technique and casting in metal from wooden patterns; J. A. H. Potratz, *Skythen in Südrussland* (Basel: Raggi, 1963), 71, fig. 49; T. Talbot Rice, *Scythians* (New York: Praeger, 1957), pl. 62 (ear).

[122]Koşay, *Alaca 1936*, 131, pls. 96, 97 (bull, Alaca III, Copper Age); *idem*, *Alaca 1937–39*, pl. 130 (bull, Tomb H), pl. 162 (bull, Tomb E), pl. 173 (bull, Tomb K): cf. Bittel, *Grundzüge*, fig. 11.

[123]Bittel, *Grundzüge*, fig. 40; Akurgal, *Phryg. Kunst*, pls. 1-6a (deer and goats from Alişar).

facing a tree-of-life but with its head reverted, and no good parallel for deer or goat with back to a tree-of-life. The artist may have encountered in his mind's eye the exigencies of space apparent in the plaques from the hüyük (i.e., BI 334,[124] 339), wherein the preference seems to be for representing a single animal, facing right or left, within a squarish frame.

Upon the reclining deer, TumP 114, the preserved portion of the legs indicates that they were folded under in an attitude of rest. The large number of tines on the antlers may be no exaggeration by the artist, as the red deer (examples of the skeletal material of which occur at Gordion) usually has five or more tines. But upon TumP 114 the whole natural system of branching is lost and the series of single tines along the beam is shown, probably not out of ignorance but for the sake of design. The broken and damaged bottom section prevents an analysis of the arrangement of the forelegs and feet.

Each animal in the group TumP 106–114 in some way retreats from realism into a schematic manner of presentation. There are at least four basic ways here of approaching the schematic; groups emerge as follows:

1. TumP 106, 112 (and the horses of TumP 40)—cylinders with bulges.
2. TumP 107—not in full round (eyes close together; cf. K-III, no. 49).
3. TumP 108, 109, 110—not in full round but back profiles gently curved; some oriental intricacy present but fierceness removed.
4. TumP 111—rectilinear (eating prey; cf. K-III, no. 49).
   (TumP 113 and 114—too fragmentary to characterize.)

The discernible system of close interrelationships with each other and with other objects found at Gordion, as discussed in the catalogue, implies, indeed demonstrates, that the miniature animals were made at Gordion and are Phrygian in concept and execution. But since every comparison appears tenuous, as though a mere memory of something somewhere else (Iran and other portions of Ana-

tolia) and long ago (Bronze Age and Early Iron Age), the artists who made these animals must have been of at least four different backgrounds but all expert Phrygian woodworkers.

SPOONS
TumP 115–119

All the spoons were found in the cauldron (TumP 1) and are not indicated on the plan.[125]

TumP 115   **Spoon**
W 16
L. 0.157   W. 0.04 m.
Pl. 25A

Complete, but the bowl warped so that it turns in on itself. Shallow oval bowl with narrow rounded point; the handle rises from the back in an arc extended at the top by a straight horizontal section. Handle round in section.

TumP 116   **Bowl of spoon**
W 68
GPL. 0.074   W. 0.042 m.
Pl. 25B

The handle broken away just above the bowl; a chip broken away at the tip. The bowl a flattish irregular oval, narrowed at the front. The handle attaches at the back just below the rim.

TumP 117   **Bowl of spoon**
W 69
GPL. 0.07   W. 0.04 m.
Pl. 25C (*R*)

Bowl much cracked; the handle broken away at its attachment. Like TumP 116; somewhat more pointed.

TumP 118   **Handle of spoon**
W 70
GPL. 0.087 m.
Pl. 25C (*L*)

Broken off at its junction with the bowl. In form like the handle of TumP 115 but shorter and heavier in fabric; the end knobbed, and the horizontal section platformed at its inner end.

---

[124]Young, *AJA* 64 (1960): 240, pl. 60, fig. 25a; also in *Dark Ages and Nomads,* pl. 20, fig. 1.

[125]See p. 290, app. III-A, Sample 3.

TumP 119   **Handle of spoon**
W 71
GPL. 0.068 m.
Pl. 25D

The bowl broken away, with the inner end of the handle. The outer part, warped, was probably straight. Similar to TumP 115; the outer end spooled.

LADLE
TumP 120

TumP 120   **Fragmentary ladle**
W 67   In cauldron TumP 1
L. (overall) 0.095   Depth 0.035 m.
Pl. 25E

Most of handle broken away; bowl badly warped. The bowl was originally round and rather deep. The handle, which attaches below the rim, arches like that of the spoon, TumP 115, but its outer end turned up rather than outward.

VESSELS AND LIDS(?)
TumP 121–147[126]

All the vessels and lids were found in the cauldron (TumP 1) unless otherwise indicated.

TumP 121   **Miniature saucer with bar handles**
W 13
L. 0.081   W. 0.047 m.
Fig. 25; Pl. 25F

Slightly warped; one handle mended. Very shallow round saucer with rim flat on top and low, raised base underneath. Flat bar handles at opposite sides bring the shape to an oblong; they are joined to the saucer just below rim level by diagonal struts forming two V's at either side, and half-rounds at the ends, each pierced by a drilled hole. Saucer and handles carved from one piece of wood. Incised decoration: crosshatching on outer body of saucer in areas between the handles; crosshatching of double lines on faces of bars of handles; at places on rim lozenge chains and diminishing triangles.

---

[126]See p. 290, app. III-A, Samples 4 and 5.

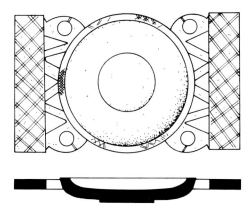

Figure 25.   TumP 121. Miniature saucer with bar handle.   3:4.

TumP 122   **Saucer with bar handles**
W 14
L. 0.128   W. 0.087 m.
Pl. 25G, H

Cracked and warped; small pieces missing. Part of a round shaft (the handle of a spoon?) stuck to the surface under one handle. Very similar to TumP 121, but larger. Four wedge-shaped panels, forming a modified Maltese cross, of crosshatching incised on outside of body; crosshatching of double lines on top of rim.

TumP 123   **Bowl of bar-handled saucer**
W 15
GPL. 0.118   GPW. 0.085 m.

Fragment, badly cracked and warped, of a saucer like TumP 121 and 122. Preserved are the central part of the saucer with its low base, part of the flat rim, and stumps of the struts of one handle.

TumP 124   **Small saucer with lug(?) handle**
W 19
H. 0.005   D. 0.04   W. rim
0.0025 m.
Fig. 26; Pl. 25I

Mended from two pieces. Slightly rounded bottom, curving up to a flat rim; the floor inside barely hollowed. A lug handle is partially preserved at the rim; shape of lug unclear. The rim at the opposite side is missing. Incised decoration of rope pattern across the underside (fig. 26).

Figure 26.   TumP 124. Small saucer with lug(?) handle. Detail: incised rope pattern.   1:1.

TumP 125   **Fragmentary lug-handled saucer**
W 18
H. 0.01   D. 0.045 m.
Pl. 25J

About half of the rim missing; mended from two fragments. Similar to TumP 124; a lug handle preserved.

TumP 126   **Saucer with cross-looped handle**
W 20
Est. D. 0.045 m.
Pl. 25K

Three joining pieces preserve nearly half of a round-bottomed, flat-rimmed saucer with double loop handles, their inner ends crossed near the bases of the loops, at rim level. The surface of the rim decorated with incised double X's; the outside below the rim shows a wedge-shaped panel of double-line crosshatching, stretching from below the handle to the center.

TumP 127   **Saucer with loop handles**
W 25
D. rim 0.09 m.
Pl. 25L

About half preserved. Saucer with convex bottom and flat rim, slightly hollowed inside; flat ribbon handle attached by both ends to rim and bent in to attach at the center, forming a double loop.

TumP 128   **Saucer fragment with T-shaped handle**
W 32
Max. dim. 0.055 m.
Pl. 26A

The fragment preserves part of the flat rim and edge of the bowl of a saucer somewhat deeper than the foregoing. The handle a flat projecting band set below rim level, with lugs oval in section projecting to either side near its outer end. Incised decoration on rim of triple-line X's separated by quadruple crossbars; and double-line crosshatching on outer wall below handle.

TumP 129   **Saucer with cut-away rim**
W 22
Est. D. 0.14 m.
Pl. 26B

Two joining pieces preserve about half of a large saucer or small plate with flat bottom, broad flat rim and slightly hollowed floor. At one side (and probably at the opposite side, now missing) the rim cut away.

TumP 130   **Saucer with cut-away rim**
W 31
Est. D. 0.16 m.
Pl. 26C

Fragment preserving part of a wide flat rim, at one point cut away. In the cut-away part of a handle: two scrolls joined near their ends by a thin bar. Dark wood.

TumP 131   **Plate with cut-away rim**
W 27
Est. D. 0.32 m.
Pl. 26D

Fragment of a flat-bottomed plate, slightly hollowed. The flat rim set off by a ridge at its inner edge. In the cut-away a scroll with a bar near its end, probably to join the end of an opposed scroll.

TumP 132   **Plate with cut-away rim**
W 23
Est. D. 0.15 m.
Pl. 26E

Two joining fragments preserve about half. Flat-bottomed plate with flat, hollowed floor; wide projecting rim with slightly raised bands at inner and outer edges. The outer band curves in to outline the edge of the cutout, and ends in a disk decoration at each side of cutout.

TumP 133   **Plate with cut-away rim**
W 24
Est. D. 0.32 m.
Pl. 26F

Not quite half preserved. Flat-bottomed plate with slightly hollowed, flat floor. Projecting rim with flat upper face, cut away at opposite sides. At the ends of the cut-aways, scrolls.

TumP 134   **Plate with cut-away rim**
W 21
Est. D. O.18 m.
Pl. 26G

About one-quarter of rim preserved. Shallow saucer. Flat rim cut away with hook at end.

TumP 135   **Plain saucer**
W 28
H. 0.004   Est. D. 0.10 m.
Pl. 26H

About one-third of rim preserved by three joining fragments. Flat bottom, slightly hollowed above, and flat projecting rim. There are no traces of handles or cut-aways.

TumP 136   **Fragments of plain plate**
W 29
Est. D. 0.20 m.

Two nonjoining fragments of a plate like TumP 135, but larger.

TumP 137   **Fragments of square bowl**
W 30
Est. W. at rim 0.12 m.
Fig. 27; Pl. 26I

Four fragments that do not join. Among them they preserve most of the square raised foot, parts of the obliquely convex walls, which were cut to form convex corners; the rim, inward-sloped and decorated with incised rings at the corners and running guilloche between them; one fragment preserves a projecting corner handle with part of the ring decoration at the corner of the rim. Incised exterior decoration of a panel at the center of each wall; three

were filled by double-line crosshatching, the fourth by latticing.

TumP 138   **Fragments of a disk (lid?)**
W 66
Est. D. 0.09 m.
Fig. 28; Pl. 26J

Two nonjoining pieces of a flat wooden disk. On the upper face elaborate incised decoration: at the center a six-petaled rosette, compass-drawn, the spaces between its leaves pricked; around it concentric rings of dots, outward-pointed triangles, and herringbone pattern. See the drawing in fig. 28.

TumP 139   **Small rectangular box**
W 12
H. *ca.* 0.045   L. *ca.* 0.055
   W. 0.045 m.
Fig. 29; Pl. 26K

Part of the bottom preserved, one end complete, and part of one side. All is so warped that measurements are approximate. Oblong box with straight thin walls and flat bottom, evidently carved from one piece of wood. The inner edge of the rim stepped to receive a lid. At the center of each side incised decoration of a compass-drawn, six-petaled rosette within a double ring, the spaces between the petals pricked.

TumP 140   **Funnel (or conical pedestal)**
W 17
Est. D. large end 0.19   Est. D. small
   end 0.035 m.
Pl. 27A

Fragment of a thin-walled object carved from one piece of wood. The preserved section mended from

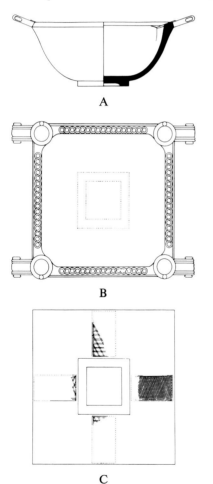

A

B

C

Figure 27.   TumP 137. Square bowl. A. Profile. B. Top. C. Bottom.   1:3.

Figure 28.   TumP 138. Fragments of a disk (lid?). 1:2.

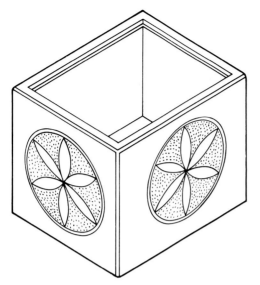

Figure 29. TumP 139. Small rectangular box, restored. 3:4.

two pieces but so badly warped as to be almost un-identifiable; but it had a tapered shape with a wide opening at one end and a narrow one at the other, funnel-like. At the wide end a plain rim (or resting surface); at the narrow end a flat raised band around the opening. A pedestal to receive a rod-shaped insertion? A funnel?

TumP 141[127] **Fragmentary shallow bowl**
    W 27
    Est. D. rim 0.11 m.
    Pl. 27B

Two nonjoining pieces. Small bowl with rounded bottom and plain rim flattened on top. No trace of handles preserved.

TumP 142 **Fragment of handled bowl**
    W 36   Southeast corner, area of painted table
    Est. D. rim 0.55   Th. 0.018–0.028 m.
    Pl. 27C

Three joining fragments of a large bowl with thick walls. The lower part missing. Rounded body slightly turned in at the rim. One sharply angular horizontal handle preserved, its ends prolonged against the body below the rim. Body and handle carved from one piece of wood.

---

[127]See p. 290, app. III-A, Sample 6.

TumP 143 **Bar-handled bowl**
    W 37   Southeast corner, area of painted table
    Est. D. rim 0.46   Th. 0.01–0.02 m.
    Pl. 27D

Seven fragments, mended to two, preserve part of the upper body, rim, and one handle of a heavy bowl probably like TumP 142. The handle, however, a horizontal bar, half-round in section, against the wall just below the rim.

TumP 144 **Bar-handled bowl fragment**
    W 38   Southeast quarter, against east wall
    Est. D. rim 0.46 m.

Small fragment from rim and handle of a bowl similar to TumP 143. The handle, better preserved, was straight, its ends cut free from the wall of the bowl.

TumP 145 **Bowl with bronze handles**
    W 33
    Est. D. rim 0.25   Est. H. *ca.* 0.15 m.
    Fig. 30; Pl. 27E, F

About half the body and rim preserved in several pieces, joined, and many nonjoining fragments which

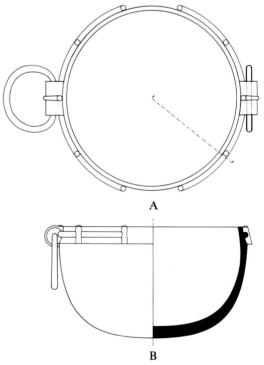

A

B

Figure 30. TumP 145. Bowl with bronze handles, restored. A. From above. B. Side view and profile. 1:5.

belong to this or to TumP 146; the mended section badly warped. Also, two bronze handles and the wooden half-bolsters from which they were suspended. Thick fabric; deep, rounded bowl with convex bottom and short rim slightly concave in exterior profile. On the outside of the rim, horizontal bars round in section, crossed at the ends and at half their length by vertical spools. The rim between the end spools left plain. The bronze handles swiveled from wooden half-bolsters at rim level on opposite sides. The bolsters have a vertical raised band around the middle and a slightly raised round platform on top beside the rim. The tops of these, and the upper ends of all the spools, show pinholes and traces of the decorative bronze studs which once capped them. Bowl, rim bands, spools, and handle bolsters all carved from the same piece of wood. This bowl was a wooden counterpart of the bronze ring-handled bowls with rim bands (MM 53–69), differing only in the greater depth of the wooden example. Dark wood.[128]

TumP 146   **Fragmentary bowl with bronze handles**
        W 34   East wall near north end
        Est. D. 0.26 m.
        Pl. 27G, H

Part of the upper body and rim of a bowl like TumP 145, and the two pendent bronze handles which belonged to it, one with a fragment of the half-bolster from which it was suspended. Heavier fabric; carved from a single piece of wood.

TumP 147   **Fragments of a bowl**
        W 35   Not on plan
        GPL. 0.14m.
        Pl. 27I

Three nonjoining fragments of a bowl like TumP 145 and 146, except that the rim band was tripled, taking up almost the full height of the spools which

crossed it (one of these is preserved). The bowl almost certainly had bronze handles; these may have been TumP 31, 32, or 33 above. Dark wood.

ATTACHMENTS*
TumP 148–150

TumP 148   **Hawk**
        W 9   In cauldron TumP 1
        H. 0.056   L. 0.109   W. 0.035 m.
        Fig. 31; Pl. 28A (*L*), B (*R*)

Feet lost. A round peglike tenon to the rear underneath the body, and a round dowel hole bored into the middle of the back, together indicate that this was an attachment that fitted into a piece of furniture. The wings outlined in overlapping planes; at rear the top plane of wings cut away to leave a peglike tail. The upper layer of the wings decorated with incised hatching, the lower with herringbone. The large head with heavy down-curved and sheathed hawk beak, has eyes hollowed for inlay.

Since this piece and TumP 149, a companion piece, were found in the cauldron, it is apparent that they had already become detached from whatever piece of furniture(?) they once adorned, before they were placed in the child's tomb.

TumP 149   **Hawk**
        W 10   In cauldron TumP 1
        H. 0.09   L. 0.093   W. 0.03 m.
        Fig. 32; Pl. 28A (*R*), B (*L*), C

The tip of the beak broken off. The legs are preserved at the front; they resemble the front legs of a lion and end in what look like paws. Hatching and herringbone decorate the wings; the eyes were inlaid. To be associated with TumP 148, whose description applies also here.

Figure 31.   TumP 148. Hawk attachment.   1:2.

Figure 32.   TumP 149. Hawk attachment.   1:2.

---

[128]See p. 290, app. III-A, Sample 7.

---

*Catalogue and discussion of attachments by Ellen L. Kohler.

The broken pegs to the rear underneath, in addition to the holes for insertion of another rod (or finial) in the middle of their backs, associate these birds with furniture (if one can imagine any pegs so thin, and angled so obliquely, as carrying much weight: the offsetting of the direction of the peg holes would lend weakness to the device). Perhaps they were suspended, legs extended in the air, near the center of the supporting rods for some light baldachino, on the analogy of one with animals from Maikop.[129]

If the hawks could have been set upon wands in the manner of those used in the ritual of Cybele, the reason for the offset angle of the finials, pegged into their backs, would remain unexplained.

The wooden figures are not truly in the round—the eyes are much too close together on the top[130]—as if the artist had considered the appearance not from the top and front but only from either side. The artist here shows less accomplishment in both conception and execution than the artists of TumP 106–114. The best parallel for the stylization of the hawks' feathers appears (e.g., fig. 19) where the similar method of lines of strokes (in oblique columns approaching an appearance of herringbone) is employed on feathered areas;[131] and for the manner of execution, compare the design upon the yoke of the ox, TumP 110 (fig. 22 E–G).

TumP 150 **Foot**
W 11   In cauldron TumP 1
H. 0.07   L. 0.098   Th. 0.026 m.
Pl. 28D, E

Warped and cracked. A semicircular arched piece of wood, round in section; its ends rest on squared

blocks connected by a straight horizontal bar. Beneath the blocks were separately added small feet or rests; at the center of the bottom of each block, a round dowel hole 0.025 m. in diameter. The semicircle within the arch bisected by a central round vertical: the quadrants to either side of this are occupied by curved, armlike or leglike pieces each of which ends in five fingers (or toes) of which one appears in relief near the bottom of the arched member at one face, four at the other face (it is difficult to tell which side is front or back). Above the arch at the center a round collar (now split in two vertically), socketed above to receive a pin 0.003–0.004 m. in diameter. Of what sort of hobgoblin this was a part, the imagination boggles to think; in any case it seems to have been a foot or base.[132]

INLAID SCREEN
TumP 151

TumP 151   **Inlaid screen**
W 60 (screen), W 61 (top, leg)
Southwest corner
Rest. H. the whole 0.805   Rest. W.
the whole 0.56 m.
Figs. 33, 34A–C, 35A–E, 36A,B;
Pl. 29A–E

At southwest corner of tomb, leaning against west wall. Now much warped, shrunken, and broken; the upper part had broken off and fallen. The top frame and leg were found behind the screen, while its upper part lay in fragments on the floor in front.

The whole had been made up from three main elements, joined: *A,* the screen proper; *B,* a frame fitted horizontally to it at the top behind; and *C,* a leg at the back fitted to the frame and supporting it from underneath. This restoration is based on the similar screens found in the Great Tumulus (MM

[129]A. M. Tallgren, *ESA* 9 (1934): 33, fig. 27.

[130]In this they resemble the miniature lion, TumP 107 (pl. 22C–F).

[131]G. Körte in *Gordion,* pl. 2 (K-III, no. 6); E. Akurgal, *Phryg. Kunst,* pls. 14a, 19a. It should perhaps be noted here that the brown-on-buff sieve-spouted jug (P 1270; pl. 96B) from the destruction layer on the hüyük was done in small-panel technique and the feathering had already been reduced to random dotting.

[132]For the use of similar divided arch designs (sometimes set upon blocks) upon a foot or base, see TumP 151 (screen), TumP 157 (stool), and MM 378 and 379 (screens). An earlier parallel for the theme of hands

grasping parts of two "belt buckles" occurs in Kültepe (Karum Kanesh Level II): one from Grave 0/19 (*Belleten* 19, no. 73 [1955]: 72 and figs. 37a, b, 93a, b) and another from a disturbed grave (*ILN,* Oct. 6, 1951, 547 and *AfO* 16 [1952/53]: 150, fig. 15). Cf. also J. H. Crouwel, "Early Belt-Buckles from Western Iran and Central Anatolia," *Iranica Antiqua* 9 (1972): 49 ff.

Cf. also two Luristan bronzes in Schaeffer, *Stratigraphie,* pl. 266:6, where the arch with central cylinder is present, with the hands of the central figure held at an angle to grasp the outer members, and pl. 266:11a,b, where fingers grasp a rein ring at the outer end of a bit. For a discussion of the dating of the latter two, see E. Porada, "Nomads and Luristan Bronzes" in *Dark Ages and Nomads,* 8–31, pl. IV and pl. VI, fig. 1.

Figure 33.   TumP 151. Reconstruction of face of inlaid screen.   Ca. 1:4.

378 and 379 below) for which the restoration is certain. The evidence that these three components belong (and once were fitted) together follows. The width of the screen (best preserved at the top of the lower openwork section) conforms almost exactly to that of the top frame: 0.56 m. The frame was fastened by two wide, flat tongues, one of which remains in its socket. These would have been fitted into sockets cut into the back face of the screen just below its upper edge, holding the frame in a horizontal position at a right angle to the screen at its top, and behind. Unfortunately the top board of the screen is fragmentary and poorly preserved at the back; though there is evidence for dowel sockets they cannot be measured or exactly placed. On the under face of the frame at the opposite side there are four dowel sockets: a central pair for wide thin tongues (one of which remains in place, and the broken-off end of the other) pinned in place by transverse pegs; and an outer pair near the ends, somewhat smaller and cut at an angle to receive tongues coming in at a diagonal. The leg must have been fitted beneath the back part of the frame: it is crowned at the top by a half-round bar with a wide thin tongue at the top of each arm to fit into the central dowel cuttings of the frame. The cuttings of frame and leg do not now match up: but this is due to warping of the leg, since the arms at its top have now spread apart somewhat. But the dowel still in place in the frame fits the dowel stump at the top of the leg, and the other dowel, of which an end is preserved at either side, seems to have broken on the line of the peg which held it in place. Below the moldings, which crown the top of the leg beneath its curved arm top, are dowel sockets, one in each side face of the leg. These were to hold the lower ends of the diagonal struts which were socketed at the top into the outer pair of holes in the under-face of the frame, and these too were cut diagonally into the side faces of the leg. Two slightly curved slats fit at their lower ends into the side cuttings of the leg. The upper ends also fit the sockets in the frame; but the slats themselves are now too shrunken to stretch the interval they once filled.

One more dowel socket, cut into the inner face of the leg, probably once held one end of a horizontal stretcher linking the leg near its bottom to the back face of the screen proper. The leg is now too short for the height of the screen; but this again is due to warping. The bottom of the foot must originally have been horizontal, to rest evenly on a flat floor; and the dowels at the top must originally have been vertical, to fit into the sockets in the under-face of the frame at the top. And, certainly, the sockets for the diagonal struts must have been in the same vertical plane as the dowels at the top. It follows that the

curvature of the leg must originally have been much sharper than it is now, and in consequence the height of the leg considerably more. This is confirmed by the cuttings of the leg itself. The struts linking the frame to the side faces of the leg must have been vertical; in consequence the upper part of the leg must be bent upward to bring the sockets which held the lower ends of these struts to the vertical. At the same time, the cutting for the strut linking the inner face of the leg to the back of the screen must be brought to the horizontal. From this it follows that the sharp curvature must have been in the thinner lower part of the tapered leg. A sharp bend near the bottom of the leg will considerably increase its height and bring it to about the height of the screen which it supported from behind, supposedly in a vertical position.

It may be noted that Tumulus P was dug one year before the Great Tumulus yielded models on which a reconstruction of a wooden screen could be based. The screen TumP 151 was dubbed a "throne back" and the other elements (even then associated with it) were placed on top, upside down, and thought to be a "canopy holder."[133]

A. **The Screen**
Rest. H. 0.805 Rest. W. 0.56
Th. 0.017–0.02 m.

The screen was made from boxwood and inlaid with yew,[134] giving a color contrast between the light background wood and the dark inlays. It was composed from about 28 separate pieces of wood, all joined together by tongues, dowels, and pegs, no doubt strengthened by liberal applications of glue. The upper part was made up from five boards placed one on top of the other, and fastened together by dowels across the joints. This is now fragmentary; but since the inlay patterns run across the joints between the boards which compose it, we must suppose that these elements were doweled together before the inlaying was done. The bottoms of the channels cut for inlay—about 0.004–0.005 m. deep—show the ends of holes bored by a fine auger or drill; no doubt a row of bored holes was linked to a continuous channel by cutting away the wood between them with a sharp knife or chisel. The channels do not appear to be undercut, wider at the bottom than at the surface; probably, therefore, the inlay strips were held in place by glue. The upper part of the

---

[133]Young, *AJA* 61 (1957): 329 f.

[134]See p. 290, app. III-A, Samples 9 and 10.

screen was framed all around by a border pattern of lozenges with triangles filling the intervals between them at either side; within this frame were three rows of small squares filled by various geometric patterns.[135]

The lower, openwork part of the screen is composed of five spaced verticals, the central one far wider than the others. Across the top of these is doweled the lowest board of the solid upper end, its face inlaid with the characteristic border framing pattern; the same border pattern runs down the faces of the outermost verticals, and part way across the bottom. The open intervals between the verticals are filled by square inserts in three rows, leaving approximately equal square openings between them. These inserts are tongued at either side, the tongues fitting into slots in the side faces of the verticals, where they were secured in place by round pegs run in from the back—run in but not through, since their ends do not appear in the front face of the screen. The faces of the inserts, and of the vertical members between them, are decorated by various inlaid geometric patterns within square frames: swastikas, X-panels and panels employing quadrants and semicircles.

The much wider central vertical, apparently a single piece of wood with cutouts and inlays, features a central round medallion ("rose window") containing six tangent rings around its edge, leaving a central opening like a six-pointed star, and six curved, triangular openings around the edge. The round frame of the medallion is raised, with flat central and sloped side faces. The square area above the medallion is framed at top and sides by checkerboard inlay; within this frame cutouts leave three tangent half-rings, all inlaid, and a bar linking the tops of the two at the sides.

Below the central medallion the panel is fish-tailed in shape, framed at the sides by the curved raised legs, inlaid with checkerboard. Between the upper ends of these a square frames inlay of linked rings with filling ornament between them. Below, the square holes may once have contained the ends of horizontal stretchers, and a continuing motive of

meander hooks defines the bottom. The curving legs, like the frame of the central medallion slightly raised above the face of the screen, end in rounded feet which project slightly beyond the sides of the screen. Pegs on their bottom faces (one is preserved) served to fasten block feet on which the whole rested.

B.   The Top Panel
       W. 0.56   Depth 0.26   Th. 0.045 m.

Broken into two pieces and so warped that they cannot be rejoined. Cut from a single piece of light wood (box). The dowel cuttings in the vertical face of one long side, and in the under-face of the opposite long side, have been discussed above.

Within the rectangular frame cut-out decoration. At either end a large ring faceted to eight faces (octagonal in section). The rings are supported by struts, round in section, from the corners of the panel. At the center between the rings the space is filled by four approximately half-rings, their open sides toward the full rings and the long sides of the panel; these are round in section. The panel, set horizontally at a height of about 0.80 m., was intended to be seen from above.

C.   The Leg
       PW. top (warped) 0.26   D. leg 0.046
       Max. dim. obliquely from top to bottom
       1.035   W. across circular element at
       bottom 0.165 m.

The leg was put together from five separate pieces of light wood[136] fastened together by dowels and

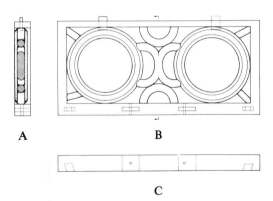

A   B

C

Figure 34. TumP 151. Inlaid screen, B, *the top panel. A. Section through the center. B. Top view, showing at the bottom (here) the holes through which the tongues at top of leg C show (see fig. 35). C. Section through slots near rear edge.   1:10.*

---

[135]The fifteen panels represent four separate designs in a subtly contrived pattern which may be expressed as:

A   B   A   B   C

B   D   B   D   B

C   B   A   B   A

Indeed, the "game" continues in the *à jour* bottom portion.

---

[136]See p. 290, app. III-A, Sample 8.

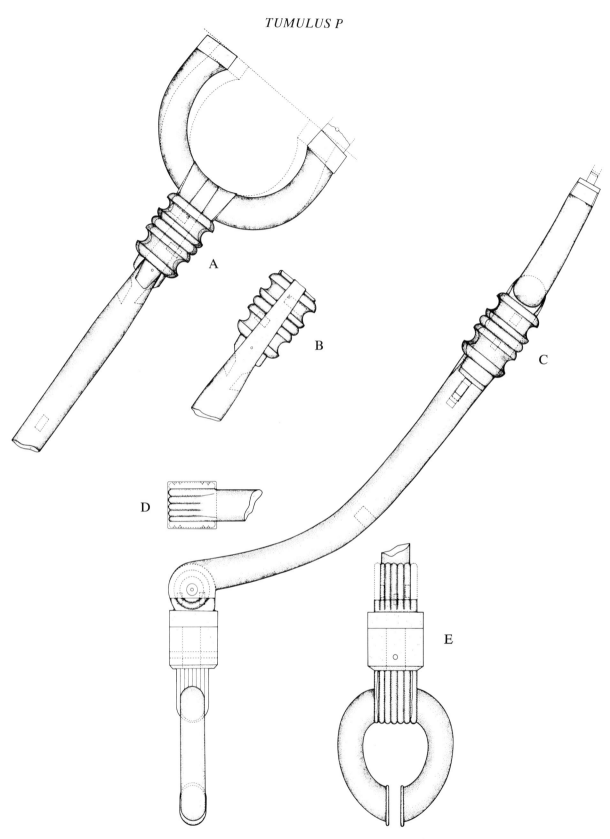

Figure 35. TumP 151. Inlaid screen, C, the leg. Views A and C show present-day warpage. 1:5.

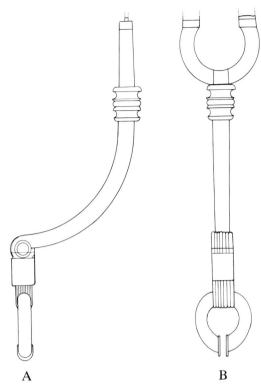

A   B

Figure 36. TumP 151. Inlaid screen, C, the leg. A. Side view. B. View from rear of screen complex. Two tongues at the top of view B fit into underside of panel B (see fig. 34). 1:10.

pegs. The leg itself, round in section and tapered downward slightly, ends at the bottom in a rounded foot, its outer face grooved and its side faces faceted in concentric circles. This circle motive is cut off at the bottom but completed in the upper part of a separate block foot which was secured by two flat dowels. The upper end of the leg, above the side sockets for diagonal struts, is sharply reduced in diameter by tapering; over it were slid the crowning moldings, separate pieces evidently hollowed at the center. These were secured in place by two tongue dowels fastened by transverse round pegs. The half-ring at the top was made of two quarter-circle arms, doweled to each side of the top of the leg proper, which extended above the top of the moldings. The original shape of the leg, and its dowel fastenings to the screen and to the top frame, have been discussed above.

———
[137]See p. 290, app. III-A, Sample 11.

TABLES
TumP 152–154

TumP 152 **Tripod tray table**
     W 40 Not on plan; pieces
      scattered in area north of
      TumP 154
     H. 0.06 D. 0.76 Th. 0.02–0.025
      W. boards 0.075–0.085 m.
     Fig. 37A, B; Pls. 6A (center), 30A

Many fragments of a nearly round table top made up from nine strips of a fine, white, brittle wood set side by side; on the underside cuttings for two of the three legs are preserved. The table top slightly hollowed within a rim which is outlined on inner and outer edges by a raised margin; at opposite sides cut-out handles. The slats that compose it show no cuttings for dowels in their side faces to fasten them together; but several show round holes with bits of dowels on the under-face, no doubt to secure a crosspiece (or pieces) underneath to hold the whole together. The top is too fragmentary to allow of any sure restoration; no doubt glue was also used. The sockets for the legs are shallow square cuttings (0.075 m. on a side) with a deeper central socket, also square, to receive a tenon (0.028 m. on a side).

Legs not identified.

TumP 153 **Tripod(?) plain table**
     W 43 Not on plan
     H. *ca.* 0.58 W. *ca.* 0.46 L. *ca.*
      0.68 W. rim 0.008 Th.
      0.071 m.
     Fig. 38A, B; Pl. 30B

Fragmentary; the top about half preserved but much broken; one leg, and the top of a second, preserved. The top made from a single slab of wood;[137] oblong with rounded corners, slightly hollowed on top with a low, rounded rim around the edge. At the better-preserved end of the top two square cuttings served to socket the tops of two legs. These cuttings are in line, and at the same distance from the table edge at opposite sides. On the underside below these cuttings the fabric of the table top is thicker, with a round socket (D. 0.066 m.). The top of the preserved leg shows a square tenon (0.026 m. on a side) which would have fitted into the cutting through the table top and the collar underneath it, and was fixed in place by a transverse dowel. The lower part of the leg is warped out of its original shape, and the foot

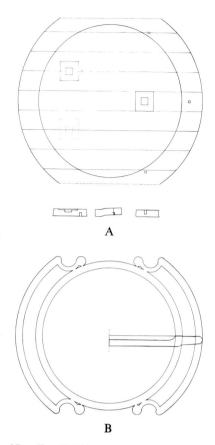

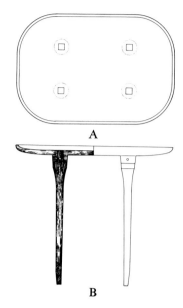

Figure 38. TumP 153. Plain table, tripod(?). A. Table top. B. Section through a leg, and side view. 1:15.

Figure 37. TumP 152. Tripod tray table. A. Underside, showing recesses for legs, and sections of sockets below. The top and bottom boards are shown here without their cutouts. B. Top of table, with cross-section. 1:15.

broken off. On the analogy of the tables from the Great Tumulus (MM 380–387) we may suppose that this table, too, had only three legs; but its other end is too broken to show any leg attachments.

TumP 154   **Table with inlaid top**
W 41   East of bed-bier
H. *ca.* 0.195   Est. L. 0.66   Est. W. 0.66   Th. top 0.025 m.
Legs: PL. from top of table 0.195 W. 0.054   Th. 0.054 m.
Fig. 39A–G; Pls. 6A (foreground), 30C, D

The roof of the tomb had crushed it in falling; most of the inlay of the table top came up stuck to the underside of the roof beams when they were lifted.

The table top was made of boards of white wood (boxwood)[138] 0.025 m. thick and 0.07–0.08 m. wide. These were fastened together in two ways: by dovetail clamps set into their under-faces across the joints (fig. 39A, B), and by horizontal dowels (fig. 39C, D). Since the pattern of the inlay runs across joints between boards of the table top, we must assume that the whole was fastened together by clamping and doweling before the channels were cut for the inlay. In a few places there are cuttings for clamps on the top face (fig. 39A, top), but since these are cut into the inlay as well as the background wood, they were cut after the inlaying had been done, and we must assume that they represent later repairs or attempts to strengthen the joints.

The channels for the inlay were made by drilling holes about 0.01 m. apart along the line of the pattern desired (the ends of the drill holes appear in the bottom of the channels), then cutting out the wood between them with a sharp knife or chisel: the channels were 0.0015–0.0017 m. in width and about 0.01 m. deep. The inlay was of dark wood, probably yew,[139] no doubt secured in place by glue. The pattern of the inlay was of diminishing squares alternately of light and dark wood, the dark squares con-

---

[138]See p. 290, app. III-A, Sample 12.

[139]See p. 290, app. III-A, Sample 13.

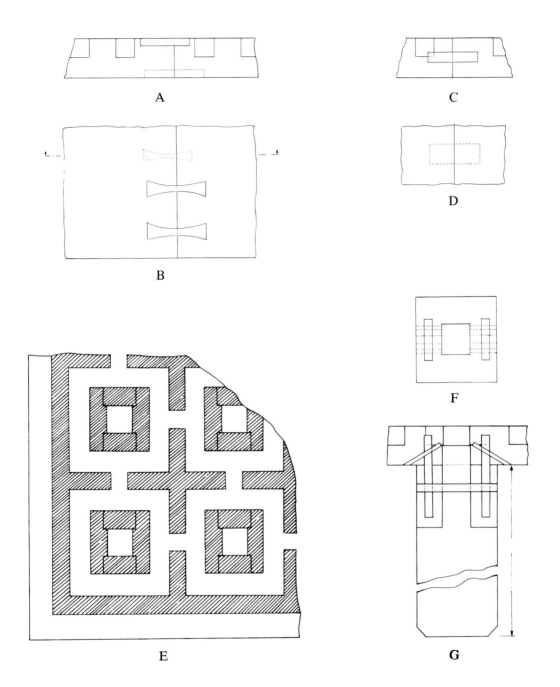

Figure 39. TumP 154. Table with inlaid top. A. Section through top showing clamp joints as indicated in B, and inlay pieces. B. Plan of clamp joints from underneath table top. C. Section through top showing dowel joint. D. Plan of dowel joint from below. E. Pattern of inlay. F. Horizontal section through leg and leg-collar joint. G. Vertical section through leg and leg-collar joint. 2:5.

nected by small dark blocks to form a diaper pattern (fig. 39E).[140]

The legs which were square in section were secured to the table top by hollow square blocks of dark wood pinned by dowels to the under-face of the top (fig. 39D). Two of these are preserved; presumably tenons at the tops of the legs fitted inside the hollow sockets and were pinned in place by cross dowels (fig. 39G). The tenons ran up through the leg sockets and into cuttings in the under-face of the table top. Again it cannot be determined whether there were four legs or three because the top is so badly preserved.

BED-BIER
TumP 155

TumP 155 **Bed-bier**
W 54, W 52   Northwest corner, head against west wall
Rest. L. *ca.* 2.30 Rest. W. *ca.* 1.10
H. leg 0.38 D. leg at top 0.08
D. leg at base 0.07 m.
Fig. 40A–F; Pls. 30E–G, 31A, B

The legs were found approximately at the four corners of the bed area, giving roughly the dimensions. Although the bed[141] was rather low, the length of its legs (0.38 m.) gave ample clearance for the dinoi that were stored underneath. The personal accoutrements of the dead child—belt and fibulae—lay fallen at the corner of the bed area; the only bones found were teeth, and since these were found in screening the filling from the bed area, there is no evidence as to the original position of the body, except that it had been placed near the center of the bed.

The legs (W 52), of which many fragments are preserved (though no complete member), show cuttings to hold the frame of the bed; just above the relief ring which encircles each leg, a socket to hold the end of a stretcher which ran across the width of the bed at head and foot; above this and near the top of the leg, a socket for the end of a rail or frame piece; and again above this and just below the top of the leg, but at a 90-degree angle to the sockets below, a socket for the end of the rail or frame piece running the length of the bed. Fragments of the rails

were found, identified by tenons to fit the sockets in the legs and by ends cut concave to fit the curve of the legs; but none was preserved to its full length to give the exact dimensions of the bed.

The top of one leg was preserved with a groove across its upper face into which was fitted a vertical cross-board, evidently the lowest member of the head- or footboard of the bed. A vertical groove near the end of this was intended to socket the end of a piece running the length of the bed, like the side of a mattress box or the rail of a crib.

Head and foot of the bed are represented by small fragments, assigned from their places of finding. A piece with a handle-like loop at one side of the top is part of the vertical support at one side of the headboard, which was evidently slotted down its inner face to receive tenons at the ends of the horizontal cross-boards. Small bits of these (there were apparently two) are preserved, one with the tenon at its end, pierced by a hole for a dowel to hold it in place. The front faces of the fragments of the headboard are decorated with a very small, cut checkerboard pattern: whether the tiny cut-out squares were ever filled by inlays is not clear. No inlays have been preserved in place, and the fineness of the pattern would have called for minute inlays. Perhaps the hollow squares gave the desired color contrast without inlay.

The footboard was crowned by a fencelike member cut from a single piece (or pieces; its full length is not preserved) of wood; square crenelations rounded at the top and linked just below it by a horizontal bar, oval in section. This crowning decoration of the footboard was doweled at either end to a framing vertical piece with a like rounded top.

The surface of the bed was evidently composed of interwoven narrow strips of heavy cloth. Traces of the cloth itself were found on the rails; and transverse indentations on the rail faces were probably caused by the pressure of the woven crosspieces.

LEGS OF FURNITURE
TumP 156

There was clear evidence in the tomb for the bed (TumP 155), the table with inlaid top (TumP 154), and a large table and a seat(?) at the southeast corner. But, with the exception of the bed, none of these was well enough preserved to allow legs to be fitted to it. Of furniture legs the tomb presented an embarrassment of riches. They are listed below, unassigned; there must have been

---

[140] A very similar table with inlaid top (W 84) was found in Megaron 3 on the city mound. See R. S. Young, *AJA* 64 (1960): 239 and here pl. 96J.

[141] See p. 291, app. III-A, Sample 14.

70

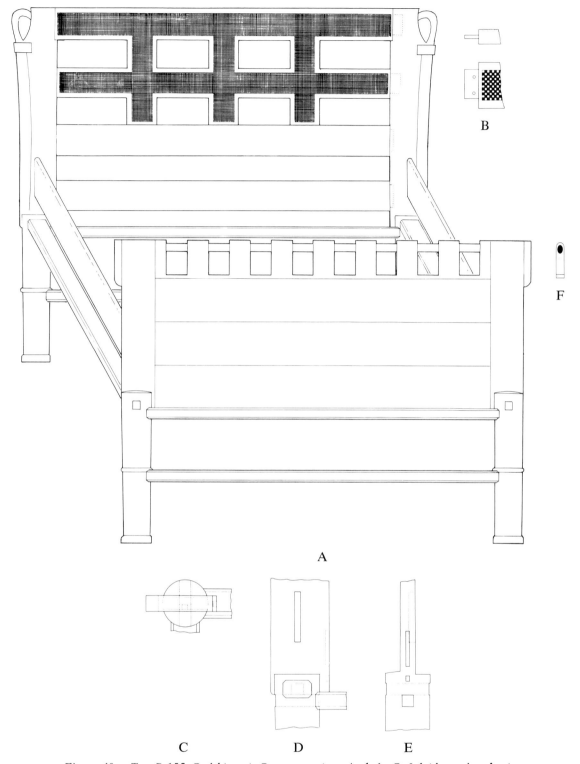

Figure 40.   TumP 155. Bed-bier. A. Reconstruction of whole. B. Inlaid woodwork of
head of bed. Fragment: front and top elevations. C. Upper portion of leg at head.
Plan with slots for long and cross rails. D. Upper portion of leg at head. Elevation
(facing foot of bed). E. Upper portion of leg at head. Inside elevation (facing other
side of bed). F. Cut-out strip at top of foot of bed. Section.   A, F 1:10; B–E 1:5.

additional pieces of furniture in the tomb, which were crushed beyond recognition in its collapse.

TumP 156   Legs of furniture

A. Pair of legs
    W 49   Under beam 4
    H. 0.30   D. base 0.045   D. top 0.06 m.
    Pl. 31C

One complete, the other in two fragments. Tapering legs, round in section, with a raised relief ring encircling them about two-thirds of the way down.[142] The lower ends thickened to a heavy straight foot; the tops shallow-domed. Just above the relief ring a long narrow oblong socket to hold the end of a stretcher. Above that and a short distance below the top, a square socket for the end of a frame piece. Above that and at 90 degrees around the face, a square socket for the other frame piece, at right angles to the first.

The socket cuttings are typical of all the legs, to hold the ends of the frame pieces and, below, a stretcher, probably across the ends.

B. Pair of legs
    W 50   One of those upright against west wall
               near southwest corner
    H. 0.375   D. base 0.12   D. top 0.14 m.
    Fig. 41; Pl. 31D

Much heavier than TumP 156*A*, but with similar socket cuttings. The same sort of relief ring occurs at about mid-height. Badly splayed and cracked. Small fragments that do not fit, but duplicate parts of these legs, suggest that there may have been a set of four.

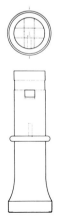

Figure 41. TumP 156. One of pair of legs B. 1:10.

C. Set of small legs
    W. 48   In southeast corner
    H. 0.125   D. top 0.025 m.
    Pl. 31E

Two legs preserved complete with tenons in the sockets; fragments of two more make a set of four. The small size of these suggests that they may have belonged to a piece of toy furniture. The legs are without relief rings and sockets for a stretcher; at the top the tenons from the frame pieces remain in their sockets.

D. Set of long legs
    W 51   Not on plan
    H. 0.48   D. base 0.09   D. top 0.10 m.
    Pl. 31F

Two legs, fragmentary and badly broken, could be put together; but leftover identical fragments suggest an original set of four. Similar to TumP 156*A* and with the same cuttings, but larger and higher. The stretcher sockets cut through the relief rings.

E. Square legs
    W 58   Center, south of cauldron, TumP 1
    GPH. 0.23   W. 0.07 m.
    Pl. 31G

The tops of two legs square in section are preserved, together with many fragments of similar legs; but it is not possible to estimate how many legs there were. One leg has a tenon at the top, which was evidently socketed into the under side of a member above (table top?). The other is plain at the top; it has a socket 0.07 m. below the top in one face, in which the tenon of a crosspiece is held by a transverse dowel. The treatment of the two legs suggested that they do not belong to the same piece of furniture.

STOOL PANELS
TumP 157–159

TumP 157   Inlaid stool panel
    W 59   Southwest corner
    Panels: H. 0.29   L. 0.505
    Th. 0.04 m.
    Fig. 42; Pl. 32A–C

Found with the screen (TumP 151). Preserved are two openwork panels, evidently (from the contrasting elaboration of the decoration) from front and back; and four seat slats whose length and

---

[142]A close parallel to the shorter legs: the ridges around their outer surfaces are probably akin to those on the

Urartian stool on wooden legs with silver sheet: T. Özgüç, *Altıntepe* II, 68 (Tomb III) and pl. XIX.

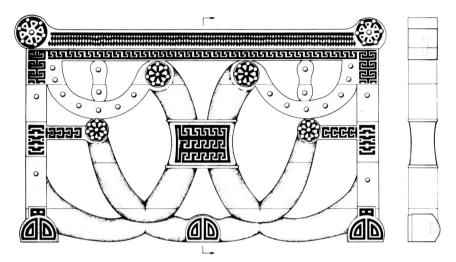

Figure 42.   TumP 157. Inlaid stool panel. Front and end elevations.   1:5.

rounded ends correspond to the uppermost members of the panels.

Each panel is composed of six horizontal crosspieces, one above the other. Since only the uppermost of each of these was secured by dowels to the pieces below them, we must assume that all the other joints were fastened by glue; as found, the panels had come apart precisely on the lines of the glued joints, so that all horizontal faces were entirely visible and the lack of doweling was glaring. Because of uneven shrinkage of the wood (probably boxwood) it was not possible to reconstitute the panels.

Doubtless the inlays of the front panel (*A*) and the back panel (*B*) could be more easily set into the separate parts before they were assembled. The joints could have been shaved down and sanded to an exact fit after the parts had been glued together. The ornamentation with stud-headed bronze pins (on Panel *A*) was perhaps added last of all. For the inlaid decoration (dark wood, probably yew) and the bronze studding see the drawing, fig. 42. We note here that the companion piece Panel *B* (pl. 32B) had inlay only in the three feet and in the central ornament; the inlay of the feet was the same as that of Panel *A*, while the central ornament has a larger, coarser geometric pattern than that of *A*. No bronze studs were added to Panel *B*.

The identity of shape, design, and dimensions of the panels makes it clear that they formed two faces, almost certainly front and back, of the same piece of furniture. The slightly hollowed top with its raised and rounded edges at the sides suggests a seat, and the length—0.505 m.—is perhaps suitable for the width of a seat. It was, moreover, a low seat, only 0.29 m. in height—perhaps a height suitable for a

small child (or for use as a footstool). Two of the four slats found with the panels, moreover, correspond exactly to their uppermost members—length 0.505 m., with rounded ends slightly raised; the other two, of exactly the same form, had shrunk somewhat in length but there can be little doubt that their original dimensions had been the same. All these slats were found covered by a pinkish powder, the residue from disintegrated textile—no doubt the cover of a cushion which once lay upon the seat.[143] Each slat, including those doweled to the top of the front and back panels, is 0.04 m. in width; together 0.24 m., perhaps rather narrow for the seat of a stool. But if we space them out with equal intervals between, we add 0.20 m. (five intervals of 0.04 m.) to a total width of 0.44 m. (less if the slats were more closely spaced). The spacing of the slats with intervals between them would seem to be suggested by their finished vertical faces; had a solid seat been intended, a single slab of wood might have been used. In any case the cushion placed on top would have made the sitter unconscious of the slatted nature of the seat.

The reconstruction of a low stool with elaborately decorated front panel and minimally decorated back panel, and a seat of spaced slats running its length, is logical and perhaps inevitable. But the difficulty is in sticking the whole together: there are sockets for horizontal dowels (to join front and back) only close to the ends at the bottom, behind the rounded feet at the corners; and these dowel holes measure 0.01 by 0.013 m. One must assume a pair of stretchers

---

[143]See p. 309, app. V, Fabric K.

joining the front and back panels at the bottom; no doubt uprights (probably doweled at top and bottom) rising from the centers of these and carrying crosspieces at the top, on which rested the ends of the seat slats. The slats were doubtless glued to the crosspieces which carried them; but the ends of these crosspieces could have been fastened to the top corners of the panels only by glue (there are no dowel cuttings). Such an arrangement sounds insecure enough; but it must be remembered that the front and back panels themselves were made up each of six horizontal members fastened together only by glue; and that the round table (TumP 152) had a top made up of nine parallel pieces which were not joined by dowels but, apparently, glued together. Quite evidently the Phrygian cabinetmakers were in possession of a particularly strong glue, or else they had a touching faith in the strength of the glue they did have and use.

TumP 158   **Stool panel with cut-out decoration**
              W 42   Not on plan
              H. 0.11   L. *ca.* 0.32 m.
              Fig. 43; Pl. 32D

Fragmentary; front, back and top carved from a single piece of wood. Front and back are flat panels with arched cutouts at sides and center of bottom. A low foot at either side supports a squared post which in turn supports the end of the seat, decorated by an oval. A slightly raised band outlines all the edges. The top was slightly concave, suggesting use as a seat rather than a footrest. Most of the top is missing, so that the depth remains unknown.

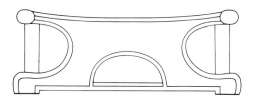

Figure 43. TumP 158. Stool panel with cut-out decoration. Front elevation. 1:5.

TumP 159   **Stool panel with cut-out decoration**
              W 62   Southwest corner
              H. 0.269   L. 0.434   Th. 0.235 m.
              Fig. 44; Pl. 32E

One panel, of a size between TumP 157 and TumP 158, is preserved complete, though slightly warped; there are several fragments of a matching panel.[144]

---

[144]See p. 291, app. III-A, Sample 15.

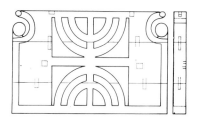

Figure 44. TumP 159. Stool panel with cut-out decoration. Front and end elevations. 1:10.

The preserved panel is composed of three horizontal pieces, one above the other, and fastened together by pairs of dowels. The cut-out decoration was probably done after the pieces had been joined; it consists of a double semicircle at the center of the top, and another, reversed, below it. Cut-out, scroll-like decoration at the upper corners. A slightly raised flat band frames the sides and bottom, and sets off the decoration of the upper corners.

Two dowel holes in the upper face could have served to secure the edge of a seat across the tops of front and back panels. But one seat slat 0.03 m. wide and preserved to a length of 0.40 m., together with fragments of other similar slats, was found with TumP 159. This suggests a slatted seat like that of TumP 157; the outermost slats could (as in the case of TumP 157) have been doweled to the tops of the front and back panels. But the problem of joining the two panels by cross-struts is again baffling. There are two dowel holes in the back of the panel at about half its height; but these are not placed symmetrically —one is slightly higher up than the other and somewhat farther from the edge. Struts joining front and back and set well in from the ends of the stool would not have been visible; nevertheless it would seem natural to place them symmetrically, and certainly at the same level.

PARASOL
TumP 160

TumP 160   **Fragments of a parasol**
              W 39   Northwest section of bed
              H. knob 0.08   GD. knob 0.065
              GPL. peg 0.155 m.
              Fig. 45; Pl. 32F, G

A cap piece round in horizontal section, and generally elliptical, above a tapering "neck," in vertical section. Into its bottom face, a large square peg (broken) enters, secured by a small round transverse dowel through the "neck." The circumference of the

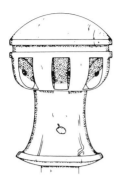

Figure 45. TumP 160. Parasol. Detail: knob. 1:2.

lower part of the cap shows eight socket cuttings, evenly spaced; each pair of these is connected by a hole bored through the wood between them. Above the socket cuttings, a groove all around the cap. With this were found long wooden pegs (one complete, and fragments of four more) pierced by a hole at either end. Presumably one end was fitted into a socket of the cap and could be secured in place by a string passed through the hole in its end, and the holes bored between the sockets; perhaps the groove above served to hold the ends of the string. Thus secured in place, each peg could move up and down through an arc of a little over 90 degrees. Since one end of the cap is convex with a finished surface, we take it to be the top of the complete object, which was supported below by a handle socketed into its lower face.

We consider the thing to be a parasol,[145] but it may also be some sort of whirligig toy.

PAIR OF FINIALS(?)
TumP 161

TumP 161   **Pair of finials**
W 63   Southwest corner of tomb
H. 0.24   W. 0.17 m.
Pl. 32H

Both pieces warped and shrunken. Each piece consists of four separate elements, joined: a central upright, its upper end rounded and grooved several times over the top, its lower a square tang around

which is fitted a hollow chamfered block secured to the tang by a round peg. The lower end of the tang protrudes beyond the bottom of the block, no doubt to serve as a dowel. To each side of the upper grooved end is doweled a half-ring, round in section; together these form a circular crowning ornament, open at the top, since the ends of the arms do not meet and are finished by slightly projecting disks.

The openings must have been at the top; the small dowels at the opposite end would have held these objects in a vertical position, presumably as finials at two corners of the object they crowned. Finding place and similarities in the techniques of cutting and assembling the parts, which resemble those used in making the back leg of the screen, suggest that these finials belonged to the same assemblage.

The illustration, pl. 32H, shows the better preserved of the two.

PAIR OF INLAID RUNGS
TumP 162

TumP 162   **Pair of inlaid rungs**
A. W 72 and *B.* W 73
A. L. 0.194 W. 0.031 m.
Fig. 46; Pl. 32I

A well preserved, *B* in two pieces, and too crushed to be measured. Identical rungs (*A* and *B*) square in section, with tenons at one end, sockets for tenons at the other. The inlaid decoration is on two adjacent faces of each rung; thus the rungs were meant to be seen from above and from one side. Possibly they were stretchers (or parts of stretchers) run between the legs of furniture. For the inlay patterns on *A*, see fig. 46.

Figure 46. TumP 162. Pair of inlaid rungs. Inlaid rung A. Top and front elevations and section. 1:4.

---

[145]Cf. scene of attendant holding parasol on the north wall of the painted tomb (525 B.C.) at Kızılbel (Elmalı):

M. J. Mellink, *AJA* 75 (1971): 248 and pl. 52, figs. 14, 15.

INLAID STRIPS
TumP 163, 164

TumP 163   **Inlaid strip**
W 45   South side, under beam 4
L. (strip of five squares) 0.334
W. 0.063   Th. 0.012 m.
Fig. 47; Pl. 33A

The plain ends show compression; they evidently served as tongues fitted into slots. Light wood with dark inlay on one face only; for the pattern see fig. 47. The drawing presents the three best-preserved squares out of five. The photograph presents the largest fragment.

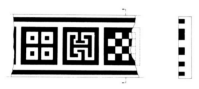

Figure 47.   TumP 163. Inlaid strip. Front elevation and section.   1:4.

TumP 164   **Inlaid strips**
W 46
L. 0.16   W. 0.047   Th. 0.02 m.
Fig. 48; Pl. 33B

One complete strip, badly warped; a second, almost complete; and four fragments. Together these suggest four or more. The four largest are published here on pl. 33B. One is drawn, fig. 48. Thin tongues projecting from the ends of the preserved strip suggest that it was socketed at either end, and round cuttings for pegs in its side faces suggest that the strips were pegged together side by side. At one end the pattern is closed, at the other it is broken in a way which suggests that it was continued on an adjacent piece.

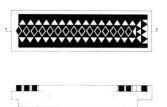

Figure 48.   TumP 164. Inlaid strip. Front and side elevations.   1:4.

ROD WITH LEATHER LOOPS
TumP 165

TumP 165   **Rod with leather loops**
W 44   On bed
GPL. 0.35   D. 0.013 m.
Fig. 49; Pls. 5B (center), 33C, D

Found on the bed, close to the belt and fibulae. Two joining fragments preserve one end of a wooden rod, now bent and twisted but probably straight originally. The end is rounded, button-like; the other end broken off. The shaft is thickened at 0.10-m. intervals and cut away to make spool-like attachment points for leather loops. One leather strap is preserved in place, its ends sewed together by three rows of stitching. Fine dark wood, the grain running the length of the rod.[146]

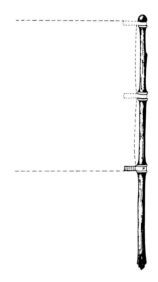

Figure 49.   TumP 165. Rod with leather loops. Fan?   1:5.

[146]Cf. the "gebogener Stab" (K-III, Holz no. 7; G. Körte in *Gordion,* 53 and fig. 14) where the rod is identified as an attribute of unknown purpose belonging to the dead. G. Körte suggests (without consideration of its warping) that it resembles the wands carried by figures on the Hittite Yazılıkaya reliefs. R. S. Young (*AJA* 61 [1957]: 327 and pl. 92, fig. 22) interpreted TumP 165 as pieces of a curtain rod. However, compare the handle of the fan held in the hand of the person attending the deceased in the recently discovered wall painting in the tumulus, Karaburun II, near Elmalı, Lycia (M. J. Mellink, *AJA* 75 [1971]: 252–253 and pl. 54, fig. 23). The length and diameter of TumP 165 seem appropriate. The possible presence of both a parasol, TumP 160, and a fan handle would bring Tumulus P into line as Western Anatolian comparanda for Karaburun and also for Kızılbel; see n. 145, p. 75. [Ed.]

SEAT(?) WITH LEGS[147]
TumP 166

TumP 166   Seat(?) with legs

> W 64   In extreme southeast
> corner
> *A*. PH. 0.48 as warped; 0.26 if right
>   angle restored.   PW. 0.42
>   Th. wall 0.04 m.
> *B*. PH. 0.17   PW. 0.20
>   Th. wall 0.04 m.
> *C*. PH. 0.41   PW. 0.19
>   Th. wall through molding 0.07 m.
> *D*. PH. 0.08   D. 0.05 m.
> Pls. 6B (upper center), 33E–G

Three main groups of fragments (*A–C*), each too warped to repair. All are in very poor condition.

A is a slab with the grain running vertically; on one long edge (taken to be the bottom) are two sockets and preserved stumps of legs, onto one of which fits one of the four bronze-sheathed legs (*D*) found in the chamber. Along the edge which received the legs, on one side face (interpreted as the inside face, see *B* below), a half-round molding extends for 0.16 m. out of the 0.42 m. width. The front edge of the slab is finished, as is the whole outside.

At a height of 0.15 m. on the inside the whole wall has now slipped into a slant, presumably away from the straight direction in which it was originally made. This could have been caused by the manner in which it was forced into the corner by the weight of the collapse.

B is a slab similar to slab *A*, preserving the bottom edge with leg socket and inside half-round molding which ceases after 0.16 m. from front edge. Perhaps *A* and *B* faced each other, molding toward molding.

C has a broken surface as if it formed a corner, but cannot join *A* or *B* so must form part of a third side. It is finished on its non-corner edge, and the lower section had a molding also.

D, four short, delicate legs, round in section; one retains the sheathing, and three show they were once wrapped in bronze sheathing.[148]

The interpretation of these pieces is very difficult. The object appears to have an overall height of 0.34 m. (*A* 0.26 plus *D* 0.08). How it is closed on top is not clear, as the top piece is lacking,[149] and there is no evidence for tacks to accommodate a cross-woven top. It must have been some sort of seat closed around three sides and open in the front, and set upon four short legs.[150]

---

[147]This catalogue entry, added and written by Ellen L. Kohler is extremely tentative, and based entirely upon the observations of Mabel Lang in the field in 1956.

[148]See p. 287, app. II-C, Sample 80. See also p. 72, n. 142. For the occurrence of bronze sheathing on legs of stools and chairs in Urartu, see C. A. Burney, *AnatSt* 16 (1966): 100 (with nn. 103, 104) and pl. XX,b.

[149]It should be noted that in many instances at Gordion the tops of tables appear to have been made of inferior wood, different from the frame and legs. Cf. the maple

---

(*Acer pseudoplatanus*) top of the three-legged table from Tumulus MM (app. III-A, p. 291, Sample 17). The top of MM 388 (*q.v.*) had also disintegrated.

[150]If the reconstruction is correct enough to be suggestive at all, it perhaps takes its place in a long series of tables and chairs derived from the tables of the XIth Dyn. in Egypt, most of which were raised upon cylindrical pegs, as ours. Cf. Tomb of Meket-Re (*ca.* 2000 B.C.): H. E. Winlock, *Models of Daily Life in Egypt from the Tomb of Meket-Re at Thebes* (Cambridge, Mass.: Harvard University Press, 1955), figs. 38, 39.

II

TUMULUS MM

THE KING'S TUMULUS

INTRODUCTION

The biggest tumulus at Gordion[1] dominates the landscape of the Sakarya and the Porsuk valleys; it is visible from miles away. No doubt this was the tumulus that drew the attention of the Körtes to Gordion in the first place. They certainly entertained thoughts of digging it, though in the end lack of technical means and time forced them to give up the project.[2] The tumulus (fig. 1) lies just across the village road to Polatlı from the second-highest mound, which the Körtes did dig (Tumulus K-III), and a short distance to the north of the child's tomb, Tumulus P.

The tumulus stands on ground which slopes gently downward to the north and west. Today its height is about 53 m., estimated from the west side, and its diameter little short of 300 m. The conical mound has obviously had its profile changed by erosion over two and a half millennia —its height decreased, its girth at the bottom augmented. In several places shallow gullies or runnels have been eaten by water running down its face (pls. 34, 35). At the top toward the south and west there is a shallow hollow or depression. The cause of this is unknown; it appears in the photograph of the great tumulus published by the Körtes, so it already existed at the turn of the century.[3]

A tumulus of this size, covering the burial (as it turned out) of a single elderly male, obviously was the monument to a very important personage, presumably a king. The assignment in ancient literature of various large tumuli at Bin Tepe near Sardis to individual kings of the Mermnad Dynasty leads to the assumption that the somewhat older tumuli at Gordion also covered the burials of kings. Hence the great tumulus, second in size in Anatolia only to the Alyattes Mound at Bin Tepe, almost inevitably became associated with Midas,

---

[1]The preliminary reports touching on Tumulus MM are: Young, *Archaeology* 10 (1957): 217 ff.; *Archaeology* 11 (1958): 227 ff.; *AJA* 62 (1958): 147–154; *TAD* 7 (1958): 4–13; *Expedition* 1, No. 1 (Fall 1958): 3–13; *ILN*, May 17, 1958, 828 ff.

[2]G. Körte in *Gordion*, 37.

[3]G. Körte in *Gordion*, 37, fig. 2. This rules out the possibility of damage from artillery fire during the Battle of

the Sakarya in 1921. At first it was thought that the depression might have been caused by settling of the mound filling after a collapse of the tomb roof, but the roof was found to be almost intact. Nor does the hollow seem to be the result of an abortive attempt by tomb robbers: the tumuli at Bin Tepe near Sardis show that rather daring tunneling was the method used by ancient robbers to reach the tombs beneath mounds of great size.

Phrygia's best-known king, and acquired the somewhat redundant nickname of Midas Mound Tumulus, or MMT. Even though the attribution of this tomb to King Midas was at times disputed, the initials "MM" have stuck and have been kept for reasons of convenience.[4]

As noted by G. Körte, the technical problems of reaching a burial beneath this mound were formidable. To work by digging trenches from the top would have entailed the removal of enormous quantities of filling and would have resulted in the virtual destruction of the tumulus, itself an impressive monument. In the course of the six campaigns at Gordion that preceded the digging of MM, the excavation of a number of smaller burial mounds (as well as the precedents of the Körte Tumuli III–V) had given us indications of what to expect. Phrygian burials were almost invariably made in tombs of wood constructed in pits sunk into the hardpan. The wooden tombs were usually packed around the outside with a filling of stone rubble and covered above their roofs by great piles of more rubble. Without doors or other means of access these tombs would seem to have been intended for one single use. Probably they were prepared in advance; when the time came, the body of the dead person was lowered into the tomb from above, the roof was laid, rubble was piled over it, and then the tumulus was built. In most cases the weight of the stone pile had eventually caused the collapse of the wooden roof. In some cases tombs had been entered and robbed, almost certainly in comparatively early times before the roof collapsed—robbing a collapsed tomb filled with rubble would have been difficult indeed. The narrow burrows through which entry had been made could usually be detected at an early stage of the digging. In no case did we find evidence for the reopening of a tomb to make a second burial in it. But, more importantly, the smaller tumuli showed that they had been so built that the peak did not lie directly over the burial, which often lay far outward from the center of the mound. Evidently the position of the center and the peak of the mound was predetermined, and it was maintained in the same place during the piling of the earth by the laying of successive lines of stones which crossed each

other at the same central point until a peak was reached. No doubt the purpose of the off-center positioning of the burials beneath their mounds was to hide them, or at least to make them difficult for robbers to find. Beneath the large tumuli the tombs were nearly at center; but here the great masses of earth to be moved (or tunneled) would have discouraged tomb robbers and rendered their activities far from inconspicuous. The mass of earth over the tombs was in itself a protection, and the procedure used in piling these tumuli was quite the opposite to that used for smaller ones. A vertical wooden mast was set up over the center of the tomb roof to be used as a center and guide for piling the earth. When the mast became buried, a second one was set up above it to mark the same spot, and earth was piled until the desired height was reached. Tumuli P, W, and K-III all showed the holes left by the decay of the masts[5] which were set up over the tombs to center the piling of the tumuli; very probably the same method of centering was used also in the case of the great tumulus. In all these cases the tombs lay slightly to the southwest of the present peaks of the mounds. The significance of this is not clear: it may be that erosion by the prevailing winds of the region has shifted the actual peaks in two and a half millennia. If, on the other hand, the builders so made their mounds that the burials lay in the southwest quadrant, they would have had to continue to pile on filling after the guide masts had been completely buried. In that case it is difficult to understand what significance, if any, this particular quadrant had and indeed what center was used for the laying out of the mound to be built. The digging of the great tumulus showed that one of the first steps taken was the laying down of a ring of filling around a pre-determined perimeter for the tumulus; the earth was piled in over this ring from all sides, so that the stratification showed uniformly a gentle slope from the perimeter downward toward center. The same kind of stratification was observed in some other tumuli. No doubt a certain amount of labor was saved in this way, for the filling material had to be carried only to the perimeter, not to the center of the mound.

---

[4]The term "MM" seems appropriate also inasmuch as there is another tumulus in the sequence on the northeast cemetery ridge bearing the designation "M." For a further

discussion of King Midas, see Conclusions, pp. 271–272.

[5]Mast in Tumulus P, p. 2; in Tumulus W, p. 196; in K-III, G. Körte in *Gordion*, 39.

THE DRILLING PROGRAM

The great tumulus covers an area of approximately 70,000 square meters. Of this the tomb itself occupies an area of only about 150 square meters. Our experience in digging smaller mounds through 1955 had shown that the burials could be far from the peak or center of the mounds which covered them.[6] It therefore seemed prudent in the case of the great tumulus to devise a means of predetermining the position of the tomb within the vast area of the mound. For this the pile of rubble stone which invariably overlay a tomb seemed to be the key. By the use of a light drilling rig which could bore through the earth or clay filling until its bit found hardpan, or was obstructed by rubble, the position and extent of the stone pile could be determined, and within it the approximate position of the tomb beneath. From the action of the drill the presence of rubble could be readily recognized, and there was no danger that the bit might penetrate the rubble and do damage to the tomb beneath. A constant flow of water through the drill was necessary to cool the bit and to soften the

material through which it bored, and ideally to return that material to the surface for examination, but as it turned out, the water that was lost was capable of damaging furniture and other objects of wood which lay in the tomb. These had in fact survived through the ages because of the constant temperature and the constant humidity of the environment in which they had been placed, sealed off from the outer world beneath huge tumuli of impermeable clay. But the survival of wooden furniture was not expected. Tumulus K-III had yielded fragments of wooden objects, but these had been sadly smashed and crushed by the inrush of rubble when the roof of the tomb collapsed.[7]

Drilling of the great tumulus was started in the autumn of 1955 and resumed in the summer of 1956.[8] A total of 96 borings was made (fig. 50) in east-west and north-south lines and spaced 5 m. apart, forming a regular grid of evenly spaced borings. Two lines were carried up the west face of the tumulus, almost from its lower margin (pl. 34B) to an enlarged area over the crest (pl. 35A). The purpose was to find and record the level of the surface of the hardpan, into which it was as-

---

[6]Many Phrygian tumuli contained burials situated off-center: Young, *Archaeology* 3 (1950): 199–200 discusses Tumuli B, C, F, G; Mellink, *Hittite Cemetery at Gordion* (1956), pl. 2, Tumulus H; Young, *AJA* 60 (1956), pl. 95, fig. 55, Tumulus N; *ibid.*, pl. 81, fig. 3, Tumulus O.

[7]The sarcophagus and other objects of wood, including fragments of furniture, are described by G. Körte in *Gordion*, 43 f.

[8]After G. Roger Edwards had completed, in late August 1955, a successful practice session on the smaller mound, Tumulus N, to train a Turkish crew for the recently imported drilling rig, Donald F. Brown, then of the Peabody Museum, Cambridge, who had previously taken cores by boring in the Sybaris plain of southern Italy and reported upon his project in *AJA* 58 (1954): 144, was put in charge of the drilling of the great tumulus (September 7 to October 8) and of Tumulus P (October 10–26). The drill used was a Hawthorne DB portable rotary rig of the wash-boring type, which was designed for light earth exploration (to stop at hardpan, rock, or even loose stone) and was manufactured by the Exploration Equipment Co. of Houston, Texas. Canonically all the water used in drilling should have returned to the surface, where the material through which the bit was boring was captured by a sieving process before the water was allowed to escape into a slush pit. However, on Tumulus MM, all the water ran away and disappeared—no doubt through cracks in

the fabric of the mound. An attempt was made to employ casing to prevent escape of the water, the casing being very generously lent through the kindness of the director of electrical projects of the Turkish government, but this method did not prove feasible mainly because of the impossibility of raising the casing with the Hawthorne DB equipment after the hole was drilled.

Toward the end of the 1955 season, after 57 holes were completed on MM, the boring of the great tumulus was abandoned, and Brown's attention turned to the smaller Tumulus P (see p. 1 and fig. 2).

When drilling began again in 1956, a trench-well (L. 20, W. 3, Depth 6–4 m.; water at –3 m.) was dug near the foot of MM at its north side and a series of three pumps run by gasoline engines, a small Marlow pump at the well, a second one at *ca.* 10 m. up the slope, and a third, larger Myers pump at a halfway station, sent plenty of water through eleven fire hoses to the top, for use in drilling. Gerret Copeland supervised the drilling in July (drill holes 58–86); after Copeland's departure, R. S. Young made a few supplementary borings at the top (drill holes 86–96).

The wooden objects from the tomb under Tumulus P, drilled in the fall of 1955 and dug in spring 1956, suffered far less water damage than those of the big tumulus, drilled 1955–1956 and dug in summer 1957. Tumulus N, drilled in 1955 and dug immediately, suffered none at all.

[This footnote was written in part by Editor]

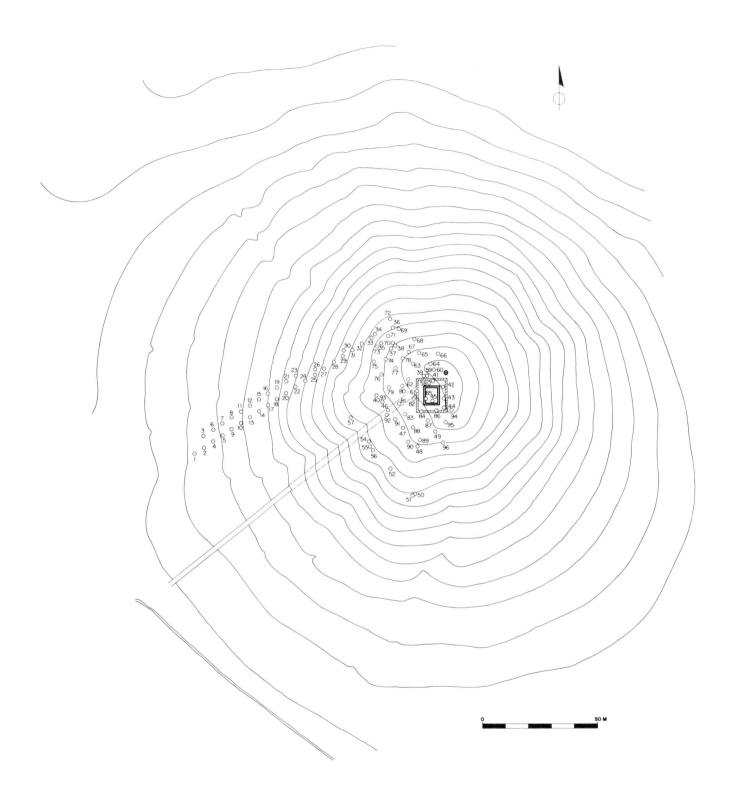

Figure 50. Tumulus MM. Plan of survey with bore holes. Contour interval 3 m.

sumed the tomb had been sunk. Naturally a fair number of drillings was aborted when the drill struck a large stone or a layer of stones in the filling at a high level: second attempts up to 2 m. away from the original boring were sometimes thwarted at the same high level. In general however most of the bores made below the peak of the tumulus in the area of the southwest struck rubble at a depth of 34 to 40 m. below the surface, and the rubble lay immediately beneath the clay filling without the empty gap which pinpointed the position of the tomb (with broken roof) under Tumulus P (see p. 4). This seemed to offer assurance that the roof of the tomb beneath Tumulus MM had held up and was intact.

During the month of July 1956 the margins of the stone pile under the great tumulus at north and south were fixed by the finding of hardpan in the drilling of the outermost rows of bores, and of rubble at a considerably higher level in the borings of the next inner rows, only 5 m. away. These indicated that the north and south fringes of the stone pile lay somewhere between the parallel rows of borings: from this could be deduced a north-south diameter of about 30 m. for the covering pile of rubble. Our impression was that the pile was more oval than round in shape, with a somewhat greater diameter east-west than north-south. But at the west all our borings were aborted by stones at high levels, and the western limit of the stone pile was not determined. It seemed, nevertheless, that we had enough data on which to proceed; and so a mast was set up near the top of the tumulus at what we calculated to be the approximate center of the stone pile. To the top of the mast, which was later used for sighting, was affixed a banner.

THE EXCAVATION

Once the general area of the tomb had been located, the plan for reaching it was to dig an open trench from the periphery as far inward as could be done safely and to tunnel the rest of the way (figs. 50, 51). The direction of the approach, from the southwest, was invited by a gully eaten in the surface by water running down the mound. This approach offered a saving in the amount of filling to be removed, and also an approach from the southwest—the shortest approach to the calculated center of the stone pile—was not directly exposed to the prevailing and often strong winds from west or south, which have at times raised such clouds of dust as to inhibit digging. Sighting up the gully toward the banner then, on April 18, 1957, we laid out a 70-m. trench on the line indicated, and work was started on April 19. The outermost 10-m. stretch was 2 m. in width (pl. 35B), enough to accommodate the Decauville railroad. The plan was to dig to the level of the surface of hardpan and to lay the railroad track on that level throughout the length of trench and tunnel, since experience had suggested that the tomb would be set down in a pit dug into the hardpan, and we wished to clear the tomb from above. At the same time the innermost cross-trench was started, 4 m. long by 8 m. wide, to allow steps to be left at each side as the depth of the trench increased (pl. 36A). In both trenches the surface was of soft, washed-down earth; in the inner trench this gave way at a depth of 1 m. to the hard clay filling of the original tumulus, while in the outer trench the soft, washed-down earth went to hardpan. On the completion of the first outer cut the railroad was laid and a

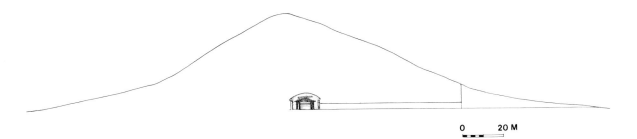

Figure 51. Tumulus MM. Section of tumulus and tomb, showing open trench and tunnel, from north-northwest.

second 10-m. stretch was opened; the process was repeated until the whole trench had been opened to the level of hardpan.

The open trench, 70 m. long at the top and 67.5 at the bottom, left a face for tunneling 11.80 m. high. The outer half to 34 m. had been cut entirely through soft earth eroded down from the tumulus itself, slightly less than 4 m. deep at the inner end. At 34 m., beneath that depth of accumulation, appeared a rather confused mass of hard clay a meter or so in height; within and above this again hard clay was found, but here clearly stratified, with a gentle downward slope from the perimeter toward the center of the mound (fig. 52). This typical stratification appeared consistently in both sides of the cut and at all levels over the whole of the inner length of the trench (33.50 m.). This stratification suggested, as already mentioned, the laying of an outer ring of clay, about 1 m. in height, around a pre-determined perimeter for the mound, and the filling in of the center by material piled in from all directions over the outer ring. The even and gentle slope of the stratification suggests a work crew, which spread the material (with rakes?) as it was dumped. The same sloped-toward-center stratification was later observed farther in, at the sides of the tunnel near the tomb. Although the fabric of the tumulus was penetrated only at this one point, we must assume that the result was typical and that the conclusion drawn from the evidence here is valid for the whole.[9]

The clay filling was extraordinarily clean: from the whole of the open trench (and from the tunnel

later) less than half a box of sherds was drawn, all of nondescript coarse ware. The exact source of the clay used for the tumulus could not be fixed; any large pits made in its removal must have filled in long since. The entire flood plain of the Sakarya, and of the side valleys leading down to it from the east, is made up of clay. The cleanness of the tumulus clay suggests that it did not come from inhabitation areas; rather, it must have come from low-lying valley areas, which were not inhabited because they were subject to flooding. Common sense would suggest that the needed clay was taken from the nearest available source.

The open trench was completed to hardpan on May 17, 1957. The natural slope of the terrain favored our enterprise: from a level of 7.57 m. above zero at the mouth of the trench hardpan rose to 10.30 m. at the tunnel face, a rise of 2.73 over a length of 67.50 m., or about 0.04 m. in the meter—a 4 percent grade, which allowed the loaded cars to roll down easily, though a trifle too fast (fig. 52).

On the day the open trench was completed the engineer and his crew of miners from the Zonguldak lignite mining region arrived; he had been bespoken ahead of time because it had seemed prudent to employ for the tunneling professionals who understood methods of shoring and propping. The tunnel was made 2.20 m. high with a width at the top of 2 m. and at the bottom of 2.50 m. Work was started on May 19 and continued around the clock in three shifts, progressing at a rate of nearly 3 m. in 24 hours. Every three meters ⊓-shaped timber

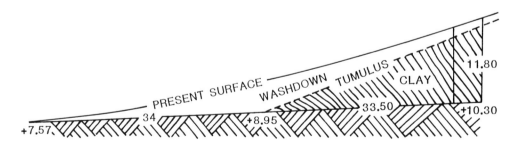

Figure 52. Tumulus MM. Section visible in northwest scarp of the open trench leading to tunnel entrance. At the inner end the 4-m. cross trench is indicated.

[9]Cf. H. H. von der Osten, *Explorations in Central Anatolia, Season of 1926* (*OIP* V, 1929), 47–48 and figs. 75–77, where he speculates upon the reasons for this method of building tumuli as demonstrated in one of the two excavated by Makridi Bey in 1926 a short distance west of the railroad station in Ankara. The tumuli are given brief mention by Hamit Zübeyr in *TTAED* 1 (1933): 6.

I. Tumulus MM from the west.

II. Tumulus MM. Screens (MM 379 and 378) *in situ*.

props were put in (pl. 36B). It had been planned to make a ceiling by sliding in planks above the crosspieces at the tops of these supports, but the hardness of the clay filling was such that it could stand up by itself, and the ceiling was omitted. Likewise it was found unnecessary to support the side faces of the tunnel with planks, and so the stratification remained visible (as far as the light allowed) throughout the length of the tunnel. The material taken from the tunnel was the same as that from the open trench, very clean hard clay, all but devoid of potsherds. There was no problem of getting air into the tunnel and the blowing machinery brought for the purpose remained unused. The length of the tunnel from the face to its inner end[10] was 67.70 m.; over this length there was a slight deviation from a beeline toward the left (north). The combined length of tunnel and open trench was 135.20 m.; of this length 101.20 m. was through the hard clay of the tumulus, 34 m. was through washed-down earth around its base. If the amount of washed-down material is constant all around the perimeter (which we cannot guarantee), the original height of the tumulus could have been as much as 70 m. or more, and its profile much steeper than it is at present.

ARCHITECTURE OF THE TOMB COMPLEX

The tunnel was stopped on June 12 by a stone wall built slightly obliquely across its line. The wall proved to be about 3 m. in height, built of roughly coursed blocks of poros stone (pl. 37A). Quite evidently we had come upon its back face: the blocks were untrimmed and of unequal thickness, so that the construction was rough indeed, and it was clear that the smooth or finished face must be at the other side. Obviously we had come upon the tomb, but was this the wall, contrary to all expectation and precedent, of a stone-built tomb rather than the expected wooden one? It seemed prudent to devise ways of testing or of by-passing the wall. A pit dug into the hardpan against its face revealed one complete course, and the top of a second, continuing the construction downward: its

foundation was evidently set down into the hardpan, and no tunneling beneath it was possible. To by-pass it by tunneling over it also proved impossible: a cutting through the roof of our tunnel, after a little less than a meter, brought down a shower of rubble stones. We were quite evidently already under the rubble heap piled over the tomb. The outflow of stones stopped after a short time; the cavity from which they had come showed a clay face above, sloping upward toward the center and at its higher side about 0.75 m. above the clay floor on which the rubble had rested. Our hole lay very near to the outer edge of the stone heap, but as our drilling had suggested that it had a diameter of about 30 m., it seemed unlikely that the stone wall could belong to the tomb proper, which should lie near the center of the stone deposit (even if not necessarily at the center of the tumulus proper). Thus there seemed to be no alternative to the direct method of breaching the wall, and at the same time it seemed safe to do so.

When this was done, there began an immediate outpouring of rubble from straight ahead, from both sides, and from above. For three days (June 13–16) the rubble was carted away as it came out. The miners were supplemented by some of our own workmen who were trained as a matter of course to collect potsherds and whatever else might be included in the rubble filling. We got half a box of nondescript coarse sherds and many fragments of broken wood. All of this belonged obviously to the rubble filling and could not be from the tomb, but at the same time all the fragments of wood bespoke the existence of a wooden tomb. On June 16 it was at last possible to enter the cavity to take stock of what had been revealed. The inner face of the wall had been cleared for about 2 m. to either side of the breach, and as had been anticipated, the trimmed faces of the wall blocks were toward the inside. But the wall face was not nicely finished as would have been the case for a face meant to be seen. The exposed wall was 0.80 to 1 m. thick and a little more than 3 m. high, with rubble resting on its top face—clearly a dam-wall to hold the rubble, and intended to be buried completely. Parallel to the wall face and about 2 m. from it lay two large, round logs resting on rubble at about the level of the top of the wall. When we scrambled up the scarp of the remaining rubble at the left (north) side of our opening, it became possible to see that the rubble had run out from

---

[10]The point taken to be the inner end of the tunnel is, specifically, the outer face of the stone wall discussed below. [Ed.]

under a great dome-shaped ceiling of compacted clay (pl. 37B); this had been so compacted by time and pressure that there seemed to be little danger of a collapse—but occasionally a stone of the rubble packing, left stuck to the under face of the clay vault, let go and fell, making life somewhat exciting. The bulk of the rubble was of fist-sized stones, but dispersed among these were many larger stones ranging in size up to that of a watermelon. All the stones of whatever size were rounded and smooth, evidently waterworn and no doubt brought from a nearby stream bed. The depth of rubble over the wall was 1.50 m.; above it the clay dome rose in an arching curve toward center, but the apex of the dome was not visible because it was still filled with rubble. The presence of rubble beneath the peak of the dome offered reassurance that no rubble had rushed down into a tomb, and that therefore the tomb roof must have remained unbroken. The rubble of the central area had been helped to stay in place by a series of large, round logs laid side by side in a direction perpendicular to that of the stone wall and at a level about 2 m. higher than its top— evidently a sort of raft or platform of logs designed to take pressure from over a tomb roof below. Some of those logs were well preserved with squarely cut ends; others had lost their ends, and occasional gaps between logs suggested the disintegration of yet others. The fragments of wood scattered through the rubble we had taken out doubtless came from this source.

For four more days until June 20 the removal of rubble continued. At the left (north) side of the opening the wall was seen to turn eastward, not at a good right angle but at a somewhat obtuse one— evidently the north wall of a somewhat irregular grave enclosure. The west wall could be followed, too, for some distance toward the south, though the corner of the enclosure in that direction remained obscured by rubble. The two great logs parallel to the wall face continued southward as far as we had cleared; they evidently rested on the rubble at the level of the wall top. The more rubble we removed, the more they became undermined toward the north. Finally timber props had to be set beneath to hold them in place (pl. 38A). But just

behind these and approximately at the same level a third log began to appear, running in the same direction but somewhat shorter toward the north, and this proved to be supported not by rubble underneath it but by yet another round log laid on the same line at a lower level. Again under these as more rubble was removed, more logs appeared until in the end a wall face 2.60 m. high was revealed, made up of eight logs piled one on top of the other. This face lay nearly 3 m. in from the stone wall and parallel to it. The logs[11] were of varying sizes and had evidently been laid in an alternation of one smaller log between larger ones above and below, so that the total was of six thick and two slimmer logs (pl. 38B). They had also been laid alternately in opposite directions so that the natural taper of the tree trunks was evened out to an approximately level horizontal surface from course to course. Branches had been trimmed off where they grew out of the trunks, but the surfaces of the logs themselves had hardly been touched and in many places the bark remained in place. Near the end of a number of the logs there was a cutting in the surface, a sort of notch with a straight vertical cut at one end, a gradually sloped face, and a deeply bored round hole at the center (figs. 53, 55, and 59). These cuttings were immediately recognized by workmen from the region of Bolu, which has remained forested and is a source of timber to this day. The end of a log so notched is raised and fitted over the axle between two wheels; a peg at the center of the axle fits into the bored hole of the cutting, and the raised end of the log can then be drawn along on the wheels.

The logs of this outer wall ended at the north each in a neat, vertical face cut by sawing, but as they were of slightly varying length, the wall's end was rather jagged and without an even vertical face. At a right angle to this end appeared the end of another similar wall of logs piled one on the other, obviously the north wall of the tomb. The logs of north and west walls were never in contact with each other at the corner, and there was no evidence that they had ever been fastened together in any way. Digging into hardpan by the corner showed the north end of the west wall to be bedded on a squared timber of some sort, but this seems

---

[11]For analyses of logs from the outer casing, see results by Kayacık and Aytuğ, p. 292, app. III-C, Samples 32–

41. See also p. 291, app. III-A, Sample 17, and p. 292, app. III-D, Sample 42.

Figure 53. Tumulus MM. Log, notched for dragging out of forest by wagon. For the position of this cutting on the west exterior facade, see fig. 59, p. 92. 1:10.

to have been only at the corner, for more digging to the south showed the lowermost log bedded on rubble—the log, in fact, set down to about half its diameter below the level of hardpan.

Protruding through the face of the topmost logs of the west wall 0.60 m. short of the corner at the north were the ends of four squared timbers cut off to an even face flush with the outer face of the log wall (see fig. 59). Those were laid in pairs, one pair on top of the other. The two parallel timbers of each layer had been bound together by a wooden clamp across the vertical joint at the end, clamps of a type that ultimately came to be known as "double-T clamps." Although the wooden clamps themselves had rotted away or fallen out and disappeared, the cuttings made to receive them were quite clear and their function unmistakable. At 2.60 m. to the south of the first appeared a second double pair of squared timbers, the ends of the pairs at the same level, again crossed over the vertical joints by cuttings for wooden clamps. The first set of clamped beams at the north was taken to represent the top of the north wall of the tomb. The second set, since the log framework through which it was mortised had been exposed southward to a distance considerably greater than that from the north wall to the corner, was taken to be the end of a central support for the tomb roof. This support measured at its end 0.88 m. in width (0.40 and 0.48 m. the widths of the two beams clamped together at their ends) by 0.79 m. in thickness

(the lower beams 0.48 m. thick, the upper 0.31 m.). This afforded material for speculation as to the inside dimension of the tomb: if the central support was actually at center, the distance from it to the south end of the tomb should equal that to the north, 2.60 m.; therefore, the total interior length of the tomb should be twice that, 5.20 m., plus the width, 0.88 m. of the central support, or 6.08 m. This calculation in the end proved to be only 0.12 m. short of the actual internal length of the tomb, 6.20 m.

A final scramble up the scarp of the remaining rubble showed the northwest part of the tomb roof sloping down from east to west and evidently one side of a gabled or double-sloped roof with the ends at north and south. Our tunnel had come upon the western long side of the tomb near its north end. Had the tunnel not deviated very slightly toward the north from a straight line, it would probably have found the center of the west side of the tomb. Since breaking through the stone enclosure wall around the tomb, we had spent a solid week removing rubble. We had gained an inkling of what the tomb was like, and a strong impression that its roof must be intact and unbroken. But during all this time we had taken out only a scant third of all the rubble within the tomb cavity. All would have to be removed eventually if the outside of the tomb was to be seen and recorded properly and if the pressure from this mass of rubble on its roof and sides was to be relieved. But at the same time the removal of all the rubble would expose completely the unsupported dome of clay which had formed and hardened over the original rubble pile. About the stability and trustworthiness of this the architects and engineers who were consulted could offer no advice based on experience, and a collapse of the dome, estimated to rise to a height of nearly 4 m. above the tomb roof, or even a partial fall of clay from it, could completely squash the tomb beneath. Our choice was to risk a collapse of the tomb roof under the weight of rubble, or a possible annihilation of the whole tomb by a collapse of the clay dome if the rubble were removed from under it. After some debate we opted for the first alternative.

From the stone enclosure wall to the face of the log wall of the tomb, a distance of a little less than 3 m., the tunnel was prolonged by wooden walls and a roof to ward off falling stones and rubble. Then borings were made with bit and brace through one of the smaller logs (the sixth from the bottom); in every case the bit struck stone at the other side. A sharp-nosed saw cut through the wood between borings, and a piece of the log was removed. Again rubble poured out through the hole. But this discouraging phenomenon lasted for only a short time; within the hour the flow ceased, and it was possible to see within the log wall the face of a second, this time built of squared timbers nicely finished and fitted together. This was clearly the wall of the tomb proper; it lay at a distance of 0.35 m. from the outer casing of logs. Our opening was enlarged to make a doorway 1.30 m. wide by about 1.50 m. high (pl. 39A); for this we had to cut through the third, fourth, fifth, and sixth logs (counting from the bottom).

It was now possible to see and to deduce something of the tomb's construction from what was visible in the narrow space between the two walls. To left and to right could be seen the beams of the top of the north wall of the tomb, and of the central roof support, mortised through the outer log casing, of which the clamped ends appeared in its outer face (figs. 54 and 59). The lower beams of the north wall did not appear. Instead, the beams of the west wall appeared to continue beyond the corner, and the inner face of the outer north wall of logs had been notched to receive their ends, though in actuality there was no contact because the beams (as far as could be seen) were not quite long enough for their ends to fit into the notches.

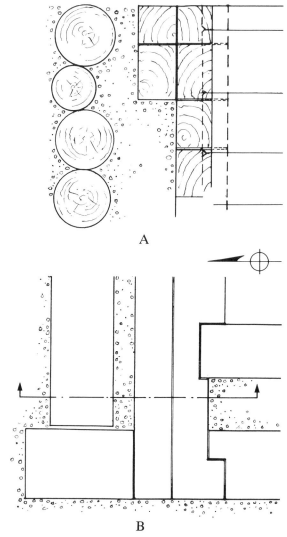

Figure 54. Tumulus MM. Exterior northwest corner of tomb chamber. A. Section through mortising, from west. B. Plan of mortising. 1:25.

But the notches suggested for the inner tomb a system of mortising which had been observed in other wooden tombs: that the inner faces of the beams of the long sides of the tomb were notched near their ends to receive the ends of the crossbeams of the shorter sides (which proved actually to be the case when it became possible to examine the corners of the tomb from the inside). In this way the tomb was capable of withstanding pressure from the outside from either direction (fig. 54): the long side walls were held apart by the end walls, and the shorter end walls were solid because the ends of their beams were secured by mortises at either side. The outer casing of logs was obviously intended to take the pressure of the rubble outside and so relieve pressure against the inner walls.

The narrow space between inner and outer walls, cleared of rubble, showed a wooden ceiling above, at a level above that of the roof support which crossed it at center. This ceiling was made up of two parallel timbers, one overhanging the outer face of the tomb wall, the other the inner face of the log wall. Although these timbers lay at slightly different levels the joint between them was tight throughout its length. This meant that the rubble between the wall faces could not have trickled down from above to fill the empty space, since the space was sealed above. It had been put in purposely. The reason for its presence was quite clear, and it offered insights into the methods used in the construction of the tomb. When we had cleared the northwest corner of the outer log walls and had found that north and west walls had no contact with each other at the corner, we began to wonder how walls of round logs piled one on top of the other to a height of eight had been induced to stand up. Wooden dowels from log to log across the horizontal joints had seemed a possibility, but in the nature of things they were not visible and could not be attested. Certainly the presence of wooden clamps across vertical joints suggested a possibility of wooden dowels across horizontal ones. But to hold up a wall of eight logs piled one above the other, such dowels (especially the lower ones) would have had to be extraordinarily strong, or extraordinarily numerous. The presence of rubble between the wall faces offered the solution: the round logs had been laid down one at a time, and as each was laid rubble had been filled in along each face to hold it in place and to prevent it from rolling. This does not eliminate the possibility of doweling; but the dowels (which, as noted, are not attested) would have had to hold only one log in place at a time, and only until rubble was filled in along both sides. In this way the walls could be built up log by log to their full height. But pre-

requisite to this was the existence of the inner tomb, whose walls held the rubble piled along the inner faces of the logs. In the other direction the stone enclosure wall held the rubble filled along their outer faces. But here we must assume a gradual course-by-course building up of the stone wall, keeping pace with the log-by-log laying of the outer casing of the tomb. The logs of the latter were, on the average, something more than 8 m. in length on the long sides, and 6.50 m. on the shorter ends, with diameters up to 0.50 m. Heavy things, difficult to move and to manipulate, certainly not easily lifted over a wall standing to a height of 3 m.! Without doubt, too, clay was piled against the back face of the stone wall as it rose course by course. This could afford a gradually sloping ramped surface over which to raise the logs to the desired level, and at the same time provide a solid backing to the wall, only one course thick, to withstand the increasing pressure of the rubble as it rose against the wall's inner face.[12]

That the inner tomb was built fully to roof level before the log casing was put around it is doubtful. The thickness of its walls (as it turned out) is 0.35–0.37 m.; but the topmost beams at both ends, which carried the gables, are double with a combined thickness of 0.85–0.90 m. Since these were laid with the inner face flush to the faces of the beams below them, there was necessarily a very considerable overhang on the outside. This overhang was supported at the ends by the log casing through which the beams were mortised, and along the center by the rubble filling between the wall faces. The wooden clamps fastening together the pairs of beams across their ends may have helped to hold the overhang, but they were probably not strong enough to hold it by themselves. The central support for the roof, too, at its west end did not exactly fit the hole through the log wall into which its end was mortised—wooden wedges had been hammered into the joint between its under-face and the log that supported it to adjust the fit of the joint.

---

[12]The piling of an inner "core" of tumulus clay against the outside of the stone enclosure wall cannot be confirmed from the record of the stratification of the clay. The light available for observation of fine detail in the tunnel was poor indeed, and while the characteristic sloping-toward-center stratification was noted in several places as far as the middle reaches of the tunnel, it was taken for granted thereafter. Since the sides of the tunnel have

been sealed by stone walls built by the Antiquities Service of the Turkish government, it is no longer possible to look at the innermost stratification behind the wall. Unfortunately one does not start to think seriously and logically about "how it was done" until all the evidence is in; and this particular bit is lacking. I think, however, that we must take it for granted.

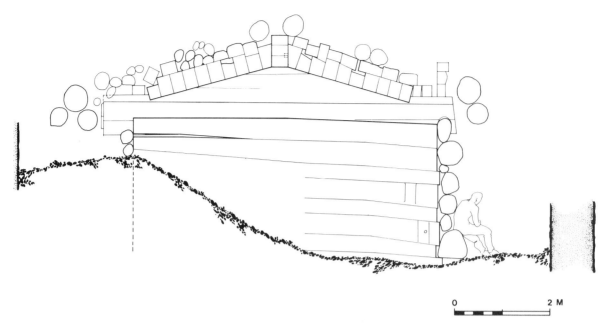

Figure 55. Tumulus MM. Elevation of north exterior facade of tomb chamber.

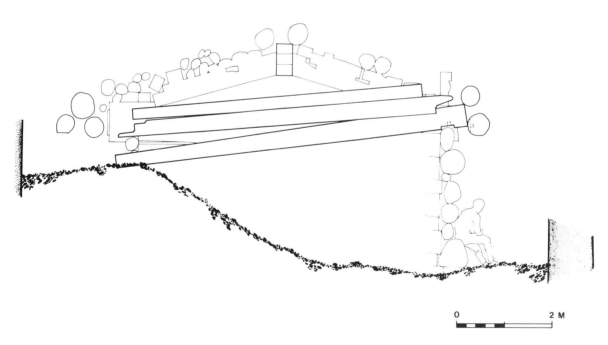

*Figure 56. Tumulus MM. North exterior facade of tomb chamber with superstruc-
ture as existing.*

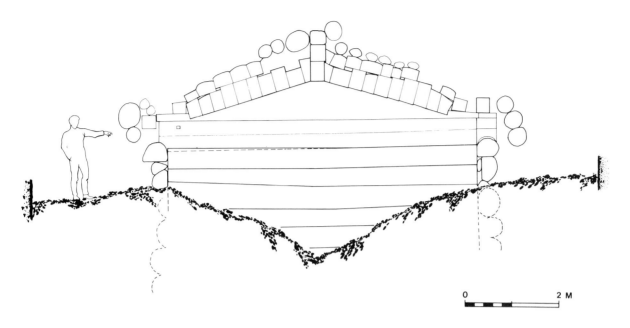

Figure 57. Tumulus MM. South exterior facade of tomb chamber.

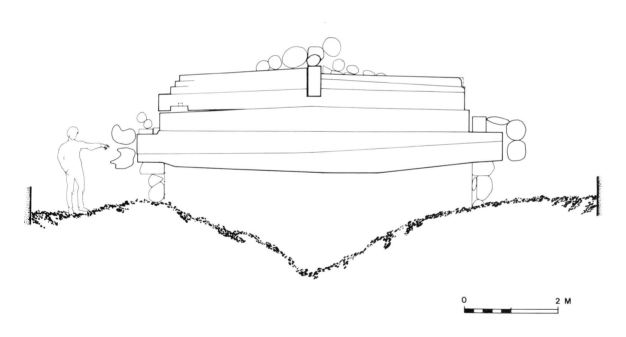

Figure 58. Tumulus MM. South exterior facade of tomb chamber with extant portion of secondary roof construction.

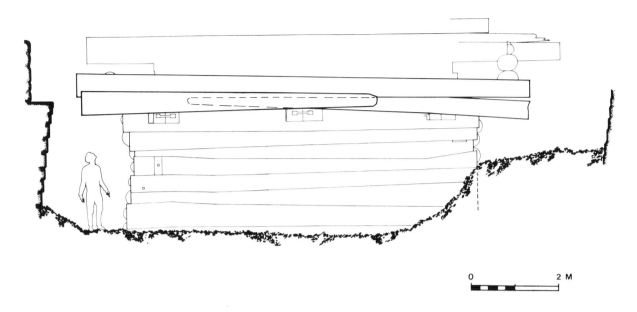

Figure 59. Tumulus MM. West exterior facade of tomb chamber with secondary roofing structure as existing.

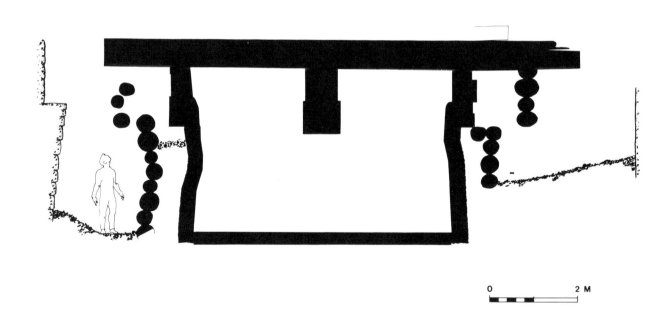

Figure 60. Tumulus MM. North-south longitudinal section of tomb chamber, from west.

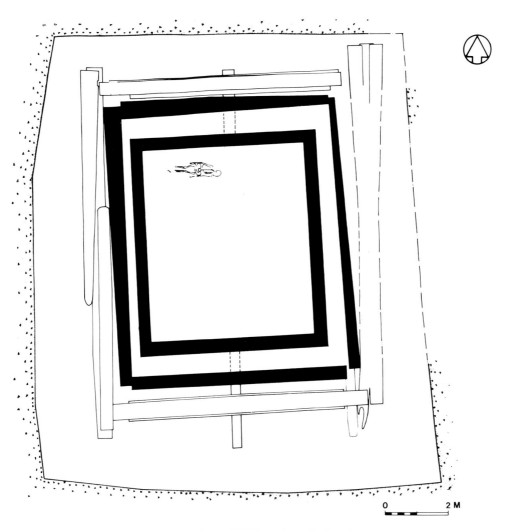

Figure 61.   Tumulus MM. Plan of tomb chamber.

Figure 62.   Tumulus MM. East-west section of tomb chamber with superstructure restored.

In any case the tomb, its protective casing of logs, and the outer enclosure of stone had all been built to the roof level of the tomb, and all the empty spaces around and between them had been filled with rubble up to that level, before the roof of the tomb was put in place. Quite probably all this work, and the laying-out of the tumulus that eventually covered it, was done during the lifetime of its future occupant. When he died at last, his body had to be lowered from above into the tomb, for there were no doorways through the stone wall or through the casing of logs or through the walls of the tomb itself to allow access. Only after the body and the grave goods had been placed in the tomb could its roof be constructed. When the tomb was roofed, and a platform of transverse logs laid above to protect the roof, rubble was heaped over the tomb to a depth of 4 m., and clay was piled over the rubble to a height of more than 40 m. It would therefore seem impossible that reuse of the tomb for later burials can ever have been contemplated. Tomb and mound belonged exclusively to the person whose skeleton lay in the tomb.

Clearly the logs observed at a high level in the rubble when we were able to enter through the break in the stone wall had been laid on top of rubble already piled in to the roof level of the tomb. At that level their function would have been to protect and take pressure from the roof of the tomb, just as did the casing below from its walls. These logs, too, must have been laid, like those of the lower casing, one on top of the other—but after the roof of the tomb had been put in place. As found, they had fallen (except the lowermost) from their original positions; and in order to fall, there had to be empty space for them to fall into. This meant that the space over the roof of the tomb had been left free of rubble—a reasonable procedure to keep weight from above the hollow space within the tomb. The shorter logs across the ends, protecting the gables, were laid well in from the ends of the long logs of the sides, their ends in contact with the inner faces so that the long logs, supported near each end, could withstand lateral pressure from the outside. The logs across the ends were to some extent relieved from pressure by the overhang of the roof above the gables.

A number of smaller timbers, squared beams, and round logs found fallen over and outside the roof have been interpreted as originating from a still higher framework of wood, probably bedded on the lower casing and designed to seal off the space above the roof at the long sides. Again these long timbers would have been held apart near their ends, and supported against lateral pressure by cross timbers or planks at the ends of the tomb. A purpose for this topmost framework may have been to give support to the platform of round logs which ran across the width of the tomb above its roof. As already noted, the ends of some 12 of these were observed still in place because their other ends were still embedded in the rubble; they ran transversely across the width of the tomb at a high level above its roof. That level turned out to be that of the top of the heavy ridge beam of the roof, itself made up from three thick beams laid one on top of the other and in sum considerably thicker than the rest of the roof, which was of double thickness. The upward-projecting ridge beam was supplemented at either side by a heavy round log laid beside it along each face. The centers of the logs of the relieving platform above were thus supported by the ridge beam and its auxiliary logs. Their ends were supported by the somewhat flimsy uppermost casing along the long sides above the tomb. But in any case these logs would have served as cantilevers, well supported at their centers. One is inclined to wonder whether the constructors realized that, and whether the relative flimsiness of the construction beneath their ends was due to a desire to keep rubble out of the area above the roof rather than a need to support the ends of beams cantilevered at their centers. In any case the greater part of the weight of the superimposed stone pile was taken by the log platform and relieved from the roof of the tomb.

In 1958 the Department of Antiquities, at the instigation of Raci Temizer and with funds supplied by the University Museum, removed the greater part of the rubble remaining in the tomb cavity. All pressure was taken from the tomb roof, and west and north sides were entirely cleared and the upper parts of the east and south sides were made visible. At this stage Charles K. Williams, II made drawings (figs. 55–62). Subsequently, after long study by Turkish engineers on the staff of the Directorate General of Antiquities and Museums, the remaining rubble was cleared out, giving passage all around the outside of the tomb, and steel posts were put in to support the timbers which had rested on top of the rubble at the level to which they had become accustomed. Twenty-eight piers of reinforced concrete were placed in a rectangle following the interior contours of the stone enclosure wall. These posts support a gabled roof of reinforced concrete above the roof of the tomb, and the space above this was refilled with rubble originally taken from the tomb, to hold the underface of the clay dome which had stood up by itself without complaint for nearly six years![13] The tomb was now secure against damage or collapse; it was open to visitors until too many of them scratched, whittled, or chalked inanities in the surfaces of wood or stone—since then visitors must look at the tomb through a metal grille.

By the time the door through the outer log wall had been cut and the ensuing observations made, it had become fairly clear that the tomb had been built at ground level or in a very shallow pit cut in its surface, rather than (as was more customary) sunk down into a deep pit. Roof level had been established at a height of about 3 m. above the surface of hardpan, and that height seemed to offer adequate headroom inside the tomb. Yet all the features of a tomb built into a pit had been reproduced or fabricated: here a built wall of stone took the place of the vertical faces of a pit, built, it seems, to contain the rubble packing around the tomb, a normal feature. This tomb presented the unusual feature of a protective wall of logs all around the tomb itself; but here the scale of the operation demanded it, and probably an estimate of the weight and the lateral pressure of the rubble which surrounded and covered it. But the level of the tomb would greatly facilitate its clearing; so too would the unbroken condition of its roof. Though always a moral certainty, the last became a fact when bit and brace were brought out again and

borings through the inner wall found nothing but emptiness on its inner side. A small window cut through the wall gave a view of the inside. The tomb was intact and its contents, though fallen to the floor and scattered, had not been crushed. An inner door was cut through the wall of the tomb; it proved to be almost at the north end of the west wall and precisely above the foot of the great bed on which lay the skeleton of the tomb's occupant.

But before considering the occupant and his grave goods (below, p. 100), it will be well to look in detail at the tomb itself. The walls were of squared timbers nicely fitted together, the wood identified as pine.[14] Subsequently, under the guidance of Burhan Tezcan, 21 wood samples were taken and identified at the Faculty of Forestry of the University of Istanbul by Professor Hayrettin Kayacık and Dr. Burhan Aytuğ.[15]

All the species seem to be native to Phrygia and the part of the Anatolian Plateau around Gordion, and it therefore seems likely that the timber for the tomb was cut in the neighborhood.[16] Since calculation indicates a total of more than 180 timbers, of which the smallest were about 5.50 m. in length, their transportation from any great distance would have presented a formidable problem.

The first beam of the outer casing to be cut (the sixth from the bottom on the west side) gave off a very strong odor of cedar when it was cut. The whole of the area outside the tomb smelled like the inside of a cedar chest, which leads us to believe that this particular log was of *Juniperus foetidissima*. The logs of the west wall below the fetid one were greater in diameter. It was realized immediately that a tree-ring chronology was a possibility for Gordion, but a limited and floating chronology

---

[13]Constructing the concrete shelter was not without its dangerous moments. Not only did a trickle of pebbles gradually loosen from the clay crust, but large flakes of drying clay also descended on the workers and the armature of the project. In the summer of 1960 part of the roof armature was damaged by a landslide, but repairs were courageously made by the Turkish team, and the clay dome held.

One can now walk around the outer casing of the tomb chamber and inspect the inner face of the limestone wall, unfinished and irregular ashlar with traces of tooling. The log casing can be inspected. The outer surface of the wall of the tomb chamber proper is visible only where the excavations cut the modern northwest entrance. The gables can be seen at the upper level. Charles K. Williams, II embodied some observations made in 1961 in

the drawings, figs. 55–62.

In 1978, the Department of Antiquities and Museums extended the protective measures by reinforcing the outer, open trench leading to the tunnel with retaining walls; an entrance room gives access from the open trench to the tunnel. [MJM]

[14]A sample of wood from the inner tomb was sent to the Forest Products Laboratory in Madison, Wisconsin, and identified by B. Francis Kukachka; see p. 291, app. III-A, Sample 16.

[15]"Recherches au point de vue forestier sur les matériaux en bois du tombeau royal de Gordion," *Istanbul Üniversitesi Orman Fakültesi Dergisi*, Series A, 18, pt. 1 (1968): 1–18. See p. 292, app. III-C, Samples 21–31.

[16]P. I. Kuniholm, *Dendrochronology*, pl. 12.

that might give us exact temporal relationships between individual features at Gordion itself but which could hardly be pinned to a fixed absolute chronology. It was not realized until Bryant Bannister, now director of the Laboratory of Tree-Ring Research, University of Arizona at Tucson, came to Gordion (in 1961) that some of these larger logs showed upward of 700 growth rings. The fact, then, that these logs used in the Gordion tomb were from trees that had already been growing at the time of the Hittite Empire opened new and wider possibilities. There exists a possibility of establishing a tree-ring chronology for the Anatolian Plateau, and this possibility is being developed.[17] In any case the prospects for establishing a relative chronology among the samples from Gordion seem at present to be hopeful.

The thickness of the tomb wall where it was cut through to make a doorway was 0.37 m. Since this was the only place where thickness could be measured, it is an assumption (though a probable one) that the thickness of the walls was uniform at all sides of the tomb. The squared beams of the walls (eight beams high on the long sides, nine at each end) were excellently fitted together and finished. Joints between beams were often so tight that they were all but invisible, their presence in some places betrayed only by slight variation in color between the timbers above and below. The inner faces of the walls had been finished with the adze and then sanded; adze marks on their faces were recognizable at places struck just right by the light. The sanding of the wall faces must have been the final

operation, done after the walls were complete. At various places, probably where there had been imperfections in the wood—rot, worm holes, knots, or the like—small areas of the wall faces had been cut out and plugged by separate pieces of wood cut to fit. There were nineteen of these plugs altogether, placed quite at random in the walls (one in the west wall, seven in the east, six in the north, and five in the south). One was diamond-shaped, the rest square or oblong, varying in size from 0.05 m. to 0.12 m. on a side. Most of the plugs had shrunk somewhat and were loose in their sockets. Unfortunately most of them disappeared during the period when the tomb was open to the public. One prefers to think that originally they had been held in place by very tight fit to their sockets rather than by glue (though that is possible); of pins or dowels to hold them in place there was no trace. It would seem likely that these plugs were put in place after the beams had been finished with the adze but before the final sanding of the surfaces.

The timbers varied greatly in height.[18] The east wall showed the largest, 0.64 m. high (the sixth from the bottom) and the smallest, 0.22 m. high, at the top. Whether the squared beams were simply stacked one on top of the other or were fastened together by dowels across the joints could not be determined. As noted above, the ends of the shorter beams across the width of the tomb were socketed into grooves in the faces of the longer pieces at the sides, and so the corners of the structure were held together. The walls rose

---

[17]Bannister took a number of cores from the outer casing of the tomb while he was at Gordion. But all the data that he had amassed from the tomb remained for a long time an isolated phenomenon, without comparanda. Peter Kuniholm, while a graduate student at the University of Pennsylvania, in Ankara on a fellowship from the American Research Institute in Turkey, undertook the project of establishing a dendrochronological chart for Anatolia, in consultation with Bannister. With the warm cooperation of the Turkish authorities and of the excavators of many sites in Anatolia, he has assembled samples of wood and of charcoal from sites as early as Acemhüyük (Middle Bronze Age) and as late as early Christian times. Comparison and coordination of this material by computer have been successful. It now seems clear that the interrelations of samples from various places and periods at Gordion will be established, yielding an exact and trustworthy relative chronology for Gordion itself (see Kuniholm, *ibid.* for details and dis-

cussion of concomitant problems). How the samples from the various other Anatolian sites may interlock with each other and with those from Gordion remains to be seen.

[18]Heights of wall timbers on interior of chamber, beginning at bottom:

West wall: (1) 0.43, (2) 0.495, (3) 0.51, (4) 0.44, (5) 0.37, (6) 0.41, (7) 0.37, (8) 0.24. Total 3.265 m.

North wall: (1) 0.40, (2) 0.45, (3) 0.415, (4) 0.345, (5) 0.33, (6) 0.36, (7) 0.36, (8) 0.32, (9) 0.28. Total 3.26 m.

East wall: (1) 0.39, (2) 0.41, (3) 0.395, (4) 0.435, (5) 0.45, (6) 0.64, (7) 0.31, (8) 0.22. Total 3.25 m.

South wall: (1) 0.44, (2) 0.385, (3) 0.425, (4) 0.42, (5) 0.365, (6) 0.35, (7) 0.335, (8) 0.28, (9) 0.32. Total 3.32 m. [Ed.]

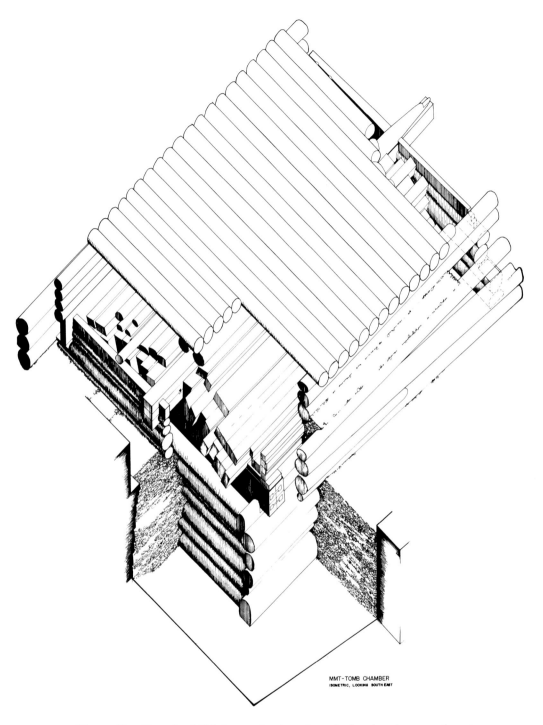

Figure 63.   Tumulus MM. Isometric view of tomb chamber, from northwest.

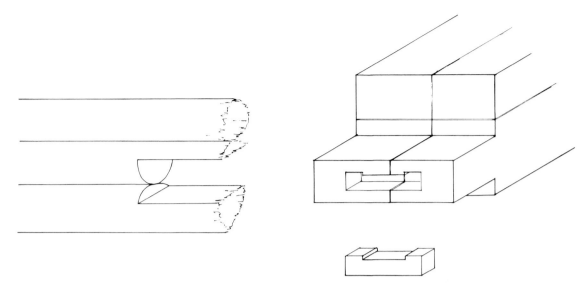

*Figure 64. Tumulus MM. End of central cross beam with mortising. Isometric
drawing.*

to a height of about 3.25 m. above the floor; the
inside dimensions of the tomb were 5.15 m. east
to west by 6.20 m. north to south.[19]

The floor, made of 14 parallel, lengthwise timbers of width varying from a maximum of 0.535
m. to a minimum of 0.205, lay entirely within the
oblong area of the tomb, its outer beams flush
against the inner faces of the beams of the side
walls, its ends against the inner faces of the end
walls. A bore drilled through the floor showed a
thickness of about 0.33 m. for the wooden beams,
and indicated the presence of a bedding of rubble
beneath them. The thickness of the rubble bedding remains unknown; but since the lowermost
log of the outer casing was bedded on rubble and

lay with about half its diameter sunk below the
surface of hardpan, it would seem likely that the
entire area to be occupied by the tomb, including
its outer casing, was hollowed into hardpan to a
certain (unknown) depth, then filled with rubble
which served as a bed alike for tomb walls[20] and
floor and for the log construction around the
outside.[21]

The condition of the tomb was generally good.
The north end had been pushed in by the pressure of the rubble outside (fig. 60); its face was
convex and bulged, and one of the beams (its
ends socketed at the corners) had cracked and its
inner face splintered. The inward bulge of the
tomb wall was reflected by an inward bulge of the

---

[19]The height of the east wall was measured at 3.25 m.;
of the west at 3.265; of the north at 3.26; and of the
south at 3.32. The slight discrepancies of measurement
may be due to minor unevenness in the settling of the
floor. The length and breadth measurements of the room,
taken at floor level, showed less discrepancy: the length
along the face of the west wall was 6.21 m., of the east
6.20 m., and the width 5.14 m. along the north wall,
5.16 along the south.

[20]Later probing by the Turkish engineers during the
restoration process (see above, p. 94) showed that the
tomb walls rested on at least two courses of ashlar
foundation.

[21]The somewhat irregular area outside the wooden con-

struction (maximum measurements *ca.* 11.50 m. east to
west by 13.25 north to south) seems to have been left at
the level of the surface of hardpan. The surrounding
stone wall was set down into hardpan to a depth of at
least two courses, but to receive its foundation, the hardpan seems to have been trenched separately. Only one
side of this wall—the north side—is straight; the rest are
variously curved or angled. Evidently construction was
started with the wooden tomb itself; then the casing of
logs around it was begun and rubble began to be piled
around it; finally the stone dam wall to contain the rubble was begun. Perhaps its contour was affected by rubble already piled in; but in any case it did not need to
be precisely lined with squared corners, since it was to
be completely buried and never to be seen.

log casing outside; both, held apart by the filling of rubble in the space between them, had been pushed inward together by the pressure from outside. The side walls of the tomb stood firm and fairly vertical; the south end wall was slightly out of plumb, its upper part pushed in a bit by pressure from outside, but no timbers were cracked or broken.

The only other damage from outside pressure was in the crossbeam which spanned the width of the tomb at its center to help support the roof. This, as will be remembered, was composed of four separate squared timbers, one pair on top of the other, carrying a shallow triangular gable to match those at the ends and to support the center of the roof timbers. Pressure from above had cracked the two lower beams of the span right through their thickness so that they sagged down as much as 0.40 m.,[22] their faces splintered, at a point somewhat east of the long central axis of the tomb. The upper (and lighter) pair of beams had also cracked at this same point; but no crack showed in the triangular gable which surmounted them. The great beam of the east wall, 0.64 m. thick, which had been notched for the passage of the spanning beams, had been somewhat splintered in its face by the downward sagging of the cracked spanners. This rather threatening situation was remedied immediately by the insertion of stout, modern propping timbers beneath the crack (pls. 39A, 49A).

The four timbers, which together comprise the central span 0.88 m. wide (0.48 plus 0.40 m.) and 0.79 m. thick (0.48 plus 0.31 m.), are about 7.40 m. in length (pl. 40A). Their ends, fastened together by wooden double-T clamps, appear at either side in the outer face of the log casing, so that they span the full width of the wooden construction (figs. 59, 64). To allow their passage, the uppermost two timbers of both east and west tomb wall were cut through, and the third timber was notched to bed them at the proper level. The bottoms of the notches lay about 2.45 m. above the floor level of the tomb, so that there was plenty of headroom to pass beneath. Since the uppermost wall beams at both sides of the tomb were completely severed for the passage of the

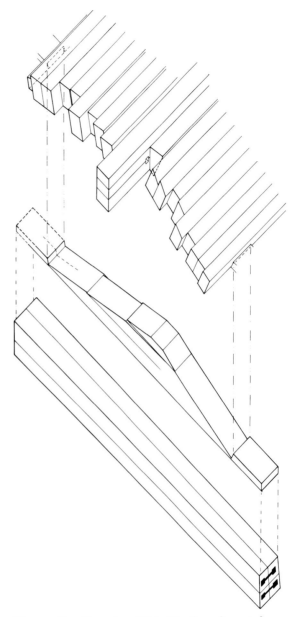

Figure 65. Tumulus MM. North pediment beam, from northwest.

spanning bridge, each became in effect two separate timbers, anchored at their outer ends by the mortises at the corners of the tomb. How their inner ends by the crossbeam were secured is not apparent: possibly by dowels run across the horizontal joints to the timbers beneath. One must assume that the builders would have been reluctant to weaken their cross-support by mortise cuttings.

The three shallow triangular gables which sup-

---

[22]The amount of sag is demonstrated by the measured heights of the central beam above the floor: at west side 2.49; at center 2.08; at east side 2.46 m. [Ed.]

port the roof (fig. 60) rest on top of the end walls and of the spanning central beam complex. The central one is slightly thinner than the beams that support it, so that each face is recessed 0.05–0.10 m. behind the face of the beam that supports it. Likewise the interior faces of the end gables are slightly recessed behind the faces of the walls below. Each gable (fig. 65) consists of three pieces of wood, which diminish in length upward with the narrowing slopes of the gable roof. Long lower pieces extend the full width of the wooden structure and are bedded, as noted, on the wall ends and the central span. Above these rest shorter pieces sloped at either side; and on those a short central piece sloped at either side and flat at the center on top to receive the ridge-beam. The total height of the tomb from floor to under-face of ridge-beam measured 3.86 m.; the height of the gable 0.61 m.

CONTENTS OF THE TOMB[23]

The door (pl. 39A),[24] which entered from the north end of the west wall, encountered the foot of the bed, between the corner blocks on which it had once rested. By putting down a plank to rest upon the raised threshold and a new block by the south end-block of the bed, we gained access to the chamber. However, before the new entryway could be made, the footboard was seen to have fallen inward (to the east) over the foot of the bed. Its north end was badly rotted away, but its south end was fairly solid, so it could be lifted out of the way. So also a "roll" of textile had to be carefully taken from the foot of the bed. Consequently these two features do not appear on Dorothy Cox's plan, fig. 66.

Immediately upon our entry, after photography

in situ and while Dorothy Cox was still drawing the plan of the finds on the floor, the three props were installed under the cracked and sagging central crossbeams: one just to the west of the break and two side by side in front of the screens on the east.[25]

Along the walls on three sides—the east (south half only), south (complete), and west (south half only)—at slightly differing heights from the floor, there is evidence that heavy iron spikes were hammered into the walls in straight rows to serve as a means of suspension for such vessels as small jugs and ring-handled deep bowls (east), ring-handled bowls (south), and "belts" and large trefoil jugs (west) (fig. 66). Many of the vessels with handles showed shallow dents at points where they hit the floor when the nails rusted off at the wall surfaces. Only stubs of nails for the most part were still embedded in the walls, but large rust stains had spread into the grain of the wood to the right and left of each original spike (pl. 40B).[26] It is thought that the bowls and other vessels without means of suspension were perhaps placed in neatly stacked piles upon the tables which were arranged to stand in the southeast quarter and the northeast corner of the chamber.

The bed in the northwest corner and extending along the north wall, and all the other individual pieces of furniture and smaller finds, are described in detail in the following catalogue where everything has been given MM numbers. There are, of course, more objects in the catalogue than could be drawn on the plan, as pieces appeared under other pieces and behind the leaning screens; these could not be indicated upon the sketch but their numbers are grouped where possible. Also, the cauldrons held many pots which were later

---

[23]The section from here, where the original manuscript breaks off, to the end of the Introduction to Tumulus MM has been adapted by the editor from R. S. Young's own words in field notes and former publications. The account of the interior of the tomb as found is based upon Gordion Notebook no. 63.

[24]Continued, as it were, from p. 95 above.

[25]Best seen in the James Whitmore photograph in *Life* 43, no. 6 (August 5, 1957): 74.

[26]Along the east wall there were three rows, at heights

1.40 m. (8 nails), 1.75 (9 nails) and 1.99 (8 nails) above the floor. On the south end wall, two rows at heights 1.83 (13 nails) and 2.10 (12 nails) above the floor, and on the west side two rows at 1.75 (10 nails) and 2.10 (10 nails) above the floor. Rodney Young constructed theoretical lists of items as hung back upon their nearest nails, and finally accounted for every object with a handle for suspension (including also the bronze and leather belts) except for a few small bronze jugs near the east wall (which could have been set upon the tables with the omphalos bowls). See *AJA* 62 (1958): 150–151. [Ed.]

mended and added to the catalogue after the clearing of the cauldrons in the workrooms.

The bed itself (figs. 112, 113; pls. 41A–43A) is described in detail on p. 188 ff. (MM 389), along with theories concerning its construction and the manner of its collapse.

The skeleton (pls. 41B, 42B), which was disturbed somewhat by the fall of the bedboards upon which it was lying, reclined on its back with feet toward the west and head toward the east. The legs were fully extended and the arms lay straight along the sides. The skull had rolled over toward its left (south), and the mandible was upside down. There was a hole in the back of the skull, and the position was slightly hunched and bent down. These minor changes were doubtless the result of the collapse of the bed platform.

The body, which lay on 0.03–0.04 m. of "mattress" (as compacted when found) evidently had been dressed in pants or a skirt of leather with fancy overlaid textiles and bronze studs on the outside. Near the feet, across the shins and to either side of the latter, we found pieces of a bronze belt (MM 180) made of plaques cut *à jour*, decorated with small bronze studs. Pieces of plain leather without cloth or studs were to be found up to and above the line of the pelvis. The leather stops at about waist level, and from there upward some bronze fibulae were found resting upon the body and embedded in the "mattress."

The fibulae on the bed are much less well preserved than those from the bag on the floor at the head of the bed (pl. 43A, and see below, p. 168 f.), probably because they had been embedded in the textiles and because they had been in contact with organic matter. One lay near the left wrist, one at and one just below the left shoulder, one on the right shoulder in its original position—that is, under where the right shoulder should have been before the body was moved by the collapse of the bed. Close above the right elbow was another. Two tufts of fine-meshed cloth near the left elbow and the right shoulder covered more fibulae. But still more lay at some distance from the skeleton to north and south, and it is difficult to guess what their original position may have been or how they could have fastened clothing on the body.

On the afternoon of July 21, Professor Muzaffer Şenyürek, then chairman of the Division of Palaeoanthropology in the University of Ankara, took up the skeleton and carried it away to Ankara. His report, from observations he made on the spot, gave us the information that the sex was male, the age 61 to 65, the height 1.59 m., and that the skull and face were long and narrow with a very heavy jaw.

Behind the head of the bed at the east, a table (MM 387) had collapsed and been in part covered by the fallen headboard (pl. 43A). Beside this a cloth bag appears to have contained fibulae, some of which had spilled out onto the floor.

In the northeast corner was a mass of rotted wooden fragments from collapsed furniture (pl. 43B).

Along the east wall, and leaning against it at center, were two large inlaid screens (MM 379, pl. 44A and MM 378, pl. 44A–C) to be compared with that found in Tumulus P (TumP 151) in 1956. Behind them were many fragments from the throne supports and a number of bronze vessels, including two situlae, one with a lion's head (MM 45, pl. 44C) and one with a ram's head (MM 46).

In the southeast corner, a great mass of bronzes lay fallen from at least two tables (pl. 45A). One table (MM 388, pl. 45A, B) was most elaborate, with inlaid panels in the faces of its frame, and openwork and inlaid supports.

Along the west half of the south wall and in the southwest corner stood three large cauldrons (MM 1–3) supported on iron ring stands (MM 357–359). The first, from the east, (MM 3, pl. 46A) has four handles, with rings in place; two of the handles are sirens (female) and two are bearded "demons." The second also has four handles, with sirens looking inward (MM 2). The rings in them are missing, but the sockets to hold them are present (pl. 46B). The one in the corner, the smallest, has two bull's-head handles (MM 1, pls. 46B, 47A).

Along the west side, from the southwest corner back to the foot of the bed, lay a series of large ellipsoidal trefoil jugs of bronze (MM 16–25), of a shape and type related to those found in the burned layers of the hüyük. Among the jugs on the floor was a series of bronze disks with accompanying studded leather plaques which have been interpreted as belts (MM 170–179). The jugs are in various positions. Two stand upright on

101

their flat bottoms, but others lie on their side. All fell from the rows of nails in the south half of the west wall (pls. 47B, C, 48A).

In the center of the room had stood at least five tables (MM 380–384) once bearing loads of bronze omphalos bowls (pls. 48B, 49A, B.) These have all collapsed, scattering their loads over the floor. The tables were oblong with rounded corners and stood on three legs. One measured 0.66 by 0.77 m. The legs remained firm, but the tops, of a different wood (one sample was maple), were damp, rotten, and often split down the center. It seemed a question whether the tops could be saved at all, but MM 384 was restorable in the end (pl. 81D, E).

CHRONOLOGY

Rodney Young did not finish the writing of this Introduction to Tumulus MM. It is clear from his other publications that he did not believe that a tumulus on this scale could have been made immediately after the Kimmerian catastrophe. He thought the tumulus belonged to Midas's predecessor on the throne of Phrygia, presumably named Gordius. Rather than rephrasing Young's historical analysis of the burial in MM,[27] the editors refer the reader to the discussion of Midas and chronology in the Conclusions (pp. 271–272).

CATALOGUE

BRONZE

LARGE CAULDRONS WITH ATTACHMENTS AND CARRYING RINGS MM 1–3

The three large bronze cauldrons stood in front of the south wall of the tomb in a row from the southwest corner, each on a footed ring stand of iron (pl. 46). MM 1, with two bull's-head attachments, stood at the corner; beside it, at the east, MM 2 with four siren attachments; and third, still farther to the east, MM 3 with two siren and two demon attachments. All three cauldrons were packed with vessels of pottery which had been placed inside them (pl. 47A), apparently containing food.[28] A number of bronze vessels with handles were also found inside the cauldrons; but probably these had been suspended originally by their handles from nails in the south wall of the tomb above and had fallen to the positions in which they were found, some in the cauldrons and others on the floor around them. Large cauldrons were used as containers for smaller offerings also in Tumuli P and W, and in K-III.

MM 1   **Cauldron with bull's-head attachments**
B 809   At southwest corner
H.-rim 0.435   D. rim 0.545   D. 0.708 m.
Figs. 67, 68A, B; Pls. 47A, 50A–C

Intact except for corrosion holes through the bottom.

The heavy rim, flat on top and slightly projecting,

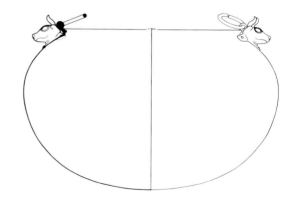

Figure 67.   MM 1.   Cauldron with bull's-head attachments.   Profile and view.   1:10.

---

[27]*Gordion Guide,* 50; *AJA* 62 (1958): 149; *Expedition* 11, No. 1, 19. The clearest statement of his thought appears in *Hesperia* 38 (1969): 260. [Ed.]

[28]For chemical analyses of the food in the pots, in cloth sacks, and loose in the cauldrons because of spillage when the pots and sacks rotted, see pp. 277–278, app. II-A, Samples 1–8.

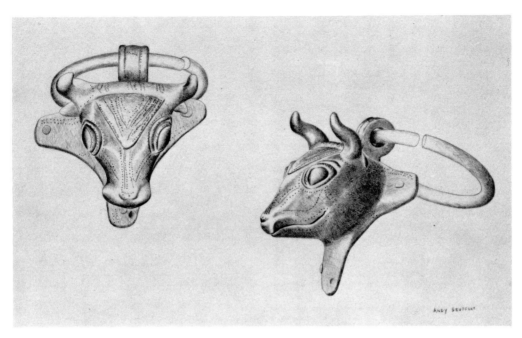

A

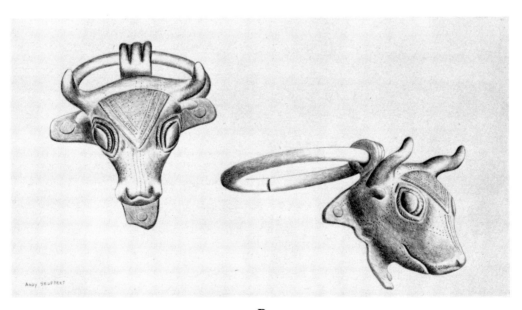

B

Figure 68. MM 1. A. Bull's head A, *front and three-quarter views. B. Bull's head* B, *front and side views. 1:1.*

with sharpened inner and outer edges, seems to be in one piece with the rounded cauldron: cast together?[29]

The handles consist of flat, T-shaped attachments fitted to the curve of the shoulder and against the face of the rim; on each of these a bull's head with a ring socket at the top behind to hold a freely swiveling carrying ring. The attachments were fastened to the shoulder, each by three dowels, one near the end of each arm, with large shallow-convex stud heads on the inside, the outside ends flattened to rivet heads by hammering. Differences in measurement and proportion suggest that the two attachments were cast in different molds. So far as can be seen each attachment—T-shaped plate, bull's head, and socket on top—was cast in one piece. The carrying handles were added by threading bronze rods through the sockets and bending them around to make circles. Attachment *B* was set slightly askew on the shoulder, slanting down a little toward one side.

Bull's-head attachments

	A.	*B.*
GW. head	0.076	0.073 m.
H. head	0.069	0.067 m.
D. rings	0.083	0.081 m.

The bull's heads have small ears set below forward-swept horns; the bulging almond-shaped eyes outlined by double raised ridges above, single ones below. The forelocks are flat, raised triangles extending down to points between the eyes. The sides of the mouths rather crudely indicated by grooves; the nostrils roughly punched. Engraved and punched decoration of lines and dots: lines with diagonal hatching between them border the forelocks; and dots in diminishing triangles fill them; hatching on the ridges around the eyes; ladders bordered by dots down the nose from forelock to muzzle; and lines bordered by dots from muzzle to inner ends of eyes.

MM 2   **Cauldron with four siren attachments**
B 786   Against south wall
H.-rim 0.485   D. rim 0.578   D. 0.775 m.
Figs. 69, 70; Pls. 51–54A

The cauldron is intact except for small holes eaten by corrosion at the bottom. All four of the siren

attachments lack their carrying rings; the socket of *A* is twisted to one side, perhaps bent when the ring was wrenched off. Two of the sirens, *B* and *D*, have lost the lower ends of their tails, broken off before the cauldron was placed in the tomb. The cauldron is rounded at the bottom; in the tomb it rested on the iron ring stand MM 358. The rim was perhaps cast in one with the cauldron;[30] its inner and outer edges were sharpened, and its flat, upper face slopes slightly inward.

The siren attachments were each fastened by three dowels below the rim, their chests covering its upper face. The dowels, two through the wings below the hands, the third through the tail, are capped on the inside by large round stud heads; on the outside their ends were spread to rough rivet heads by hammering, and these overlap the feather patterns engraved on the surface of the attachments. Probing with a wire shows the busts to be solid inside; but their position as fixed to the cauldron rim makes it impossible to determine whether they were solid-cast, or hollow-cast and filled with lead as were the cores of the bulls' heads of TumW 1 and 2 (see pp. 200–201).

The lower parts of the attachments are thick plates of bronze bent to conform to the curves of the cauldron shoulder and set close against the outer face of the rim. At either side the ends are notched at the edges to leave six scallops representing the ends of wing feathers; at the bottom *A* is notched to seven, *B* and *D* apparently to six scallops, to show the ends of the tail feathers. The feathers themselves are engraved in three tiers on wings and tails, the wing feathers running out nearly horizontally in parallel lines, the tail feathers spreading with the outward taper of the tail. The innermost tier of short feathers forms a continuous semicircular band radiating from an inner ring decorated with triangles alternately hatched and dotted. This inner decorated ring or zone encloses two oval openings and between them a strut (the body of the bird) from which rises the flat ring socket from which the (missing) carrying handle was suspended. In low relief along the upper edges of the wings lie the outstretched forearms and hands of the sirens, decorated above the wrist and below the elbow with engraving to represent bracelets.

The busts that rise above the rim, cast in one

---

[29]Ann K. Knudsen (*Phryg. Met. and Pot.* [1961], 295–297) believed these three cauldrons, MM 1–3, to have been cast, together with their rims, because she could find no hammer marks on them. A. Steinberg (*Bronzes of the Bernardini Tomb* [1966], 570–573) published them as cast because his analyses found so high a percentage of

tin in them that he believed that it would have been too difficult to hammer them. More recently, Steinberg (see app. II-C, pp. 286–289, Samples 81–90, and his footnotes) has come around to the position that MM 1–3 were hammered and annealed. [Ed.]

[30]See above, n. 29.

Attachment *A*
  Front: Necklace

                  Neck edge

                  Chest strip

                  Sleeves   (*L*)   (*R*)

                  Bracelets   (*L*)   (*R*)

  Back: Neck edge

                  Tail circle

Attachment *B*
  Front: Necklace

                  Neck edge

                  Chest strip

                  Sleeves   (*L*)   (*R*)

                  Bracelets   (*L*)   (*R*)

  Back: Neck edge

                  Tail circle

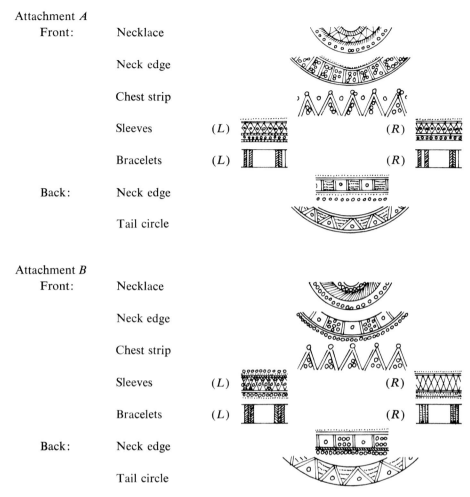

Figure 69.   MM 2. Cauldron with four siren attachments. Siren attachments A *and*
B. *Details: incised decoration of their garments.   Not to scale.*

with bird-shaped attachments, represent the heads and shoulders of humans, usually taken to be women and conveniently (though not necessarily accurately) called sirens. The hair, usually parted in the middle, falls to the shoulders, separated at the bottom into seven or eight ringlets. At the front across the forehead a series of short, vertical engraved lines represents a fringe or bang of hair, above this the hair runs to either side, to be represented by horizontal lines across the ringlets around the lower part. The eyebrows are raised ridges, hatched; the eyes outlines above and below by ridges more finely hatched to represent the eyelashes. On the chin of each figure are two tiny punched circles.

The sirens wear bodices with short sleeves to above the elbow; the sleeves show only at the back where engraved bands represent the decoration at their ends. At either side where sleeve decoration meets a decorative band across the front of the bodice the pattern changes. The decoration of the bodice at front and back comes together along the shoulder, turning downward in what may be intended to be the representation of a shoulder seam. At the front the lowest pattern (above the rim) is usually a row of double triangles with small punched rings between them and above their points; a second band, above, is of panels divided by double verticals and irregularly filled by small punched rings varying in number from panel to panel. Above this, bands of combinations of punched rings, zigzag and "fringing" at the base of the neck.

Variations in profile, in expression and in engraved detail give each figure individuality, and differences in measurement show that each was

105

Attachment *C*
Front:

Necklace

Neck edge

Chest strip

Sleeves (*L*) (*R*)

Bracelets (*L*) (*R*)

Back: Neck edge

Tail circle

Attachment *D*
Front:

Necklace

Neck edge

Chest strip

Sleeves (*L*) (*R*)

Bracelets (*L*) (*R*)

Back: Neck edge

Tail circle

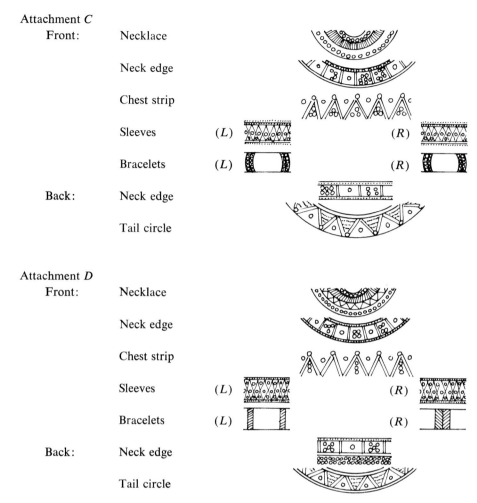

*Figure 70. MM 2. Cauldron with four siren attachments. Siren attachments C and
D. Details: incised decoration of their garments. Not to scale.*

cast separately in its own mold which was apparently not used for a second casting. The dimensions follow.

Siren attachments

	A.	*B.*	*C.*	*D.*
H. or P.H.	0.212	0.193	0.212	0.195 m.
H. from rim	0.08	0.095	0.07	0.082 m.
W. across wings	0.265	0.277	0.275	0.275 m.
W. head	0.055	0.055	0.051	0.055 m.

A. Fig. 69; Pls. 51B, 53B, 54A[31]

---

[31]See also Akurgal, *Kunst Anat.,* 39, *Abb.* 17; 303, fig. 10.

Hair in seven ringlets, parted in center, carelessly delineated. Tail has seven scallops and three tiers of feathers below the tail circle. Tiers of feathers on wings arranged as two short, one long. For details of the designs upon her garment and her jewelry, expressed by incision, see fig. 69.

B. Fig. 69; Pls. 52A, 53C, 54A

Hair in eight ringlets, parted in center, done in soft wavy lines. Tail broken across above end at bottom, preserving one and a half tiers of feathers. Wing arranged in two short tiers and one long tier of feathers. *B* has straighter nose than *A, C,* and *D.* The details of her jewelry and garment are to be found in fig. 69.

C. Fig. 70; Pls. 52B, 53D, 54A

The figure leans far forward to peer into the

cauldron. Hair is arranged in seven ringlets with no parting and is etched with short, choppy lines. The tail is finished in a straight line across the bottom, with the feathers in three almost equal tiers. The wings are not identical in treatment: the left ends in three scallops and a vague continuation, the right in four scallops plus continuation. The tiers of feathers are one short, one medium, and one long. Her chest is shorter where she seems to lean over the rim. See fig. 70 for the details of design on her jewelry and on her garment.

D. Fig. 70; Pls. 53A, E, 54A

Hair arranged in seven ringlets, finely etched. Tail is broken, preserving one and a half tiers of feathers. The wing feathers arranged in tiers, two short and one long. Details of the designs upon her garment and jewelry are seen in fig. 70.

MM 3   **Cauldron with two sirens and two demons as attachments**
　　　　B 842   Against south wall
　　　　H.-rim 0.515   D. rim 0.58–0.587
　　　　　　D. 0.782 m.
　　　　Pls. 54B–57

Intact; spots of corrosion on bottom inside.[32]
Slightly larger than MM 2 but similar in shape; in the tomb the cauldron rested on the iron ring stand MM 357. The rim like that of MM 2, evidently cast in one with the cauldron.[33] The attachments consist of two sirens and two bearded demons, the members of each pair (*A, C* and *B, D*) set opposite and facing each other, all fastened to the shoulder of the cauldron by three dowels with round shallow-convex stud heads inside, hammered rivet heads outside. The dowels through the wings are set high and far out, beyond the ends of the hands. The carrying rings remain in their sockets, hanging down to cover approximately the ends of the dowels that fasten the tails to the wall. The handles are lengths of heavy bronze rod, round in section, bent around to form circular rings. The ends do not quite meet, leaving narrow gaps between.

In form and general appearance the bird's wing and tail attachments, though slightly larger, are much like those of MM 2; all may well have been cast in the same workshop. The engraved decoration of MM 3 is, however, much more precisely and carefully planned than that of MM 2, probably by a different artisan. We may note, for example, that the feather

ends of wings and tail are properly scalloped, not merely beveled and notched as on MM 2*A*, or left straight across the bottom of the tail as on MM 2*C*, suggesting that the tails were cast straight across the bottom, then scalloped by filing. The feathers themselves are more precisely rendered by engraving than those on MM 2: a heavy line separates each from each, a double line down the center suggests the quill or spine, and diagonals at each side complete the feather pattern. The wings show four tiers of feathers, the outer running horizontally outward, the innermost a semicircular radiating tier with feather ends set off by double outline, the feathers themselves unengraved. This innermost tier, as on MM 2, encloses a decorative zone (pendent triangles filled by punched dots) around the strut, which carries the handle socket between oval openings. The inner semicircle of feathers forms the topmost of three tiers on the tail. The outstretched arms of the figures wear bracelets at the wrist only, the loose flesh at their elbows is rendered by small concentric arcs, a detail ignored by the engraver of MM 2. The patterns that decorate the ends of the short sleeves (these vary from figure to figure) are carried over the shoulder and down to the bottom in front.

The sirens (*B* and *D*): the hairdo is approximately the same as that of the sirens of MM 2; here each siren wears seven ringlets. The eyebrows have fine hatching, and the eyelashes are suggested by fine hatching on the ridges above and below the eyes. The lips are tighter and thinner on *B* than on the rest. There are five to six punched, shallow dots on the chins of the MM 3 sirens. The lower edges of the bodices are simply decorated with a row of single triangles filled by punched dots; on *D* the triangles diminish in height from right to left as though the bust, already decorated, had been filed down at the (observer's) left to fit it to the rim of the cauldron. At the base of the necks double and triple narrow bands of decoration, the lowest representing the neckline of the bodice, the upper a necklace.

The demons (*A* and *C*): these differ from the sirens only in the bearded heads. The waved or crimped hair lies in five wedge-shaped rolls on top of the head, decorated by engraved lines running from side to side. Below at the sides and back are five more waves with vertical engraved lines; a sixth wave at the bottom behind rests on the back. At the front at either side a ringlet decorated with vertical engraving hangs to the shoulder. Both demons wear long beards hanging to the chest and cut square at the bottom; neither has a mustache. The beard of *A* is decorated with spiral hooks made probably with a punch; the beard of *C* with engraved herringbone pattern.

―――――――――
[32]For analysis of corrosion product, see p. 285, app. II-B, Sample 73.

[33]See p. 104, n. 29.

Again the members of each pair were cast in individually made molds, apparently never reused for a second casting.

	Demon attachments		Siren attachments	
	A.	C.	B.	D.
H.	0.189	0.187	0.189	0.183 m.
H. from rim	0.067	0.069	0.068	0.065 m.
W. across wings	0.295	0.302	0.296	0.297 m.
W. head	0.048	0.047	0.05	0.0495 m.

Demons

A. Pls. 55A, 57A, E

Sleeves: lozenges outlined by double lines; single punched rings inside the lozenges and between their points above and below. Double-line borders.

Chest: row of single triangles filled with punched dots.

C. Pls. 56A, 57C, G

Sleeves: two bands of ladder pattern, punched circles between the rungs, bordered above and below by rows of punched circles.

Chest: no decoration.

Sirens

B. Pls. 55B, 57B, F

Sleeves: lozenge chain, lozenges with double outline; a punched dot in each and between the points above and below. Borders of punched dots between lines at each side.

Neck at front: zone of herringbone bordered above and below by punched dots.

D. Pls. 56B, 57D, H, I

The tail is of thinner metal than the wings and central complex, so that there is a second curving arc across the base of the tail where the metal steps down from the thicker to the thinner part of the plate; in this the curved ends of the innermost tier of feathers are lost.

The sleeve, neck, and chest decoration as on *B*. On the chest the triangles at the left are truncated below.

The literature on siren and demon attachments (*Assurattaschen*) is already great, and rapidly becoming greater.[34] These have aroused keen interest among archaeologists in Greek lands because they have been found in numbers among the early votives at Olympia, Delphi, and Athens, and because they are tangible links between the Orient and Greece in the late Geometric and early Orientalizing period, since it is agreed among scholars that a majority of them are imports from Near Eastern lands. They have been found hitherto detached from their cauldrons which, because they were of thin bronze, have disappeared altogether; but recently a cauldron was found at Olympia together with some of its attachments: a reconstruction shows two demons, three griffin- and three lion-protomes.[35] Neither the new cauldron from Olympia nor any of the attachments found individually at the various Greek sanctuaries comes from a stratigraphically significant environment; the dating must depend on external evidence.

The Gordion cauldrons found in the tomb under the Great Tumulus were the first to be found intact with their attachments and in an environment which may suggest a firm dating.[36] For reasons cited above (p. 102 and n. 27) we

[34]They were first gathered together by E. Kunze, *Kretische Bronzereliefs* (1931), Anhang 2, 267 ff. and supplemented by the same author in *Reinecke Festschrift* (1950), 100–101. One of the latest treatments, based on the specimens found at Olympia, is by H. V. Herrmann in *Ol. Forsch.* VI (1966). An unpublished dissertation of 1959 is cited: M. A. Brandes, *Orientalische und archaisch-griechische Kesselattaschen aus Bronze in Gestalt geflügelter Menschenprotomen* (Heidelberg). An article by Oscar Muscarella, "The Oriental Origin of Siren Cauldron Attachments," *Hesperia* 31 (1962): 317–329, appeared too late for use by Brandes or Herrmann. All references to 1962 may be found in Herrmann, *Ol. Forsch.* VI. See also E. Akurgal, *Urart. altiran. K.* (1968), 20 ff.

[35]Olympia No. B 4224; Herrmann, *Ol. Forsch.* VI, 11–17 and pls. 1–4. The reconstruction pl. 4; the demon attachments, Herrmann nos. A3–A4.

[36]In 1966 the cauldrons from Tomb 79, Burial 1, in Salamis (no. 202 with griffins and janus-headed warrior demons, and no. 203 with bulls' heads and Hathor heads) were found in clear context, datable to *ca.* 700 B.C. Cf. Karageorghis, *SalRDC*, 89–91 and pls. 40, 41 (cauldrons as found); *idem, ENS* III, 97–114 and pls. X–XIII, also app. II, 214–221, including figs. 1–4 (restoration of no. 202). The style of the bulls' heads on no. 203, however, relates in no way to that of the heads on MM 3 at Gordion.

have indicated the years beginning the last quarter of the eighth century for the time of the closing of the tomb: specifically, the years between 725 and 720 to 717 B.C. If this date is acceptable, then the cauldrons, and especially MM 2 which had seen use and been damaged before it was placed in the tomb, must have been made somewhat earlier, probably at some time in the third quarter of the century, between 750 and 725 B.C. They take their place, then, as fixed points in the development of the various types of bull, siren, and demon. Other specimens, found without context, must be dated with reference to the Gordion examples.

In the form found in the Gordion attachments, the personification of the demon or deity, male or female, has evidently taken over the major role (as seen from behind) and all but eclipsed the original symbol, the sun disk. The bust and spread wings obscure the upper part, and the body strip, which unites bust and tail and carries the socket for the ring handle, cuts across the lower half of the circle leaving of the original disk only two more or less oval openings at either side. We may note, however, that in the earlier examples the surviving half-circle of the rim surrounding the sun disk, now having become a circle *à jour,* is usually a true half-circle and that it is decorated with formal geometric patterns which have nothing to do with the bird anatomy of wings and tail that surround it. On the Gordion attachments the second tier of decoration, which encloses this innermost ring, becomes the innermost circle of feathers of wings and tail. This half-circle of feathers demands a continuation by tiers of feathers ranged out from the same center. For the slightly spread tail there was no problem; but for the wings which, in the Hittite tradition, were feathered horizontally, there was difficulty, and the lower rows of feathers show an obtuse-

angled break in their alignment where the outer tiers meet the innermost. This difficulty holds for the attachments of both Gordion cauldrons, and presumably also for an attachment from Van attributed by Herrmann to "Werkstatt A."[37] But on the Van attachment the wings, like those of the Gordion sirens and demons with horizontal and parallel upper and lower edges, end in curves, nearly quarter-circles, without an indication of feathering. The feather ends were first indicated, it would seem, by notches in the wing ends, as on MM 2 (pls. 51–53A), separating the end feathers of each row. One of the figures (Siren *C,* pl. 52B) on MM 2 has actually no indication at all of feather ends across the bottom of the tail, which ends in a straight line. We may further note that the wing fragment from Olympia attributed to "Werkstatt A"[38] has the ends of the feather rows separated by notching, not cast as separate rounded ends. On MM 3 (pls. 55, 56) this detail is better rendered and the feather ends of each row (and of the tails) were distinguished in the casting. On the *later* examples the problem of wing feathers raying out from a single center was taken care of by continuing the rounded feather end silhouettes inward along the underside of the wing in the casting.

So established has been the opinion that, in general, siren and demon attachments are to be attributed to Urartu[39] that Herrmann takes up several pages disproving it;[40] to his arguments may be added the observation made above that the only attachments which can be proved to be Urartian are the bull's-head group which lack carrying rings. The alternative is the Syro-Hittite area; the clinching argument is a comparison of the siren and demon heads with contemporary reliefs from neo-Hittite towns, Carchemish and Sakçegözü.[41] The art of these towns, often referred to as North Syrian, is more properly called

---

[37]H. V. Herrmann, *Ol. Forsch.* VI, pl. 25:1,2.

[38]*Ibid.,* pl. 21:2 (A 17).

[39]As late as 1961 E. Akurgal labels all the siren attachments he illustrated as Urartian, and divides them between two styles: a "ringel-" and a "strichelstil": *Kunst Anat.,* 35 f. A connection with "späthethitisch-aramäisierend" (i.e., North Syrian) style is recognized; it is suggested (p. 68) that, after the Assyrian conquest of the cities of North Syria, bronze smiths migrated to Urartu.

[40]"Urartu oder Nordsyrien," in *Ol. Forsch.* VI, 59 f. In

demolishing the Urartu mirage, and even though he twice concludes positively that the Nimrud example in the British Museum is truly Assyrian, he cannot refrain from toying with the possibility that this piece may be Urartian.

[41]Herrmann, *Ol. Forsch.* VI, pl. 28. This had been done before by E. Akurgal, *Kunst Anat.,* 43 f. and elsewhere, who recognizes a strong Hittite and North Syrian influence, then unnecessarily complicates the situation by transferring the whole operation to Urartu. We might

neo-Hittite and in its later phase *späthethitisch-aramäisierend.* The iconography of the demon attachment, as pointed out by Herrmann and Akurgal, is Hittite.

To return to the Gordion sirens and demons: Could they have been Phrygian? I think it has been established that the prototype for both the siren and demon series was neo-Hittite through intermediate Assyrian and West Syrian developments. We shall see that the local smiths had the skill to make them; but then it is possible that some of the smiths working in Phrygia may have been Syro-Hittite craftsmen working abroad and teaching the Phrygians their craft. We can demonstrate that neo-Hittite art was one of the major influences on Phrygian; and we know that in 718–717 B.C., at least, relations must have been close between Midas of Phrygia and Pisiris of Carchemish, as they had been without doubt somewhat earlier between the Phrygians and Urballa/Warpalawas of Tyana.

RING-HANDLED SMALL CAULDRONS WITH T-SHAPED ATTACHMENTS
MM 4–9
(See also pp. 223–224.)

All the small cauldrons were found along the east wall of the tomb: three behind screen MM 379, one behind screen MM 378, two to the south of screen MM 378. No doubt they had been suspended by one handle from nails in the wall above, probably in pairs. Dimensions and details of finish, as well as finding places, indicate that MM 4 and 5, MM 6 and 7, and MM 8 and 9 were companion pieces or pairs.

MM 4   **Ring-handled small cauldron with T-shaped attachments**
B 797   Behind screen MM 379
H.-rim 0.187   D. rim 0.163   D. 0.241
   W. rim 0.016   L. handle attachment
   0.083 m.
Pl. 58A, C

Intact except for a small corrosion hole in the wall. Heavy fabric, evidently cast. The body squat spherical, slightly pointed toward the bottom. The rim wide and flat on top, its outer edge squared, its sharper inner edge overhanging. A thin horizontal seam is visible at several places on the straight face of the outer edge, suggesting that the rim itself was a flat hoop of bronze separately made and applied on top of the everted lip of the cauldron. It was probably fastened by brazing, since there are no visible traces of pins or dowels.

The handle attachments, T-shaped and half-round in section, were cast in one with the ring sockets for the handles, which stand at the crossings of the T's. The end of each arm is flattened and thin, disk-shaped to bed the round head of a pin fastening the attachment to the cauldron. The ends of the pins appear on the inside, cut off and flattened to rivet heads. The handles were made from bronze rods uniformly round in section (not tapered) about 0.007 m. thick, threaded through the sockets and bent around to make rings *ca.* 0.045 m. in diameter.

MM 5   **Ring-handled small cauldron with T-shaped attachments**[42]
B 798   Behind screen MM 379
H.-rim 0.187   D. rim 0.163   D. 0.241
   W. rim 0.0195   L. handle attachment
   0.0725 m.
Pl. 58B

Two large corrosion holes in the shoulder. Exactly like MM 4; minor variations in the dimensions. The rim again seems to be a separately made hoop added to the lip of the cauldron.

MM 6   **Ring-handled small cauldron with T-shaped attachments**
B 801   Behind screen MM 379
H.-rim 0.175   D. rim 0.159   D. 0.223
   W. rim 0.022   L. handle attachment
   0.07 m.
Pl. 58D, F

Intact. Heavy fabric, cast. The body squat spherical slightly pointed at the bottom. The rim heavy and squared off at its outer edge, thinner and over-

---

note that the time he suggests for this transfer, 710–675 B.C., must be considerably later than the early attachments from Van and Toprakkale, the latter of which Akurgal dates to the end of the eighth century. On the dating suggested for the Gordion cauldrons, the productions of "Werkstatt A" (p. 109, n. 37), which include two specimens from Van, can go back to the third quarter of the century. The same comparison and ensuing conclu-

sion attributing the attachments to North Syria were made independently by O. Muscarella, *Hesperia* 31 (1962): 318–329 and pl. 104.

[See also Young's discussion in *JNES* 26 (1967): 150, in which he appears to ascribe the Gordion siren attachments to North Syria even more strongly. Ed.]

[42] See p. 287, app. II-C, Sample 91.

hanging but also squared at its inner; probably a flat hoop added to the cauldron lip though it is not possible to detect the seam. The handle attachments like those of MM 4 and 5, except that the arms of the T are finished at each end and bottom by a raised ridge or molding above the flat end tabs which bed the heads of the pins.

MM 7   Ring-handled small cauldron with T-shaped attachments
B 802   Behind screen MM 378
H.-rim 0.171   D. rim 0.156   D. 0.224
    W. rim 0.022   L. handle attachment
    0.072 m.
Fig. 71; Pl. 58E

Intact. Exactly like MM 6, with small variations in the measurements. Cloth was found attached on the exterior.[43]

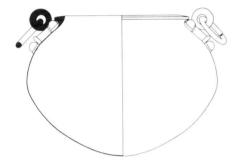

Figure 71. MM 7. Ring-handled small cauldron with T-shaped attachments. Profile and view. 1:4.

MM 8   Ring-handled small cauldron with T-shaped attachments
B 799   Behind table MM 388
H.-rim 0.124   D. rim 0.138   D. 0.17
    W. rim 0.0155   L. handle attachment
    0.0645 m.
Pl. 58G

Intact. Heavy fabric, cast. MM 8 and 9 smaller than 4–7. The body squat spherical, rounded at the bottom. The rim flat on top, everted and sharpened at its outer edge, slightly overhanging and blunt at its inner. The rim appears to have been cast in one with the bowl and finished by filing. Handle attachments plain as on MM 4 and 5.

MM 9   Ring-handled small cauldron with T-shaped attachments
B 800   South of screen MM 378
H.-rim 0.12   D. rim 0.139   D. 0.171
    W. rim. 0.014   L. handle attachment
    0.068 m.
Pl. 58H, I

Exactly like MM 8, with slight variations in measurements.

SMALL CAULDRONS WITH BUCKET HANDLES
MM 10–13

Four small cauldrons similar to the preceding (MM 4–9) but with bucket handles instead of carrying rings were found at the east side of the tomb. Identity in shape and dimensions marks them as two pairs. The first, MM 10 and 11, with plain rings and T-attachments, was found behind screen MM 379 and the second, MM 12 and 13, with bull's-head attachments, behind MM 378. All had evidently been suspended from iron nails in the wall face and had fallen when the nails broke. Clearly they had hung originally in pairs above the two screens and in their fall had broken through the top members of these. The vessels are of heavy cast bronze.[44]

MM 10   Small cauldron with bucket handle
B 805   Behind screen MM 379
H.-rim 0.143   D. rim 0.141   D. 0.181
    W. rim 0.014   L. handle attachments
    0.043 and 0.045 m.
Pl. 58J

Intact; heavy fabric, cast. Spherical body slightly pointed toward the bottom; a low neck below the everted rim which is slightly convex on top and rounded at its inner edge, evidently cast in one with the bowl. T-shaped handle attachments fitted to the neck under the rim, half-round in section, a fine platform molding along the upper section. The lower end of the T thinned and rounded to make a tab to bed the large round stud which caps the pin fastening it to the shoulder. Dowels, their ends carefully smoothed and polished, fasten the crosspiece near its ends. At the crossing of the T a small vertical ring

---

[43]See app. V, p. 304, Fabric F.

[44]For analyses of the contents of MM 10 and 13, see pp. 278, 284, app. II-A, Samples 9 and 10.

socket, cast in one with the attachment; a larger carrying ring attached through this. The bucket handle is octagonal in section, thick at the center and tapering to thin round wire at the ends. It is bent to fit and rest on the curve of the rim; its ends, threaded through the carrying rings, are bent back and wound around its lower part to form eight spirals at one side, nine at the other.

MM 11   Small cauldron with bucket handle
B 806   Behind screen MM 379
D. rim 0.141   W. rim 0.0135
    L. handle attachments 0.048, 0.047 m.
Pl. 58K

The bowl is broken all around at the level of greatest diameter, and the edges of the break so corroded that the upper and lower pieces cannot be fitted together. The stud from the lower end of one handle attachment is missing. Exactly like MM 10; the handle coiled to eight spirals at each end.

MM 12   Small cauldron with bucket handle and bull's-head attachments
B 803   Behind screen MM 378
H.-rim 0.138   D. rim 0.165   D. 0.21
    W. rim 0.009   L. across handle
    attachments 0.07 m.
Fig. 72; Pl. 59A, B

Intact. The body squat spherical with rounded bottom. Projecting rim flat on top, its outer edge sharpened, its inner grooved underneath: probably a flat hoop of bronze brazed to the lip of the cauldron as in MM 4–7. The handle attachments T-shaped flat plates of bronze, their ends broadened slightly and rounded to bed the large stud heads of the pins which fasten attachments to cauldron at shoulder and under rim. The ends of the pins flattened and spread inside. At the crossing of each attachment a short plain cylindrical neck; to these are attached (by brazing?) small ornamental cast bulls' heads.

Bulls' heads	W. across horns
A.	0.035 m.
B.	0.041

These have short outward-projecting ears below curved horns, and flat, rounded forelocks, raised. The eyes are bulgy bumps outlined by almond-shaped incisions. One head has a rounded nose, the other a nose ridged down the center. The heads in profile are remarkably blocklike, not tapering toward the muzzle; incisions along the side faces indicate the openings of the mouths.
Behind the bulls' heads, ring sockets for attach-

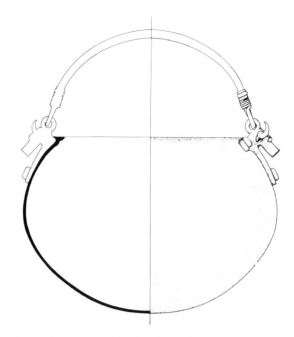

Figure 72. MM 12. Small cauldron with bucket handle and bull's-head attachments. Profile and view. 1:3.

ment; through these are threaded the ends of the bucket handle, which are turned back and spiraled around the lower handle five times at each side. Above the spirals a bead-and-reel molding around the handle. The central part of the handle octagonal in section, tapered from the center and bent to approximate the curve of the cauldron rim.

MM 13   Small cauldron with bucket handle and bull's-head attachments
B 804   Behind screen MM 378
H.-rim 0.134   D. rim 0.161   D. 0.209
    W. rim 0.008   L. across handle
    attachments 0.063, 0.069 m.
Pl. 59C

Just like MM 12 in every detail except that the handle ends are spiraled six times around the lower part at each side. Complete, but the handle broken at one end.

Bulls' heads	W. across horns
A.	0.037 m.
B.	0.036

Remains of textile were associated with the food remains found inside it.[45]

---

[45]See app. V, p. 302, Fabric A.

JUGS WITH SIDE SPOUT, SIEVED
MM 14, 15

MM 14 was found at the foot of the east wall of the tomb, from which it had fallen. MM 15 lay close to the west wall not far from the southwest corner; it could have fallen from the south wall and rolled to the place at which it was found.

MM 14　　**Jug with side spout, sieved**
　　　B 816　　Against east wall, upside down
　　　H.-rim 0.103　H.-h. 0.137　D. rim
　　　　0.065　D. 0.102　D. base 0.04 m.
　　　Pl. 59D, E

Complete and in good condition. Thin fabric: hammered? The base a low round ridge, concave within the ring; the body squat spherical. The neck ringed at half its height by a rounded ridge hollow inside; above, a shallow cuplike echinus mouth. There is no sign of a seam at the curving junction of shoulder and neck, or of neck and mouth. The ridge around mid-neck is hollow inside and therefore purely decorative; it does not mask a seam. The whole vessel seems to have been made in one piece by hammering; handle and spout were separately made and added.

The handle is of two plates of thin bronze folded together. The edges of the inner piece, dovetailed at both ends, are bent up to hold the outer in place. At the top both plates end in a pair of rounded tabs; those of the outer plate overlap the inner face of the lip, of the inner the outer face of the lip; all are pinned together by dowels with round stud heads inside the lip, the ends outside flattened by hammering to rivet heads. A pin with a stud head fastens the lower end of the handle.

The spout, of heavier bronze and evidently made by casting, is attached to the shoulder by three fine pins through a flange or collar around its base; the ends of these pins can be felt on the inside, but on the outside they have been so carefully smoothed and polished as to be all but imperceptible. The wall at the shoulder where the spout is attached was pierced by many fine holes to make a sieved opening. The inner end of the spout is tubular, the longer outer part is widened and troughed to a half-round open at the top. The tip of the spout rises above the level of the rim of the vessel; it was doubtless finished by hammering. The spout was set at something less than 90 degrees to the left of the handle.

MM 15　　**Jug with side spout, sieved**
　　　B 1099　　Against west wall, partially
　　　under MM 16
　　　H.-top of knob 0.135　H.-h. 0.154
　　　　D. base 0.052　D. lid 0.07　D. 0.121
　　　　L. body and spout 0.228 m.
　　　Fig. 73A–C; Pl. 59F

The state of the vessel was so corroded that cleaning seemed too risky; it was left uncleaned. One side of the lid and its knob, part of the rim and neck below, and a huge hole in the wall at one side, also one corner of the spout eaten away. The body squat spherical on a ring base, the bottom concave within the ring. A short straight neck below a rim stepped horizontally outward, then turned straight up to

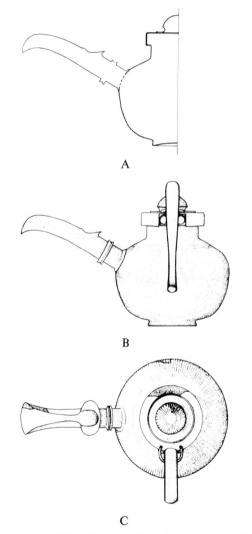

A

B

C

Figure 73. MM 15. Jug with side spout, sieved. A. Profile. B. Side. C. Top.　1:4.

113

form a collar over which the flange of the lid fits exactly. The handle two thin sheets of bronze folded together at the edges, the inner dovetailed at both ends to hold the outer. A pin with a large round stud head fastens the lower end to the wall, two similar studs the tabbed upper end to the rim.

The spout set somewhat less than 90 degrees to the left of the handle; the shoulder sieved at that point by many fine holes. A spreading collar at the base of the spout was attached to the wall by ten small dowels of which the ends, hammered to flat rivet heads, show on the inside. The outer ends of the dowels are not visible on the uncleaned surface of the bronze outside; no doubt they were carefully smoothed and polished. The inner end of the spout is tubular, with a grooved molding around it; beyond the molding a trefoil mouth of which the central lobe projects to form a long flaring trough spout widened and rounded at the end.

The flat lid has a down-turned flange around its edge to fit closely over the collar rim of the jug, the flange notched to fit around the studs which fasten the upper end of the handle. The lid has its own central omphalos-like knob handle, radially ribbed; a raised half-round molding midway between handle and edge. A U-shaped hoop of wire, its ends flattened and pinned to the edge of the lid on top, passes around the handle of the jug and serves as a keeper to prevent the lid from becoming separated and lost; the loop is wide enough to pass over the widest part of the jug handle. The omphalos-like knob handle of the lid contains a brownish, soft substance, probably a mixture of beeswax and sawdust; in places the surface of this shows in reverse the radial ribbing of the bronze where it is missing. The lid would thus seem to have been raised in one piece by hammering, and the ribbed decoration of its knob handle by hammering and chasing. The waxy substance that remained inside the handle served, no doubt, as a bed for the decoration of the knob. The lid was closed beneath by a flat disc of bronze fitted tightly and covering the opening to the knob handle; the disc was fastened in place by the two pins holding the wire keeper to the lid outside; these pins passed through wire, lid, and liner.

The body of the vessel is of thin fabric evidently made by hammering; it is decorated overall by fine reeding (or grooving). Three horizontal ridges encircle it high on the shoulder; below them a zone of vertical reeding, about to the level of the lower handle attachment, then a zone of horizontal reeding to just above the base. The inside face of the wall, which can be seen through the large hole at one side, is perfectly smooth and does not show the reeding in reverse. Evidently then the reeded decoration was

not made by hammering; it could have been made with a fine gouge. That the vessel could have been hammered from the inside into a reeded mold seems altogether unlikely. The lower, horizontal reeding was evidently done before the handle was attached: it runs uninterrupted beneath the lower attachment. The vertical reeding of the upper body was made apparently after the spout had been attached (it does not run under the flange of the spout, where it could have caused leakage), and again before the handle was put on; it is regular and uninterrupted beneath the handle. The spout was evidently made by casting, its long trough end later thinned and flared by hammering.

LARGE GLOBULAR JUGS WITH TREFOIL MOUTH
MM 16–25
(See also pp. 224–227.)

The ten large globular jugs all lay on the floor along the west side of the tomb. One of them, MM 22, had rolled some little distance after falling from the wall, and it lay partially under the central bronze cauldron MM 2 at the south end. Five of the jugs have large dents in their walls, made perhaps when they fell. The iron nails in the west wall of the tomb were arranged in two rows of ten each, and the only objects found at the foot of the west wall were the ten bronze jugs and the ten studded plaques of leather (belts?), MM 170–179, with their bronze-disk decorations. We may then assign these twenty objects to the two rows of ten nails, the jugs probably hanging by their handles from the upper row, since their height is less than the length of the leather plaques, and the space between the rows of nails is only 0.35 m. wide. There was no evidence to indicate whether the jugs were empty when they were hung up, or filled with some liquid.

MM 16   **Large globular jug with trefoil mouth**
B 787   West wall
H.-h. 0.357   D. 0.315   D. base
0.143 m.
Pl. 60A

Hole in wall; stained. Made from five separate pieces: the globular body; the disk base; the neck and trefoil mouth; and two plates, which form the handle. The body was evidently made by hammering; its thickness is 0.001 m. or less. Neck and mouth were cast in one piece; the lip is squared off on the edge. The joint between neck and shoulder is masked on the outside by a raised ridge all around the base of the neck. Through the hole in the wall it is possible to see the edge of the separately made floor piece around the bottom. The bottom is slightly concave beneath and set off from the wall above by a shallow groove; another groove around its outer edge underneath leaves a slightly raised resting-ring all around. The hollow handle is made from two plates folded together, its outer face grooved down the center. Two studs decorate its upper attachment, two more its lower. Between the latter appears the end of a dowel, carefully smoothed and polished but with a circular groove in the face of the bronze around it to indicate that there was once a third, smaller stud. The careful smoothing of the pins indicates that its head was lost in antiquity and that the vessel had been in use before it was placed in the tomb.

MM 17 **Large globular jug with trefoil mouth**
B 794   Southwest corner
H.-h. 0.32   D. 0.291   D. base 0.138 m.
Pl. 60B

A small dent in the right side near the bottom. Similar to MM 16, the body slightly more squat and less globular; a low resting-ring beneath. A raised ridge at the base of the neck all around. The handle made in the same way as that of MM 16, but not grooved down its outer face; slightly convex in section.

MM 18 **Large globular jug with trefoil mouth**
B 792   West wall
H.-h. 0.337   D. 0.306   D. base
        0.145 m.
Pl. 60C

A large dent in the wall below the handle attachment. Similar to MM 16; again the body slightly more squat and less globular, with a resting-ring underneath. A raised ridge all around the base of the neck. The handle grooved down the center of its outer face.

MM 19 **Large globular jug with trefoil mouth**
B 788   West wall
H.-h. 0.341   D. 0.33   D. base 0.163 m.
Pl. 60D, E

Intact. The body again more squat, the level of greatest diameter below the handle attachment, the shoulder high and rounded, the lower part shallow. Base a low round ridge with under-floor slightly concave. Raised ridge all around the base of the neck. The handle grooved down its outer face.

MM 20 **Large globular jug with trefoil mouth**
B 789   West wall
H.-h. 0.345   D. 0.349   D. base 0.17 m.
Pl. 60F

No dents. The body again more squat, with a sharp curve at the level of greatest diameter where the shallow body and the high, rounded shoulder meet. A resting-ring underneath around a slightly concave under-floor. A raised ridge at the base of the neck. The handle grooved; at its lower attachment a dowel end, carefully smoothed and polished, between the two studs. There is no trace of a stud cap around it as on MM 16; perhaps here merely an extra pin to strengthen the attachment.

MM 21 **Large globular jug with trefoil mouth**
B 790   South end, partially under
   MM 1
H.-h. 0.337   D. 0.335   D. base 0.16 m.
Pl. 60G

Two large dents, one in the right side, the other just to left of center at the front. The body similar to that of MM 20. A resting-ring underneath and a raised ridge around the base of the neck. The handle grooved. On the inside it is possible to see a small plain plate of bronze applied against the wall, and in its face the flattened ends of the pins which hold the lower end of the handle.

MM 22 **Large globular jug with trefoil mouth**
B 791   South end, partially under
   MM 2
H.-h. 0.36   D. 0.348   D. base 0.165 m.
Pl. 60H

A large dent at one side of the handle attachment. The body squat like that of MM 20. A resting-ring underneath; a double ridge at the base of the neck all around. The edge of the lip, squared off, 0.005–0.0055 m. in thickness. The handle grooved.

MM 23 **Large globular jug with trefoil mouth**
B 796   West wall
H.-h. 0.30   D. 0.306   D. base 0.147
   Th. lip 0.004 m.
Pl. 60I–L

No dents. The body squat like that of MM 22. Base a slightly raised ring, concave underneath. The upper part of the shoulder covered by a wide plate with a raised ridge at its center; another raised ridge around the base of the neck. The outer edge of the plate appears to be folded under; the plate is evidently a separate piece, a sort of collar joined at its outer edge to the shoulder by a folded seam, and to the base of the neck by the usual seam. The face of the handle slightly convex, ungrooved.

MM 24   Large globular jug with trefoil mouth
B 793   Near foot of bed
H.-h. 0.34   D. 0.353   D. base 0.167 m.
Pl. 60M, N

A large dent in the body at the left side. The body squat. A low raised base, concave underneath; a raised ridge around the base of the neck. The handle grooved.

MM 25   Large globular jug with trefoil mouth
B 795   West wall
H.-h. 0.316   D. 0.322   D. base 0.156 m.
Fig. 74; Pl. 60O, P

No dents. Squat body, a resting-ring underneath. Raised ridge at base of neck. The outer face of the handle plain and slightly convex, ungrooved; its lower attachment strengthened by an added plate of bronze on the inside, as with MM 21.

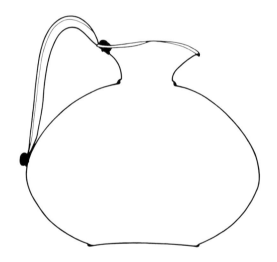

Figure 74.   MM 25. Large globular jug with trefoil mouth. Profile.   1:5.

SMALL JUGS WITH TREFOIL MOUTH
MM 26–44
(See also pp. 224–227.)

In addition to the ten large jugs, nineteen smaller ones of various shapes were found, most of them lying on the floor of the tomb at the south and east sides. Because all ten larger jugs were found along the west wall and their number

corresponds to that of the ten nails in the face of the wall, it seems reasonable to assume that they had originally been suspended against the wall by their handles. That the smaller jugs were once hung up in like manner from the south and east walls seems likely, and dents in the sides of some of them attest a fall. Four jugs were found close to the east wall of the tomb from which they presumably had fallen; ten lay close to the foot of the south wall. The other five were in the corner, or had rolled toward the center of the tomb on landing. Three jugs at the south side were found inside the large cauldrons: two, MM 30 and 32, in MM 3, and MM 39 in MM 1. Their good state of preservation suggests that they had fallen into the cauldrons rather than been placed there at the time of burial. The pottery vessels inside the cauldrons had been badly flaked and rotted by the food which they contained, and the bronze vessels would have been affected, too, had they been exposed to whatever chemical reaction took place; clearly they came after it was finished.

MM 26   Small jug with trefoil mouth
B 1095   South end, near MM 2
H.-rim 0.122   H.-h. 0.135   D. 0.125m.
Pl. 61A

Intact. Low base, the bottom slightly concave and hollowed, the body squat; short narrow neck and trefoil mouth. Three horizontal ribs around the body; two more, smaller, around the base of the neck. The fabric thin, shaped by hammering and fitted together in three pieces: neck and mouth, shoulder and body to central rib, and lower body with base. The handle was also separately made and added. The two pieces of the body were fastened together at a folded seam along the central ridge, the seam secured by short pins run through all around at intervals of about 0.008 m. apart. The ends of the pins, carefully smoothed and polished, barely show in the upper and lower faces of the rib. Of the three ribs around the body only the middle one is functional, the other two decorative. In the same way one of the ribs around the base of the neck conceals a seam secured by a single pin at the back under the handle; the other rib is decorative.

The handle is of the usual Phrygian type in two plates folded together and half-round in section; the tabs inside and outside the lip are fastened by pins run through and flattened to rivet heads at both ends. A similar pin fastens the lower end of the handle.

116

MM 27   **Small jug with trefoil mouth**
      B 1097   Near center, under table
      MM 381*B*
      H.-rim 0.147   H.-h. 0.185   D. 0.125 m.
      Pl. 61B, C

Intact; the edge of the foot roughened by corrosion. Heavy fabric; no seams can be seen on the outside (or felt on the inside) at the levels where neck and foot meet the body. It therefore seems likely that the vessel was cast in one piece. Globular body on a short stem spreading below to a flat base with a central hollow underneath, in which appears a flat rivet head. Short neck and trefoil mouth, thickened and squared at the lip. Inside, a round plate of bronze separates the body from the hollow stem and foot below, evidently held in place by the pin of which the head appears at the bottom. The base is filled by some heavy substance, probably clay or wax. Whether this false bottom was original or a later addition is not clear; the round-mouthed jug TumW 6 affords a parallel. It is possible that the bottoms of MM 27 and TumW 6 were filled in order to add weight at the base and thus improve stability; both are rather wide, high vessels on stemmed bases with disproportionately small resting surface and likely to be top-heavy.

The handle made in the usual way of two plates folded together, but decorated by three slightly raised oblong areas, one above the lip of the jug, the second at the top of the curve, the third just below the top of the back face. Each of these areas is ornamented by ten vertical grooves. Large, round stud heads decorate the tab at the base of the handle and the two tabs inside the lip; the pins of the latter hammered to rivet heads over the outside tabs at the top.

MM 28   **Small jug with trefoil mouth**
      B 1096   Not on plan; southwest
         corner, under MM 1
      H.-rim 0.105   H.-h. 0.133   D. 0.10 m.
      Pl. 61D

The bottom cracked; a corrosion hole in the handle, and the stud head at its base lost. Heavy fabric, probably cast in two pieces, the join between them masked by a raised ridge at the shoulder. Flat bottom and spherical body; short wide neck and trefoil mouth thickened and squared at the lip. The handle two plates folded together; both plates end at the bottom in a half-round tab pinned to the wall by a dowel which has lost its stud head. At the upper end two round studs above the rim inside, the pins capped by similar studs outside.

MM 29   **Small jug with trefoil mouth**
      B 1098   Near southeast corner
      H.-rim 0.157   H.-h. 0.208
         D. 0.1565 m.
      Pl. 61E

Intact. The body squat globular flattened at the bottom; rather thin fabric, perhaps made by hammering. The shoulder, neck, and trefoil mouth heavier, the lip thickened and squared—evidently cast. The edge of the shoulder overlaps the upper edge of the body and is turned in, probably to a folded seam, which can be felt on the inner surface. The usual handle of two plates folded together; at its lower end a double tab, each part a three-quarter circle held to the wall by a pin with a large round stud head. Pairs of studs cap the pins fastening the tabs at the top, both inside and outside the rim.

MM 30   **Small jug with trefoil mouth**
      B 1091   Inside cauldron MM 3
      H.-rim 0.15   H.-h. 0.173   D. 0.136 m.
      Fig. 75; Pl. 61F, G

Intact. Evidently made in three pieces as were the large jugs MM 16–25 (above). The body, of thin fabric, hammered and closed at the bottom by a flat disk base fastened by brazing or by solder; the neck and trefoil mouth, thickened and squared at the lip, cast and joined to the top of the shoulder by a folded seam masked by a raised ridge at the base of the neck. The seam can be felt on the inside.

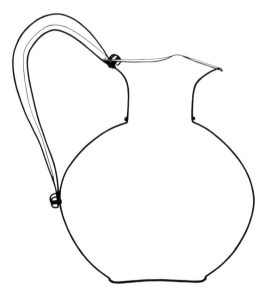

Figure 75. MM 30. Small jug with trefoil mouth. Profile. 1:3.

The handle of the usual folded type, its lower end T-shaped with the ends of the crosspiece rounded to the contour of the studs capping the pins which fasten it to the wall. The lower end of the handle was further secured by a third pin between the studs, its end flattened. At the top two stud heads on the inside above the rim, their pin ends flattened on the outside below.

MM 31   **Small jug with trefoil mouth**
          B 1094   Center, near table MM 383
          H.-rim 0.168   H.-h. 0.196   D. 0.157 m.
          Pl. 61H

Intact except for a stud lost from the base of the handle.

Like MM 30 made from three pieces: the low raised base a separately made disk brazed or soldered to the bottom of the body; traces of the solder may be observed. A double raised ridge at the base of the heavier, cast neck masks the joint with the shoulder, a folded seam which can be felt on the inside.

The usual folded handle. At its lower end the inner plate cut off above the attachment, the outer ending in three-quarter circle tabs, each fastened by a large round stud (one missing). At the top two studs inside above the rim, the flattened ends of their pins outside at the back.

MM 32   **Small jug with trefoil mouth**
          B 1092   South wall, inside cauldron
          MM 3
          H.-rim 0.143   H.-h. 0.152   D. 0.123 m.
          Fig. 76; Pl. 61I

Intact; a dent in the wall at the handle level. Like MM 30 and 31 made in three pieces: a squat, hammered, spherical body closed at the bottom by a disk with a slightly raised ring foot around its edge, brazed to the body; the heavier neck and trefoil mouth with its squared lip cast and joined to the body by a seam concealed by a raised ridge around the base of the neck. Folded handle, its lower end fastened to the wall by two round studs and a third pin of which the flattened end appears between them. At the top two studs above the rim, the flattened ends of their pins at the back.

MM 33   **Small jug with trefoil mouth**
          B 1093   Not on plan; southeast
          quarter, under MM 52
          H.-rim 0.154   H.-h. 0.165   D. 0.133 m.

Intact. Like MM 32: low ring foot, globular body, raised ridge at base of neck with a seam on the

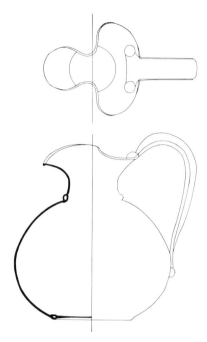

Figure 76.   MM 32. Small jug with trefoil mouth. Top view and profile.   1:3.

inside; lip thickened and squared. Heavy fabric, made probably from three cast pieces joined by a seam at the base of the neck and by brazing at the bottom. Folded handle; at its lower end both plates terminate in half-round tabs pinned to the wall by pins with large stud heads. The end of an extra pin, flattened, between the studs. At the top two studs above the rim inside, the flattened ends of their pins at the back outside.

MM 34   **Small jug with trefoil mouth**
          B 1082   Beside table MM 388
          H.-rim 0.16   H.-h. 0.19   D. 0.15 m.
          Pl. 61J

Small dents in the body and a hole in the handle near its top. Globular body flattened at the bottom; short neck flaring to a trefoil mouth with squared thickened lip. No traces of a seam at shoulder or base; perhaps cast in one piece, or more likely in two with a brazed seam at the base. The usual folded handle; the inner plate cut off above the lower attachment, the outer ending in two rounded tabs which bed the stud heads of pins fastening them to the wall. At the top two round studs on the inner face above the rim, the flattened ends of their pins on the outer face.

MM 35   **Small jug with trefoil mouth**
B 1081   Southeast corner, inside
MM 68
H.-rim 0.10   H.-h. 0.132   D. 0.109 m.
Fig. 77; Pl. 61K

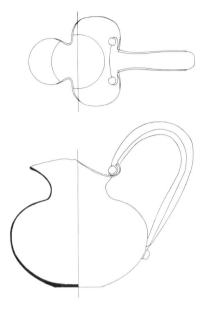

*Figure 77.   MM 35.   Small jug with trefoil mouth.
Top view and profile.   1:3.*

Intact. Like MM 34 without visible seams. The
base flat, the body more squat than that of MM 34,
and the trefoil mouth slightly more beaked. Folded
handle with both inner and outer plate ending in
rounded tabs pinned to the wall by pins with round
stud heads. At the upper end two round studs above
the rim, the spread ends of their pins behind.

MM 36   **Small jug with trefoil mouth**
B 1090   In front of screen MM 378
H.-rim 0.134   H.-h. 0.173   D. 0.135 m.

Intact. Like MM 34 and 35 without a trace of a
seam between neck and shoulder; but the base is
slightly oval rather than round, and shows many
hammer marks on the inside and traces of a brazed
or soldered seam around the edge. The trefoil mouth
thickened and squared at the lip, evidently cast. The
fabric of the body, perhaps cast in one with the
neck and mouth, and the vessel closed by a hammered disk plate brazed to the bottom. Folded handle, both plates ending below in a rounded tab fastened to the wall by a stud-headed pin. At the top
two round studs above the rim, their pins capped at

the back by two more. The hollow of the handle is
filled inside by a yellowish substance, perhaps beeswax.

MM 37   **Small jug with trefoil mouth**
B 1088   East of cauldron MM 3
H.-rim 0.123   H.-h. 0.168   D. 0.117 m.

Intact. Like MM 36 but smaller and with a raised
base. Heavy fabric; body and neck with squared
trefoil mouth probably cast in one piece, the base
added and brazed on. Folded handle, the inner plate
cut off above the lower attachment, the outer ending
in rounded tabs fastened to the wall by two large
studs. At the top two round studs above the rim inside, their pins capped also by studs at the back
outside.

MM 38   **Small jug with trefoil mouth**
B 1089   Not on plan; under cauldron
MM 3
H.-rim 0.108   H.-h. 0.115   D. 0.104 m.
Pl. 61L

Intact; one side dented. Like the preceding: squat
body and flat bottom. The edge of the lip thickened
and squared. The handle folded, both plates ending
below in a single round tab fastened to the wall by
a pin with a large flat head on the inside, capped by
a stud outside, the end of the pin visible at the center
of the stud. At the top studs cap both ends of the
pins fastening the tabs to the rim.

MM 39   **Small jug with trefoil mouth**
B 1083   Inside cauldron MM 1
H.-rim 0.124   H.-h. 0.160   D. 0.109 m.

A small hole through the wall, and a dent. The
lower end of the handle disintegrated in cleaning; it
was fastened by a single stud, of which only the pin
remains. Low ring foot hollow inside, and biconical
body with a rather tall neck. The lip thickened and
squared. Folded handle, fastened at the top by two
pins capped at either end by round studs. The inner
studs above the rim plain; the outside ones at the
back show in their surfaces the ends of the pins,
smoothed and polished.

MM 40   **Small jug with trefoil mouth**
B 1085   East wall, north end
H.-rim 0.144   H.-h. 0.169   D. 0.127 m.
Pl. 61M

Disease has opened up holes in the handle. Several dents in the lower body. Globular body flattened
at the bottom; tall, slightly flaring neck, lip thickened

and squared. Folded handle, its lower end two rounded tabs fastened by studs. At the top two pins capped each by studs both inside and out; the ends of the pins show, smoothed and polished, in the faces of the outer studs. When found, the handle was filled inside with a "yellow substance" (wax?).

MM 41   **Small jug with trefoil mouth**
         B 1087   Near southeast corner
         H.-rim 0.122   H.-h. 0.147   D. 0.103 m.
         Pl. 61N, O

Intact. An ancient repair at the back of the neck under the handle: two dowel holes through the neck were covered by a flat oblong bronze plate laid against the outer face of the vessel and neatly fitted to it, fastened to the neck by a dowel at each corner —two at one of the upper corners—no doubt to prevent leakage. Tall globular body, flat bottom, trefoil lip thickened and squared. Folded handle, its lower end rounded and fastened by a single stud; the upper end fastened by studs inside above the rim, the ends of their pins spread by hammering at the back outside.

MM 42   **Small jug with trefoil mouth**
         B 1086   South of table MM 388
         H.-rim 0.128   H.-h. 0.158   D. 0.10 m.
         Pl. 61P

Corrosion has eaten a large hole at the top of the handle. Low ring foot and globular body; rather long neck with trefoil mouth thickened and squared. Folded handle: both plates at the bottom end in two round tabs superposed, pinned to the wall by a stud. At the top two studs inside above the rim, their pins flattened and spread at the back outside.

MM 43   **Small jug with trefoil mouth**
         B 1084   South of table MM 388
         H.-rim 0.172   H.-h. 0.205   D. 0.138 m.

Intact. Globular body on a rather high ring foot hollow inside; long narrow neck and trefoil mouth thickened and squared at the lip. The handle folded, its lower end two rounded tabs secured by studs, its upper end fastened by two pins capped at both ends by studs. The ends of the pins, smoothed and polished, show in the surfaces of the outer studs.

MM 44   **Small jug with trefoil mouth**
         B 817   Under MM 2
         H.-rim 0.147   H.-h. 0.177   D. 0.125 m.
         Fig. 78; Pl. 62A, B

Intact. A raised base, slightly concave underneath, and squat body with a central rib around its widest

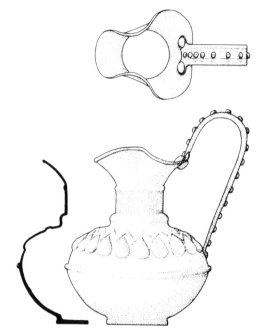

Figure 78. MM 44. Small jug with trefoil mouth. Top view and profile. 1:3.

part. Relief decoration, repoussé, on the shoulder: a series of 19 drop-shaped petals, their pointed ends upward to fit the recesses of a large, raised, zigzag band. A rounded ridge at the base of the straight narrow neck, and a smaller one at the top; between these fine vertical ribbing. Spreading trefoil mouth, the lip thickened and rounded. Flat handle rising above the rim.

The fabric of the vessel is thin; irregularities indicate that it was made by hammering. The jug was made in three pieces joined together; the cast handle was added. The base and lower body to the rib form one piece, the shoulder and neck to its upper ridge a second. The central rib where these pieces are joined shows in places around its outer face a fine seam. The pieces are held together by fine dowels run vertically through the rib as on MM 26; the ends of these are barely visible on the under-face of the rib, though most—and especially its upper face—were so carefully smoothed and polished that it is not easy to detect them. The third piece, the trefoil mouth, is prolonged downward by an open cylinder of thin bronze fitted closely inside the ribbed neck, the lower end no doubt hammered down to fit into the ridge around the base of the neck where it was secured by two fine dowels run vertically down through the base rib at front and back.

The strap handle, a thick flat strip of cast bronze, is slightly wider at the front (above the rim) than at the back. At the front two grooves with incised hatching to make herringbone pattern between them decorate the two edges; at the back single grooves with diagonal hatching at one side only along the edges. The flat central strip between the grooves is ornamented by 16 round studs of which the pins show, hammered flat, on the under face. At its lower end the handle is tongued, the tongue slipped into a notch in the inner face of a small bolster attached to the wall of the jug, apparently by pins run into it from the inside of the vessel, since their ends do not show in the face of the bolster. At its upper end the handle has two rounded tabs at the front, fitted over the inner face of the rim and secured by two round studs. The tabs and upper end of the handle are only half the thickness of the handle proper, and an extra plate with round tabs was added at the back, held to the handle by the pin of the first ornamental stud on its face, and by the pins of the two studs which fasten the handle to the rim at the front—these pins capped also at the back by round stud heads.

SITULAE
MM 45, 46

Both situlae were found lying on the floor behind MM 378, the lion-headed one, MM 45, partially emerging beyond its right edge (pl. 44C). Both had been wrapped in linen cloth, of which tatters still adhered to their surfaces (pl. 44C and 63B); and originally both had doubtless been hung in cloth bags on nails on the east wall of the tomb.[46] Although there are differences between the two vessels, there can be little doubt that they were offered as a pair in the tomb, although not necessarily made as a pair. The ring- and bucket-handled small cauldrons, as we have already noted, were made and offered in pairs.

MM 45   **Lion's-head situla**
    B 810   Partially behind screen
      MM 378
    L.-rim 0.225   L. inside 0.17
      D. rim 0.113 m.
    Lion's head: H. 0.119   W. 0.116 m.
    Pl. 62C–F

Complete, but with small cracks and dents; the handle broken. The bronze corroded, particularly

around the eyes and at a large spot on the mane below the right ear. The white filling of the eyes has crystallized and partly eroded away.[47] Thin fabric.

A hammered vessel of two thicknesses, the inner with concave rounded bottom and smooth walls without ridges. A yellowish, waxy substance, perhaps beeswax, fills the lower end between the lion head and the bottom of the liner. The inner piece was slid down into the outer and secured in place by folding its upper edge over that of the outer to form a narrow projecting rim. The joint was further secured by the pins, which fasten the handle attachments to the wall. These are flat sheets of thin bronze cut to the shape of birds with spread wings and tails; rounded tabs pierced by holes to hold the handle project above the edge of the rim (see MM 46, fig. 79). The attachments overlie the projecting rim and the first series of raised ridges below it; they are fastened each by two pins capped by round studs inside the rim, their ends hammered to flat rivet heads on the outside. Parallel incisions in the surface of the bronze suggest the feathering of wings and tail. The handle, square in section at the top, tapers to a round wire at either end, the ends threaded through the eyes of the attachments, then turned back and coiled spirally 14 times around the lower handle at each side. The handle was made to the same radius as the rim so that when folded down, it lies flat on top.

The outer wall is cylindrical, increasing slightly upward toward the mouth. It is ornamented by four sets of triple raised encircling ribs, half-round in section. The lowest of these may conceal a seam where collar and lion head are joined; if so the patina, which cannot be cleaned away, hides it.

The lower end is in the form of a lion head with mane and ears above and ruff below setting it off from the collar above. A latticework of fine incision indicates the locks of hair on mane, ruff, and neck; a suggestion of individual hair is given by finer incisions within the latticing. The same decoration is carried over the laid-back ears, which are conventional projections, not hollowed.

The lion is represented as snarling with open mouth, protruding tongue, and wrinkled face. A rounded knob above the inner end of each eye; above these the forehead is furrowed on top by four ridges running back to the base of the mane. Below them the muzzle is furrowed on top by three curving ridges which are carried to the corners of the eyes. Four round-ended, petal-like ridges at each side of the muzzle and two more on the cheek below each

---

[46]See app. V, p. 304, Fabric F.

[47]For contents, see pp. 278, 284, app. II-A, Sample 11;

for identification of inlays and corrosion products, see p. 285, app. II-B, Samples 74–76.

eye. The jawbone outlined by an S-shaped raised area from the base of the ear to the chin. The edge of the mouth framed all around by a flat raised lip. With the exception of the four sharp canines, the teeth were blocked out by raised squared ridges with punched or incised lines to separate the individual teeth. The tongue, protruding between the canines, hides the incisors of the lower jaw. The eye hollows surrounded by fine raised rims and filled with white material with round pupils inlaid of polished black stone.

MM 46 **Ram's-head situla**
B 1060   Behind screen MM 378
L.-h. 0.293   L.-rim 0.205   L. inside
0.149   D. rim 0.125 m.
Ram's head: H. 0.087   W. across horns
0.113 m.
Fig. 79; Pl. 63

Complete, but with cracks and small dents and spots of corrosion. The white inlay almost completely gone from one eye; the pupil was found separately. Thin fabric.[48]

Similar in construction to MM 45, with inner and outer pieces folded together at the rim and filled between at the lower end by a waxy substance. The handle attachments flat bird-shaped plates (fig. 79) fastened to the rim by dowels with stud heads inside, flattened rivet heads out. The handle round in sec-

Figure 79. MM 46. Ram's-head situla. Detail: handle attachment. Not to scale.

tion throughout and tapered, its outer face transversely ribbed at the thicker central part. The ends coiled 13 times around the base at either side. The radius slightly greater than that of the rim.

The flaring cylindrical body surrounded by six raised encircling single ribs, half-round in profile; between the topmost two eight rosettes in relief, evenly spaced but not spaced in relation to the handle attachments.

At the lower end a ram head, the mouth closed. The junction with the neck masked at the top by the horns, at the sides and bottom by five rows of curled snail-shell locks. Behind these the tips of the ears are represented by small V-shaped ridges. Between the horns at the front a triangular area of snail-shell curls. The horns, laid close to the head, take nearly complete loops, their ends turned up and out just short of their bases. The horns segmented by parallel curved grooves.

The eyes, almost almond-shaped, are outlined by fine raised ridges all around; above them sets of three more raised arcs (like eyebrows), all tooled with fine parallel grooves across the tops. Three parallel curved grooves above the nostrils; below them a Y-shaped groove down to the mouth. The end of the muzzle punched with fine round dots to represent whiskers. The mouth and chin plain; a groove down the center of the underside of the lower jaw. The eyes inlaid like those of MM 45, but between the white material of the eyeballs and the polished black stone of the pupils there seem to have been rings of a yellow material somewhat harder than the white, to represent the irises.

If the bronze situlae are compared with other bronze vessels from the tomb, even though they appear finer and more elaborate than the rest, it appears that they could have been made in Gordion workshops. It is their animal form and their style which indicate another source of inspiration. The lion-situla has its only parallel in the relief (now lost) from the palace of Sargon II of Assyria, at Khorsabad.[49] On two slabs, servants are shown carrying to the members of a banquet lion-situlae, which they are filling from a cauldron. The bronze examples from Tumulus MM share

---

[48]For contents, see pp. 278, 284, app. II-A, Sample 12.

[49]Botta and Flandin, *Mon. Nin.*, I, pl. 16; K. R. Maxwell-Hyslop, *Iraq* 18 (1956): 152, fig. 2; and Young, *Archaeology* 11 (1958): 231. In this article Young discusses in detail his reasons for the dating of the situlae and con-

sequently the tomb to pre-718 B.C. Cf. also Young, *AJA* 62 (1958): 152 and n. 27 where comparisons are made with Urartian bronzes and with the bronze weight in the form of a lion now in the Louvre: P. E. Botta, *op. cit.*, vol. II, pl. 151; Frankfort, *AAAO*, pl. 115.

many details with those on the relief: gaping jaws and sharp teeth, threefold wrinkles on the jowls, wavelike creases above the muzzle, raised lumps above the inner corners of the eyes, the ruff-locks around the face. But immediately calling these situlae Assyrian may not take into consideration the situation at that period in Sargon's court. These could be Urartian (loot from the capture of Muṣaṣir, 714); they could be Phrygian (tribute from King Midas, 718). The inspiration, however, appears to be Assyrian. The ram would appear to be of like origin.[50]

A parallel for the ram's-head situla (H. 0.218 m.), allegedly from Luristan, is in the Teheran Museum. This vessel has a bucket handle with twisted wire ends and Assyrian friezes on the body (top and bottom are lotus bud friezes; the two central friezes are running animals).[51] Pottery ram's-head vessels were found at Ziwiyeh.[52]

Situlae of this type are also known from Samos: B 275 is a smaller bull's-head situla (H. 0.132 m.) with groups of incised lines on its sides.[53]

P. Calmeyer has recently published a comprehensive listing of situlae including these ram and lion types.[54]

LADLES
MM 47, 48
(See also pp. 227–229.)

The two ladles were found on the floor associated with the wooden screens (MM 378 and 379), where they had doubtless fallen from nails in the east wall of the tomb. The small ring- and bucket-handled cauldrons MM 4 and 5 and 8–13 were found in the same place. Evidently the ladles were for use in conjunction with the small cauldrons and had been placed with them at the time of burial; compare Tumulus K-IV, where a ladle was found inside a small cauldron.[55]

MM 47 Ladle
B 808   Behind screen MM 378
L.-h. 0.205   D. bowl 0.084 and 0.097 m.
Pl. 64A

Intact. Thin fabric; bowl, tang, and handle all in one piece, evidently hammered. The lip of the somewhat oval hemispherical bowl thickened and flattened on top. The tang concave at each side below squared upper corners, at the top curving to the long flat handle, slightly tapered and recurved at the top to form a hook. Above its end the handle is narrowed, then flared to suggest a broad-billed bird's head. The edges of the tang set off by an outlining groove, probably made by punching, since it is perceptible as a slightly raised band at the back. The groove continues up the handle from each end, dividing its face into three flat ribs. At the top behind the curve a small added bolster, its round ends projecting beyond the sides of the handle, evidently held in place by a dowel.

MM 48 Ladle
B 807   North of screen MM 379
L.-h. 0.24   W. bowl 0.092 m.
Pl. 64B

Intact. Similar to MM 47, with longer, narrower handle. Thin fabric; bowl, tang, and handle hammered from one piece. The tang is straight across the top, with concave sides and sharp-angled upper corners. The outlining groove uninterrupted below the base of the handle; two parallel grooves, springing from it, decorate the face of the handle. Two tiny bolsters ornamented with grooves near their projecting round ends are doweled across the handle just below its top at front and back.

BOWLS
MM 49–169

SPOUTED BOWLS WITH HORIZONTAL HANDLE
MM 49, 50

Both were found close to the south wall of the tomb, from which they had presumably been suspended by their handles.

[50]Ann Knudsen in *Phryg. Met. and Pot.* (1961), 260–272, discusses these animal-headed situlae in detail and concludes that they are of Phrygian workmanship, probably made at Gordion.

[51]*7000 Years of Iranian Art* (Washington, D.C.: Smithsonian Institution, 1964), p. 147, no. 424.

[52]A. Godard, *Le Trésor de Ziwiyè (Kurdistan)* (Haarlem:

Joh. Enschedé, 1950), 68 f., figs. 57 and 58.

[53]Jantzen, *Samos* VIII, 71, 74 and pl. 73.

[54]In W. Kleiss, *Bastam* I, *Ausgrabungen in den urartäischen Anlagen 1972–1975* (Berlin: Gebr. Mann, 1979), 197–199.

[55]G. Körte in *Gordion*, p. 101, Bronze no. 4, and fig. 74.

MM 49   **Spouted bowl with horizontal handle**

B 836   Upside down on floor, near south wall

H. 0.065   D. 0.222   L. with spout 0.291 m.

Pl. 64C

In good condition; not cleaned. Heavy cast fabric, thickened to 0.003 m. and flattened at the rim. The bowl with rounded bottom, slightly shallower than hemispherical and somewhat oval at the rim, wider from side to side than across from front to back. The rim is not level; it slopes slightly upward toward the spout, which was cast in one with the bowl. The open spout a trifle deeper than a half-circle, short, and flared outward all around at the end, the corners squared. Opposite the spout a horizontal handle round in section and tapered from the middle. The ends are waisted spools with a raised central molding, rounded, to approximate a bead and reel profile. The handle attached at either end by a dowel of which one end appears, carefully smoothed and polished, inside the rim; the outer ends of the dowels are not visible in the face of the handle, and they may not come all the way through its thickness.

MM 50   **Spouted bowl with horizontal handle**

B 837   South wall

H. 0.055   D. rim 0.197   L. with spout 0.267 m.

Pl. 64D

Intact. Heavy cast fabric, thickened and flattened at the rim, which is slightly overhanging on the inside. Shallow round bowl convex at the bottom. At the back a horizontal handle round in section and with squared ends set flush to the rim and attached by dowels. Opposite at the front a semicircular spout open at the top, flared at its end and squared at the corners. The spout proper seems to have been finished by filing and hammering; it is part of a cast half-round attachment with a bar across the top to bridge the inner end of the spout. The attachment fastened to the bowl by six thick, round dowels, their ends inside and out (like those of the handle dowels) so smoothly finished and polished as to be all but invisible. Within the spout the wall of the bowl pierced by ten small round holes which served to strain liquids poured from it. The holes are not quite centered to the spout, which was probably attached after they had been drilled. The strainer holes are somewhat smaller than the dowels; evidently drills of two different sizes were used.

*BOWLS WITH LIFTING HANDLES
MM 51–53*

MM 51 was found close to the south wall of the tomb, from which all had probably fallen. A second (MM 53) lay on the floor where it could have fallen from the south wall, a meter away, or from the table (MM 385) just to the east of it. The third (MM 52) lay in a stack of bronzes which had evidently fallen from the same table.[56]

MM 51   **Bowl with lifting handles**

B 813   Southeast corner

H.-rim 0.056   H.-h. 0.106   D. rim 0.2175   W. handle 0.09 m.

Pl. 64E

Intact. Rim slightly thickened, flat on top; walls curved and bottom flattened but not to true horizontal, so that the bowl sits a bit crooked. Lifting handles consisting of curved end brackets below a straight horizontal rod with ends projecting beyond the brackets; cast. The handle round in section except at the lower ends of the brackets, which are undercut to half-round section so that the full-round part above rests half on top of the rim, the half-round part below against the outer face of the bowl; attachment is made by dowels through bowl rim and lower ends of brackets.

MM 52   **Bowl with lifting handles**

B 815   North of table MM 385

H.-rim 0.075   H.-h. 0.11–0.12   D. rim 0.279   W. handles 0.112 m.

Pl. 64F

Intact. Heavy fabric, probably cast. Shallow bowl rounded at the bottom; the rim thickened and flat on top, plain on the outside, overhanging in a sharp ridge on the inside. Two lifting handles, each consisting of a straight rod, round in section, with nail-head ends projecting beyond curving brackets which attach below to flat attachment plates. The plates are scalloped along their lower edges and curved to fit the rim, set flush to its upper edge and fastened each by three dowels with hemispherical stud heads inside the rim, flattened and polished outside. These handles are apparently secondary, for at each side there are six holes below the rim arranged in two triangles—three holes equally spaced, two above and one be-

[56]For analyses of contents of MM 51–53, see pp. 278, 284, app. II-A, Samples 13–15. See p. 140, n. 69 for an explanation of the presence of food in these bowls [Ed.]

III. MM 45. Bronze situla in form of a lion's head.

IV. MM 46. Bronze situla in form of a ram's head.

low. All the lower holes have been plugged with bronze—perhaps the remains of the dowels, which fastened on the original handles—to prevent leakage. Of the upper holes only three are similarly plugged; the other five are concealed, or partly concealed, on the outside by the plates of the existing handles. They are visible inside the rim except for one, which is entirely covered by a stud of the present handle attachment. The axis of the original handles was slightly off that of their replacements. The bowl clearly was at some time remodeled, the original handles removed and the existing ones substituted for them.

MM 53 **Bowl with lifting handles**
B 814   Southeast quarter
H.-rim 0.074   H.-h. 0.095
    D. rim 0.25 m.
Pl. 65A

The bowl intact; two of six (three at each side) attached spools missing. Heavy fabric, probably cast. Shallow bowl rounded at the bottom, with erect rim thickened and flat on top. The lifting handles square in section, very slightly arched at the top, and cast together with their attachment plates, which are long narrow strips with rounded ends projecting beyond the roots of the handle brackets. Each attachment fastened to the bowl by a central and two end dowels. The central dowels are carefully smoothed and polished at the inner ends, hammered to rivet heads on the outer; three of the four end dowels are hammered to rough rivet heads both inside and out, the fourth capped at both ends by stud heads. It seems unlikely that the three dowels with rivet heads could ever have been capped by studs now lost; therefore either the three rivet-headed dowels, or the dowel capped by studs at both ends, must represent a later repair, probably the former.

Attached at each side were three half-spools of which two are now missing; the dowel holes through the wall indicate their positions, and the spools were evenly spaced. In shape they are waisted (their sides slightly concave), rounded at the bottom and flat on top where they were decorated by hemispherical studs, three still in place, the fourth represented by a hole for its pin. The spools were fastened in place by dowels run through the wall and spool, their ends smoothed flat and polished.

BOWL WITH LIFTING HANDLES
AND FIXED RINGS
MM 54

Similar to the three bowls above, MM 51–53, but perhaps transitional to those with swiveling ring handles, MM 55–69 below, is a bowl with ring handles fixed in an upright position. This was found lying on the floor partly beneath the cauldron, MM 2; it must have fallen from one of the nails in the south wall.

MM 54 **Bowl with lifting handles and fixed rings**
B 1032   Partially under MM 2
H.-rim 0.071   H.-h. 0.135
    D. rim 0.242 m.
Pl. 65B

Heavy fabric, cast. The shallow bowl rounded at the bottom, its wall thickened to a rim flat on top and 0.0035 m. thick at the edge. The ring handles made to look as though held upright by curved tubular holders with raised moldings at the ends; actually the rings, tubes, and rim attachments were cast together as single pieces. The attachments are narrow flat bands fitted to the face of the bowl rim; above they are thickened inward so that the tubular handle holders rest also in part on top of the rim. Each was fastened to the rim by three dowels with decorative stud heads inside, the outer ends cut off and hammered to rivet heads. One of the six dowels is missing.

BOWLS WITH SWIVELING RING HANDLES
AND BANDED RIM
MM 55–69

Fifteen bowls banded with added strips of bronze below the rim outside, the strips crossed by vertical semispools at their ends and in some cases also at their centers, and with ring handles suspended from bolster attachments, were included among the offerings in the tomb. Fourteen of these lay along the south and east walls, no doubt as they had fallen when the iron nails from which they had been suspended gave way.[57] The fifteenth (MM 60) lay among bowls of other

---

[57]Samples of the *contents* of some of these bowls (MM 56, 60, 61, 63) were kept: see pp. 278, 284, app. II-A, Samples 16–19. The dried food found in these bowls must have dropped into them after they were lying on the

floor. One possible source is the small cauldrons, which also fell from the nails, scattering their already dried contents. [Ed.]

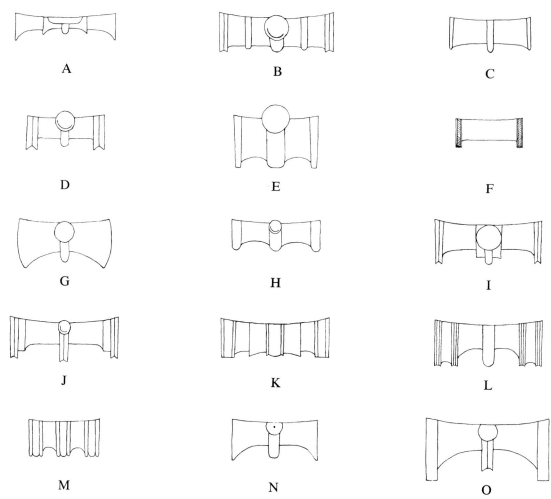

Figure 80. *Forms of bolsters (as seen from above) on bowls with ring handles and banded rim. A. MM 55. B. MM 56. C. MM 57. D. MM 58. E. MM 59. F. MM 60. G. MM 61. H. MM 62. I. MM 63. J. MM 64. K. MM 65. L. MM 66. M. MM 67. N. MM 68. O. MM 69. 2:3.*

shapes which had evidently been stacked one inside the other on the wooden tables in the southeast corner.

Three of these bowls (MM 67–69) bear smears of beeswax on the rim beside the handle attachment with alphabetical inscriptions scratched in the wax.

MM 55 Bowl with swiveling ring handles and banded rim (four spools)
B 1031 Partially under MM 2
D. rim 0.275 H. 0.08 L. bolster 0.043
GW. across rings 0.072 m.
Fig. 80A; Pl. 65C

Intact; heavy fabric, cast. Slightly thickened rim, flattened on top, barely flaring. The half-bolsters attached each by four dowels in pairs, one above the other. Bolster, fig. 80A. A compass prick at the center of the floor.

The rim bands high in profile, with straight sides and half-round top; four vertical spools, one at each end of the rim bands, each fastened to the rim by a dowel. The spools nearly cylindrical in profile, with flaring ends. Rim bands and spools evidently cast in one.

The handle is oval, round in section, and tapered from the middle.

MM 56   **Bowl with swiveling ring handles and banded rim (four spools)**

B 1039   Southeast corner, east wall
D. rim 0.25   H. 0.09   L. bolster 0.047 m.
Figs. 80B, 81; Pl. 65D

Figure 81.   MM 56. Bowl with four spools at rim. Profile and view.   1:5.

Intact; cast. The bolsters attached each by two dowels near their outer ends. The ends of the dowels, cut flush to the surface and polished, appear both in the bolster faces and inside the rim of the bowl. Bolster, fig. 80B.

The rim bands rectangular in profile, their height greater than their width. Four vertical spools, one at each end, fastened to the rim each by a dowel: the dowel ends inside the rim all show, but only one appears in the outer face of a spool. The spools nearly cylindrical, flared at the ends.

Decorated with six small, round-headed studs, one on top of each spool. One on the platform at the top of each bolster. Five are still in place, the sixth lost.

The handle round in section and tapered from the middle.

MM 57   **Bowl with swiveling ring handles and banded rim (four spools)**

B 1042   Southeast corner, partially under MM 51
D. rim 0.25–0.255   H. 0.063
L. bolster 0.034 m.
Fig. 80C; Pl. 65E

Intact. One of the bolsters is attached to the rim by a single dowel with a flat, nail-like head, which appears inside the bowl rim; evidently a repair. The other bolster shows a dowel hole in its outer face which was apparently never used, since there is no trace of a dowel. Bolster, fig. 80C.

The rim bands seem to have been cast in one with the bolsters. A small dowel fastens the inner end of each close beside the end of each bolster. The bands are half-round in section, with four vertical spools,

one at each outer end, all fastened to the rim by dowels. The spools are cylindrical with flat projecting nail-like heads at top and bottom. A compass prick at the center of the floor.

The handles round in section, not tapered.

MM 58   **Bowl with swiveling ring handles and banded rim (four spools)**

B 1034   Southwest corner, partially under MM 2
D. rim 0.273   H. 0.082   L. bolster 0.034 m.
Fig. 80D; Pl. 65F

Intact. Short flaring rim slightly set off from body. The bolsters are fastened to the rim each by two dowels; they appear to have been cast in one with the rim bands. Bolster, fig. 80D.

The rim bands half-round in section with four end spools, each fastened to the rim by a dowel. The spools cylindrical.

Decorated with six small round-headed studs, one on top of each spool, one on the top of a platform above each bolster. The studs overlap the upper face of the rim; all are still in place.

The handles round in section and tapered from the middle.

MM 59   **Bowl with swiveling ring handles and banded rim (four spools)**

B 1033   Southeast corner, partially under MM 68
D. rim 0.223   H. 0.063   L. bolster 0.035 m.
Fig. 80E, 82; Pl. 66A

Intact. A compass prick at the center of the floor. The bolsters fastened each by two dowels of which the inner ends appear cut flush to the face of the bowl rim inside and polished; only one dowel end (of four) is visible in the outer face of a bolster: perhaps the bolsters were in this case solid-cast. At the top of each bolster a round button which in part overlaps the upper face of the rim; the buttons do not carry decorative studs. Bolster, fig. 80E.

The rim bands rectangular in section, with rounded edges. The bands and the four vertical spools of this bowl were (uniquely) separately made, the inner faces of the spools notched to fit over the bands and to hold them in place against the rim. The spools, of shallow concave profile, were set over the bands and doweled to the rim.

The handle round in section and tapered from the middle.

MM 60   **Bowl with swiveling ring handles and banded rim (four spools)**
B 841   In pile west of table MM 388
D. rim 0.286 H. 0.081 L. rings 0.072
    and 0.075 L. bolster 0.028 m.
Fig. 80F; Pl. 66B, D

Intact. The bolsters attached each by a single dowel; the central and end-moldings cabled. Bolster, fig. 80F.

The rim bands rectangular in section with four spools, one at each end, fastened each to the rim by a dowel. The spools cylindrical with flat projecting ridges around top, center, and bottom.

The handles faceted to eight flat faces: octagonal in section. Not tapered.

MM 61   **Bowl with swiveling ring handles and banded rim (four spools)**
B 1041   Behind screen MM 379
D. rim 0.269–0.272 H. 0.079
    L. bolster 0.04 m.
Fig. 80G; Pl. 66C, E

Intact. A compass prick at center of floor. The bolsters attached each by a single dowel with a round stud head at its inner end; the outer, cut flush and polished, shows in the face of the central molding of the bolster. A button at the center of each bolster on top (like MM 59); no studs. Bolster, fig. 80G.

The rim bands half-round in section, with four spools, each fastened by a dowel with a stud head inside the rim, similar to those that fasten the bolsters. Four additional stud-headed dowels set halfway between bolster and spool secure the rim band and bring the total of studs decorating the inner face of the rim to ten.

The handles round in section, very slightly tapered from the center.

MM 62   **Bowl with swiveling ring handles and banded rim (four spools)**
B 1043   Not on plan; southwest corner under MM 17
D. rim 0.265 H. 0.057 L. bolster
    0.0375 m.
Fig. 80H; Pl. 66F

Intact. A compass prick at the center of the floor. The bolsters attached each by two dowels, their ends cut flush to the inner face of the rim and to the surface of the bolster faces. Bolster, fig. 80H.

The rim bands half-round in section; the four spools, doweled to the rim, cylindrical in profile. Decorated with six round-headed studs, one on top

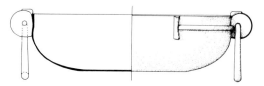

Figure 82. MM 59. Bowl with swiveling ring handles and banded rim. Profile and view. 1:5.

of each spool, one set into the top of the central molding of each bolster (there are no platforms). Three of the studs still in place, the other three lost.

The handles round in section and tapered from the middle.

MM 63   **Bowl with swiveling ring handles and banded rim (eight spools)**
B 1036   South wall, between MM 2 and 3
D. rim 0.257 H. 0.072 L. bolster
    0.045 m.
Fig. 80I; Pl. 66G

Intact. The bolsters attached each by two dowels run through from the bolster face to the inner face of the rim, the ends cut flush and polished. Bolster, fig. 80I.

The rim bands half-round in section, each with four vertical spools, two at the ends, two halfway from end to bolster. Each spool fastened to the rim by a dowel of which only one end is visible in the inner face of the rim. The spools cylindrical in profile.

The handles round in section and tapered from the middle.

MM 64   **Bowl with swiveling ring handles and banded rim (eight spools)**
B 1037   East wall, behind table MM 388
D. rim 0.229 H. 0.071 L. bolster
    0.046 m.
Fig. 80J; Pl. 66H

Intact. The bolsters attached each by two dowels set close together near the center; the ends of these, cut flush to the surface and polished, show inside the rim and on the bolsters. Bolster, fig. 80J.

The rim bands half-round in section, each with four evenly spaced spools. The spools, nearly cylindrical in profile but with flared ends, are fastened to the rim by dowels run right through spool and rim, both ends showing. There are traces of solder at the junctions of bolsters and rim.

Decorated with ten small hemispherical studs, one

on top of each spool, one set into the central molding of each bolster at the top (there are no platforms). The studs overlap the upper face of the rim. All but one, which has been lost, are still in place.

The handles round in section and tapered from the middle. In proportion to the bolsters, which are long, the handles are small and sharply curved; they turn in their sockets with difficulty.

MM 65   **Bowl with swiveling ring handles and banded rim (eight spools)**
B 1038[58]   Not on plan, east wall under MM 161
D. rim 0.247   H. 0.076   L. bolster 0.046 m.
Fig. 80K; Pl. 67A

Intact. The bolsters attached each by two dowels with round stud heads which decorate the rim inside; the points do not show in the bolster faces. Bolster, fig. 80K.

The rim bands half-round in section, each with four evenly spaced vertical spools. The spools cylindrical in profile, each fastened to the rim by a dowel.

The handles round in section and tapered from the middle.

MM 66   **Bowl with swiveling ring handles and banded rim (eight spools)**
B 1035   East wall, behind screen MM 379
D. rim 0.306   H. 0.085   L. bolster 0.045 m.
Figs. 80L, 83; Pl. 67B

Intact. The bolsters fastened each by two dowels, their ends inside and out cut flush to the faces of the bronze and polished. Bolster, fig. 80L.

The rim bands high, with straight side faces and half-round top. Four vertical spools, evenly spaced, on each; their profiles slightly concave. Each fastened to the rim by a dowel. The flared upper ends of the spools overlap the upper face of the rim. The bol-

sters notched on their inner faces to fit over the rim bands.

The handles round in section and tapered from the middle.

Three bowls (MM 67–69) of the normal type with swiveling ring handles and banded rim (eight spools; see foregoing) bear smears of beeswax on the outer face of the rim beside one handle; on the wax are scratched alphabetical inscriptions. Because of the presence of the wax, it was not possible to clean the bronze,[59] and therefore some of the details are not as clear as they are on the bowls which could be cleaned. On the inscriptions, see pp. 273–277, and fig. 134A–C, and pl. 97A–C.

MM 67   **Bowl with swiveling ring handles, banded rim (eight spools), and wax inscription**
B 1040   Not on plan; under table MM 388
D. rim 0.25   H. 0.067   L. bolster 0.03 m.
Figs. 80M, 134B; Pls. 67C, 97B

Intact; not cleaned. The bolster at one side was cast in one with the rim band; it was not doweled directly to the rim but held in place by dowels through the rim band close beside its ends. At the other side the bolster was separately made, the separately made rim bands added against its ends. How this bolster was attached does not appear. Bolster, fig. 80M.

The rim bands short, half-round in section, and crossed each by four spools slightly concave in profile and flattened on their outer faces. Each spool doweled to the rim.

The handles round in section and very slightly tapered from the middle.

A wax inscription was packed into the space between two outer spools under the rim band.[60]

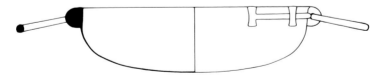

Figure 83.   MM 66. Bowl with swiveling ring handles and banded rim. Profile and view.   1:5.

[58]See pp. 286–287, app. II-C, Samples 92 and 93.
[59]For analysis of corrosion product on MM 68, see app.

II-B, p. 285, Sample 77.
[60]R. S. Young, *Hesperia* 38 (1969): 262, no. 32.

MM 68   **Bowl with swiveling ring handles, banded rim (eight spools), and wax inscription**
B 818   Southeast corner
D. rim 0.2775   H. 0.079   L. bolster
    0.036 m.
Figs. 80N, 84, 134A; Pls. 67D, F, 97A

Intact but for spots of corrosion.[61] The bolsters attached each by single dowels near the center; it is not possible to see whether bolster and rim bands were separately made or cast in one. Bolster, fig. 80N.

The rim bands half-round in section, with eight vertical spools attached to the rim each by a dowel. The spools slightly concave in profile. At the top of each spool and on the platform at the top of each bolster a small hole for the pin of a hemispherical stud; but no studs were still in place when the bowl was found. Either the studs were all lost before the bowl was placed in the tomb, or they were never added despite the provision made for them. There are no signs of pins broken off inside the holes.

The handles round in section, not tapered.

The inscription was incised upon a bed of wax impressed in the space above the rim band between the end of a bolster and the first spool.[62]

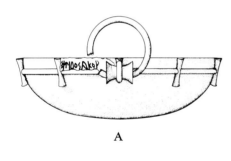

A

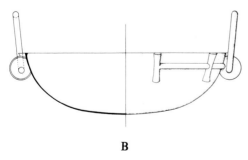

B

Figure 84. *MM 68. Bowl with inscription on wax. A. From side, with inscription. B. Profile.* *1:5.*

MM 69   **Bowl with swiveling ring handles, banded rim (eight spools), and wax inscription**
B 819   Behind screen MM 378
D. rim   0.252   H. 0.076   L. bolster
    0.052 m.
Figs. 80O, 85, 134C; Pls. 67E, G, 97C

Intact. The bolsters pinned to the rim by single dowels; it is not possible to see whether they were separately made or cast together with the rim bands. Bolster, fig. 80O.

The rim bands half-round in section; eight spools, each pinned to the rim by a dowel. The spools cylindrical in profile, with flat projecting nail-like heads at top and bottom.

The inscription was incised in wax which had been pressed into the space above the rim band between the bolster and the first spool.[63]

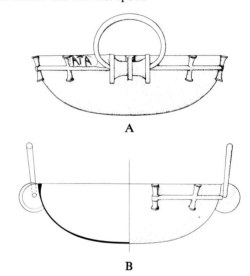

A

B

Figure 85. *MM 69. Bowl with inscription on wax. A. From side, with inscription. B. Profile.* *1:5.*

See the general discussion of bowls with swiveling ring handles and banded rims on pp. 229–233.

OMPHALOS BOWLS
MM 70–167
(See also pp. 233–236.)

Ninety-eight omphalos bowls (*phialai mesomphaloi*) were found in the southern and eastern

---

[61]For analysis of corrosion product, see p. 285, app. II-B, Sample 77.

[62]R. S. Young, *op. cit.*, 260, no. 25.

[63]*Ibid.*, 262, no. 33.

areas of the tomb. They had been stacked one inside the other and placed in piles on the six tables (MM 380–385) that stood free in the southern half of the room; other stacks had rested on two tables (MM 386, 388) that stood against the east wall. The tops of the tables, especially MM 380 and MM 383, the best preserved, showed discolored rings where the bowls had once rested, but with the collapse of the tables the bronzes which rested on them had been dumped to the floor. The way in which the bowls were found overlapping in rows on the floor, especially in front of cauldron MM 3 and by the table MM 388, showed that they had been stacked, the smaller bowls within the larger. A number of these bowls do not appear on the plan because they were covered by others or by the tops of the collapsed tables. No omphalos bowls were found in the north half of the tomb or along its west side.

Common to all the bowls are the large central omphalos, hollow underneath, and the raised ridges, sharp or rounded in profile and varying in number, which surround its base. Otherwise the bowls fall into three groups: 54 with relief decoration of petals (MM 70–123), 7 with horizontal grooving or ribbing on the inside (MM 124–130), and 37 with plain walls (MM 131–167).

PETALED BOWLS WITH DECORATED OMPHALOS
MM 70–73

MM 70   **Petaled bowl with decorated omphalos and lugs on rim**
B 843   Under table MM 388
H.-rim 0.057   D. rim 0.195   D. omph.
0.044   Th. rim 0.004 m.
Pl. 68A

Intact. The rim thickened and flattened on top.

The bowl rather deep with sharply flared rim and flat bottom above the lower bulge of the relief petals, on which the vessel rests. Mushroom-shaped omphalos with plain concave stem and reeded cap, a groove around a compass prick at the center. The reeding of the top appears in reverse on the other side, which suggests that it was made by chasing. Around the base of the omphalos three ridges, triangular in profile.

The relief pattern of petals is normal (see p. 140, fig. 90A), with 16 rounded petal bases around the bottom, multiplying to 64 pointed tips below the rim. On the outside the petals are plain at the bottom, their points at the top are defined by a raised zigzag band. On the inside a similar raised zigzag band above the petal tips; below, defining their rounded lower ends, fine hollowed arcs, probably made by engraving, tangent at their ends. The raised zigzag bands both inside and outside the rim could have been made only by casting.

On the rim five added lugs, evenly spaced. These are oval at the top, slotted beneath to fit over the rim, and pointed below. The upper ends (above the rim) decorated by double raised bands crossing at the top, the four angles between the arms filled by incised concentric circles (two) with compass pricks at the center. The lower points of the lugs are pinched together against the inner and outer wall faces of the bowl to hold them in place on the rim, which thickens to the lip. At either side of each lug a round stud caps each end of a pin run through the rim of the bowl. These pins do not fasten the lugs to the bowl, but prevent them from sliding to either side along the rim, and their stud heads add decoration.

MM 71   **Petaled bowl with decorated omphalos**
B 840   Not on plan; under table
MM 382
H. 0.075   D. rim 0.225   D. omph.
0.046   Th. rim 0.004 m.
Fig. 86A; Pl. 68B

A large corrosion hole in the top of the omphalos, and a dent in one petal. The bowl rather deep with nearly straight rim flattened on top. Mushroom-shaped omphalos with plain concave stem on a high platform. On the cap grooved decoration: four sets of diminishing chevrons, their points tangent at the center; around them two rings of radiating short strokes, and plain grooves on the vertical face of the omphalos. The grooved decoration appears in reverse on the underside.

Around the base of the platform under the omphalos seven ridges, sharp triangular in profile. The petal pattern normal except that the rounded lower ends of the 14 petals of the first tier are so spaced that the pointed ends of the intermediate tier are carried to bottom between them. The upper tier of short petals brings the total of points below the rim to 56. The tips and lower ends of the petals plain both inside and out.

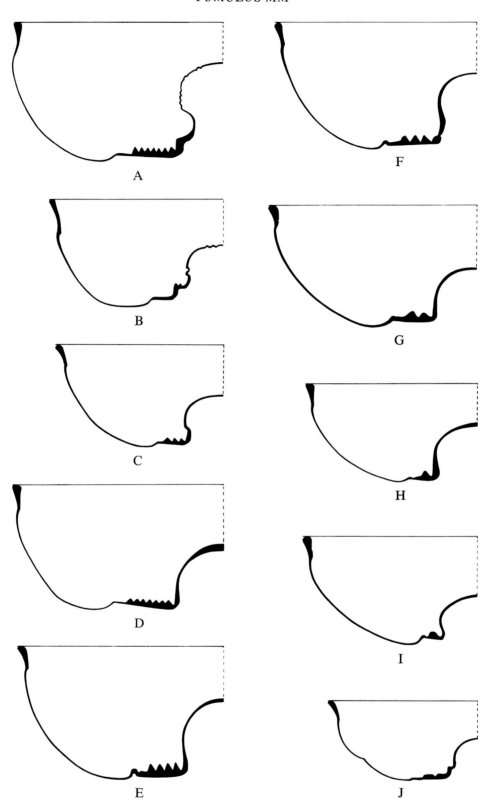

*Figure 86.   Profiles of omphalos bowls. A. MM 71. B. MM 72. C. MM 73. D. MM
74. E. MM 75. F. MM 84. G. MM 89. H. MM 100. I. MM 109. J. MM 123.   1:2.*

MM 72 **Petaled bowl with decorated omphalos**
B 844   East wall, behind table
MM 388
H. 0.059   D. rim 0.182   D. omph.
0.039   Th. rim 0.003 m.
Fig. 86B; Pl. 68C

Intact. The rim offset and flared, the lip flattened on top. Mushroom-shaped omphalos on a platform bordered around its edge by two raised ridges. The stem of the omphalos concave below a raised ridge and a groove; the cap grooved: three rings around a compass prick at the center, reeding below. The relief decoration appears in reverse on the underside. The step from platform to floor is hollow underneath; at its lower edge there are faint traces of a seam where body and platform were joined, and perhaps of solder or brazing.

The petal pattern normal: 18 petals with rounded lower ends multiplying to 72 points below the rim. The tips and bases of the petals plain both inside and out.

MM 73 **Petaled bowl with decorated omphalos**
B 881   Partially under MM 3
H. 0.053–0.054   D. rim 0.178
D. omph. 0.04 m.
Fig. 86C; Pl. 68D

Intact. The bowl rather shallow; rim offset inside and flared. Mushroom-shaped omphalos with thick stem and reeded cap, a compass prick at the center. The relief appears in reverse on the underside. Three triangular ridges around the base of the omphalos.

The petal pattern normal; 15 petals with rounded lower ends multiplying to 60 points below the rim. In section the petals are spined or ridged down the middle, rather than rounded. Their upper and lower ends plain both inside and out.

PETALED BOWLS WITH
PLAIN OMPHALOS
MM 74–123

MM 74 **Petaled omphalos bowl**
B 894   On table MM 384
H. 0.064–0.0655   D. rim 0.223
D. omph. 0.051   Th. rim 0.004 m.
Fig. 86D; Pl. 69A

Intact. The rim slightly flared, offset on the inside; the thickened lip flat on top. The omphalos hemispherical, slightly stilted; a compass prick at the center underneath. Seven small ridges around its base, blunt triangular in profile.

The petal pattern normal, 14 base petals multiplying to 56 points below the rim. The petals spined.

Their upper and lower ends plain both inside and out.

MM 75 **Petaled omphalos bowl**
B 891   East of table MM 383
H. 0.07–0.071   D. rim 0.222
D. omph. 0.045 m.
Fig. 86E; Pl. 69B

Intact. Large omphalos, slightly more than hemispherical; a compass prick at center on top and underneath. Around its base four ridges triangular in section; farther out, where the floor joins the wall, another ridge, blunted and grooved underneath.

Normal petal pattern, 16 base petals multiplying to 64 tips. The upper ends of the petals are plain inside and out; the rounded lower ends are set off by deep grooved arcs on the outside, by slightly raised arcs flat on top on the inside.

MM 76 **Petaled omphalos bowl**
B 886   On table MM 382
H. 0.07   D. rim 0.219   D. omph.
0.039   Th. rim 0.004 m.
Pl. 69C

Intact; the omphalos hemispherical, slightly stilted; lip flattened. Like MM 75: 4 triangular ridges, 16 petals multiplying to 64, their lower ends set off by grooves on the outside and by slightly raised ridges on the inside; but here the tips of the petals are outlined by an engraved zigzag both inside and out.

MM 77 **Petaled omphalos bowl**
B 888   Under table MM 382
H. 0.07–0.071   D. rim 0.207–0.209
D. omph. 0.041   Th. lip 0.003 m.

Intact. Omphalos hemispherical, slightly stilted. Precisely like MM 76 in every detail.

MM 78 **Petaled omphalos bowl**
B 887   Partially over table MM 384
H. 0.0675–0.07   D. rim 0.217–0.221
D. omph. 0.042   Th. lip 0.003 m.
Pl. 69D

Intact; the omphalos hemispherical, slightly stilted. Exactly like MM 76 in every detail except that on the inside shallow arcs, perhaps made with a punch, outline the lower ends of the petals.

MM 79 **Petaled omphalos bowl**
B 885   On tables MM 382, 384
H. 0.0635–0.066   D. rim 0.219
D. omph. 0.041   Th. lip 0.004 m.

Intact. Omphalos hemispherical, slightly stilted. Precisely like MM 78 in every detail.

MM 80   **Petaled omphalos bowl**
     B 889   South of table MM 383
     H. 0.068–0.071   D. rim 0.222–0.223
          D. omph. 0.043 m.
     Pl. 69E

Intact. Precisely like MM 77 and 78 in every detail.

MM 81   **Petaled omphalos bowl**
     B 890   South of table MM 383
     H. 0.063   D. rim 0.218   D. omph.
          0.041   Th. lip 0.003 m.

Intact. Omphalos hemispherical, slightly stilted. Like MM 79 and 80 in every detail except that on the inside the lower ends of the petals are set off by grooved arcs made probably in the casting rather than with punches.

MM 82   **Petaled omphalos bowl**
     B 892   South of table MM 383
     H. 0.068–0.07   D. rim 0.223
          D. omph. 0.041   Th. lip 0.003 m.
     Fig. 87A; Pl. 69F

Intact. Omphalos hemispherical, slightly stilted. Like the foregoing except that the tips of the petals are not set off by engraved zigzags inside or out, and that their lower ends are not outlined on the inside; the deep outlining groove outside remains to define the petal bases.

MM 83   **Petaled omphalos bowl**
     B 893   South of table MM 383
     H. 0.061–0.064   D. rim 0.214
          D. omph. 0.044   Th. lip 0.003 m.
     Pl. 69G

Intact. Omphalos hemispherical, slightly stilted; a compass prick at the center underneath. Like MM 82 in every detail except that, of the four ridges surrounding the omphalos, the three inner are triangular in profile, the outermost is half-round.

MM 84   **Petaled omphalos bowl**
     B 882   South of table MM 383
     H. 0.067–0.07   D. rim 0.214
          D. omph. 0.04   Th. lip 0.003 m.
     Fig. 86F; Pl. 69H

Intact. The rim offset on the inside and slightly outward-tilted. The omphalos slightly more than hemispherical; a compass prick at the center of its underside. Three ridges triangular in profile; the omphalos itself rests on a very narrow raised ledge.
Petal pattern normal with 16 base petals multiply-

ing to 64 points below the rim. The tips plain both inside and out; the rounded lower ends outlined outside by deep grooved arcs (cast rather than punched or engraved) and inside by a low raised ridge.

MM 85   **Petaled omphalos bowl**
     B 880   On south edge of table
     MM 383
     H. 0.058–0.062   D. rim 0.208
          D. omph. 0.049   Th. lip 0.004 m.

Intact. The bowl rather shallow, the rim offset on the inside and flared, the lip squared. Omphalos somewhat more than hemispherical, a compass prick at center on top. Three ridges triangular in profile. The petals spined, 16 multiplying to 64. Their upper ends plain inside and out, their lower ends plain on the inside, outlined by grooved arcs outside.

MM 86   **Petaled omphalos bowl**
     B 883   East wall, south of table
     MM 388
     H. 0.051   D. rim 0.168   D. omph.
          0.0375   Th. lip 0.003 m.
     Pl. 69I

Intact.[64] The rim offset and slightly flared. Omphalos a little more than hemispherical; a compass prick at the center on top. Three ridges, triangular in profile. The petals spined, 14 multiplying to 56. The petal tips plain inside and out; the rounded lower ends set off by grooves on the outside, by raised ridges inside.

MM 87   **Petaled omphalos bowl**
     B 884   East wall, behind table
     MM 388
     H. 0.0545   D. rim 0.173   D. omph.
          0.037 m.
     Pl. 69J

Intact. Exactly like MM 86 in every detail. Petals spined.

MM 88   **Petaled omphalos bowl**
     B 875   South of table MM 383
     H. 0.07   D. rim 0.222   D. omph.
          0.046   Th. lip 0.0045 m.
     Pl. 69K

Intact. The rim slightly flared. Omphalos a trifle more than hemispherical, with central compass pricks on top and underneath. Two rounded ridges, the inner one higher than the outer. The petal pattern

---

[64]For analysis of contents, see pp. 278, 284, app. II-A, Sample 20.

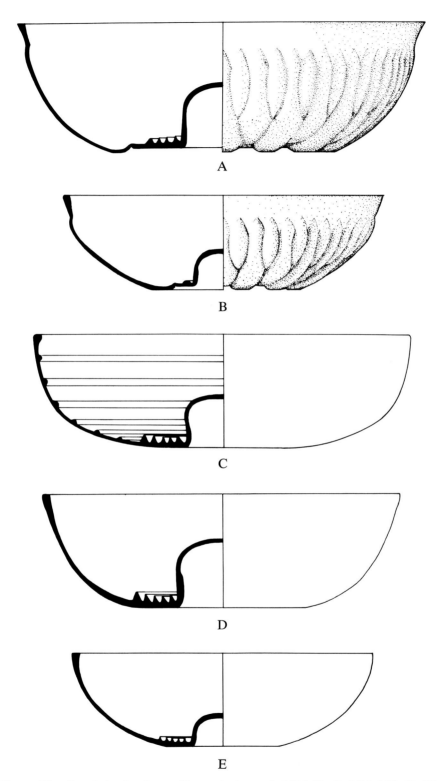

Figure 87. Omphalos bowls, profiles and views. A. MM 82. B. MM 116. C. MM 130. D. MM 135. E. MM 136. 1:2.

normal, but the lower points of the middle tier extend down almost to the floor. Fourteen petals multiplying to fifty-six, their tips and bases plain both inside and out.

MM 89   **Petaled omphalos bowl**
             B 876   Southwest of table MM 388
             H. 0.064–0.065   D. rim 0.223
             D. omph. 0.046   Th. lip 0.0045 m.
             Fig. 86G; Pl. 70A

Intact. The rim slightly flared. Omphalos hemispherical, slightly stilted, with central compass prick on top. Two rounded ridges, the outer one slightly higher than the inner. Petal pattern normal, 14 petals multiplying to 56. Their ends plain outside, top and bottom; their tips defined inside by an engraved zigzag, their lower ends by fine engraved arcs tangent to each other.

MM 90   **Petaled omphalos bowl**
             B 877   Partially under MM 3
             H. 0.059–0.061   D. rim 0.204
             D. omph. 0.043   Th. lip 0.004 m.
             Pl. 70B

Intact. Omphalos hemispherical, slightly stilted, with central compass pricks on top and underneath. Like MM 89 in every detail except that the petals are spined.

MM 91   **Petaled omphalos bowl**
             B 878   South of table MM 388
             H. 0.061   D. rim 0.220   D. omph.
             0.045   Th. lip 0.004 m.

Intact. Omphalos hemispherical, slightly stilted, with central compass prick on top. The outer of the two rounded ridges slightly wider, but not higher, than the inner. The ridges stand on a low raised platform which steps down to the floor; a barely visible ring at this point on the under-face suggests a seam where bowl and omphalos-ridges complex were joined. Petal pattern normal, 14 petals multiplying to 56. The tips and bases plain on the outside; inside the tips defined by a fine engraved zigzag, the bases by low raised arcs flat on top.

MM 92   **Petaled omphalos bowl**
             B 879   Standing at foot of screen
             MM 378
             H. 0.063–0.065   D. rim 0.236
             D. omph. 0.047   Th. lip 0.005 m.
             Pl. 70C

Intact. Omphalos more than hemispherical; central compass pricks on top and underneath. Two rounded ridges on a low platform, as on MM 91; a barely visible seam ring on the underside around the margin of the step. Fourteen petals multiplying to fifty-six. The lower ends of the petals plain outside, defined by fine engraved tangent arcs inside. Their tips outlined by a fine engraved zigzag inside, by a low raised zigzag outside. As the points of the petals of the two lower tiers are wider than those of the fillers between them, both zigzags are irregular, with wider zigs above the petal ends alternating with shorter zags above the fillers.

MM 93   **Petaled omphalos bowl**
             B 850   On table MM 384
             H. 0.045   D. rim 0.169   D. omph.
             0.043   Th. lip 0.0045 m.

Intact. Shallow bowl with slightly flared rim; flat lip. Omphalos hemispherical, slightly stilted, a central compass prick on top. Around its base a single ridge with rounded profile. Normal petal pattern, 18 petals multiplying to 72. The tips of the petals plain inside and out; their lower ends plain outside, set off by low raised arcs inside.

MM 94   **Petaled omphalos bowl**
             B 852   South of table MM 383
             H. 0.045–0.047   D. rim 0.174
             D. omph. 0.043   Th. lip 0.005 m.

Intact. The lip flattened. The omphalos hemispherical, slightly stilted; a central compass prick on top. Just like MM 93 in every detail except that the lower ends of the petals are plain inside, not set off by raised ridges.

MM 95   **Petaled omphalos bowl**
             B 858   East wall, behind table
             MM 388
             H. 0.057–0.06   D. rim 0.18   D. omph.
             0.0465   Th. lip 0.005 m.
             Pl. 70D

Intact.[65] The rim flat on top. The omphalos hemispherical with a central compass prick on top. Around its base one large ridge with rounded profile. Normal petal pattern, 17 petals multiplying to 68. The petals spined. Their upper and lower ends plain both inside and out.

---

[65]For contents, see pp. 278, 284, app. II-A, Sample 21.

MM 96 Petaled omphalos bowl
B 866   South of table MM 383
H. 0.051–0.0525 D. rim 0.19
D. omph. 0.0415 Th. lip 0.005 m.
Pl. 70E

Intact. The rim rather sharply flared. Omphalos hemispherical, with central compass pricks on top and underneath. A single large ridge, rounded in profile. Normal petal pattern, 16 petals multiplying to 64. Their tips and bases plain, both inside and out.

MM 97 Petaled omphalos bowl
B 874   North of table MM 388
H. 0.055–0.058 D. rim 0.213
D. omph. 0.06 Th. lip 0.0025 m.
Pl. 70F

Some small holes eaten by corrosion. Rim short, not offset. Omphalos slightly more than hemispherical; at its center on top and underneath a patch, as if the compass point had made a hole which had to be plugged. Inside the omphalos, which is very big, remain smears of wax, probably put in to prevent leaking. A large ridge rounded in profile around its base. Normal petal pattern, 16 multiplying to 64. Their tips and bases plain outside; inside an engraved zigzag defines their tips, low flat raised arcs their lower ends.

MM 98 Petaled omphalos bowl
B 849   Southeast corner, south of
table MM 385
H. 0.047–0.049 D. rim 0.175
D. omph. 0.033 Th. lip 0.0035 m.

Intact. Bowl shallow, rim slightly flared. Omphalos hemispherical and rather small, a central compass prick on top. A single rounded ridge. Petal pattern normal, 15 multiplying to 60. The ends of the petals plain outside; inside their tips defined by an engraved zigzag, their bases by engraved arcs tangent to each other at the ends.

MM 99 Petaled omphalos bowl
B 860   Under east section of table
MM 381
H. 0.057–0.059   D. rim 0.197
D. omph. 0.051 Th. lip 0.0035 m.

Intact. Bowl shallow, rim slightly flared. Omphalos hemispherical, large in proportion to the bowl, and with a central compass prick on top. Like MM 98 in every detail, with engraving to set off the 15 petal ends on the inside only.

MM 100 Petaled omphalos bowl
B 863   South of table MM 380
H. 0.053 D. rim 0.182 D. omph.
0.046 Th. lip 0.004 m.
Fig. 86H

Intact. Profile like that of MM 99. The omphalos hemispherical, slightly stilted; a central compass prick on top. The single ridge around its base rather pointed in profile. The 15 petals spined, plain at both ends outside; inside their tips are plain, their bases set off by low raised arcs.

MM 101 Petaled omphalos bowl
B 872   Between screen MM 378
and table MM 388
H. 0.057–0.06 D. rim 0.199
D. omph. 0.046 Th. lip 0.004 m.
Pl. 70G

Intact. The rim slightly flared. Omphalos hemispherical with compass prick on top. The lower ends of the 15 base petals plain outside, their tips defined by an engraved zigzag with a second parallel to it on the rim above. On the inside, engraved zigzag defines the petal tips, engraved arcs their bases.

MM 102 Petaled omphalos bowl
B 873   South of table MM 380
H. 0.045–0.047 D. rim 0.195
D. omph. 0.049 Th. lip 0.003 m.

Intact. Shallow bowl with a lightly flared rim. Omphalos hemispherical, slightly stilted; compass prick on top. The 60 petal ends plain on the outside; inside their tips defined by a low relief zigzag, their bases by low raised arcs.

MM 103 Petaled omphalos bowl
B 846   Not on plan; under table
MM 382
H. 0.051–0.055 D. rim 0.185
D. omph. 0.042 Th. lip 0.0025 m.

Two holes eaten by corrosion. The rim flared. Hemispherical omphalos, a central compass prick on top. A single ridge, round in profile. Petal pattern normal, 14 petals multiplying to 56. The ends of the petals plain both inside and out. The lower part of one of the large petals is covered by a rectangular patch of thin bronze hammered to fit its profile; no doubt a repair. Since no pins or dowels are visible, the plate was probably attached by brazing or by soldering.

MM 104   **Petaled omphalos bowl**
         B 847   South of table MM 388
         H. 0.05–0.053   D. rim 0.164
             D. omph. 0.04   Th. lip 0.003 m.

Intact.[66] The rim slightly flared. Omphalos hemispherical. Like MM 103 with plain petal ends on the outside; inside their tips defined by an engraved zigzag, their bases by low raised arcs tangent at their ends.

MM 105   **Petaled omphalos bowl**
         B 857   On south edge of table
                 MM 383
         H. 0.04   D. rim 0.152   D. omph.
             0.037   Th. lip 0.003 m.
         Pl. 70H

Intact. Omphalos hemispherical; central compass prick on top and underneath. Incised outlines on bases of petals outside. Otherwise precisely like MM 104 in every detail.

MM 106   **Petaled omphalos bowl**
         B 865   Not on plan; under MM 70,
                 northeast corner table MM 388
         H. 0.04–0.042   D. rim 0.155
             D. omph. 0.039   Th. lip 0.003 m.

Intact. A central compass prick on top of hemispherical omphalos. Precisely like MM 104 in every detail.

MM 107   **Petaled omphalos bowl**
         B 871   Not on plan; in pile under
                 table MM 388
         H. 0.06   D. rim 0.202   D. omph.
             0.044   Th. lip 0.0035 m.

Intact. Hemispherical omphalos. Exactly like MM 104 in every detail; larger.

MM 108   **Petaled omphalos bowl**
         B 853   West of table MM 382
         H. 0.054   D. rim 0.184   D. omph.
             0.04   Th. lip 0.0035 m.
         Fig. 88

Intact. Omphalos somewhat more than hemispherical; a central compass prick on top. The petal tips plain outside, their 14 bases outlined by grooves; inside a low raised arc around the base of each petal, the tips above plain.

This bowl, uniquely, once had a handle. Three dowel holes were drilled through the rim in a triangular pattern, and a triangular sinking was filed

[66]For contents, see pp. 278, 284, app. II-A, Sample 22.

Figure 88. MM 108. Petaled omphalos bowl. Detail: scar of lost attachment at rim. Not to scale.

in the inner face of the rim; on the outside the thickened projection of the rim was also filed away (fig. 88). The end of the handle, which must have been either slotted or made from two pieces, was fitted into these sinkings and secured in place by dowels. The handle seems to have been a later addition to the bowl, but it was evidently lost before the vessel was offered in the tomb.

MM 109   **Petaled omphalos bowl**
         B 861   Southeast of table MM 383
         H. 0.055   D. rim 0.185   D. omph.
             0.041   Th. lip 0.004 m.
         Fig. 86I

Intact. Omphalos a little more than hemispherical somewhat squat in profile; a compass prick on top. The ends of the petals plain outside; inside low raised arcs define their 14 bases, low relief pointed arches (or zigzags of curved lines) set off their tips.

MM 110   **Petaled omphalos bowl**
         B 859   In front of screen MM 378
         H. 0.056–0.058   D. rim 0.209
             D. omph. 0.0425   Th. lip 0.003 m.

Intact. Omphalos a little more than hemispherical, a compass prick at the center of its top. The petal tips are plain on the outside, their 14 lower ends outlined by grooved arcs; inside, the tips defined by an engraved zigzag, the bases by low relief arcs.

MM 111   **Petaled omphalos bowl**
         B 870   Under west edge of the
                 table MM 388
         H. 0.0575–0.06   D. rim 0.213
             D. omph. 0.042   Th. lip 0.003 m.

Intact. Omphalos slightly more than hemispherical, with compass prick on top. Exactly like MM 110 in every detail.

MM 112   **Petaled omphalos bowl**
         B 869   North of cauldron MM 3
         H. 0.049–0.051   D. rim 0.172
             D. omph. 0.044   Th. lip 0.003 m.
         Pl. 70I

Some holes eaten by corrosion. The shallow omphalos less than a hemisphere; a compass prick on top. A large ridge rounded in profile around its base. Petal pattern normal, 13 multiplying to 52. Their extremities plain both inside and out.

MM 113   Petaled omphalos bowl
        B 851   South edge table MM 383
        H. 0.049–0.054   D. rim 0.176
            D. omph. 0.048   Th. lip 0.004 m.

Small holes eaten by corrosion. Omphalos hemispherical, with a compass prick on top. The ends of the petals plain outside; the tips plain inside, the 13 bases outlined by low arcs in relief.

MM 114   Petaled omphalos bowl
        B 839   Between tables MM 380
        and 383
        H. 0.048–0.052   D. rim 0.172
            D. omph. 0.044   Th. lip 0.004 m.

Spots of bronze disease; this bowl has not been cleaned.[67] Omphalos hemispherical. As far as can be seen, exactly like MM 113 in every detail.

MM 115   Petaled omphalos bowl
        B 856   South of table MM 383
        H. 0.05   D. rim 0.172   D. omph.
        0.042   Th. lip 0.004 m.
        Pl. 70J

Intact. Omphalos hemispherical, with compass prick on top. The same in every detail as MM 113.

MM 116   Petaled omphalos bowl
        B 848   South of table MM 388
        H. 0.047   D. rim 0.17   D. omph.
        0.037   Th. lip 0.0035 m.
        Fig. 87B

Intact. Omphalos hemispherical, with compass prick on top. The petals outside plain at the tips, outlined by grooved arcs at the 13 bases; on the inside engraved zigzag defines the tips, low relief arcs, the bases.

MM 117   Petaled omphalos bowl
        B 864   Inside fallen table MM 388
        H. 0.048–0.049   D. rim 0.168
            D. omph. 0.043   Th. lip 0.002 m.

Large holes eaten in the wall by corrosion. The rim plain and rounded at the edge. The omphalos hemispherical, a central compass prick on top. The petals spined. On the outside their 13 bases plain,

their tips outlined by an engraved zigzag; on the inside engraved arcs outline their bases, engraved zigzag their tips.

MM 118   Petaled omphalos bowl
        B 854   East of table MM 385
        H. 0.055–0.056   D. rim 0.166
            D. omph. 0.038   Th. lip 0.003 m.

One large and several small holes in the wall. The rim almost vertical. Omphalos a little more than hemispherical, with a compass prick on top. The 13 petals rounded in section at the bottom, semispined in the upper part. On the outside their tips defined by an engraved zigzag, their bases by grooved arcs; on the inside their tips defined by zigzag in low relief, their bases by arcs in low relief.

MM 119   Petaled omphalos bowl
        B 855   Not on plan; south of table
        MM 388, under MM 104
        H. 0.058–0.06   D. rim 0.176
            D. omph. 0.045   Th. lip 0.003 m.
        Fig. 134D

An inscription lightly scratched on the bottom between the omphalos and the petal bases; see p. 275 and fig. 134D.[68]

Small holes eaten by corrosion. Lip flat on top. Omphalos slightly less than hemispherical. The 13 petals rounded at their bases, semispined above. On the outside the lower ends of the petals plain, their tips defined by an engraved zigzag. Inside their lower ends defined by fine tangent engraved arcs, their tips plain.

MM 120   Petaled omphalos bowl
        B 867   South of screen MM 378
        H. 0.045–0.046   D. rim 0.155
            D. omph. 0.032   Th. lip 0.003 m.
        Fig. 89

Small holes in wall. The lip thickened and rounded on the outside. Omphalos hemispherical, stilted. A large ridge, rounded in profile, around a narrow plat-

Figure 89. MM 120. Petaled omphalos bowl. Detail: patch on rim. Not to scale.

---

[67]For composition of bronze, see p. 287, app. II-C, Sample 94, and p. 290, app. II-D, Sample 102.

[68]See also R. S. Young, *Hesperia* 38 (1969): 260, no. 30.

form below the omphalos. The petal pattern normal except that the petals of the lowest tier do not touch at the bottom, leaving the intermediate petals open at their lower ends and without lower points. Twelve petals multiplying to forty-eight. On the outside the petal tips plain, the bases outlined by grooved arcs. Inside the petal tips plain, the bases outlined by raised arcs.

On the rim a thin plate of bronze has been folded over the lip and against the inner and outer faces of the rim (fig. 89). There are no dowels or dowel holes; the plate was probably held in place by hammering tight against the wall faces. The purpose of this patch is not certain; perhaps to cover dowel holes for the attachment of a handle, like those on MM 108 (see p. 138, fig. 88).

MM 121   Petaled omphalos bowl
B 868   Behind table MM 388[69]
H. 0.049   D. rim 0.16   D. omph.
0.042   Th. lip 0.003 m.

Intact. The lip thickened and flat on top. Omphalos hemispherical, slightly spread toward the bottom; a compass prick on top. The rounded ridge surrounded by a raised lip and a deep groove outside. Petal pattern normal, 12 multiplying to 48. On the

outside the petal tips plain, their bases set off by grooved arcs. Inside the tips plain, the bases defined by low relief arcs.

MM 122   Petaled omphalos bowl
B 862   Not on plan, under table
MM 384
H. 0.054–0.057   D. rim 0.195
D. omph. 0.045   Th. lip 0.004 m.
Pl. 70K

Intact. The lip flat on top. The omphalos somewhat more than hemispherical; central compass pricks on top and underneath. Below it a narrow flat platform with stepped outer edge. The petal pattern normal, 17 petals multiplying to 68 tips. The tips plain on the outside, the bases defined by fine engraved arcs. Inside, tips and bases plain.

MM 123   Petaled omphalos bowl with variant petal pattern
B 845   Not on plan; east wall
between MM 86 and MM 56
H. 0.038   D. rim 0.157   D. omph.
0.025   Th. lip 0.003 m.
Figs. 86J, 90B; Pl. 70L

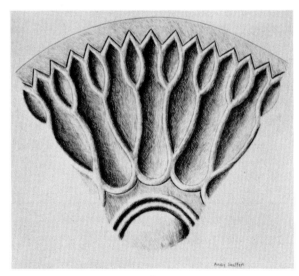

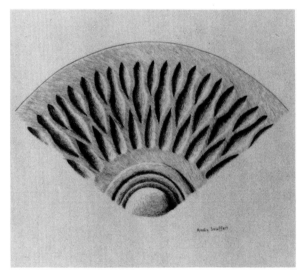

A

B

Figure 90. Petal patterns on omphalos bowls. A. Normal. B. Abnormal, MM 123.

[69]Some of the omphalos bowls, MM 121, 123, 128, 129, 137, 141, 144, 155, 157, and 162, all of which were found in the southeast corner near tables MM 386 and 388, contained dried foodlike material. See pp. 278 f., 284, app. II-A, Samples 23–32. Since it seems likely that, as Young claims, these were *stacked* on the tables and fell when

the tables collapsed, they could hardly have held food until some later time. It is possible that these, as well as the ring-handled bowls (see p. 125, n. 57) received their contents at the time the small cauldrons MM 4–13 dropped to the floor and perhaps flung abroad the already dried food they contained. [Ed.]

One large and several small holes eaten by corrosion at one side. The bowl shallow, flat at the bottom, flared at the rim. The omphalos, hemispherical and slightly stilted, shows a central compass prick on its upper and lower faces. Around it a narrow platform stepping down to a wider platform with a deep groove ring at its center; another shallow step to the flat floor. Around the floor 32 short petals in relief, their lower ends rounded, their upper ends pointed. Between the tips of these a second tier of 32 longer petals pointed at top and bottom, their upper points elongated to the rim. Between the tops of these a third tier of 32 small petals pointed at both ends, so that there are 64 points below the rim (fig. 90B). The rim thickened and flat on top. Inner and outer faces plain.

The petals of the middle tier are shaped like those of the normal bowls. The profile, fig. 86J, is taken through the upper and lower tiers, giving a double convex silhouette quite unlike that of the normal bowls. This, too, is the only specimen on which the number of petal bases is half, instead of a quarter, of the number of points below the rim.

GROOVED OMPHALOS BOWL
MM 124

MM 124   **Grooved omphalos bowl**
　　　　 B 834　　 Not on plan; south of table
　　　　　 MM 383, covered by MM 82, 83
　　　　 H. 0.067–0.07　 D. rim 0.184
　　　　　 D. omph. 0.038 m.
　　　　 Fig. 91A; Pl. 71A

Intact. The rim nearly vertical, with a sharp engraved groove near its lower edge outside. The omphalos is stilted hemispherical, resting on a low platform stepping down in three degrees to the floor. The omphalos and platform were added separately a little off-center. The wall, of thinner bronze than rim or omphalos, shows five wide shallow convex ribs on the inside (grooves on the outside), evenly spaced. The six interspaces are flat, showing only the curve of the bowl wall. Unless the bowl was cast, it is difficult to see how this grooving, which shows both inside and out, could have been made other than by hammering or filing/scraping. The latter is shown by the contrasting roughness of the ribs/grooves.[70]

OMPHALOS BOWLS RIBBED ON THE INSIDE, PLAIN OUTSIDE
MM 125–130

MM 125   **Ribbed omphalos bowl**
　　　　 B 833　　 South of table MM 388
　　　　 H. 0.054–0.056　 D. rim 0.166
　　　　　 D. omph. 0.041 m.
　　　　 Pl. 71B

Intact. Heavy fabric, the outside perfectly plain. Omphalos a trifle more than hemispherical. Around its base one large ridge, rounded in profile. On the wall inside, seven raised horizontal ribs, evenly spaced, all the same size, rounded in profile but smaller than the central ridge around the omphalos.

MM 126   **Ribbed omphalos bowl**
　　　　 B 829[71]　　 Southwest corner of table
　　　　　 MM 384
　　　　 H. 0.056　 D. rim 0.21　 D. omph.
　　　　　 0.054　 Th. rim 0.005 m.
　　　　 Pl. 71C

Intact. The outside perfectly plain. Omphalos a trifle more than hemispherical; beneath it a low narrow platform surrounded by three ridges triangular in section. On the wall six more horizontal ribs, evenly spaced and sharp in profile.

MM 127   **Ribbed omphalos bowl**
　　　　 B 835　　 South of table MM 383
　　　　 H. 0.065–0.068　 D. rim 0.20
　　　　　 D. omph. 0.042 m.
　　　　 Fig. 91B; Pl. 71D

Intact. Heavy fabric, the outside perfectly plain. Omphalos hemispherical, stilted, a compass prick on top. Around its base four ridges triangular in profile and increasing in size from the center outward. On the wall five low-spined horizontal ribs with wide, shallow concavities between them; the rim thickened.

MM 128   **Ribbed omphalos bowl**
　　　　 B 831　　 Not on plan; south wall,
　　　　　 under MM 68
　　　　 H. 0.047　 D. rim 0.156　 D. omph.
　　　　　 0.04 m.
　　　　 Fig. 91C; Pl. 71E

Small holes eaten by corrosion. Heavy fabric, thickened at the lip; the outside plain. Omphalos

---

[70]These observations were made in the Ankara Museum by Ann K. Knudsen. See her *Phryg. Met. and Pot.*, 170.

[71]See p. 287, app. II-C, Sample 95.

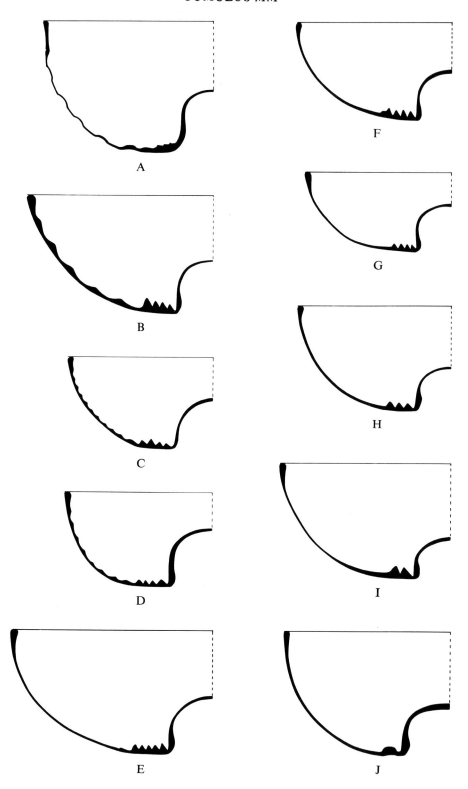

Figure 91. Profiles of omphalos bowls. A. MM 124. B. MM 127. C. MM 128. D. MM 129. E. MM 133. F. MM 138. G. MM 141. H. MM 145. I. MM 148. J. MM 156. 1:2.

hemispherical, slightly stilted; a compass prick on top, surrounded by an incised ring. Around the base of the omphalos four ridges triangular in section. On the wall ten low, pointed horizontal ribs with wider, concave flutes between them. The spacing of the ribs, wide at the floor, becomes increasingly closer toward the rim.

MM 129   Ribbed omphalos bowl
  B 832   Not on plan; south of table MM 388, under MM 104, 152
  H. 0.0485   D. rim 0.157   D. omph. 0.042 m.
  Fig. 91D; Pl. 71F

Intact. Heavy fabric, the outside perfectly plain. Omphalos hemispherical, slightly stilted. A compass prick on top. Around its base four ridges, triangular in section. On the wall seven low horizontal ribs, pointed, with shallow concave flutings between; an eighth rib at the base of the rim inside. Spacing of ribs approximately equal.

MM 130   Ribbed omphalos bowl
  B 830   North of cauldron MM 3
  H. 0.055–0.056   D. rim 0.203
  D. omph. 0.042   Th. lip 0.004 m.
  Fig. 87C; Pl. 71G

Intact. Heavy fabric. The outside perfectly plain. Omphalos hemispherical, slightly stilted; a compass prick on top. Five fine ridges triangular in section around its base. On the wall six horizontal ribs, evenly spaced, rounded in profile; between them slightly concave shallow flutes.

PLAIN OMPHALOS BOWLS
MM 131–167

MM 131   Plain omphalos bowl
  B 1078   North of table MM 385
  H. 0.062–0.065   D. rim 0.225
  D. omph. 0.056   Th. lip 0.0035 m.

Intact. Bowl shallow, its curve unbroken to rim. Thickened at the lip, which is flattened on top. The omphalos hemispherical, stilted. Around its base six fine ridges triangular in section, the outermost slightly larger than the others. The omphalos was lined with smears of wax, which were lost in cleaning.

MM 132   Plain omphalos bowl
  B 1076   North of cauldron MM 3
  H. 0.064–0.066   D. rim 0.23
  D. omph. 0.049   Th. lip 0.003 m.

Intact. Omphalos a little more than hemispherical; central compass pricks on top and underneath. Around its base five fine ridges triangular in profile; these rise from a low circular platform which steps down to the floor of the bowl, leaving a flat raised margin around the outermost ridge.

MM 133   Plain omphalos bowl
  B 1077   On table MM 384
  H. 0.067–0.069   D. rim 0.23
  D. omph. 0.0485   Th. lip 0.0035 m.
  Fig. 91E; Pl. 72A

Intact. Omphalos hemispherical, a central compass prick on top and underneath. Like MM 132 with a low platform spreading beyond the five surrounding ridges.

MM 134   Plain omphalos bowl
  B 1073   South of table MM 388 under MM 42
  H. 0.057   D. rim 0.176   D. omph. 0.049   Th. lip 0.004 m.

Intact, but not cleaned. Omphalos hemispherical; around it five ridges triangular in profile, the outermost somewhat larger and more rounded than the others. No platform.

MM 135   Plain omphalos bowl
  B 1074   East of table MM 380
  H. 0.054–0.056   D. rim 0.19
  D. omph. 0.047   Th. lip 0.0035 m.
  Fig. 87D

Intact, but not cleaned. Omphalos a little more than hemispherical, a compass prick on top. Five ridges as on MM 134.

MM 136   Plain omphalos bowl
  B 1075   Southeast corner, on table MM 386
  H. 0.047–0.049   D. rim 0.158
  D. omph. 0.033 m.
  Fig. 87E

Intact, but not cleaned. Small omphalos, stilted, hemispherical. Like MM 134, 135.

MM 137   Plain omphalos bowl
  B 1072   Northeast of table MM 385
  H. 0.047   D. rim 0.17   D. omph. 0.043   Th. lip 0.002 m.
  Pl. 72B

Intact. The rim flat on top. Omphalos a little more than hemispherical; central compass pricks on top and underneath. Around its base four fine ridges, triangular in profile; these rise from a low platform which steps down to the floor beyond the outermost ridge.

MM 138   **Plain omphalos bowl**
       B 1069   South of table MM 388
       H. 0.051–0.054   D. rim 0.177
         D. omph. 0.041   Th. lip 0.003 m.
       Fig. 91F

Intact. Omphalos a little more than hemispherical. Like MM 137: four ridges on platform.

MM 139   **Plain omphalos bowl**
       B 1071   Not on plan; southeast
         corner, under MM 386
       H. 0.06   D. rim 0.157   GD. 0.159
         D. omph. 0.0335   Th. lip 0.004 m.
       Fig. 92A; Pl. 72C

A large corrosion hole in the wall. The bowl deep, its wall curving continuously and slightly inward to the rim. Omphalos hemispherical and slightly spread at the base. Around it four fine ridges, triangular in profile, the outermost wider and shallower than the others.

The omphalos was closed at the bottom by a round flat disk of bronze 0.049 m. in diameter. This was held in place by a dowel run through it and through the top of the omphalos, its ends spread by hammering and polished. The upper end fine and barely visible in the top of the omphalos; the lower more coarse and less carefully polished. There are traces of cracking and discoloration (by fire?) in the bronze around the disk on the bottom, and these suggest that the plate was added as a repair, perhaps to stop leakage, after the bowl had suffered damage.

MM 140   **Plain omphalos bowl**
       B 1068   Between tables MM 380
         and 383
       H. 0.059–0.060   D. rim 0.195
         D. omph. 0.055   Th. lip 0.004 m.

Intact. The large omphalos hemispherical, with a compass prick on top. Four ridges triangular in profile; no platform.

MM 141   **Plain omphalos bowl**
       B 1070   West of table MM 388
       H. 0.041–0.045   D. rim 0.163
         D. omph. 0.041   Th. lip 0.003 m.
       Fig. 91G; Pl. 72D

Intact. Omphalos a little more than hemispherical; a compass prick on top. Four fine triangular ridges.

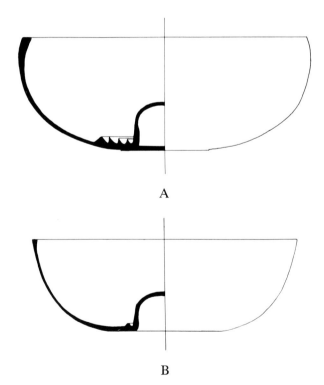

Figure 92. Profiles and views of omphalos bowls. A. MM 139. B. MM 157. 1:2.

MM 142   **Plain omphalos bowl**
           B 1067   On table MM 380
           H. 0.052–0.055   D. rim 0.20
           D. omph. 0.0415   Th. lip 0.003 m.

Corrosion holes in wall. Small omphalos, hemispherical, with compass prick on top. Four ridges triangular in profile, the outermost larger and more rounded than the others.

MM 143   **Plain omphalos bowl**
           B 1066   North of cauldron MM 3
           H. 0.065   D. rim 0.211   D. omph.
           0.046   Th. lip 0.003 m.

Intact. Omphalos hemispherical; central compass pricks on top and underneath. Three ridges, triangular in profile.

MM 144   **Plain omphalos bowl**
           B 1064   Partially under table
           MM 388
           H. 0.06   D. rim 0.192   D. omph.
           0.039   Th. lip 0.0025 m.

Intact. Omphalos a little more than hemispherical; compass prick on top. Three fine ridges, triangular.

MM 145   **Plain omphalos bowl**
           B 1062   North of tables MM 382
           and 384
           H. 0.054–0.057   D. rim 0.175
           D. omph. 0.04   Th. lip 0.003 m.
           Fig. 91H; Pl. 72E

Intact. Omphalos hemispherical, slightly spread at the base. A compass prick on top. Three fine triangular ridges.

MM 146   **Plain omphalos bowl**
           B 1063   South of table MM 383
           H. 0.059–0.062   D. rim 0.171
           D. omph. 0.0425   Th. lip 0.003 m.

Intact. Omphalos hemispherical, with central compass pricks on top and underneath. Of the three ridges around the omphalos, the outer ridge heavier than the other two.

MM 147   **Plain omphalos bowl**
           B 1065   South of table MM 384
           H. 0.062–0.065   D. rim 0.206
           D. omph. 0.038   Th. lip 0.0025 m.

Intact. Omphalos slightly more than hemispherical, a compass prick on top. Two fine ridges trian-

gular in profile, and an outer ridge lower and more spreading.

MM 148   **Plain omphalos bowl**
           B 1060   On table MM 380
           H. 0.058–0.062   D. rim 0.192
           D. omph. 0.039   Th. lip 0.003 m.
           Fig. 91I; Pl. 72F

Intact. Omphalos shallow hemispherical, slightly stilted; compass pricks on top and underneath. Two rather large, sharp, triangular ridges around the base.

MM 149   **Plain omphalos bowl**
           B 1061   Under fragment of table
           MM 381
           H. 0.08–0.083   D. rim 0.23
           D. omph. 0.048   Th. lip 0.005 m.

Surface pitted by corrosion. Omphalos a little more than hemispherical, a compass prick on top; around its base two rather large ridges rounded in profile.

MM 150   **Plain omphalos bowl**
           B 1054   On southeast corner of
           table MM 380
           H. 0.05–0.053   D. rim 0.179
           D. omph. 0.042   Th. lip 0.003 m.
           Pl. 72G

Intact. The rim slightly thickened but convex on top. Omphalos slightly more than hemispherical, a compass prick on top. A single heavy ridge, triangular in profile, close in toward the base of the omphalos.

MM 151   **Plain omphalos bowl**
           B 1048   West of table MM 388
           H. 0.058–0.061   D. rim 0.187
           D. omph. 0.049   Th. lip 0.003 m.

Intact. The omphalos tall and nearly flat on top; its straight side walls swell outward from the base. A compass prick on top. Around its base a single ridge triangular in profile.

MM 152   **Plain omphalos bowl**
           B 1044   South of table MM 388
           H. 0.039–0.041   D. rim 0.163
           D. omph. 0.04   Th. lip 0.003 m.

Intact. Bowl shallow. Omphalos a little more than hemispherical. A large ridge rounded in profile around its base.

MM 153 **Plain omphalos bowl**
B 1045   Southeast corner of table
MM 380
H. 0.063   D. rim 0.202   D. omph.
0.046   Th. lip 0.004 m.
Pl. 72H

Intact. Omphalos hemispherical. Exactly like MM 152, but larger.

MM 154 **Plain omphalos bowl**
B 1046   Not on plan, south of
table 388
H. 0.045   D. rim 0.159   D. omph.
0.039   Th. lip 0.002 m.

Intact. Omphalos hemispherical, a compass prick at center of underside. Similar to MM 152–153.

MM 155 **Plain omphalos bowl**
B 1047   Not on plan, with
fragments of table MM 386
H. 0.039   D. rim 0.142   D. omph.
0.035   Th. lip 0.003 m.

A large corrosion hole in the wall. Omphalos hemispherical, a prick on top. Like the foregoing.

MM 156 **Plain omphalos bowl**
B 1049   Wedged between tables
MM 382 and 384
H. 0.066–0.068   D. rim 0.188
D. omph. 0.05   Th. lip 0.003 m.
Fig. 91J, Pl. 72I

Intact. Omphalos hemispherical, a compass prick on top. Rounded ridge; on the underside a shallow, hollowed ring surrounds the omphalos beneath the ridge.

MM 157 **Plain omphalos bowl**
B 1050   Not on plan, under table
MM 386
H. 0.048   D. rim 0.145   D. omph.
0.036   Th. lip 0.0025 m.
Fig. 92B; Pl. 72J

Intact. Omphalos hemispherical, its base slightly spreading. A compass prick on top. Like MM 152–155.

MM 158 **Plain omphalos bowl**
B 1051   South wall, near table
MM 386
H. 0.044–0.05   D. rim 0.169–0.172
D. omph. 0.041   Th. lip 0.003 m.

Intact; not cleaned. Omphalos a little more than hemispherical. Similar to MM 157.

MM 159 **Plain omphalos bowl**
B 1052   Southeast corner, near
table MM 386
H. 0.044   D. rim 0.171   D. omph.
0.044   Th. lip 0.003 m.

Intact. Just like MM 158.

MM 160 **Plain omphalos bowl**
B 1053   Not on plan, southeast
corner, under MM 386
H. 0.05   D. rim 0.182   D. omph.
0.04   Th. lip 0.004 m.

Intact. Omphalos small, slightly more than hemispherical, with a compass prick on top.

MM 161 **Plain omphalos bowl**
B 1055   East wall, south of table
MM 388
H. 0.042–0.044   D. rim 0.168
D. omph. 0.041   Th. lip 0.0025 m.

Intact; not cleaned. Just like MM 160.

MM 162 **Plain omphalos bowl**
B 1056   Southeast corner, with
table MM 386
H. 0.046–0.048   D. rim 0.156
D. omph. 0.0415   Th. lip 0.0035 m.

Intact. Omphalos more than hemispherical, with compass prick on top. Just like the preceding.

MM 163 **Plain omphalos bowl**
B 1057   West of table MM 388
H. 0.068   D. rim 0.24   D. omph.
0.06   Th. lip 0.002 m.
Pl. 72K

Intact. Omphalos hemispherical, with a central compass prick on top.

MM 164 **Plain omphalos bowl**
B 1079   Not on plan, southeast
corner, under MM 68
H. 0.038   D. rim 0.155   D. omph.
0.037   Th. lip 0.0035 m.

Intact. Omphalos hemispherical, with central compass pricks on top and underneath.

MM 165 **Plain omphalos bowl**
B 1059 Southwest of table MM 388
H. 0.051–0.054 D. rim 0.159
D. omph. 0.036 Th. lip 0.0025 m.

Intact.[72] Omphalos a trifle more than hemispherical, a compass prick on top. The omphalos rises from a low, raised platform which projects beyond its base, stepping down at its outer edge to the floor of the bowl.

MM 166 **Plain omphalos bowl**
B 1058 In southeast corner.
H. 0.048–0.05 D. rim 0.171
D. omph. 0.044 Th. lip 0.003 m.
Pl. 73A

Intact.[73] Omphalos hemispherical, a compass prick on top. Precisely like MM 165 with low platform; bowl slightly larger.

MM 167 **Plain omphalos bowl**
B 838 Under west side of table MM 383
H. 0.07–0.075 D. rim 0.223
D. omph. 0.04 Th. lip 0.0025 m.
Pl. 73B

Intact; not cleaned. The omphalos tall and narrow, with three wide, shallow, horizontal grooves around it, which appear in reverse on the underside. The low platform wide, with four fine ridges, each defining a shallow step down toward the outer edge.

PLAIN DEEP BOWLS
MM 168, 169[74]

MM 168 **Plain deep bowl**
B 811 Southwest of table MM 388
H. 0.06 H. collar 0.016 D. rim 0.141 Th. lip 0.0035 m.
Fig. 93; Pl. 73C

Dented, otherwise intact. Bowl nearly hemispherical, with convex bottom. Heavy cast fabric, thick at

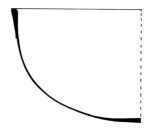

Figure 93. MM 168. Plain deep bowl. Profile. 1:2.

the base and thickened at the rim, which is collared on the outside, the lower edge of the collar standing up from the surface of the wall. The inside plain.[75]

MM 169 **Plain deep bowl**
B 812 Not on plan, southeast corner, under MM 89
H. 0.063 H. collar 0.015 D. rim 0.138 m.
Pl. 73D

Intact; not cleaned.[76] Exactly like MM 168; slightly deeper.

BRONZE AND LEATHER BELTS
MM 170–180
(See also pp. 236–240.)

Nine wide bands of leather[77] of multiple thickness, decorated at the surface by bronze studs arranged in varying patterns, were found at the foot of the west wall of the tomb. They had evidently fallen from one of the two rows of iron spikes (probably the lower row) driven into the west wall. Associated with these decorated leather plaques or bands was in each case a round disk of bronze hammered repoussé and decorated with studs of various sizes. Of these nine were found (MM 170–178). In four cases small oblong plaques of bronze decorated *à jour* and by studding were found within the folds of the leather after it was straightened. These must have

---

[72]For contents, see pp. 279, 284, app. II-A, Sample 33.

[73]For contents, see pp. 279, 284, app. II-A, Sample 34.

[74]Young, in his inventory of bronze vessels, in *AJA* 62 (1958): 150, mentions the 170th vessel—the plain bowl resting near the northwest corner post of the bed—as having been too corroded to save. It remained uncatalogued and is unnumbered on the floor plan, fig. 66. [Ed.]

[75]For contents, see pp. 279, 284, app. II-A, Sample 35.

[76]For analysis of contents, see pp. 279, 284, app. II-A, Sample 36; for corrosion product, p. 285, app. II-B, Sample 78; for composition of bronze, p. 290, app. II-D, Sample 103.

[77]For chemical analyses of leather from belts MM 170–176, see pp. 279–280, 284, app. II-A, Samples 37–43.

been decoration perhaps from the ends of the leather belts opposite the bronze disks. Five more similar oblong bronze plaques (MM 179*A–E*) were found on the floor by the west wall. They must originally have been associated with the other five pieces, but from their finding places there was no evidence on which to assign any of them to a specific belt.

There has been much discussion as to the identification of these objects. On the average their width is 0.19–0.20 m. The full length was nowhere completely preserved: the longest piece, MM 173, was about 0.80 m. in length. These dimensions seemed both too wide and too short for belts to be worn with any degree of comfort; nor was anything found that could be identified as a belt clasp. Nevertheless, fragments of a similar object (TumW 25, pp. 207–208) were found on the floor of the tomb under Tumulus W just at the waist of the skeleton, and these were interpreted as parts of a belt. Wide belts of the sort are sometimes shown in wear on reliefs from Hittite through Assyrian times. Perhaps the most apposite of these is the İvriz relief in which the god Tarhu and the king Urballa/Warpalawas are shown wearing wide belts evidently decorated with bronze studs.[78] The central disk "stomacher" at the front, included on all the Gordion examples, does not appear in the reliefs; it may have been a Phrygian addition.

The belts were hung up on the wall of the tomb with the disk ends (the strongest parts) at the top;[79] the lower ends could have gradually frayed away and fallen. MM 193 preserves four squares of studded decoration to a length of about 0.80 m., and with the ends, one covered by the disk "stomacher" and the other by an oblong decorated plaque of bronze, the original length must have been about 1 m., sufficient (in most cases) for a belt. A count of the loose and fallen studs found in association with each belt suggests a restoration of four squares of decoration in addition to the ends covered by bronze; probably the original length of these belts averaged about a meter. How the ends were fastened together we cannot say, as there is no evidence. See the restored drawings, fig. 94 A–G, which are based on

the details of MM 170.

A tenth bronze and leather belt (MM 180), of a type without a disk and resembling the end-plaques found with MM 170–178 (a majority of which are grouped as MM 179), was found lying across the ankles of the skeleton.

MM 170   Bronze and leather belt
  B 1128, 1137   West wall, central
  Figs. 94, 95A; Pl. 73E–G

Three separate pieces: *A*, the disk; *B*, the belt; *C*, the end-plaque.

A. Disk
  D. 0.21   D. central hole 0.06   GPW. disk incl.
  lugs 0.252   GPW. lugs 0.09   D. studs
  0.006 m.

A circular disk cut from a sheet of very thin bronze with projecting squared lugs at opposite sides. The lugs were bent back on themselves to serve as clamps to hold together the layers of backing material and to secure the disk to the belt (*B*). One lug remains bent, the other is partially flattened and shows its edge which is pierced by a row of holes for sewing.

The face of the disk decorated by concentric raised ridges, probably hammered up repoussé. Of these there is an outer group of four and an inner group of three, separated by a wide, flat ring. The flat inner and outer margins are decorated by added studs, hemispherical: 46 around the outer edge, 16 around the open circle at the center. A few of the studs are missing. Beneath the outer rim, and fastened to it by the pins of the studs that decorate it, were two semicircles of thin bronze which were folded lengthwise down the middle and bent back on themselves to make a clamplike frame which did not extend across the lugs (fig. 94C). These semicircles held together the edges of the three or so thicknesses of leather which were cut to fit the back of the disk. The last thickness of the backer was made from three scraps of leather sewn together (fig. 94E). Where the leather backing is exposed by the central round hole of the covering bronze disk, an extra layer of leather in the form of a square patch reinforced the back of the central "doily" (fig. 94D). The doily is itself decorated by a large central bronze stud surrounded by two rings of much smaller ones. All the space between was occupied by incredibly small bronze studs with heads only two, one, and even one-half of one millimeter in diameter. All the studs, in-

---

[78]Illustrated in E. Akurgal, *Kunst Anat.*, 61, fig. 38; *idem, Kunst Heth.*, pl. 140 and color plate XXIV.

[79]With MM 170 was preserved the point of an iron spike resting under the disk. [Ed.]

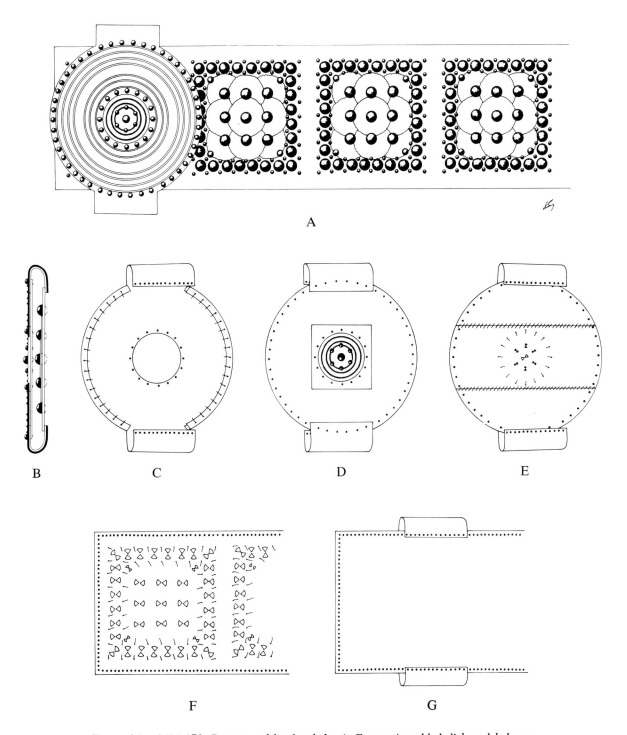

Figure 94. MM 170. Bronze and leather belt. A. Front of studded disk and belt, restored. B. Section taken through center of disk and showing belt in place behind.
Bronze is indicated in black. C. Back of bronze disk. D. Front of first leather backer,
with central portion of studded decoration at center, and first lining for disk lugs. E.
Back of last separate leather backer for disk, made from three smaller pieces. More
leather interlining is provided for lugs. F. Back of first leather backer of belt. G. Back
of final belt backer, fastened to back of bronze disk lug. 1:5.

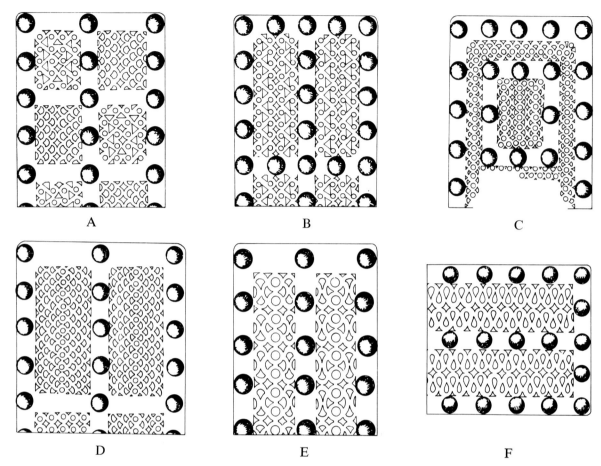

Figure 95. A–E: selection from the end-plaques on the wide leather belts, MM 170–179, to illustrate the variety of à jour *decoration. A. MM 170C. B. MM 171C. C. MM 177C. D. MM 179D. E. MM 179E. F. Plaque from the narrow belt. MM 180. 2:3.*

cluding the smallest ones, except for those with D. 0.0045, were made with prongs at either side, which were put through tiny slits in the leather and were then bent toward each other like the ends of a staple.[80] It seems incredible that such fine work could have been done without some sort of visual magnification.

B. Belt
   W. *ca.* 0.19 (the frayed and broken edges
      allowed only approximate measurement)
   L. *ca.* 0.76 (see below)   D. studs 0.015,
   0.0075, 0.0045 m.

The leather belt behind the bronze disk was cut squarely at both ends and was *ca.* 0.19 m. wide and

of unknown length. The layers of leather were held together by sewing along all the edges; the sewing holes are visible. All but the final layer (next to the body) were held together by the staple-like prongs of the decorative studs at the surface (fig. 94F). These were arranged in a repeating pattern of squares; the last of these was covered in part by the terminal disk. Each side of a square was formed of a row of eight of the largest studs framed by inner and outer rows of the smallest studs; in the center of each square a three-by-three arrangement of the largest studs.[81] Each of the nine interior studs was surrounded by a circular band or collar of the tiniest studs (as on the central doily) and those collars appear to overlap so that the one around the central stud is complete,

---

[80]L. Bellinger, *BullNBC* 46, pts. 1 and 2 (1962): 12.
[81]For an analysis of the corrosion product on the bronze

studs of *one* of the belts MM 170–180 (B-number unknown), see p. 285, app. II-B, Sample 79.

and those around the outer studs are shown as if partly covered by it. At the four inner corners of each square, one of the middle-sized studs. Straight strips of the fine doily technique were used as margins on all four outer edges of the belt and between the squares.

Each square-complex thus had 9 inner large studs and 28 more in the framing square; a total of 37. Enough loose and fallen studs were found on the floor of the tomb with and around the belt to give assurance that there had been altogether four squares of decoration. We thus reach a length of 0.76 m. (0.19 m. on a side of each square). An additional 0.06 m. to bed the bronze end-plaque would bring the total length to the requirements for a belt length; and an additional square of studded decoration, which is within the realm of possibility, would bring the total length to a little more than 1 m.

C. End-plaque
L. *ca.* 0.20   W. 0.058   D. studs 0.008 m.

Found beneath the belt. Broken into many pieces; somewhat tenuous joins made the measurement of length only approximate.

An oblong plaque of bronze, with flat border around the edges, a lengthwise band at center, and five flat cross-bands. The area is thus divided into two rows of six small squares. These are decorated *à jour* by a network of variously shaped small holes. The central and long-edge bands are decorated by studs, 13 in each row (fig. 95A).

MM 171   **Bronze and leather belt**
B 1135   West wall (*B* and *C* under
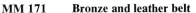   MM 18)
Figs. 95B, 96A; Pl. 73H, I

A. Disk
D. 0.19   D. central hole 0.038   W. across lugs
0.215   W. lugs 0.095   D. studs 0.008 m.

Rings of studs around inner and outer margins as on MM 170; between them six raised ridges, with a flat central ring between each set of three, as on MM 170; but here the central ring is decorated by studs rather than left plain. The extra layer of leather backing the central doily was round instead of square as in MM 170.

B. Belt
W. *ca.* 0.185   L. *ca.* 0.90+ m.

The studded squares framed by seven studs at each side; within, three rows of three, as on MM 170, with overlapping collars of tiny studs around them. Four squares preserved, plus the equivalent of a fifth covered by a disk.

C. End-plaque
L. 0.185   W. 0.057 m.

Similar to that of MM 170. Two rows of three oblongs decorated *à jour*; thirteen studs down long edges and center, but five at each end (instead of three). A fragment of leather, held in place by the

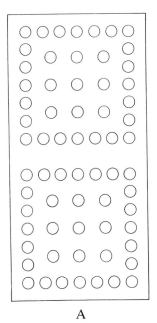
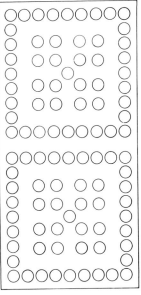

A   B

Figure 96. Pattern of arrangement of studs on bronze and leather belts. A. Found on MM 171, 173, 176. B. Found on MM 175 and 178.

stud pins, remained at the back; no doubt part of the belt end.

MM 172   **Bronze and leather belt**
          B 1130   Belt in southwest corner;
          disk not on plan
          Fig. 97; Pl. 73J

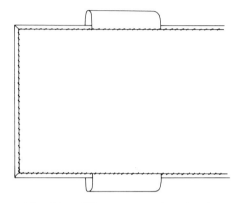

Figure 97.   MM 172. Bronze and leather belt. Alternative method of closing final leather backers of belt. 1:5.

A.   Disk
          D. 0.20   D. central hole 0.048   D. studs
          0.008 m.

Much broken and corroded; about one-third missing, and the lugs incomplete. Three rings of studs; three raised ridges between the inner pair, four between the outer. The doily within the central hole had disintegrated.

B.   Belt
          W. 0.19   L. 0.76⁺ m.

Four squares of studded decoration, plus a blank area of 0.04 by 0.19 m. Eight studs at each side of the squares, framing four rows of four.

C.   End-plaque

See MM 179*A–E.*

MM 173   **Bronze and leather belt**
          B 1129   West wall
          Fig. 96A; Pl. 73K

A.   Disk
          D. 0.195   D. central hole 0.056   D. studs
          0.0075   W. across lugs 0.215   W. lugs
          0.092 m.

Broken and mended, with gaps. Many studs lost.

Three rings of studs, with three raised ridges between each pair.

B.   Belt
          Full width not preserved.

Four studded squares, each framed by squares with seven studs to a side; within, three rows of three studs. Collaring of tiny studs, overlapping, around the large ones. At the end a plain area of leather 0.07 m. wide remains between the first studded square and the row of sewing holes which fastened the layers of leather together at the end. Once covered by an end-plaque?

C.   End-plaque

See MM 179*A–E.*

MM 174   **Bronze and leather belt**
          B 1136   West wall, central
          Pl. 74A

A.   Disk
          D. 0.195   D. central hole 0.082   W. across
          lugs 0.215   W. lugs 0.09 m.

Three rings of studs, three raised ridges between the outer and the central ones, two between the central and inner. On the doily framed by the central hole there was a central large stud surrounded by a ring of eight more; diameter of studs 0.011 m. In the space around these, the usual decoration in tiny studs.

B.   Belt

In very poor preservation, unmeasurable.
Framing squares of decoration probably had seven studs on a side.

C.   End-plaque

See MM 179*A–E.*

MM 175   **Bronze and leather belt**
          B 1140   West wall, belt not on plan
          Fig. 96B; Pl. 74B

A.   Disk
          D. 0.208   D. central hole 0.07   D. studs 0.007
          W. across lugs 0.22   W. lugs 0.095 m.

Three rings of studs, with three raised ridges between each pair. The doily that appears through the central hole was decorated by three rows of three studs arranged in a square; filling of tiny stud decoration around and between these.

B. Belt
  W. 0.20   GPL. 0.50 m.

Three studded squares preserved, or partly pre-served. Each framed by a square with nine studs on a side; within it four rows of four studs arranged in pairs, with a central stud in the wider space be-tween the two pairs. Space between and around filled by decoration of tiny studs.

C. End-plaque

See MM 179*A–E.*

MM 176   **Bronze and leather belt**
  B 1144   West wall, disk not on plan
  Fig. 96H; Pl. 74C

A. Disk
  D. 0.195   D. central hole 0.057   D. studs
  0.006, 0.008   W. across lugs 0.23 m.

Broken and mended from many pieces; gaps. Three rings of studs: those of the central one larger than the studs of the inner and outer rings. Two raised ridges between the inner pair of stud rings, three between the outer.

B. Belt
  W. 0.195 m.

The greater part of two squares preserved. Fram-ing squares seven studs on a side; within, three rows of three. There are evidences to suggest that the tiny stud background decoration had been made in one piece within the frame—that is, not a decoration of separate and overlapping collars around the separate studs within the square.

C. End-plaque

See MM 179*A–E.*

MM 177   **Bronze and leather belt**
  B 1139   West wall, south of bed
  Fig. 95C; Pl. 74D, F

A. Disk
  D. 0.20   D. central hole 0.056   W. across lugs
  0.225 m.

Inner and outer margin rings of studs. Next to each row of studs three sharp ridges. Inner area *à jour* in sections formed by eight spokes which are plain strips each holding three studs. Pattern of each section; a central line of contiguous circles with lateral scale design. A very large stud (D. 0.025 m.)

found beneath the central hole had probably deco-rated the middle of the doily.

B. Belt

The measurements, and the pattern of studded decoration were irrecoverable.

C. End-plaque

One corner was found. The margin at three sides decorated by studs; within the squarish area enclosed by these *à jour* decoration, with a studded reserved oblong around its center, three studs across top and bottom.

MM 178   **Bronze and leather belt**
  B 1141   West wall
  Fig. 96B; Pl. 74E, G

A. Disk
  D. 0.215   D. central hole 0.072   D. studs
  0.0075   W. across lugs 0.24 m.

Disk badly cracked; exactly like that of MM 175. The doily within the central hole also the same; nine studs in three rows.

B. Belt

Fragmentary; about two and a half studded squares preserved. Framing squares of seven studs on a side; within, four rows of four studs, perhaps with a central stud as on MM 175.

C. End-plaque
  L. *ca.* 0.17   W. 0.049 m.

Found curled around upon itself; measurements therefore approximate. *À jour* decoration, evidently square or oblong central panels framed by flat bands decorated by studs, as on MM 177.

END-PLAQUES OF BELTS
MM 179A–E

Five oblong bronze plaques decorated *à jour* and with studding were found on the floor at the west side of the tomb. These are so similar in proportions, form, and decoration to the end-plaques found with four of the belts that it seems unquestionable that they must be associated with the other five, but in no case did circumstances of finding make it possible to assign any particular plaque to a particular belt.

MM 179A–E   End-plaques of belts
Not on plan, scattered
along west wall
Pl. 74H–L

A.   B 1138
GPL. 0.112   W. 0.055 m.
Pl. 74H

A little more than half the plaque is preserved, including one end. The plaque had studs all around its edges, and a central lengthwise row down the middle. The cross-rows (one preserved) would have divided it into six equal panels, in two rows of three each, as above. The panels decorated *à jour.*

B.   B 1142
GPL. 0.11   W. 0.058 m.
Pl. 74I

Broken obliquely across; one end preserved. The same as *A* above.

C.   B 1143
GPL. 0.138   W. 0.059 m.
Pl. 74J

More than half the plaque preserved, mended. The same as *A* and *B* above.

D.   B 1145
L. 0.192   W. 0.056 m.
Fig. 95D; Pl. 74K

Complete; mended, but many studs missing. Studded decoration along the long edges and down the center; plain flat cross bands, unstudded, divide the area into six equal oblong panels. Five of these are decorated *à jour*; the sixth is cut out to a clean, open blank.

E.   B 1146
GPL. 0.135   W. 0.058 m.
Fig. 95E; Pl. 74L

Mended; one end preserved, and perhaps about half the length. The long edges and a lengthwise central strip studded; there is no evidence for cross bands dividing the area into panels. At each side of the central studded band, *à jour* decoration, apparently in long strips running the length of the plaque.

BRONZE BELT
MM 180

MM 180   Bronze belt
B 1127   On bed, feet of skeleton

Two plaques of bronze with *à jour* decoration, and a heavy bronze buckle. With these were found scraps of leather, surely from the backing, with the imprint of the *à jour* decoration of the bronze on one face. One of the plaques seems to preserve both its ends; hence the bronze part of the belt would seem to have been made up of separate pieces sewn end-to-end to the leather backing, rather than of continuous strips, as in the belts from Tumulus P (TumP 34–36). The buckle implies a double hook at the other end of the belt.[82]

A.   Plaque
L. 0.155   W. 0.056 m.
Fig. 95F; Pl. 74M

Studs across one end, and down center and long edges; *à jour* decoration in two strips between the three rows. No cross bands.

B.   Plaque
PL. 0.10   W. 0.054 m.
Pl. 74M

Studs across the preserved end; the other broken off. Like plaque *A.*

C.   Buckle
L. 0.044   W. 0.044 m.
Pl. 74M

Heavy bronze, probably cast in one piece. The buckle itself bolster-shaped, but grooved to each side of the center, which runs back to join the flat attachment plate, pierced by three holes, two round and one triangular.

JEWELRY: BEADS, PENDANTS, ETC.*
MM 181–184

The small bits of bronze jewelry were all found among the fibulae scattered over the floor at the head of the bed. They had evidently been wrapped in the same cloth and set on the table MM 387, falling and becoming scattered on its collapse. No doubt they had originally been strung together on thread (or wire, see MM 181C). Probably many of the tiny beads, too, had disappeared, either fallen down cracks in the floor or eaten by corrosion. We publish, therefore, samples that represent original totals that cannot be calculated.

---

[82]An alternate method of closure is discussed on p. 237. [Ed.]

*Catalogue and discussion of jewelry by Ellen L. Kohler.

MM 181   Beads
　　　　　B 1131 (*A, B*), 1989 (*C*)
　　　　　Northeast corner, scattered

A.　Nine beads
　　　D. 0.0075–0.010　W. 0.004–0.0095 m.
　　　Pl. 75A

Spherical to flattened spherical in shape, with holes, and evidently graduated in size. All decorated with fine hand-done milling in lines radiating from around the string holes; the larger beads show fine transverse grooving around the middle. From a necklace?

B.　Four beads
　　　D. 0.008–0.009　W. 0.004–0.006 m.
　　　Pl. 75B

Plain depressed-spherical beads with large string holes. These are undecorated, but appear to be graduated in size.

C.　Three beads on a fragment of bronze wire
　　　D. round beads 0.01　W. squared bead 0.013
　　　　GPL. wire 0.024　Present D. wire 0.002 m.
　　　Pl. 75C

All plain. Two spherical beads with a blocklike rectangular bead between them. Strung on wire.

MM 182   Six pendants
　　　　　B 1134　　Northeast corner, scattered
　　　　　L. 0.021　W. 0.0045　Th. 0.0025 m.
　　　　　Pl. 75D

Long thin clapper-shaped pendants with rectangular bottom ends and long, flat shafts, slightly tapered and decorated with fine striations on one face (the other face plain). At the upper ends, above varying types of hollow neckings, tangs pierced for stringing. Several of these pendants were found with their tangs lying inside the wider openings of the sockets MM 183.

MM 183   Seven sockets
　　　　　B 1133　　Northeast corner, scattered
　　　　　H. 0.008–0.0115　D. 0.009–0.012 m.
　　　　　Pl. 75E

Short, hollow cylindrical tubes, again apparently graduated in size. Their outer faces show varying moldings: bead, reel, hollow scotia, etc. All are domically capped at the upper end, which in some cases is finely milled. The holes which pierce them are tapered from a fine string hole at the top to a wider opening at the bottom. A string passed through the top may have held the ends of a number of pendants like MM 182 suspended through the other opening, but with their upper, pierced ends concealed in the lower part of the opening.

MM 184   Socketed cubes and spheres
　　　　　B 1132　　Northeast corner, scattered

Fifteen pieces with a round socket bored into one face to receive the end of a stem (pin? or shaft of pendant?).

A.　Seven approximately spherical pieces
　　　Ave. D. 0.0045 m.
　　　Pl. 75F

B.　Eight cubes or elongated cubes
　　　Cubes ave. dim. 0.004 on a side; elongated cubes
　　　　0.004 x 0.003 m.
　　　Pl. 75F

There is the strong possibility that these beads, sockets, and pendants (MM 181–183, possibly even 184), termed by R. S. Young "jewelry," were originally combined to form tassels for the double-pinned fibulae.[83]

---

[83] R. S. Young observed, p. 159, that upon all double-pinned fibulae a hole runs lengthwise through the half-spool above each spring, and also that a wire "bumper" is attached on the rear face of each lock-plate. Oscar Muscarella also observed the hole running behind the spool on MM 185 when it was traveling in the Art Treasures of Turkey Exhibition, and believed that the hole must have accommodated wire or yarn for perishable tassels on the analogy of a gold fibula (L69.12) which was lent anonymously to the Metropolitan Museum in New York and which is published in *JNES* 30 (1971): 49–63. Muscarella expressed an uneasiness concerning the presence of the metal tassel, unknown (heretofore) on the Gordion examples; he feared it might provide a reason to doubt the genuineness of the fibula he was publishing (*ibid.,* 49, n. 2).

However, his tassle (*ibid.,* pl. I, figs. 1–3) features a cylindrical molded keeper, striated over its domical end and closely resembling the seven "sockets," MM 183. The long pendants (MM 182) were found partially fitted into the blunt end-faces of those "sockets." The beads, MM 181*A* and *B*, were separated in the cataloguing into "plain" and "hand-milled" spherical beads and could have possibly been strung, two or three at a time in graduated groups, upon the cord or wire above the keepers. MM 181 through 183 were all found inside the rotting cloth which contained, among other things, all the double-pinned fibulae. The numbers in each category of bead, pendant, etc., are not now enough to fit out complete tassels for all the double-pinned fibulae, but as Young observed above, a few of these tiny elements could, as time passed, have disappeared completely or

FIBULAE
MM 185–356

The many bronze fibulae were found in two groups. The greater number, 145, lay scattered over the floor to the east of the head of the bed, together with the piece of linen cloth in which they had been wrapped.[84] This package had evidently been placed, at the time of the burial, on the wooden table (MM 387) which stood at the head of the bed; the collapse of the table had thrown the package to the floor, and scattered its contents. The fibulae of the second group were found on top of the bed, around the skeleton, and over the surface of the bed, where they had no doubt fastened the bed clothes. Twenty-seven of these are published here; ten more were so corroded that they disintegrated in cleaning. The fibulae of the first group were in general in very good condition; those of the second for the most part in very bad condition due no doubt to chemical reaction induced by the decomposition of the body on the bed. All the fibulae belong to one or another of five types of Blinkenberg's Group XII (Asia Minor).[85]

FIBULAE WITH DOUBLE PIN, SHIELDED MM 185–194

Among the fibulae found scattered over the floor at the head of the bed were ten very large specimens, each with a double pin shielded by a removable bronze plate, which served to hide the pins and in most cases to cover their sharp points. Apart from their double pins and shields and

their extraordinary size and weight, these fibulae conform to the normal Blinkenberg types: two (MM 185, 186) of Group XII,14; one (MM 187) of Group XII,13; and seven (MM 188–194) of Group XII,7. They were not, however, made in pairs as were the smaller fibulae. Every one of the ten was made with the catch at the same end, the left.[86] Variations in the shape and decoration of the shield plates, no two of which are exactly alike, also show that these fibulae were intended to be worn singly. Their unusually heavy weight must have tended to pull down the clothing that they fastened; again, for practical reasons, they must have been worn one at a time. If we follow the suggestion implied from the finding places of MM 343, 344 and MM 349, 350, we will infer that fibulae with the catch at the left were worn at the left side of the body, the catch outward; and therefore that all ten of the double-pinned fibulae were intended to be worn at the left. Their size and elaborate decoration suggest a garment of heavy material fastened only at the left, perhaps some sort of robe of state. A fibula of the double-pinned sort (actually Blinkenberg's Group XII,9 with studded decoration)[87] is shown in wear on the rock relief at İvriz,[88] where it fastens one corner of a heavy outer garment, passed over the right shoulder, to the vertically hanging edge at the left side near the left elbow. Although all the details of the fibula are not clear because of the surface wear on the rock, there can be little doubt that the carver has translated to stone relief a fibula of the shielded Phrygian type.

We may note that two specimens were found in a Phrygian tomb near Ankara.[89] They are not a

---

fallen between the floor boards of the tomb.

The tassles strung on yarn or twine, supporting bronze jewelry, if attached to a fibula which was worn bow-down in life, would have hung to the side of the bow, down from the half-spool which is situated on the (wearer's) right side of the pin. And if attached to both the hole in the spool and to the bumper on the lock-plate, as Young suggests on p. 159, it would, if able to run easily in and out, indeed serve the purpose he proposes of holding the lock-plate to the arc while the hook was not closed over the pin tube. (See fig. 99, p. 159, showing MM 185 with such a tassle made up of jewelry pieces MM 181–183). [Ed.]

[84]L. Bellinger, *BullNBC* 46, pts. 1 and 2 (1962): 13.

[85]Blinkenberg, *Fibules,* 204 ff. See above, p. 20, n. 27, and below, pp. 239–249.

[86]I.e., the wearer's left, the observer's right.

[87]The only extant example of a double-pinned fibula of Group XII,9 from Gordion has been added to the catalogue since the author's completion of this portion of his manuscript. See p. 160, n. 95 concerning MM 187A. [Ed.]

[88]E. Akurgal, *Phryg. Kunst,* pl. C,1–2; also *idem, Kunst Anat.,* 61, fig. 38.

[89]H. Zübeyr, *TTAED* (1933): 14–15, (Gazi Orman Çiftliği), nos. 9–10. Both photographs were taken from the back of the fibulae and so look reversed, with the catch at the wearer's right. Akurgal illustrates one (no. 10), from the front and after cleaning, in *Phryg. Kunst,* pl. 60b. There the catch would be at the wearer's left if the arc were hanging down.

pair; they differ in type (one is XII,14; one is XII,7) and both have the catch at the wearer's left. The Ankara grave would seem from its contents to be about contemporary with our Gordion group.

Twelve fibulae, then, of the fourteen known to me of the double-pinned type, are from Phrygia: ten from Gordion and two from Ankara. Two more must also have been of Phrygian origin, exported to east and to west. The first, another example of Group XII,7, was found in a house of the Phrygian period at Boğazköy;[90] the other at the Heraeum in Samos,[91] again of Group XII,7.

Each of these fibulae was put together from a multiplicity of separate parts. As noted above, the fibulae themselves are of the normal Asia Minor types which may be identified now as specifically Phrygian. Because the pins were double, a shield was needed, since only one pin (the one nearer the bow) could be put under the catch[92] and no fibula with a double catch is known.[93] The shield, a most ingenious mechanism, must therefore have been an invention of the Phrygian smiths.

Double-pinned fibulae without shields have been found in Tumuli W, P, and K-III at Gordion; we may assume with probability that these too once had shields, now lost. The mechanism and the elaborate construction of these Phrygian fibulae is described below in the catalogue (see especially MM 185).

MM 185 **Double-pinned fibula with shield**
B 900
H. 0.065 L. 0.067 W. shield 0.016 m.
Figs. 98A–C, 99; Pl. 76A–C

The fibula a normal XII,14 type, very large. A milled bead between two doubly grooved reels at the center of the arc; two milled beads alternating with doubly grooved reels at either end, and a sharply pointed ridge around the arc at each side between center and end moldings. The moldings are all slightly flattened or blunted at the back, and the milling and grooving are not carried around to the backs of the beads and reels. The fibula was cast; perhaps the mold was not entirely filled when the bronze was

poured. The arc, round in section, probably required a two-piece mold. The milling of the beads, which seems too fine to have been produced in the casting, was probably added later with a fine graver, and any traces of webs left by a two-piece mold were removed in the final filing and polishing. The catch, at the wearer's left, appears to have been cast in one with the arc. It is spurred (or "horned") and has a flat central spine with two deep grooves between spine and outward-turned edges. The catch rises directly from the last reel at the end of the bow; it must have been cast flat with the bow, its end turned over afterward to make the hook.

The spring was made separately and attached to the other end of the bow. Because the spring is shorter than the catch, it was necessary to insert an extra molding, or "button," between the spring and the end of the arc. This served not only to equalize the length of the legs of the bow but also to increase the tension on the spring when the pin was closed. In this case the extra molding or button was cast in one with the spring; in other examples it was cast sometimes together with the bow as an extra molding at one end, or it was a separate piece inserted between bow and spring. The spring is fastened to the fibula by a wire tenon made in one with it, which was run into a socket drilled to receive it at the end of the bow. Here the socket was drilled diagonally through the end of the bow from its end-face to the back face of the bow, where a small round hole appears in the lower bead and was prolonged upward in the back face by a groove that runs through the reel above and into the face of the top bead. Evidently the wire tenon was heated and thrust through the socket until its end came out of the hole at the back of the bow; then the end was bent upward and hammered into the groove, thus holding the spring securely in place. On other fibulae the attaching was done less crudely. At the back of MM 193 the oblong end of a wire tenon is visible in a small round hole in the back face of the first molding below the spring; and on MM 187 the ribbing of the large bead below the spring is interrupted by an irregular round blob of bronze at the back, the end of a wire tenon which has been cut and hammered flat. On MM 188 the attachment was made more neatly (if less securely): the end of the tenon was cut off flush to the back face of the central block molding near its upper edge, and so polished that even today it is barely visible.

---

[90]P. Neve in Bittel *et al.*, *Boğazköy* IV, 32 f. and pl. 20:6.

[91]U. Jantzen, *Samos* VIII, 48, no. B 1513, and pl. 44. Also illustrated by G. Kopcke, *AthMitt* 83 (1968): 294, no. 126, and pl. 127.

[92]All the fibulae from MM were found closed, with the

inner pin in the catch.

[93]The (restored) double catch of a fibula published by U. Jantzen in *Festschrift Matz*, 39–40 and pl. 8:1,2, is bent down at the top, not up (as is the lower catch) to cover the upper face of the upper pin.

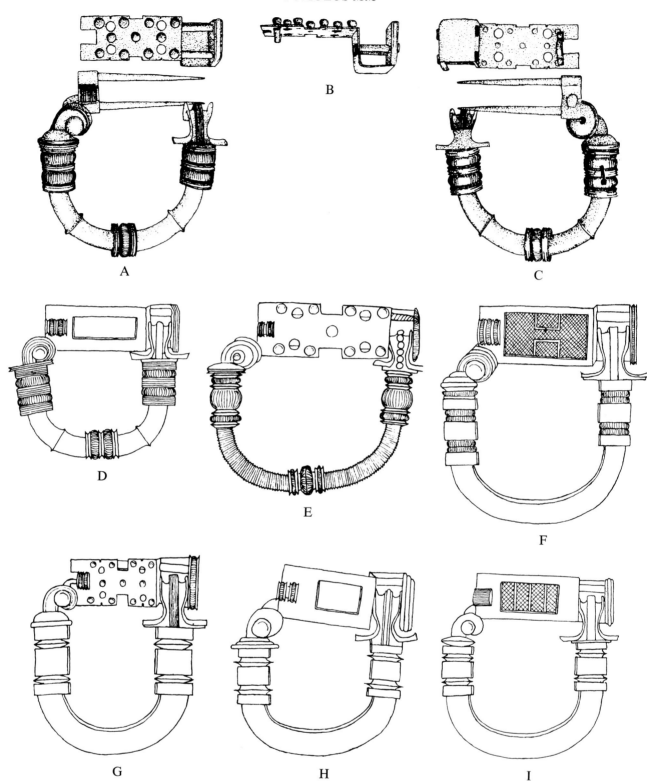

Figure 98. *Fibulae with double pin, shielded. A. MM 185, with shield detached, front. B. MM 185, detail of shield, side view. C. MM 185 with shield detached, back. D. MM 186. E. MM 187. F. MM 188. G. MM 189. H. MM 190. I. MM 191.   3:4.*

The same processes are to be noted in the decoration of the spring. A round-headed stud was used to mask the hole at the center of the spring, its head covering the opening at the front, the pin running through to the back where its end was bent over to hold it tightly in place. At the back of MM 190 the end of the pin has been cut and hammered to a rivet head which cannot be pulled through the hole of the spring.

The heavy spring, cast, makes three coils which are finely grooved along the edges. It ends in a flat oblong vertical plate from which the two pins project at a right angle, one above the other. The tenon, the button above it, the spring, the plate and the two pins seem to have been cast in one piece, the pins finished afterward by hammering and filing. The front of the pin-plate is decorated by an added half-bolster of bronze ribbed around its outer face and grooved beneath its upper and lower edges. The half-bolster is fastened to the face of the pin-plate by a dowel run through from the back; the end of this appears at the back halfway between the two pins, hammered to a flat rivet head.

The bolster serves to hold in place the inner end of the bronze shield-plate which conceals the pins. The end of the plate is notched to slide into the grooves beneath the upper and lower edges of the bolster, and in this way it is held firmly. The outer end of the shield is bent in three right angles to form a recess to fit around the catch of the fibula. This recess is crossed by two hollow tubes, one above the other, which contain the sharp points of the double pin. The tubes, separate pieces, are cylinders closed at one end. In some cases, as here, the closed ends of the cylinders appear in the outer face of the shield-end, carefully fitted and polished. In other cases where they do not appear, we must assume that they have been countersunk into shallow beds sunk into the inner face of the bronze. The open ends of the tubes invariably show in the other face of the bronze recess as rings carefully fitted and polished, into which the ends of the pins disappear. The shield was put in place by slipping one end over the points of the pins and sliding the other into the grooves under the bolster; the fibula was then closed by hooking the lower cylinder under the catch, which was thus enclosed within the recessed end of the shield. The same mechanism is common to all of the large double-pinned fibulae; but only MM 185 was still flexible enough when found to allow the removal of the shield for an examination in detail. All these fibulae were closed when found.

The shield-plate is notched at the center of its upper and lower edges as well as at its inner end, and a pair of round holes is added at either side of the central notches. Its decoration consists of eleven round studs in two rows of four and a central row of three. The pins of these studs, cut off and hammered flat, appear in the back face of the plate. The two pins at the inner end served also to secure to the back face an arc of bronze wire added across the end of the notch (fig. 98B, C). The ends of this wire, hammered flat, were fastened by the pins; the wire itself served as a bumper or stop against the face of the pin-plate between the roots of the pins. The base of the bolster (between the grooves into which the end of the shield slides) is pierced lengthwise by a round hole. It is possible that a fine string or thread, passed through this hole and once tied to the bumper-stop at the end of the shield, could have been used to prevent the shield from sliding backward when the fibula was open; when it was closed with the catch recessed in the niche, such sliding was impossible. All the shielded fibulae from MM have a lengthwise hole through the bottom of the bolster.[94]

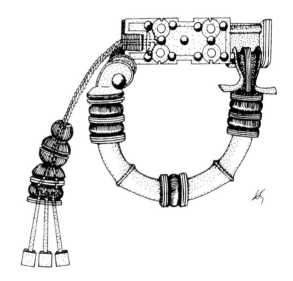

Figure 99. MM 185. Double-pinned fibula with shield. Complete with an imaginary tassle assembled from bits of bronze jewelry, MM 181–183. The tassle acted as a keeper for the shield while the pins were out of the hook. 3:4.

[94]See p. 155, n. 83. Note that the lack of a bolster on the double-pinned fibulae of Tumulus W and Tumulus P is probably responsible for the loss of the shields; or perhaps the idea of a shield had not yet been developed. [Ed.]

MM 186   **Double-pinned fibula with shield**
B 822
H. 0.057   L. 0.065   W. shield
0.016 m.
Fig. 98D; Pl. 76D

Fibula Group XII,14. Two milled beads alternate with three reels, grooved at their edges, at the center of the bow; the same at either end, but the reels much heavier with four grooves in their edges. The profiles of the larger moldings flattened or blunted at the back; the milling of the beads not carried around the back. The button below the spring is a separate piece held in place by the tenon of the spring. The faces of the spring grooved; its central hole masked by a stud with the pin bent at the back. On the bolster at the front two beads alternating with three double reels. An oblong opening through the face of the shield is backed by a thin sheet of bronze added behind; the sunken panel may once have held inlay. The tubes covering the pinpoints do not show in the outer end of the shield; probably they are countersunk. A step or bumper at the back at the inner end of the shield.

MM 187   **Double-pinned fibula with shield**
B 901
H. 0.069   L. 0.076   W. shield 0.02 m.
Fig. 98E; Pl. 76E

Fibula Group XII,13. The bow finely ribbed throughout its length. At the center a triple molding of central bead, milled and grooved down the middle, and triple reels at either side, the central reel rounded and milled, the outer ones sharp. The end moldings the same, except that the central bead is larger and ribbed. The heavy spring grooved on its front and back faces; a stud masks its central hole. The end of the wire tenon that fastens spring to bow is visible as a small blob of metal on the ribbing at the back face of the nearest large bead. The bolster decorated by two triple reels, the rounded central moldings milled. The central spine of the catch decorated by studs; the upper of the two cylinders which contain the pinpoints is spirally fluted. The shield notched at its upper and lower edges and pierced by four round holes; decoration of eleven studs (one

now missing) in rows of four, three, and four as on MM 185. A fine wire stop, or bumper, at the back of the inner end.

MM 187A[95]   **Double-pinned fibula with shield**
B 1987
H. 0.069   L. 0.066   W. shield
0.019 m.
Pl. 76F

Fibula Group XII,9. Lacks many studs, most of two pins, the studded pin through the spring, and the bolster. The bow rectangular in section with studded decoration. The end moldings: three blocks, the center one thicker than the others, separated by single very sharp reels.[96] Edges of the spring finely grooved. The shield has square cutouts in long sides, and four holes near edges. Large studs: six on bow, one each on central blocks. Small studs: three on each smaller block, four on spine of hook. Several on shield, but positions no longer clear.

MM 188   **Double-pinned fibula with shield**
B 820
H. 0.075   L. 0.076   W. shield 0.02 m.
Fig. 98F; Pl. 76G

Fibula Group XII,7. The bow nearly square in section. The end moldings—single large blocks separated from smaller blocks above and below by double reels—are carried around fully at the back. The button beside the spring is a separate piece held in place by the tenon of the spring. The faces of the spring grooved; its hole masked by a stud, the end of its pin turned over at the back. The bolster decorated by three rounded moldings, milled, alternated with four sharp reels. The catch was made separately and fastened by a wire tenon the end of which shows in the back face of the central block below. The ends of the tubes covering the pinpoints appear in the end face of the shield. The lower corner of the shield was cut away to fit the curved face of the spring.

The shield decorated by a sunken oblong panel; at its bottom a raised diaper pattern of circles, interrupted at the center of top and bottom by oblong notch areas defined by relief bands. A wire bumper at the inner end of the back.

---

[95]MM 187A and MM 310A–D (below) were catalogued in 1973, too late to be included by O. Muscarella in his studies. Young inadvertently omitted them from his catalogue of the fibulae from Tumulus MM. These have been inserted according to their Blinkenberg groups by the editor, but it must be noted that they have not been in-

cluded in any simple totals or statistics heretofore or here published. [Ed.]

[96]The basic bow of MM 187A most resembles that of MM 189 (Group XII,7), but the additional studs place it here.

MM 189 **Double-pinned fibula with shield**
B 821
H. 0.068 L. 0.065 W. shield
0.017 m.
Fig. 98G; Pl. 76H

Fibula Group XII,7. Similar to MM 188; the reels between the blocks single and sharp, projecting beyond the faces of the blocks. The back perfectly flat and the reels blunted; the fibula could have been cast in an open mold. The button made in one with the spring; the catch cast with the bow. The edges of the spring ribbed front and back; a stud with its pin, bent over behind, masks the hole. On the bolster two milled beads alternated with three sharp reels. The tubes containing the pinpoints were socketed; their ends do not appear in the end face of the shield. The upper and lower edges of the shield notched at the center, with smaller notches to either side; four round holes, one near each small notch. Decoration of eleven studs as on MM 185. Fine incised grooves outline the central notches and the round holes. A wire bumper at the back.

MM 190 **Double-pinned fibula with shield**
B 895
H. 0.066 L. 0.069 W. shield
0.017 m.
Fig. 98H; Pl. 76I

Fibula Group XII,7. Bow similar to that of MM 189, but the moldings are carried around to the back though the edges of the reels are slightly blunted. The button cast with the spring, the edges of the spring finely ribbed. A stud masks the hole, the end of its pin behind hammered to a flat rivet head. The catch cast in one with the bow. The bolster decorated at either end with a bead and reel, the beads finely milled. The ends of the tubes containing the pinpoints appear in the end face of the shield. The shield-plate was made from two pieces of bronze, layered; at the outer end these were turned down, and held in place by the tube cylinders. At the front an oblong opening through the outer plate shows the plain face of the inner; perhaps there was inlay. A wire bumper at the back.

MM 191 **Double-pinned fibula with shield**
B 896
H. 0.064 L. 0.066 W. shield
0.014 m.
Fig. 98I; Pl. 77A

Fibula Group XII,7. Similar to MM 189–190; the back flat. The button below the spring was cast in one with the bow. The edges of the spring finely ribbed; the pin of the central stud hammered flat at the back. The bolster a plain half-round, horizontally ribbed. The end of the tenon holding the spring in place shows in the back face of the upper reel. The catch cast with the bow. The shield without tubes to contain the pinpoints; its face decorated by an oblong sunken panel divided into four by raised vertical bands and ornamented by fine latticing in relief. A large bumper at the back.

MM 192 **Double-pinned fibula with shield**
B 897
H. 0.068 L. 0.065 W. shield
0.014 m.
Fig. 100A; Pl. 77B

Fibula Group XII,7. Bow and moldings like those of MM 190; the back flat. Both faces of the spring

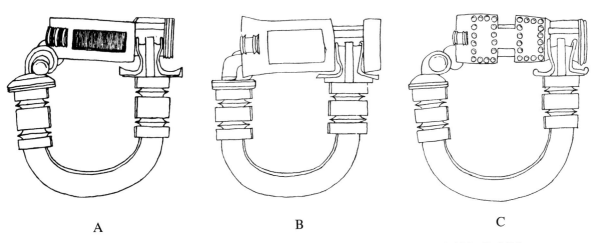

A   B   C

Figure 100. Fibulae with double pin, shielded. A. MM 192. B. MM 193. C. MM 194. 3:4.

grooved; the button below it finely ribbed. A stud masks the hole, the end of its pin bent over at the back. The bolster decorated by three double reels. Tubes contain the pinpoints. A plain sunken panel, oblong, in the face of the shield; a wire bumper at the back.

MM 193   **Double-pinned fibula with shield**
B 898
H. 0.062   L. 0.0635   W. shield
0.022 m.
Fig. 100B; Pl. 77C

Fibula Group XII,7. Bow and moldings like those of MM 190; the back flat. The edges of the spring raised front and back; no central stud. A round hole in the back face of the top block shows the end of the wire tenon, square in section, which fastens spring to bow. The bolster plain, with two raised ridges at each end. Tubes contain the pinpoints. The face of the shield decorated by a sunken panel, oblong and waffled at the bottom.

MM 194   **Double-pinned fibula with shield**
B 899
H. 0.065   L. 0.065   W. shield
0.017 m.
Fig. 100C; Pl. 77D

Fibula Group XII,7. Similar to MM 190–193; the reels between the end blocks squared instead of round. The back flat. The button cast in one with the spring. The pin of the masking stud turned over at the back. A hole near the top of the central block at the back shows the end of the tenon which holds the spring in place. The bolster decorated with pairs of fine raised ribs at the ends, a single one at the center. The catch cast in one with the bow. No tubes to contain the points of the pins. The shield notched at the center of its upper and lower edges, the rectangles at either side of the notches outlined by closely set small studs. Two of these hold the ends of the bumper wire at the back.

FIBULAE WITH SINGLE PIN
MM 195–356

GROUP XII,7
MM 195–234
Fig. 101A and Pl. 77E–L

All Group XII,7 fibulae were spilled over the floor by the head of the bed. Of the 40 specimens 20 have the catch at the right, 20 at the left. For this reason it seems likely that they were intended to be worn in pairs, and we have attempted to match them, using as criteria close correspondence in dimensions and small variations among the end moldings. Since, however, the fibulae were found in a confused scatter, the matching of pairs has in many cases been arbitrary, based solely on internal evidence.

The type of all these fibulae is the same: flat arc oblong in section, with two block moldings separated by single or double cushions at either end. The end moldings are not usually carried around to the back, which is sometimes flat, sometimes slightly raised at the ends, and which often shows traces of finishing with the file. In many cases, and especially before cleaning, the back surface was slightly concave with low convex rises along the edges, suggesting the surface tension of bronze poured into open molds. In addition to their numbers the reels or cushions between the end blocks show variations in their decoration by milling, grooving, and so on. The buttons at the top of the arc at the spring end also show variations in shape and detail; they were for the most part cast in one with the fibula bow. The pins with their springs were made separately with a wire tenon at the end, which was inserted into a hole drilled to receive it in the end of the bow. In almost every case the catch was cast in one with the bow. The catches are spurred at the top and spined on their outer faces, with outward-turned edges like those of the shielded fibulae. Variation among the catches occurs in the occasional decoration of the central spine. The catch, the only part of the fibula with a definite front and back face (spine at the front) and always cast in one with the bow, demonstrates that it was not possible to cast the two fibulae of a pair (right and left) in the same mold.

It does not seem necessary to illustrate every one of these very similar fibulae. The type is illustrated in the drawing, fig. 101A, made from MM 195. Distinctive variants are shown; the rest are listed by pairs in tabular form, so that comparative measurements may be seen at a glance; and comments on particular specimens are added.

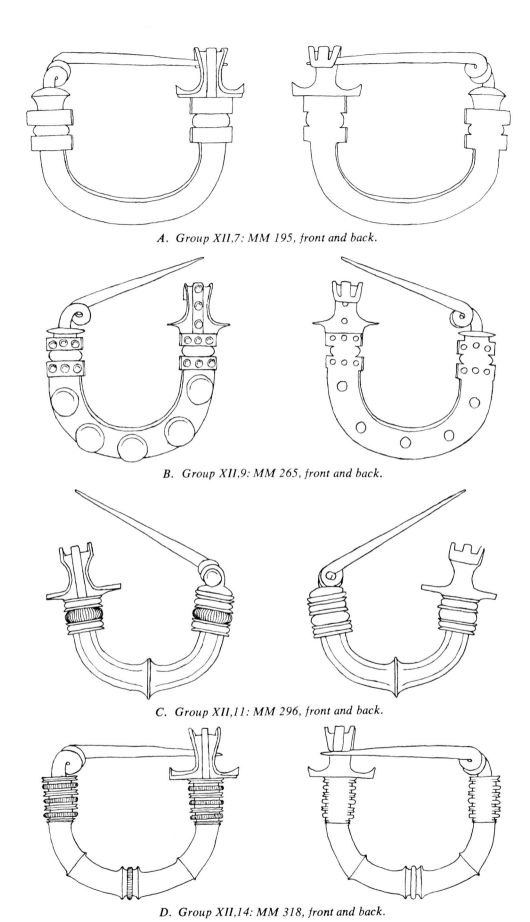

A. *Group XII,7: MM 195, front and back.*

B. *Group XII,9: MM 265, front and back.*

C. *Group XII,11: MM 296, front and back.*

D. *Group XII,14: MM 318, front and back.*

Figure 101. Fibulae of Group XII.   1:1.

		H.	L.	Comment
MM 195 (B 992)	L	0.047	0.059 m.	Single cushion, plain. Spring-button high, undecorated.
		Fig. 101A; Pl. 77E		
MM 196 (B 993)	R	0.048	0.057	
		Pl. 77F		
MM 197 (B 994)	L	0.0475	0.0575	The same as MM 195, 196
MM 198 (B 995)	R	0.05	0.0575	
MM 199 (B 996)	L	0.047	0.057	The same as MM 195, 196. MM 200 lacks half of its pin.
MM 200 (B 997)	R	0.0465	0.0575	
MM 201 (B 998)	L	0.042	0.0525	The faces of the springs grooved.
MM 202 (B 999)	R	0.044	0.053	
MM 203 (B 1000)	L	0.047	0.058	Faces of springs grooved. Spring-buttons striated. Pin of MM 204 missing.
MM 204 (B 1001)	R	0.05	0.055	
MM 205 (B 1003)	L	0.0475	0.058	Two cushions between blocks. Faces of springs grooved.
MM 206 (B 1002)	R	0.05	0.057	
MM 207 (B 1004)	L	0.05	0.0595	Two cushions between blocks. Spring-buttons striated.
		Pl. 77G		
MM 208 (B 1005)	R	0.046	0.061	
		Pl. 77H		
MM 209 (B 1006)	L	0.0475	0.055	The same.
MM 210 (B 1007)	R	0.048	0.054	
MM 211 (B 1008)	L	0.05	0.056	Cushions between blocks milled. Spring-buttons striated.
MM 212 (B 1009)	R	0.046	0.055	
MM 213 (B 1010)	L	0.048	0.057	Between blocks: single cushions, milled, between sharp disks (bead and reel).
		Pl. 77I		
MM 214 (B 1011)	R	0.048	0.057	
		Pl. 77J		
MM 215 (B 1012)	L	0.052	0.06	The same. Spring-buttons striated.
MM 216 (B 1013)	R	0.051	0.061	
MM 217 (B 1015)	L	0.052	0.0615	The same.
MM 218 (B 1014)	R	0.051	0.059	
MM 219 (B 1017)	L	0.049	0.059	The same. Spring-buttons plain.
MM 220 (B 1016)	R	0.044	0.059	
MM 221 (B 1019)	L	0.0485	0.055	The same. Springs grooved, buttons striated.
MM 222 (B 1018)	R	0.05	0.059	
MM 223 (B 1020)	L	0.039	0.053	The same. Spring-buttons short.
MM 224 (B 1021)	R	0.043	0.0525	
MM 225 (B 1023)	L	0.0435	0.0535	The same.
MM 226 (B 1024)[97]	R	0.044	0.053	
MM 227 (B 1026)	L	0.046	0.0515	The same. Spring and pin of MM 228 missing.
MM 228 (B 1025)	R	0.044	0.053	
MM 229 (B 1028)	L	0.044	0.055	The same. MM 229 lacks half the pin; MM 230 lacks spring and pin.
MM 230 (B 1027)	R	0.045	0.054	
MM 231 (B 1030)	L	0.035	0.0445	Single cushions, milled, between blocks. Catch of MM 231 missing.
MM 232 (B 1029)	R	0.034	0.047	
MM 233 (B 826)	L	0.05	0.06	Between blocks, milled cushions between reels. Springs grooved, buttons striated.
		Pl. 77K		
MM 234 (B 1022)	R	0.049	0.0565	
		Pl. 77L		

[97]See p. 287, app. II-C, Sample 96.

GROUP XII,9
MM 235–284
Fig. 101B; Pl. 78A–L

Like the XII,7 fibulae, the fifty specimens of XII,9 were found in the scatter on the floor at the head of the bed. The two groups are essentially the same in form, with flat arc ending in moldings of blocks separated by reels or cushions. Like the XII,7 fibulae, the XII,9, flat at the back, could have been cast in open molds. The catch was cast in one with the bow, the spring made separately and attached by a wire tenon. The XII,9 fibulae, however, are invariably smaller than the other type, and are elaborately decorated with round-headed studs of different sizes. Large studs decorate the arc, their pins cut off and hammered flat at the back, where they are clearly seen (fig. 101B). Of the 50 specimens found, 49 have five studs on the bow; one has only four. Smaller studs were used to decorate the blocks at the ends of the arc, usually three to the front face of each block though in some cases only two were used, set at the ends of the block with empty space between them. Again, the pins of these smaller studs run right through the thickness of the blocks, and their flattened ends appear at the back. Similar small studs—sometimes three, sometimes two— were used to decorate the central spine of the catch. These must have been attached before the

hook was turned round to make the catch, as the flattened ends of their pins appear in its inner face. It would seem certain that the holes into which the pins were set in the catch, in the block moldings, and in the bow, were drilled through the bronze after it had been cast. Fibulae ornamented in this way are vulnerable to damage, and many have now lost one or more of their studs. Where the heads have been lost, the holes through which their pins were set are visible, in some cases with the decapitated pins still in place and the area once covered by the stud head clearly defined on the surface of the bronze around the pin hole.

Of the 50 specimens 25 have the catch at the right and 25 at the left. Again it seems that they were intended for use in pairs. Since from the circumstances of finding there was no external evidence, the criteria used for the matching of pairs are, again, close similarity in the dimensions and in the small variations in the end moldings and the studding. The pairing is, therefore, arbitrary; in some cases it is fairly obvious and certain, in others less so. The last two fibulae, right and left as required, do not otherwise match: the single fibula with four studs on its arc (MM 284) is mated to the smallest of the five-stud fibulae, evidently a substitute in the tomb for the proper mate of MM 284 which had perhaps been lost or broken before burial.

FIBULAE WITH THREE STUDS ON EACH BLOCK: MM 235–266

		H.	L.	Comment
MM 235 (B 917)	L	0.0435	0.0485 m.	Rounded cushion between blocks. Mushroom-shaped spring-
MM 236 (B 915)	R	0.0435	0.049	button
MM 237 (B 927)	L	0.04	0.048	The same. Spring-buttons radially striated.
MM 238 (B 926)	R	0.04	0.0465	
MM 239 (B 913)	L	0.041	0.0475	The same. Spring-buttons plain.
MM 240 (B 921)	R	0.041	0.048	
MM 241 (B 924)	L	0.04	0.0475	The same. Cushions between blocks small. Two studs lost from
MM 242 (B 911)	R	0.039	0.048	MM 242
MM 243 (B 906)	L	0.042	0.054	The same. The cushions small.
		Pl. 78A		
MM 244 (B 823)	R	0.0425	0.054	
		Pl. 78B		
MM 245 (B 908)	L	0.042	0.052	Similar.
MM 246 (B 928)	R	0.0415	0.0515	
MM 247 (B 914)	L	0.042	0.051	Similar; small cushions. One stud lost from MM 247.
MM 248 (B 910)	R	0.043	0.053	
MM 249 (B 923)	L	0.042	0.049	Similar. Two large and eight small studs lost from MM 250.
MM 250 (B 929)	R	0.04	0.048	

FIBULAE WITH THREE STUDS ON EACH BLOCK: MM 235–266 cont.

		H.	L.	Comment
MM 251 (B 919)	L	0.042	0.052	A small additional cushion between block and spring-button.
		Pl. 78C		
MM 252 (B 903)	R	0.041	0.051	
		Pl. 78D		
MM 253 (B 918)	L	0.041	0.0485	Like MM 251, 252. Two large studs lost from MM 253 and one
MM 254 (B 920)[98]	R	0.041	0.048	from MM 254.
MM 255 (B 909)	L	0.042	0.051	The same; spring-buttons radially striated.
MM 256 (B 907)	R	0.041	0.052	
MM 257 (B 916)	L	0.042	0.053	Cushions between blocks and above spring-button horizontally
MM 258 (B 904)	R	0.043	0.053	grooved.
MM 259 (B 925)	L	0.036	0.042	Like MM 257, 258.
MM 260 (B 825)	R	0.0375	0.0415	
MM 261 (B 931)	L	0.041	0.051	Spring-buttons flat plates ground at the edge, cast in one with the
		Pl. 78E		bow.
MM 262 (B 930)	R	0.039	0.051	
		Pl. 78F		
MM 263 (B 905)	L	0.044	0.05	Not a pair; MM 263 with plain, MM 264 with cushioned spring-
MM 264 (B 912)	R	0.04	0.045	button.
MM 265 (B 902)	L	0.046	0.05	Not a pair: see MM 263, 264.
		Fig. 101B		
MM 266 (B 922)	R	0.042	0.047	

FIBULAE WITH TWO STUDS ON EACH BLOCK: MM 267–284

		H.	L.	Comment
MM 267 (B 941)	L	0.047	0.0565 m.	Narrow cushions; small cushion between spring-button and near-
		Pl. 78G		est block. Two studs on spine of catch.
MM 268 (B 942)	R	0.046	0.056	
		Pl. 78H		
MM 269 (B 940)	L	0.045	0.0525	Like MM 267, 268.
MM 270 (B 944)	R	0.046	0.0525	
MM 271 (B 936)	L	0.04	0.0485	Spring-buttons plain. Two studs on spine of catch.
MM 272 (B 938)	R	0.04	0.0485	
MM 273 (B 933)	L	0.045	0.056	Like MM 271, 272. Two large studs lost from MM 274.
MM 274 (B 934)	R	0.044	0.056	
MM 275 (B 946)	L	0.045	0.056	The same. Two large studs lost from MM 275 and one from MM
MM 276 (B 945)	R	0.0475	0.0575	276.
MM 277 (B 943)	L	0.045	0.056	The same.
MM 278 (B 939)	R	0.046	0.054	
MM 279 (B 935)	L	0.0395	0.046	The same. Three large studs lost from each.
MM 280 (B 937)	R	0.039	0.045	
MM 281 (B 947)	L	0.039	0.047	Not a pair. Triple reels between the blocks. Spring-button of MM
		Pl. 78I		281 flat, fitted to stilt above bow; a button between bow and
MM 282 (B 948)	R	0.044	0.05	spring on MM 282.
		Pl. 78J		
MM 283 (B 932)	L	0.038	0.045	Not a pair: MM 283 with five studs on the arc, three on each
		Pl. 78K		block, two on the catch-spine; MM 284 with four studs on arc
MM 284 (B 949)	R	0.034	0.038	and three on catch.
		Pl. 78L		

---

[98]See p. 287, app. II-C, Sample 97.

GROUP XII,11
MM 285–317
Fig. 101C and Pl. 79A–F

Thirty-three specimens, of which twenty-six came from the mass on the floor, seven more from the bed itself.

FIBULAE FROM THE FLOOR: MM 285–310

This group has 12 fibulae with catch at the wearer's left, 14 at the wearer's right. By the criteria of size and variant minor detail, 11 roughly matching pairs can be mated arbitrarily; a twelfth, though made up of right and left, is not otherwise matched; and two are left over, both with the catch at the right end.[99]

The curved arcs are usually fairly shallow, their faces faceted to eight flat planes, the faceting varies from sharp to blurred; it is not possible to determine whether it was made in the casting or by filing afterward. The group is set apart from other types by a swelling at the center of the bow. This swelling may vary from a rather shapeless thickened lump to a fine, sharp rib standing up from the surface all around the arc. The ends of the bow are invariably decorated by a triple molding—a central bead, usually milled, between three reels above and below, the middle one sometimes sharp, sometimes thickened and rounded. The flat spring-buttons, sometimes plain but more often radially striated, were cast in one with the bow or were separate pieces brazed to its end. The springs were held in place by wire tenons run into sockets drilled in the ends of the bows, see MM 308. The central hole of the spring is always masked by a round stud of which the pin is flattened and spread to a rivet head at the back. The type is a variant of Blinkenberg's XII,13, set apart by the central swelling (instead of moldings) and by the octagonal section of the arc, though the end moldings are usually the same. On the typology, see p. 246 f.

	H.	L.	Comment
MM 285 (B 954)	L 0.0385	0.046 m.	Little swelling of arc, sharp central rib. Section octagonal, spring-button plain.
	Pl. 79A		
MM 286 (B 955)	R 0.038	0.0425	
	Pl. 79B		
MM 287 (B 971)	L 0.042	0.049	Central rib a rounded swelling. End beads large, milled at front and sides, grooved down the middle. Spring-button striated.
	Pl. 79C		
MM 288 (B 970)	R 0.042	0.0505	
	Pl. 79D		
MM 289 (B 973)	L 0.042	0.048	The central hump vestigial. Spring-buttons radially striated.
MM 290 (B 972)	R 0.041	0.05	
MM 291 (B 959)	L 0.04	0.047	The octagonal arcs have little central swelling: instead a low central rib. End-beads milled all the way around the back; spring-buttons milled only at the edges.
MM 292 (B 828)	R 0.039	0.048	
MM 293 (B 963)	L 0.042	0.046	Arcs octagonal, central humps mere sharpened ridges. Milled end-beads large, with nearly straight faces. Spines of catches grooved. Spring-buttons radially striated. Stud through spring of MM 294 lost.
MM 294 (B 962)	R 0.043	0.049	
MM 295 (B 953)	L 0.041	0.05	Arcs octagonal, with sharp central rib. An extra cushion at the spring-button.
MM 296 (B 952)	R 0.0415	0.051	
	Fig. 101C		
MM 297 (B 957)	L 0.0425	0.051	Sharp central rib around the octagonal arcs. Spring-buttons plain.
MM 298 (B 956)	R 0.043	0.0485	

---

[99]See n. 100, p. 168, concerning the addition of four more examples. [Ed.]

FIBULAE FROM THE FLOOR: MM 285–310 cont.

	H.	*L.*	*Comment*
MM 299 (B 951)	L 0.039	0.049	Central ribs sharp; arcs octagonal. Spring-buttons plain.
MM 300 (B 950)	R 0.041	0.047	
MM 301 (B 965)	L 0.042	0.0455	The central humps rounded; arcs octagonal. Spring-buttons
MM 302 (B 964)	R 0.042	0.049	radially striated.
MM 303 (B 969)	L 0.041	0.046	Vestigial central ribs around octagonal arcs. Spines of catches
MM 304 (B 960)	R 0.041	0.0475	grooved. Spring-buttons radially striated.
MM 305 (B 968)	L 0.0415	0.045	Central swellings vestigial, rounded. Arcs octagonal. Spring-
MM 306 (B 966)	R 0.043	0.047	buttons striated.
MM 307 (B 827)	L 0.0415	0.05	Probably not a pair. Both have pointed central swelling, octag-
	Pl. 79E		onal arc, and grooved central spine of catch, but the end mold-
MM 308 (B 958)	R 0.0415	0.046	ings differ and the radially striated spring-buttons vary in shape.
	Pl. 79F		Spring and pin of MM 308 have come loose, showing the wire tenon which runs into the leg of the fibula. The spring-button remains in place, either cast with the bow or (more likely) brazed to it.
MM 309 (B 961)	R 0.042	0.05	Octagonal arc without central swelling; instead a very sharp rib. Spring-button flat, and plain.
MM 310 (B 967)	R 0.039	0.045	The central bulge a blunter rib. Spine of catch grooved. Spring-button striated.
MM 310A (B 1986)[100]	R 0.044	0.043	Moldings: bead between four sharp reels. Beads finely milled. Spine grooved four times. Spring-button striated.
MM 310B (B 1985)	L 0.038	0.0425	Pin missing. Bulge modified. Spring-button finely milled all the way around. Spine flat.
MM 310C (B 1984)	R 0.038	0.041	Pin missing. Bulge modified. Beads and spring-button finely milled all way around. Spine flat. Possibly a pair with MM 310B.
MM 310D (B 1983)	L 0.036	0.042	Pin missing. Bulge modified. Beads and spring-button finely milled in front only. Spine flat.

FIBULAE FROM THE BED: MM 311–317

Of the seven specimens of Group XII,11 four have the catch at the left, three at the right. Because of corrosion and loss of detail there can be no certainty about the matching of pairs.

	H.	*L.*	*Comment*
MM 311 (B 1121)	L 0.039	0.042 m.	Found near the right elbow. Pin missing, stud through spring.
MM 312 (B 1125)	R 0.04	0.046	Found in a mass of cloth near the right shoulder. Spring and pin missing. Both MM 311 and MM 312 have a rather sharp central rib, milled beads between triple reels at the ends. Arcs octagonal. Perhaps a pair.
MM 313 (B 1124)	R 0.04	0.045	Found in a mass of cloth near the right shoulder. Spring and pin missing.

[100]MM 310A–D, from the floor near the linen cloth, were inadvertently omitted by the author in his listing of fibulae of Group XII,11. These are inserted here in the approximate order of their size. These four (and MM 187A above) have not been included in either Muscarella's or Young's statistics. [Ed.]

FIBULAE FROM THE BED: MM 311–317 cont.

	H.	L.	Comment
MM 314 (B 1123)	L 0.039	0.047	Finding place same as for MM 313. Spring and pin missing. Both MM 312 and MM 313 have a swelling at the middle of the octagonal arc. Milled between triple reels at the ends. MM 313 much bent.
MM 315 (B 1126)	L 0.039	0.0435	Found in a clump of textile near the foot of the bed. Spring and pin missing.
MM 316 (B 1122)	R 0.041	0.0425	One of a group of three beside the left shoulder. Spring and pin missing. MM 315 and MM 316 have faceted arcs swelling at the center, and milled beads between triple reels at the ends.
MM 317 (B 1120)	L 0.03	0.04	Found in a crack between two bed planks, at shoulder level. Pin and catch missing, and most of spring. Sharp rib at center of faceted octagonal arc. Milled beads between triple reels at ends.

GROUP XII,14
MM 318–356
Fig. 101D and Pl. 79G

Nineteen examples of Group XII,14 were found on the floor by the bed; twenty more lay about the skeleton and scattered on top of the bed.

The first group may be matched to make eight reasonably certain pairs, with three (two right and a left) remaining over. Two of these could, of course, be worn together though they do not actually match; there remains a single "spare," MM 336.[101] The variations among the moldings at the center of the arc and at its ends are sufficiently numerous and divergent so that the (again arbitrary) matching of pairs is more sure with this fibula type than with those that have preceded.

For the fibulae found on the bed matching is more difficult. The preservation of these is far less good than that of the ones found on the floor. All the fibulae from the bed lack their pins, many lack their springs, and the catches of most are badly corroded. These fibulae were found well scattered over the whole area of the bed. There were thirty-two altogether, seven of Group XII,11 (MM 311–317 above) and five that disintegrated in cleaning, as well as the twenty of Group XII,14. Unfortunately neither the type nor the direction of the catch was recorded for the five specimens that disintegrated. A hopeful but dubious hypothesis might suggest that one of these was of Group XII,11, four Group XII,14; for the twenty speci-

mens of the latter type may be tentatively matched to make eight pairs, with four single fibulae (all with the catch at the wearer's left) remaining over.

The scattering of these over the surface of the bed must have been caused to some degree by its collapse. The planks of the bed lay, as found, on the floor of the tomb to which they had fallen when the supports at the ends gave way. This collapse no doubt shifted the positions of many of the things on top of the bed; several of the fibulae were found, in fact, in cracks between the planks. None of the fibulae could have traveled very far horizontally as a result of the collapse; yet a number were found at some distance from the skeleton. We must therefore assume that while some of these fibulae had been used to fasten the garments of the dead man, others may have been used to fasten the bedding. In any case 32 fibulae would have been an excessive number for fastening the grave clothes, even those of a king.

The importance of the finding places of these fibulae lies, of course, in the evidence they afford as to the nature of the garments worn, how they were fastened, and how the matched pairs were used. This evidence is, for the most part, ambiguous, and suggestions drawn from it can be tentative only. Fibulae at the shoulder are to be expected, since this is the natural place to fasten a garment open at the top. MM 349, found at the (proper) left shoulder, has its catch at the wearer's left and may be paired (on internal evidence as well) with MM 350 found at the right shoulder, its catch at the wearer's right. This suggests that the fibulae were worn in pairs, the catch outward at each side, the spring toward the center of the

[101]See p. 171, n. 106.

body.[102] The suggestion is strengthened by the evidence of another pair, MM 343–344, found at the elbow at either side, MM 344 at the right elbow with the catch at the wearer's right, MM 343 (found between the left arm and the ribs, slightly above the elbow level) with its catch to the left. One more, MM 355, was found between the (proper) left forearm and the femur of the skeleton, just above the level of the hand; a fibula again with the catch at the left and which may well have been originally at the left wrist. All the aforementioned fibulae taken together suggest a garment with sleeves fastened at shoulder, elbow, and wrist; and those from the (proper) left side consistently have the catch at the left, those from the right side with catch at the right. This does not hold for all the fibulae found on the bed, since many with the catch at the right were found on the left side of the bed, and vice versa.[103] The five fibulae discussed nevertheless seem to be the ones most intimately related to the body as it was found, and the ones that can reasonably be assigned to their places on the clothing worn by the dead man. On the plan (fig. 66) fifteen of the fibulae found on the bed are shown; the rest lay underneath or in masses of cloth, or in cracks between the planks, and were not visible when the plan was made.

The Group XII,14 fibulae were made with the arc round in section and with widely projecting sets of moldings at the top and at either end as well as raised ribs, sharp in profile, around the arc halfway between the moldings. In every case the moldings are carried around to the back, though on many specimens they are blunted or flattened behind. The intermediate ribs, which have less projection, are usually sharp and complete at the back. These fibulae must have been cast in closed molds, probably two-piece molds, which were not entirely filled by the molten bronze when it was poured—hence the complete arcs and ribs, the flat or blunted moldings. The springs with their pins were made separately and added as in the other types. Some of the fibulae from the bed, lacking their springs entirely, show a hole in the end of the bow into which a wire tenon fastening spring to bow had been set.

FIBULAE FROM THE FLOOR: MM 318–336

	H.	*L.*	*Comment*
MM 318 (B 974)	L 0.045	0.053 m.	Single milled cushion between reels at center; three, alternated
	Fig. 101D; Pl. 79G		with double reels, at the ends.
MM 319 (B 975)	R 0.043	0.052	
	Pl. 79H		
MM 320 (B 976)	L 0.047	0.054	Similar; all the reels double.
MM 321 (B 977)	R 0.046	0.053	
MM 322 (B 978)	L 0.048	0.06	Two milled cushions alternated with sharp reels at center; the
	Pl. 79I		same at the ends, the central reels doubled. Spines of the catches
MM 323 (B 979)	R 0.046	0.061	grooved.
	Pl. 79J		
MM 324 (B 980)	L 0.041	0.048	Similar to MM 322, 323.
MM 325 (B 824)[104]	R 0.042	0.052	
MM 326 (B 990)	L 0.043	0.056	Reels at center of arc, doubled. At the ends blocks between
	Pl. 79K		cushions, and reels above and below.
MM 327 (B 989)	R 0.044	0.0545	
	Pl. 79L		

---

[102]See above, n. 27, p. 20, where the author presents his reasons for publishing fibulae with pins at top, as they were worn in life. [Ed.]

[103]This is natural, as someone at the last probably walked around the bed and kept pinning his upper coverings to his lower coverings before the bed was let down into the corner of the tomb. [Ed.]

[104]See p. 290, app. II-D, Sample 104.

FIBULAE FROM THE FLOOR: MM 318–336 cont.

	H.	L.	Comment
MM 328 (B 982)	L 0.04	0.052	At center of arc a concave reel with a milled rib down the middle; double reels to either side. At the ends two cushions alternating with double reels.
MM 329 (B 983)	R 0.041	0.051	
MM 330 (B 985)	L 0.039	0.057	Similar to MM 328, 329. The end of the pin missing from MM 330.
MM 331 (B 984)	R 0.043	0.056	
MM 332 (B 986)	L 0.043	0.059	Two cushions alternating with three sharp reels at center of arc. At the spring end two cushions between reels, at the catch end three.
MM 333 (B 987)	R 0.045	0.054	
MM 334 (B 988)	L 0.04	0.044	Not a pair. MM 334 with milled cushion between double reels at center of arc, triple reels at the ends. MM 335 with double cushion and three reels at center of arc, double cushion and double reels at the ends.
MM 335 (B 981)[105]	R 0.034	0.0465	
MM 336[106] (B 991)	R 0.04	0.048	Plain single cushions between double reels at the center of arc, and between blocks at the ends.

FIBULAE FROM THE BED: MM 337–356

	H.	L.	Comment
MM 337 (B 1111)	L 0.03	0.038 m.	Both found to right of skeleton, in cracks between planks: MM 337 at shoulder level, MM 338 at pelvis. Both lack their pins, MM 338 its spring and part of its catch. Center and end moldings of milled cushion between double reels.
MM 338 (B 1113)	R 0.032	0.042	
MM 339 (B 1109)	L 0.035	0.042	Both found in area of right shoulder, in a mass of cloth. Like MM 337, 338. MM 339 lacks spring and pin, MM 340 pin and part of catch.
MM 340 (B 1108)	R 0.032	0.041	
MM 341 (B 1117)	L 0.03	0.036	Both found in area of left shoulder. Cushions between double reels at center of arc, pairs of cushions alternated with double reels at ends.
MM 342 (B 1116)	R 0.033	0.042	
MM 343 (B 1103)	L 0.035	0.044	MM 343 found just below left and shoulder between arm and ribs. MM 344 at right elbow. Milled cushion between double reels at center of arc, and at ends.
MM 344 (B 1106)	R 0.034	0.043	
MM 345 (B 1101)	L 0.0325	0.039	MM 345 found in area of left shoulder, MM 346 in a mass of cloth near right shoulder. Similar to MM 343, 344. Both lack their pins, MM 346 its spring.
MM 346 (B 1110)	R 0.033	0.045	
MM 347 (B 1119)	L 0.031	0.038	MM 347 found in a mass of cloth in area of left elbow, MM 348 in a mass of cloth by right elbow. At ends, milled cushions alternated with double reels. Both lack their pins, MM 347 its spring, MM 348 most of its catch.
MM 348 (B 1118)	R 0.03	0.036	
MM 349 (B 1104)	L 0.034	0.043	MM 349 found on left shoulder of skeleton, MM 350 on right. Similar to MM 343, 344; both lack their springs and pins.
MM 350 (B 1112)	R 0.033	0.041	
MM 351 (B 1107)	L 0.038	0.041	Both found to right of skeleton, MM 351 at elbow level. Single

---

[105]See p. 287, app. II-C, Sample 98.

[106]MM 336, which was mentioned as a "spare" on p. 169 above, is in the strictest sense a member of Group XII,13.

as it has no moldings in the quarters of the arc. MM 187 and MM 336, then, are the two examples of XII, 13 from Gordion mentioned in Muscarella, *Phryg. Fib. Gordion,* 22, and listed in his appendix A, p. 78. [Ed.]

FIBULAE FROM THE BED: MM 337–356 cont.

		H.	L.	Comment
MM 352 (B 1114)	R	0.033	0.042	cushions, milled, and double reels; the end cushions large. Both lack spring and pin.
MM 353 (B 1100)	L	0.03	0.04	Three found to left of skeleton, one (MM 356) to right. MM 355 by left wrist. All with single milled cushion between double reels, and catch at left. All lack their pins, MM 353 and MM 356 their springs, MM 353 and MM 354 much of their catches.
MM 354 (B 1102)	L	0.034	0.044	
MM 355 (B 1105)	L	0.033	0.043	
MM 356 (B 1115)	L	0.028	0.045	

IRON*

RING STANDS
MM 357–359
(See also pp. 250–251.)

The three ring stands that supported cauldrons MM 1–3 at the southwest corner of the chamber were the only objects of iron found in the tomb. Apparently the stands had suffered greatly from oxidation; beneath each on the floor was a deposit of rust, up to 0.10 m. deep, which had flaked and fallen from the iron rings. The preserved iron of the stands, much thinned by this flaking, is too oxidized to make the details of manufacture visible. However, at the points where the legs join the carrying rings, there is invariably a slight thickening or swelling of the iron. Either the rings were slotted at these points to receive the upper ends (or tenons on the upper ends) of the legs or they were set into notches formed in the upper ends of the legs. The carrying rings are iron rods of round section, bent into circles, with ends forge-welded together. The legs are straight iron rods of square, or flattened oblong section, tapering to a point or bent outward and then down into pronglike feet.

MM 357 **Tripod ring stand**
　ILS 258　　Not on plan; south wall,
　　under MM 3
　OD. ring 0.5075　Th. 0.02　GPH.
　　0.37 m.
　Pl. 80A

Supported the bronze cauldron with two sirens and two demons, MM 3 (GD. 0.782 m.). There is a gap of about 0.10 m. in the ring, where the iron has

---

*Section on iron by Joanna F. McClellan.

rusted away completely. Two feet are missing. The legs, once nearly square in section, are straight, turning out and then down at the bottom in a sharp double curve, to form feet.

MM 358 **Tripod ring stand**
　ILS 259　　Not on plan; south wall,
　　under MM 2
　OD. ring 0.45　Th. 0.02　GPH.
　　0.42 m.
　Pl. 80B

Supported the bronze cauldron with four sirens, MM 2 (GD. 0.775 m.). The ring and one leg are complete. One leg is broken off, the third lacks its foot. Legs about square in section, are straight but curved out and then down at the lower end to form feet.

The broken leg preserves at the top a trace of the tongue, which originally fit into a rectangular hole in the underside of the ring.

MM 359 **Tetrapod ring stand**
　ILS 260　　Not on plan; southwest
　　corner, under MM 1
　OD. ring 0.655　Th. 0.03　GPH.
　　0.388 m.
　Pl. 80C

Supported the cauldron with bulls' heads, MM 1 (GD. 0.708 m.). The ring is complete, and round in section. The legs, square in section, are straight. Their lower ends have corroded away to different lengths, and are now thinned to sharp points. There is no evidence that these legs once had turned-out feet like those of the tripods above.

A swelling at the joint of legs and ring may indicate the legs were notched at the top and welded to the outside of the ring.

POTTERY

The tomb contained only eighteen vessels of pottery: twelve dinoi (MM 360–371), and six small amphoras (MM 372–377). All had been packed into the three large bronze cauldrons at the southwest side of the tomb, six in each. MM 1 contained five dinoi and an amphora (MM 360–364 and MM 372); MM 2 the same (MM 365–369 and MM 373); and MM 3 two dinoi and four amphoras (MM 370–371 and MM 374–377). It seems to have been customary to pack small offerings into the cauldrons: in the other tombs included in this study, P and W, as also in K-III, the smaller offerings of pottery, bronze and wood had been so packed. The capacity of the MM cauldrons was great enough to contain more than six pottery vessels of moderate size; but the amphoras and dinoi had been carefully set in place with their open mouths upward, evidently because they had contained offerings, probably of food, at the time of burial (pl. 47A). The contents had largely dried up by the time the tomb was opened; yet, practically all the pottery vessels provided samples which upon analysis suggested food remains.[107] The contents had affected the fabric of the pottery; all the vessels were badly split and flaked on both inner and outer surfaces, and some of the amphoras were represented below shoulder level only by masses of thin flakes that could not be fitted together. The pottery placed in the tomb was of everyday utilitarian fabric intended simply as containers; in the case of MM a full bronze dinner service was evidently considered more suitable to the eminence of the dead man than pottery could have been. Nevertheless three of the pottery vessels are of interest to us because they bear graffiti scratched in their surfaces: one (MM 362) with a Phrygian alphabetic inscription, another (MM 370) with a conventional pattern. MM 361 has an **X** incised on its bottom.

All the vessels are black polished with a markedly lighter biscuit. The dinoi vary considerably in quality, from fine to coarse, whereas the small amphoras are of a homogeneous, medium fine fabric.

DINOI
MM 360–371

MM 360   **Dinos**
     P 1826   Inside MM 1
     H. 0.216   D. 0.232   D. rim 0.14 m.
     Pl. 80D

Mended; large body fragment missing; surface almost totally deteriorated and flaked away. Coarse, reddish brown clay, heavily micaceous; originally a fairly good black polish mottled with a lighter colored mica film. Body spherical on a flattened resting surface; wide, abbreviated neck; flaring rim flattened on top.

MM 361   **Dinos**
     P 1822   Inside MM 1
     H. 0.221   D. 0.244   D. rim 0.147 m.
     Pl. 80E

Mended; much of surface flaked off in huge chips. Fabric and body shape similar to MM 360. Everted rim, broad and flattened on top, above a very abbreviated neck. On bottom, a cursorily incised **X**.

MM 362   **Dinos**
     P 1825   Inside MM 1
     GPH. 0.16   GPD. 0.227   Est. D. rim
     0.155 m.
     Fig. 134E; Pls. 80F, 98B

A fragment: the lower part missing entirely, and about half of the upper. Interior surface wholly deteriorated. Fine, reddish brown clay; surface unevenly burnished to a medium luster. Apparently spherical body, like MM 360–361; short neck below a small, everted rim rounded on exterior and top. An incomplete graffito incised on the shoulder after firing.[108]

MM 363   **Dinos**
     P 1824   Inside MM 1
     PH. 0.20   D. 0.245   D. rim 0.18 m.

Fragmentary; entire lower part missing. Fabric like MM 360. Body either spherical or a plump ovoid; short neck below a broadly flaring rim.

---

[107]See app. II-A, pp. 280–281, 284, Samples 44–60.

[108]R. S. Young, *Hesperia* 38 (1969): 258 ff. and fig. 1, no. 31. Here see p. 274, fig. 134, and p. 275.

MM 364   **Dinos**
P 1823   Inside MM 1
Rest. H. 0.199   D. 0.219   D. rim
0.158 m.

Mended; bottom and lower body missing; much of surface flaked and chipped. Medium fine, micaceous clay, fired light reddish brown; slipped and burnished to a medium luster and fired with blushes of brown. Spherical or plump ovoid body; abbreviated neck; flaring rim rounded on top.

MM 365   **Dinos**
P 1804   Inside MM 2
H. 0.214   D. 0.233   D. rim 0.152 m.
Pl. 80G

Mended, with many large flakes missing from the surface and a hole near the base. Fabric like MM 364. Body like MM 360 and 361; short flared neck with groove at base; small everted rim, wide and flat on top.

MM 366   **Dinos**
P 1803   Inside MM 2
H. 0.206   D. 0.221   D. rim 0.139 m.
Pl. 80H

Mended; few gaps in body; wall inside almost entirely flaked away. Moderately coarse, micaceous clay, reddish brown; surface like MM 364. Spherical body; short, wide neck below a flaring rim rounded on its edge.

MM 367   **Dinos**
P 1802   Inside MM 2
H. 0.211   D. 0.248   D. rim 0.151 m.
Pl. 80I

Complete; much of surface split and flaked away. Coarse fabric, like MM 360. Plump ellipsoidal body resting on a low ring foot with convex outer profile; everted rim, broad and flattened on top, above a very abbreviated neck.

MM 368   **Dinos**
P 1805   Inside MM 2
H. 0.192   D. 0.234   D. rim 0.17
D. base 0.095 m.

Mended; small fragments missing; much of surface chipped and flaked. Fabric like MM 364. Ellipsoidal body resting on a disk base; everted rim, wide and shallowly convex on top, set directly upon shoulder with no real neck below.

MM 369   **Dinos**
P 1806   Inside MM 2
H. 0.19   D. 0.233   D. rim 0.132
D. base 0.099 m.

Mended; large fragments missing; surface badly flaked. Fine, (now) laminated clay fired light brown; slipped and well polished to a medium luster and fired a quite uniform black. Disk foot supporting a plump, spherical body; very short neck below a flaring rim, rounded on its edge.

MM 370   **Dinos**
P 1830   Inside MM 3
H. 0.184   D. 0.211   D. rim 0.135
D. base 0.085 m.
Fig. 102; Pl. 80J

Complete; surface split and flaked away over large areas. Fabric like MM 366. Low disk foot grooved at juncture with plump ellipsoidal body; short, wide neck below a small, everted rim flattened and outward-sloping on top. Low on the shoulder a doodle, scratched after the vessel was fired: herringbone or pine tree pattern, pointed downward; its upper part chipped away.

Figure 102.   MM 370. Dinos. Detail: incised doodle.

MM 371   **Dinos**
P 1828   Inside MM 3
PH. 0.185   D. 0.26   D. rim 0.155 m.

Fragmentary; only the rim and about one-third of the upper body remain. Fabric like MM 362. Body apparently spherical or a plump, depressed ovoid; short neck below a flaring rim like that of MM 364.

SMALL AMPHORAS
MM 372–377

MM 372   **Small amphora**
P 1827   Inside MM 1
H. 0.245   D. 0.222   D. rim 0.142
D. base 0.083 m.
Pl. 80K

Mended; large holes in the body; much of surface flaked and chipped away. Medium fine, micaceous clay, fired reddish brown; slipped and burnished to medium luster, and fired black with lighter blushes. Plump piriform body with flattened resting surface; narrow straight neck; wide everted rim, overhanging and flat on top. Handles oval in section, from shoulder to middle of neck.

MM 373   **Small amphora**
P 1807   Inside MM 2
H. 0.244   D. 0.225   D. rim 0.124 m.
Fig. 103A; Pl. 80L

Mended, with several gaps; surface flaked. Fabric like MM 372. Piriform body with flat bottom; neck and rim like preceding; double-round handles from mid to upper shoulder.

MM 374   **Small amphora**
P 1831   Inside MM 3
H. 0.25   D. 0.221   D. rim 0.124 m.
Fig. 103B; Pl. 80M

Complete but for large gap in rim; surface flaked away over about half of the body. Fabric like MM 372. Body and neck similar to MM 373; everted rim, ledged; oval neck handles like MM 372.

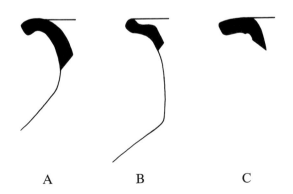

Figure 103. Rim profiles of small amphoras. A. MM 373. B. MM 374. C. MM 376. 1:2.

MM 375   **Small amphora**
P 1829   Inside MM 3
PH. 0.103   D. rim 0.132 m.

A fragment preserving neck, rim and both handles; surface badly flaked. Fabric like MM 372. Neck and rim also like MM 372; double-round handles to mid-neck.

MM 376   **Small amphora**
P 1832   Inside MM 3
PH. 0.132   D. rim 0.139 m.
Fig. 103C

A fragment like MM 375; rim with part of neck and both handles. In fabric and shape like MM 372; single rolled handles.

MM 377   **Small amphora**
P 1833   Inside MM 3
PH. *ca.* 0.16   D. 0.213   D. rim 0.123 m.

Fragmentary; upper part of body with neck, rim, and handles. Fabric like MM 372. Narrow neck; everted, ledged rim like MM 374; narrow strap handles from mid-shoulder to mid-neck.

SUMMARY OF POTTERY*

The ceramic offerings of Tumulus MM mark a considerable departure from the attitudes toward pottery that are observable in other wealthy tombs of the period. For all its opulence, the chamber yielded only two shapes, dinoi and small amphoras, neither of better than medium quality reduced fabric (cf. p. 173). Ordinarily such shapes as these (in the case of the amphoras, their larger counterparts) would have been relegated to the floor, but instead all had been carefully placed upright in the three cauldrons (MM 1–3). Sizable pottery containers, like those included in Tumuli W, K-III, P, and even more modest burials of the time, are here very noticeable by their absence. Perhaps even more conspicuous is the total omission of vessels of fine wares, either reduced or painted. In Tumuli W and K-III it was vessels of this category, rather than larger and coarser shapes, that saw special placement in the cauldrons, while in Tumulus P the obvious im-

_____

*Summary by G. Kenneth Sams.

portance attached to fine ceramics is emphasized by the large grouping against the south wall. The underlying reason for this exclusion was thought by R. S. Young to have stemmed from notions that bronze was a medium more suitable than clay to the rank of the deceased (p. 173); yet, the revised dating of the tomb introduces the possibility of other factors as well (*v. infra*, p. 270).

Together with these discrepancies in the use of pottery occur distinctions of a typological nature. As observed elsewhere (p. 254), the dinoi are of two varieties, ellipsoidal and spherical. The former (MM 367–368, 370) maintains associations with early Gordion through parallels in Tumuli K-III, P, and the destruction level, whereas the dominant spherical type (MM 360–363, 365–366, 369) is without parallel in either early settlement contexts or decidedly early tombs. Close associations are to be found in Tumuli S-2 and F, the latter of which can be no earlier than the third quarter of the seventh century. This is also the type of dinos encountered in Anıttepe I and II in Ankara, cremation burials that may well postdate the destruction of Gordion. The amphoras, too, by reason of their shape and small size, constitute an anomaly among early tomb groups, nor are good parallels forthcoming from the early city proper. Their closest counterparts at Gordion are from the post-destruction Tumuli S-1 and B, while Anıttepe II offers a very close parallel in both form and scale.

These patterns of association are difficult to reconcile with either the traditional, *ca.* 725–720 date for MM or its early placement in relation to Tumuli K-III and P. A far more plausible and likely environment for the pottery is that provided by K. DeVries's proposal for a lowered dating of the great tomb, a revision based on the development of certain bronze types (p. 198 f.). In a horizon that is subsequent to Tumuli K-III and P, and also roughly coeval with the city's destruction, the spherical dinoi and the small amphoras can assume an innovative, forward-looking aspect rather than one that is both anomalous and anachronistic. Likewise in such a context, the severely diminished range of shapes together with the absence of fine wares may, instead of merely reflecting views on the relative baseness of pottery, anticipate a spirit of ceramic frugality that is observable in certain post-destruction tombs. It is at the same time perhaps more than coincidental that MM and the two Anıttepe tumuli possess the same limited variety of shapes, as though there was some consensus as to what the absolute essentials of an abbreviated ceramic assemblage ought to be.[109] That these later tendencies are *previews* of future developments, rather than features fully absorbed into a late scheme, is suggested by certain other considerations. The placement of the vessels in cauldrons perpetuates an earlier practice that is seen in Tumuli W and K-III and may indicate a tomb that is innovative in its ceramic contents, yet mindful of immediate tradition. Perhaps more significant in this regard is the presence of ellipsoidal dinoi. Until this type can be proven to have survived considerably beyond the time of the destruction (p. 255), it would seem to caution against too low a dating and suggest instead that MM is still close to the date of P and the time of the early city's end.

WOOD

INLAID SCREENS
MM 378, 379

The two wooden screens stood near the center of the east side of the tomb, leaning against the east wall. Originally they had been set up, while still intact, side by side in front of the wall face; but they had been damaged by the falling of bronze vessels hung from nails in the wall face above them: their back supports and the horizontal openwork frames at the top had been knocked out by the falling bronzes, so that the screens

---

[109]Anıttepe I apparently contained only dinoi, while Anıttepe II included at least one small amphora. In both tombs some of the dinoi served as ash urns, whereas the others presumably held foodstuffs. At Gordion, Tumulus B emphasizes small amphoras and wide-mouthed jars related to spherical dinoi, thereby perpetuating the pattern seen in MM. Tumuli F and S-2 show a propensity for spherical dinoi. The evidence is admittedly equivocal in post-destruction Gordion. For example, Tumulus H, dated by its East Greek bird bowl to about the third quarter of the seventh century, contained bowls and jugs, mostly of fine wares, instead of dinoi and small amphoras.

proper were found not standing upright but slanted back with their tops resting against the face of the wall. One sidepiece of the frame behind MM 379 at its top remained in place, holding the right upper corner away from the wall and the screen nearly in its original vertical plane. The bronzes which had fallen from the wall, including the relatively heavy small cauldrons (MM 10–13) and the two situlae (MM 45–46), were found on the floor behind the screens, together with the fragments of the wooden back frames and supports of the screens themselves. The last could be accurately fitted together at the time of finding.

The screens were left in place for as long a time as possible in the hope of a slow and gradual drying. But after a month they began to grow a green mold, which had to be wiped off. They were placed in tanks of alcohol to dry the wood, then in a solution of paraffin dissolved in benzine. The operation was not altogether a success, probably because the wood (boxwood) was too dense to absorb the paraffin; in any case after they were removed from the solution, the various parts began to shrink and warp. The paraffin solution also darkened the light-colored background wood and greatly lessened the color contrast between background and inlay of dark wood. Consequently, the best pictures of the screens are the ones taken while they were in situ after the tomb was opened (see pl. 44A, B and color pl. II). Nevertheless these screens were well enough preserved that an accurate reconstruction on paper could be made, and they served as models to solve the mysteries of restoration for the two similar screens found in Tumuli P (TumP 151) and W (TumW 80).

Despite small variations between the two, discussed in the catalogue entries, it is evident that the two screens were planned and made as a pair.

MM 378   Screen
W 81   Against east wall
Figs. 104–106; Pls. 44A–C, 80N–P
A. Screen: H. 0.95   W. 0.80
      Th. 0.025 m.
      Depth inlay 0.003–0.004   W. inlay
         0.0025–0.003   Inlaid lozenges
         0.0025 square   D. rose window
         0.10   OD. rose window raised
         ring 0.168 m.
B. Frame: H. at rear 0.14   W. 0.80
      Depth 0.24 m.

Pl. 80N–P
C. Back support or leg: L. oblique
      slats 0.38   W. 0.042   Th.
      0.02 m.
Pl. 80P

The complete assemblage consists of three main elements: *A*, the screen proper, a flat oblong in one plane with overall inlaid decoration at the front; *B*, the horizontal, boxlike frame at the back of the screen at its top; and *C*, the back support or leg beneath the back piece of the frame. In combination these elements make a portable unit that can stand upright by itself without tipping forward or backward.

A.   The Screen (Fig. 104)

The screen proper, its face perfectly flat except for the raised ring around the "rose window" near its center and the inlaid curving legs below, was put together from eleven pieces of wood joined together by dowels set into slots cut in the thickness of the wood and secured in place by pegs run in from front or back. Since the inlaid designs of the screen face run right across the joints between its component pieces, we must assume that the whole was doweled together before the inlaying was done; in any case in some places the inlays run across the ends of the dowel pegs. On the analogy of the screen from Tumulus P (TumP 151), of which pieces were submitted for analysis, we assume that the light background wood is boxwood and the darker wood of the inlay, yew.

The components of the screen are two long framing pieces at the sides; between them in the upper part three crosspieces. The center below is occupied by the rose window with the half-circle decoration above and the squared volute decoration below, and an extra, separate piece to eke out the bottom. At either side of this central complex two vertical pieces (a broad and a narrow one) fill the spaces to the side frames. The pairs of pegs run in to hold in place the ends of the dowels that held all together were apparently inserted indifferently from the front or the back: thus the three pairs which attest three dowels fastening the upper part of the framing piece at the right to the ends of the three crosspieces beside it are not balanced by corresponding pegs at the other ends of the same dowels, for those were run in from the back and did not come through to the front. It is likely that the three cross boards at the top were doweled and pegged together before inlaying; likewise the side panels below, and the central panel with its lower addition. These four sections were then joined together, and finally framed by the long ver-

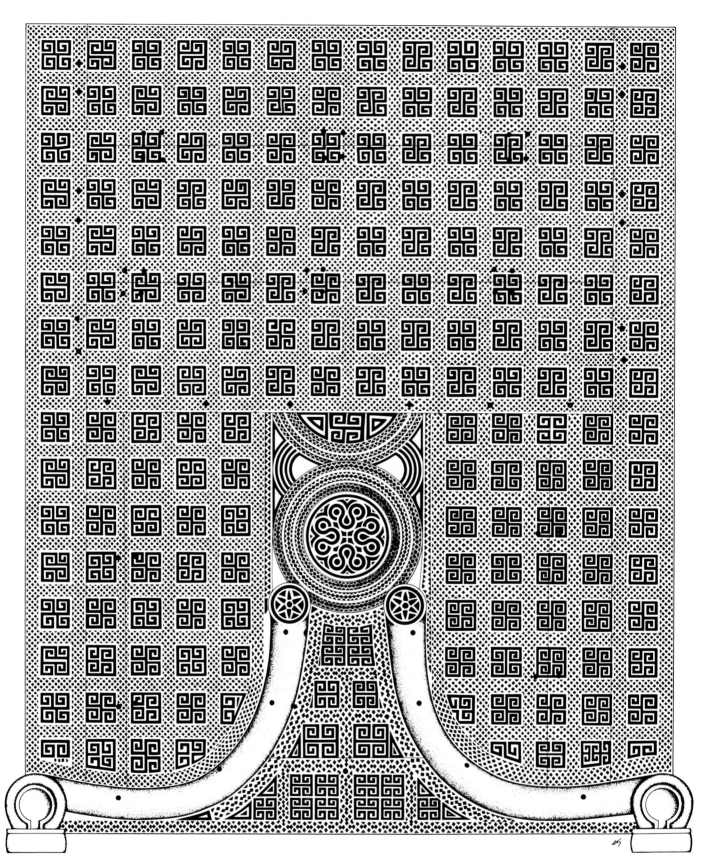

Figure 104. MM 378. Reconstruction of face of inlaid screen. Ca. 1:4.

178

tical strips to either side. The clearest indication that separate pieces were joined before inlaying is in the third swastika to the right of the rose window where the lower left vertical arm of the swastika may be seen to run across the end of a dowel-peg (pl. 44C). The inlays remain for the most part firmly in place, so that it is not possible to observe the methods of inlaying,[110] but it is probably safe to assume that they were the same as for the screen TumP 151: rows of borings by a fine awl, later joined by cutting away the wood between bores with a sharp knife. On TumP 151 there was no evidence for undercutting to hold the inlays in place; we must assume that they were probably held by glue. We must also assume that the whole surface was finished by sanding, probably after all the separate parts had been assembled into one.

The decoration of the upper part of the screen is of swastikas and other geometrical forms in squares, fourteen units across the width horizontally in eight vertical rows: 112 in all. The same decoration is applied at each side of the lower part, seven rows of five squares at each side with a shorter row of four at the bottom—altogether 190. The most common decoration is the swastika; but of that there are variations of color (the swastika proper of dark inlaid wood, or of the light background wood)[111] and of direction (running clockwise or counterclockwise). The long framing piece at the right side shows fifteen swastikas alternating (from the top) in dark and light color, and all running clockwise. At the bottom a half-square is filled by a squared volute in light background wood. In many places squares are made up by two squared volutes opposed or addorsed, set either horizontally or vertically; and there are other complicated variations of the swastika pattern. It may be said that no two of the nearly 200 inlaid squares are exactly alike, though the variations of actual pattern may be only six or eight in number.

All of the space around and between the square inlays is occupied by tiny inlaid lozenges and triangles, usually three rows of lozenges bordered to each side by a row of triangles to each strip. On occasion the lozenges are inlaid into the ends of the round pegs which hold the dowels in place.

At the center of the lower section is the rose window, defined by a raised circle of wood with beveled edges. Both the flat upper face and the two sloping faces of this ring are inlaid with lozenges and triangles of dark wood, leaving a double zigzag of the light background wood. Within it is a circle of four curved double hooks opening outward at top and bottom and to either side. Outside their openings and between their ends eight short brackets, each with a tiny triangle near its center, give a flowerlike effect; the whole design of the rose window seems to be a conventionalized floral pattern.[112]

The space above the ring is filled by about one third of an inlaid circle, pendent, with a border of zigzag patterns like those of the relief rings in the segment above, a squashed swastika in the middle, and quarter-circles filled with triangles at the corners. Bridging the space between the rose window and the upper pendent half-circle, on both sides, quadruple concentric arcs.

Below the rose window are panels of squared double volutes: at the top a cluster of four, turned alternately downward and upward; in the middle, four squared double volutes spaced apart and increasing in size in the lower row. The joined piece across the bottom shows the same patterns, smaller, but in two clusters of four, with triangles at the outer edges.

The curved legs below the rose window are of a soft, light-colored wood like those of the tables, and evidently like them bent by steaming or soaking to a curve. They terminate at the top in medallions inlaid with a star or rosette pattern, the edges of those

---

[110]At the bottom of inlay channels (when inlay is missing) are closely spaced round pocks: they are the ends (or bottoms) of holes made by a fine drill. These occur when the slot is with the grain as well as when it is across it.

No traces of glue are now visible, though there must have been such.

[111]The white wood, which was inlaid into, is part of the background. In the swastikas it is often cracked across with the grain, almost never across it.

The dark wood—the inlay—seems to have been cut across the grain, as the ringing can sometimes be seen in its surface. It is cracked in any direction. It comes in long and short pieces: straight, L, U, and even ⊓. No doubt pieces cut across the grain could be driven

more tightly into the inlay slots.

[112]The rose window was laid out with a compass: the prick of its stationary arm shows at the very center. Its diameter is 0.10 m.; that of the raised ring enclosing it 0.168 m. Probably its decoration, too, was laid out with a compass. At the bottom of the diamond-shaped insertions, where the inlay is missing, are larger round marks from the end of an awl. The smaller circles were probably laid out with a compass too, but the centers are now occupied by inlay. The lateral circles above the rose window were laid out with a compass; the central prick is visible at the left (not at the right). The upside-down arch above is also probably compass-drawn, but the center of the circle lay well over on the separate piece above, and the prick was probably obliterated by inlay.

overlap the beveled face of the ring around the rose window. The legs were cut at the back to flat faces and fastened by pairs of pegs at different levels to dowels or struts at the back, apparently anchored in sockets cut into the side faces of the wood at one or both sides. At their lower (and outer) extremities the legs end in scroll feet.

B. The Frame (Figs. 105, 106)

The sidepieces of the frame show eight square cut-out openings in two rows of four each; around and between these holes the surface is decorated by inlay in straight lines and rows of tiny lozenges. The horizontal strips which frame the cutouts above and below and divide them into two rows have tenons at their inner ends which fit into sockets in the back face of the screen near its top, so that the top faces of screen and of frame behind it are at the same level. The back strip of the frame is narrower than the side pieces and is decorated by a single row of 13 square cut-out openings; again it has end tenons to socket into the inner faces of the side frames. There is no inlaid decoration in the outer face of the back frame.

The long narrow area within this frame, an oblong approximately 0.75 m. long by 0.20 m. wide, was filled by an elaborately carved horizontal panel se-

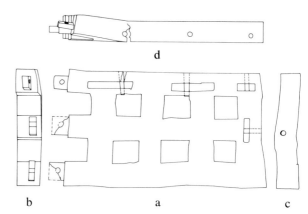

Figure 106. MM 378. Detail showing mortising and crosspegging: a, interior of side face of frame B; b, top view; c, front end; d, back end.

cured in place by three dowels along its long sides and one at each end. This panel, carved *à jour* from a single piece of soft light-colored wood, had suffered very badly in the fall of bronze vessels from above; they must have broken right through it, reducing it to small bits, which lay on the floor behind the screen. It was possible, however, to recover the main elements of the design (the "three burner stove") of the carving, though not in every detail. Two straight flat crossbars divided the length of the oblong into three panels, a longer central and two slightly shorter end ones. In each of these was a large ring open at the center. Lengthwise flat bars linking the edges of these rings again divide the three panels into six. Around the large rings these panels were filled by small rings carved *à jour*, tangent to each other and held together at their points of contact by flat raised bands, which resemble wrappings tying the rings together. Evidently the outer edges of the panels were filled by half-rings because there was not room for full ones. The two outer large rings were tangent to the two ends of the frame, and were supported by diagonal struts from the corners and by short struts to the long sides of the frame. In the shattered state of the wood it was not possible to tell whether or not the spaces between these struts had been filled by *à jour* decoration of small rings, and therefore these areas have been left open in the restored drawing.

C. The Back Support, or Leg (Fig. 105)

This was incompletely preserved. The lower end remained, square in section, and the scroll foot like those at the front of the screen; quite possibly the foot has been turned the wrong way in the restored drawing (fig. 105). A dowel hole at the center of the under-face of the back strip of the frame must have

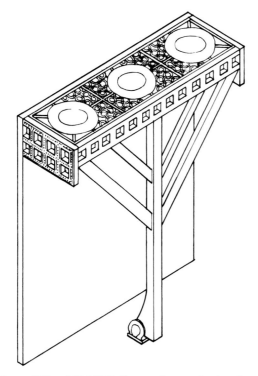

Figure 105. MM 378. Screen. Isometric drawing of the frame, B, and the leg, C.

held a tenon (or a dowel: a dowel is still in place in the corresponding socket of MM 379) at the top of the back leg. Two diagonal struts at either side of the leg gave support to the frame along its whole length, giving the supporting back member the form of a double Y. These struts are well preserved with tenons at both ends, to fit vertically into slots in the under-face of the back frame, and horizontally into slots in the side faces of the central leg. Thus support for the frame at the back was sturdy and well distributed along its length.

MM 379   **Screen**
        W 82   Against east wall, north of
            MM 378
        Dimensions the same as those of
            MM 378
        Fig. 107; Pl. 44A

As found, the right sidepiece of the back frame at the top was still in place, holding one corner of the screen away from the wall face and approximately in its original position.

MM 379 was put together in the same way as MM 378, the component elements being the same: *A*, screen proper, *B*, back frame, and *C*, upper supports and back leg. The inlaid decoration of the face was almost exactly the same except that variations in the pattern occur in the rose window, where the four separate recurved double hooks of MM 379 are linked together at their ends by crosspieces to form a continuous outline, and the brackets around the outer edge are replaced by shallow triangles, as shown in fig. 107. Above: pendent half-circle in flat design made of rings inlaid with lozenges; inner part of half-circle filled with vertical rows of lozenges and triangles.

Figure 107. MM 379. Screen. Detail: "rose window," front, and rendering of contour of face.

PLAIN TABLES WITH THREE LEGS
MM 380–387

Five plain tables, MM 380–384 on the plan, occupied the open space in the south half of the tomb, MM 380–382 in a row from north to south, MM 383 and MM 384 in a second row to the east of them. MM 386 had stood in the southeast corner, MM 385 between it and MM 384, the southernmost of the second row of the group. MM 387, at the head (east end) of the bed, had borne the mass of bronze fibulae, wrapped in a cloth, which was found scattered on the floor. The other tables had borne omphalos bowls and other bronze vessels, which had been placed upon them stacked one within the other. The weight of these stacks had in some cases been sufficient to make impressions in the surface of the rather soft wood of the table tops, and undoubtedly the weight of the bronzes had contributed to the collapse of the tables which bore them. These were all found lying on the floor, their tops partially covering the fallen legs, and the bronzes scattered but in several places preserving unmistakably the pattern of fallen stacks.

In most cases the table legs, of light, buff-colored wood, were well preserved though in some cases broken; the tops, of a soft, dark-brown wood (maple)[113] were usually less well preserved. The dark wood had become flaked and spongy and in many places had shredded. Consequently, in many cases the dimensions of the tables could be estimated only approximately because the legs had to some extent become warped. This was evident because when the flattened ends of the legs, beveled to rest flat on the floor, were held flat to the floor, the tenons at the tops of the legs were not at a true vertical. Nevertheless, all the tables were the same in form and construction and must have been very close to the same in their dimensions. An approximate mean of these suggests a height of about 0.50 m. and a length of about 0.75 m. by a width of about 0.60 m. for their tops. All the tables had three legs, which assured that they rested firmly on the floor without wobbling.

The table tops are oblong with rounded corners, each of one piece which is about 0.01 to 0.015 m. thick cut lengthwise to follow the grain of the wood. The upper faces are very slightly

---

[113]See p. 291, app. III-A, Sample 18.

dished, leaving a low, rounded rim all around the edge. Each shows three approximately square holes or cuttings arranged in a triangular pattern to receive the tenons at the tops of the three legs. The legs are downward-tapered and round in section, each with a plain decorative raised band at its upper end and a tenon, approximately square (about 0.03 by 0.03 m.) and about 0.06 m. long, at the center of its top. The lower ends of the legs curve rather sharply outward, the curve beginning well down toward floor level. Since the grain of the wood follows the curve of the legs, it seems evident that the wood was artificially bent by pressing, by soaking, or by steaming. At the bottom the rounded undersurface of each leg was cut away to leave a flat face to rest on the floor.

Legs and table tops were fastened together by the tenons at the tops of the legs, fitted in to the holes cut through the tops. But there was always an intervening member: a collar of soft wood about 0.05 m. thick and equal in diameter to the top of the leg. A central hole in this was fitted to the leg-tenon, and the collar fixed in place by a transverse peg through collar and tenon. The collar served to hold the tenon securely and to spread the bearing surface for the table top; no doubt it made a firm joint and prevented wobbling which might have damaged the table top where the end of the tenon passed through it. The length of the tenon must have equaled the thickness of collar plus the thickness of top, so that the end of the tenon was flush with the surface of the table. It is likely that the joint was reinforced in each case with glue.

Figure 108. Theoretical reconstruction of a three-legged table, based on MM 384.

MM 380   **Plain table with three legs**
W 79   Center floor
Est. H. *ca.* 0.515   L. top *ca.* 0.77
W. top *ca.* 0.61 m.
Pls. 48B, 49A, 81C

MM 381   **Plain table with three legs**
Not catalogued   Center of floor
H. not estimated   L. top 0.77
W. top ±0.63 m.
Pl. 49A, B

The top was broken and scattered. See MM 381*A* and 381*B* on floor plan.

MM 382   **Plain table with three legs**
Not catalogued   South of center
Est. H. *ca.* 0.50   L. top *ca.* 0.75
W. top ±0.61 m.
Pl. 49B

MM 383   **Plain table with three legs**
Not catalogued   East of center
H. not estimated   L. top *ca.* 0.72
W. top *ca.* 0.58 m.
Pl. 49A

MM 384   **Plain table with three legs**
W 78   Southeast of center
Est. H. *ca.* 0.45   L. top *ca.* 0.735
W. top *ca.* 0.60   Th. 0.017   Legs:
GD. (where tenon begins) 0.069
Tenon: L. 0.03   W. 0.027
H. 0.058 m.
Fig. 108; Pls. 49B, 81D, E

From the pieces recovered, as seen in pl. 81D, the table was restored in the laboratories of the Museum of Anatolian Civilizations in Ankara.

MM 385   **Plain table with three legs**
Not catalogued   Southeast corner
L. top 0.68   W. top 0.57(?) m.
Pl. 45A

MM 386   **Plain table with three legs**
Not catalogued   Deep southeast corner
L. top 0.82 m.   W. top unmeasurable
Pl. 45A

Crushed beneath a heap of bronzes.

MM 387   **Plain table with three legs**
Not catalogued   Northeast corner
L. top unmeasurable   W. top ±0.52 m.
Pl. 43A, B

Complete dimensions not preserved; one side was crushed beneath the fallen headboard of the bed.

INLAID TABLE WITH THREE LEGS
MM 388

The ninth table had stood by the east wall of the tomb, just to the south of the two screens (MM 378, 379). It, too, had collapsed; its appearance as found is shown in pl. 45A, B. It had kept its shape well enough so that the construction of this extraordinary piece of furniture was clear. All its pieces were found in a reasonably good state of preservation, and most of them could be fitted to their original places on the evidence of tenons fitting exactly to the holes made to receive them, or breaks across tenons fitting exactly to the stubs that remained in their sockets. The table was made of light-colored wood, probably boxwood, with lavish inlays of dark wood (yew?). Only the top was lost; it was of soft flaked dark wood, badly crushed and broken by the bronzes that overlay it.

MM 388   "Pagoda" table
            W 80   East wall
            Est. H. *ca.* 0.65   Frame: L. *ca.* 0.70
            W. *ca.* 0.58 m.
            Figs. 109–111; Pls. 45A, B, 82, 83

The *top,* of which only shreds and small fragments were preserved, must have overhung the frame at both sides and ends giving the table a somewhat larger bearing surface than the size of the frame implies. The table was supported by three legs. Tenons at the tops of these, stepped to smaller tenons near their tops, are about 0.06 m. in height; the lower and larger parts of these, 0.045 m. high, must have been collared by added pieces of wood as were those on the plain tables MM 380–387. The smaller top tenons, 0.015 m. long, suggest the thickness of the table top if they were fitted to holes cut through it as were the leg tenons of the plain tables. Their upper faces would then have been flush with the surface of the table, and the thickness of its top, 0.015 m. In addition, the top was supported all around near its edge by 18 struts and handles which rose above the frame and which are finished at their tops by shallow tenons, 0.006–0.007 m. high, which must have been socketed in cuttings in the under-face of the table top. Tenons on the lower ends of the struts and handles were in turn socketed in cuttings in the upper face of the frame. The frame was itself supported by a large prop beneath each corner. On one long side there were two direct props rising from just behind the feet at the ends of two of the legs, and on the other long side (which is taken to be the front),

where the third leg was set at the middle of the table length, by props rising from the two ends of a rocker mortised across the third leg just behind its foot.

The *legs* show dowel cuttings in their front faces just below the ornamental top moldings. These bedded dowels ran to the back faces of the frame; two of the dowels remained in place on the legs when the table was found (pl. 45A, B). Other cuttings farther down the legs toward their backs suggest stretchers running from leg to leg to give greater rigidity to the support of the table. These stretchers were not found (or were not recognized as such if they were preserved), but the cuttings in the legs must assure us that they once existed. If these are included, the whole rickety structure was put together from about 44 separate pieces all doweled (and let us hope also glued) together. Since the props which supported the corners of the frame ran vertically upward from sockets just behind the feet of the table, and the depth of the feet was about 0.10 m. (the projection of the handles about 0.085 m.), we may reasonably assume that the overhang of the table top was at least equal to the projection of the feet beyond the frame: this would give top dimensions at least 0.20 m. greater than those of the frame.

The *frame* was made up from four separate pieces of wood (fig. 110; pl. 82A), the front and back ones slightly longer than the sidepieces. The longer pieces (*A* front, *B* back) are tongued at both ends to fit into slots in the ends of the shorter (*C, D,* sides); the joints were secured by pegs above and below the tongues. Each side (*C, D*) consists of a number of square panels or medallions linked by two horizontal bars round in section, and each carved from a single piece of wood. The long sides (*A, B*) show five panels each about 0.06 m. square; the shorter sides (*C, D*) four panels with a half-panel to the edge of the slot for the corner joint at either end. The panels are all of the same size; the round bars that link them are shorter on the short sides of the frame than on the long. All the panels were elaborately inlaid with dark wood in various characteristic geometric patterns, including multiple lozenge panels, swastikas, and checkerboard. In the top face of each panel a cutting was made to secure the tenon of the lower end of a strut supporting the table top. Two of these, at opposite sides of the frame, were found still in place with the tenons at their lower ends embedded in their sockets (pl. 45B).

The *struts* (fig. 111A–G; pl. 82B–E), bedded in the upper faces of the panels of the frame, supported the table top close to its outer edge all around. They are approximately 0.20 m. high overall, through the tenons at top and bottom. The upper tenons, 0.006–0.007 m. long (as compared with the 0.015 m.

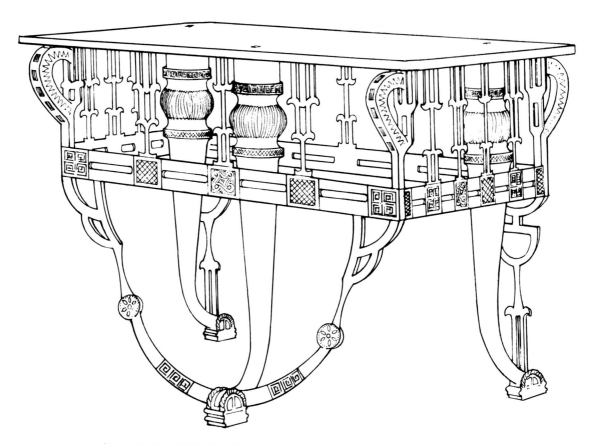

Figure 109.   MM 388. Theoretical reconstruction of inlaid "pagoda" table.

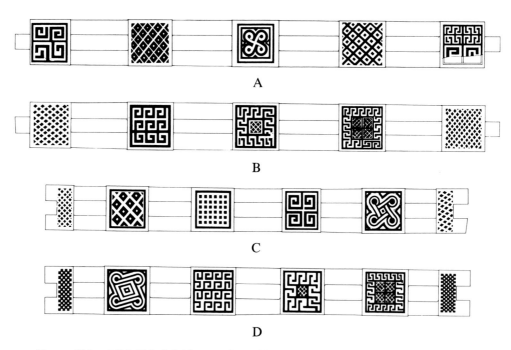

Figure 110.   MM 388. Inlaid "pagoda" table. Details: four frame pieces. A. Frame, front panel. B. Frame, back panel. C. Frame, side panel. D. Frame, side panel.   1:5.

184

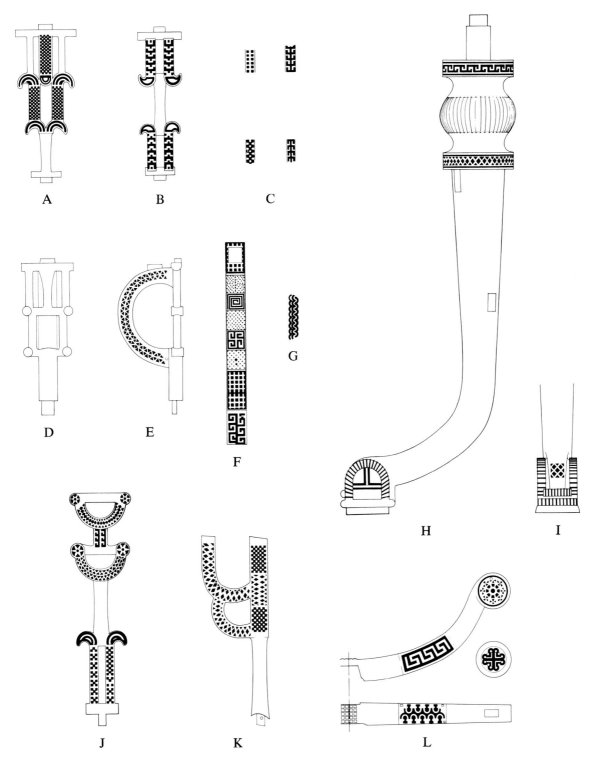

Figure 111. MM 388. Inlaid "pagoda" table. Details: A. Strut, Type 1. B. Strut, Type 2. C. Strut, Type 2, designs of outer faces. D. Strut, Type 3. E. Strut, Type 3, side view, with handle. F. Design on exterior of the handle at E. G. Strut, Type 3, design on side. H. Leg, side view. I. Foot, front view. J. Rear leg prop. K. Front leg prop. L. "Rocker," front and top views. 1:5.

tenons at the tops of the legs) were evidently bedded in sinkings in the under-face of the table top; the visible height of the struts which separated frame and table top must have been about 0.185 m. Though all necessarily of the same height, the struts are of three different types.

Most numerous (eight examples: see fig. 111A; pl. 82C) are struts of the first type with a half-round horizontal member at the bottom; from the center of this rises a single vertical member, square in section, which divides toward its top to form a Y shape, the ends of the branches curved outward and downward, volute-like. From the tops of these rise two similar verticals which in turn support a third tier of three verticals, the central one rising between the upper ends of the two below, the outer ones most often round in section. Across the top is again a half-round horizontal. There are tenons at the center, top, and bottom. Seven of the eight struts of this type are the same; the variant eighth shows upward-turned ends at the bottoms of the verticals of the two upper tiers.

The second type (six examples: see fig. 111B, C; pl. 82D) shows two verticals rising from the horizontal half-round at the bottom; these end at their tops in outward-turned volutes, between which rises a single plain vertical, usually round in section. This is crowned by two more verticals like those below, but reversed and with their volutes upward-turned at the bottom. The whole is finished at the top by a horizontal half-round, and again has tenons at top and bottom.

The outer faces of both types of strut are decorated by dark wood inlays in various patterns. The first type shows inlays on the two verticals of the central tier, and the central vertical of the uppermost. Curvilinear strips outline the volutes, and a circular star or wheel pattern often decorates the bottom of the central piece of the top tier. The most common pattern is checkerboard, and it illustrates the skill and unending patience of the craftsmen who made this table: the strut illustrated in the drawing fig. 111A has 194 inlaid squares of dark wood, each very slightly more than 0.002 m. on a side. On struts of the second type the verticals of the uppermost and the lower tiers are inlaid, usually with a pattern of squared brackets, stacked. Variant patterns are shown on fig. 111C.

The third type of strut (four examples; see fig. 111D–G; pl. 82E) supported the handles placed at each corner of the table. The struts proper resemble those of the first type in that the tiers of verticals increase upward from one at the bottom to the three

at the top; but the lowermost vertical is a heavy, squared member to which the lower end of the handle is pinned by a dowel, and the central member of the top tier is spread at its upper end to receive a dowel fastening the upper end of the handle. With the exception of the lowest, all the verticals (as well as the horizontal crosspieces) are round in section, so that there is no flat surface for inlaid decoration; instead there are projecting round knobs like spool ends at the intersections of the horizontal and vertical members. A small round hole in the side face of the handle (fig. 111E) at its lower end indicates the position of a peg fastening it to the dowel that held the handle to the face of the strut behind it.

The arrangement of the struts, then, seems to have been: the four struts of type three, which carried the handles, at the four corners of the frame; the six struts of type two over the central square panels of the long sides of the frame, and over the outer panels at either end; and the eight struts of type one, two at each side, alternated with the struts of type two (see pl. 82B).

The *handles* (fig. 111E; pl. 82B, E), doweled at top and bottom to the faces of the corner struts, projected at both ends of the long sides of the table. Each is a vertical loop-shaped piece with a flat outer and a rounded inner face. A tenon at the top of each handle gave support to the overhanging edge of the table top. The flat outer face of the handle is decorated with elaborate inlay in square panels of various geometric patterns; this decoration is continued downward on the outer face of the strut to which the handle is fastened; see fig. 111F. The side faces of each handle were also decorated with inlays, usually rows of interlocking triangles, but in one case with triple curved, wavy lines (fig. 111G).

Each of the three *legs* (fig. 111H, I) is made up of two separate pieces: the leg proper with the foot, fastened by a tenon at its upper end to a decorated top piece or "capital." The upper member consists of a central convex bulb vertically reeded all around, with flat projecting disk moldings above and below, their faces inlaid with meander-like patterns or lozenges and triangles (see fig. 111H; pl. 83A). These pieces served to spread the bearing surface at the tops of the legs; into their tops were set vertical dowels stepped inward at their upper ends. Round rings of wood, or "collars," must have been set around the thick lower parts of the dowels, giving support to the table top from underneath, while the smaller tenons above were bedded in cuttings in the under-face of the table top, or through it.

The legs proper are of light-colored wood, round in section, downward-tapered, and artificially bent outward at the bottom like those of the plain tables. Dowel cuttings (pl. 83A) at their tops held stretchers, round in section, whose other ends were anchored in the back faces of the frame panels. Two of these were still in the leg sockets when the table was found (pl. 45A).

The feet, square and flat underneath to rest horizontally on the floor, are arched above at each side with two half-round horizontal moldings across the front. Arches and moldings are decorated by crossing strips of dark-wood inlay; within the arches and between them at the front is more inlaid decoration (fig. 111H, I). The vertical inlay strips across the front moldings must curve with the contour of the half-rounds into which they were inlaid; these then must have been secured in place by glue.

The legs were placed two at one long side of the table at the corners, the third at the middle of the opposite long side. From their outer ends just behind the feet rose props to support the frame at its corners. The legs at the corners of the table bore similar props, doweled at their lower ends to the upper face of the out-turned legs just above the feet.

The two straight *props* (each a single piece of wood) have two vertical lower members, square in section and inlaid at the front, with voluted tops (fig. 111J; pl. 83B, C), above them a single vertical, round in section, and at the top two U-shaped members, one above the other. The uppermost of these was doweled to the under-face of the table frame. Inlay patterns are checkerboard, rows of triangles and lozenges, meander hooks, and rosettes in the roundels at the ends of the topmost members.

The third and fourth props which supported the front corners of the frame are again a pair: vertical members round in section surmounted by R-shaped pieces square in section and decorated at the front with inlays. The upper members are inverted with their open ends upward; crosspieces which were doweled to the under-face of the frame close them at the top (fig. 111K; pl. 83D, E). These two props were supported at their lower ends by a "rocker" which crossed, and was mortised to, the third leg which was set at the center of that side of the table. The rocker (fig. 111L; pl. 83F), a curved piece of wood round in section but in part squared to receive inlaid decoration on its front and upper faces, ends at either side in a roundel to which the lower end of a prop was doweled and pegged.

BED
MM 389
(See also pp. 259–260.)

MM 389 **Bed**

(No field number) Northwest corner

L. (overall) 2.93 W. 1.90
W. platform, *ca.* 1.40 m.
Figs. 112, 113; Pls. 41A–43A

The bed lay along the north wall, its foot against the west wall. The footboard—which matched the headboard— was found fallen inward, over the lower end of the bed; as it lay immediately in front of the doorway cut through the wall of the tomb, it was necessary to remove it in order to gain access, and therefore it is merely suggested on the plan of the chamber. The headboard, fallen outward at the other end, lay on the floor at the opposite end of the bed (pl. 43A). Both had evidently been supported on crossbars of iron; a large quantity of iron rust was found along the length of the underside of the footboard when it was lifted, and subsequently a similar band of iron rust was found on the lower face of the headboard. These iron bars were set between the corner blocks of the bed at both ends—probably their ends had been fitted into cuttings in the side faces of the blocks, though the condition of the wood was so bad that no traces of cuttings were discernible. Iron crossbars at each end would have supported the ends of the planks of the bed platform, as well as the end boards. The platform would then have had a width equal to the space between the inner faces of the corner blocks which presumably supported the iron crossbars, about 0.95 m. Close examination of the remains, however, indicated that the platform had been wider—about 1.40 m., including an outer plank at each side, extending between the east and west inner faces of the corner blocks and evidently supported beneath by lengthwise planks set on edge. All the planks, fallen to the floor, were in extremely bad preservation, but it could be ascertained that their thickness was about 0.04 m., and that the central one (on which the skeleton rested) was wider than the rest—about 0.58 m. in width. The rather shapeless edge planks at north and south, which appear on the plan, would then have been the supporting members; they originally stood on edge and had now fallen over. The inner planks, which they supported between the corner blocks, would have been the edge planks of the bed platform; and these in turn would have supported the rails along the sides of the bed. These were found beneath, at both sides (pl. 42B):

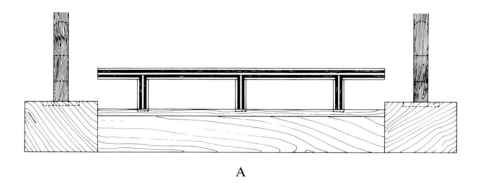

A

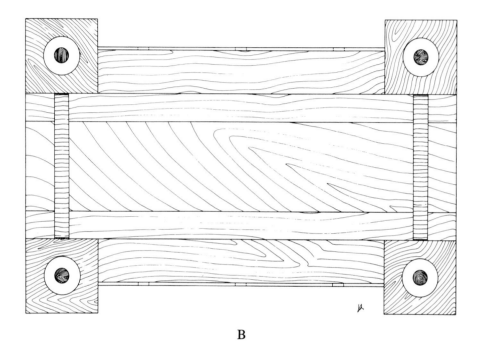

B

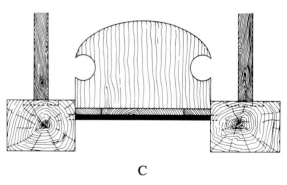

C

Figure 112. MM 389. An attempted reconstruction of the bed, following the author's text. Where methods of fastening by slotting or nails are unknown, they are ignored in reconstruction. A. Elevation of the south side, with the vertical supporting board in place. B. Plan. C. End elevation. The iron rod, evidenced only by rust on the bottom of the headboard, is drawn as supporting the boards of the bed platform, with the headboard resting on both.   1:25.

rails 0.075 m. thick were made up of thin (0.015 m.) strips of dark and light wood sandwiched together and evidently secured by nails. There were two layers of dark wood, which was well preserved, alternated with three layers of light (fig. 113), which had shredded and shriveled badly. No nails were preserved, but corresponding nail holes could be seen running through the dark strips. The rails were supported in three places by vertical struts 0.22 m. high and notched at their upper ends to receive the rail that they carried. The vertical supports were themselves sandwiches of five layers of alternated light and dark wood, like the rails they carried and of the same dimensions, 0.02 m. thick by 0.075 m. wide. The longest piece of bedrail found was 1.35 m. in length; its width of 0.02 m. corresponds to the 0.02 m. thickness of the prop, and its (calculated) thickness to the width of the prop. Cuttings in this piece allow a calculation of the total length of the bedrail. One end is preserved, nicely squared; 0.28 m. from the end begins a notch 0.075 m. long in each side face of the rail, where it was fitted in to the notched upper end of its support; and 0.60 m. beyond there is a second similar notch. We may then suppose that the rail had three supports each 0.075 m. wide, spaced 0.60 m. apart, and that it overhung its supports by 0.28 m. at each end. The total length of the bedrail then would be 1.985 m., which corresponds almost exactly with the distance between the inner faces of the corner blocks. The outer planks were too rotted to show cuttings to receive the lower ends of the three supports for the bedrail. It is pos-

sible that there were holes through the outer plank, and that the supports were bedded in the edge of the supporting plank beneath. The platform of the bed was thus enclosed by rails 0.22 m. high along the sides, and by head- and footboards at the ends. Its height above the floor cannot be exactly calculated; probably 0.25 to 0.30 m. The corner blocks are 0.33 m. high above floor level; the level of the platform must have been somewhat lower.

The end boards, of dark wood about 0.10 m. in thickness, were curved at the top and notched by semicircular cutouts into each side. The wood resembled the black pine used for the cover beams of Tumulus P. As mentioned above, both end pieces showed much iron rust along their lower faces.

The corner blocks, of similar wood, were nearly square (0.50 by 0.48 m.) and 0.33 m. high. In the top face of each was a circular sinking 0.25 m. in diameter and 0.03 m. deep. On or near each of these sinkings was a piece of black wood, round in section and 0.10 m. in diameter; the longest of these was preserved to a length of 0.60 m. It is likely that these are remnants of corner posts of the bed; the positions in which they lay suggest it, and they are not to be assigned to any other pieces of furniture. The discrepancy between diameter of bedposts and sinkings made to hold them (0.10 and 0.25 m.) suggests that there were collars of soft wood set into the sinkings in the corner blocks, and that the posts were held upright by these, their lower ends held at their centers. The use of such collars is attested in the attachment of legs to table tops through collars of soft wood (MM 380, 388).

The platform of the bed, then, consisted of seven lengthwise planks, and these were found fallen to the floor and resting flat on it. The bed in Tumulus P showed no such planks; in their absence we inferred, from scraps of heavy clothlike webbing, a surface of interwoven strips of cloth stretched between the sides and the ends of the frame (TumP 155) above. These would make a surface more comfortable to rest on than the planks of the MM bed (we assume that both beds were brought from the palace, where they had been used in life, rather than that they were specially constructed as tomb furniture).[114]

The hardness of the MM bed was mitigated by thick layers of blanket-like cloth laid as a mattress on which the skeleton rested; these reached a thick-

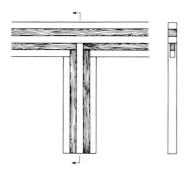

Figure 113. MM 389. Detail of the rail, in contrasting woods. A section through the rail (R). 1:8.

[114]Samples of textiles from Tumuli MM and P and burned pieces from Megaron 3 in the city were studied by Louisa Bellinger of the Textile Museum in Washington and published in *BullNBC* 46, pts. 1 and 2 (1962): 4–33. Bellinger lists the fibers used as being wool and mohair, flax and hemp; there was no cotton. The animal

fibers were no doubt taken from the local sheep and goats, the vegetable fibers and in particular the linen (flax) must have been imported, probably in the form of spun thread. Wool and mohair would have been felted or spun and woven to cloth locally.

ness of 0.04–0.05 m. and were made from many layers of a combination of gauzelike stuff, appearing yellowish, brownish, and pinkish, and of coarsely woven cloth, some apparently felted.[115] This had covered all but the corner blocks. It lay in irregular oblongs because the individual planks of the bed had fallen and shrunk so that there were long trenches between them (pl. 41A, B). The mattress material was also broken crosswise in many places. Along the inner (north) edge the material seemed to have been folded or doubled over; we could see the curve as it bent back on itself. At the head of the bed it was evi-

dently attached to the headboard partway up, as some of it still clung to the face of the headboard (pl. 43A). The fall of the headboard had torn it away, however, and most of the material rested on the iron bar or below it. It formed a concave arc along its upper edges as if it had been festooned at the two ends and allowed to sag down between them. Below this turn-up against the headboard the material was thicker and ended in a roll. A roll was left also near the footboard (removed as the tomb was being entered; see p. 100).

---

[115]See, in addition, R. Ellis' Fabrics A, C, D, F, and I (app. V), pp. 301 ff. [Ed.]

III

TUMULUS W

INTRODUCTION

Keith DeVries

Tumulus W[1] lies a kilometer and a half to the east of MM along the old road to Polatlı (pls. 1B, 84A).[2] With an imposing height of some 22 m. and a base of about 150 m. across, it is the largest of the tumuli of the area after MM (fig. 114).

Before excavation, the surface of the mound was undisturbed, except for fox burrows and a gully at the southwest, which villagers identified as a crater made by a shell during the Battle of the Sakarya in 1921 and subsequently enlarged by erosion.

THE EXCAVATION OF THE TUMULUS

The drilling rig employed on Tumuli P and MM had proved effective in locating the burial chambers and thus had reduced both the labor needs and the damage to the outer form of the

tumuli. However, Professor Young judged that the flow of water required for the drilling operation had been harmful to the chambers and the wooden objects within. He decided, therefore, not to use the drill on W. The cleanness of the clay of P and MM, with only a very few sherds found in that of both tumuli, did, however, point to the practicality of digging the outer clay fill with another labor- and time-saving device: a bulldozer. He placed advertisements in the Ankara newspapers, which resulted in the hiring of a driver and an Allis-Chalmers HD-6 Diesel.

The work, with the machine doing the digging, began on May 15, 1959. The fact that the chambers in the tumuli dug previously had lain to the south of the center[3] prompted the positioning of the trench there and specifically in the southwest quadrant where it was possible to take advantage of the already existing gully. The trench was laid with its open end to the southwest and extending

---

[1]This account of Tumulus W is based on the following sources by Rodney S. Young: his record of the excavation in Gordion Notebooks 78 and 84, his initial discussions in "The Gordion Campaign of 1959: Preliminary Report," *AJA* 64 (1960): 228–232 and *TAD* 10 (1960): 3–4, his remarks on the chronology in *Gordion Guide*

(1968), 42–43 (52–53 in unchanged text of 1975 edition), and his revealing comments in the catalogue of objects.

[2]Presumably an ancient road followed the same route, judging from the tumuli along each side from MM to W. Cf. G. Körte in *Gordion*, 36–37.

[3]See p. 5, fig. 3 (P) and p. 82, fig. 50 (MM).

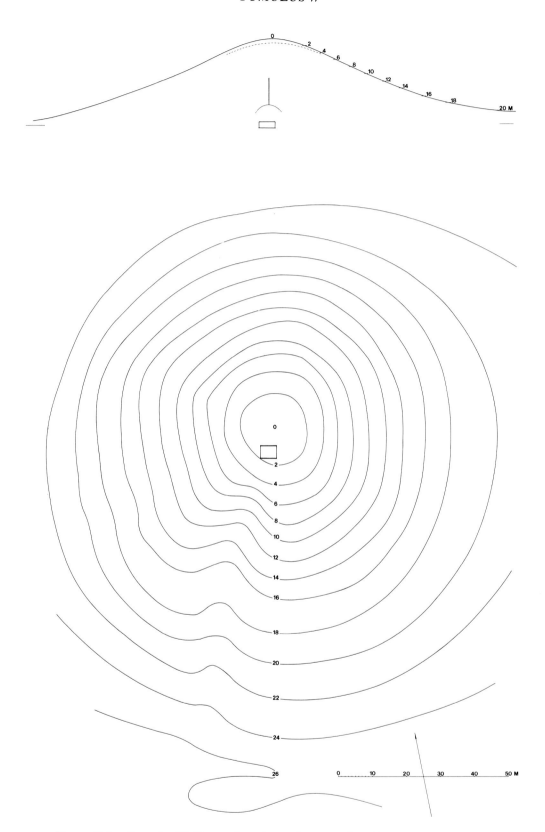

Figure 114.   Tumulus W. Restored section and survey plan. Contour interval 2 m.

to the northeast 4 m. beyond the top point of the mound; wedge-shaped, the trench reached its maximum width of 16 m. at its open end (pl. 84B).

At 11 m. below the surface appeared the topmost remaining traces of a hole for a mast, like those which in K-III and P had risen directly above the chamber.[4] There was thus confirmation that the trench had been correctly positioned.

Young had the machine pulled from service at a depth of 13.62 m. because of concern that, with its weight of about nine tons, it might break through into the chamber if it got too near. With the slower digging by hand that now commenced it was possible to confirm that the clay fill was indeed clean: from the 260 cubic meters of clay that were removed in the ensuing work the only find was a fragmentary animal bone.

For the altered digging, a new trench, with the mast-hole as its center, was laid out on the surface to which the machine had cleared. The trench, which measured 6.50 by 8 m. after secondary expansion, again had a southwest-northeast orientation. As digging proceeded, the original mast-hole terminated at 17 m. below the surface, but at a meter above that point a second mast-hole, immediately to the west, began and continued down.

At 18.62 m. the workmen began to reach the end of the clay, which was found to curve outward and downward from a central high point. Below was loose rubble of small, fist-sized stones at an irregular level, not corresponding to the curve of the clay. At the west and south the rubble was high and lay in part directly under the clay, but at the east and north it sloped away drastically to form a cavity with a diameter of 6 to 6.50 m. and a surface 1.20 m. below the clay (pl. 84C, D). Clearly, the usual rubble packing around a tomb chamber had been found, and the deep cavity within it indicated that as in P the ceiling of the chamber had given way, pulling stone down with it, while the clay shell above had maintained its original form.

Some serious threats soon became apparent, which were to inspire a nickname of "Pauline" for the tumulus, after the old-time movie serial *The Perils of Pauline*. The clay was found to have cracked, apparently from the fall of the roof, since

a line of cracking ran parallel to the circumference of the cavity in the rubble, and when the loose, small-stone rubble was dug from a spot, other rubble would pour down into the resulting depression and leave a hollow space below the already weakened scarps. As a result of these conditions, the clay scarp at the west began to collapse, and the danger was checked only by a successful digging back to beyond the line of cracking. Three days later the clay at the south, which had been left high as a shoveling platform, gave way. Young sprained his ankle from either the collapse or from the resulting turmoil, and he recorded in his notebook the "great deal of terror" that there had been in the trench.

Cutting back the clay at the south was a partial remedy; a more thoroughgoing one was building a frame to check the rubble and to keep it from further emptying out below the scarps. A box left open at the top and bottom was assembled from four planks of the largest size available: 5 m. long, 0.05 m. thick, and 0.25–0.40 m. wide. The sides were for damming the rubble, and within was a free working space (pl. 85A). A major difficulty was posed by the restricted five-meter-square dimensions, which considerably reduced the size of the trench and made it questionable if the full tomb chamber would be encompassed.

The installation of the frame required some finesse. It was found that, by shoveling out from below the planks and putting weight on them from above, the frame could be sunk as desired, and the delicate position was reached in which the top was at a sufficient level to hold back the high rubble at the west and the bottom low enough to check seepage from below.

As the excavation proceeded, rubble was regularly taken out from below the frame so that the box would continue to sink in accord with the deepening trench. For the essential extension of the sides of the box upward, a second and a third frame were added, and as a further step and partly to relieve the pressure that the first frame was bearing, a fourth frame was driven down lower than and inside the first; small vertical planks were inserted at the north and east to take up a small gap between the two frames (pl. 85B). For added strengthening, crosspieces were put within the entire set of frames.

With the initial uncovering of the top of the tomb chamber came confirmation that the ceiling

---

[4] K-III: G. Körte in *Gordion,* 39–40; P: above, p. 2.

had fallen in, with no beams still in place. It also became clear that the tomb chamber was at a pronounced angle to the trench, with an almost exact east-west orientation, and was not in fact totally within the protective set of frames: the corners all protruded to varying degrees beyond. Those areas of the chamber would thus be subject, as clearing proceeded, to having rubble rain down on them.

To cope with the problem, Young had a ceiling slipped down onto the southeast corner, the one that most seriously extended beyond the frames. The first step of the operation was to put down a one-layer raft of planks on top of the rubble and above the corner. As the rubble was removed it was put on top of the raft, and the latter sank from both the weight and the falling level of rubble below until it reached the bottom of the first frame. Additional planks were then worked between the top of the low inner frame and the bottom of the first frame, and they passed below the raft to act as a second thickness and to catch any rubble that the raft might not stop.

At the northeast corner, it was found sufficient to put in large stones along the outside of the set of frames to check the surge of small-stone rubble (pl. 85B). Young judged that the northwest and southwest corners did not extend far enough beyond the frames to need attention.

By this time there had come the comforting realization that the rubble packing around the walls of the chamber was made up of fairly large stones that were not exerting a dangerous pressure on those walls. Work now began on clearing both the rubble and the fallen roof beams within the chamber. At one point the operations were disrupted by a flow of small rubble at the southwest corner. A raft, as at the southeast, was sunk to act as a ceiling here too, and as at the northeast large stones were put in to check the small ones (pl. 86A).

Most of the beams were found to have fallen directly down onto the floor, but the first two at the west still had their north ends up and the last three at the east, their south ends. With the lifting of the beams came the explanation: it was at those spots that the grave goods were more intact than they were elsewhere.

The way was now free for the study and removal of the objects in the tomb. However, because of the restricted working space and the threat of landslide, relatively little exploration was done beyond the interior of the chamber, except for auger borings through the walls and some limited probes below the floor.

During a day-and-a-half break that preceded the final day of work, rubble leaked down at the west and filled up that end of the chamber; luckily most of the floor there had previously been cleared and all objects already noted had been removed. The incident, with its implications that the stone could not be kept out for long, influenced Young in his decision to have the structure refilled. He saw in fact some positive advantages in doing so; the wood of the frames and rafts could be retrieved for further uses and the ancient wood of the chamber would get protection from the sun and rain and from accidental damage like the fire that had destroyed the chamber of Tumulus P.[5] Once the floor at the center and east had been completely cleared, he had the wooden barriers pulled up; the stone poured in at once and again sealed off the chamber.

STRUCTURE OF TOMB CHAMBER AND MOUND

As normal in the early Phrygian tumuli (MM being an exception), the hardpan had been cut down to make a shallow pit for the tomb chamber. Young estimated the depth of the pit to be 1 m. but could not ascertain the other dimensions. A clear feature was rubble, which had been laid in the pit as a bedding for the chamber floor. There were also timbers, which seem to have been logs split lengthwise and embedded in the rubble with their broad surfaces turned up. One such log, with a radius of about 0.20 m., was found lying below the west wall and projecting 0.12 m. beyond it; as a counterpart a probably similar timber underlay the east wall, and Young hypothesized in his notebook that a third such log might be below the center of the floor. The tomb chamber itself, which had an almost exactly east-west orientation (figs. 114, 115), had an interior length of 4.62 m., a width of 3.30 m.,

[5]Early in the spring of 1957 the still exposed timbers of the Tumulus P chamber were accidentally set on fire by

the discarded match or cigarette of a careless tourist. [Ed.]

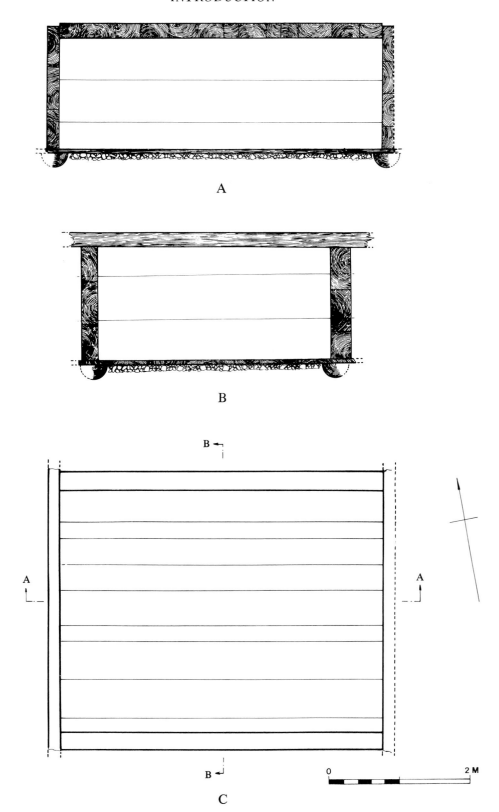

A

B

C

*Figure 115.   Tumulus W. Tomb chamber. A. Section A–A, from south. B. Section
B–B, from east. C. Floor plan. Darker lines are walls; lighter lines are floor planks.*

and a height of 1.55 m. The floor was made up of a single layer of planks 0.05 m. thick, with widths ranging from 0.19 to 0.54 m. Resting directly on the rubble and split logs, the planks ran the length of the chamber and extended beyond the two short end walls at the east and west. Similarly the edges of the planks extended beyond the walls along the north and south sides. The floor thus seems to have encompassed a larger area than the chamber and to have formed a broad base for the walls. Nine planks were within the room, and Young supposed that there might be eleven in all.

The north and south side walls rested against the east and west end walls, with no evidence of mortising, and the side walls were lower (1.54–1.57 m.) than the end ones (1.72–1.74 m.). All were built of large beams identified at the time of excavation as pine, with thicknesses of 0.18 to 0.30 m. and heights of 0.33 to 0.62 m.; four beams were used in the east wall and three each in the others. The beams had been skillfully squared off and smoothed and had been so well fitted together that the joints were not always immediately apparent.

The roof consisted of a single layer of 13 beams with widths from 0.21 to 0.48 m. and thicknesses of 0.22 to 0.24 m. Running perpendicular to the length of the chamber, they originally had their ends resting on the relatively low north and south walls, and the entire set of beams was held between the high east and west walls. The comparatively weak construction, with no layer or layers of upper timbers such as were present in K-III, P, and MM, may have brought about an early collapse.[6]

A long mast, positioned just slightly to the east of the center of the chamber and detected from the hole left when it rotted out, rose above the roof to guide in the piling up of the mound, and it was succeeded by another mast, nearly superimposed upon it; as noted above, similar masts had been used in Tumuli P and K-III. The holes of the two masts of Tumulus W still had the impressions of wood within them; the upper mast, as measured from the hole, was 0.12 m. in diameter high on its shaft, and it broadened out to 0.15 m. toward its base.

In the heaping up of the tumulus, the chamber was kept within the southwest quadrant in the usual manner. Again as normal, a dome-shaped core of rubble was packed around the chamber and here reached a height of 5 m. above the roof. The rubble around the walls and apparently that originally just above the roof was made up of fairly large stones; the rubble higher up was the small, loose fill that caused such serious difficulties during excavation. Since the side walls of the chamber with their considerable length showed no signs of buckling from the pressure of the rubble, Young suspected that there might be protective walls beyond them, somewhat in the manner of MM: "Possibly longer beams outside [the side walls] were braced against the ends of the end walls, thus taking the pressure against the sides of the tomb and forming a sort of double wall filled between by rubble. We have [however] no evidence for such outer beams; the augers which bored through the walls in each direction found only rubble on the other side."[7] He considered it likely enough, though, that the full weight of the rubble pressed unchecked against the end walls, which showed no signs of the pressure but which, because of their shorter span and their support from the side walls, would not be expected to be as affected. He thought, in fact, that the direct pressure would be what was holding the end walls firmly against the side ones in the apparent absence of mortising.

Beyond the rubble and constituting by far the greatest mass of the tumulus was the great clay fill, 18.62 m. thick at the point directly over the one-time peak of the rubble core. Within the clay was an isolated dump of stone and a few pockets of gravel; the only other distinguishing features were the contrasting colors of the various clay components.

THE CONTENTS OF THE TOMB

In the center of the tomb (fig. 116) lay the skeleton, badly crushed by the fall of the roof but traceable for a length of 1.38 m. Little of the skull was intact other than teeth and the lower jaw, and the bones of the body were thoroughly smashed.

---

[6]K-III: G. Körte in *Gordion,* 41; Tumulus P: above, p. 4; MM: above, p. 89.

[7]Gordion Notebook 84, 22.

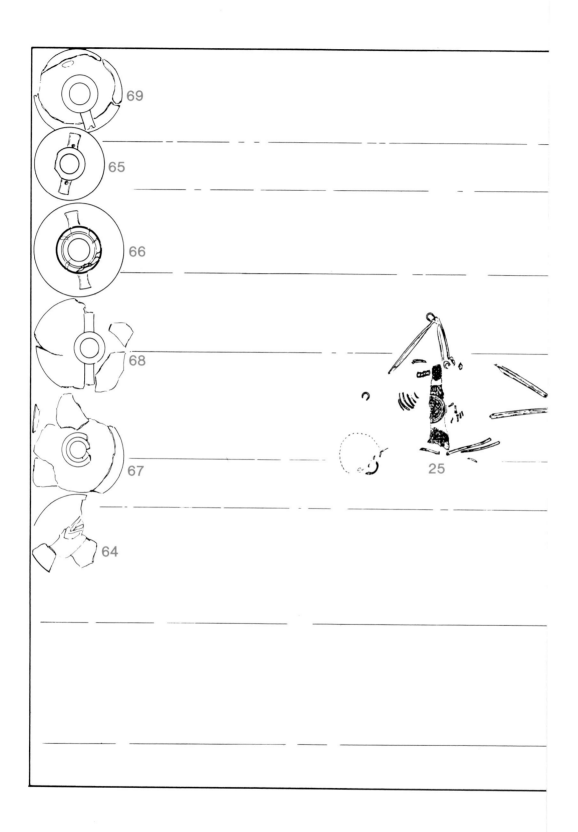

Figure 116.   Tumulus W. Floor plan of ton

From the sparse evidence available, Professor Muzaffer Şenyürek of the University of Ankara identified the skeleton as that of a small, fairly young adult and was inclined to think it male, although he could not be certain.[8]

There were no traces around the skeleton of any wood that might have belonged to a bed or coffin. The body looks instead to have been put onto the floor on top of several layers of cloth, including what appear to have been felt and a coarsely woven linen or hemp,[9] and laid in an extended position with the head toward the west, the right arm stretched along the side, and the left arm bent with its hand resting on the stomach. None of the textile remains at the spot could be definitely identified as parts of garments, and clothing is best ascertained from its fastenings. Two fibulae (probably the pair TumW 29 and 30) were at the shoulders, a normal spot for the pinning of garments (albeit female) in Geometric Greece, and a place where fibulae were found in the burial of MM; TumW 27 was by the left elbow, much like the fibula securing the overgarment of King Warpalawas on the İvriz relief and reminiscent of the fibulae by the elbows of the skeleton in MM; and TumW 28 was in a position suitable for having fastened clothing at the neck.[10] By the ribs and perhaps still *in situ* were two fibulae, probably the pair TumW 31 and 32; two further fibulae, TumW 33 and 34, were by the body, but their exact relation to it was not clear.

Worn over the clothing would have been the handsome, bronze-studded leather belt, TumW 25, part of which was found still in place at the waist and part of which had become stuck to the underside of a fallen beam and was lifted with it. Young suggests in the following catalogue that the now disintegrated fragment of studded bronze with a leather backing, TumW 26, which lay below the left elbow and would have been approximately in line with the waist, may have been part of the same belt.

The tomb goods, nearly all badly smashed, were ranged along or close to the east and west walls. Included among them were 26 more fibulae, TumW 35–60, which were loosely scattered in apparently random groups along much of the east side, as detailed in the catalogue. The other goods seem to have been arranged with more care and separated into distinct classes. The most valuable objects were concentrated in the southeast corner: two bull's-head cauldrons (TumW 1, 2), two small cauldrons with bird attachments (TumW 3, 4), an elaborate piece of wooden furniture (TumW 80), an ivory pendant (TumW 81), and a pair of bronze handles (TumW 24), perhaps from a wooden bowl. The two bull cauldrons were themselves pressed into service as containers for further objects. In TumW 1 were the two painted pottery jugs (TumW 61, 62), and the second cauldron (TumW 2) held a remarkable collection of small bronze vessels (TumW 5, 6 and 9–23) as well as two bronze ladles (TumW 7, 8), two wooden disks (TumW 74, 75), and the black polished pottery jug (TumW 63). Unlike the large cauldrons of MM and P, the ones here were not on stands but had been set directly onto the floor. Extensive bits of loosely woven linen or hemp on the outsides of the two cauldrons make it probable that they had been wrapped in

---

[8]From a letter of M. Şenyürek to R. S. Young dated August 17, 1959: "The features of the cranial fragments (receding forehead, strong postorbital constriction, rounded upper margin of the orbit, largish mastoid process and large widths of some teeth) indicate a male individual. On the other hand, the postcranial bones, especially those of the lower extremity, are rather small. This, while not incompatible with a small male, still inserts an element of uncertainty in the sexing. As you know, in the absence of a pelvis (a few small fragments of ilium are present, but no part of the characteristic pubic bone is preserved), the sexing by crania involves a margin of error which is certainly greater in a fragmentary collection like this. Hence, while the cranial fragments indicate a male individual, the small size of the postcranial bits, while not incompatible with a small male, still need to be more closely studied. . . . I consider it safer to leave the sex, in spite of the appearance of the cranial fragments, as an open question for the moment, until I have compared the fragments of all bones with the Gordion collection in order to assess the significance of various deviations. . . . As for the age . . . it was an adult who was not old. . . . He was relatively small."

[9]For the difficulty in determining whether the loose-weave Gordion textiles are linen or hemp, see L. Bellinger, *BullNBC* 46 (1962): 13.

[10]MM fibulae: above, pp. 168 f., 179. Fibulae as shoulder fasteners in Geometric Greece: K. DeVries, *Hesperia* 43 (1974): 82. Warpalawas' fibula: E. Akurgal, *Kunst Heth.*, pl. 140 and color plate XXIV; *idem, Phryg. Kunst*, pl. C; O. Muscarella, *JNES* 26 (1967): 83–84; R. M. Boehmer, *AA* 88 (1973): 149–152, fig. 3.

the cloth, and fragments of linen or hemp inside TumW 2 prompted Young's suggestion in the catalogue that the individual small vessels it contained were wrapped as well.

Intruding into the rich furnishings of the corner was the storage amphora TumW 72, the southernmost of a line of such pots along the east wall. There were at least three others, of which it was possible to mend two (TumW 70 and 71); in TumW 70 were yellowish brown lumps of organic matter, which may be food remains.[11] By the amphoras, along with fibulae, were five fragmentary wooden plates (TumW 75–79). Corresponding to the row of amphoras was a similar line of six storage vessels (five amphoras, TumW 65–69, and a jar, TumW 64) along the west wall (pl. 86B). TumW 65–68 contained further organic material that might be the remains of food, while TumW 69 had inorganic matter that may include red ocher.[12]

At three places on the north wall there were pieces of loosely woven linen or hemp clinging to the wood. Thus, as in Tumulus P, there may have been wall hangings.[13] Young recorded in his notebook evidence for painted decoration as well: "In the northwest corner there is a substance that adheres to the faces of the north and west walls, and can be peeled off in thick layers with a whitish back. As this in places runs across and covers the joints between wall beams, it would seem to be some sort of wall covering— the workmen suggest leather, but paint is more likely as there is no trace of tack or nail holes to fasten leather to the wall."[14]

CHRONOLOGY

Young noted several relatively early chronological pointers among the material of the tomb.

In his 1968 guidebook to Gordion he cited the lack of panels and figured decoration on the fine jug TumW 6 as making it earlier than the otherwise comparable pottery of Tumulus K-III and, by extension, Tumulus P.[15] Another indicator noted in the guidebook was the presence of bronze vessels that had been hammered rather than cast, and a further indicator was the rather high date judged likely for two objects with parallels in the East: the bronze bowl, TumW 9, with its network of lozenge-shaped petals corresponds to an Assyrian bowl inscribed with the name of Assurtaklak, perhaps the eponymous official of 806 B.C.,[16] and the bowl, TumW 10, had a rosette in its center, a detail Young saw as having "early" correspondences in Assyria.[17] In his summary of the fibulae for this volume (pp. 246–247) he cited an additional indicator. The Group XII,13 fibulae of Tumulus W are, with their block moldings at ends and middle, in a formative stage of the type, while those of K-III, with "cushions and reels" substituted in the middle, are more advanced, and those of K-IV, with cushions at the ends as well, still more developed.

One can add further evidence for an early date for Tumulus W. Among the fibulae there are other signs of evolution, and consistently the fibulae of Tumulus W show the earliest traits. Within type 13 not only are blocks replaced by "cushions," but the moldings become more fully shaped and grow increasingly broad in relation to the bow; the sequence is that given by Young but with the material of MM distinguishable as later than that of K-IV: thus, W, K-III, K-IV, and MM. Among the type 3 fibulae a sequence of increasingly crisply shaped moldings is likewise traceable, with the progression being W, K-III, and P. More broadly there is a trend among the fibulae in general toward increasing complexity

---

[11]For contents of TumW 70, see pp. 282, 284, app. II-A, Sample 72.

[12]Contents of TumW 64–68: see pp. 282 and 284, app. II-A, Samples 66–70. Contents of TumW 69: pp. 282, 284, Sample 71.

[13]Tumulus P: above, p. 7.

[14]Gordion Notebook 84, 7. Two samples of "leather" were sent for analysis: see pp. 281 and 284, app. II-A, Samples 61 and 62.

[15]*Gordion Guide*, 42–43 (52–53 in unchanged text of 1975 edition).

[16]H. Luschey, *Phiale*, 34 and fig. 13a–c. D. D. Luckenbill, *Anc. Records* II, 433. It is in its decoration rather than its shape that TumW 9 is close to the Assyrian bowl.

[17]Young was drawing upon remarks in Luschey, *op. cit.*, 31–33, who noted that the rosette decoration of bowls begins in the second millennium B.C. and continues into the first, as seen in the Assurtaklak piece, but disappears at some time in the Late Assyrian period. The decoration seems still to have been current as late as the advanced eighth century, however, to judge from a bowl in a grave at Nimrud: M. Mallowan, *Nimrud and Its Remains* I (London: Collins, 1966), 116.

of ornamentation, and in their plainness the fibulae of Tumulus W stand at the head of the development. Fibulae of types 3 and 7 acquire a more elaborate form with the addition of studs (becoming types 8 and 9), as seen embryonically in K-III and fully developed in K-IV and MM but not at all in Tumulus W. Also fibulae of type 13 can take on an additional molding to either side of the central one, thus becoming type 14, as represented in K-IV and MM but again not W.

Similarly the omphalos bowls of Tumulus W display earlier characteristics than do those of the other excavated Gordion tumuli. As discussed below on p. 266, the bowls show a development in overall size, in the size of the omphalos, and in the articulation of the ridges, with the sequence being W, K-III, P, and MM.

Possibly chronologically significant, too, is the single ceiling of Tumulus W in contrast to the double one of Tumulus P and the complex arrangement of MM with a ceiling, a shell of logs above, and a horizontal platform of logs still farther up. The structures in the latter two tumuli could represent evolving remedies to cope with the fragility of a single ceiling under the weight of rubble, and Tumulus W could belong to a phase before solutions to the problem began to be attempted.

A final factor, one to be cautiously noted, is the siting of the tumuli of the area. Those of periods after the destruction of the citadel are concentrated toward the edges of the bluff overlooking the flood plain and distinctly to the west and south of the central cluster containing K-III, K-IV, P, and MM (see fig. 1), tumuli of pre-destruction to destruction periods.[18] It would seem consistent with the overall pattern for Tumulus W, at the eastern extremity of the zone, to be the earliest yet known.

Young in the guidebook account assigned to Tumulus W a date at the end of the ninth century or "slightly later," although in his fibula summary below (p. 242) he implies a date of about mid-eighth century. In any case a variety of evidence indicates that the tumulus is perceptibly earlier than the others published here and that it thus should belong to a period decades if not some generations before the catastrophe that struck Gordion and the Phrygian kingdom.

CATALOGUE

BRONZE

CAULDRONS WITH BULL'S-HEAD ATTACHMENTS
TumW 1, 2
(See also pp. 219–223.)

The two cauldrons were found side by side at the southeast corner of the tomb, each packed with smaller offerings: in TumW 1 the pottery vessels of finer ware (TumW 61–62); in TumW 2, to the west of TumW 1, the smaller bronzes (TumW 5–23), the black polished jug (TumW 63), and the two wooden disks (TumW 74–75). The cauldrons had evidently been set directly on the floor without ring tripods to support them. Both had been badly crushed by the collapse of the roof; their walls had been shattered to many fragments but had held their shape largely because of the objects packed inside and also in part because both had been wrapped in fine linen cloth, of which large wads were found around each. The bull's-head cauldrons appear to have been made as a pair.

TumW 1 Cauldron with bull's-head attachments
    B 1250   In southeast corner, mouth
      to east wall
    Rest. D. rim 0.26–0.27 W. rim
      0.011 m.
    Fig. 117A; Pl. 87A–D

Large cauldron shaped like MM 1, with squat sperical body open at the top and thick, flattened rim

---

[18]Other tumuli within the same cluster yielded scanty finds but ones indicative of the same general period. Tumulus R had no grave goods at all, but Q had fibulae that seem intermediate between those of W and K-III, and S contained a single fibula that belongs within the range of W to K-IV.

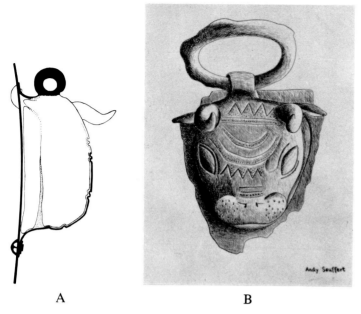 

A B C

Figure 117. Details: bull's-head attachments from cauldrons. A. TumW 1, section through attachment A. *B. TumW 2, attachment* A. *C. TumW 2, attachment* B. *1:2.*

slightly everted. It was not possible to tell whether the cauldron had been made by casting or by hammering.

Two bull's-head attachments with carrying rings set at opposite sides, fitted close under the everted rim, but they were badly damaged across muzzles and jaws. The rings are attached in the usual way through ring sockets at the tops of the heads. Both attachments (as those also of TumW 2) were made in the same way. Each consists of a cast core on which the major details of the bull's face, for example the grooves around the eyes and the wrinkles above the muzzle, were worked out in the cast. Applied outside this was an envelopment of thin bronze, evidently hammered over the cast core to pick up the details of the casting; finer details of dots and strokes were then worked in the surface of the envelopment with punch and graver. The horns and ears appear to have been made together in one piece at each side, then socketed in to the head; the ring socket at the top was also made separately and attached to the head. The envelopment was apparently not carried over these added pieces, which could have been attached after it was hammered over the core. At the sides and top it was carried back beyond the depth of the core, then bent out to a U-shaped flange all around the edge. Through this flange the attachment was fastened to the shoulder of the cauldron by three dowels, at the upper corners and the bottom. The dowels had hollow, flattened hemispherical heads in-

side the cauldron, rivet heads outside. Before attaching, and in order to hold the cast core in place within the envelopment, the back was filled with lead to occupy the space between cast and cauldron shoulder. The attachments thus became very heavy and broke away from the thin bronze of the shoulder.

Bull's-head attachments

	A.	B.
H. chin to base of ring socket	0.072	0.069 m.
W. across ears	0.078	0.083
OD. carrying ring	0.062	0.062

The horns extend forward, first downward then up at the tips. The ears, set behind the horns, extend outward to the sides. The eyes almond-shaped, with raised arc ridges above and below. The forelock is indicated by two necklace-like arcs hanging from below the horns: each a double engraved line enclosing punched dots. A similar band, horizontal, runs across from horn to horn; above it a zigzag, the punched dots above it, runs horizontally between the inner corners of the eyes. The muzzle set off by curved engraved lines; across its base above, triple engraved lines with punched dots between the lower two. On the muzzle punched dots and short engraved lines to suggest the nostrils. The opening of the mouth a fine engraved line.

200

TumW 2 **Cauldron with bull's-head attachments**
B 1251[19]   In southeast corner,
        upside down to west of TumW 1
Fig. 117B, C; Pl. 88A

The cauldron was so fragmented that no attempt was made to put it together, particularly since it seems to differ in no way from TumW 1.

The attachments exactly the same as those of TumW 1; attachment *B* preserves much of the flange around the edge of the hammered envelopment, together with two of the holes for pins by which it was attached to the cauldron.

Bull's-head attachments

	A.	*B.*
H. chin to base of ring socket	0.073	0.068 m.
W. across ears	0.0855	0.079
OD. carrying ring	0.064	0.0625

SMALL CAULDRONS WITH BIRD ATTACHMENTS AND BUCKET HANDLES
TumW 3, 4

The two vessels with bird attachments to hold the ends of bucket handles were completely crushed by the collapse of the roof. It was not possible to put either together again; as far as could be seen, however, they were alike in every detail, again made as a pair. The cauldrons appear to have been squat spherical in shape, perhaps flattened at the bottom. The rims thickened and flattened on top, sloped slightly inward; the fabric very thin, perhaps hammered. In shape the vessels seem to have been much like the bucket-handled small cauldrons MM 10–13.

TumW 3 **Small cauldron with bird attachments and bucket handle**
B 1249   Southeast corner, north of
        TumW 2
Est. D. rim 0.12 W. rim 0.0045 m.
Pl. 88B

Attachments in the form of birds with spread wings and short tails squared across the bottom. These were fastened to the shoulder of the vessel by dowels through wings and tail, their ends hammered

flat inside and out and smoothed. The birds face outward, their thin curved necks growing from heavy bulbous bodies, which are hollow behind. The heads have long downward curving beaks. There is no engraving to indicate eyes, feathering, or feet. Behind the heads standing ring sockets set transversely. Through these were threaded the ends of the bucket handle, squared in section at the center and tapering at the ends to heavy round wire which, after being threaded through the sockets, was turned back and wound around the lower parts of the handle ten to thirteen times.

Bird attachments

	A.	*B.*
H.	0.069	0.068 m.
W. across wings	0.093	0.082

TumW 4 **Small cauldron with bird attachments and bucket handle**
B 1252   Southeast quarter
Est. D. rim 0.165 W. rim 0.0045 m.
Fig. 118; Pl. 88C

Evidently exactly like TumW 3 in every detail;[20] one of the bird attachments (*B*) appears somewhat smaller than the other.

Bird attachments

	A.	*B.*
H.	0.072	0.072 m.
W. across wings	0.091	0.07 as preserved

JUGS
TumW 5, 6

TumW 5 **Sieve-spouted jug with round mouth**
B 1244   Southeast corner, in
        TumW 2
H.-rim 0.115–0.118 H.-h. 0.157
D. rim 0.095 D. 0.123 D. base
0.061 m.
Pl. 88D

Two holes in the body. Many corroded areas; not cleaned. Heavy fabric throughout; probably cast in one piece before the addition of handle and spout. The low straight base slightly concave, leaving a resting ring around the edge; there is no trace of a

---

[19]See app. II-C, p. 287, Samples 99 and 100; also app. V, p. 308, Fabric H.

[20]See p. 287, app. II-C, Sample 101.

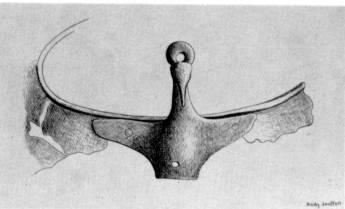

Figure 118. TumW 4. Small cauldron with bird attachments and bucket handle. Attachment A, front and side views. 1:2.

seam where base and body join. The body plump ovoid with a wide, straight neck flared outward at the rim; the lip grooved around its inner edge, flat on top, and 0.003 m. thick. There is no trace of a seam where body and neck join. The handle is a rod of bronze, round in section and cast in one with the transverse rotelle which crosses its top, and bent to join the vessel at rim and shoulder, rising in a high loop above the rim. Its upper end is notched at the front to fit on top of the lip, spread behind to a fishtail shape fitted against the outer face of the rim and secured by two dowels capped by shallow round heads inside and out. The lower end of the handle spreads to a round tab secured to the shoulder by a dowel with a flat round head outside, a flattened rivet head inside.

The spout, set at an angle of slightly less than 90 degrees to the handle, was separately cast and added. The wall of the jug at the base of the spout is pierced by many small holes to make a strainer. The holes were bored or drilled rather than punched, since the surface of the bronze is perfectly smooth around them. The spout is flanged around its inner end; 11 dowels with rivet ends inside and out fasten the flange to the shoulder of the jug. Above the flange the spout is tubular, decorated by a half-round ridge in relief, its ends at one side represented as a T-shaped crosspiece drawn through a loop. This decoration is evidently in imitation of the knotlike fastening of a string or thin rope. Above the string decoration the upper part of the tube is cut away, leaving a U-shaped channel, which continues out to a squared-off end.

TumW 6 **Footed jug with round mouth**
B 1245   Southeast corner, in
    TumW 2
H.-rim 0.14   H.-h. 0.16   D. rim
    0.087   D. 0.113   D. base 0.058 m.
Pl. 88E

Intact. The base is a low cone with a flat ring resting surface formed by a shallow sinking at the center underneath. No trace of a seam at the stem outside; foot and body were evidently made in one piece —probably cast, judging by the weight. Squat ovoid body and high neck flaring slightly outward to a plain round mouth. Hollow handle made from two bronze plates folded together. At their upper ends the plates fit against the inner and outer faces of the rim and are secured by two rivet-headed pins. At the bottom both plates are rounded off and secured by a single rivet-headed dowel, off-center. A small, flat, round plate of bronze divides body from base inside; a pin through its center is continued downward by a wire which was bent at its lower end to form a T-shaped anchor which was embedded in wax, which fills the inside of the base and so holds the anchor in place. This repair or addition was perhaps made to remedy a leak or to achieve greater stability for the vessel by increasing the weight at its narrow bottom.

The small bronze jug (with trefoil mouth), MM 27 (pl. 61B), affords a parallel for the weighting of the foot. This round-mouthed class of jug is represented in pottery in great numbers on the city mound among the burned debris of the megara and the terrace rooms. Cf. example, pl. 96F.[21]

---

[21]Black polished footed round-mouthed jug (P 2359) from burned debris on the floor of Megaron 3 on the city

mound. H.-h. 0.25; D. 0.191 m. Mended complete; discolored to yellow and black. Handle a double rolled loop.

LADLES
TumW 7, 8

TumW 7 **Ladle**

B 1246 Southeast corner, in TumW 2

GPL.-top of handle 0.235 D. bowl 0.102–0.105 m.

Pl. 89A

The handle swollen and opened by corrosion, its upper end broken away; the bowl split and very corroded. As the condition of this ladle precluded cleaning, all its details are not clear. The heavy fabric and the presence of three raised ridges across the face of the handle at its lower end and its top (below the missing elbow) suggest that this ladle was cast rather than hammered; but it is not clear whether bowl, tang, and handle are in one piece or were assembled from separate parts. The bowl shallow and slightly oval; the tang a simple oblong; the handle thick and nearly square in section.

TumW 8 **Ladle**

B 1247 Southeast corner, in TumW 2

L.-top of handle 0.251 D. bowl 0.092 m.

Pl. 89B–D

The handle broken across and mended; otherwise intact. The bowl of thin fabric, shallow and a trifle oval in outline, its thickened plain lip very slightly overhanging on inside. The plain, nearly square tang in one piece with the bowl, which seems to have been made by hammering. The heavier handle was cast, its long central stem, rectangular in section, finished

at either end by a heavier, cylindrical section above a rectangular block. The ends of the blocks were slotted across to grip the tang of the bowl at the lower end, the elbow of the handle at the upper. Since no pins or dowels are visible, it is probable that these joints were secured by solder. Each end was decorated by punching and incising to form a conventionalized animal head (probably a lion), the end block making the head and the cylinder above it the neck; the slot that gripped the tang made the mouth so that the animal appears to grip the edge of the tang in its jaws. The eyes are represented by punched dots within single punched rings, the hair on the neck of the upper animal by grooves made with a curved punch. The rest of the decoration was made by incising: nose stripes of fine crosshatching for both animals, parallel zigzags with rows of dots between them for the neck of the lower animal. The face of the handle is decorated with fine incised crosshatching from top to bottom. The elbow and bird's-bill-shaped upper end of handle, of thinner bronze than the stem, were perhaps finished by hammering. The handle of the bronze belt, TumP 36, offers a parallel for the animal's-head finials.

BOWLS
TumW 9–23

All 15 bronze bowls were found inside the cauldron TumW 2, some of them stacked one inside another, and quantities of shreds of netlike linen cloth found with them suggested that they had once been wrapped in cloth, either individually or by stacks. Of the fifteen, two (TumW 9–

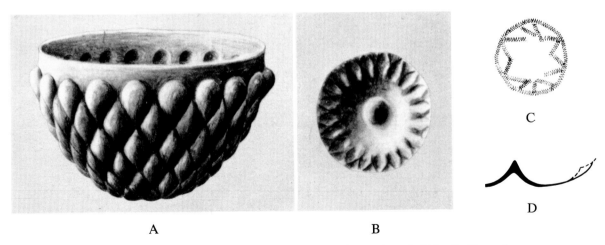

A   B   C

D

Figure 119. TumW 9. Bronze bowl with relief decoration. A. Side. B. Base, showing lower rows of petals. C. Incised design around omphalos on interior. D. Profile of lower portion.   1:2.

Figure 120. TumW 9. Omphalos bowl with relief decoration. Profile. 1:2.

10) have relief decoration; one (TumW 11) is ribbed on the inside; five (TumW 12–16) are plain omphalos bowls with ridges around the omphalos; and two (TumW 17–18) are hammered omphalos bowls without ridges or other decoration. In addition there are five (TumW 19–23) plain bowls without omphalos.

OMPHALOS BOWLS
TumW 9–18

OMPHALOS BOWLS WITH RELIEF DECORATION
TumW 9, 10

TumW 9   **Omphalos bowl with relief decoration**
B 1229   Southeast corner, in TumW 2
H. 0.073   D. rim 0.124   D. through relief 0.135 m.
Figs. 119, 120; Pl. 89E

Intact. The shape deep and somewhat pointed, flattened at the bottom, with a short, straight verti-cal rim. The metal reddish and coppery, the fabric thin: thickness at lip 0.002 m. The omphalos small and conical, a compass prick on top of its point; it is not quite round and shows traces of hammer marks. Lightness of fabric, hammer marks on the omphalos, and minor asymmetries in contour and among the petals of the repoussé decoration, together with the reddish color, suggest that this is a hammered bowl of copper. The body decorated in relief by six tiers of lozenge-shaped petals interlocking in a net pattern; 20 tiny petals at the base increasing in size through the intermediate tiers to 20 large, drop-shaped petals with rounded upper ends below the plain rim.

There are no ridges on the floor around the base of the omphalos; instead the floor is decorated with a design of impressed strokes within an engraved ring: a rough zigzag within the circle, resembling a crude six-pointed star (fig. 119C). It cannot be determined whether the strokes were made individually with a sharp punch or graver, or by use of a rouletting instrument; in any case the punched (or rouletted) ornament does not show in the outside face.

TumW 10   **Omphalos bowl with relief decoration**
B 1230   Southeast corner, in TumW 2
H. 0.044   D. rim 0.15   D. omph. 0.015 m.
Figs. 121, 122; Pl. 89F

One side much corroded, with holes eaten through the highest relief of the petals. The bowl low and spreading, with flattened bottom and barely curved wall; a short, slightly flared rim. The bronze brownish rather than red; the fabric heavy, with 0.002 m. thickness at the lip. The relief decoration of the outside appears throughout as hollows on the inside except at the rim, which is perfectly smooth and plain inside, while on the outside relief arcs above the tops

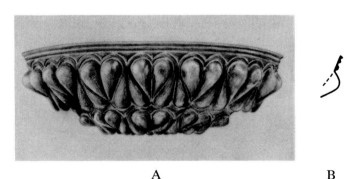
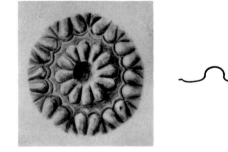

A   B   C   D

Figure 121. TumW 10. Bronze bowl with relief decoration. A. Side view. B. Profile of rim. C. Base and lower rows of knobs. D. Profile of base. 1:2.

of the petals form a continuous scalloping below two raised horizontal ridges, rounded in profile, with a groove between them. The omphalos squat hemispherical, very small, and hollow beneath. Instead of ridges it is surrounded by 12 radiating petals to make a rosette with convex center surrounded by hollowed petals. Above, petaled decoration in two tiers separated by a plain zone. In the lower tier eighteen pairs of drop-shaped petals, nine with the pointed ends upward, nine (slightly larger) with the pointed ends down, alternating. The upper tier has the same decoration on a larger scale and with 28 pairs of petals, 14 with points upward alternating with 14 pointed downward. The rounded bases—or tops—of the petals are outlined throughout on the floor, and twice in the central zone, by relief arcs which form continuous scalloping, as on the rim. This raised scalloping does not appear as corresponding grooves on the inside, which is perfectly plain; and this must suggest that the bowl was made by casting rather than hammered repoussé.

Figure 122. TumW 10. Bronze bowl with relief decoration. Profile. 1:2.

RIBBED OMPHALOS BOWL
TumW 11

TumW 11 **Ribbed omphalos bowl**
B 1236   Southeast corner, in TumW 2
H. 0.036   D. rim 0.16   D. omph. 0.028 m.
Fig. 123; Pl. 89G

Complete. Surface pitted by corrosion, a crack at the rim. The bottom shallow convex, the wall nearly straight, outward tilted. Heavy cast fabric. Omphalos hemispherical, slightly flared at the base. Around it two ridges triangular in profile. The floor flat; on the wall inside eight closely spaced, low, rounded horizontal ridges with shallow grooves between them. The outside plain.

PLAIN OMPHALOS BOWLS
TumW 12–18

TumW 12 **Plain omphalos bowl**
B 1237   Southeast corner, in TumW 2
H. 0.038   D. rim 0.147   D. omph. 0.028 m.
Pl. 90A

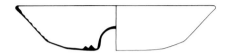

Figure 123. TumW 11. Ribbed omphalos bowl. Profile and view. 1:3.

Intact. The bottom flattened; wall rising in convex curve to plain lip. Omphalos hemispherical, slightly flared at the base; a compass prick on top. Around its base three sharp ridges triangular in profile.

TumW 13 **Plain omphalos bowl**
B 1238   Southeast corner, in TumW 2
H. 0.039–0.042   D. rim 0.146   D. omph. 0.017 m.
Pl. 90B

Intact. Shape like TumW 12; heavy fabric. A small round hole just below the rim may have been used for suspension by a string. Tiny omphalos, hemispherical. Three fine sharp ridges as on TumW 12, but set closer in toward omphalos.

TumW 14 **Plain omphalos bowl**
B 1240   Southeast corner, in TumW 2
H. 0.045   D. rim 0.174   D. omph. 0.026 m.
Pl. 90C

Corrosion holes and cracks below the rim at one side. Omphalos high, slightly more than hemispherical; a compass prick on top. Ridges as on TumW 12–13.

TumW 15 **Plain omphalos bowl**
B 1239[22]   Southeast corner, in TumW 2
H. 0.043–0.048   D. rim 0.157   D. omph. 0.031 m.

Not cleaned. The wall cracked at one side from

---

[22]Fragments of textile were found adhering to this bowl. See app. V, p. 304, Fabric E.

rim to base and then right around the central ridges probably on the line of a seam where the bowl was joined to its omphalos and surrounding ridges. The omphalos hemispherical, surrounded by two ridges triangular in profile, the outer slightly larger than the inner.

TumW 16   **Plain omphalos bowl**
             B 1241   Southeast corner, in
             TumW 2
             H. 0.048   D. rim 0.186   D. omph.
             0.032 m.
             Pl. 90D

Not cleaned. Badly cracked in three places, and lacking small fragments. Wide, shallow bowl flattened at the bottom. Just below the rim a bronze stud with flat, round head on the outside, its pin hammered flat on the inside—perhaps a plug to close a suspension hole like that on TumW 13. The omphalos hemispherical, flared slightly at its base; two sharp ridges around it.

TumW 17   **Hammered omphalos bowl without ridges**
             B 1242   Southeast corner, in
             TumW 2
             H. 0.045–0.048   D. rim 0.144
             D. omph. 0.021 m.
             Fig. 124; Pl. 90E

*Figure 124.   TumW 17. Hammered omphalos bowl
          without ridges. Profile and view.   1:3.*

Intact except for one small corrosion hole. Thin fabric of reddish coppery color; hammer marks are visible. The rim slightly thickened inside and rounded at the lip. The omphalos conical, not quite round at its base, drawn up at the top and truncated. The thin fabric, coppery color, absence of ridges, and irregularities of profile indicate that this bowl was hammered in one piece, probably by sinking.

TumW 18   **Hammered omphalos bowl without ridges**
             B 1243   Southeast corner, in
             TumW 2
             H. 0.041–0.045   D. rim 0.136–0.138
             D. omph. 0.024 m.
             Pl. 90F

Intact. Very thin fabric showing hammer marks; metal reddish and coppery. Omphalos shallow hemispherical, not perfectly round at its base. The rim thickened inward, flat on top: thickness 0.0025 m. Omphalos and bowl hammered together from one piece of metal.

PLAIN BOWLS
TumW 19–23

TumW 19   **Plain bowl**
             B. 1231   Southeast corner, in
             TumW 2
             H. 0.045   D. rim 0.147–0.150 m.
             Pl. 90G

Complete but cracked; not cleaned. Thin fabric. The bottom flat, the low wall convex and surmounted by a short sharply flared rim above a deep groove. Irregularities in the profile, lightness of the fabric, and the deep groove below the rim suggest that this bowl was made by hammering.

TumW 20   **Plain bowl**
             B 1232   Southeast corner, in
             TumW 2
             H. 0.041   D. rim 0.151 m.
             Pl. 90H

Intact, but with a nick in the lip. Heavy fabric, the lip slightly thickened and rounded; the metal brownish. Wide, shallow bowl with convex bottom forming a continuous curve with the wall; profile about one third of a sphere.

TumW 21   **Plain bowl**
             B 1233   Southeast corner, in
             TumW 2
             H. 0.046   D. rim 0.145 m.

Intact. Heavy fabric of brownish metal. Lip slightly thickened on the inside. Just below it a small, round hole for suspension, now plugged by a metal pin with flattened and polished ends. Shape as TumW 20.

TumW 22   **Plain Bowl**
             B 1234   Southeast corner, in
             TumW 2
             H. 0.045   D. rim 0.138 m.

Part of rim and wall at one side eaten away by corrosion. Thin fabric; yellowish metal. Like TumW 20–21 in shape, but slightly outward-flared at the top. The lip thickened on the inside. This bowl probably hammered rather than cast.

TumW 23   **Plain bowl**
　　　B 1235　　Southeast corner, in
　　　TumW 2
　　　H. 0.047　D. rim 0.139 m.
　　　Pl. 90I

Intact; the surface slightly pitted. Heavy fabric with lip 0.002 m. thick. The bowl slightly less than hemispherical but flattened at the bottom. Two compass pricks close together in the floor at center inside. The bowl was probably cast.

BOWL HANDLES
TumW 24

Found in cleaning the floor of the tomb, near center at the east side. There was no trace of a bronze bowl to go with these handles, so we assume that they belonged to a bowl of a material which has perished, presumably wood. In contour the handles are oval rather than round, and they are not closed. They could not, then, have been carrying handles of cauldrons or the like; rather their ends at either side of the gap must have been fitted into slots in the ends of a bolster. They may have come from a bowl of the shape of MM 55–69, but made of wood and fitted with bronze handles. Bronze rings like these were found together with wooden bolsters in Tumulus P (TumP 31–33).

TumW 24   **Pair of bowl handles**
　　　B 1287
　　　A. W. (across) 0.089　Th. 0.01 m.
　　　B. W. (across) 0.09　Th. 0.01 m.
　　　Fig. 125

A intact but diseased; *B* mended at ancient break.
　Pair of elliptical ring handles which are not closed, a gap left between the ends at the center of a long side. Bronze rods round in section, tapering very slightly from the center to the ends, which are cut off squarely.

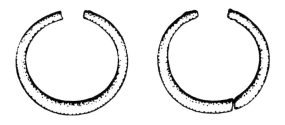

Figure 125. TumW 24. Pair of bowl handles. 1:3.

BRONZE AND LEATHER BELT
TumW 25, 26

The fragments of a leather belt decorated with bronze studs of various sizes were found lying across the skeleton about at the waist (fig. 116). The materials of which it is made as well as the position in which it was found indicate that it must have been worn around the waist as a belt, and contemporary representations in reliefs of wide belts decorated by round studs are not infrequent. The fragment found in Tumulus W was ornamented (probably at the front) by a flat bronze ring, encircling an open central circle elaborately decorated with curvilinear designs in small studs placed directly on the leather behind it. In this it is like the bronze and leather objects found in Tumulus MM and identified as belts (MM 170–178). The central disk at the front, which does not appear in the Assyrian or the North Syrian reliefs, may have been a special Phrygian feature. The belt TumW 25 is so fragmentary that it yields no clue as to how it was fastened or what its exact original dimensions were. The width of the belt must have been approximately the same as the diameter of the central disk: *ca.* 0.135 m. There were several thicknesses of leather, the outermost of which showed traces of bright vermilion color.

TumW 25   **Bronze and leather belt**
　　　B 1289　　At waist of skeleton
　　　GPL. as it lay *ca.* 0.35 m.
　　　Fig. 126; Pl. 91A

Preserved are about half of the central disk with one lug still attached at the edge (the opposite lug was also found, broken off), and fragments of the edges of the belt at either side; also two non-joining fragments of the belt itself.

A.　The central disk
　　　Est. D. *ca.* 0.136　D. lgst. studs 0.009 m.
　　　Fig. 126 (center); Pl. 91A (center)

A ring of thin flat bronze about 0.02 m. in width all around; the center open. The ring had a plain flat outer margin turned under all around at the edge except where the lugs joined. The outer face of this ring margin is decorated by a ring of half-round knobbed projections, a triple ring of much smaller ones, a second ring of knobs somewhat smaller than the outermost, and an innermost triple ring of tiny projections. All this decoration seems not to have

Figure 126. TumW 25. Bronze and leather belt. Fragment C (L); disk A (center); fragment B (R). 1:3.

been made by adding studs of various sizes but by punching or hammering up the bronze sheet repoussé from the back. At four points—top and bottom and the two sides—the inner row of larger knobs is interrupted by genuine hemispherical-headed studs of which the pins were bent over behind to hold a leather backing in place. The lugs at top and bottom, folded over and pierced by pins with stud heads, likewise served to hold the backing in place.

The central opening was filled by leather dyed or painted vermilion and decorated in an elaborate pattern of large and tiny studs. At the center a Maltese cross, the corners of each arm touching a pair of tangent circles shaped like a volute design with an outward-pointed triangle between their outer sides. Each circle has a large stud as a central eye and is made up of a quintuple row of tiny studs, each about 0.001 m. in diameter.

The belt itself to either side of the central medallion was evidently divided into square or oblong panels similarly decorated by small and large studs on a background of vermilion leather.

B. Fragment of belt
    Max. dim. 0.135   D. lgst. studs 0.008 m.
    Fig. 126 (*R*); Pl. 91A (*R*)

Part of one border, like that of the central medallion consisting of two rows of tiny studs (here studs, not repoussé). At one point it is joined by a vertical band of cross-decoration, evidently a border between two panels with variant decoration: at the left a braided or guilloche pattern, at the right tangent circles.

C. Fragment of belt
    Max. dim. 0.070   D. lgst. studs 0.0075 m.
    Fig. 126 (*L*); Pl. 91A (*L*)

An oblique pattern, the openings pointed by large

studs. The lattices themselves made by triple rows of tiny studs.

END-PLAQUE
TumW 26

Found under the left elbow of the skeleton, and perhaps originally part of the belt, a fragment of an oblong plaque of bronze worked *à jour*.

TumW 26   **End-plaque**
                   B 1290
                   GPL. 0.095   GPW. 0.029 m.

The bronze thin and diseased. A section along one edge only was preserved. The margin plain, with three hemispherical stud heads in place, securing it to a leather backing—traces of leather were still adhering to the pins. Within the margin, part of a design *à jour* of spaced half-circles along the edge, full circles within. Similar bronze plaques decorated *à jour* were found with the very similar belts in Tumulus MM (pl. 73G, I, 74F–M);[23] these may have been end pieces or parts of fastenings at one end of the belt.

FIBULAE
TumW 27–60

Of the 34 fibulae found in Tumulus W, 8 lay on or about the skeleton at the center of the grave, the rest in groups in various parts of the tomb, or scattered. Most were poorly preserved,

---

[23]MM 170*C*, 171*C*, 177*C*, 178*C*, 179*A–E*.

either broken by the collapse of the tomb roof or eaten by corrosion. Three subtypes of Blinkenberg's Group XII were represented: two specimens of XII,3, twenty-six of XII,7A,[24] and six of XII,13. Due to their scattered positions and poor state of preservation, the combining of these fibulae into pairs was difficult and dubious; nevertheless, it seems that some at least were made in pairs with catches to left and right, though not to such an extent nor so clearly as those found in Tumulus MM.

end moldings made up of blocks and blunt reels; more moldings below the spring end than below the catch, in order to raise the spring and so increase tension on the pin when the fibula was closed. The catches spurred at the base, double grooved down the outer face; probably cast together with the bows and then bent round. The springs separately made and fastened to the bows by wire tenons in drilled sockets. Studs mask the central holes through the springs. Pins double, one above the other.

FIBULAE FOUND ON OR NEAR
THE SKELETON
TumW 27–34

GROUP XII,3
TumW 27, 28

These fibulae are not a pair since both have catch to wearer's left. The arcs are thin, rectangular in section, and nearly semicircular. The

GROUP XII,7A
TumW 29–33

Group XII,7 fibulae have an arc rectangular, nearly square, in section and finished at the ends by square blocks alternated with reels, varying in number. The blocks are always wider than the bow, their sides projecting beyond its edges inside and out: compare MM 195–234 (pl. 77E–L). The variant and probably earlier subtype, isolated and labeled 7A by O. Muscarella (see above, n.

	H.	L.	Comment
TumW 27 (B 1253)	L 0.068	0.07 m. Pl. 91B	Left elbow. End of catch, upper pin, and all but stud of lower missing.
TumW 28 (B 1254)	L 0.065	0.079 Pl. 91C	Arc and catch complete. Stubs of both pins, and plate from which they spring, preserved.

	H.	L.	Comment
TumW 29 (B 1255)	L 0.06	0.071 m. Pl. 91D	The arc a flat band; above it two reels and a small bead.
TumW 30 (B 1256)	R 0.061	0.072 Pl. 91E	
TumW 31 (B 1258)	L 0.057	0.0695 Pl. 91F	The arc a flat band; above it single reel between grooves.
TumW 32 (B 1257)	R 0.059	0.07 Pl. 91G	
TumW 33 (B 1286)	L 0.025	0.028 Pl. 91H	At ends of arc two reels, grooves below and between them.

[24]A variant of Blinkenberg's Group XII,7 isolated by Oscar Muscarella, *Phryg. Fib. Gordion,* 17 f. The subtype is characterized by a flat (rather than square) arc, wide and sometimes crescent-shaped. Often the block moldings at the ends of the XII,7 arcs are dispensed with and displaced by grooves; usually spring and catch are cast in one with the arc.

24) has a wider, flatter, thinner arc, sometimes crescent-shaped, which ends in various combinations of beads and reels without square blocks; the end moldings usually continue upward the width of the bow. The molded ends, moreover, are thicker than the arc proper; the transition from the arc thickness to the molding thickness is made by a concave upward curve at the end of the arc, usually on front and back. Characteristic of these also is a rather high button below the spring, inserted to increase the tension on the pin when it was closed.

The first four fibulae of this type found on the skeleton may well form two pairs, TumW 29–30 and TumW 31–32: details of end moldings and dimensions correspond. The fifth, a miniature, cannot be paired. All have lost their pins, most of their springs, and large parts of their catches.

GROUP XII,13
TumW 34

Again a variant of Blinkenberg's subtype, with arc round in section and nearly semicircular, a cubed block at either end and at the center. A groove at either side sets off the block from the arc; compare TumW 56–60 below.

		H.	*L.*	*Comment*
TumW 34 (B 1285)	R	0.03	0.04 m.	Pin missing. One spur abraded.
		Pl. 91I		

		H.	*L.*	*Comment*
TumW 35 (B 1273)	L	0.046	0.058 m.	The arc a flat band; at the ends a reel between grooves.
		Pl. 91J		
TumW 36 (B 1274)	R	0.043	0.056	
		Pl. 91K		
TumW 37 (B 1276)	L	0.047	0.061	At the ends three reels with grooves between. High cylindrical buttons below the springs.
		Pl. 91L		
TumW 38 (B 1275)	R	0.053	0.058	
		Pl. 91M		
TumW 39 (B 1260)	R	0.047	0.055	Arc slightly lunate, narrowing to ends. Moldings three-reeled, grooves between. Three singles.
TumW 40 (B 1259)	R	0.046	0.06	
TumW 41 (B 1261)	R	0.047	0.055	

FIBULAE FOUND ON FLOOR NEAR NORTHEAST CORNER OF TOMB
TumW 35–41

GROUP XII,7A
TumW 35–41

A group of seven fibulae, all of subtype XII,7A, found scattered but in a group evidently fallen from the same place. Five with catch to the right; two to the left; it is possible to suggest two pairs (TumW 35, 36 and TumW 37, 38) and three odd items, but the pairs cannot be certain.

FIBULAE FOUND AT EAST END OF TOMB
BETWEEN TumW 70 AND TumW 71
TumW 42–48

GROUP XII,7A
TumW 42–48

Seven more fibulae of subtype 7A lay among sherds between pots TumW 70 and 71. Four of these have the catch at the wearer's right, three at the left; possibly two pairs and three odd pieces.

210

		H.	L.	Comment
TumW 42 (B 1271)	L	0.055	0.063 m.	End moldings a reel between grooves.
TumW 43 (B 1268)	R	0.057	0.064	
		Pl. 91N		
TumW 44 (B 1272)	L	0.051	0.059	The arcs slightly lunate. End moldings a reel between grooves.
TumW 45 (B 1270)	R	0.051	0.06	
TumW 46 (B 1269)	L	0.044	0.059	Not a pair; TumW 47 much larger than TumW 46. End mold-
TumW 47 (B 1267)	R	0.058	0.07	ings a reel between grooves.
TumW 48 (B 1266)	R	0.06	0.076	Much of pin preserved. End moldings as above.
		Pl. 91O		

FIBULAE SCATTERED ON FLOOR AT EAST END OF TOMB
TumW 49–51

GROUP XII,7A
TumW 49–51

Three fibulae found in cleaning the floor, all of subtype 7A. Two with catch at wearer's left, one at right. Probably not a pair.

FIBULAE FOUND UNDER BIRD BOWLS TumW 3, 4
TumW 52–55

GROUP XII,7A
TumW 52–55

Four fibulae, all subtype 7A, possibly once contained in one of the bird bowls under which they were found. Three with catch to the right, one to left: a possible pair TumW 52–53.

		H.	L.	Comment
TumW 49 (B 1278)	L	0.046	0.057 m.	Reel between grooves at ends.
TumW 50 (B 1279)	R	0.036	0.046	Rounded bead between grooves at ends.
TumW 51 (B 1277)	L	0.062	0.076	Pin preserved. End moldings reel between grooves, blocks below. Cylindrical button below spring.

		H.	L.	Comment
TumW 52 (B 1263)	L	0.05	0.064 m.	End moldings reel between grooves. Arc a flat band.
		Pl. 92A		
TumW 53 (B 1264)	R	0.05	0.06	
		Pl. 92B		
TumW 54 (B 1265)	R	0.053	0.063	Much corroded; ends a reel between grooves.
TumW 55 (B 1262)	R	0.05	0.066	Pin and most of spring missing. Moldings as above.

FIBULAE FOUND AT EAST END OF
TOMB NEAR NORTHEAST CORNER
TumW 56–60

GROUP XII,13
TumW 56–60

Five fibulae of Group XII,13 found together

on the floor about 1 m. south of the northeast corner. Three with catch to the right, two at the left: two possible pairs and an odd fibula. Arc round in section with cubed blocks at ends and center like TumW 34.

		H.	*L.*	*Comment*
TumW 56 (B 1280)	*R*	0.046	0.056 m.	Ends of pins missing. Surfaces pitted. Cylindrical buttons above
		Pl. 92C		springs. Fine incised lines encircle arc at edges of cubes.
TumW 57 (B 1282)	*L*	0.045	0.054	
		Pl. 92D		
TumW 58 (B 1281)	*R*	0.048	0.055	Like TumW 56–57.
TumW 59 (B 1283)	*L*	0.045	0.056	
		Pl. 92E		
TumW 60 (B 1284)	*R*	0.031	0.0435	Small; spring and pin missing.
		Pl. 92F		

POTTERY

FINE WARE
TumW 61–63

JUGS WITH SIEVED SPOUTS
TumW 61–63

TumW 61　　**Brown-on-buff sieve-spouted jug**
P 2283　　Southeast corner, in
　　TumW 1
H.-rim 0.081　H.-h. 0.11　D. rim
　　0.059　L. spout from bridge
　　0.138 m.
Pl. 92G–I

Intact except for mended spout; small chips missing. Fine buff clay; surface well polished over brown paint. Spherical body flattened at bottom to a resting surface; short flaring neck with plain rim flattened on top. To this have been added a long, open spout bridged at its inner end where it meets the body, and, at an angle of slightly less than 90 degrees to the spout, a vertical strap handle rising above the rim and crossed at the top by a small transverse bolster. The extremely long spout, trough-shaped and slightly flared toward its end, completely overbalances the

jug which will not stand upright unless weighted inside. At the base of the spout the wall is pierced by many small round holes to make a strainer. Six low steps ("waterfalls") in the floor of the spout between its base and its end. The overall zoned decoration employs the following motives: dotted crosshatching (lower body, shoulder and neck; bridge of spout; sides of spout inside, and one band near the outer end of its floor, and another near its end outside); dotted latticing (bolster and a square panel between handle and spout); parallel chevrons, dotted (widest part of body, and shoulder below the neck; the ends of the side walls of the spout inside, and five zones across its floor—four of double, one of single dotted chevrons; one band across exterior of spout); plain checkerboard of alternating oblong and square rows of checks (on exterior spout); checkerboard of three rows with solid checks replaced in the middle row by dot filling (three rows on interior spout and one each at base and at end of exterior; four on the handle); a lozenge chain on exterior spout. Spanning bottom and lower body is a large, open lattice pattern formed from pairs of dot rows between lines; the intersections of the lines are developed into small checkerboards. All the zones except those within the spout's waterfalls are bordered by dot rows between lines; almost all are separated by reserved bands of varying width, including the waterfall zones where the bands mark the individual steps. On the flattened surface of the rim is a double row of dots, while the side faces of the handle have transverse dot rows between lines.

TumW 62   **Bichrome sieve-spouted jug**
           P 2282   Southeast corner, in
           TumW 1
           H.-rim 0.116   H.-h. 0.148   D. 0.125
           D. rim 0.099 m.
           Pl. 92J, K

Intact, but the surface peeled at one side. Fine, clean clay fired yellowish buff; matt dark brown and dark red paint over burnished surface. Low base, slightly convex inside an outer ring so that the vessel does not sit upright. Depressed ovoid body; tall, slightly flaring neck ending in a plain rim. Vertical band handle from level of greatest diameter to a flat platform projecting behind the rim; a small bolster at the top of its curve. At about 90 degrees to the left of the handle a shallow spout has been added outside the rim and running down to the shoulder; the wall finely sieved within the spout. Wide bands of red at rim, junction of shoulder and neck, below lower handle attachment, and around lower body; over each of these, fine brown lines. Similar bands of brown-on-red, vertical, divide the neck and the shoulder into panels. On the neck three of the panels are filled by horizontal wavy lines, alternated of brown and red; two (on the spout and beside the handle) are filled by vertical wavy lines similarly alternated. On the shoulder below the spout a panel filled by an hourglass, latticed; to each side (beyond blank panels) a panel crosshatched in brown, with red dots within the diamonds; a similarly decorated panel to right of the handle. In the remaining shoulder panel, nearly opposite the spout, a large, red-filled Saint Andrew's cross with dotted red chevrons in the triangular fields. Flanking this panel are narrow isosceles triangles, each containing a vertical wavy line in red; the same motive borders one side of the panel to the left of the spout.

TumW 63   **Black polished sieve-spouted jug**
           P 2284   Southeast corner, inside
           TumW 2
           H.-rim 0.08   H.-h. 0.117   D. 0.106
           L. spout from bridge 0.066 m.
           Pl. 93A, B

Intact but for mended handle; surface flaked away and chipped in many places, especially at the lower part of the handle. Fine, micaceous clay, fired light brown; thick-walled and rather heavy for its size; surface slipped and burnished, and fired black with blushes of brown. Broad, elliptical body on a flat resting surface; short, flaring rim set atop the shoulder. Rolled vertical handle rising above the rim and curving down to join the body at level of greatest diameter. Open-trough spout set about 90 degrees to the left of the handle; at its inner end a pointed bridge; the shoulder sieved by small holes within the base of the spout.

COARSE WARE
TumW 64–72

Six coarse pottery storage vessels (TumW 64–69) had been placed upright along the face of the west wall of the tomb, extending from the northwest corner to more than half its width. No doubt at the time of burial these had contained offerings of food or liquid (see pp. 198, 282). They were found crushed down upon themselves by the collapse of the roof, the position of the fragments showing very clearly that they had been placed upright against the wall. A similar row of at least four coarse storage vessels had stood along the east wall, but these had been more crushed and scattered than those at the west when the roof collapsed, and it was possible to put together recognizable fragments of only three of them (TumW 70–72).

With the exception of TumW 72, all are of black polished fabric with a biscuit that is considerably lighter in color.

STORAGE JAR
TumW 64

TumW 64   **Storage jar**
           P 2285   West wall, south end
           H. 0.42   D. 0.38   D. rim 0.163 m.
           Fig. 127A; Pl. 93C

Mended, with fragments missing; surface worn. Micaceous clay fired reddish brown; surface black with summary polish; mica film. Broad ellipsoidal body flattened at the bottom to make a resting surface; straight, rather narrow neck with four evenly spaced ridges, the lowest at transition from shoulder; everted ledged rim.

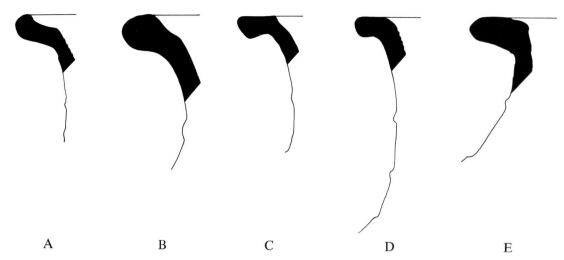

Figure 127. Rim profiles of coarse pottery. A. TumW 64, storage jar. B–E. TumW 66, 67, 71 and 72, amphoras. 1:2.

AMPHORAS
TumW 65–72

TumW 65   **Amphora**
P 2286   West wall
H. 0.527   D. 0.333   D. rim 0.143 m.
Pl. 93D

Mended, with small fragments missing; much of surface flaked away. Fabric like that of TumW 64, but with brown blushes. Elongated ovoid body with flattened resting surface; straight neck tapered slightly to an everted rim. Band handles shoulder to midneck, each with a large knob at its elbow.

TumW 66   **Amphora**
P 2287   West wall
H. 0.515   D. 0.422   D. rim 0.206 m.
Fig. 127B; Pl. 93E

Mended; scratches on lower body. Clay like TumW 64; slipped and burnished with a burnisher which made broad strokes; thin mica film and blushes of lighter color. Plump ovoid body flattened at the bottom, the shoulder curving continuously through the neck to the everted ledged rim. Three raised decorative ridges: around middle of neck, at base of neck, at level of upper handle attachment. Vertical strap handles on shoulder.

TumW 67   **Amphora**
P 2342   West wall
PH. 0.332   D. 0.397   D. rim
0.16 m.
Fig. 127C

Mended; the lower part missing. Reddish yellow

clay, heavily micaceous; slipped, polished, and fired black with lighter blushes. Narrow neck with blunt ridge at base; second ridge at midway; everted rim; strap handles from shoulder to angle between shoulder and neck. The handles ridged down the middle on their outer faces, and with a deep finger impression at their lower attachments.

TumW 68   **Amphora**
P 2344   West wall
H. 0.415   D. 0.435   D. rim 0.162 m.
Pl. 93F

Mended with gaps; surface deteriorated. Reddish brown clay; matt surface. Broad ovoid body on flattened bottom; narrow neck; everted ledged rim. Strap handles from shoulder to neck.

TumW 69   **Amphora**
P 2345   Northeast corner
H. 0.467   D. 0.395   D. rim 0.175 m.

Fragmentary; surface of lower body and rim badly deteriorated. Reddish yellow clay, heavily micaceous; thin slip, polished to a low luster and fired black with lighter blushes; mica film. Ovoid body; narrow neck with thick ridge at base and two more placed above and below midway; everted rim. Handles as on TumW 67.

TumW 70   **Amphora**
P 2343   East wall, north half
Rest. H. 0.443   D. 0.397   D. rim
0.175 m.

Mended; base, fragments of body and one handle missing; surface deteriorated in places. Fabric similar to TumW 69, but without mica film. Elongated, biconical body; narrow neck with thick ridge at base and a second just below midway; everted rim with incipient ledge. Strap handles from shoulder to lower neck; ridged down the middle with shallow channel to either side; short horns trail obliquely from each side of lower attachments, while small knobs flank the upper.

TumW 71   **Amphora**
P 2365   Body east wall; neck
fragment south wall
PH. 0.202   D. rim 0.143 m.
Fig. 127D; Pl. 92G

Fragmentary; from mixed sherds. Part of shoulder, neck, and rim preserved with one handle; scratches on shoulder. Light reddish brown clay; slipped and polished but now practically matt; mica film. Body perhaps elongated like TumW 65; tall, narrow neck with ridge at base and two more ridges placed at quarter and mid-height; everted rim; plain strap handles from shoulder to middle of neck.

TumW 72   **Red polished amphora**
P 2346   Southeast corner, north of
TumW 1
H. 0.475   D. 0.445   D. rim 0.212 m.
Fig. 127E; Pl. 93H

Mended; many fragments missing; surface almost totally deteriorated. Coarse red clay with many lime bits; red polished surface, perhaps with a mica film. Pointed ovoid body with flattened resting surface; low neck with ridge at midway; everted rim. Horizontal handles, round in section but twisted to make a spiral surface, set upright high on shoulder. Low, raised bands placed just below greatest diameter, low on shoulder and at top of shoulder.

SUMMARY OF POTTERY*

In range and variety, the pottery of Tumulus W presents a far less impressive group than that which is encountered in either K-III or P; moreover, the quantity of ceramic vessels is here the lowest among the early series of wealthy tumuli. At least ten storage vessels, nine of which were inventoried, served the important function of containers (TumW 64–72), while three spouted sieve jugs betray some limited and very particularized interest in pottery of good quality (TumW 61–

63). The sieve jugs of clay were supplemented by one of bronze (TumW 5), and all were divided equally between the two cauldrons, TumW 1 and 2. TumW 2 contained a total of 20 vessels, all bronze but for the black polished TumW 63. The deposition is reminiscent of the pottery service contained by the bronze cauldron no. 49 of Tumulus K-III, and is perhaps analogous to the concentration of pottery vessels in the south central area of Tumulus P (p. 32).

Although the sieve jugs and amphoras have been examined elsewhere in connection with their counterparts in other tombs (pp. 251 f., 255 f.), it will be worthwhile to reiterate certain observations. TumW 61 is of fine brown-on-buff ware like that encountered in both P and K-III; its style is closest to that of K-III, no. 10. The black polished sieve jug TumW 63, although a little heavier in weight, is of fabric similar to that of the fine reduced wares of P, while the amphoras TumW 65–72 parallel in technique and certain aspects of form the coarser reduced ware vessels of the same tomb. This can be said as well of the storage jar TumW 64. While an uncommon shape in these early burials, it is clearly related in form and presumably in function to the large amphoras of Tumuli W and P; its broad ellipsoidal body with one half much less convex than the other (i.e., bicurved) is otherwise not seen among the large vessels of W, although close parallels are to be found among P's amphoras. TumW 62 seems by reason of its bichrome fabric, style, and shape to have been an import; neither the early tumuli nor settlement contexts of the early city provide comfortable parallels. Certain of the larger vessels show signs of wear from previous use, as differentiated from the deterioration which seems to be a result of conditions in the tomb (TumW 64, 66, 71).

The relative earliness of Tumulus W manifests itself more readily through its bronzes than through its pottery.[25] Nevertheless, certain features and conditions of the ceramic assemblage may perhaps be interpreted as symptoms of an early date. Thus the absence of dinoi may be more than fortuitous in view of the shape's abundance and apparent importance in the later tombs P and MM. It is conceivable that the ceramic

---

*This summary written by G. Kenneth Sams.

[25]Above, pp. 198–199.

form had not yet become part of the traditional funerary ensemble at the time of W and that its function was served by the tomb's small bronze cauldrons, the shape of which may well have inspired the ceramic counterpart. The absence of animals on TumW 61 may also have chronological implications, as Rodney Young believed, since they do appear later on vessels of the same fine ware from K-III and P.[26] A purely geometric, prefigural phase of brown-on-buff ware seems both likely and reasonable, but it must be emphasized that the absence of animals in itself cannot be used as a sure indication of relative date for several vessels from K-III are totally geometric. The storage amphoras of W may indicate a further mark of earliness, at least within funerary

contexts: they favor ovoidal forms and in fact never display the double-contoured or bicurved ellipsoidal shape that is found in K-III and P (p. 256); the latter profile is, however, encountered in the storage jar TumW 64 and may here reflect an early use of the body shape that was eventually to be extended to amphoras.[27] A final chronological indication may be the scarcity of vessels of fine ware in the tomb. Aside from the three sieve jugs, TumW 61–63, pottery is relegated to storage purposes, whereas both K-III and P offer impressive arrays of fine ceramics. MM, judged latest of the group on the basis of its bronzes, may belong to the early stage of a new trend for it displays a total disregard for elegant pottery (cf. pp. 175–176).

WOOD

DISKS
TumW 73, 74

Both were found in the cauldron TumW 2.

TumW 73   **Disk**
W 101
D. 0.055–0.061   Th. 0.01 m.
Fig. 128

A flat disk (now warped and nearly elliptical—originally round) of polished dark wood with plain back and side faces. The front decorated by incision: five concentric bands, each consisting of four fine lines, and at center a small dotted ring.

TumW 74   **Disk**
W 102
D. 0.035–0.0375   Th. 0.008 m.

A flat disk of polished dark wood, now slightly warped toward the elliptical. All surfaces plain.

PLATES AND FRAGMENTS OF PLATES
TumW 75–79

The fragments of five different plates or trays were found together near the east end of the

tomb, just north of center. The first two, TumW 75 and 76, are strips from across the centers of shallow, flat-rimmed plates; the other three consist of two to four side (not central) strips from other plates. The varying diameters and widths of the surrounding flat rims assure us that we are

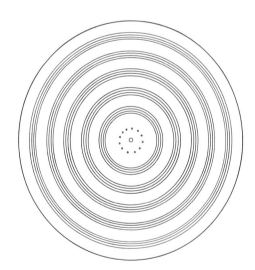

Figure 128. TumW 73. Disk with linear decoration. Restoration to its original round form is here based on its greatest preserved diameter. 1:1.

---

[26]Cf. R. S. Young, *Gordion Guide* (1975), 52.

[27]Pre-destruction evidence from the city mound, by rea-

son of its fragmentary nature, is of no help in determining the profile's popularity during early periods that may be contemporary with W.

dealing with five separate objects. Since the preservation of the pieces recovered is relatively good, it is difficult to explain the complete disappearance of the missing fragments. However, the side faces of each strip, well enough preserved, in no case show holes for dowels to fasten piece to piece; they must, therefore, have been fastened together by glue. It is possible that when the glue gave way, the component pieces became scattered and that some of them were destroyed when the roof of the tomb fell.

TumW 75　**Fragmentary(?) plate**
　　　　　　W 103　　Near east wall
　　　　　　L. 0.345　　W. fragment 0.139
　　　　　　　　W. rim 0.054 m.
　　　　　　Pl. 94A, B

A central section of a plate cut along the grain of the wood. The plain, flat rim at either end slightly raised above the shallow, flat floor, the transition a gentle curve. The outside plain with an upward curve toward the rim; the plate now rocks slightly on its rounded bottom.

TumW 76　**Fragmentary(?) plate**
　　　　　　W 104　　Near east wall
　　　　　　L. *ca.* 0.348　　W. fragment 0.123
　　　　　　　　W. rim 0.052 m.
　　　　　　Pl. 94C, D

Similar to TumW 75.

TumW 77　**Fragments of a plate**
　　　　　　W 105　　Near east wall
　　　　　　L. 0.328　　W. fragments 0.05 and
　　　　　　　　0.051　　W. rim. 0.047 m.
　　　　　　Pl. 94E

Two fragments that belonged at either side of a central section like TumW 75–76.

TumW 78　**Fragments of a plate**
　　　　　　W 106　　Near east wall
　　　　　　L. 0.34　　W. rim 0.067 m.
　　　　　　Pl. 94F

Three slats. Wide rim. One must assume (probably) two pieces missing: a central piece and an inner piece next to one edge.

TumW 79　**Fragments of a plate**
　　　　　　W 107　　Near east wall
　　　　　　D. 0.362　　W. rim 0.068 m.

Four pieces, one evidently a narrow central slat. The wide rim remains constant in width on all the pieces.

SCREEN
TumW 80

TumW 80　**Screen**
　　　　　　W 109　　Near southeast corner
　　　　　　GPL 0.77　　W. as found *ca.* 0.20
　　　　　　Th. 0.018 m.
　　　　　　Fig. 129; Pl. 94G

Found on the floor of the tomb lying just to the west of the bronze cauldrons TumW 1 and 2 (see fig. 116), Two fragments: a large piece and a small

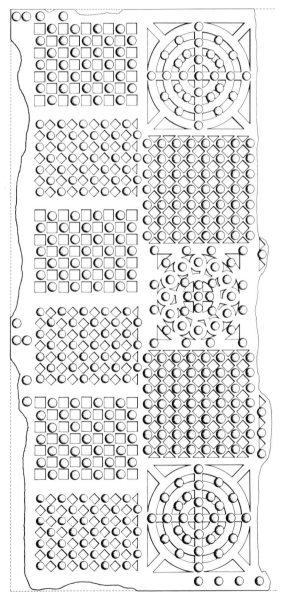

Figure 129.　TumW 80. Screen.　Approx. 1:5.

one. Considerable splintered wood, unidentifiable, lay about the fragments, and a large handful of bronze studs which had once decorated it, was gathered from the floor. The screen (if such it was) was made from three long strips of wood fastened together on the long sides by dowels in much the same way as were the component pieces of MM 378–379. The large fragment consists of two strips once in the same plane but now buckled to a V shape; the dowel holes may be seen in the wrenched-apart edges. A third strip is attested at the broken right edge, fig. 129; the small fragment must have belonged to this. The borders at the left side and at the top and bottom could be recognized: the left border decorated by cut-out perforations in patterns. The outer (left) strip shows six oblong panels, one above the other; for these two patterns were alternated: a checkerboard of solid and cut-out squares, and a lattice of the same, somewhat smaller and running obliquely. On the checkerboard the center of each solid square was decorated by a large bronze stud; on the lattices the solid squares at the crossings of the oblique rows were similarly decorated with slightly smaller studs. The right edge of the central strip shows four studs still in place in positions corresponding to those of the studs at the ends of the latticed panels of the left side. These indicate latticed panels at the right, and their levels suggest that the outer strip at the right duplicated that at the left with alternated checkerboard and lattice panels, but with a lattice panel (instead of checkboard) at the top. The small non-joining fragment is from a lattice panel and must have belonged to the right side of the screen.

The central strip shows five panels, each approximately square. Three patterns of openwork cutouts were used to decorate these: at top and bottom concentric rings joined by spokes, the spokes ornamented by bronze studs; above and below these a lattice of solid and cut-out diamonds, the solid ones again decorated by studs; and at the center again concentric rings, a cross at the middle of the inner one and curlicues faced counterclockwise joining the inner and outer rings. This rather elaborate cut-out pattern of the central panel was generously embellished with bronze studs.

The missing strip at the right side would have brought the width of the whole to about 0.54 m. (each strip approximately 0.18 m. wide). Though smaller, the proportions of the whole (0.77 m. high by 0.54 m. wide) are comparable to those of the screens from MM (0.95 m. high by 0.80 m. wide) and from P (about 0.80 m. high by 0.56 m. wide). Just to the north of TumW 80 was found an arched foot much like those of the MM screens; though in horrible condition (it disintegrated later), it was entirely recognizable. This piece, in addition to the flat character of the other pieces that were preserved, suggested that we were dealing with another screen. Since the "screen" from Tumulus W does not have in its face the inlaid curving legs of the screens from Tumuli P and MM, the foot must have belonged at the bottom of the leg behind, which enabled a screen to stand upright. No fragments of the leg itself, or of a back-frame that it supported, were recognizable. Nevertheless, the identification of this piece of furniture as another screen remains probable.

IVORY

PENDANT
TumW 81

TumW 81 **Globular pendant**
BI 366
H.-loop 0.04   D. 0.031 m.
Pl. 94H

Found on the floor in the area of the screen, TumW 80. Mended from several chips and laminations; small bits missing. A well-cut globular pendant of ivory with a pierced loop at the top, round in section, for suspension.

IV

COMMENTARY

BRONZE

BULL'S-HEAD ATTACHMENTS*,[1]
MM 1, 12, 13   TumW 1, 2

The large cauldron found intact with its four bull's-head attachments in an Urartian tomb at Altıntepe in eastern Anatolia, together with its tripod rod stand, has been universally accepted as a product of Urartian bronze smiths.[2] The Altıntepe cauldron agrees in details of style, moreover, with four bull's-head attachments, which are perhaps from a single cauldron; of them two are known to have been found in the old excavations at Toprakkale by Lake Van.[3] Four further attachments of the same general type may again be from one cauldron, and two of these pieces have an assured provenience of Guşçı on the northwestern shores of Lake Urmia;[4] a smaller but

---

*This section written by Keith DeVries.

[1]Rodney S. Young had completed the first two paragraphs of his projected discussion of the bull's-head attachments, and in the text that follows the paragraphs are left substantially in their original form; the first is the more modified, because of an adjusted count of Urartian protomes. Notes 2–4 are also basically his.

The whole text is organized in accordance with his apparent intention: a consideration of the different classes of bull attachments and the degree to which each is represented among the material from the tumuli published here and from Gordion as a whole. It is clear enough that he would have ruled out the possibility of any of the Gordion heads being Urartian, but it is not certain to what extent he would have altered an early view that the Tumulus W and Cumae bull cauldrons as well as the MM ones may be Phrygian (*AJA* 64 [1960]:231). However, since in his later work he helped define the North Syrian school of bronze production and emphasized its

importance (*JNES* 26 [1967]:145–167), it is likely that he would have accepted or independently made a North Syrian attribution for TumW 1 and 2 and the Cumae cauldron.

[2]Best illustrated in E. Akurgal, *Kunst Anat.*, figs. 30–32. The tomb was a chance find by road builders in 1938; the cauldron was reserved for the Ankara Museum by H. H. von der Osten. In 1959 Tahsin Özgüç reopened and cleared the tomb, as well as two contemporary ones (*Altıntepe* II, 10–27, 65–72).

[3]R. D. Barnett, *Iraq* 12 (1950): 19, pl. 16, paired two heads in the British Museum from the Toprakkale excavations. P. Amandry in *Aegean and Near East,* 239, pls. 24–26, added to them a head in the Walters Art Gallery in Baltimore and another in a private collection in Paris.

[4]G. M. A. Hanfmann, *AnatSt* 6 (1956): 205–213, pls. 17–19, associated heads in the Fogg Museum, the Louvre, and private collections in Cincinnati and Cleveland.

again generally similar piece is also said to be from near Lake Urmia.[5] Further comparable attachments (the precise number not published) come from a tomb by the Araxes River in northwestern Iran.[6] Thus we have more than 14 bull's-head attachments of consistent type coming with certainty or some likelihood from the Urartian region and probably belonging to five cauldrons.[7]

Common to all but (apparently) the small Urmia bull's head and at least one of the Araxes attachments is a two-piece construction: the heads proper end in circular or oval openings which could be slipped over collars cast together with the attachment plates having the schematic form of birds; in some cases the heads are fastened in position by dowels. The join was to some degree masked by a raised and decorated band of bronze encircling the front and sides of the neck and ending (on the Altıntepe and Toprakkale attachments) below the ears. None of the bulls' heads carries holders for ring handles at the back on top; instead the forelock, a slightly raised rectangle, is carried over the head and down the neck at the back for a certain distance. The forelocks are squared at the front between the eyes (as also at the back) and divided usually into six long tresses which end in spiral snail-shell locks. The horns, rather long, sweep outward, then up and back; in some cases they were separately made and socketed to the head, a band of engraved decoration around their bases serving to mask the joins. The ears, too, fairly large and extended horizontally to each side below the horns, seem in some cases to have been separately made and joined. The bony structure of the nose is emphasized, set off from the cheeks in some cases by modeling, in others by grooves or engraved lines. The eyes are round, surrounded by a raised ridge, which in some cases shows a tear duct at its inner

end; above, on all but the small Urmia piece, large lunate or bean-shaped swellings indicate eyebrows.

These attachments may have had a considerable chronological range. A bell with an inscription of Argishti I (ca. 786–764 B.C.) in the Araxes tomb and a metal vessel bearing the name of the Cilician king Urikki (ca. 740–732) in the Altıntepe tomb indicate dates well before the end of the eighth century for the bull's-head cauldrons and other material of the two grave deposits.[8] If Toprakkale was indeed founded by Rusa II (ca. 685–645) rather than Rusa I (ca. 735–714), then the attachments from that site probably go into the seventh century.[9]

A few bull attachments associated with Urartu show only a minimum of the standard characteristics. One from Karmir Blur has in common with those considered above only the treatment of the horns and a rendition of a squared forelock with tresses, but the forelock itself differs by being shrunken and vestigial.[10] In addition, the attachment has the atypical element of a spool mounting for a ring handle. A very late date may explain the unusual features of the piece: it was found in the destruction level of the site and thus in a context of the late seventh to early sixth century.[11] Three bull's-head attachments among a large group of Urartian bronzes in the University Museum stand even further apart, since they have smooth, rounded forelocks and have left as standard only the horns that project first outward and then upward; one of the heads, like that from Karmir Blur, has a spool mounting. Lack of information on the find circumstances of the pieces and the resulting lack of knowledge of the extent to which they and other material with them belong to a single coherent group from a single spot make it difficult to assess their significance.[12]

[5] *Aegean and Near East,* 260, pl. 32:3.

[6] B. Piotrovskii, *Iskusstvo Urartu* (Leningrad, 1962), 3, fig. 1, pl. 1; while the specific number of attachments is not cited, the plural is used. G. Azarpay, *Urartian Art,* 53, pl. 34.

[7] Further studies dealing with Urartian and other bull's-head attachments include H. V. Herrmann, *Ol. Forsch.* VI, 114–130; Van Loon, *Urartian Art,* 104–107; O. Muscarella, *MMJ* 1 (1968): 7–18; *idem* in *Art and Technology,* 111–112; H. Kyrieleis, *AthMitt* 92 (1977): 71–89.

[8] Araxes tomb: Piotrovskii, *Iskusstvo Urartu,* 7; Van Loon, *Urartian Art,* 104. But cf. Azarpay, *Urartian Art,*

25. Altıntepe tomb: F. Steinherr, *Anatolia* 3 (1958): 97–102; Van Loon, *loc. cit.* The reading of Urikki's name on the Altıntepe vessel is considered incorrect (H. G. Güterbock).

[9] For the problem in determining the ruler, see M. N. Van Loon, *Urartian Art,* 30.

[10] B. Piotrovskii, *Karmir-Blur* I (Erevan, 1950), 70, fig. 44; G. Azarpay, *Urartian Art,* 53, fig. 15.

[11] O. Muscarella, *AJA* 69 (1965): 237.

[12] O. Muscarella, *MMJ* 1 (1968): 18, n. 29, has a brief discussion of the material, based on a photographic ex-

The Urartian attachments have value as the best understood of the groups and the class from which definitions of others must still proceed, but for the purposes of this volume the most important aspect of the pieces is a negative one: their absence from the Gordion tumuli and the citadel mound as well. The alliance between the Phrygians and Urartians in the period of King Midas[13] and whatever earlier relations there may have been did not bring to the Phrygian capital any known cauldrons with attachments of this sort or for that matter any other bronzes found to date, although to judge from Assyrian records and finds from Urartu the Urartian craftsmen were proficient at fine bronze production.[14]

A set of bull's-head attachments that has long been recognized as Near Eastern but as differing distinctly from the Urartian group is the pair fitted onto a cauldron now in Copenhagen and said to have been found at Cumae:[15] the bull attachments are characterized by a one-piece construction of head and bird-shaped plate, a mounting for a ring handle, a compact but rounded head, short horns which curve inward over the head, a rounded forelock which instead of tresses has incised decoration around its border, and a fully modeled muzzle.

While an identification of the region of manufacture did not come as readily as for the Urartian class,[16] H. V. Herrmann[17] and, more recently and with fuller evidence, H. Kyrieleis[18] have been able to demonstrate convincingly a homeland in the North Syrian area, on the basis of other bronze bull attachments found there (one perhaps from

the Aleppo area[19] and one, less close, from Zincirli[20]) and of stone bull sculptures from Carchemish[21] and, once more not quite so close, a stone bull's-head weight from Zincirli.[22]

Most significant for Gordion is the presence at the site of cauldrons with North Syrian bull attachments in contrast to the absence of the Urartian. H. Kyrieleis has already published the attachments of TumW 2 (pl. 88A) as North Syrian,[23] and the closely similar ones of TumW 1 join them (pl. 87). Both these Gordion sets differ somewhat from other attachments of the group in having triangular rather than bird-shaped plates and in having an upward turn to the horns after the initial curve across the head, but they are fully canonical in their handle mounting, curved forelock, articulated muzzle, and especially in the broad, rounded form of the head, a feature which is at its most pronounced in these pieces. A bull attachment found in Megaron 4 of the citadel in debris of the early seventh-century destruction of the site quite possibly belongs to the group too, but heavy damage prevents certainty (pl. 95D).[24] As North Syrian imports, the bull cauldrons are not isolated at Gordion, other objects from the region being ivory horse trappings found in Terrace Building 2 of the destruction level[25] and, in all probability, the cauldrons with "siren attachments," MM 2 and 3, from the great tumulus (above, pp. 104–110; pls. 51–57).

Dating criteria for North Syrian bull attachments are vague, unless it should be that the Copenhagen cauldron, which being complete presumably was in a tomb, really is from Cumae; no

---

amination. The group was bought by the University Museum in 1967; Engin Özgen has studied part of it for his doctoral dissertation for the University of Pennsylvania, *The Urartian Bronze Collection at the University Museum: The Urartian Armor* (1979).

[13]D. D. Luckenbill, *Anc. Records* II, sections 11, 55.

[14]M. N. Van Loon, *Urartian Art,* 84–87.

[15]P. Amandry in *Aegean and Near East,* 242–244, pl. 28. E. Akurgal, *Kunst Anat.,* figs. 33–34. The style was first analyzed by Amandry, and his distinction between the Cumae cauldron and the Urartian ones has been accepted by the writers on the subject cited in n. 7.

[16]Van Loon, *Urartian Art,* 106, suggested "some workshop intermediate between Urartu and Greece, perhaps Cyprus." R. S. Young, as cited in n. 1, hypothesized in 1960 that its bronze working school might be Phrygian. O. Muscarella in *Art and Technology,* 112, suggested a

"Near Eastern" but non-Urartian category that might comprise both Phrygian and North Syrian centers.

[17]*Ol. Forsch.* VI, 122.

[18]*Ibid.,* 74–76.

[19]R. Dussaud, *Syria* 11 (1930): 366, fig. 2. H. Kyrieleis, *AthMitt* 92 (1977): 74, pl. 29, figs. 4–5.

[20]F. von Luschan, *Ausgrabungen in Sendschirli* V (Berlin, 1943), 107, pl. 49g.

[21]C. L. Woolley and R. D. Barnett, *Carchemish* III (London, 1952), pls. B 34 and B 47. E. Akurgal, *Kunst Heth.,* pl. 108.

[22]F. von Luschan, *op. cit.,* pl. 11b, 12f.

[23]*AthMitt* 92 (1977): 75–76, pl. 31:1–3.

[24]Gordion inventory number B 1445.

[25]R. S. Young, *AJA* 66 (1962): 166–167, pls. 46–47. R. S. Young, *JNES* 26 (1967): 149, pl. 21.

known graves of the Greek colonists there predate the Early Protocorinthian period, beginning *ca.* 720 B.C.[26] It could be that the unusual[27] triangular plates on the attachments from Tumulus W, a relatively early tomb at Gordion (above, pp. 198–199), are a sign of their belonging to an initial phase, before the bull-protome type may have been influenced by the "siren" attachments (or for that matter bird-headed attachments like those of TumW 3), for which bird bodies are likely to have been an integral part from the beginning of the series. The unparalleled technique of manufacture of the Tumulus W pieces, with their having a cast inner part and a hammered and incised shell, could also perhaps be understood as an early feature.

A third group of bull attachments, first identified by M. van Loon and Herrmann and now more fully by Kyrieleis, is Phrygian, with the class represented almost entirely by examples from Gordion.[28] Defining characteristics include the attachment plate, which has generally dwindled from a bird body to a "T,"[29] the geometric abstraction of the head, and the appliqué-like raised eyes. One can note as forming a particularly close group the pairs of attachments on two small cauldrons of the great tumulus, MM 12 and 13 (pl. 59A–C) and a pair, presumably from a single small cauldron, in Terrace Building 1 of the destruction level (pl. 95B):[30] on them the geometricization is heightened to the degree that the muzzle is flattened and a ridge runs down the center of

the nose. For those two features there is a fair parallel in the wooden lion TumP 107 (pl. 22C–F) and a much better one in the lion of an orthostate sculpture from the citadel mound;[31] the parallels help give assurance that the style is indeed Phrygian, particularly since the orthostate must certainly have been worked at Gordion.

The pair of heads on the large cauldron MM 1 (pl. 50) are rather different from those just considered and are less rigidly geometricized, perhaps because their larger size allowed more modeling; the muzzle is shaped and rounded, there is only a hint of a nose ridge, and the eyes are large, gogglelike members, encircled by two high ridges. As Van Loon has noted, however, there is a close correspondence between those eyes and the ones on the lion of the orthostate cited above, and one can add the overall similarity of outline and proportions between the two bulls' heads and the lion's, with the total resemblances being enough to justify a Phrygian identification here, too.

At least one Phrygian bull cauldron traveled beyond its home area. Herrmann and Kyrieleis have both recognized a bull protome found at the Heraeum on Samos as Phrygian.[32] The identification appears certain, since the piece matches in all key particulars those of the tight group comprised of MM 12 and 13 and the pair from Terrace Building 1.

The handle mounting on all the Phrygian bull attachments except for those from Terrace Building 1 and the rounded forelock on all but those of

---

[26]J. N. Coldstream, *Greek Geometric Pottery* (London, 1968), 325–326.

[27]With the possible exception of the incomplete Zincirli attachment (Von Luschan, *op cit.*, pl. 49g), no other bull attachments clearly belonging to the North Syrian group have triangular plates. One does occur on an attachment in Greece with some North Syrian characteristics (C. Waldstein, *The Argive Heraeum* II [Boston and New York, 1905], pl. LXXV, 25), but Kyrieleis suspects that the piece may be a Greek product (*AthMitt* 92 [1977]: 87).

None of the extant Urartian bull attachments has such plates either, but on the Cypriote and (eventually) Aegean Greek pieces (below, p. 223) triangular and elliptical plates are common (Herrmann, *Ol. Forsch.* VI, pls. 47–52; Kyrieleis, *AthMitt* 92 [1977], pls. 32–33, 35–37). If these do indeed reflect the original plate form, then it lingered longer in the Cypriote class than it did in the North Syrian and Urartian groups.

[28]Van Loon, *Urartian Art*, 105, n. 119. Herrmann, *Ol.*

Forsch. VI, 122, where MM 12 and 13 are thought to be Phrygian, but MM 1 is thought to be linked to the Cumae group and North Syria. Kyrieleis, *AthMitt* 92 (1977): 76, 87. Not taken into account here is Young's early view on a Phrygian class of bulls' heads (p. 219, n. 1).

[29]Such a plate also occurs on the late Urartian bull attachment from Karmir Blur (Piotrovskii, *Karmir-Blur* I, 70, fig. 44). Small T attachments without protomes are present at Gordion on the small cauldrons MM 4–11 (pl. 58).

[30]Gordion inventory numbers B 1398*A,B*. G. R. Edwards, *Expedition* 5, no. 3 (1963): 45, fig. 22. Muscarella, *MMJ* 1 (1968), fig. 10.

[31]R. S. Young, *AJA* 62 (1957): 144, pl. 21, fig. 4.

[32]U. Jantzen, *Samos* VIII, 77, 79, pl. 77, B 1266. H. V. Herrmann, *Gnomon* 47 (1975): 400. Kyrieleis, *AthMitt* 92 (1977): 87.

the cauldron MM 1 suggest an influence from the North Syrian type, a natural enough occurrence in view of the import of that class into Gordion.

A fourth group of bull attachments that Kyrieleis has defined is characterized by wide flaring horns that form a crescent, a raised bridge between the horns, and the lack of a forelock.[33] The type was produced on Cyprus from at least the late eighth century and was adopted by Aegean Greek craftsmen in the seventh century. As with the Urartian bulls' heads the significance for Gordion is a negative one, since no examples have turned up either in the tumuli or on the citadel, although some trade ties during the period with Cyprus or with the broader Levantine cultural zone of which it was a part are suggested by the black-on-red juglet (TumP 59), the Egyptian blue objects (TumP 46 and 47), and a bronze bowl with lotus handles from Tumulus K-III.[34]

SMALL CAULDRONS WITH T-SHAPED ATTACHMENTS
TumP 3-5   MM 4-9

To these may be added:

Gordion: K-III, nos. 51–54[35]

Compare also:

Gordion: K-III, nos. 47, 48 (pottery)[36]
K-III, nos. 49, 50 (large cauldrons)[37]

Small cauldrons with freely swiveling ring handles fastened to T-shaped attachments were found in three of the Gordion tumuli: P, MM, and K-III. The handles, rods of bronze threaded through the ring sockets and bent to form circular rings, fitted loosely and swung freely. They may be distinguished easily from the oval or flattened rings of which the ends, often separated by a gap, were fitted into bolsters at the rims of bowls, so that they could swivel only upward or downward (MM 55–69). The attachments of K-III, nos. 51, 52, were evidently plain flat plates of bronze doweled to the wall at either end. There could doubtless be numerous variations in the shape of the attachments; the T-shaped ones, however, are sufficiently distinctive to form a class and seem to have been Phrygian. The lower pin through the base of the stem of the T gave added support.

The small cauldron form was popular and useful. Such a cauldron could be hung up by one handle out of the way, or easily transported when full by turning up both handles and thrusting a carrying stick through them. Remains of the carrying sticks were found in TumP 5 and in K-III, no. 51. The form, though imitated in wood (TumP 145) and in pottery (K-III, nos. 47, 48) was essentially a metallic one since ring handles of clay or wood were inherently too fragile to bear much weight. Perhaps it is significant that of the two pottery vessels from K-III one (no. 47) is round-bottomed, the other (no. 48) has a low base ring. Without a resting surface no. 47 would not stand up; and doubtless its ring handles, of clay, could not bear the weight of the whole if it were hung up. Thus no. 48 would seem to have been an improved version of no. 47.

Cauldrons could be used for the storage of liquid or dry foodstuffs, or as mixing bowls, and also no doubt for cooking. For the last purpose, of course, wooden vessels would not serve, and the pottery vessels that have survived in K-III are of fine black polished rather than coarse cooking ware. The bronze cauldrons with handles that could be trusted for suspension over the fire would have been most suitable for cooking, but none of the specimens from MM or from P shows traces of discoloration by fire. They may have been placed in the tomb in new condition, or, if used before being offered, used only for purposes of storing or serving. It is interesting to note that these cauldrons seem often to have been made in pairs. The six found in MM may be matched with

---

[33] *Ibid.*, 76–86.

[34] G. Körte in *Gordion,* 72, no. 57, fig. 51.

[35] *Ibid.,* 70–71 and figs. 47, 48.

[36] *Ibid.,* 67, fig. 43.

[37] *Ibid.,* 68–70 and figs. 44–46.

assurance into three pairs: shape, dimensions, and treatment of detail are identical within the pairs and diverge between them. Thus MM 4 and 5 are almost identical in size and profile, and in having flat hoop-rims added over the lips of the cast vessels. MM 6 and 7, again identical in size and profile, have been more carefully finished at the rim so that it is not easy to determine whether the rims were cast together with the vessels or added; and this pair shows the added feature of raised moldings at the ends of the T attachments. MM 8 and 9, smaller in size and different in profile from the other four, are identical to each other. The same correspondences of size, shape, and detail indicate that TumP 3 and 4 were a pair. On the other hand TumP 5 lacks a mate and none of the specimens found in Tumulus K-III can be matched. Of the last the two with T-shaped attachments (nos. 53, 54) had ring handles of bronze while the others (nos. 50–52 large cauldrons) carried rings of iron as well as strengthen-

ing bands of iron below the rim, and no. 50 had its attachments fastened by iron rivets. G. Körte[38] interpreted these features as repairs; he concluded that the bronzes found in Tumulus K-III had been imported from Cyprus and later repaired with iron by the natives at Gordion. Recent discoveries at Gordion as well as elsewhere in Phrygia, and the rarity of similar bronzes in Cyprus, make this hypothesis no longer tenable. The great majority of the bronzes found at Gordion were undoubtedly made there, or nearby. Whether the use of iron bands and rivets and ring handles on vessels of bronze was original, or the result of repairs made later, we cannot tell with certainty. The only bronze vessels to be found in the more recent excavations at Gordion which show traces of iron fittings are the cauldron TumP 2 (pl. 7B), and fragmentary remains in TB-1 (ILS 384, 400, 419) and TB-2 (ILS 386) on the city mound (pl. 95E, G), and B 426 in Tumulus E and B 470 in Tumulus F.

JUGS WITH TREFOIL MOUTH
TumP 6, 7   MM 16–44

The jug with trefoil mouth (oinochoe) is virtually a closed vessel with swelling body and a small opening at the top, sometimes with a fairly long, narrow neck. Its handle is a separately made piece attached by pins or dowels to the back of the rim at the top and to the shoulder below. The ingeniously made handle of most of the Gordion specimens, described below, would seem to have been a Phrygian specialty. Its attachment at the top to the rim of the jug was easily possible at any time, but the pinning of its lower end to the wall of the vessel at the shoulder would seem to have required access from the inside, especially in the case of two jugs (MM 21 and 25) inside which a small, separate reinforcing plate is visible at the point of attachment, the flattened ends of the dowels showing in its face. In most cases the outer end of the pin is capped by a decorative round stud head, its inner end flattened by hammering to a rivet-like head. These manipulations —the threading of the pin through holes drilled in the wall and handle, the insertion of plates to strengthen the join on the inside, and the hammering down of the inner ends of the pins, could not have been done through the narrow opening

at the top. Further, all the large jugs, MM 16–25, show a seam at the base of the neck, concealed by a raised ring, at the point where neck and mouth (usually cast) are joined to the vessel (usually hammered). Exactly how these seams were made is not visible because all the jugs are too well preserved; but an overlapping edge may in most cases be felt around the top of the shoulder inside. Probably the raised ring at the base of the neck, a part of the neck itself, was intended not only to conceal the seam but also to prevent the neck from slipping down inside the body. A margin below the neck ring—the overlapping edge that can be felt on the inside—was fitted into the hole at the top of the body and then turned out and hammered flat under the inner face of the shoulder at its edge, thus preventing the neck from pulling out. The resulting seam was thus secure; it may have been strengthened with solder on the inside to cement it and to seal the join against leakage. This seam, whether soldered or not, could have been made only from the inside.

It is evident, then, that the bodies of these ves-

---
[38]*Ibid.,* 92 f.

sels must have been put together from more than one piece and that the joining operation was done last, after the neck had been attached to the shoulder and the lower end of the handle had been pinned in place. Two of the smaller jugs, MM 26 and MM 44, both made by hammering, show a ridge around the middle of the body in which appears the seam where the upper and lower parts were joined, and also the ends of the pins—carefully smoothed and polished, often almost invisible—run through the rib to hold the pieces together. In these cases simple mechanical means were used with the utmost skill to make all but invisible and (we hope) leak-proof joins. Some of the large jugs, MM 16–25, show faint traces of a seam at the bottom where base and body join. These traces are visible mostly on the inside (when the inside is visible at all) and suggest a soldered rather than a folded join, which would have had to be made from the inaccessible inside of the vessel. A soldered join here at the bottom would be in any case more proof against leakage than a folded one, and all traces of it could be polished away on the outside.

It has been mentioned that the bodies of the large jugs were made by hammering. Their walls are usually a millimeter or less in thickness, and this fineness of fabric, together with certain slight irregularities of profile (e.g., in many cases the curve from lower body to shoulder is sharper at one side than at the other, and at a different level), is indicative of a hammering rather than a casting process in manufacture. The bodies were probably hammered by a combination of the sinking and the raising techniques: a disc of bronze was hammered by the first method up to the level of greatest diameter, then by the second after the wall starts to curve in toward the base.[39] It is apparent that the bodies were made upside down: that is, with the wide opening which became the bottom of the finished jug upward. In consequence after the hammering of the body a hole had to be cut at the bottom (which became the top) into which the base of the neck could be fitted. The hole could be exactly centered and measured to fit the neck by use of the compass. The next step must have been the fitting of the neck and the hammering down of the flange at its

bottom to hold tightly the edge of the shoulder between neck-ring and hammered seam.

The neck and mouth were usually made in one piece, probably by casting; they are of much heavier fabric than the hammered body. The trefoil mouth is usually thickened at the lip and squared off to a flat edge often four millimeters or more in thickness—evidently a product of casting rather than of hammering. An exception is the neck of MM 44, a hammered cylinder closely fitted inside a hammered and chased outer cylinder and pinned in place at the bottom.

After the joining of neck and body, the handle must have been added and pinned in place while the bottom was still open. With only one exception (again MM 44, with a flat, cast handle) all the jugs from MM and P have the typical Phrygian handle made from two plates of bronze folded together (pl. 60J–L). The lower or inner plate was a long, tapering strip of bronze with a T head at the top to fit against the outer face of the jug mouth at the back. The head could be a straight bar of bronze, or it could have a rounded tab at either side: the first where the ends of the pins holding it in place were flattened to rivet heads by hammering, the second when they were capped by decorative hemispherical stud heads. The lower end of the inner plate was sometimes squared off, sometimes slightly flared to a dovetail. In most cases it was prolonged below the dovetail by a round tab or by a three-quarter-round tab at each side, but in some cases there was no tab. The upper or outer plate, similarly shaped, was hammered to a convex profile, sometimes with a groove down the center of its outer face to give the effect of a double-rolled handle. At the top it ended in a tang, usually a three-quarter circle at each side, which was fitted against the inner face of the trefoil mouth opposite the spout and pinned in place by two stud-headed dowels, one at each side. The pins of these were run through the tabs of the outer plate, the wall of the jug, and the under plate and either flattened to rivet heads or capped with studs at the back. At its lower end the outer plate was finished by a single rounded tab, or more often by two three-quarter-round tabs, for fastening to the wall by either one or two round-headed studs, the ends of their pins flattened on the inside of the vessel. The outer handle plate was fitted over the inner and the overlapping edges of the inner bent

---

[39]These processes are described by H. Maryon in *AJA* 53 (1949): 93 ff.

up to hold it in place; the seam where the edge of the lower plate is turned over the margin of the upper always appears along both sides of the handle. At the bottom the squared or dovetail end of the lower plate covers more of the face of the upper, curving to fit its convex face and gripping it firmly. Where the inner plate has no tang at the bottom, its end is held against the wall by the outer; where there is a tang, it exactly matches that of the outer plate and the dowels were run through both as well as through the wall. As noted above (p. 224) in two cases (MM 21 and 25) the wall was strengthened at this point by a separate plate added against its inner face.

A handle made from two plates folded together in this way was hollow inside. The handles of two of the smaller jugs, MM 36 and 40, seem to have had a yellowish filling. This substance seems to have been soft, hardly a core over which the bronze could have been hammered; perhaps beeswax poured in in a liquid state after the handle had been finished to give solidity. Before filling, the handle must have been heated and bent to span exactly the space from rim to shoulders; no doubt the holes for the dowels were drilled through tabs and wall together while the handle was somehow held temporarily in place. After the drilling the stud-headed dowels could be slipped through the holes from the outside, their ends flattened by hammering from within. The final operation was soldering on the base, a hammered disk of bronze, usually slightly concave on its underside. By means of a compass it could be measured and made to fit exactly. The lower edge of the wall seems (as far as we can see) to have been turned inward at a right angle, offering a flat surface to which the edge of the base could be soldered. Once the base had been fastened in place, no more work could be done from the inside, and all that remained was the filing and polishing of the outside of the vessel.

This method of manufacture was used for all the large globular jugs and for most of the smaller ones. Of these, MM 30–33, with raised ring around the base of the neck, must have been made with a neck-to-shoulder join like that of the large jugs. MM 28 and 29 had the upper shoulder made in one with the neck and overlapping the upper cap of the body where there must be a seam out of reach of fingers feeling on the inside of the vessel. On the rest, MM 34–43, there

is no trace of a seam at shoulder or base of neck. Some are of heavy fabric, and others of light. Possibly in the case of the former, body and neck were cast in one piece, of the latter, hammered in one. In every case, however, the bottom must have been separately made and attached last after the lower handle end had been pinned in place. Exceptions are MM 26 and MM 44 which, as we have seen, were joined at a rib around the middle of the body. These two vessels, however, are exceptions altogether, most interesting from a technical point of view and masterpieces of craftsmanship. There remains MM 27, which shows no trace of a seam at the neck, inside or out, or at the base outside. The improbable suggestion was made above that it had been cast in one piece, since the fabric is heavy. If the high foot was separately made and joined by a seam that we cannot see, our problem may be alleviated somewhat: the opening in the bottom, even smaller than that at the neck, must have been difficult to work through for attaching the handle, though it was done somehow. But MM 27 with its false bottom above the stemmed foot affords us direct evidence for the use of separate bronze disks such as must have been used for the bases of almost all the other jugs. The means of attaching this were mechanical: a long dowel whose outer head appears at the center of the bottom. The inside of the jug was not accessible for soldering the disk in place.

In shape the majority of the small jugs are essentially the same as the large, with flat bottom, squat or globular body, short neck, and wide trefoil mouth (MM 27–38). The rest are fundamentally the same, but from MM 39 to MM 43 we progress through a heightening of the body from the squat or globular to (MM 41) an almost ovoid shape, and a lengthening of the neck to an almost straight cylinder (MM 42, 43). The two jugs from the child's tomb, TumP 6, 7, have a shape all their own with flaring funnel-like neck, but the necks of these were hammered, not cast. It is interesting to compare the only trefoil jugs of pottery found in these tumuli, TumP 64 and 65 (pl. 18E, F); TumP 64 is of metallic shape and has a raised ring around the base of its neck that is entirely nonfunctional in pottery and bespeaks direct imitation from a bronze model.

Large globular jugs of the type of MM 16–25 seem to have been rather rare in bronze. Only one parallel can be cited, a fragment from one of the roughly contemporary tumulus burials at Ankara, which would seem to have belonged to a jug of this shape.[40] But pottery jugs of this type, normally 0.30 to 0.40 m. in height and thus comparable in size, were evidently a useful and popular part of the Phrygian household equipment. Numerous specimens have been found in all the buildings of the Phrygian city, buildings destroyed with their contents in the general conflagration of the early seventh century. The clay is usually well polished at the surface, the color varying from buff through brown and red to gray or black; this color variation is doubtless the result of secondary firing. The shape must have been a useful one for pouring liquid or for storing it—probably water for everyday use—in fairly large quantities; the capacity of each jug is close to a gallon.[41] A

characteristic pottery jug of this type is shown on pl. 96E.[42] The pottery jugs often have double-rolled handles, and these may have been imitated by the bronze jugs with the handle grooved down its outer face to give the same effect. The type, whether in pottery or bronze, seems to have been purely Phrygian though it is not unlike somewhat coarser Urartian jugs found at Karmir Blur.[43] Jugs of pottery, common at Gordion, were probably widespread throughout Phrygia, though few examples can be cited. A jug found in stratum IV at Alişar[44] and a fragment of a jug painted with bichrome decoration at Boğazköy,[45] of the same type but probably much later in date, give some indication that this Phrygian type spread over a wide area and continued to be made through the seventh century and perhaps into the sixth.

LADLES

TumP 8, 9   MM 47, 48   TumW 7, 8

To the ladles listed above, the following may be added:

Gordion: Tumulus K-III, no. 91.[46]

Tumulus K-IV, no. 4.[47]

Ankara: Tumulus at Gazi Orman Çiftliği, nos. 7, 8.[48]

Ephesus: Outside the basis. Only handle and tang preserved.[49]

Gordion: Burned debris in Megaron 3 in the city. Badly burned. Stepped tang, a

smaller rectangle above a larger. Not catalogued.

Tumulus S-1 (seventh century). Fragments of two ladle handles decorated with added bolsters. B 194, 195, unpublished.

Of the fourteen specimens cited, eleven are from Gordion, two from nearby Ankara, and one from Ephesus. Eleven were found in eighth-century—or at least in pre-Kimmerian—context and three, including the one from Ephesus, in seventh-

[40]E. Akurgal, *Dergi* 8 (1950): 89 and pl. A,2. The upper end of the handle was fastened by a bolster rather than by the two stud-headed pins common at Gordion. Mouth and neck are preserved, with top attachment for the handle. The clean break all around the base suggests that here as at Gordion, body and neck were made in separate pieces. This fragment was not illustrated in the original publication, *Belleten* 11 (1947): 27 ff.

[41]R. Johnston experimented at Gordion with the capacities of pottery trefoil jugs. See his *Pottery Practices*, 208–211.

[42]Black polished trefoil jug (P 1639) from Megaron 2 (Mosaic Building) on the city mound. H.-h. 0.346; D. 0.323 m. Found on the floor northwest of the hearth, in the burned stratum. Mended from many fragments. Dis-

colored from its second firing. Flat base, double rolled handle.

[43]B. B. Piotrovskii, *Urartu*, 190, fig. 51.

[44]E. F. Schmidt, *The Alishar Hüyük, Seasons of 1928-1929 (OIP 19)*, 252–253 and fig. 330, no. *a* 1049.

[45]Illustrated by E. Akurgal, *Phryg. Kunst*, pl. 27b.

[46]G. Körte in *Gordion*, 75 and fig. 59.

[47]*Ibid.*, 101 and fig. 74.

[48]H. Zübeyr, *TTAED* 1 (1933): 13–14. No. 7 also in Akurgal, *Kunst Anat.*, color plate IIIa,b facing p. 108, where it appears grouped in IIIa with MM 68 (above) and in IIIb with MM 12 (above).

[49]Hogarth *et al., Ephesus*, pl. XIX,7 and p. 152.

century or later context. Thus the focal point and center of production would seem to have been Phrygia and probably Gordion itself; and the period of greatest popularity the latter part of the eighth century.

Implements of this form were obviously useful and more neatly adapted to their purpose than were the bucket-handled situlae (MM 45, 46, above) and their Assyrian counterparts, which had to be plunged deeply into the liquid to be bailed (rather than dipped) from a large container to a smaller one. The long ladle handle kept the hand well above the food or liquid to be served; its recurved upper end formed a hook by which it could be hung conveniently from the rim of the cauldron or from one handle. Cauldron and ladle seem indeed to have been inseparable partners: in Tumulus MM the ladles were placed with the smaller cauldrons in the same part of the tomb; in K-IV the ladle was found inside a small cauldron; and all of the other burials (P, W, K-III, and Ankara) contained both types of vessel. The ladles, in fact, seem generally to have been offered in sets of two. This was the case in MM, P, W, S-1, and the Ankara tomb. In no case were the paired ladles twins, exactly alike, as were the small cauldrons in MM and P.

The finding places and early contexts of these ladles, as well as their numbers, give the impression that they were of Phrygian origin. Other characteristics strengthen this impression. The tang, which serves as a transition from bowl to handle, is a feature common to all the Phrygian ladles and one that serves to bind them together as a definite type. This tang may assume various shapes: the simple rectangle or oblong (TumW 7, 8; TumP 8; K-III, no. 91; Ankara 7); or the oblong with concave vertical sides (MM 47, 48; K-IV, no. 4); the stepped form of two oblongs (Gordion city, uncatalogued); the crescent (Ankara 8); or the disk (TumP 9, Ephesus). In most cases the tang seems to have been made in one with the bowl, whether by hammering or by casting. In many cases it was made in one with the handle. MM 47, 48, TumP 8, K-IV, no. 4 (cast, according to G. Körte) seem to have been made each in one piece, with bowl, tang, and handle cast together or hammered from a single block of bronze. The tang was often decorated: sometimes by a simple outlining border groove (MM 47, 48; K-IV, no. 4), or with *à jour* ornament of

round holes near the edges (Ankara 7). When grooved outline decoration was used, it was carried up the face of the handle, giving the impression of ribbing. The *à jour* disk tang of TumP 9, elaborately decorated with punched and incised ornament, was obviously cast, separately made and added. The binder used was evidently solder; there are no traces of pins or dowels, no overlapping edges, no folds. Solder was used (according to G. Körte) to fasten the handle of the ladle in K-III to its tang, where the two pieces of bronze are overlapped and held together though there are no traces of pins or dowels. Likewise the animal-head jaws of TumW 8, which are slotted to grip the edges of the tang and the upper handle, must have been reinforced with solder; no pins were run through to hold the parts together. The Phrygian ladles thus attest that the techniques of casting and hammering, of fastening by solder and of decorating by the punch and the graver were all known to and used in the Phrygian bronze-working industry.

Characteristic of Phrygian bronze work, too, is a fondness for ornamentation by the addition of bolsters and rotelles. This tendency is illustrated in a number of specimens among the ladles—MM 47, 48, K-IV, Ankara 8—which have small bolsters added across the handles at various points, usually below the curve of the elbow at front or back, sometimes both; and once (Ankara 8) across the middle as well. The handles are usually narrowed above their ends, then flared and rounded off at the tip, by this silhouette giving the impression of a conventionalized bird's head with broad, flat bill. That this effect was intended and not the result of mere chance is demonstrated by TumP 9, of which the handle-end is a fully modeled bird's head with eyes once inlaid and with feathers indicated by punching. The Phrygian artisans seem to have been fond of birds' heads as terminal decoration; animals, whether painted on pottery or carved in ivory,[50] are often shown with the tail ending in a bird's head. For ladle handles a rather wide head was required with a broad bill ending in a curve, and waterfowl such as ducks, geese, or swans were appropriate. The bird's-head terminal later became completely conventional; many a Greek *kyathos* of bronze or of silver

---

[50] E.g., *AJA* 64 (1960), pl. 60, fig. 25, center.

shows a duck's or a swan's head at the end of its handle. Though the Greek *kyathoi* eliminate the tang, joining a handle directly to the wall of the bowl, they were probably derived ultimately from the earlier Phrygian ladles. The specimen from the Artemision at Ephesus is a link; with its discoid tang and conventional silhouette bird's-head terminal, it would seem to be typically Phrygian and probably an export from the plateau to the coast. The Greeks, then, would seem to have taken the Phrygian ladles as models for their own, ultimately adapting the form to their own needs and taste. No doubt more of the Phrygian ladles, which served as models, will turn up at early Greek sites along the coast and in the islands immediately offshore, especially in Samos where there was a well-attested early Greek bronze-making industry.

The majority of the Phrygian ladles are simple enough in form and simple in their decoration. One, slightly more elaborate than the rest with its animal-head handle decoration (TumW 8), would seem to be purely Phrygian;[51] the animal heads

that grip tang and elbow end in their jaws are typical of the Phrygian fondness for animal decoration and are products, surely, of the same imaginative humor that could create the goose-shaped vessels of Tumulus P (TumP 49, 50).[52]

The most elaborate of the ladles, TumP 9, with its fully modeled bird's-head terminal illustrates the same tendency. That it was made by Phrygian artisans and probably at Gordion is further suggested by the elaborate moldings, some of them milled, that terminate the ends of the handle shaft. These in form and decoration bring immediately to mind the moldings of the Phrygian fibulae. The disk-shaped tang, which has its counterpart in the Ephesus fragment, matches technically the other parts; it was probably cast and decorated in Phrygia, but its form was quite possibly derived from sources farther to the east. The decoration *à jour* with its rayed inner disk may well have had more than mere decorative significance, at least in origin: it was perhaps a solar symbol.

BOWLS WITH RING HANDLES AND BANDED RIM

Bronze

Gordion:	Tumulus MM. MM 55–69. Here, pls. 65C–67G.
	Tumulus J. B 405, fragments of complete bowl. Seventh century. Here pl. 95A.
Ankara:	Gazi Orman Çiftliği. Three bowls.[53]

Manisa:	Izmir Museum. Two bowls from a tomb.[54]
Curium:	Metropolitan Museum, New York. Two bowls from the Cesnola Collection.[55]

Pottery

Gordion:	Tumulus K-III, no. 46.[56]

[51] See p. 238 for discussion of similar decoration employed on the belt TumP 36.

[52] Ladles of large sizes occur in Early Iron Age context in Iran, e.g. at Marlik: E. O. Negahban, *Iran* 2 (1964): 15; idem, *Marlik*, 43 and figs. 34, 36. A pair of long-handled bronze ladles accompanies a pair of large bronze vessels (D. 0.50 m., shape unspecified). Also at Hasanlu: an iron ladle from Burnt Building III (ninth century) in the University Museum (HAS. 62-240; D. bowl 0.09 m.). Its handle is square in section and meets the bowl directly, without an intervening tang. In Cemetery B at Sialk (Tomb 3) a bronze ladle with twisted handle and a hook on its end: R. Ghirshman, *Sialk* II, pl. XXIV, 8 (S.545a)

= C. Schaeffer, *Strat.,* fig. 255:2. Ladles from Marlik and Sialk have handles at right angles to the lip; those from Hasanlu and Gordion are in a straight line with erect lip.

[53] H. Zübeyr, *TTAED* 1 (1933): 10–11, nos. 1–3; E. Akurgal, *Phryg. Kunst,* 81–86, pls. 57–59.

[54] E. Akurgal, "Bayraklı," *Dergi* 8 (1950): 87 and pl. B,2 facing p. 81; idem, *Phryg. Kunst,* 81, pl. 60a.

[55] G. M. A. Richter, *Greek, Etruscan and Roman Bronzes in the Metropolitan Museum* (New York, 1915), 203–204, nos. 537–538.

[56] G. Körte in *Gordion,* 66–67, fig. 42.

Boğazköy:	Ankara Museum. Large sherd with bolster.[57]
Samos:	North Cemetery, outside Grave 45. Buff bowl with red bands.[58]
Sardis:	West of Artemis Temple, Grave 61.2: Lydian marbled-ware bowl, P. 61.5. *Ca.* 600 B.C.[59]

Wood

Gordion:	Tumulus P. TumP 144–146. Here pls. 27E–H.

Bronze Attachments from Lost Bowls of Bronze, Pottery, or Wood

Gordion:	Tumulus P. TumP 31–33. Here pl. 10K.
	Tumulus W. TumW 24. Here p. 207, fig. 125.
Ankara:	Anıttepe, Tumulus I. Two handles with bolsters and three without bolsters.[60]
Samos:	B–494, B–413. Rim bands, spools and ring handles.[61]
Lindos:	Votive deposit. Three bronze bolsters, slightly resembling MM 62, 65, and 67.[62]
Argive Heraeum:	Bronze handles with and without bolsters: nos. 2087–2190. No. 2141 could well be Phrygian, the rest Greek imitations. See also fragments of rim bands nos. 2215–2217.[63]

Perachora:	Hera Limenia. A pair of ring handles, and some single[64] examples.
Olympia:	Handle in bolster.[65]
Athens:	Acropolis. Three handles in bolsters.[66]
Delphi:	A handle, Inv. 3146.[67]

Ivory

Ephesus:	A bowl held in the hand of the carved ivory "Hawk Goddess," now dated by Jacobsthal and others to the second quarter of the sixth century.[68]

The popularity of this type of bowl, so widespread over so long a period, must have been due to its usefulness and convenience both in carrying about and for hanging out of the way when not needed. The largest number of bowls at Gordion are of bronze; but these had been placed in the tomb of a royal personage. The wooden specimens from Tumulus P, the handles of wooden bowls which had perished from P and W and from Ankara, together suggest that the shape was widely made and used in humbler materials. Nevertheless the type must have been of metallic origin, imitated in cheaper materials for everyday use. The raised bands of the rim could have had no use in pottery or wood; the swiveling pendent handles were invariably of bronze because pottery handles of this sort would have been impossibly fragile and wooden ones impossibly difficult to

---

[57]E. Akurgal, *Dergi* 8 (1950): 87, figs. 3, 4; K. Bittel, *IstMitt* 5 (1942): 72, no. 51.

[58]J. Boehlau, *Nekropolen*, 46, no. 7, and 150, pl. VIII, 2. Grave 45 was a stone sarcophagus of a young girl; bowl a miniature: D. 0.082 m. See also E. Akurgal, *Dergi* 8 (1950): 88.

[59]G. M. A. Hanfmann and A. H. Detweiler, *ILN*, April 7, 1962, 543, fig. 10; Hanfmann, *BASOR* 166 (Apr. 1962): 24, fig. 20; A. K. Knudsen, *Berytus* 15 (1964): 59–69, pls. VIII, IX,2.

[60]T. Özgüç and M. Akok, *Belleten* 41 (1947): 42, 72, pl. XXI, fig. 43.

[61]U. Jantzen, *Samos* VIII, 54 and pl. 50; J. Birmingham, *AnatSt* 11 (1961): 190.

[62]Chr. Blinkenberg, *Lindos* I, 220, pl. 30, nos. 718a,b

and 719.

[63]C. Waldstein, *The Argive Heraeum* II, 289–293, pls. 121–122; 294, pl. 123.

[64]H. Payne, *Perachora* I, 161 f., pl. 65, nos. 1–2 (pair) plus others.

[65]A. Furtwängler, *Olympia* IV, 134 and pl. L, no. 843.

[66]A. D. Keramopoullos, *Deltion* 1 (1915), Parartema 25, fig. 16, nos. alpha, gamma, epsilon.

[67]P. Perdrizet, *Delphes* V, 78, no. 370, fig. 270.

[68]Cecil Smith in Hogarth *et al.*, *Ephesus*, 156, no. 1, pls. XXI,6 and XXII,1a–c. See Jacobsthal, *JHS* 71 (1951): 92. Jacobsthal believed the bowls to be Greek, but this was before the opening of the Gordion tomb. See also E. Akurgal, *Kunst Anat.*, 207–210 and *Abb.* 169–173, agreeing with Jacobsthal's dating.

make. The making of the bronze bowls themselves was complicated enough, since they were
usually put together from seven or more separate
pieces.

The bowls proper, shallow with rounded convex bottom and slightly flared rim, are of thick
fabric, evidently cast rather than hammered. The
rims, somewhat thickened, vary from 0.003 to
0.005 m. in thickness at the lip, which is finished
to a flat upper face. There are slight variations in
depth and in profile of the bowls and their rims,
but the type remains constant. Small variations in
dimensions of the bowls show that no two could
have been cast from the same mold; all were
made individually. After casting the bowls were
filed and polished. Many show the prick of a
compass at the center of the floor inside; the compass was evidently used for truing the shape in
polishing, and probably also for measuring off the
spacing of the handle bolsters and rim attachments.

After the bowls had been cast and polished,
separate bands of bronze were applied to their
rims outside and pinned in place by bronze
dowels. Two, or perhaps four (as in the case of
the bowl from Tumulus J, pl. 95A), bands were
applied to each bowl, covering about two-thirds
of the circumference of its rim at opposite sides,
and leaving gaps between their ends at front and
back, perhaps to facilitate pouring or drinking
from the vessel. The rim bands from bowls in P,
MM, and W vary in section and profile. Most are
half-round; others are rectangular, high or low,
one with beveled corners, two with high, straight
faces and rounded top. All are crossed by vertical
spool-like pieces at their ends, some by additional
spools spaced halfway between the ends and the
central bolster. The bands and the spools that
cross them were usually cast in one; in the single
exception (MM 59) band and spools were made
separately, the latter grooved in their inner faces
to fit over the bands and hold them in place
against the rim. The spools show variations in
shape and profile: some are nearly cylindrical;
others are "waisted" with slightly concave profile;
still others cylindrical with flared ends; and three
have flat projecting heads (like nail heads) at top
and bottom. In some cases, especially when round
studs were set on top to give added decoration,
the upper ends of the spools were made to overlap and cover the upper face of the rim of the
bowl. Attachment to the bowl was usually by a
dowel run through the wall and into or through
each spool.

Since all the bowls from MM are intact, with
the bolsters carrying the handles still in place and
covering the centers of the rim bands, it is not
possible to see whether the bands were single
pieces at either side bent to fit the curve of the
bowl and covered at the middle by the bolster. In
two cases, MM 57 and MM 67, it appears that
rim bands, spools, and bolster at each side may
have been cast in one piece; in one other, MM
68, we cannot be certain that the method was the
same because it was not possible to clean the
bowl. In every other case the rim band is covered at its center by the bolster which is grooved
in its inner face to fit over it. The bolsters, then,
were usually applied after the rim bands had been
fastened in place. They were pinned to the wall
of the bowl by single or double large dowels,
sometimes with decorative stud heads on the
inner face of the bowl. More often simple pins of
bronze were used, run through the rim and bolster, their ends cut flush to the face of the bronze
and polished inside and out. Where the ends of
the dowels appear in the outer faces of the bolsters, we must probably assume that the bolsters
were hollow-cast; in other examples where the
dowel ends do not show, we might assume the
bolsters to be solid. The bolsters, then, like the
bowls themselves and the rim bands with their
spools, were cast. They show great variety in the
numbers and the profiles of the raised moldings
which decorate them. Each bolster was cast separately, and while the two attachments of each
bowl are always matched slight variations in
measurement between them show that they were
not cast from the same mold. The bolsters are
always nicely fitted to the curve of the bowl rim;
they may have been adjusted by filing, or perhaps
an impression of the curve was used in making
the mold for each bolster. In some cases the central rib of the bolster is finished at the top by a
platform overlapping the upper face of the lip,
occasionally carrying a decorative stud or ornamented with a flat, round button.

At either end of the bolster a hole or socket
served to receive one end of the oval ring handle,
which could thus swivel upward and outward
around the bolster. The sockets are of necessity
off-center, since the bolsters are in any case only

semicylindrical, flattened at one side to fit against the rim, and notched at the center to fit over the rim band. The pivots of the handles were therefore displaced outward or downward from center. The handles, usually round in section though one pair (MM 60) is faceted to eight flat faces (octagonal in section) were bars of bronze bent to an oval shape, the ends brought into line so that the ring could swivel freely in its socket. In some cases the handles are tapered, thick at the middle and diminishing toward the ends; in others they have the same thickness throughout. In most cases the width across the handles at center is greater than the depth of the bowl so that the handles cannot hang vertically when the bowl is laid on a flat surface; these bowls were intended to be hung up against the wall by one handle. No examples were found at Gordion of handles with knobbed decoration like those on one of the bowls from Koşay's tumulus in the Gazi Orman Çiftliği at Ankara.[69]

Supplementary decoration in the form of round-headed studs was added to many of the bowls, set at the top of each of the spools and at the center of each of the bolsters on top—in some cases as many as ten studs. The dowels that fasten the separate pieces together also on occasion have stud heads to decorate the inner face of the bowl rim. Sometimes stud heads have come off the spools, but small pinholes remain as a sign of attachment.

It seems obvious that this elaborate type of bowl was metallic in origin and that specimens in pottery or in wood are merely conventional imitations.[70] The purpose of the bands at the rim, apart from mere decoration, must originally have been to give extra support at a point of strain, the handle. It may be that the bands were at one time cast in one with the bolsters (as appears to be the case with MM 67), the pins that secured the spools to the bowl rim giving additional (or alternative)

support to the dowels holding the bolster. On MM 67 the bolsters are not doweled to the rim directly; instead, the rim band, which must be cast in one with the bolster, is pinned to the bowl close beside the bolster at either side. If this was the original intent, it seems to have been abandoned after the type became established, for most of the specimens show the bolsters pinned over the bands and covering them. The bolsters, when applied in this way, can derive no additional support from the pins fastening the spools to the bowl. In any case, whatever its original purpose may have been, the rim-banded bowl with swiveling handles[71] seems to have become very popular in Phrygia and to have been widely disseminated from there.

Listed above (p. 229 f.) are all the specimens known to me in bronze, in pottery, and in wood. The earliest and the most numerous are those from Tumulus MM at Gordion, belonging to the latter half of the eighth century. Approximately contemporary must be those from the Gazi Orman Çiftliği at Ankara. Only slightly later and still pre-Kimmerian would be the wooden bowls from Tumulus P and the pottery one from K-III.[72] The tomb at Manisa was perhaps later. The bowls from Curium in Cyprus in the Metropolitan Museum cannot be dated from context; in shape they would appear to be more developed than the Gordion ones. The pottery bowl from Sardis is a Lydian imitation reported to come from a grave to be dated around 600 B.C. The ivory lady from Ephesus, who carries the latest of these bowls, has been dated ca. 575–550 B.C.

The span of production and use of these bowls, then, would seem to have been from the second half of the eighth through the first half of the sixth century. In the present state of our knowledge all of the earlier, eighth-century, specimens come fom Phrygia; the rest, from the islands, from Cyprus, from Ephesus, and from Greece,

---

[69]H. Zübeyr (Koşay), *TTAED* 1 (1933): 11, no. 2 and fig. 2; E. Akurgal, *Belleten* 8 (1950), pl. B, 1 right (facing p. 81).

[70]A. K. Knudsen treats the subject of pottery imitations of bronze ring-handled bowls in depth: *Berytus* 14 (1965): 59–69.

[71]The bowl handles, usually with a gap between their ends and flattened across the top to fit into their bolster sockets, are oval as a result and can be distinguished eas-

ily from the rounder closed rings of the cauldrons. I am inclined to attribute all the handles found singly or in pairs without bolsters (or bowls) to wooden vessels; one pair was found in Tumulus P with wooden bolsters still attached to bronze handles. We are often told that pottery is indestructible; bronze, too, would leave some trace, whereas wood can vanish completely.

[72]G. Körte in *Gordion*, 66–67, no. 46, fig. 42.

perhaps later. Since no earlier examples have been cited from Urartian lands (Toprakkale, Van, Altıntepe, Karmir Blur) or from Assyria, the form would seem to have been a Phrygian invention rather than an Oriental type taken over and transmitted westward by the Phrygians.

Nor did the type entirely die out in Phrygia itself with the invasion of the Kimmerians. The Gordion fragment cited above (p. 229) came from a post-Kimmerian burial of the seventh century (Tumulus J); and fragments of pottery vessels, bearing the relief bands at the rim or bolster handles, have been found in post-Kimmerian city levels. The bronze fragment is technically interesting, since it affords us details that are not visible on the better-preserved bowl from Tumulus MM. It includes a bolster and two of the rim bands together with their vertical spools (pl.

95A). The bolster was hollow-cast and fastened to the bowl by two dowels for which the holes are preserved. The rim band was not a single piece spanned at its center by the bolster, but two short pieces notched into its ends. The spools were cast in one with the bands; their upper ends were not only flared but brought to full round and notched underneath at the inner side to fit over the bowl lip, so that they needed to be pinned to the rim only at the bottom. This fragment shows not only that the ring-handled bowls continued to be made after the Kimmerian catastrophe but also that there was a development in technique. But it must have been the pre-Kimmerian bowls of the eighth century that made their way to the Greek settlements of the west coast, from there to be exported to Greece itself and to serve as models for imitations by the Greek bronze smiths.

OMPHALOS BOWLS*
TumP 11–28 MM 70–167 TumW 9–18

Bronze omphalos bowls were deposited in increasing quantity, size, and elaboration in the early tumuli at Gordion. Tumulus W had 10 omphalos bowls (and 5 plain bronze bowls), wrapped in cloth, stored in cauldron TumW 2 in the southeast corner of the tomb chamber; in P, 18 omphalos bowls (and 2 plain bronze bowls) were found fallen from a table along the west side of the south wall; these, too, had been wrapped in cloth before being deposited in the tomb. The glass omphalos bowl TumP 48 (pl. 15A, B; fig. 18, p. 32) was stored in one of the bronze bowls. The original disposition in K-III is not known in such detail; 13 omphalos bowls (and 14 plain bowls), wrapped in cloth, were among the gifts in the south half of the tomb chamber. In MM, 98 omphalos bowls (and 2 plain bowls) were stacked in piles on eight tables in the southern and eastern part of the chamber.

These bowls were carefully deposited in the tombs as drinking vessels, customarily filled with liquids from cauldrons with the aid of ladles or jugs. In shape they take an intermediate position between Near Eastern forerunners and the Greek

mesomphalic phiale. The pedigree of the phiale has been studied thoroughly by Heinz Luschey, but at the time of his study he had only the K-III examples from Gordion with which to assess the Phrygian elements in the complex history of the shape.[73] The discoveries in Tumuli W, P, and MM have widened our horizon, along with new finds from tumuli in Ankara.[74]

We can see the omphalos bowl developing from Tumulus W to MM. Tumulus W contains some tentative examples, such as the hammered TumW 17 (pl. 90E; fig. 124, p. 206) and TumW 18 (pl. 90F) with conical and shallow bosses respectively; but Tumulus W also has bowls with functional omphaloi surrounded by two or three rings, the best example of which is TumW 14 (pl. 90C). Such bowls are plain on the outside, but have a simple elegance in their interior medallion of raised boss with concentric ridges. The omphalos offers a safe finger grip for the person holding the bowl, and was designed and developed for this purpose. Most of these bowls are cast, probably in two pieces with a seam around the centerpiece of boss and rings.[75]

---

*This section written by Machteld J. Mellink.

[73] Luschey, *Phiale* (1939).

[74] T. Özgüç and M. Akok, *Belleten* 41 (1947): 64–66,

figs. 18, 45–49; Mellink, *AJA* 73 (1969): 214.

[75] A. K. Knudsen, *Phryg. Met. and Pot.*, 81–82.

In Tumuli P and K-III the assortment is bolder in size and execution. The centerpiece becomes more elaborate. Nine bowls in Tumulus P are of the type with four concentric ridges around a functional omphalos (e.g., TumP 14, pl. 9F, G); seven have three rings each. The type is beginning to be standardized although sizes still vary. This standard type of Phrygian omphalos bowl is still found in large numbers in Tumulus MM: six-ridged (MM 131, p. 143, much larger than any in Tumulus P), also with five, four, three, or two ridges, sometimes with a platform effect for the central medallion (MM 137, pl. 72B; MM 138, fig. 91F, p. 142). At this stage the type with just one single ridge makes its appearance; a single rounded ridge becomes popular. MM has the most impressive series of these practical, basic Phrygian "medallion phialai" (MM 150-166). Standard omphalos bowls of this type are also known from the Ankara tumuli and from the Afyon region. They continue in use even when more elaborate versions of Phrygian omphalos bowls begin to be produced.

The concentric ring ornament is sometimes accompanied by further grooving in the interior of the bowl. This type of decoration appears in a small number of instances. TumW 11 (pl. 89G; fig. 123, p. 205) is a heavy cast bowl with a flattish base; the interior has two firm ridges around the omphalos and eight low ridges and grooves along the rim. Concentric grooving appears over the entire interior surface of TumP 12 (pl. 9D, E), a heavy bowl with three sharp ridges setting off its omphalos. In the extensive collection of omphalos bowls from MM, concentric interior ribbing occurs in seven instances, the majority combined with ridges around the omphalos (MM 124-130, pl. 71A-G; figs. 91A-D, 87C). This type, although it has its decorative logic and a local origin, did not become popular in Phrygia.

Potters and workers in faience, glass, and metal in Egypt and western Asia had long experimented with the decorative combination of bowl shape and calyx or blossom. The petaled bowl appealed to the Phrygians as it did to the Near Easterners, and they developed their version of a petaled omphalos bowl. The best preserved forerunners of

Phrygian petaled bowls are from Assur, as explained by Luschey. Yet the beginning of relief-decorated metal bowls in TumW 9 is not of a familiar pedigree. TumW 9 (pl. 89E; figs. 119, 120), a hammered bowl of thin reddish copper, is embossed with a network of drop- and lozenge-shaped elements, interlocking to create a pine-cone effect. The rim is straight and firm; the omphalos is a conical point in a plain zone, with a curious rocker pattern engraved on the interior (fig. 119C). The comparison with the bowl from Assur *Gruft* 30, which carries the name of Assur-taklak[76] is apt for the network of bosses, but the profile of the Assyrian bowl is quite different with its flaring rim extending over the bulge of the large upper lobes, and with its flat base and rosette ornament as a central medallion. TumW 9 is an experimental piece, a deep bowl to which an oriental surface pattern is applied. It could be a local product, but we do not know if it had Phrygian counterparts.

TumW 10 (pl. 89F; figs. 121, 122) has a more clearly floral design with its central rosette and concentric zones of antithetical paired petals. The bowl is perhaps cast rather than hammered. A very small omphalos forms the heart of the 12-petaled rosette (the petals sunk in the interior); the design is more elaborate on the exterior with ample inspiration in the Assyrian series,[77] but the drop-shaped petals dominate the friezes in an abstract arrangement not quite matched at Assur, and related at Gordion only to TumP 11, not to the numerous petaled bowls from MM. TumP 11 (pl. 9A-C; fig. 8) also makes a playful ornamental use of drop- and diamond-shaped petals, interlocking them in concentric zones and varying their sizes. The design is freer and more complicated than that on TumW 10. The upper drops form large knobs projecting well beyond the rim, which is grooved on the outside. This cast bowl has a tiny dimple in a blank lobed field on the exterior, a firm small omphalos on a platform with two ridges in the interior.

The metal workers who produced TumW 10 and TumP 11 may not have been based at Gordion, to judge by the novelty and proficiency of the design and the lack of continuity in this line.

---

[76]Luschey, *Phiale*, 41; Arnt Haller, *Die Gräber und Grüfte von Assur* (*WVDOG* 65, Berlin, 1954), 110, pl. 22c,d,e; see also the illustration in F. Matz, *Klio* 30

(1937): 112, pl. 1. This bowl may indeed date to 805 B.C.

[77]Luschey, *Phiale*, 40; Matz, *Klio* 30 (1937): 112-113.

It is difficult at present to assign these pieces to another workshop, but there are many centers of Anatolian metallurgy in the eighth century B.C., especially in the region of Tabal and Kummuh.

Tumulus P contained a much more conventional petaled design on the glass bowl TumP 48 (pl. 15A, B; fig. 18). The omphalos, set on a disk in the interior, is surrounded by 32 radiating petals, their rounded tips neatly fitted below the rim in botanical order. This arrangement is in harmony with many Near Eastern designs of *Zungenphialai* and with the presumed Assyrian manufacture of TumP 48.

The great tomb MM, on the other hand, with its 54 petaled omphalos bowls (MM 70–123) introduces a clearly Phrygian variant of the radiating floral design. These bowls are hybrids of the basic Phrygian ringed omphalos bowl and the oriental blossom bowl. The omphalos of the Phrygian phiale had grown to a size and had acquired an ornamental status which prevented its being seen as the heart of a flower when oriental fashions entered the metal workshop. The petals of the blossom bowl could not be attached to the omphalos or its platform. Instead, the petals' rounded lower ends are separated by a blank zone from the omphalos and its Phrygian rings, which may be as many as seven or, more normally, fewer (often just a single ring is common at this time for standard bowls). These petals radiate and taper toward the rim, and are interleaved in their upper parts with smaller pointed petals, which make a regular zigzag fringe with the tips of the main petals and the tips of the main interstices (which represent a second, outer layer of large petals). None of the tips reaches the rim, and a plain rim zone is invariably maintained. The petals appear embossed on the exterior and sunk on the interior. The lower parts of the large outer petals bulge out so that the bowl stands on them, but the petals taper off as they curve up with the profile of the bowl. The lower ends of the petals may be set off by grooves or arcs on the outside (and ridges on the inside); a zigzag may be engraved to mark the fringe of tips on the inside; the petals may be spined or ridged down

the middle. Such linear effects may be achieved in the mold or by tooling. A certain variety also exists in the number of petals. The basic system is 16 petals multiplying to 64 tips at the rim, but systems of 12, 15, 17, and 18 occur. The design is regularized and although the blossom bowl is at the origin of the type, the Phrygian product develops an ornamental logic of its own, with calligraphic base lines and zigzags (cf. MM 80, pl. 69E), and a clear separation between the relief design and the structural elements of rim and omphalos.

The combination of ridges, omphalos medallion, and floral petaling, as noted above, is a typically Phrygian creation. The omphalos itself may occasionally become the center of ornamental attention. MM 70 is unusually elaborate (pl. 68A). Its mushroom-shaped omphalos has rosette patterning on its surface; three grooves surround the centerpiece, and the petals as usual keep their distance. The five grooved lugs on the rim add exceptional ornament. MM 72 (pl. 68C; fig. 86B) is a variant of MM 70 with denser petals (18/72); MM 73 is simpler (15/60). MM 71 (pl. 68B; fig. 86A) has a platform with seven sharp ridges around a mushroom omphalos; the grooved design on the cap is based on a familiar Anatolian cross with corner fillers. In rare instances a plain omphalos bowl may have an elaborate centerpiece. MM 167 (pl. 73B) has a tall omphalos profiled with grooves both inside and out and set on a low platform with four step-ridges. Even in K-III, no. 72, we have an odd experiment, both in the profile of the bowl and in its lead-filled mushroom-shaped omphalos.[78]

From the series of omphalos bowls in MM we learn that workshops in Gordion had started a regular production of semi-orientalizing, but characteristically Phrygian, petaled bowls. One measure of the wealth of the king buried in MM is the profusion of petaled bowls in his chamber. Other examples of this type are rare outside of tomb groups. There are two petaled bowls from Gordion Tumulus S-1, one from S-2, a bit later than the MM series. Outside of Gordion, the Ankara tumuli contained Phrygian petaled bowls;[79] later

---

[78]G. Körte in *Gordion*, 73. A. K. Knudsen, *Phryg. Met. and Pot.*, 79, with comments on wax and lead filling in omphaloi.

[79]T. Özgüç and M. Akok, *Belleten* 41 (1947): 64–65 figs. 18 and 22.

Phrygian specimens come from Boğazköy and Kerkenes Dağ.[80]

The relationship of these Phrygian omphalos bowls to East and West has become clearer through the excavation of Tumuli W, P, and MM. The development of a large, hollow omphalos as a finger hold may be interpreted as a Phrygian functional modification of what used to be a solid ornamental centerpiece in Assyrian bowls. In the present state of affairs, we do not know the oriental production as well as we know the Gordion workshops, nor do we have archaeological substance for the lists of metal tribute that went from southeastern Anatolian kingdoms to Assyria.

As for Phrygian connections with the West, Phrygian phialai had a clear influence on the shapes of mesomphalic phialai dedicated in Greek sanctuaries from the early seventh century on. An occasional import may have found its way to Greece earlier.[81] Among the 200 votive phialai excavated in the sacred pool at Perachora are petaled bowls that are clearly derived from the Phrygian MM type, and an occasional copy of the basic medallion type.[82] The discoveries at Gordion allow us to modify Luschey's conclusions with the working hypothesis that the origin of the omphalos bowl proper is to be sought no longer in Greece but in Phrygia.[83] Phrygian metal workers created their own variants of the Near Eastern repertoire in the case of the phiale, as they did in the categories of handled bowls, cauldrons, jugs, and ladles. The bowl with a functional hollow omphalos became a standard Phrygian vessel in the eighth century B.C. Its context suggests that it was a drinking vessel, not a special instrument of libation. When the Greeks introduced the mesomphalic phiale for libations, they adopted a versatile bowl shape, not a Phrygian drinking custom.

BELTS*

TumP 34–36   MM 170–180   TumW 25

The earliest of the belts from the tumuli, TumW 25 (fig. 126, p. 208), seems ancestral to those from Tumulus MM in several ways. Its disk is a circular frame of bronze worked repoussé in knobs and ridges very finely executed. Except where lugs are placed, it is bent back all round to protect and hold the edges of a large roundel of studded leather dyed vermilion. The disk is separate from and set in front of the studded leather belt itself; the lugs, separately attached to the disk, are bent back to fasten the disk to the belt at some point selected by the maker. The basic elements of design on the leather roundel of the disk are looped circles forming volutes with pointed extensions (stems) at the center over the top of each; a stud occurs at the center of each circle. On the belt itself we see a system of straight strips of fine studding forming panels, with continuous strips along the straight edges; the panels were filled with figure-eight loops or single guilloches (as on the disk) made of tiny studs and filled with large studs. One fragment of the belt (TumW 25C), with its obliquely crossing studded strips and *à jour* squares featuring larger studs, is reminiscent of the studded *à jour* wood work on the screen (TumW 80). An end-plaque in bronze sheet cut *à jour* (TumW 26) accompanied the belt proper. It is disappointing that there was no evidence for the means of fastening. The only method that seems possible is a lacing-up between the end-plaque and the other leather end of the belt, both of which were provided with sewing holes.

The belt fragments from Tumulus K-III[84] consist only of the circular leather backing for a disk, and fragments of the end-plaque with studded

---

[80]K. Bittel, *Boğazköy* I, 53 and pl. 21:2; E. Schmidt, *AJSL* 45 (1929): 274, K80, figs. 73–74.

[81]Luschey, *Phiale,* fig. 7, from Olympia, but even this has a later profile.

[82]T. J. Dunbabin in H. Payne, *Perachora* I, 148–156: petaled bowls pl. 52, basic type pl. 55:4. For derivative petaled bowls, cf. Furtwängler, *Olympia* IV, pl. 52, no. 880.

[83]Luschey, *Phiale,* 37, 144.

*This section written by Ellen L. Kohler.

[84]G. Körte in *Gordion,* 48, figs. 7, 8.

bands going obliquely with reference to the edge bands, as proved by the triangular and lozenge-shaped *à jour* work. One edge band of the K-III belt has rows of very fine beading (repoussé or studded?).

Most of these elements of a bronze and studded leather belt survive in one way or another on the ten much larger and simpler versions (MM 170–179; fig. 94, pls. 73E–74L) which were hung on the west wall of the king's tomb. Here the disks have a wider bronze frame with a separate rim piece attached in the rear and bent back all round to hold the leather backers of the disk; the lugs are cut in one with the sheet of the disk (p. 149, fig. 94C). The central openings are much smaller than those in Tumulus W for exposure of the studded leather behind them, the design upon which in the case of MM 170 was reduced to one central stud surrounded by three rings of smaller studs in a field of densely placed tiny studs. The bronze disk itself, studded concentrically on inner and outer edges of the front face, probably is a sturdier version of the fine studding and ridging of the narrower disk on TumW 25, adding and adapting some of the design from the larger leather roundel in the center of it. The rougher ornaments on the MM disks are made by repoussé hammering which needed more space. On the leather belts themselves the use of fine studding in straight strips continues along all edges and forms square panels; these panels are each outlined by rows of large studs, and large studs are used for the interior patterns in squares of 3 by 3, or 2 by 2 several times (p. 151, fig. 96). Each stud appears to have its own collar of very fine studding although all lie in one plane. Each leather belt had a bronze end-plaque like that found with TumW 25. These outsize examples of old fashioned belts, much too large for wear by the small gentleman on the bed nearby, have no visible means of fastening. Perhaps they were meant as funereal gifts for the king, part of his

traditional possessions and equipment. The type, as belt, seems to disappear after this.[85] The style of craftsmanship seems a survival past its time, too, as the screens and other furniture in MM no longer employ studding.

However, the belt represented by MM 180, found lying on the bed as if placed across the king's ankles, was probably of the kind he actually wore. This represents the beginning of something new—the use of the familiar end-plaques, but laid end-to-end with a heavy bronze toggle at one end of the belt and sewing holes all around the edges and at the other end. Young believed this toggle would require a double-hook fastener at the other end,[86] but it is hard to believe that such a large item could be completely lost in the textiles on the bed. Another suggestion for the type of closing occurs on the reliefs of Carchemish whereon King Yariris and his son, Kamanis, are wearing belts secured by a number of strings which lead from the sewing holes at the end of the belt and are then either simply gathered into a thick cord or are knotted into a sort of net before being gathered into the cord, which then disappears around the corner on all sculptural representations, but which had to be fastened somehow.[87] The easiest method of securing the cord, adaptable to our toggle, would be a simple knot of the clove-hitch type (completely adjustable to the size of the waist at each tying) with the remaining ends hanging down in a tassle; or else let the cord be formed into a loop at the time of the first lacing through the sewing holes, the loop to go over the points of the T-shaped toggle (completely unadjustable method after the initial setting of the cords). However it was fastened, the belt appears to be a whole new departure at Gordion, employing the old idea: end-plaques, here possibly secured with cords to the toggle.

The three solid bronze belts found on and near the child's bed in Tumulus P seem completely unrelated to the studded and *à-jour*-cut belts of

[85]Only once a few scattered fragments from one disk (B 1514) were found on the Gordion city mound, in the fill of a cellar (South Cellar) dug deep into the clay layer. On the cellar, see Young, *AJA* 70 (1966): 268–269. Another example of an end-plaque (B 1670), more fragile in form, having no central band for studding, occurred in the first layer above clay.

[86]See p. 154.

[87]Hogarth *et al., Carchemish* I, pl. B.4*a,b*; pl. B.5*a,b* (strings bunched); pl. B.7*a* (strings netted). The sculptures B.4, 5, and 7 belong to the "Royal Buttress" of Yariris and his son, Kamanis. J. D. Hawkins, in *Iraq* 36 (1974): 72–73, basing his work upon a study of the links between the inscriptions at Carchemish and Assyrian chronology, places Yariris-Kamanis in the first half of the eighth century B.C.

Tumuli W and MM. They furnish a solid field for fine incised decoration and, by means of the new manner of fastening with hook-and-eye, are completely adjustable. Perhaps for the craftsmen of Gordion this, too, is a new departure, the original idea for which is to be found outside Gordion.[88]

Of the three, TumP 34 (fig. 9) appears perhaps the earliest. Fairly gross punching, which remains unrelated to the techniques used on the rest of the belt, is used to achieve the zigzag on the catch-plate. Heavy compass incising is used to form the guilloche that runs around the margin of the belt. The roundel found at the base of the hook is a simple compass-drawn circle. Only two choices for the hook are built into the catch-plate. The two circular cutouts at the base of the fibula and the hook, as also at the base of the catch-plate, are entered by narrow channels (as if for the leading in of a cord); perhaps there was some sort of secondary safety feature such as a tie to back up the hook-and-eye method, which may have been still in the trial-and-error stage of development at Gordion. The nature of the fibula-like handle above the hook, with its arc rectangular in section, its blocks as moldings, and singularly underdeveloped reels, is to be found on the fibulae from Tumulus W and upon those from P, which are scarcely further developed.

The second of the three is probably TumP 35 (fig. 10), which has abandoned the heavy compass drawing, and uses only very light freehand incision. More extensive use of zigzag filling is seen. The two large oblongs between the squares of design on TumP 34 are here seen to be reduced to mere strips between the squares. The hook now has four choices in the catch-plate. The *à jour* circles no longer have thin thread slots, but are opened up as if the cord mechanism is seen to be unnecessary, perhaps due to the increased number of "eyes" in the catch-plate. The fibula upon the hook is still rectangular in section, but

it has decorated blocks, and chamfered reels still to be compared, however, with the handles of the ladle, TumW 7 (pl. 89A). The roundel at the base of the hook has become a large and very complicated floret (indeed a "rose window") and found in company with the same sets of back-to-back half-circles as found on the screen, TumP 151 (fig. 33; pl. 29B); these are also to be found on the screens MM 378 and 379, but the half-circles are turned about.

The most advanced of the three is TumP 36. The incised decoration is light and very fine, but not so well rendered as that on TumP 35. New X-in-square and checkerboard designs are introduced. The hook has four choices and the catch-plate looks stronger. The usual *à jour* circles, at the base of the fibula handle and the hook, have become mere open notches and the fibula handle on the hook uses an animal juncture very closely related to that of the ladle TumW 8 (pl. 89B–D). This ladle also shows a handle rectangular in section like all the fibulae of W and P, and these have blockish moldings and reels that are earlier than the very complicated bead and reel of the fibulae of Tumulus MM. On the belt area itself, the oblongs between squares of design have now become merely extra strips of margin for the squares and between these we begin to see three studs (with holes for heavy pins) with their incipient sketched-in collars, which were to become all-important on the large studded belts hung on the wall of MM.

Obviously these three belts comprise a small individual group, forming part of a long series of solid belts running parallel in time with the soft disk and studded leather wrap-arounds of both W and MM. The beginning of this solid type is hard to account for, but the continued use of this type on the city mound after the Kimmerian destruction[89] and the spread of the type down to the Ionian seacoast[90] seem to speak for the popular-

---

[88]Long tongue-shaped strips of silver sheet, with up to eight rectangular holes in them, cut *à jour* in a ladder-like pattern, have been found in the cemetery at Karataş in Lycia (M. J. Mellink, *AJA* 73 [1969]: 325). They occur in Tomb 307 (B 55) and Tomb AQ-367 (B 105). They appear to be *à jour* diadems or else belt ends, and if they are belt ends, they would imply that a type of adjustable hook(?)-and-eye belt was native to western Anatolia in the Early Bronze Age.

[89]From the post-Kimmerian strata on the city mound

there are many examples of solid bronze belts or fragments from them: four complete belts (B 677, B 1320, B 1605, B 1669); four detached fibula-like buckles (B 1147, B 1195, B 1638, B1685); one hook (B 1606); five fragments of catch-plate (B 1392, B 1670, B 1493, B 1509, B 1510). Most of these were in the first layer above clay, but they also spread upward into the Hellenistic levels.

[90]See below, p. 239, nn. 92 and 93.

ity of the improvements to be seen in the form, and especially the efficiency, of the hook-and-eye locking mechanism.

As to the dating, obviously Tumulus W comes first and we know that MM continues that tradition, but it seems that the links discussed above among the three belts from Tumulus P and between them and other crafts at Gordion are significant. It is as if the craftsmen who made the ladles from Tumuli W and P were working hand in hand with the fibula makers and the belt makers, and the advances in fibula type are greater in the series of handles from TumP 34 to TumP 36 than they are between the fibulae of W and those of P.

It appears, when one looks at the patterns within the squares on all the belts from Tumuli W and P, that W and early P prefer oblique diaper patterns within the square, whereas late P shows only one small lingering usage of it, and Tumulus MM belts abandon the oblique altogether in their geometric decoration.[91]

The evidence, then, seems to form a style sequence for the belts: Tumulus W, K-III, P, MM, or, since the patterning on the disk belt in K-III

is unknown, another possible sequence is W, P, K-III, MM.

The type of belt represented by TumP 34–36 continued to be worn on the west coast of Anatolia; several groups, of slightly divergent development, were found in levels II-V at Emporio on Chios.[92] The fibula-like buckles in that collection seem to be linked to the Blinkenberg types for Anatolia rather than to the Greek fibulae made contemporaneously on the island.[93] The strap ends have as many as eleven holes to receive the hook, and are made of tongue-shaped sheets of metal actually hinged to the belt at the inner ends. Such hinges, and the number of holes, are developments from perhaps outside Gordion, or else later than the Tumulus P group.[94]

Boardman argues cogently that since all illustrations of these belts in wear show them on female bodies, the votives he finds in his Harbor Sanctuary at Emporio are gifts from women to the goddess. He cites *Olympia* IV, pl. 38, a *potnia therōn* wearing such a belt, as an illustration. However, one would not like to take this to mean that the occupant of Tumulus P had to be a young girl.

FIBULAE
TumP 37–39   MM 185–356   TumW 27–60

In his study *Fibules grecques et orientales,* published in 1926, C. Blinkenberg isolated a group (his Group XII), which he assigned to Asia Minor. This group was divided into seventeen subtypes, all of which share certain characteristics: (1) an arc or bow approaching a semicircle in outline, (2) at one end a simple, turned-up hook catch in almost every case spurred or voluted at the base, usually with its outer face grooved or otherwise decorated, and (3) a repertory of moldings to decorate the ends, and sometimes the center, of the bow. By far the greater

number of the specimens listed were found (or bought) in Asia Minor; of those found outside, a majority came from the islands just off the coast, particularly from Rhodes (Lindos). Of the ones found in Asia Minor nearly half came from the tumuli at Gordion dug by Gustav Körte in 1900, another quarter from the Artemis sanctuary at Ephesus. The finding places are revealing: fibulae were considered appropriate tomb gifts for the dead to take with them to the other world; they were also considered appropriate votives to be offered to the gods at their sanctuaries. Blinken-

---

[91]Tumulus MM contained no painted pottery, but the principle of less and less emphasis upon the oblique seems also to hold true for the pottery from W, K-III, and P (in that order). The screens from W and P include many instances of oblique diaper patterns, those from MM none. See, however, p. 184, fig. 110.

[92]J. Boardman, *Greek Emporio* (1967), 214–221.

[93]Boardman discusses the Anatolian ancestry of his belts in *Anatolia* 6 (1961): 184–186.

[94]Only one example of such a hinge has come out of the upper levels on the city mound at Gordion (on belt B 1605 from "South Cellar"; cf. p. 237, n. 85). There are three, however, from Tumulus S-1 on the south cemetery ridge.

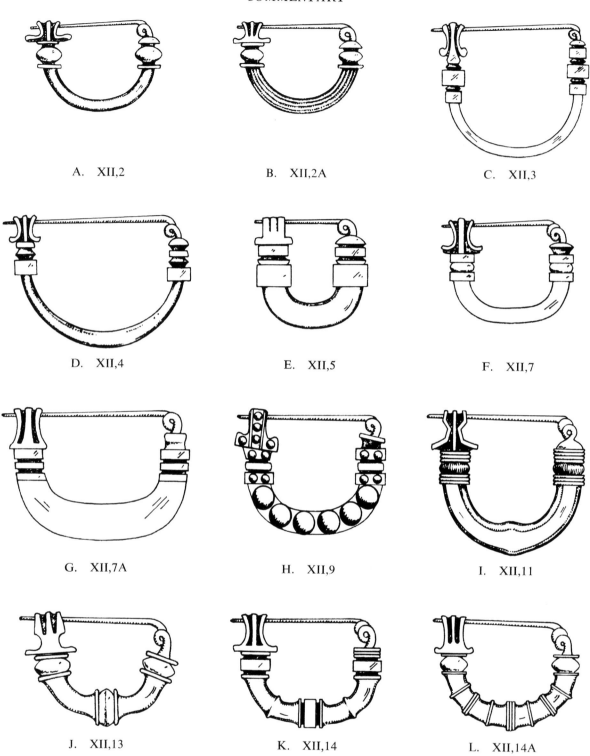

A. XII,2

B. XII,2A

C. XII,3

D. XII,4

E. XII,5

F. XII,7

G. XII,7A

H. XII,9

I. XII,11

J. XII,13

K. XII,14

L. XII,14A

Figure 130. Fibulae of Group XII according to Blinkenberg and Muscarella. All examples are chosen from Gordion collections, but they are regularized and not drawn to scale. A, B, H, J, K, L from Tumulus S-1. C, E from Tumulus K-III. D from Tumulus E. F, I from Tumulus MM. G. from Tumulus J.

berg notes that the great sanctuaries were frequented by strangers from many places and as a result they abound in many different types of fibulae from all over the eastern Mediterranean world. On the other hand the fibulae offered in graves were almost exclusively of types locally current, which had no doubt been used in life. Thus of the forty-odd highly characteristic fibulae of the Italic type that have been found in Greece and listed by Blinkenberg (his Group XI) all come from the great sanctuaries where they were offered as votives—Olympia, the sanctuary of Artemis Orthia at Sparta, the Argive Heraeum, the sanctuary of Zeus at Pherae, at Aegina, and Lindos; not one was found in a grave. The distribution of the Group XII fibulae follows the same pattern: in the homeland (Gordion, Ankara) they are found in graves, in foreign parts as votives at sanctuaries—at Ephesus, Samos and Lindos, at Olympia, Athens, the Argive Heraeum, Perachora.[95]

Blinkenberg's fibulae of Group XII, then, hold together typologically as a group, and his assignment of it to Asia Minor on various grounds—the numbers found in Asia Minor, their early date, and their use as grave offerings—is convincing and has been generally accepted.[96] Excavation at Gordion since 1950 has vastly increased the volume of the material in hand and has confirmed its Asia Minor origin. A more precise and specific classification of the various subtypes, and their geographical assignment to the several regions of Asia Minor as well as a clarification of their chronological sequence and an approximate dating for each subtype, is now within reach. Oscar Muscarella, in his study, *Phrygian Fibulae from Gordion*,[97] gives the count of fibulae found at Gordion in the course of the present excavations through the 1961 campaign as 609 specimens plus many fragments, almost all from graves or tumuli but including a scattering of lost or mislaid fibulae from the various levels of the city itself.

Our present study of the three pre-Kimmerian tumuli P, MM, and W accounts for 209 of these, and an additional 65 were found by G. Körte in

Class	W	MM	K-III	P	K-IV	Total from Tumuli	Total found at Gordion through 1961
Group XII,3	2	—	6	3(+)	—	11(+)	12(+)
XII,4	—	—	6	—	—	6	11
XII,5	—	—	2	—	—	2	5
XII,7[98]	26	40	24	—	10	100	114
XII,9[99]	—	50	1	—	5	56	73
XII,11[100]	—	33	—	—	—	33	40
XII,13	6	—	2	—	2	10	133
XII,14	—	39	—	—	6	45	135
With shield	—	10	—	—	—	10	10
Unclassified	—	—	—	—	1	1	1
TOTALS	34	172	41	3(+)	24	274(+)	534(+)

[95]C. Blinkenberg (*Fibules*, 204 f., Types d'Asie Mineure) lists some exceptions, e.g., a fibula found in a girl's grave on Samos (XII,13m) and one found in Schiff's grave at Thera (XII,13n). But the Theran grave was in itself an exceptional environment.

[96]Except, somewhat naively, by A. M. Snodgrass, *Dark Age of Greece*, 347.

[97]Ph.D. thesis, University of Pennsylvania, 1965. However, Muscarella in *Phryg. Fib. Gordion* (1967), 12, extends the statistics for fibulae from Gordion through the campaign of 1965. About 200 fibulae have been found on

the city mound in subsequent campaigns; their contexts still need to be analyzed.

[98]Muscarella justifiably divides this group into two subtypes, XII,7 and XII,7A (see below, p. 244); here they are lumped together for the sake of simplicity.

[99]The fibula from K-III, classified XII,8 by Blinkenberg, was reclassified XII,9 by Muscarella because it has moldings at the ends of its arc.

[100]I have preferred to assign these to Blinkenberg's Group XII,11 rather than to create an additional subtype, XII, 13A, as does Muscarella.

Tumuli III and IV, of which the former is certainly, the latter is probably, to be dated before the Kimmerian catastrophe. The subtypes of Group XII represented in these tombs must, therefore, have been current already by the end of the eighth century and the beginning of the seventh. A table will show at a glance the subtypes represented in each of the early tumuli, and their numbers.

Numbers and earliness of date lead to the conclusion that some of these subtypes must be not merely Asia Minor but specifically Phrygian products: they are approached neither in number nor in earliness of environment by other fibulae found in Anatolia. Koşay's Phrygian tomb at the Orman Çiftliği near Ankara, about contemporary with MM at Gordion, contained more fibulae of the same type,[101] and Blinkenberg lists a number of similar specimens about which he can be no more specific as to provenience than "région d'Ankara," "région d'Eskishehir," or "Dorylaion." This, however, suffices; for both of these regions lie in the heartland of ancient Phrygia, to the east and to the west of Gordion. Finding places thus pin down certain of the subtypes to Phrygia, and numbers not merely to Phrygia but probably to Gordion itself as their place of origin. These subtypes are obviously XII,7, 9, 11, 13, and 14; among these may be included also the ten[102] large shielded fibulae from MM.

On our table, above, the Gordion tumuli are arranged in their apparent chronological order.[103] These are all pre-Kimmerian and therefore to be dated before *ca.* 690/685 B.C. The total of pre-Kimmerian specimens of each subtype is given, and in the final column the total for each subtype found at Gordion through 1961. With the exception of a scattering found in the burned Phrygian city (most being of subtype XII,7) the rest were found in post-Kimmerian environments—in the upper levels of the city mound, and in tumuli or graves of the seventh and sixth centuries. The Kimmerian destruction would appear to be in a

sense pivotal: some types (the eighth-century ones) were perhaps on the wane in popularity before the catastrophe, and disappear after it; others (the late eighth- and seventh-century ones), however, appear in smaller numbers before the destruction, but wax in popularity (and in numbers) after it.

Thus we may see that the number of examples of subtype XII,3 in Tumuli W (pl. 91B, C), K-III,[104] and P (pl. 12E–G), is increased by only one specimen (a fibula found in the fields and turned in by a villager); we may reasonably infer that this type was popular in the eighth century but was displaced by others in the seventh. Of this subtype Blinkenberg in 1926 was able to cite only the six specimens from K-III, plus one in the Stockholm Museum that had been found in Asia Minor. To Blinkenberg's list Muscarella in 1965 was able to add the supplementary specimens from Gordion Tumuli W (TumW 27, 28) and P (TumP 37–39), and again only one other—a fibula without known provenience or date in the Ankara Museum, though its presence there must presuppose a finding place in central Anatolia. And so, of 14 specimens of XII,3 fibulae known, all were found in Asia Minor, 12 at Gordion, 11 of the last in a pre-Kimmerian environment. We may conclude, as does Muscarella, that this is a definitely Phrygian fibula type made most probably at Gordion through the second half of the eighth century and probably discontinued in the seventh.

Subtype XII,4 (fig. 130D) cannot be so clearly defined. Blinkenberg lists only the six specimens from K-III at Gordion,[105] an environment that offers a dating toward the end of the eighth century. Of the five additional XII,4 fibulae found at Gordion, two were in a grave under a small tumulus (Q) along with a fragmentary fibula of Group XII,13.[106] Two more were found in the earth piled to make another tumulus (E),[107] which lay in an area used as a common cemetery of cist graves and pithos burials from the time of the

[101]H. Zübeyr, *TTAED* 1 (1933): 14–15, nos. 9–10.

[102]See nn. 95 and 96 on p. 241.

[103]In the course of the further research and writing for this volume, other options and arguments regarding the chronological order of the tumuli in the table on p. 241 have presented themselves. See the conclusions in each section of "Commentary" (pp. 219–262) and the chapter

entitled "Conclusions" below (pp. 263–272). [Ed.]

[104]G. Körte in *Gordion*, 77, nos. (bronze) 2–7, figs. 62, 63.

[105]*Ibid.*, 78, nos. (bronze) 32–37, fig. 66.

[106]Muscarella, *Phryg. Fib. Gordion*, 22.

[107]*Ibid.*, 15 and pl. II, no. 10.

Hittite Empire through the Lydian period, and again in the time of the early Roman Empire. The tumulus itself was piled in the sixth century; the earth used to make it was taken from the surrounding cemetery so that many objects (as well as parts of human skeletons) from earlier graves were included in its filling. The two fibulae of Group XII,4 must have come from graves disturbed as this project was being carried out; all that can be said about them is that they must be at least as early as the sixth century. The fifth specimen of this subtype was found by a villager and turned in; it can add no information. To this list Muscarella adds three more: one each from Ališar and Boğazköy, and one from Antissa in Lesbos. None of these affords chronological evidence for dating; but of 14 specimens known, 11 were found at Gordion (6 in an environment of *ca.* 700 B.C.), 13 in Asia Minor, and the last on a Greek island just off the coast. In K-III, subtype XII,4 overlaps with XII,3; it is not represented earlier. It would seem definitely to be a type made in Phrygia and probably at Gordion from the late eighth century into the seventh. The poverty of Tumulus Q (which contained only three fibulae), contrasted with the wealth found in the earlier burials, suggests that it belongs to post-Kimmerian times.

Approximately contemporaneous must be subtype XII,5. Again two specimens were found in K-III,[108] carrying the type back to the end of the eighth century. But in addition to these, Blinkenberg was able to list eight more: one from Troy, one from Ephesus, two more from Asia Minor in the Stockholm Museum (one of these found in the Ankara region), three from Lindos, and one from the Argive Heraeum. The preponderance is again Anatolian: six of ten from Asia Minor, three from a sanctuary at Lindos in Rhodes, just off its coast, and one from a Greek sanctuary. To Blinkenberg's list Muscarella adds an indefinite number, more than eight: three from Gordion;

one in the Metropolitan Museum bought in Istanbul and evidently from Asia Minor; one from Kato Phana in Chios; "several" from Antissa in Lesbos; one from the Artemis Orthia sanctuary at Sparta; and one from a group of votives found at Aetós in Ithaca. Chronologically some of these additions are helpful. Two of the Gordion fibulae of this type (J 130, 132) were found in the burned debris of Terrace Building, Room 2, in the Phrygian city, which makes them pre-Kimmerian in date; of these one is of gold, the other of silver (pl. 95H, I).[109] The third specimen from Gordion had no helpful environment. The votive fibula from Sparta seems also to have been found in a late eighth- to early seventh-century context. On the other hand the specimen from Kato Phana was found in a deposit dated to the sixth century. The type would thus seem to begin in the late eighth century and to continue throughout the seventh, possibly continuing into the sixth. Of more than eighteen examples cited, five are from Gordion, five more from Asia Minor, more than five from islands just off its coast, and three from Greece. The preponderance of numbers here is not so great as to suggest that this particular subtype was made at Gordion[110] or even that it was necessarily a Phrygian type; but it does seem sufficient to justify Blinkenberg's assignment of the XII,5 fibulae to the Asia Minor group.

With the XII,7 fibulae we return to surer ground. From four pre-Kimmerian tumuli (W, MM, K-III, K-IV) at Gordion, there are 100 specimens. Of these the 34 found by G. Körte in Tumuli K-III and IV were known to Blinkenberg, who adds a later specimen from the earth filling of Tumulus K-I, which covered a cremation of the first half of the sixth century. He adds also two fibulae in the Stockholm Museum, found in Asia Minor, and five from Lindos. Of 42 fibulae cited 37 are from Asia Minor, 34 of them pre-Kimmerian. In the case of this group the eighth-century dating can be confirmed on external evi-

---

[108]G. Körte in *Gordion,* Tumulus III, no. (bronze) 38, p. 78, fig. 67; and no. 39.

[109]Gold (J 130), silver (J 132) on pl. 95H,I. See Muscarella, *Phryg. Fib. Gordion,* 16 and pl. III, nos. 12 and 13.

[110]The gold and silver fibulae (cf. n. 109 above) found in the burned Terrace Building in the Phrygian city were

accompanied by a third, of electrum: *AJA* 66 (1962), pl. 48, fig. 23: Group XII,7A (see below). We do not know the sources of precious metals found at Gordion; electrum may have come from Lydia or from elsewhere. But the electrum fibula is of a common Phrygian subtype very probably made at Gordion; the fibula itself may have been made at Gordion of electrum imported from elsewhere.

dence: a tribute bearer depicted in relief in the friezes of King Sargon's palace at Khorsabad is shown wearing an enormous fibula of Blinkenberg's Group XII,7.[111] Khorsabad and its palace were created by Sargon II in the late eighth century as his capital; a fibula type current at the time was represented. Characteristic are the squared bow and the end moldings; the sculptor had a Phrygian fibula in mind. Forty specimens were found in Tumulus MM, evidently enough earlier than Sargon's relief so that the type was known and available to be copied (or adapted) by Sargon's sculptors. The XII,7 fibulae of Tumulus MM have a flat arc, thick and oblong in section (sometimes nearly square): the end moldings are of flat squared blocks projecting inside and outside the ends of the bow, and alternated with cushions or reels. The type is quite characteristic and almost unchanging.

There is, however, a variant form which unfortunately G. Körte failed to notice (Tumuli K-III and K-IV evidently each contained fibulae of both forms) and which cannot be distinguished in the cursory descriptions of their publication. Blinkenberg, too, did not make a distinction; and on our table (p. 241) we have lumped all together because we cannot tell how many of each variant type were found in K-III and in K-IV. The distinction was made by Muscarella[112] who noted a type with a thin, flat arc, sometimes lunate in outline, tapering to ends which usually have a simple reel or cushion next to the catch and the spring; the last are always made in one with the arc. The ends of the arc are often thickened, the flat rather thin bow forming a concave curve toward its thicker ends; the front faces are flattened (as in almost all the fibulae from Tumulus W) to give the appearance of the front face of a block molding which, however, is never wider than the end of the arc below. This subtype is differentiated as Group XII,7A. Two fibulae noted by Blinkenberg were attributed to Boeotia (his Group IX,1, examples a,b) probably because of the lunate outline of the arcs; both are in the Stockholm Museum, both were bought in Smyrna, and both can now be matched by early fibulae

found at Gordion. The type is Phrygian, not Boeotian, and it differs from the other early lunate fibulae of Blinkenberg's Group IX (Types béotiens divers) in having moldings at the ends of its arc.

Evidently we have in this group three phases in a sequence of development: first, the lunate or narrow arc tapering toward its ends where simple moldings set off the spring and catch, second, the thickening of the ends and the squaring of their front faces, giving the impression of end blocks (as on the fibulae from Tumulus W). The first phase, and probably the second, could be made as well by hammering as by molding; the more elaborate third phase, as represented by the fibulae from MM, could have been made only by casting. Evidently the XII,7A fibulae from Tumulus W are earlier typologically than the XII,7 fibulae from MM; but the two variants, once differentiated, seem to have run parallel through the later eighth century and into the seventh: both appear in K-III and K-IV. The whole group is specifically Phrygian and probably was manufactured at Gordion where we are able to glimpse the various phases of its development and their differentiation into two subtypes.

With the Group XII,9 fibulae we again have outside evidence for dating. The type is presumably a variation of XII,7 with thick arc oblong in section and block moldings separated by reels at the ends. But the XII,9 fibulae are usually smaller and are elaborately decorated on the front of the arc by hemispherical studs of which the pins are normally hammered to flat rivet heads at the back. Smaller studs decorate the front faces of the block moldings at the ends, and in many cases more small studs are added down the central spine of the catch. Evidently holes were drilled through arcs and end blocks for the pins to pass through; to leave holes in the casting would have involved a rather intricate process of mold making. At Gordion 56 pre-Kimmerian specimens were found in MM, K-III, and K-IV. The pre-Kimmerian dating is confirmed by a fibula worn by King Urballa/Warpalawas of Tyana on a rock relief at İvriz east of Konya; the fibula has long

[111]Botta and Flandin, *Mon. Nin.* II, pls. 103, 106; also illustrated in Barnett, *JHS* 68 (1948): 9, fig. 7. See also Muscarella's discussion in *Phryg. Fib. Gordion*, 68, and

in *JNES* 26 (1967): 82 and pl. II, fig. 1.
[112]*Phryg. Fib. Gordion*, 17 f.

been recognized as Phrygian.[113] The king is identified by the hieroglyphic inscription of the relief itself; he is also named in the Assyrian records as a payer of tribute to Tiglath-Pileser III in 738 B.C.[114] It is suggested that he may have had a long reign and that the Ivriz relief was carved only toward the end of it—that is, fairly late in the eighth century.[115] It is perhaps a point worth consideration, however, that King Urballa/Warpalawas might have been better able to afford the carving of large-scale rock reliefs in the years before rather than those after he was obliged to pay tribute to the Assyrian king. In any case at Ivriz we have a representation of a Phrygian fibula carved in the years around 738 B.C., more probably before than after. The type represented is obviously one of those decorated with hemispherical studs—Blinkenberg's Group XII,8, 9, or 10. The width of the bow excludes the first alternative and brings to mind immediately the fibulae of Group XII,9 from Tumulus MM and elsewhere at Gordion. But the fibula on the relief would seem to have a double pin, or a double transverse bar, across its open side—in the present state of the relief it is not clear which. The most probable guess as to what the stone carver was trying to represent is that it was a very large XII,9 fibula equipped with a sliding shield to cover a double pin like those of the fibulae MM 185–194. Among these last, three different subtypes of Blinkenberg's classification are represented; there is no reason why a XII,9 fibula could not have been similarly equipped.[116] In like manner Blinkenberg's fibulae of Group XII,10 are pulled together only by the presence of a fixed transverse bar that runs horizontally between the ends of the bow to cover the pins; the specimens he cites are a collection of at least three different subtypes in all other respects normal: his XII,10a,b, from Olympia are of Group XII,9; his example "c"

from Ine in the Troad is of Group XII,5; and his "d," from the Argive Heraeum, is of Group XII,13. No fibula with a fixed transverse bar across its open side has yet been found in Phrygia. The fixed bar is probably an adaptation influenced by the Phrygian sliding shield; the studded fibulae of Group XII,10 were perhaps first made locally at Samos and later elsewhere in Greece. U. Jantzen has recently published[117] a studded fibula with two transverse bars, now in Hamburg but of unknown provenience. Parallels are cited and illustrated from Olympia (including the two noted by Blinkenberg) and from Samos. With the exception of two pieces from the Samian Heraeum,[118] the rest would seem to be adaptations made locally in Samos or in mainland Greece under the influence of Phrygian models. All the Gordion specimens of fibulae from Group XII,9 have wide arcs with double blocks at the ends, cast; the ornamentation with studs of two sizes is done neatly, the pin-ends at the back cut off and the studs hammered to rivet heads rather than crudely turned over and hammered down. If, then, our supposition that the Olympia and Samos fibulae of Blinkenberg's Group XII,10 are Greek adaptations influenced by Phrygian models with shielded pins is correct, there can have been no model with a fixed transverse bar for the North Syrian stone cutter to copy on the Ivriz relief, and our suggestion that his model was a large XII,9 fibula with a sliding shield stands. Every minute detail of the bronze could hardly have been rendered in carving stone, and the present state of the relief is worn, so our supposition must remain an educated guess.

The distribution of the Group XII,9 fibulae was fairly wide; with their decorative studs they must have had a certain appeal. Blinkenberg mentions (in addition to 13 from Asia Minor) specimens from Lindos, Paros, Olympia, and the Ar-

---

[113]First noted (as an Asia Minor rather than a Phrygian type) by Blinkenberg (*Fibules,* 29); brought out of the decent obscurity of specialist treatises and given wider notice by Barnett, *JHS* 68 (1948): 8 f. and 7, fig. 6; better illustrated by E. Akurgal (*Kunst Anat.,* 61, fig. 38) and by Frankfort (*AAAO,* pl. 154).

[114]D. D. Luckenbill, *Anc. Records* I, 276. Also noted by Barnett; see n. 113.

[115]E. Akurgal, in *Kunst Anat.,* dates the relief *ca.* 720. But he is under a compulsion to squeeze all the develop-

ment of Phrygian art (the "reif" style) into the years between 725 and 676—a dating that is no longer tenable.

[116]See MM 187A and n. 95, p. 241. [Ed.]

[117]Jantzen in *Festschrift Matz,* 39 f. and pl. 8:1–2.

[118]*Ibid.,* pls. 9:1–2 and 10:5–6; but the latter, a fragment, would seem to have had a transverse bar, made in one with the fibula. Certainly we have no Phrygian fibulae like the one from Samos, *ibid.,* pl. 11:1–3, put together from several flat sheets of bronze held in place by the pins of the studded decoration which act as dowels.

give Heraeum; he cites a total of 21. Muscarella can add more than 10 from Anatolia apart from Gordion: examples from Boğazköy, Midas City, and Manisa, as well as "several" from unspecified sites. Examples have been found outside at Mytilene, Samos, and Perachora in Greece, and one from Italy (Latium). At Gordion Group XII,9 fibulae have also been found in tombs of the seventh century and perhaps continue into the sixth. The type, then, flourished over a long period, perhaps from the mid-eighth century into the early sixth. Its Phrygian origin can hardly be doubted; of the 104 specimens known to Muscarella, 73 were found at Gordion, which may well have been the center of their manufacture and distribution.

The Group XII,11 fibulae are distinguished by bead-and-reel end-moldings in various combinations, a bow round in section and swollen at the center. The central swelling may vary from a great hump to a barely perceptible thickening crowned by a central reel. In most cases the round arc has been faceted to an octagonal profile with eight flat faces; all the specimens from Tumulus MM were further elaborated by studs concealing the central eye of the spring, the pin ends turned back behind. Blinkenberg cites only two specimens, from Bursa in Bithynia and from Ephesus; to these may now be added the 33 from MM and 4 from one seventh-century tumulus (S-1), 3 from another (N) at Gordion. Muscarella[119] lists one more, found in a seventh-century votive deposit in the island of Siphnos. The type is evidently at home in Asia Minor and probably at Gordion in Phrygia; it flourished from the time of Tumulus MM until well into the seventh century.

The most numerous of the Asia Minor groups is Blinkenberg's XII,13. This is the case not only at Gordion, where 133 specimens were found to the end of the 1961 campaign, but also in other places: Muscarella lists a total of more than 300

known examples. The great numbers that have been found are evidently due not to an intense popularity over a limited period but rather to an enduring and widespread popularity over a very long period; the group continues, it seems, into the fifth century. Nevertheless, it was evidently Phrygian in origin, and perhaps at Gordion we can observe the initial stages of its development. The earliest tumulus, W, contained six specimens: TumW 34 (pl. 91I), TumW 56–60 (pl. 92C–F). These are of normal type with semicircular bow round in section, and central and end-moldings.[120] But the moldings are not the usual rounded combinations of reels and cushions; instead they are cubical blocks both at the ends and the center. The two specimens found in K-III[121] have normal central moldings of rounded cushions and reels; the end-moldings on the other hand are simple cubical blocks like those of the earlier Tumulus W fibulae, and Blinkenberg remarks in discussing them that one must doubtless see in these a more archaic element. The slightly later specimens from K-IV have normal rounded moldings throughout, and so do all XII,13 fibulae. If the development was (as it appears to have been) from the Tumulus W type with block moldings to the K-III type combining end blocks with central reel, then to the transitional MM example (MM 336)[122] with central reels, but blocks with reels at the ends, and finally to the K-IV phase with normal reel moldings throughout, then the normal type was developed at Gordion, which must have been its home. One of the large shielded fibulae (MM 187) from the great tumulus is in other respects a normal XII,13 specimen, though greatly elaborated; its arc is ribbed throughout and its end-moldings are ribbed globular beads.

It seems hardly worthwhile to list the numerous finding places of Group XII,13 fibulae in Anatolia and in the Greek world.[123] The type became

---

[119]Muscarella tries to make a distinction between fibulae with a central swelling on the arc (XII,11) and those with a small reel at its center, which he calls XII,13A. I fail to see where a line can be drawn between the two species; the 33 specimens from MM show all possible shades of variation between, and usually the central reel rises from a slight swelling. I have preferred to lump all together under Blinkenberg's XII,11 rubric.

[120]See also above, p. 198, for DeVries' presentation of

the arguments for dating of tumuli by their fibulae. [Ed.]

[121]G. Körte in *Gordion*, 78 and fig. 68, nos. 40–41; Blinkenberg, *Fibules*, 219–220, Group XII,13a.

[122]See p. 242, n. 106.

[123]They are listed by Muscarella in *Phryg. Fib. Gordion*, appendices A–C, 78 ff., and included are two specimens from as far afield as the Pithecusae excavations on Ischia.

so widespread and its popularity lasted so long that there probably came into being several centers for its manufacture. Blinkenberg notes three specimens in silver and electrum from the archaic base under the Artemision at Ephesus,[124] and these may suggest a center in Lydia producing fibulae of Phrygian type as early as the first half of the seventh century. In any case the type seems to have originated at Gordion, probably near the middle of the eighth century.

The Group XII,14 fibulae are as numerous at Gordion as the XII,13, and almost as early. Thirty-nine specimens were found in Tumulus MM, and two of the large shielded group (MM 185, 186) are of this subtype. No doubt it was created as a variation and elaboration of XII,13 by the addition of simple blunt reels between the central and the end-moldings. If this is the case, on typological grounds Group XII,14 should be slightly later than XII,13. At Gordion we have 45 specimens from the pre-Kimmerian tumuli, MM and K-IV. The total found at Gordion through 1961 is 135; Muscarella lists a total of slightly over 200 known specimens.[125] Priority of date and preponderance of numbers suggest that this type, too, was a Phrygian member of the Asia Minor group, originated and developed at Gordion from the simpler XII,13 group. The XII,14 fibulae were used through the seventh and sixth centuries, and perhaps into the fifth. The type became as widespread as did XII,13, and no doubt was imitated and produced at several centers from the seventh century onward.

The fibulae from our tumuli suggest that seven (XII,3, 4, 7, 9, 11, 13, and 14) of the subtypes of the Asia Minor group were of Phrygian origin. Probably two more should be included—XII,5 and XII,8. Muscarella, who included in his study all the fibulae of the Asia Minor group, assigns to Phrygia also XII,2, not represented in the tumuli

in this volume.[126] The lion's share of the Asia Minor group, then, seems to be Phrygian: 10 out of 17 subtypes.[127] This is not so surprising as it might at first seem. Phrygia in western Asia Minor was the first to develop a high level of culture in the Early Iron Age, and was therefore in a position to influence the rest and to supply models to them. Lydia and the western coastal areas were subject to influence from the Aegean islands as well as from the Anatolian hinterland. The finds from the Artemision at Ephesus show among them Phrygian as well as Greek influences, and much of the fine jewelry and gold work will likely be proved by the Sardis excavations to be of Lydian origin. The southwest of Asia Minor and Cilicia were, on the other hand, more closely linked to Cyprus.

We have been able to set up a fairly secure sequence for the various Phrygian subtypes of the Asia Minor group. Unfortunately this will not be very useful for close dating. Only the Group XII,3 type seems, according to our present knowledge, to be limited to the pre-Kimmerian period and to Anatolia itself; no specimens have been found outside, which may in itself be significant. The rest of the subtypes discussed begin before the Kimmerian destruction but continue to be made and used into or through the seventh century, some even through the sixth and into the fifth. Unless, then, a particular fibula shows some characteristic that is obviously early in the development of a type (as the XII,13 fibulae from Tumulus W), these small bronze objects will be useful for dating only in a very general way. Each type was used over too long a period. At Gordion it has been observed that late specimens (of the late seventh and sixth centuries) are often carelessly made; but this does not necessarily hold true for other sites, and the XII,13 and 14 fibulae must have come to be made in a number of places.

---

[124]Hogarth *et al., Ephesus,* pl. V, 3–5.

[125]Muscarella, *op. cit.,* appendices A–C.

[126]*Ibid.,* 14, 37. The Group XII,5 fibulae he divides, assigning some to Phrygia, others elsewhere (unspecified).

[127]Of the remaining seven subtypes, we have noted above that XII,10 is not truly a subtype: the group includes fibulae of types XII,5, 9, and 13, with the addition of a bar across the open side in front of the pins. The same may be the case with Group XII,1, essentially the sim-

plest form of bent wire safety pin. Blinkenberg's basic criterion, a simply or spirally ribbed arc, is actually a decoration rather than a typological one. Two subtypes, XII,16 and XII,12, have not been found at Gordion or in Asia Minor; both show an arc flat-oval in section, and most of the specimens cited were found in Paros or at Lindos. The last three subtypes, XII,15–17, are late, obviously influenced by Asia Minor models but not necessarily themselves of Asia Minor origin. Most of them were found outside Asia Minor.

A random analysis of three fibulae from Gordion showed them to have an abnormally high content of zinc; to be, in fact, of brass rather than of bronze.[128] The fibulae, as it turned out, were the only bronzes among those tested from Gordion to show this high zinc content, and one is inclined to assume that their makers were aware of the different properties of the ore alloyed with copper for their fibulae, and used it to achieve the more golden color and the shinier surface of brass, which more closely resembles real gold than does bronze.

It seems to have been customary among the Phrygians to offer large numbers of fibulae in important tombs. Although the great Tumulus MM contained perhaps an exaggerated number—more than 30 in use on the body and on the bed as well as 145 "spares" wrapped in a linen cloth—the others also included fibulae in respectable numbers. In Tumulus P there was a minimum of fourteen, though only three survived complete enough for publication. It has been noted in the catalogues above that there was strong evidence for the pairing of fibulae, left and right, in MM and to some extent in W also. The early type XII,3 was not made in pairs; almost invariably the catch lies at the wearer's left side. These fibulae are very wide and high and could contain a considerable amount of heavy cloth. Probably they were made (like the shielded fibulae MM 185–194 and the one shown on the İvriz relief) to fasten a heavy outer garment which was so worn that it needed to be secured at one side only. This, too, may have had something to do with the doubling of

the pins to two, one above the other, found almost exclusively on the XII,3 fibulae and on the elaborate shielded specimens found in MM, which have their counterparts in a tomb at Gazi Çiftliği near Ankara. The Gordion shielded fibulae (all ten have the catch at the left) were all found closed, the upper pin hooked over the catch. The point of the lower pin was not exposed, since it too was covered by the shield. Possibly the double-pinned fibulae of Group XII,3 were also provided with some kind of a shield to prevent the wearer from being scratched by an exposed upper pin—shields which have not been found or were not recognized as such, or more likely which were of some perishable material—leather or wood—that has not survived. But the other subtypes with single pins were evidently meant to be worn in pairs.[129] How they were worn, with the catch outward, is suggested by the finding places of some of the fibulae about the shoulder in Tumulus MM, discussed above pp. 156, 169 and in reference to MM 343–344 and MM 349–350.

With the possible exception of some of the Group XII,7A specimens, which could conceivably have been made by hammering, all the Gordion fibulae were cast. For those with the arc round in section (XII,5, 11, 13, 14) a closed mold had to be used, possibly a single mold, more likely a two-piece mold. No fragment of a fibula mold has yet been found at Gordion; but at Bayraklı half of a two-piece mold was found for local imitations of fibulae of Phrygian type,[130] and it is likely that the techniques of casting came together

---

[128]Analysis done at Oxford for Arthur Steinberg, to whom I am indebted for the information. The fibulae in question were MM 226, 254, and 335 (see pp. 287–288 below, app. II-C, Samples 96–98). An extremely high zinc content was noted also in Urartian bronzes from the Ankara Museum submitted for analysis at the same time. Since zinc, a highly volatile element, was presumably not isolated until the time of the Roman Empire, we must assume that the alloy was accidental and that a natural ore with a very high zinc content was available and was used, in Phrygia at least, to make jewelry for personal wear such as fibulae. Tests of bronze vessels from the Gordion tumuli showed an alloy of copper and tin in varying proportions, and trace elements; there was no noticeable or significant amount of zinc. One assumes a source of natural ore with high zinc content in eastern Anatolia, available alike to Phrygia and Urartu. But the fibulae are Phrygian, not imports from Urartu, where

fibulae seem to have been rarely worn, and then were of entirely different types: see O. Muscarella, "A Fibula from Hasanlu," *AJA* 69 (1965): 233 f., also E. R. Caley, "Investigations on the Origin and Manufacture of Orichalcum," in M. Levey, ed., *Archaeological Chemistry* (Philadelphia: University of Pennsylvania Press, 1967), 62–68.

[129]In the tumuli dug by G. Körte, too, there are some evident pairs: in K-IV (*Gordion*, 101–102) there were two pairs of Group XII,9 fibulae, nos. 1–2 and 3–4; and the XII,7 or 7A fibulae included five with catch to the left and six to the right (if fibulae are held arc down). Tumulus K-III (*Gordion*, 77–78) contained twenty-four Group XII,7 or 7A fibulae, eleven rights and thirteen lefts (arc down).

[130]Muscarella, *Phryg. Fib. Gordion*, 48–49 and pl. XVI, 83, 84.

with the models from the same source. In the great majority of cases at Gordion arc and catch were cast in one, the catch cast flat and later turned up to make the hook. Since the outer face of the catch was invariably spined and grooved, the two fibulae of a pair could not be made from the same mold merely by turning up the hooks in opposite directions after casting; each member must have had its own mold. The spring with its pin was usually added after casting, attached by a wire tenon from the spring which was inserted into a hole drilled in the end of the arc opposite the catch. Most of the shielded fibulae, MM 185–194, show the end of the tenon in place; and in many cases where spring and pin have pulled out and been lost, the drilled hole for the wire appears above the moldings at the end of the arc. An extra molding or button (Muscarella calls it a spring-plate) was usually added at the spring end between spring and arc, above the end-moldings. In some cases this was cast together with the arc, in others together with the spring, and in a few clear cases it was a separate piece inserted between them and held in place by the wire tenon. The purpose of this was evidently to raise the spring which in any case was usually shorter than the catch, and by so doing to increase the pressure on the spring when the fibula was closed for purposes of security. After the casting and the adding of the spring and pin, the fibula was finished by filing and polishing, in some cases by engraving also. Many of the end and central moldings, often the surface of the button facing the spring, are ribbed or finely milled; the milling in particular seems too fine to have come through from the mold in a casting process. The milling was probably added afterward by the use of a fine graver. In most cases this fine decoration is limited to front and side faces and not carried around to the back. On many of the fibulae, indeed, it could not have been done at the back through lack of the metal surfaces, since the

moldings are often deficient or blunted behind, as though the molds had not been entirely filled with metal in the casting. The fibulae with square or oblong arc (XII,3, 7, 9) usually show the same blunting of end-moldings at the back; in some cases their back faces are completely flat, suggesting that these may have been cast in open one-piece molds. Holes were evidently drilled through the arcs and the block moldings at the ends of XII,9 fibulae for the insertion of the pins of the stud decoration. The ends of these at the back were usually cut off a short distance above the face behind, then heated and hammered down to neat rivet heads which could not pull out. In general the fibulae were so finely and carefully finished that no evidence was left to show the methods of manufacture; not a single one, for example, shows any trace of a web left by a two-piece mold.[131] Molds of this sort made of stone, perhaps with impressions for casting two or more fibulae at a time, could doubtless have been used over and over again. The lack among the Gordion fibulae of exact replicas such as might be expected among casts from a single mold may have resulted from the finishing and polishing process after casting, which could account for minor variations of dimensions and profile. Evidently the bronze smiths were workmen so skilled and conscientious that it is useless to speculate about their methods of casting until one of the workshops in which they produced their fibulae (and other bronzes) is found and excavated. Prime examples of their skill and ingenuity are the large, shielded fibulae from MM, described above in detail under MM 185. These are masterpieces of precise tooling and demonstrate, since they have been found only at Gordion or at Ankara, what the Phrygian craftsmen in bronze could do. It would indeed seem that smiths who could produce fibulae like these were capable of producing almost anything in bronze.

---

[131]A fibula from no clear context (B 2000), of Group XII,14, is unfinished. It shows a webbing of bronze along all longitudinal edges; in this case the evidence for the use of a two-piece mold is unmistakable. [Ed.]

IRON*

RING STANDS

TumP 43   MM 357–359

To the four examples above, the following may be added:

Gordion: ILS 350, ILS 385, burned debris in TB-2 on the city mound, unpublished.

ILS 303, burned debris in TB-3 on the city mound, unpublished.

Tumulus K-III, nos. 99–101.[132]

Ankara: Anıttepe, Tumulus I.[133]

Anıttepe, Tumulus II.[134]

Archaeological Museum, METU, no. 604, from the Phrygian tumulus on the Çiftlik Road.[135]

Rust and corrosion have obscured the technique used to attach the legs to the ring of three of the four ring stands published here. Traces of a tenon on the top of one leg of MM 358 and slots on the underside of the ring into which the legs were inserted were noticed by R. S. Young during a careful examination of the stand after its excavation. A similar joining technique can be seen on a contemporary iron tripod from the Phrygian tumulus on the Çiftlik Road, excavated by the Middle East Technical University and now displayed in its museum, and may have been used on the four tripods found on Anıttepe in Ankara. Such a joining technique would have been fairly easy to perform. The tenon would have been formed by heating the end of the tripod leg, and then hammering it into shape on the anvil, and a hammer-driven punch would have been used on the heated iron ring to form the rectangular notch into which the leg's tenon was inserted.

Swelling at the joints of the legs and ring, noticed on most of the tripods from Gordion, in-dicates the possibility of an alternate welding technique in which the top of the leg was notched, the ring set in the crevice, and the laps of the notch forge-welded to the ring by heating and hammering. G. Körte suggests that such a procedure was used in manufacturing the tripods from Tumulus K-III.[136]

It is possible that the pronglike feet were meant to be stuck in the ground to provide a more secure support for the weight of the cauldrons they carried. Alternately, small blocks of wood may have been wedged under the feet to provide additional support. When MM 359 was removed from the tomb, R. S. Young, the excavator, noted in his fieldbook "round spots on the wooden floor under two of the feet, suggesting that the legs may have been finished with wooden blocks for feet."[137] The four tripods from the Anıttepe tumuli apparently had similar pronglike feet, while the tripods from the city mound at Gordion and no. 99 from Tumulus K-III had wide, flat feet. No distinctive feet are preserved on the legs of TumP 43.

In the Near East, iron became a common material for tripods, supporting stands, and braziers by the eighth century. The Near Eastern tripod stand was made of bronze or iron rods with bronze feet and decorative attachments. Frequently these stands supported bronze cauldrons with animal protomes and decorative handle attachments similar to those from Gordion, MM 1–3.[138]

The ring stands from Gordion are decidedly less decorative than the Near Eastern rod tripods and may be considered purely functional items, meant to support cooking pots over the fire. There is no doubt that they were local products.[139]

---

*This section written by Joanna F. McClellan.

[132]G. Körte in *Gordion*, 80–81, 68.

[133]Özgüç and Akok, *Belleten* 11 (1947): 62–64 and fig. 17.

[134]*Ibid.*, 71–72.

[135]Noted by Mellink, *AJA* 73 (1969): 214.

[136]*Gordion*, 80.

[137]Gordion Notebook 63, 100.

---

[138]Salamis: Karageorghis, *SalRDC*, pl. I; Altıntepe: Akurgal, *Phryg. Kunst*, 50, fig. 30; Nimrud: Pleiner and Bjorkman, "The Assyrian Iron Age," *ProcAPS* 118 (1974): 300, fig. 12:4.

[139]Over 130 objects of iron were found in the nearly contemporary burned level on the city mound. The large number of objects, the duplication of shape, and the presence of iron ore and slag suggest that there was an active iron industry at Gordion in the late eighth and early seventh centuries.

Whether the ring stands in Tumuli MM and P were originally made to support the cauldrons with which they were buried, or were ordinary kitchen utensils borrowed for this special purpose, is unknown. In size and shape they are no different from the iron tripods that were used as kitchen equipment in the Terrace Building on the city mound. These were found standing against the walls of rooms containing a central hearth and many plain pottery jars, bowls, and cooking vessels.

The more decorative Near Eastern rod tripods and Greek tripod cauldrons, on the other hand, stood at least 0.30 m. higher than the largest iron ring stand from Gordion, making them a convenient height to support serving vessels, whereas the lower Gordion ring stands probably supported cooking kettles over the fire.

POTTERY*

SIDE-SPOUTED SIEVE JUGS
TumP 72–78   TumW 61–63

The side-spouted sieve jugs of Tumuli P and W adhere to the same basic formula of design that characterizes all other examples of the shape from early Gordion: the spout is attached to a sieved area on the body and a vertical handle is invariably placed to the right of the spout at an interval not exceeding 90 degrees. It has elsewhere been argued that the shape served the function of a beer drinking vessel.[140] The sieve would have strained the grain husks of a coarse brew, while the relation of handle to spout would have put the latter at a convenient angle for the mouth when the jug was held by the right hand.[141]

The shape is one of the few represented in either pottery or bronze in all four of the major early tumuli. The seven of Tumulus P are all of pottery, while of the four from W one is of bronze (TumW 5). MM possessed no small vessels of fine ware, but the shape is represented by two examples among its extensive bronze offerings (MM 14, 15). The greatest quantity comes from Tumulus K-III where all fifteen specimens are of clay (nos. 4–11, 16–22). A single pottery example from Tumulus X (P 3136) shows that even modest burials of the time could occasionally include the shape among their furnishings.[142] In Ankara evidence for the sieve jug's use in a funerary context is provided by a black polished pair from the large tumulus on the Çiftlik Road excavated by the Middle East Technical University and as yet unpublished. Anıttepe I in Ankara contained a single bronze example, as did a tomb excavated in 1932 in the present-day Atatürk Orman Çiftliği.[143] At Gordion the practice of including sieve jugs in tumuli seems to have waned soon after the city's destruction; in fact, the shape is not to be found in any tumuli of appreciably post-destruction date. MM may well indicate the trend, at least in respect to ceramic types.

The evidence of deposition within the early tombs at Gordion reveals intentional groupings of the shape and at the same time says a little about its role in the funerary setting. In Tumulus W the four sieve jugs were divided evenly between the two cauldrons, TumW 1 and 2. In K-III all but one of the fifteen had been placed in the large cauldron no. 49 together with other vessels.[144] In both cases it is clear that the jugs would have

---

*This section written by G. Kenneth Sams.

[140]*Archaeology* 30 (1977): 108–115.

[141]Upon observing the sieve jugs of Tumulus K-III, Gustav Körte in *Gordion*, 82–86, proposed their use as dippers for beer which was then strained into cups, in this case nos. 26–32. Crucial evidence for interpretation of the vessel as a beer-drinking device is provided by a fragment of Archilochos (preserved in Athenaeus, *Deipnosophistai* X.447b) wherein the poet likens *fellatio* to a Thracian or a Phrygian drinking beer through an αὐλός. Although the passage is usually taken as a reference to sipping beer through straws (primarily on the evidence of

Xenophon, *Anab.* IV.v.26–27), the analogy seems much more appropriate, and anatomically more cogent, for the thick spouts of the jugs. One may argue further that the evidence of sipping straws and sipping bowls (cf. TumP 70–71) strongly suggests that Phrygians and other Anatolians were not given to drinking their beer from the equivalent of a mug or stein.

[142]For the tomb, see *AJA* 70 (1966): 267–268.

[143]Cf. *Belleten* 11 (1947): 67 and fig. 52; *TTAED* 1 (1933): 15–16, no. 11 a–c.

[144]*Gordion*, 83–84.

been empty, having seen prior use in some graveside rite, as supposed by Gustav Körte,[145] or intended for use in the afterlife, or both. In Tumulus P the pattern differs, for all seven were found together in a tight cluster in the south central area of the tomb (see fig. 5), as though they had once been set in a group with other pieces of a service on the theoretical table, which collapsed (p. 32). Some may have been set full on the table, to await the pleasure of the deceased, while others undoubtedly must have been empty (v. *infra*). It is perhaps more than fortuitous that the seven sieve jugs of Tumulus P provide a numerical correspondence with the two groups of seven each, painted and black polished, from Tumulus K-III's cauldron.

Three fabrics are represented by the sieve jugs of Tumuli P and W. Of these, two are standard in the early tombs, the black polished of TumW 63 and all seven from Tumulus P, and the brown-on-buff painted fabric of TumW 61, which is the prevailing painted ware of Tumulus K-III's sieve jugs. TumW 62 is of a bichrome ware that is otherwise unknown in the early tumuli. With the exception of this same example, the sieve jugs of Tumuli P and W are of a particular type wherein the mouth opening is relatively wide and defined by either a low neck (TumW 61 and 63, TumP 72–75) or a low, thickened rim resting directly atop the shoulder (TumP 76–78). This is also the predominant type found in Tumulus K-III (nos. 6–11, 16, 18–22). In bronze it can be seen in TumW 5. TumW 62 differs in having a *tall*, wide neck and a spout that does not project but rather is affixed vertically, its mouth flush with the rim; the body type is essentially that of a round-mouthed jug like TumP 54.

Within the predominant type, considerable variety is imparted by the differing lengths, attitudes, and forms of the spouts. Due to the off-balancing effect of this appendage, most funerary sieve jugs cannot stand alone when empty; design determined whether they could stand when filled. The spouts of TumW 61 and TumP 75 are so extraordinarily long in relation to body size that it would have been impossible for the vessels to stand. A full measure of beer could not have

countered the weight for, since their spouts are attached horizontally and span mid-body, the jugs could have been filled only to about halfway before the liquid would spill through the spout (in the case of TumP 75, not even halfway). It seems clear that the vessels had to be held at all times when filled, and at an angle with the spout up for anything more than half a measure. The same kind of attachment is seen in the twins TumP 76 and 77; although their spouts are not so disproportionately long, it still seems doubtful that they could have stood alone with half a measure of beer as counterbalance. On TumP 72, 78 and TumW 63, the spouts are slanted and attached higher up on the shoulder, thereby increasing the amount that the jugs could hold if standing upright. TumW 63 stands alone even when empty due to the somewhat heavy fabric of its body; the others could perhaps have stood free when filled, the weight of the brew providing a sufficient counterpoise. Most practical in this regard are the very similar pair, TumP 73, 74, where the spout is placed high, spanning shoulder and neck, and is nearly flush with the rim. Both could have been filled to the top, and would most likely have stood alone. The same is true of the anomalous TumW 62 whose compact, chimney-like spout obviates any problems of balance and capacity.

The spouts themselves may be completely open troughs (TumP 72–74), but more normally a bridge encloses the spout at the point of attachment to the body. If the bridge had a function, its purpose is obscure. Equally ambiguous are the stepped waterfalls within the spout of TumW 61. The intent may lie solely in the visual effect created as the brew came cascading out. The analogous treatment of TumP 74, 75 would have been a much less successful amusement, if such it was, for the steps of the former are somewhat hidden away at the spout's base, while those of the latter are no more than shallow channels at mid-length. Sieve jugs from Tumulus K-III reveal a similar detailing of the spout: no. 19 is closest to the idea of TumW 61, while no. 21 recalls the more cursory channeling of TumP 75.[146]

A final noteworthy feature of design is the

[145]*Ibid.*, 85.

[146]Sieve-spouted jug K-III, no. 6, was anciently trimmed

to make a neat new edge after breakage. Is this a sign of usage before deposit in the tomb? See E. Akurgal, *Phryg. Kunst*, pl. 20b.

sieved disk covering the mouth of TumP 72, seen again on two of the fourteen sieve jugs from Tumulus K-III's cauldron (nos. 11 and 22). In all three cases it becomes one of a group of seven, if the equal division of painted and black polished examples in the cauldron is not fortuitous. While the intention of double straining is clear, the addition seems superfluous from a practical point of view.[147] Since the device is found only in funerary contexts, its purpose may lie in some notion of hyper-purification.

The painting style of TumW 61 parallels that of the sieve jugs from Tumulus K-III and is closest to no. 10 in its use of narrow zones and in the total coverage of the body, including the bottom, with decoration. The bichrome painted style of TumW 62 is as unparalleled among the tombs as is its distinctive fabric. In Tumulus P, where the absence of painted examples is most conspicuous if compared with K-III, three of the black polished jugs are decorated in relief. The garlanding of the twin jugs, TumP 76 and 77, is effected partly by repoussé, a technique that in itself suggests influence from metalwork. The motif as well may have been inspired by the relief designs of bronze vessels, although no close parallels in metalworking are known. The reeded relief of TumP 78 may likewise have been derived from metal ware; a ready parallel is provided by MM 15 (pl. 59F). Tumulus K-III has no parallels for the relief garlanding of TumP 76 and 77, although an idea similar to that of TumP 78 is provided by the broad channeling of no. 21. Furthermore, it and no. 19 as well display a similar furrowing of the handle between bolster and rim. TumP 76–78 have also a type of low relief formed by a shallow cutting away of the background. This is seen on the bridges of all three and on the inner handle sections of TumP 76 and 77. The same technique and the same basic elements of semicircles and bars impressed with rows of tiny squares are seen on nos. 19 and 21 from Tumulus K-III. The forms are so close, in fact, as to admit the strong possibility of a single hand or pottery for them all. Here, too, the inspiration

of metalwork may be in evidence, for similar designs are to be seen on the openwork disk of one of the two bronze ladles from Tumulus P (TumP 9, pl. 8I).

The ubiquity of the sieve jug in early burials is at variance with its degree of frequency in the destruction level where it is one of the least often encountered of the standard Phrygian shapes. The variety with low, wide mouth, which predominates in the early tombs, is known through no fewer than five examples, and is in fact the least frequently occurring of three principal types that can be distinguished in the early city.[148] The shape's placement in quantity in wealthy tombs combined with its relative dearth in the city proper suggest that it was a luxury item in early Phrygian times. This impression is upheld to some extent by the high concentration of the shape in Megaron 3 (seven examples), a building of the Palace Area whose contents bespeak a far greater opulence than do the more domestic service buildings. If indeed the shape was a luxury item, there seems to have been more than a single grade of luxury. The examples from the city are almost always of ordinary, albeit fine quality, monochrome wares which offer considerable contrast with the elegant painted and relief sieve jugs of the tumuli. Brown-on-buff ware, in itself rare within the early city, is encountered in only a single sieve jug from the destruction level,[149] while the type of body relief seen on TumP 76 and 77 is totally unknown for sieve jugs and other shapes as well; the same is true of the shallow relief seen on bridges and handles. The reeded relief of TumP 78 has some distant analogies in the early city, but in general this is a technique which does not become popular at Gordion until archaic times. Moreover, the stepping and channeling of spouts seem a feature restricted to the more elegant assemblages from the tombs, for not a single instance is recorded from settlement contexts of the early city. A similar case may be made for the sieved tops of TumP 72 and nos. 11 and 22 from Tumulus K-III. The bichrome jug, TumW 62, already seen to be an anomaly among

---

[147]It should be noted that the spout sieve of TumP 72 is not preserved, yet is assumed on the analogy of Tumulus K-III, nos. 11 and 22.

[148]The others are a narrow-necked variety, as seen in

Tumulus K-III, nos. 4 and 5, and a type whose body is like that of a round-mouthed jug such as TumP 54.

[149]*Archaeology* 30 (1977): 112.

the types from the tumuli, is also unparalleled in the early city proper. While corresponding in basic form to a round-mouthed jug, a standard Phrygian shape, the form of its spout is unique. Furthermore, both the technique and the style of its bichrome painting differ considerably from what is known of early bichromy at Gordion, where a light ground coat is normally employed as a contrasting base and where the use of red paint is very sparing. In every regard, the jug seems quite clearly to be an import, perhaps from another Phrygian center.

DINOI

TumP 79–87 *bis*   MM 360–371

The term "dinos" is here used to indicate a type of medium-sized jar with a low, wide-mouth opening; "lebes" or "hole-mouthed jar" are equally appropriate terms. Although lacking in a rigorously formal standardization, the vessels of this description, known from both funerary and settlement contexts, create a visibly related group. Furthermore, their shared characteristics bespeak a shape derived for a particular function, that of a container whose low, wide opening would allow for easy and unobstructed access to the contents. As observed by R. S. Young (p. 173), the upright position of the dinoi in the three large cauldrons of MM suggests their use as food containers, as does analysis of their contents (cf. app. II-A, Samples 44–54). A similar purpose is presumed for those placed on the floor and under the bed in Tumulus P.

The dinos, whatever its particular contents, became a standard furnishing in the tombs of early Gordion. Tumuli P and MM have produced the greatest quantities, 10 and 12 respectively. Tumulus K-III, however, contained only two (nos. 47, 48), as did both X and Y, burials of more modest proportions which may or may not antedate the city's destruction.[150] In Ankara as well the dinos appears to have been a common constituent of the Phrygian tomb, known in quantity from Anıttepe I and II and from the large tumulus on the Çiftlik Road excavated by the Middle East Technical University.[151] The absence of the shape in Tumulus W, seemingly the earliest of the excavated series, may indicate that the dinos had

not yet become standard equipment for the grave. Conceivably the two smaller cauldrons of bronze, TumW 3, 4, fulfilled the desired function. The metal shape is at any rate allied to the ceramic and could have served as the prototype for a less expensive version in clay.

All examples so far retrieved from early tombs at Gordion are of characteristic black polished ware with a lighter colored biscuit; those of MM are in general of better quality than those of Tumulus P. Two basic types may be distinguished among the dinoi of these two tombs: the first is a broad, ellipsoidal form usually with a low, everted rim placed directly atop the shoulder; the other inclines more toward a spherical body and favors flaring rims, often above a short or abbreviated neck. The first variety is found in both tumuli, yet only in P, where the type was employed almost exclusively, do there occur exaggeratedly ellipsoidal forms whose diameters exceed the body height by a fourth to over a third (TumP 79, 81, 83, 87). Examples of this category from MM are not as pronounced in their width (MM 367, 368, 370); in their proportions they parallel less emphatic ellipsoidal dinoi from Tumulus P (TumP 80, 84–86). The second type is seen only in MM where it is the predominant form (MM 360, 361, 365, 366, 369); MM 362–364 and 371, although fragmentary, would appear on the strength of their abbreviated necks and flaring rims to belong to this variety as well. Of these, MM 365 is particularly noteworthy by reason of its articulated collar neck; from a typo-

---

[150]Cf. *AJA* 70 (1966): 267–268.

[151]Anıttepe I produced eight, Anıttepe II at least five dinoi; in each burial there was evidence to indicate that the shape combined the functions of ash urn and storage container. Cf. *Belleten* 11 (1947): 62–63, 71 and figs.

14–16, 34–36. The Çiftlik Road tumulus, as yet unpublished, contained six black polished dinoi and four painted; for a brief notice of the excavation see *AJA* 73 (1969): 214. Publication by Sevim Buluç: *Ankara Frig Nekropolünden Üç Tümülüs Buluntuları*, forthcoming.

logical point of view it could perhaps be argued that the vessel is not a dinos; yet, at any rate its function parallels that of the others. The anomalous TumP 82 combines the spherical body of this type with the low mouth opening of the ellipsoidal group, and may represent an intentional compromise between the two. In its dimensions it is among the broadest of the dinoi (0.295 m.), and may in this respect as well be emulating the ellipsoidal type with its more capacious bodies.

The ellipsoidal variety and the related balloon-like spherical shape of TumP 82 find ready parallels in the destruction level. Two black polished dinoi from Megaron 3 within the Palace Area are particularly close to the ellipsoidal type (P 2575; P 2602, pl. 96H), while a few painted dinoi correspond well to the dimensions and proportions of TumP 82. The dinoi of Tumuli X and Y are also of the ellipsoidal variety favored in Tumulus P, as are the exceptional ring-handled specimens from Tumulus K-III (nos. 47, 48). There is no clear evidence to indicate whether this type continued in funerary or domestic use much beyond the time of Gordion's destruction.[152] The spherical dinoi of MM present a different pattern of associations, one which corresponds to that of the tomb's amphoras (pp. 256–257). It is a type that finds only general analogies, and no convincing parallels, in the destruction level. The closest correspondences are from Tumulus S-2, a tomb whose date in relation to the destruction is ambiguous, and Tumulus F, a cremation burial that can be no earlier than the third quarter of the seventh century on the basis of imported Greek pottery. Furthermore, MM 365, with its distinct collar neck, seems the precursor of a jar type which was common in later burials and which may have supplanted the dinos as a traditional funerary container.[153] The dinoi of Anıttepe I and II in Ankara,[154] at least those illustrated, belong as well to the MM variety and thereby offer further indication of a type whose *floruit* was after the destruction of Gordion rather than before (cf. p. 176).

AMPHORAS

TumP 91–104   MM 372–377   TumW 65–72

The importance of the amphora as a funerary item is revealed by the fact that it is the only pottery shape common to all four of the early wealthy tumuli. Of these, Tumulus K-III has produced the least (nos. 1, 2), while P, with no fewer than 14, ranks highest. Modest burials of the time also included the shape among their furnishings, as indicated by single examples in Tumuli G, X, and Y; later tombs continued the practice. Amphoras from tombs in Ankara suggest that the shape, like the sieve jug and the dinos, was widely used by the Phrygians as a traditional funerary furnishing.[155] The widespread use of the amphora in early burials at Gordion was due no doubt to its value as a container for food.[156] The narrow necks of all the funerary examples may be indicative of a concern for prolonged storage if compared with the wider mouths of the dinoi which seem more adapted to ready and frequent access. Furthermore, the height

---

[152]Rim sherds of black polished dinoi from the rubble fill overlying the chamber of Tumulus Z, a burial tentatively dated to about 650 B.C., display low, everted rims like those characteristic of the ellipsoidal types; yet the spherical MM 361 exhibits a similar rim, as does TumP 82. Were this ambiguous evidence to prove positive, the life of the ellipsoidal dinos could be extended to as much as a generation or so beyond the destruction. There are otherwise no indications of the type's continuation. A fragmentary bichrome example with plastic animals from Tumulus J seems more akin to the balloon-shaped variety represented by TumP 82: *UMB* 17, 4 (Dec. 1953): 34–35, fig. 28.

[153]For a jar of similar type used as a cremation urn in

Boğazköy, see Hartmut Kühne in Kurt Bittel *et al., Boğazköy* IV, 42, fig. 9a.

[154]See n. 151 above.

[155]Anıttepe II contained a single example: *Belleten* 11 (1947), pl. 19, fig. 37. At least one amphora had been placed in the large tumulus on the Çiftlik Road, excavated by the Middle East Technical University and as yet unpublished.

[156]Tumulus III, no. 1 contained what was analyzed early in this century as butter: *Gordion*, 53–54. For analysis of the contents of amphoras in MM and W, see pp. 281–284, app. II-A, Samples 55–60 and 68–73 respectively.

range (0.40–0.50 m.) of most of the amphoras from Tumuli P and W suggest common notions about the ideal size of a large funerary container; the roughly commensurate dimensions may even reflect a loose system of volumetry. Such is even more apparent with the small amphoras of MM, for all are of a closely uniform size which is about half that of the amphoras from Tumuli P and W.[157] Both their smaller scale and their upright placement in cauldrons rather than on the floor may imply contents different from those of their larger counterparts. As suggested elsewhere (p. 175), the amphoras of Tumulus MM may also reflect changing attitudes about ceramic funerary repertories.

With but two exceptions, the amphoras are of reduced ware. The small examples of MM are of finer fabric and finish than the others, a grading that is probably in direct proportion to scale; but all share the common technique of a two-step firing process, oxidation followed by short-term reduction, which resulted in a dark surface and a light biscuit. In many cases a micaceous film overlies the surface (cf. p. 47). The technique is the normal one for the reduced wares of the early tumuli, and also saw widespread use in the early city. TumP 94 appears to have been painted dark and polished over a light ground, while TumW 72 is of a red polished fabric that is otherwise unknown among monochrome vessels of the early tombs. The former is quite clearly betrayed as an import by reason of a fabric that is unique to early Gordion. That of TumW 72, however, finds copious parallels in light monochrome wares from the early city.

Typologically, the amphoras allow of a broad division into two principal categories, neck- and shoulder-handled. Neck amphoras are overall of most frequent occurrence within the tombs. The type predominates among the small amphoras of MM (MM 372, 374–377), while in Tumulus W it is the most recurring form (TumW 65, 68, 70, 71). In Tumulus P it is the more frequent of two principal types (TumP 91–96, 98, 101). Tumulus G, a less grand burial of the time, contained a single neck amphora (P 179). Almost as numerous as neck amphoras in Tumulus P are shoulder-

handled amphoras (TumP 97, 99, 100, 102–104), a variety that is rare in MM and Tumulus W (MM 373, TumW 66) yet the type of both amphoras from K-III (nos. 1, 2). TumW 72 also belongs to this latter category, but it represents a distinctly different idea of attachment with its horizontal handles set upright on the shoulder. TumW 67 and 69 belong to neither of the major categories, for their upper handle attachments, as though in compromise between the two principal types, are directed to the angle formed by shoulder and neck. This intermediate variety is likewise encountered on the single amphoras from Tumuli X and Y (P 3135, P 3163), thereby dispelling any notions that the type is an accidental one due merely to careless handle attaching.

Among the neck amphoras, only those of MM present a homogeneous group, for their similarities in size and form of handles are augmented by close affinities in fabric and overall profile. The group is in fact so closely integrated as to suggest the possibility of a single potter or pottery for all. Such uniformities are not to be found among the larger neck amphoras of Tumulus P or W where individualistic forms seem the rule. In contrast, the large amphoras of shoulder-handled type from Tumuli P and K-III comprise a more formally interrelated group by reason of their ellipsoidal, bicurved profiles, usually with the upper body contour more convex than the lower. Seen again on the neck amphoras TumP 94 and 96, the body type is predominant among the amphoras of Tumulus P. In Tumulus W, on the other hand, ovoid bodies prevail, even among the shoulder-handled specimens (TumW 65, 66, 68, 69, 72); the ellipsoidal type of Tumulus P is not to be found among the tomb's amphoras, although the storage jar TumW 64 betrays the profile's currency at the time of W (cf. p. 215).

Despite their various typological differences, the amphoras of Tumuli W, K-III, and P, as well as the smaller specimens of MM, betray certain likenesses of a familial nature. All, for example, are narrow-necked, a distinction that is seemingly less cogent in funerary contexts than it is in the early city proper where a large class of wide-mouthed amphoras exists side by side with narrow-necked types. A sense of extended family relationship is also imparted by the common feature of a broadly everted rim, although details of forming vary considerably. In Tumulus P about

---

[157] Although three of the six are fragmentary, the rim diameters of all are within a narrow, two-centimeter range.

half of the rims are stepped or ledged on the interior, as if to support a missing lid (cf. TumP 92, 95, 96, 99, 100). This highly popular characteristic of Phrygian pottery is found also in MM and Tumulus W, although in each tomb the frequency is less (MM 374 and 377, TumW 66 and 68). The storage jar TumW 64 likewise has a ledged rim, one which is practically identical to that of TumP 95. Furthermore, the unledged rims of the nearly identical pair TumP 98 and 101 are very similar in profile to that of TumW 72. Other grounds for comparison between the amphoras of Tumulus P and those of Tumulus W are few. In both groups there is a similar approach to the refinements and nuances of form, such as ridges used decoratively and architectonically, handles with central spines or ridges along their lengths, and the quirk of implanting finger hollows at the base of handles. On TumP 93 and TumW 70, the potters had the same idea of punctuating the handle attachments with flanking knobs, a touch inspired perhaps by metalworking.

In the destruction level, large, narrow-necked amphoras of the same general types as those found in W, K-III, and P are common. Due to lack of statistics and incomplete retrieval, however, it is impossible to determine either the total range of their variety or their frequency. Likewise, the fragmentary nature of pre-destruction settlement material obviates a proper analysis of the shape's earlier history at Gordion. It is, nevertheless, very clear that the forms of rims and many of the niceties of design found among the tumulus amphoras had long been constituent parts of the Phrygian ceramic tradition at Gordion. The ellipsoidal, shoulder-handled variety that is characteristic of Tumuli K-III and P continued in funerary use for some time after the destruction, as is witnessed by two examples from Tumulus KY (P 1350, P 1367); there are no indications that the same was true of the large-neck amphora. The smaller amphoras of MM find analogies for their size category in the destruction level, but comfortable parallels are, overall, lacking in the early city. The closest correspondences at Gordion come from Tumulus S-1, a tomb whose bronzes indicate a date later than MM,[158] and from Tumulus B, a double inhumation burial whose painted pottery supplies an unquestionably post-destruction date. Two amphoras (P 37, 38) and possibly a third (P 41) from the latter tomb, while not providing exact parallels, do conform in size, basic shape, and their overall homogeneity to the pattern seen in MM. Further indication that the small funerary amphora was a relatively late phenomenon may be provided by the single amphora from Anıttepe II, as yet the closest parallel to the MM type. If the chronological scheme that holds for Gordion is applicable as far east as Ankara, Anıttepe II, as a cremation burial, would be no earlier than the second half of the seventh century. When assessed against other considerations (p. 176), the evidence implies that MM 372–377 represent an innovative category of amphoras, one which was to be perpetuated locally and employed as far afield as Phrygian Ankara.

WOOD

RECTANGULAR SAUCERS, TRAY-PLATES AND TABLES*
TumP 121–134, 152   MM 380–387   TumW 75–79

All the saucers and tray-plates were made of either a single wooden board or a plaque of several strips glued together along their thin long edges. All are oblong and somewhere near a 3:2 proportion. Once the board was cut to length, or the plaque was assembled, the plate was designed by its maker in one of two ways. Method A employed two concentric circles drawn by compass to a diameter greater than the width of the plaque (fig. 131A). The long sides were left straight and truncated. The short sides were trimmed to follow the circles, and an inner edge was cut to form

---

[158]Personal communication from K. DeVries.

*This section written by Ellen L. Kohler.

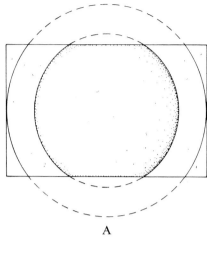

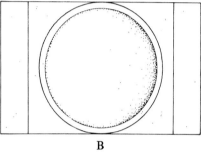

Figure 131. Schematic drawing to illustrate methods of making the two basic types of wooden plates.

the rim of the plate. Decoration was sometimes added by cutting away a shallow design from along the straight sides. By the second method, B, a circle was inscribed between the two long edges of the rectangle (fig. 131B). This circle then became the plate or bowl proper, and the area left over from plate to ends of board or plaque was available to become a decorative handle area.

The plates TumW 75–79, on the evidence of the absence of the round top and bottom edge pieces, were apparently restricted to Method A, and were differentiated from each other only by the widths of their raised rims. They were left plain along the long edges of the rectangle, and were, as a result, the simplest of all the forms retrieved

in the early tumuli. None of these could be shown to have been mounted on legs.

Type A trays are seen also in Tumulus P and in MM. In Tumulus P, grouped under method A are the saucers and plates with "cut-away" rims, TumP 129–134, which show a number of decorative ways of treating the side edges of the plaque: cut-away areas featuring scrolls and scrolls joined by a bar. The plain table (TumP 153) is merely rectangular with rounded corners and narrow rim, but it is fairly deeply dished in the manner of the plates. The shape of its legs is unknown. But on the large tripod-tray table (TumP 152) the details along the straight edges are developed to S-scrolls ending in disks on the rim. The margins are everywhere raised ridges. This is basically the Tumulus W method with added decoration, but with evidence for the addition of legs and braces under the tray, although the legs were never identified.

In MM eight examples of Type A trays of the simplest type were found mounted on legs, forming tables (MM 380–387), more or less alike. The legs were inserted into the tops via a square tenon through a cylindrical collar as in Tumulus P. The tops were similarly dished but the legs show evidence of the advancement seen in a knowledge of pressure-bending.[159]

Type B trays appear only in Tumulus P. Here the ends of the rectangle leave room for a variety of handles, bars strutted to the plate rim (TumP 121–123), lugs (on saucers TumP 124, 125), loops (on saucers TumP 126, 127), and T handle (on saucer TumP 128).

As in the case of the bronze belts (see above pp. 236–239), Tumulus P contains innovative forms alongside the older forms prevalent in Tumulus W. And in MM the tables appear to follow those in Tumulus W, and not to take cognizance of the inventions to be found in Tumulus P.

In Samos Type A survives in, for example, a plain three-legged table top[160] although it remains undished on the upper surface. It came from the flood-deposited sediment in the South Temenos. Type B plates of a developed bar-handled type

[159]R. S. Young, *Expedition* 16, no. 3 (Spring 1974): 7; cf. also p. 24 above.

[160]G. Kopcke, *AthMitt* 82 (1967): 135, no. 24, figs. 15–16 and *Beil.* 75:1–2. Three holes for tenons at tops of legs.

are from the same provenience.[161] These also continue to have incised decoration on the exterior. One wooden piece[162] appears somehow related to TumP 121 and 122, but some edges have been straightened and the size is greatly increased. If it is truly a finished piece, then it must have

been pegged in or glued in as part of a large tray of some kind.

It seems that again, as in the case of the belts (see pp. 238–239), the innovative forms appearing in Tumulus P survive, to be carried to the Greek cities of Western Anatolia.

FURNITURE[163]

In MM and Tumulus P, the impression was strong that the tomb chambers were arranged as far as possible to reproduce rooms in the palace, which the deceased persons had occupied in their lifetime, and that everything was included that might be required by their spirits for use in the other world.

In the king's tomb, then, there were a bed (MM 389), two screens (MM 378, 379), and nine tables (MM 380–388); also a number of smaller items which could be neither identified nor restored, but which had evidently been stacked one on top of the other in the northeast corner. The tomb would seem to our taste to have been rather overcrowded with furniture and

other things, but doubtless it was less spacious than the king's bedroom in the palace had been.

In the child's tomb the original arrangement of the furniture was less clear, but again there was a large bed in one corner on which the body had been placed, a screen in another corner together with a number of stools and tables against the wall of one long side. Thus there was a certain duplication of the material from the king's tomb, and at the same time, variation in type and in arrangement.[164]

As for the beds, the king's, though uncomfortable, was rather large and grand. It had the virtue too, of being easy to disassemble and move from one place to another. No doubt it was used by the

---

[161]*Ibid.*, 118, no. 8 (inv. H 36) fig. 5 and *Beil.* 60:1–2. The rolled ridges on the bar of the handle continue under the curved wall of the dish. See also D. Ohly, *AthMitt* 68 (1953): 98–101, where on figs. 11–12, the author convincingly restores the tray-plates Holz 14 and Holz 15 with bar handles ending in volutes; they are, however, no doubt like Kopcke's no. 8 (Kopcke, *op. cit.*, 119).

[162]D. Ohly, *AthMitt* 68 (1953): 107–110, nos. 21,22, figs. 22–25, and pl. 33. The stiffening of the lines and the use of ivory inlays in the bar handle show developmental changes, but these objects appear to follow upon the bar-handled pieces, TumP 121–122.

[163]A few of R. S. Young's own comments of a general nature, not included in the catalogue, have been directly lifted, or paraphrased only slightly here, from his article, "Phrygian Furniture from Gordion," in *Expedition* 16, no. 3 (Spring 1974): 2–13. [Ed.]

[164]In all three tombs there appears to have been wasted space in the middle or on the edges of the floor, left clear although sometimes objects which had in the beginning been hung on nails or stacked on tables had later fallen to the floor. An L-shaped clear space is apparent on the floor of MM (fig. 66), north-south near the west side and east-west on the north; in Tumulus P (fig. 5) a straight space runs west-east in the west half; in

Tumulus W (fig. 116), east-west along both north and south walls. What could these cleared spaces be except areas covered by the ramp-planks let down into the chambers after the walls were built up to eaves- or roof-height? Probably a good many persons had to enter MM in single file via one plank, place their offerings and leave via another plank, in order that 379 objects could be hung on nails or set upon the floor. The bed itself (MM 379) was probably let down from above with the body already laid out upon it, judging from the fact that the fibulae which tucked in his textile coverlets were formally placed and closed along the north (wall) side.

As a result of the exigencies of the method of filling the chamber, the arrangement in the tomb probably has to depart in minor details from the pattern of arrangement to be found in real life in the megara on the city mound. An effort may have been made to keep it as close as possible, but in the end the blank areas of floor were left after the drawing up of the planks. It is true that objects were hung up also in the megara. The ivory horse trappings found in TB-2 (called TB-"East room" in 1961; *AJA* 66 [1962]: 166–167 and pls. 46 and 47) were thought to have been hung on pegs in the wall. In all these buildings of the city mound, larger items were lined up against the walls to leave circulation space in the centers, and so it happened in the graves, but for a different reason. [Ed.]

king while he was alive, then placed in the tomb for further use in the other world. The child's bed, on the other hand, while much too big for its occupant, was smaller than the king's, and was probably of more normal type. Beneath the bed were many large pottery bowls in which were the remains of food; these had been placed under the bed from the side where there was no stretcher to impede access. The bed surface must have been 0.40–0.45 m. above the level of the floor. At the surface, the sides were closed by planks on edge, their ends slotted into the head- and footboards, serving to reinforce the stability and rigidity. Although not all the pieces were found, the regularity of the crenelations in the headboard made possible a calculation of the total width, and it accorded very well with the approximate measurement of the width of the bed yielded by the sagged and broken frame piece at the head. Probably in life the child slept in a crib of some sort or in a much smaller bed. For some reason this was not used for the entombment; rather, a full-size bed from the palace was substituted for it. With its elaborate, carved decoration, this was a palatial bed, perhaps more representative of the beds in use in well-to-do Phrygian households than the king's bed is. Certainly it must have been more comfortable to sleep in, and we may guess that bed surfaces made of interwoven strips stretched within the frame were more favored than wooden planking.

The inlaid table (TumP 154) in the child's tomb had its counterpart on the city mound stratified in the burnt level (W 84 in Megaron 3; see pl. 96J). Even the design of the inlay is similar.

The eight plain tables found in the king's tomb (MM 380–387) are all alike and must give us a picture of what Phrygian tables were like. At about 0.50 m., the tables were not of a height that people of normal stature could have fitted their knees under with comfort. Evidently the Phrygians did not sit up to their tables. No proper chairs were found, and the stools from the child's tomb, about 0.35–0.40 m. in height, would have again been too high for use with the tables. Probably people sat on thick cushions or hassocks on the floor. The tables must have been serviceable: having only three legs (as did most of their Egyptian and Greek counterparts), they were stable without wobbling.

The ninth table (MM 388), infinitely more elaborately made than the others, although collapsed, could be fitted together from all its pieces, with each in its proper place. The dowels and tenons and mortises afforded the clues that enabled us to reconstruct the whole and reveal it in its full intricacy. Although we may be surprised, it must be admitted, nevertheless, that the table is from a technical point of view a masterpiece of the cabinetmaker's craft. Though somewhat higher than the other tables, the frame below its top, the corner supports—especially the rocker on one long side—would have made sitting at it uncomfortable (if not impossible), whether for dining or for writing.

The screens and the extraordinary ninth table give us some inkling of the strength of the glue that was available to the Phrygian cabinetmakers. In many cases tenons were used without cross-pegging, and they must have been secured with glue. The inlays of the screens, inasmuch as they were not countersunk, must have been glued in place. The gluing process was widespread throughout the area of the Eastern Mediterranean at an early time, and perhaps it emanated originally from Egypt; thus we have the Eighteenth Dynasty cabinetmaker at work cutting wood while his gluepot stands at a nearby fire for the glue to be thinned by heating so that it can be used to join the pieces of wood.[165]

Also widespread must have been the other techniques of furniture-making—the turning of legs on the lathe, their bending to a curved profile by steaming or by soaking, the use of mortise-and-tenon or dowels, inlaying of surfaces with decorative patterns of wood or ivory or other materials. Thus the Phrygians had all this to their hand, and made the furniture as it is only as a result of their personal taste in design.

Near the beginning of his history, Herodotus[166] tells us that "Gyges was the first foreigner we know to have sent offerings to Delphi, after Midas, Son of Gordios, King of Phrygia. For Midas dedicated the royal throne whereon he was accustomed to sit and administer justice, an object well worth looking at." The throne by Herodotus' day must have become rather venerable; because, being foreign, it was somewhat exotic; and be-

---

[165]H. S. Baker, *Furniture*, 302, fig. 464.

[166]I.14 2–3.

cause being royal, it was probably elaborately made of rich materials. But at the time of its dedication before 700 B.C. (if its dedicator was that King Midas who died as a consequence of the Kimmerian raid early in the seventh century) the throne could have been of considerable interest, from a technical point of view, to the emerging Greek cabinetmakers of the time.

Quite obviously the construction and decoration of screens such as TumW 80, TumP 151, and MM 378 and 379 must have been extremely time-consuming; they could not have been made to put in the tomb after the king died, but must have been brought from the palace where they had been in use before his death. They were not, then, special pieces made for funerary use, but were representative of normal (though palatial)

Phrygian furniture. Though the proper restoration of all these screens is assured and their original appearance is now clear, their use is still obscure. That they were not thrones is certain; but in the absence of parallels we are reduced to guesses as to how they were used. Perhaps the best guess is that they were sumptuous backgrounds—throne backs, if you will—before which a magnate could sit in glory on a stool or on a hassock. Thus they served the psychological, if not the physical, functions of a throne. But the throne at Delphi would have been other in design, perhaps made to be sat upon "properly"[167] as were the Assyrian thrones shown on reliefs of the ninth and eighth centuries, which could well have served as models to be copied or adapted by Phrygian furniture makers.

---

[167]Herod. I.14.3: ". . . ἐς τὸν προκατίζων ἐδίκαζε," literally "*into which* seating himself, he was wont to pronounce judgment" as if in a chair with arms. [Ed.]

V

CONCLUSIONS

Machteld J. Mellink

The three early tumuli selected by their excavator for the first volume of the new Gordion publications are representative of early Phrygian history and its problems. Rodney Young centered his work in the tumulus cemetery, after preliminary exercises, on the group of tumuli dominated by the great landmark of MM. Gustav Körte had excavated K-III, the largest neighbor of MM, but could not undertake the technical assault on MM. Rodney Young explored new techniques of drilling in his investigations of Tumulus P, and in the course of its excavation learned also of the conservation problems that awaited the excavator of tomb chambers with furniture and wood carvings. His planning and execution of the tunneling of MM and the exploration of the tomb chamber were courageous and consistent. His description of the enterprise allows the reader to read between the lines that the discovery of the tomb chamber in MM was a rare confrontation with an intact part of the past, in this case with the past of a people forgotten or distorted by historical tradition and with a king who belonged to its greatest period.

The later excavation of Tumulus W was a deliberate attempt to move away from the cluster of prominent burials, which seemed to belong to the pre-Kimmerian period, and to extend the Phrygian archaeological record further into the past. This attempt was successful in that it reached an

unmistakably earlier burial. At this stage of analysis it is unlikely that any of the other excavated tumuli belong in a stage antedating W.

TOMB CONSTRUCTION

The Phrygian burial custom of building a wooden chamber to house the body of a prominent individual and covering the chamber with a stone pile and tumulus has become better known through the study of Tumuli W, P, and MM, along with K-III and K-IV. We know from the regular cemetery in the area to the south and west of the MM, P, K-III, K-IV complex that commoners received simple inhumations and later, cremations, without giant tomb markers. Tumuli were reserved for the privileged class, whether noblemen or relatives of the ruling family. The chamber of Tumulus W is relatively large (interior measurements 4.62 by 3.30 by 1.54/1.57 m.) and roofed with a single layer of beams. The timbers are enormous and carefully selected. We note, if this is the beginning of the burial custom at Gordion, that it follows an established formula. The same formula appears in Tumulus K-III, and in Tumulus P, except that the roof is given double thickness in each case, as a strengthening device. The chambers of Tumuli P and W are of about the same size and not tall enough to be considered the equivalents of living rooms. K-III and K-IV are deeper, but the entire series belongs together as a group that varies only in details of size and execution. MM, on the other hand, has a chamber carefully prepared and put together as a cabin with gabled roof and a construction that, but for the lack of a doorway, may be the replica of an existing timber house. The emphasis on the interior of the chambers is the same throughout the series of tombs. The timbers are smoothly finished on the interior, whereas the outside is of only structural concern. In the case of MM, the exterior reinforcement of the tomb chamber, the extra casing and the tying-in of casing and cabin are carefully planned *ad hoc*. The knowledge of the carpenters who put together the chamber in MM must derive from a long-standing tradition of building log cabins and wooden houses. Gabled roofs were characteristic of Phrygian eighth-century architecture.

The tomb chamber of MM, then, is a special construction improving upon the standard type of low, flat-roofed burial chamber, and replacing it with a room more similar to the living rooms of

Phrygian aristocracy. So far as we can judge, this is an exceptional tomb chamber for an exceptional king.

The standard type of flat-roofed, low burial chamber appears fully developed in W, our earliest tumulus. Even if we date the burial in W to the very beginning of the eighth or the end of the ninth century B.C., it appears to us as a sudden introduction of a well-developed burial custom into Western Anatolia. We do not know where the Phrygians practiced this burial custom before they came to Gordion (and Ankara), and in which part of Anatolia, Europe, or Asia we have to recognize the immediate ancestry of these Gordion tombs and their occupants. The generic connection with South Russian and later, Scythian, burial customs has to be admitted, but the manner of introduction into Anatolia is uncertain. On the other hand, we may wonder if the remodeling of the flat-roofed timber grave into a gabled room in MM was the beginning of a Phrygian contribution to the development of stone-built gabled tomb chambers in tumuli of Western Anatolia, some of which betray their Phrygian affinities.

Table of Measurements

Tumulus	Weathered height tumulus	Weathered diameter tumulus	Interior length chamber	Interior width chamber	Interior height chamber	Type of roof
W	22 m.	150 m.	4.62 m.	3.30 m.	1.54/1.57 m.	one layer
K-III	23	75	3.70	3.10	1.90	two layers
P	12	70	4.57	3.48	1.54	two layers
K-IV	8?	30	3.70	2.50	1.70	one layer
MM	53	250	6.20	5.15	3.25/3.86	gabled, with outer casing

CONTENTS OF THE TOMBS

FURNITURE

The wooden furniture in the tomb chambers has given us a chapter of Phrygian art and craftsmanship hitherto barely suspected on the basis of the contents of K-III and K-IV and the passage in Herodotus I.14. Most of the burials were laid on beds (except for Tumulus W, whose occupant lay on layers of textile). Wooden trays and tables appear in increasing numbers, and there is evi-

dence in all tombs, but best of all in Tumuli P and MM, of the peculiarly Phrygian screens or throne backs which we now come to understand as decorative backrests meant to be set up behind a person seated on a rug or cushion. One such screen was found on the floor of Megaron 3 on the city mound, burnt in the Kimmerian raid.[1] The construction and decoration of these screens are unparalleled in the eighth century. The manner in which they are set up in MM shows that

---

[1] *AJA* 64 (1960): 239–240.

they need not rest against the wall of a room, but can be used in outdoor settings, tents, or even chariots. The holes in the top of the rear frame may have allowed standards or awnings (parasols) to be erected. The arrangement in the tomb chamber of MM, with open space left in front of the screens but tables with drinking vessels nearby, suggests that the place for guests of honor was in front of the screens. Thrones as such were not part of the furnishings of the tomb. The screens are appropriate to customs in which even the most prominent members of the group are seated at ground level, distinguished by their location and backdrop, and surely also by the splendor of rugs and cushions which prepared their place.

The absence of an oriental throne is matched by the absence of orientalisms in the decoration of the furniture. Here we see no lion's claws, bull's hoofs, ivory bands with sphinxes and palmettes (although the latter begin to make their appearance on the city mound in the pre-Kimmerian level), but we note a tradition of openwork and inlay combined with metal studding. The dominant characteristic is geometric patterning in which swastikas and meander are freely used in single and combined versions by craftsmen whose colleagues in the textile and metal workshops are drawing on the same authentic Phrygian ornamental repertoire. Curvilinear ornament is not absent, but it is used sparingly, for example, in the "rose windows" of the screens. Some of the craftsmen who were making these screens may have seen oriental furniture and oriental ornament, but it had little effect on what must have been a long-standing Phrygian idiom. There is no indication of a borrowing of ornament from the Greek geometric repertoire, although there may indeed have been common roots to the developments on either side of the Aegean.

The textiles preserved in the tomb chamber are giving us a beginning of understanding of a great medium of traditional design and polychromy. The original appearance of the chambers at the time of their closure is hard to reconstruct, because even now we lack the full evidence for the extent and coloring of the textiles in the tombs. The chamber in Tumulus P provided the clearest evidence for the fastening of textiles to pegs along the top of the walls; traces of similar cloth were found in W (along with what may have been

paint). Designs of the geometric tradition have been recovered from pieces of Fabric G (p. 305, figs. 144–148) in Tumulus P, beginning to confirm physically what had been postulated on the basis of indirect illustrations such as the costume of Warpalawas in the İvriz relief. The analysis of Phrygian textile patterns will allow a study also of the connections between the Phrygian art of eighth-century Gordion and the rock carvings of Western Phrygia with the monumental versions of geometric ornament.

METAL WARE

The vessels used for the real or symbolic food and drink provided in the tombs are to an important extent of bronze, as befits the prosperity of the privileged tomb owners. In this category the Phrygians are not drawing on an exclusively native tradition. We know that the Near Eastern aristocrocy of the Iron Age, whether in Assyria, Urartu, the neo-Hittite kingdoms, or Cyprus, was provided with enormous quantities of large and small bronze cauldrons, drinking and pouring vessels, some of them decorated. Such metal ware was used in trade to the West and East and as tribute sent by smaller kings to the Assyrian ruler, or it was captured as booty in conquered territory. The Phrygians in their metal ware betray an awareness of Near Eastern decorative fashions. The large and small cauldrons are provided with figural attachments as early as the stage of Tumulus W, with bulls' heads made in North Syrian or neo-Hittite tradition and birds functioning as finials for basket handles. MM with its more openly orientalizing ornament, siren and bearded demon attachments on the cauldrons, wherever the particular workshop may have been located, displays an immediate dependency upon Near Eastern fashions which were at that time also finding their way beyond Phrygia to the West. It is difficult to identify the precise origin of even those metal vessels which are admittedly imports, such as the lion's- and ram's-head situlae, MM 45 and 46. The special sources from which these fine objects came will have historical importance in the sense that "imports" often are exchange gifts among ancient royalty; specific alliances may be documented archaeologically even if the written record does not exist.

We see a general trend of orientalizing metallurgy also in the development of Phrygian omphalos bowls, which start in Tumulus W, in small format, to emphasize the plain omphalos and soon develop into the typical Phrygian vessel with ridged, prominent omphalos, and combine this with the oriental blossom bowl to create the series of petaled bowls from MM. Again, it is easier to show the Phrygian reaction to a general orientalizing trend than to determine the specific place of inspiration (or manufacture) of the earliest relief-decorated omphalos bowls TumW 9 and 10 and TumP 11. The handled bowls in the Phrygian tombs are clearly a regional transformation of a wooden prototype with metal fittings into an all-metal bowl or basin, with characteristic decorative treatment of functional details: ring handles, bolsters, bands, knobs. Trefoil jugs are perhaps a translation from local pottery rather than a borrowing from the East. At the same time, a one-handled jug with flaring rim and separate foot (TumW 6) maintains its popularity in pottery and metal.

Phialai were used as drinking vessels, to be filled with the aid of pitchers or ladles. Ladles are not a common implement of early Near Eastern drinking parties. Large, awkward iron ladles are known from Iran, in Marlik and Sialk.[2] TumW 8, the first ladle known at Gordion, has a peculiarly primitive zoomorphic juncture between handle and cup; the incisions and modeling look awkward either because a Phrygian is imitating a more accomplished (Iranian?) example or because the ladle itself comes from a peripheral workshop. The small ladle, precursor of the Etruscan *kyathoi* and the elegant Achaemenid ladles of precious metal, seems early to become a regular part of the metal drinking equipment in Phrygia (W through MM). Situlae like MM 45 and 46 are exotic oddities. The ladles would have dispensed wine rather than beer. If beer indeed is the beverage drunk from the vessels with strainers, it was less popular than wine. Strainer jugs with side spout start in metal with TumW 5, an accomplished piece with a spool decorating the top of its handle. Perhaps we should not forget that the jar with strainer spout and a handle set at right

angles to it was an Anatolian pottery vessel known in the Old Hittite days at Gordion.[3]

In any case, the metal workshops of Phrygia prove themselves to be active and ready to make their own designs translated from local pottery forms or adapted from Near Eastern embellishments of basic shapes. The Phrygian designs are durable and in turn begin to influence the West, whether in Lydia, Greece, or Etruria.

POTTERY

With the emphasis on wealth and metal ware, the pottery inventory of the newly excavated tumuli cannot be a fair selection of the best from Phrygian workshops. A certain amount of storage equipment went into the tombs, black polished handleless jars (dinoi), kraters, and amphoras, of regular functional types which will ultimately give a good standard for comparison with habitation levels. Imitation of metallic features is noticeable in the pottery "cauldrons," K-III, nos. 47 and 48. Black polished, "reduced" ware is the normal fabric for most Phrygian pottery, whether for the household or for some more elegant destination. Painted vessels are exceptional, but tend to be put into tombs for that reason, as is noticeable in Tumuli W and P. Tumulus W, with its two strainer-spouted jugs, proves that somewhere within reach of Gordion potters went to work on brightening these normally monochrome jugs. TumW 61 is a very fine example of the delicate dark-on-light decoration, polished over the paint, which is a rarity on the city mound, and which may have its home in the southern region of the Phrygian domain rather than at Gordion.[4] TumW 62, with its matt bichrome decoration and its odd attachment of the spout to the collar, is so far unfamiliar in Phrygian territory, and even in Anatolia.

In Tumulus P we see the fine painted ware of the class of TumW 61 developing beyond the stage represented even in K-III, where in small panels typical Phrygian animal motifs appear (hawks, goats); the larger panels on the Tumulus P jugs make room for such exotic hybrids as a sphinx

[2]See p. 229, n. 52.

[3]Mellink, *Hitt. Cem.*, pl. 14e (P 368).

[4]Akurgal, *Phryg. Kunst*, 21–22; G. K. Sams, *AnatSt* 24 (1974): 175. The sherds are from the 1941 excavations of Alaettintepe.

with bird's-head tail. It is remarkable that the painted pottery from Iron Age Ali̇şar and vicinity, often labeled Phrygian, is entirely absent from these tumuli, although variants and allusions appear in the Kimmerian destruction level of the city mound. The preference of taste goes in the direction of Konya and the Taurus area rather than Ali̇şar (and Iron Age Kültepe). The fine painted ware, in addition to its compromise with figural ornament, also introduces running and stacked meanders in a context which presumably remains purely Phrygian. Its linear panels, like those on the engraved metal belts of Tumulus P and presumably many textiles, include oblique diamond patterns.

Tumulus P, more so than its counterpart K-III, welcomes foreign matter. The juglet, TumP 59, in Cypriote style, is clearly an import: it may come from Cilicia. Its Egyptian blue counterpart, TumP 46, belongs in the same Levantine orbit, as does the dish TumP 47. The glass omphalos bowl TumP 48 may point to a specific Assyrian origin, and a date to the last quarter of the eighth century B.C.

Pottery parallels found in the destruction level of the city mound include for Tumulus P a checkerboard askos (P 2364) from Room TB-4 (pl. 96G);[5] also a painted fine ware strainer jug with tall neck (P 1270; pl. 96B).[6] These comparisons bring the date of the latest material in Tumulus P close to the time of the Kimmerian raid.

PERSONAL EQUIPMENT

Apart from the textiles, the drawings and analysis of which are beginning to reconstruct an important aspect of the Phrygian appearance, belts and fibulae are characteristic belongings. The belt, TumW 25, has such fine and intricate studded work that, as in the case of the furniture, we must admit that a long technical tradition stands behind it. The ornament is in part curvilinear, as in the roundels on furniture from Tumuli P and MM. There may be a variant of the lotus motif in the four designs surrounding the cross in the center of the disk. The expertise with which the curvilinear

motifs are combined and braided into quadruples is perhaps to be compared to the fine interlacing of linear design on a carved furniture panel (W 89) from Megaron 3 on the city mound.[7] Studded belts remain in use to the period of Tumuli K-III and MM. The engraved belts of Tumulus P represent an artistic counterpart of the finest painted pottery, but the technique of the engraver surpasses that of the painter. The system of adjusting and fastening of this type of belt must have had its development separate from that of the studded series; the metal workers and fibula makers contributed to the making of a Phrygian belt which became attractive to the West Anatolian and East Greek world.

If the belt is an essential piece of equipment to hold the Phrygian robe tight around the waist, fibulae appear to have served for fastening of the garment near the shoulders. The pairing of many (but not of the largest) fibulae is demonstrated most clearly in the sets found by the head of the bed in MM. Secondarily fibulae were used to pin the bedclothes around the body of the king in MM. The types and variants of the bronze fibulae found in the series of tumuli, including K-III and K-IV, are discussed in detail under Commentary and under Tumulus W, chronology. Apart from the chronological aspect, the fibulae of the Gordion tumuli need to be appreciated as another characteristic Phrygian way of reshaping a metal form not exclusive to their culture. The Phrygian development remains functional and abstract. No special ornamental adjuncts or spaces for engraving are developed; instead, the arc of the fibula and the structural connection with the spring and catch are places of simple ornamental elaboration of the juncture. The moldings are blocklike in the beginning but, along with the section of the arc, can become rounded and diversified. Places for decoration can be increased by emphasizing the center of the arc, and the centers of its bent ends, or the surface of the arc, which can be studded. A minimum of engraving or studding can be applied to the shield-plate, a Phrygian invention for double-pinned fibulae.

The surplus number of fibulae given to each of the persons buried in this series of tumuli sur-

---

[5]See also *AJA* 64 (1960): 342 and pl. 58, fig. 29.

[6]See also *AJA* 60 (1956): 263 and pl. 94, fig. 50.

[7]*AJA* 64 (1960), pl. 61, figs. 23, 24.

passes that of the extra belts considerably; we may wonder if a collection of fine fibulae (from special Phrygian workshops) was made by persons during their lifetime, perhaps partly through gifts of appropriate and elaborate sets.

Phrygian fibulae are known to have been carried to East and West. They are illustrated on Assyrian reliefs and on the rock relief of Warpalawas at İvriz, and appear in Greek sanctuaries from Samos to Perachora.

The absence of more precious jewelry from the tumuli is to be noted. Electrum (J 131),[8] gold, and silver fibulae (J 130, 132; pl. 95H, I) were found in the Terrace Building on the city mound at Gordion. In general we have no indication of a profusion of precious metals in Phrygia, unlike the situation in Lydia and the Persian Empire, including its Anatolian districts.

Among the other types of equipment absent from the Gordion tumuli are weapons and defensive gear such as helmets and shields. In this respect the Phrygians seem to be consistent as a matter of principle. Horse gear and chariots may have been buried outside the chambers in places as yet undiscovered, but so far no chance discovery in any of the five tumuli of the group discussed would point to such customs for the early period.

ART

In many ways, the Phrygians through their burial customs and funeral equipment appear to us as a people different from their Greek or Near Eastern neighbors. The tombs are closed, doorless chambers; the tumuli are anonymous markers without stelai or commemorative monuments (in spite of the epigram quoted by Plato, *Phaedrus* 264 D). We do not find the Phrygians interested in representing themselves in any of the decorated objects in the tombs. Representational art is coming in on the painted pottery, presumably through the connection with neo-Hittite neighbors and via southeastern Phrygia, the Konya and Taurus regions. There is also an earlier kind of animal style, which brings in the bird attachments on the small cauldrons TumW 3 and 4, the zoomorphic juncture on the ladle, TumW 8, a bird's-head

finial on that of TumP 9, and the small pottery bird motif on the spout of K-III, no. 20. These ornaments seem to belong with a nonoriental component in Phrygian arts and crafts, at least with one that does not come from the old cultural *koine* of the Near East. In the wood carvings (TumP 106–114, 148, 149) and bronze quadriga (TumP 40), which may have been left as toys for the child buried in Tumulus P, we see this different artistic component more clearly, especially in the series of bird carvings, in the oddly angular griffin eating a fish, in the stag and deer figures, which transform reality in a manner that may belong to an old native strand in Phrygian culture, wherever it was practiced. Several of the wood carvings show the compromise between the local manner of seeing animal forms and the Near Eastern traditional motifs: especially the lion carvings and the bull-and-lion fight (TumP 109). In the art found in the pre-Kimmerian citadel more of the compromise is achieved, in architectural sculpture (lion brackets and orthostates) and, on a miniature scale, in the small ivory panel representing a Phrygian warrior on horseback.[9] In these works also the differences between Phrygian and neo-Hittite (or other Near Eastern) art cannot simply be attributed to the inexperience of a beginning artist.

The strength of Phrygian arts is in their abstract decorative tradition combined with careful craftsmanship. The nonfigural designs of the furniture and the metal work are most characteristically Phrygian and part of a tradition the antiquity of which is hard to estimate.

We see the Phrygians in these tumuli at a moment when they are increasingly in contact with their neo-Hittite, Urartian, and Assyrian neighbors, and a few direct results of these contacts are visible in the tombs. Gifts such as the situlae (MM 45 and 46), the glass bowl (TumP 48), the Egyptian-blue miniatures (TumP 46 and 47) come from the Near Eastern world, and the cauldron attachments of MM 2 and 3 are at least members of the Near Eastern family.

The question of Greek contact with Phrygian art does not receive any enlightenment from the present group of tumuli. No Greek objects were deposited in the tombs as imports or gifts, and, as

---

[8] *AJA* 66 (1962): 166 and pl. 48, fig. 23.

[9] R. S. Young, *AJA* 64 (1960), pl. 60, fig. 25c (BI 333), and see logo for this volume.

explained above, the geometric repertoire of the Phrygian arts appears entirely indigenous. Contact with the Greeks is suggested by stray Greek pottery fragments of *ca.* 720–690 B.C. from the citadel mound. The presence of alphabetic writing in MM may have to be seen as the most striking sign of interaction with the Greeks of the eighth century B.C. But in material and artistic culture Tumuli W, P, and MM reveal considerable autonomy and a beginning temptation on the part of the Phrygians to look toward the world of the Near East.

CHRONOLOGY

The discussion of the contents of the tumuli has made clear that Tumulus W is generally agreed to be the earliest of the three published here, and also earlier than K-III and K-IV. The relative order of the other tumuli is a matter of some debate, principally concerning the place of MM. Rodney Young considered MM earlier than Tumuli K-III, P, and K-IV on the basis of his analysis of the fibulae; in the further study of the fibulae and other categories of metal ware, the likelihood that MM is the latest in the series was proposed by K. DeVries and discussed in the introduction to the catalogue of Tumulus W.

The relative chronology of the fibulae, which are found in large number in each of the tumuli in question, should indeed be considered one of the keys to internal chronology. It is possible that MM contained a greater variety of fibulae from workshops outside of Gordion and that we are not observing a development strictly in one direction. On the other hand, some confirmation of the chronology of fibula types (and not just of refinements within the details of individual types) comes from the analysis of the fibulae found at Phrygian Boğazköy, where Blinkenberg Groups XII,3, 4, 5, and 7A have not been found, presumably because they antedate the Phrygian occupation of Boğazköy.[10] Fibula Groups XII,3, 4, 5, and 7A are absent from MM (see the tabulation on p. 241). The development of the form and number of moldings on fibulae from Group XII,13 and 14 in MM is the strongest indication

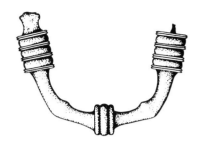

Figure 132. B 1764. Fibula (XII,14), from TB-8. 1:1.

of progress and refinement among the fibulae in this tomb.

The fibulae found in the destruction level on the city mound are in general remarkably different in assortment from those put in the tumuli and show a preponderance of flat arcs, Group XII,7A, and of foreign fibulae of Cypriote and leech types. B 1764 (fig. 132) from TB-8 is of Group XII,14 type, perhaps developed just a little beyond the specimens from MM, but it is an exceptional piece on the mound.

The progress seen in the shaping of fibulae from MM may be matched by improvements in other categories of metalwork. The phialai of MM are larger in size and bolder than those of Tumulus P, which in turn are advanced beyond the stage of Tumulus W. The production of a local series of petaled bowls is amply attested by the series of 54 such bowls in MM (MM 70–123), whereas there is no evidence of locally made blossom bowls in Tumulus P, K-III, or K-IV. The phialai of the destruction level on the citadel are of basic ridged omphalos type, with the exception of one bowl from TB-6 with interior ribbing (B 1488; fig. 133). The small cauldrons of Tumulus P have rather simple, flat T-shaped attachments (TumP 3, pl. 8C); the contours of the attachment may be elaborated but the surface stays flat (TumP 5, pl. 8D). MM 9 (pl. 58I) has a pro-

Figure 133. B 1488. Omphalos bowl from TB-6. 1:2.

---

[10]Boehmer, *Kleinfunde,* 49, 54.

filed attachment, MM 4 (pl. 58C) has a convex section for the stems of the T, and ends in flat tabs for the studs; MM 6 and MM 7 have additional moldings on the stems of the T's.

The conclusion with reference to the metalwork is that we are watching progress from Tumulus W to P to MM and that even in the local workshops degrees of refinement increase. We cannot always be sure of the age of the object deposited in a tomb, and we may see different workshops in the types of belts and some of the fibulae. MM had access and claim to more metal wealth than any of the other tumuli discussed here, but the balance of the differences in execution of most of the metalwork would confirm the relatively later status of the tomb. The citadel has yielded too few metal finds to allow a comparative tabulation of statistical value, except in the case of the fibulae which, however, belong in a different category of elegance and practicality and need to be analyzed for their foreign content.

The second criterion for relative chronology is ceramic. Here also we have to cope with different purposes and different needs. The series of painted vessels from Tumulus W to Tumulus K-III and Tumulus P illustrates the presence of a well-developed fine style on an established strainer-spouted shape in TumW 61. The jugs in K-III are still close in style, although they open up small panels for animal design. The fine style in Tumulus P (TumP 54–57) is loosened considerably, with the large panels and orientalizing sphinxes, even beyond the stage seen in P 1270 from Room CC-2 in the destruction level of the citadel (pl. 96B). On the other hand, simpler painted vessels of what may be the local Gordion style make their appearance in Tumuli K-III (K-III, nos. 4, 5, 11, 12) and P (TumP 54, 58) and have general counterparts in the destruction level, again perhaps with a touch of precision in K-III that is lost gradually. Bichrome ware of the white-ground kind, which begins to appear on the citadel before the destruction,[11] is absent from Tumuli K-III and P.

Black polished dinoi show a development in shape from ellipsoidal in Tumulus P to spherical in MM; the small amphoras in MM are related to

specimens in Tumulus S-1, a somewhat later burial.

Absolute chronology by archaeological criteria can come only from the foreign imports in Tumulus P and MM, and from datable contexts of Phrygian exports with counterparts in these tumuli. This leaves us with the glass bowl TumP 48, which is tentatively associated with Assyrian glass manufacture from the time of Sargon (722–705 B.C.), with the situlae MM 45 and 46, which have counterparts in reliefs from Sargon's palace in Khorsabad, and with the somewhat less direct comparison of the relief bowl TumW 9 with the bowl from Assur inscribed with the name of Assurtaklak, who may be the eponymous official listed for 806 B.C.

This would give us a potential range from the beginning to the end of the eighth century B.C. for the tumulus series from W to MM. Confirmation comes from the appearance of Phrygian fibulae of Group XII,7 at Khorsabad[12] and of XII,9 on the relief of Warpalawas at Ivriz. The date of the Ivriz relief may be as early as 738 (the date of his tribute to Tiglath-pileser III) or as late as 709 (if the Nimrud letter to be discussed below is dated this late). Both types of fibula are well represented in MM.

Phrygian exports found in Greek sanctuaries have so far not occurred in sufficiently precise chronological association to help in dating the Phrygian sequence rather than vice versa. The same applies to Phrygian metal ware in Lydia.

Carbon-14 and dendrochronology are not yet in a position to offer more precision to the chronology roughly established with the aid of Assyrian correlations. The preliminary results of the radiocarbon determinations (app. IV, p. 293) are in general agreement with the historical estimates. A precise historical determination of MM will be of great value to the method of dendrochronology, which may be able to attach the special date of the construction of MM to the last preserved tree rings on the outer logs of the casing around the tomb chamber. Unfortunately most of the timbers of Tumuli W and P are trimmed, so that an overlap of the sequence of tree rings for any one tumulus still will not reveal the year in which the trees were cut and taken to the burial sites.

[11]R. S. Young: *AJA* 60 (1956), pl. 94, fig. 51; *AJA* 64 (1960), pl. 58, fig. 21; *AJA* 68 (1964), pl. 88, fig. 19.

[12]O. Muscarella, *JNES* 26 (1967): 82, pl. II,1.

HISTORICAL IDENTIFICATION

MM is the largest tumulus in Gordion, at least twice as large as W and K-III. The tumulus dominates the area of Gordion and is visible from afar. It was built to be a landmark for a person whose memory was to be lastingly honored, and to cover a tomb chamber which was unique in construction and equipment. The tomb had been planned carefully, and the building of the tomb chamber had presumably been started before the actual death of the person buried in it.

There is little doubt that MM is a royal tumulus. The identification of the king buried here as Midas presented itself before excavation, and was expressed in the name "Midas Mound," current through the years of excavations at Gordion and used in this volume. The date of the tomb, as recapitulated in this chapter, is probably not earlier than the last quarter of the eighth century B.C. It is the tomb with the most explicit Near Eastern associations in its display of large cauldrons with siren and demon attachments and situlae of oriental manufacture, and in its style of petaled omphalos bowls. Yet, the man buried here was surrounded by authentic Phrygian equipment, wooden furniture, textiles, and personal paraphernalia that characterize him as a typical representative of the Phrygian West. A few graffiti reveal that the alphabetic script was used in his lifetime for the Phrygian language, his idiom. His burial customs are those of his ancestors, although on a more glorious scale.

The skeleton on the bed was that of a man about 65 years old, who could have ruled as king for 40 or more years. The only king known to us as a historical ruler of Phrygia, whose fame reached the Greeks and whose actions were recorded by the Assyrians, is Midas. The Greek tradition is mythologized, but Herodotus may be right when he attributes a fine piece of furniture, a throne in the Corinthian treasury at Delphi, to the Phrygian king Midas as the earliest foreign

dedication made at the sanctuary (I.14). The Assyrian tradition is precise. Midas, referred to as Mita of Mushki, an ethnic designation that may refer to Midas' rule over tribes beyond the Phrygian West, is a minor but persistent adversary of Sargon on the western boundaries of the Assyrian realm. He is referred to in Sargon's annals from the fifth to the thirteenth year (717–709). Mita's connections are with Pisiris of Carchemish, Ambaris of Tabal, Matti of Atuna, and Rusa I of Urartu, and he is well enough known to be sought out by Assyria's opponents as an ally. He is active in Que-Cilicia and captures towns there which have to be retaken by the Assyrian governor. According to Sargon's annals, Mita finally requested an alliance and offered tribute in 709 B.C.

A letter found in Nimrud in 1952 refers to another pro-Assyrian move of Mita, who had intercepted messengers sent by Urikki of Que to Urartu and delivered them to an Assyrian governor of Que. The same letter makes it clear that a messenger from Warpalawas came along with the Phrygian messenger. The date of the letter is usually assumed to be 710 or 709 B.C.,[13] although an earlier date in the rule of Tiglath-pileser III, *ca.* 735 B.C., has also been advocated.[14] In either case, the connections of Midas are indirectly extended to Warpalawas, the king of Tuhana-Tyana, who in his İvriz relief displays his Phrygian associations and in whose city Midas left an alphabetic inscription on the (now lost) black stone of Tyana.[15] The minimum chronology for the Assyrian connections with Mita-Midas is 717–709 B.C., the maximum at present 735–709 B.C. The king most directly concerned with Midas' actions is Sargon.

The historical and archaeological evidence converge strongly. The archaeological dates for the equipment of the MM burial fall in the rule of Sargon. The age of the king (65) buried in MM makes it possible that he is the Midas whose connections with Warpalawas and Urikki may have started in the rule of Tiglath-pileser III,

---

[13] J. N. Postgate, "Assyrian Texts and Fragments," *Iraq* 35 (1973): 21–34, Nimrud Letter no. 39. Cf. also H. W. F. Saggs, *Iraq* 20 (1958): 182–187.

[14] Houwink ten Cate in *Fischer Weltgeschichte: Die altorientalischen Reiche* III: *Die erste Hälfte des 1. Jahrtausends* (Frankfurt am Main: Fischer Bücherei, 1967) 122 and 346, n. 10.

[15] J. Garstang, *LAAA* 1 (1908): 10–16; Friedrich, *Kleinasiatische Sprachdenkmäler* (Berlin: De Gruyter, 1932), 127–128, no. 19; M. J. Mellink, "Midas in Tyana," in E. Masson and Cl. Brixhe, eds., *Florilegium Anatolicum, Volume offert à Emmanuel Laroche* (Paris: E. de Boccard, 1979), 249–257.

about 735 B.C. The Assyrian record provides the background for Midas' political and cultural association with neo-Hittite kings from Carchemish to Tabal and with the Urartians as well as the Assyrians.

The death of Midas is not reported by the Assyrian annals. The Greeks have the story that he committed suicide by drinking bull's blood at the time of the Kimmerian invasions (Strabo I.61). Eusebius put his accession at 738, his death at 696; Sextus Julius Africanus puts his death 20 years later. Eusebius' dates agree well with the Assyrian record, and can include an earlier contact with Warpalawas under Tiglath-pileser III. According to Eusebius, Midas ruled 42 years.

If we associate the destruction level on the citadel of Gordion containing the burnt megara on the south side of the great plaza and the terrace buildings with the Kimmerian raid that drove Midas to despair and death, the relative chronology is in order. There is no appreciable gap in the time between the surviving inventory of the burnt citadel and the latest elements in the MM series. The citadel has some more evidence for contacts with neo-Hittite cultures in the form of architectural sculpture and ivory horse trappings, neither of which needs to put the date of the destruction level far from that of the closing of the MM chamber.

We do not know the real history of the end of Midas' rule, and we shall have to interpret the raids of the Kimmerians by a careful reading of the record of the citadel. Preliminary analysis supports the interpretation of the occupant of MM as Midas. The effect of the Kimmerian raids was not such as to destroy the city of Gordion or its dynasty. Tumuli continued to be erected in the seventh century, and the rebuilding of the citadel started gradually under the protection of the mudbrick fortification of Küçük Hüyük. That major building projects in the citadel and the tumulus cemetery could be brought to completion after a Kimmerian raid is not inherently improbable. Midas had a vast realm and his citadels were not all looted at the time when Gordion suffered destruction. The objects put in his tomb could have been assembled from his other strongholds.

The assumption that the tomb of Midas has been recovered is presented here as the most probable combination of various strains of evidence, some of which, especially the story of his suicide, are poorly attested. The archaeological facts of MM agree with the Assyrian and Herodotean record in presenting evidence for a great king of Phrygia, the greatest known in East and West, and the greatest buried at Gordion.

Identification of the occupants of Tumuli K-III and P is difficult. We can assume on the basis of their proximity to each other and to MM, and of the relatively close archaeological sequence of their contents, that the child in P and the unknown occupant of K-III ("nur geringe formlose Reste fanden sich vor"[16]) were relatives of Midas. Where Midas' father and predecessor was buried, we cannot tell. In Tumulus W we may have the tomb of a person of the generation before Midas, buried in a sizable chamber under a large mound. He remains anonymous, but he is a representative of the cultural and perhaps also historical tradition which continues in the era of Midas. The contents of W show a beginning of contact with the Konya-Taurus region and with the orientalizing metal workshops (TumW 9–10). The child in Tumulus P was privileged to receive the greatest number of items of foreign manufacture, and seems to have been buried with a certain lavishness.

We shall continue the analysis of the history and occupants of the Gordion tumuli in Volume II of this series.

---

[16]G. Körte in *Gordion,* 45.

APPENDICES

I. INSCRIPTIONS

LES GRAFFITES DU GRAND TUMULUS

Cl. Brixhe, Université de Nancy II, Nancy, France

Bibliographie

Haas = O. Haas. *Die phrygischen Sprachdenkmäler* (Linguistique balkanique X). Sofia, 1966.

Lejeune, *SMEA* = M. Lejeune, "Discussions sur l'alphabet phrygien," *Studi micenei ed egeo-anatolici* 10 (1969), 19–47.

Lejeune, *REA*[1] = M. Lejeune, "Notes paléo-phrygiennes," *Revue des études anciennes* 71 (1969), 287–300.

Lejeune, *Kadmos* = M. Lejeune, "Les inscriptions de Gordion et l'alphabet phrygien," *Kadmos* 9 (1970), 51–74.

Young = R. S. Young, "Old Phrygian Inscriptions from Gordion: Toward a History of the Phrygian Alphabet," *Hesperia* 38 (1969), 252–296.

1. Parmi les plus anciens tumuli, seul MM, le Grand Tumulus, a fourni des inscriptions, sous la forme de graffites sur vases[2]:

MM 68 (Fig. 134A; Pl. 97A)

Dans de la cire, sur le bord d'une sorte de grand bol en bronze, *siꜛidosakor* (dextroverse), lecture de Lejeune (*SMEA*, 22 et 42; *REA*, 289 et 292; *Kadmos*, 58 sq. et 71); Young (260 et 262, nº 25) lisait *siꜛidozakor*.[3]

MM 67 (Fig. 134B; Pl. 97B)

Dans de la cire, sur le bord d'un bol de bronze identique au précédent, *uzd* (sans doute dextroverse),[4] Young, 262, nº 32; cf. Lejeune, *REA*, 289, et *Kadmos*, 71.

MM 69 (Fig. 134C; Pl. 97C)

Dans de la cire, sur le bord d'un récipient en bronze semblable aux deux précédents, *ata* (prob-

---

[1]Dans cet article, comme dans le suivant, M. Lejeune reprend tous les documents publiés par R. S. Young (*Hesperia*) avec la même numérotation que ce dernier.
[2]Par la suite les textes seront simplement désignés par le numéro que leur donne Young dans *Hesperia*.
[3]Pour ce graffite, voir encore R. S. Young, *AJA* 62

(1958): 153 et pl. XXV, 21; le même, *ProcAPS* 107 (1963): 362 et fig. 20; Haas, 198, nº. XXV. On trouvera là un dessin ou une photo sans translitération.

[4]Plus pour des considération phonétiques qu'en raison de la forme des lettres, qui n'est pas pertinente.

Figure 134. Inscriptions from Tumulus MM. A. MM 68, Young n° 25. B. MM 67, Young n° 32. C. MM 69, Young n° 33. D. MM 119, Young n° 30. E. MM 362, Young n° 31. 1:1.

ablement dextroverse),[5] Young, 262, nº 33; cf. Lejeune, *REA*, 289, et *Kadmos*, 71.

MM 119 (Fig. 134D; Pl. 98A)

Sur le fond d'un petit plat en bronze, *eies* (dextroverse), Young, 260, nº 30; cf. Lejeune, *REA*, 289, et *Kadmos*, 71.

MM 362 (Fig. 134E; Pl. 98B)

Sur le flanc d'une jarre sphérique très endommagée, *aladis url*, Lejeune, *REA*, 289, et *Kadmos*, 57 et 71; Young (260, nº 31) proposait *agadis urg*, sans exclure la leçon retenue par Lejeune.[6]

2. Selon Young (p. 259),[7] "many of the bronzes from the Gordion tomb show damage and repairs, the damage suffered no doubt during a period of use in the palace before they were placed in the tomb." Serait-ce le cas des nº 25, 30, 32 et 33? Je ne le crois pas; ceux que j'ai pu voir sont en excellent état.[8] D'ailleurs, si l'interprétation proposée *infra* pour les textes est exacte, les objets inscrits n'appartenaient pas, de son vivant, au prince défunt, mais à des individus qui les lui ont offerts après sa mort, ce qui paraît exclure qu'ils aient été usagés. Ils peuvent avoir été d'une fabrication déjà ancienne; mais, comme leurs propriétaires n'avaient aucune raison d'y apposer leur nom tant qu'ils étaient en leur possession,[9] il est vraisemblable que les graffites ont

été gravés[10] au moment de l'offrande, c'est-à-dire à l'époque de la fermeture du tombeau. Si l'on excepte le texte Young nº 29, trouvé dans les ruines de la cité et susceptible d'être antérieur à 750, nous sommes en présence des documents paléo-phrygiens les plus anciens. On en aperçoit immédiatement l'intérêt pour l'histoire de l'alphabet utilisé: ils sont contemporains des plus anciennes inscriptions grecques[11] et, comme le fait remarquer Young (p. 253), ils précèdent largement les plus vieux textes ioniens ou éoliens (milieu du VIIe s.). De ces constatations, jointes à des considérations géographiques,[12] Young (p. 254–256) croit pouvoir conclure à l'indépendance des écritures phrygienne et grecque, empruntées selon lui à une source commune, un alphabet sémitique adapté à des langues indo-européennes quelque part sur les côtes ciliciennes ou nord-syriennes, auxquelles les Phrygiens avaient accès par l'intérieur des terres. Une thèse inverse, fondée sur l'emploi ou la forme de certains caractères, est défendue par M. Lejeune.[13]

Quel que soit le chemin emprunté par l'écriture pour parvenir en Phrygie, il est raisonnable de placer son importation à la fin du IXe ou au début du VIIIe siècle; on ne peut expliquer autrement l'autonomie partielle qu'elle manifeste à l'égard de son modèle, grec ou sémitique, dès ses premières apparitions:

a. Comme l'a relevé Young (p. 266 sq.), alors

---

[5] A cause de l'orientation de la barre du *t* et du *a*, qui n'est cependant pas pertinente. Quelle que soit la direction de l'écriture, la lecture, notons-le, est la même.

[6] Discussion générale sur les signes Γ et Ϝ chez Lejeune, *SMEA*, 23 sqq.

[7] Cf. encore le même, *Gordion Guide* (1968), 42.

[8] Voir les photos données par Young, pl. 68 (nos. 25, 32, 33) et ici pl. 97A–C.

[9] Si les propriétaires ont gravé leur nom sur les poteries trouvées dans les ruines de la ville, n'est-ce pas parce qu'à l'occasion de leur utilisation les objets pouvaient passer entre d'autres mains et risquaient d'être dérobés.

[10] Quelquefois dans une languette de cire déposée sur le bord, pour faciliter le travail et éviter d'entamer le bronze.

[11] Le célèbre graffite sur vase du Dipylon, qui passe généralement pour l'inscription grecque la plus ancienne, est attribué à la première moitié du VIIIe siècle par quelques auteurs (cf. G. Klaffenbach, *Griechische Epigraphik*, Göttingen, 1957, 34); la plupart le situent vers 725 (L. H.

Jeffery, *The Local Scripts of Archaic Greece*, Oxford, 1961, 76, nº. 1; M. Guarducci, *Epigrafia greca* I, Rome, 1967, 135, nº. 1); mais voir maintenant J. N. Coldstream, *Greek Geometric Pottery*, Londres, 1968, 358, qui le place vers 740 (référence aimablement communiquée par le Prof. K. DeVries).

[12] A l'ouest, la Lydie aurait constitué une barrière entre la Phrygie et les cités grecques de la côte, tout comme, au sud-ouest, la Carie aurait interdit toutes relations suivies avec Rhodes et les Grecs de cette région.

[13] *SMEA*, 40 sq., et *Kadmos*, 64: la dépendance de l'alphabet phrygien à l'égard du grec lui semble assurée (*a*) par le dédoublement du *wāw* sémitique en Ϝ et Ϝ, (*b*) par la forme rectiligne (Ι) qu'a prise l'avatar du *yod* employé pour noter *i*, (*c*) par l'utilisation (dans les premiers temps seulement, pour les parties occidentale et centrale du domaine, toujours dans les autres zones) de ce même signe pour symboliser *y*, ce qui impliquerait un emprunt au système graphique d'une langue qui avait perdu ce phonème. Cf. Cl. Brixhe, dans *Le déchiffrement des écritures et des langues* (présenté par J. Leclant), Paris, 1975, 67.

que les inscriptions grecques comparables (monostiques) de la même époque sont sinistroverses conformément au modèle sémitique, sur les six textes phrygiens les plus anciens (les cinq du Grand Tumulus et le n° 29), quatre sont dextroverses et les deux autres ont toutes chances de l'être.

b. Avec le n° 32, il est possible que nous ayons le premier exemple de *zêta* (cf. Young, p. 262; Lejeune *Kadmos,* p. 58 et 60). Pour rendre compte de son tracé (Ⴥ), si l'identification est correcte, on peut songer à une évolution interne, cf. la forme prise par le même symbole sémitique en lydien, où il note la sifflante dite normale (Ⴥ, forme courante, à côté de I, plus rare, dont elle dérive sans doute). Un graffite inédit (n° d'inv. I 520), trouvé dans les ruines de la cité (remblai du IIIᵉ siècle), nous livre peut-être, dans un contexte obscur (*mezi*), un second exemple de la lettre: son tracé serait intermédiaire entre le *zêta* grec archaïque et celui, d'origine cursive, qui apparaît à l'époque hellénistique. La valeur exacte du caractère resterait à déterminer. Si, comme le suggère M. Lejeune (*Kadmos,* p. 59 sq.), il n'avait dû servir qu'à noter la variante voisée de *s* devant consonne sonore[14] (ici, *uzd < *usd?*) ou n'être utilisé que pour quelques mots, tel le nom de la "terre" (cf. le radical néo-phrygien ζεμελο-; *mezi* pourrait appartenir à cette catégorie), on comprendrait aisément qu'il eût été rare, mais, en raison de sa médiocre utilité, on devrait s'étonner de sa présence—peu économique—dans le système graphique.

c. ↑, inconnu du grec[15] et des écritures sémitiques, paraît avoir été ajouté très tôt, puisqu'il figure déjà dans notre graffite n° 25. Sur ses occurrences (Phrygie occidentale, Gordion, Tyane) et sur sa valeur possible, voir Young, p. 265 sq., Lejeune, *SMEA,* p. 42, et *Kadmos,* p. 63. Après avoir ajouté au dossier deux emplois isolés in-

édits rencontrés sur des tessons de Gordion (n°ˢ d'inv. I 369 et 457), qu'il me suffise de rappeler trois points: (1) le signe connaît dans la Cité de Midas une variante Ψ, cf. *k*Ψ*iyanaveyos* en face de *k*↑*ianaveyos* (Haas, p. 190 sq., n°ˢ II et III); (2) sauf, naturellement, s'il est isolé, il précède toujours un *i* (cf. *si*↑*idosakor*)[15a], ce qui fait penser à une palatale ou au produit d'une dépalatalisation (voir Haas, p. 178, et Lejeune, *l.c.*), (3) sa présence après *k* semble, pour des raisons articulatoires évidentes, exclure qu'il recouvre une occlusive palatale ou affriquée; elle nous oriente plutôt vers une spirante, palatale ou issue d'une dépalatalisation.

3. Les objets retrouvés dans les tumuli sont sans doute le plus souvent des offrandes destinées à être utilisées dans l'au-delà par le défunt. Quand ils sont inscrits, on peut raisonnablement s'attendre à y retrouver le nom de ceux qui les ont donnés.

Les graffites les plus modestes paraissent, en effet, se réduire à un nom de personne. *Eies* (n° 30) est un *Lallname* à mettre probablement aux côtés du gréco-anatolien Εια (Bithynie, confins phrygo-lyciens et phrygo-pisidiens, Pisidie) et du pisidien épichorique Εια/Ειη.[16] *Ata* (n° 33),[17] qui peut être un masculin, est un autre *Lallname,* tiré d'un de ces noms familiers que tous les peuples utilisent ou ont utilisés pour désigner le père, cf. hittite *attas* ou turc *ata. Uzd* (n° 32) devrait, représenter une abréviation, voir Lejeune, *REA,* p. 291, et *Kadmos,* p. 60.

Le n° 31 présente un texte un peu plus complexe, composé de deux séquences séparées par un espace. On est apparemment en présence de deux "mots," l'un complet (*aladis*), l'autre abrégé (*url,* cf. Lejeune, *REA,* p. 291, et *Kadmos,* p. 57). Cette différence de "traitement" devrait correspondre à une différence de statut. *Aladis* pourrait être le nom du donneur, nominatif singu-

---

[14]Notons qu'à l'époque de l'adoption de l'écriture par les Phrygiens le *zêta* grec valait *dz* ou *zd* selon les régions.

[15]A moins qu'il n'ait quelque rapport avec le *sampi* ionien (suggestion de Young, p. 266); mais il faut souligner que, parmi les variantes de ce signe, seule Τ est attestée comme lettre, ↑ apparaissant uniquement dans le système numéral dit milésien (= 900; voir M. Guarducci, *o.c.* 102 et 422 sq.).

[15a]Ceci était vrai au moment de la rédaction de cet appendice. Mais, dans trois textes récemment trouvés au

S.O. d'Afyon, le signe apparaît devant *e. e* étant, comme *i,* une voyelle palatale, les nouvelles découvertes ne remettent pas en cause les hypothèses avancées ici quant à la valeur du symbole discuté.

[16]Cf. L. Zgusta, *Kleinasiatische Personennamen,* Prague, 1964, §319.

[17]Attesté à Gordion par le n°. 45 de Young et par deux graffites inédits (n°. d'inv. I 455 et 484); cf. à l'époque gréco-romaine Ατα/Αττα (fém.) et Ατας/Αττας (masc.), Zgusta, *o.c.,* §119.

lier d'un thème en -*i* (Lejeune, *REA*, p. 292), sans parallèle dans l'onomastique anatolienne, donc peut-être proprement phrygien. Toute hypothèse sur la signification de *url*, susceptible de le déterminer d'une manière ou d'une autre, semble ɔctuellement inutile.

Avec le n° 25, enfin, nous pourrions avoir affaire à une phrase (nominale ou verbale). M. Lejeune (*REA*, p. 292) suggère la possibilité d'une lecture *siîidos akor*.[18] Pour le premier mot (un anthroponyme?) on peut hésiter entre un génitif singulier athématique déterminant *akor* (idée de Lejeune) et un nominatif singulier thématique, sujet de la phrase. Quant à *akor,* ce serait

la première personne du singulier d'un verbe médio-passif (avec finale -*or* en face du -*tor* de la troisième personne néo-phrygienne) ou un substantif neutre en *-r̥* ou *-ōr* (plutôt). Ces deux hypothèses sont de M. Lejeune (*ibid* p. 294), qui avoue sa préférence pour la seconde. Si celle-ci se révélait exacte, il serait possible, au cas où *siîidos* représenterait le nom du donneur au nominatif, que le verbe ("donner," "offrir" *vel simile*) fût sous-entendu et qu'*akor* fût un accusatif, complément d'objet[19] ou attribut du complément d'objet, lui aussi sous-entendu.[20]

Nancy, 1975

II. CHEMICAL ANALYSES

A. ANALYSES OF SPECIMENS FROM TUMULUS MM (1957) AND TUMULUS W (1959)

A. E. Parkinson, Museum Chemist, University Museum, Philadelphia, Pennsylvania

Sample	Description			Results[21]				Text ref.
					Ignition Residue			
		Vol. at 105° C %	*Behavior during Ignition*	*% of Dried Sample*	*Constituents of Acid-soluble Portion*	*% Insoluble in Acid*	*Elem. Organic Anal.*	
1	MM 1. Outside pots in cauldron	5.23	Much smoke, easily ignited	10.9			N	p. 102
2	MM 1. Contents of sack	3.92	Smoke ignited	35.76	Cu,Fe,Al, Ca,Mg	23.7	N,Hal	p. 102
3	MM 1. Hardened food clump, from sack	4.50	Much smoke, easily ignited	11.8			N	p. 102
4	MM 2. Part of clump, from sack	4.97	Much smoke, burnt with smoky flame	10.6			N	p. 104
5	MM 2. Outside pots; containing wood	6.71	Some smoke, woody odor	17.40	Cu,Fe,Al, Ca,(Mg)	23.1	N	p. 104

[18]Suggestion déjà implicitement chez Young (p. 266)?

[19]Désignant la chose offerte, c'est-à-dire le bol de bronze.

[20]Voir, à propos d'une autre inscription paléo-phrygienne, Cl. Brixhe, *Mélanges Mansel*, Ankara, 1974, 249 et n. 85–86, où l'on trouvera des parallèles grecs pour ces deux

éventualités.

[21]See p. 283 for A. E. Parkinson's account of his analytical procedures and analytical results, p. 284 for conclusions and identifications.

II. CHEMICAL ANALYSES—*continued*

Sample	Description	Results						Text ref.
				Ignition Residue				
		Vol. at 105° C %	Behavior during Ignition	% of Dried Sample	Constituents of Acid-soluble Portion	% Insoluble in Acid	Elem. Organic Anal.	
6	MM 3. Outside pots; ball of food	7.13	Much smoke, burnt with sooty flame	8.94			N	p. 107
7	MM 3. Outside pots	4.42	Much smoke, burnt with smoky flame	12.3			Neg.	p. 107
8	MM 3. Outside pots	4.47	Much smoke, burnt with smoky flame	12.13			N	p. 107
9	MM 10. Contents	0.72	No smoke	88.52	Cu,*Fe*	0.28		p. 111
10	MM 13. Contents, possibly including scraps of textile bag	0.50		87.43				p. 112
11	MM 45. Contents	0.40	No smoke; particles glowed	87.80				p. 121
12	MM 46. Contents	1.32	No smoke	85.63				p. 122
13	MM 51. Contents	0.99	Protein odor initially; no smoke	86.83				p. 124
14	MM 52. Contents	1.31	No smoke	86.57				p. 124
15	MM 53. Contents	1.01	No smoke	86.15				p. 125
16	MM 56. Contents	0.77	No smoke	86.84				p. 127
17	MM 60. Contents	0.81	No smoke	89.78				p. 128
18	MM 61. Contents	0.93	Some particles glowed	85.69				p. 128
19	MM 63. Contents	0.75	No smoke	87.26				p. 128
20	MM 86. Contents	0.61		85.55				p. 134
21	MM 95. Contents	0.69	No smoke	86.57				p. 136
22	MM 104. Contents	1.33		78.50	Cu,*Fe*	1.40		p. 138
23	MM 121. Contents	0.44		86.91				p. 140
24	MM 123. Contents	0.68		84.43				p. 140
25	MM 128. Contents	1.3	No smoke or odor	84.57				p. 141
26	MM 129. Contents	1.1		80.22				p. 143
27	MM 137. Contents	1.23	Particles burnt	80.36				p. 143

II. CHEMICAL ANALYSES—*continued*

Sample	Description	Results						Text ref.
				Ignition Residue				
		Vol. at 105° C %	Behavior during Ignition	% of Dried Sample	Constituents of Acid-soluble Portion	% Insoluble in Acid	Elem. Organic Anal.	
28	MM 141. Contents	2.88	No smoke	73.28				p. 144
29	MM 144. Contents	0.89	Few particles glowed; slight protein odor	85.15				p. 145
30	MM 155. Contents	0.59	Particles glowed	83.26				p. 146
31	MM 157. Contents	0.64	Particles glowed; slight odor of burning wood and protein	83.46				p. 146
32	MM 162. Contents	0.72	No smoke or odor	85.48				p. 146
33	MM 165. Contents	1.03		83.51				p. 147
34	MM 166. Contents	1.60		82.47				p. 147
35	MM 168. Contents	0.94		82.88				p. 147
36	MM 169. Contents	2.02	Slight smoke	83.38	Cu,*Fe*,Al, Ca,(Mg)	6.82		p. 147
37	MM 170. Leather, partly intact pieces and partly powdered material		Little smoke, indeterminate odor; few particles glowed	70.68	Cu,*Fe*	Small		p. 148
38	MM 170. Leather, intact pieces only		Little smoke, indeterminate odor; few particles glowed	50.7				p. 148
39	MM 170. Crumbly purple-black metal (?) in clumps under belt, near "belt plaque"	1.56	No apparent change	85.36				p. 148
40	MM 172. Leather, partly intact pieces and partly powdered material		Little smoke, indeterminate odor	51.79				p. 152

II. CHEMICAL ANALYSES—*continued*

Sample	Description	Results						Text ref.
				Ignition Residue				
		Vol. at 105° C %	*Behavior during Ignition*	*% of Dried Sample*	*Constituents of Acid-soluble Portion*	*% Insoluble in Acid*	*Elem. Organic Anal.*	
41	MM 173. Leather	5.77	No smoke; suffocating odor vaguely suggesting protein	65.83	Cu,Fe,(Ca, Mg,Al,PO$_4$)			p. 152
42	MM 175. Leather, partly intact pieces and partly powdered material		Little smoke, strong odor	57.46				p. 152
43	MM 176. Leather, partly intact pieces and partly powdered material		Little smoke, stifling odor	59.73				p. 153
44	MM 360 (in MM 1). Contents	4.67	Burnt; smoke ignited; waxy odor	53.59	Cu,Fe,Al, Ca,Mg	63.23	N	p. 173
45	MM 361 (in MM 1). Contents	5.65	Burnt; smoke ignited; waxy odor	9.05	Fe,Ca,Mg, (Cu,Al)	0.4	N	p. 173
46	MM 362 (in MM 1). Contents	9.50	Much smoke, waxy odor; ignited	10.9			N	p. 173
47	MM 363 (in MM 1). Contents	4.83	Burnt; smoke ignited; waxy odor	17.71			N,Hal	p. 173
48	MM 364 (in MM 1). Contents	3.41	Softened, puffed up; heavy black smoke burnt; waxy odor	12.0			Neg.	p. 174
49	MM 365 (in MM 2). Contents	11.2	Much smoke, burnt with sooty flame	12.4			N	p. 174
50	MM 366 (in MM 2). Contents	15.91	Much smoke, waxy odor, burnt with sooty flame	10.4			N	p. 174
51	MM 367 (in MM 2). Contents	3.28	Much smoke, easily ignited; woody odor	6.73			N	p. 174

II. CHEMICAL ANALYSES—*continued*

Sample	Description	Results						Text ref.
				Ignition Residue				
		Vol. at 105° C %	*Behavior during Ignition*	*% of Dried Sample*	*Constituents of Acid-soluble Portion*	*% Insoluble in Acid*	*Elem. Organic Anal.*	
52	MM 368 (in MM 2). Contents	7.11	Much smoke, burnt with sooty flame	11.3			N	p. 174
53	MM 369 (in MM 2). Contents	4.86	Much smoke, easily ignited	14.48			N	p. 174
54	MM 370 (in MM 3). Contents	3.91	Much smoke, burnt with smoky flame	7.36	Cu,Fe,Al, Ca,Mg	0.5	N	p. 174
55	MM 372 (in MM 1). Contents	4.95	Burnt; smoke ignited; waxy odor	12.93			N	p. 175
56	MM 373 (in MM 2). Contents	4.52	Much smoke, easily ignited	10.4			N	p. 175
57	MM 374 (in MM 3). Contents	9.64	Smoke tended to ignite	11.9			N	p. 175
58	MM 375 (in MM 3). Contents	5.18	Much smoke, burnt with smoky flame	9.60			N	p. 175
59	MM 376 (in MM 3). Contents	8.06	Smoke tended to ignite	11.7			(N)	p. 175
60	MM 377 (in MM 3). Contents	4.89	Smoke ignited	11.2			N	p. 175
61	Tum. W, south wall near west corner. Leather (?), brown flakes, soft and brittle	4.0	Smoke with strong, indefinable odor	4.2	Fe,Mg,(Al, Ca)		N,Hal	p. 198
62	Tum. W, north-west corner. Leather(?), brown flakes, soft and brittle	3.5	Smoke with woody odor; part fused, ignited, burned with smoky flame	2.9			N,Hal	p. 198
63	TumW 1 and 2. Material between lead backing and cast core bull's head, bitumen(?), black gritty material	0.61	Not much smoke; particles glowed	77.60	Pb,Cu,Fe, Al,Ca,Mg, SiO_2	13.3	(N),Hal, S,P	p. 199

II. CHEMICAL ANALYSES—*continued*

Sample	Description	Results						Text ref.
				Ignition Residue				
		Vol. at 105° C %	*Behavior during Ignition*	*% of Dried Sample*	*Constituents of Acid-soluble Portion*	*% Insoluble in Acid*	*Elem. Organic Anal.*	
64	TumW 6. Inside base of jug; small lumps and yellow powder containing brown particles	0.48	Some part ignited; heavy smoke with waxy odor did not ignite	91.29	Fe,Al,Cu, (Ca,Mg)	92.6[22]		p. 202
65	TumW 25. Leather, soft brown lumps	10.59	Smoke with possible protein odor	33.07	*Cu*,Fe,Al,P, Ca,Mg	9.97		p. 207
66	TumW 64. Contents, brown powder and lumps	7.92	Some spots glowed; smoke	28.7			N,Hal	p. 213
67	TumW 65. Contents, yellow-brown powder and crusty lumps	4.87	Heavy smoke tended to ignite; spots glowed	12.7			N,Hal	p. 214
68	TumW 66. Contents, brown powder and fragments including wood	8.58	Carbonized without much smoke; some particles glowed	37.00			N,Hal,P	p. 214
69	TumW 67. Contents, brown fragments and powder containing pieces of wood	10.8	Carbonized without much smoke	41.27			N,Hal,S,	p. 214
70	TumW 68. Contents, soft brown lumps	8.13	Some particles glowed, heavy smoke did not ignite	13.4	*Fe*,Al,Ca, (Cu),P?		N,Hal	p. 214
71	TumW 69. Contents, brown powder and flakes	3.73	Carbonized without much smoke	69.71	Fe,Al,Ca, Mg,Mn	74.2	N,Hal	p. 214
72	TumW 70. Contents, yellow-brown lumps	4.95	Smoke with waxy odor; spots glowed	9.28			N,Hal	p. 214

[22]This residue contained SiO_2, Fe, Al, Mg, K, and possibly Na.

Analytical Procedures

Most specimens did not appear to be homogeneous, at least in physical form. To obtain a strictly representative sample for analysis it would have been necessary to grind up and mix the whole specimen or a large part of it thoroughly, thus destroying the specimen physically. Instead, a roughly representative sample was used. For example, if a specimen was partly earthy lumps and partly powder, usually parts of each were taken and mixed. It must be recognized, however, that other samples from the same specimen might give different results, quantitatively if not qualitatively, especially if the specimen were heterogeneous in chemical composition, or a mixture of two or more different materials. If it contained obviously foreign material, this was excluded as far as possible.

The procedure usually followed in analyses was as follows: the sample was powdered (occasionally this was difficult to accomplish completely), weighed and heated at 105° C for at least several hours to expel incidental moisture, then weighed again. Generally, organic materials absorb and hold more moisture than inorganic ones, and the amount at any one time depends on external conditions of temperature and humidity, so the object of this operation was to bring all samples to a basic, "dry" condition. This is especially important if the sample weight is to be used in quantitative calculations, which otherwise would not give comparable results. The dried sample was then ignited to burn off organic matter, and the residue was weighed.

The ignition residues of certain samples were digested with acid in order to dissolve them as much as possible and were analyzed qualitatively for metallic elements and sometimes for other constituents, and often the part that was insoluble in acid was dried and weighed. Sometimes the amount of silica was determined also. These qualitative and quantitative analyses were made on selected samples which, for example, had high, medium, or low organic matter, as indicated by the amount of ignition residue, or whenever it seemed they might provide useful information.

Samples from a few specimens that were obviously inorganic or predominantly inorganic were analyzed without being ignited.

Specimens that contained a large amount of organic matter were also analyzed for elements that might be part of organic compounds. This elementary organic analysis required a separate sample in each case, and shows the presence of nitrogen, halogens (chlorine, bromine, iodine), sulphur, and phosphorus. The analysis as made does not clearly distinguish between the three halogens, but chlorine is by far the most common and the most likely to be present.

Analytical Results

As far as practical these are presented in tabular form.

The percentage figures given under "Volatile at 105° C" are based on the weight of the sample as received.

The amount of the ignition residue, given as a percentage of the dried sample, is important. A high ignition residue indicates little or no organic (carbonaceous) matter in the sample; conversely a low ignition residue points to a large amount of organic matter.

For purposes of brevity chemical symbols are used to show constituents found through analysis, viz.: Cu, copper; Pb, lead; Sn, tin; As, arsenic; Fe, iron; Al, aluminum; Mn, manganese; Ca, calcium; Mg, magnesium; Na, sodium; K, potassium; P, phosphorus; PO_4, phosphate; SiO_2, silica; SO_4, sulphate; CO_3, carbonate; Cl, chlorine; Hal, halogen; N, nitrogen; S, sulphur. A symbol in *italics* indicates that that constituent was predominant or occurred in large quantity, while parentheses indicate that the elements within them were present only in very small amounts or in traces. The fact that a constituent is represented as the element does not mean, of course, that it was present in that form; more likely it was present as an oxide or other compound, but these distinctions usually are not made by the analysis.

The acid-insoluble residue was frequently granular or crystalline and usually composed mainly of silica or undecomposed silicates. A small amount of inorganic residue in a predominantly organic specimen may have come from the original material, but a large amount is probably from contamination from the surrounding material, such as earth.

The presence of organic nitrogen is particularly

important because nitrogen is contained in all amino acids, the basic constituents of proteins, and therefore points to the original presence of such animal products as meat, cheese, fur, or skin, although these may have been degraded or completely changed in form and appearance through the years. Sulphur also is present in some amino acids, and chlorine and phosphorus may come from animal material. Fats and carbohydrates contain only carbon, hydrogen, and oxygen and would contribute to the carbon content of a specimen. The production of much heavy smoke, and especially a waxy odor, during ignition could be an indication of the original presence of fatty matter.

Conclusions and Identification

In some cases the analysis provided enough information to identify the specimen or at least to give a reliable indication of its nature. In many cases, especially those largely organic specimens that presumably had suffered considerable change from their original condition, positive identification was not possible.

Samples 1–36, 39, and 44–60:

On the basis of the amount of ignition residue almost all the specimens fall into two well-defined groups: mainly organic and mainly inorganic. All except two of the organic specimens contained nitrogen, and it is possible that all were largely food remains of some kind. The inorganic specimens were not further identified, but the ignition residues of nos. 9 and 22 were ferric oxide containing black copper oxide, and it is probable that these specimens themselves had a similar composition. All the ignition residues which were analyzed contained large amounts of iron and some copper, and it seems likely that all the inorganic specimens contained considerable iron. The iron was probably derived from the many iron nails and other objects in the tomb that had partly

rusted. The copper was probably from corroded bronze objects or, in those cases where the specimens were found in bronze containers, possibly from corrosion of the containers. Elements such as aluminum, calcium, and magnesium are common constituents of clay and other earthy material, and probably such material formed a large part of the inorganic specimens, such as pottery.

Samples 37, 38 and 40–43:

Rather heavily mineralized leather.

Samples 61, 62:

Probably partly decomposed leather.

Sample 63:

The ignition residue was probably mainly lead oxide (PbO) and black copper oxide (CuO) with siliceous material. The original sample probably had a similar composition but with a little organic matter; not bitumen.

Sample 64:

The part of the ignition residue insoluble in acid (92.6 percent) was probably a potassium and possibly sodium silicate containing iron, aluminum and magnesium. Specimen probably mainly clay.

Sample 65:

Probably leather, partly mineralized.

Samples 66–70 and 72:

All were mainly or largely organic, and nitrogen was found in all of them. On the basis of the results, it is not possible to say definitely what the specimens were originally, but they could have been wholly or partly food of one kind or another.

Sample 71:

Largely inorganic; cannot be positively identified on the basis of the results. May contain some red ochre.

Philadelphia, 1967

B. PRELIMINARY REPORT ON THE TECHNICAL EXAMINATION OF SAMPLES TAKEN FROM VARIOUS BRONZE OBJECTS FROM GORDION (1959)[23]

R. J. Gettens, Curator, Research Laboratory, Freer Gallery of Art
Smithsonian Institution, Washington, D.C.

Sample	Description	Results	Text ref.
73	MM 3. Blue-green crystalline corrosion product from thickly corroded area on interior	Identified provisionally as *basic copper nitrate*; it is the most perfectly crystalline of the three samples of this material studied. Preliminary studies by M. Mrose of the U.S. Geological Survey in Washington show this corrosion product identical with a synthetic *basic copper nitrate*.[24]	p. 107
74	MM 45. "White" of left inlaid eye; white crystalline substance	Identified provisionally by microchemical methods as *magnesium carbonate* similar to the mineral "magnesite."	p. 121
75	MM 45. Material from outer rim of left eye	Identified provisionally as *decomposed glass* or similar vitreous material; sample was not large enough for adequate identification; it was observed, however, that the fragments have conchoidal fracture, are isotropic in character, but have a wide range of refractive index (estimated $n = 1.45$–1.50).	p. 121
76	MM 45. Blue corrosion product from left side	Identified microscopically as *azurite* (basic copper carbonate).	p. 121
77	MM 68. Green corrosion product	Identified by X-ray diffraction analysis as *malachite* (basic copper carbonate).	p. 130
78	MM 169. Blue-green crystalline corrosion product from exterior	Identified provisionally as *basic copper nitrate*.	p. 147
79	MM 170-180. Blue-green corrosion product on bronze bosses on leather	Identified by X-ray diffraction and microchemical analysis as *basic copper sulphate*; identical in crystal structure to the copper sulphate mineral "brochantite."	p. 147

Comment: The identification of *malachite* and *azurite* (basic copper carbonates) among the copper corrosion products is expected; the finding of basic *copper nitrates* and *sulphates,* however, is quite unexpected and they raise many questions relevant to the atmospheric conditions and corrosive agencies in the Gordion tomb [MM]. The presence of rare and unusual minerals suggests strongly that, henceforth, all metal objects from this tomb should be carefully examined for rare and unusual mineral corrosion products. . . . It is presumed that these bronzes found in the Gordion tomb were never in direct contact with the earth, hence the corroding environment was entirely gaseous.[25]

Washington, D.C., 1959

[23]These were exhibited at the Walters Art Gallery in Baltimore on February 2, 1959. Samples were made available through the interest and courtesy of several persons: Rodney S. Young and A. Eric Parkinson of the University Museum; Burhan Tezcan of the Archaeological Museum, Ankara, and Dorothy K. Hill of the Walters Art Gallery.

[24]Described by W. Nowacki and R. Scheidegger in *I. Acta Crystallographica* 3 (1950): 472–473.

[25]See R. J. Gettens, "The Corrosion Products of Metal Antiquities," *Smithsonian Report, 1963* (1964), 547–568, especially 556; see also *idem*, "Patina: Noble and Vile," in *Art and Technology*, 56–72. [Ed.].

C. ANALYSES OF SELECTED GORDION BRONZES

Arthur Steinberg, Anthropology/Archaeology Program,
Massachusetts Institute of Technology, Cambridge, Massachusetts

While working on a group of Etruscan and imported bronzes from the Bernardini Tomb (found at Palestrina, near Rome, in 1876) during the early 1960s, I thought it advisable to do some spectrographic analyses of those bronzes and stylistically related ones (including samples from Gordion) in an attempt to fix their proveniences more precisely and to determine something about trade in such large exotic ritual goods.[26] The underlying theory of doing such analyses on archaeological objects is that the impurities patterns of trace elements (Pb, As, Sb, Ni, Bi, Fe, Zn, Ag) will be different for objects from different areas because the ores from which they are made should have different places of origin. As it turns out now, both from this project and many others,[27] even though the basic theory may be correct, emission spectroscopy with its limits of resolution, and this series of trace elements (common to most ores) give far too general a characterization of the bronzes to be of any help in locating them more precisely. But beyond these limitations are such problems as: the ancient remelting and reuse of bronzes from various sources in one object; uncertainty about which trace elements come with the copper and which with the tin, so that their absolute values are not useful; difficulties of sampling cast bronzes due to segregation of various elements during solidification; difficulties of getting a good representative sample from a corroded bronze. But even if the sampling problems can be overcome, it seems to me that the metallurgical uncertainties enumerated are sufficiently grave that this approach cannot be used for the purpose intended. On the whole, I have little confidence in what the analyses themselves show,[28] but publish them here for the use of others, and because they do reveal some interesting metallurgical characteristics of these fine bronzes.

Sampling of the Gordion bronzes concentrated on the cauldrons with various kinds of handle attachments ranging from simple ring handles to those with elaborate cast figures of sirens, demons, and bulls' heads, which usually had rings fastened to loops on their backs. The reason for this focus was that several similar objects had been found in Etruria as well, and though we could show no kinship on the basis of these analyses, we did note that several of the Gordion cauldrons had unusually high tin contents. So, for example MM 3 (with two sirens and two demons) had 17.6 percent tin, MM 2 (with four sirens) had 23.4 percent tin, and MM 5 (ring-handled deep bowl) had 24.2 percent tin. The other cauldrons TumW 2 (with bulls' heads on a lead core) and MM 1 (with bulls' heads) contained only 13.3 percent and 10.4 percent respectively. The omphalos bowls (MM 114, 126) and ring-handled bowl (MM 65) tested range between 9.3 and 16.1 percent tin.

What is unusual about all these vessels is that their tin content is generally above 10 percent, but even more unusual is that the largest cauldrons have those enormously large amounts of 17 to 24 percent. The reason for astonishment is that these vessels are hammered: raised up from bronze ingots by continued hammering and annealing. This is a reasonable process when the tin content is around 10–12 percent or less, but the difficulty increases as the tin content rises because the bronze tends to become brittle and requires excessive annealing and even working while it is hot in order to avoid cracks and breaks. Hot-forging such enormous cauldrons, if that is what was done, is an extraordinary feat for these an-

---

[26]Analyses were made by Anne Millett at the Research Laboratory for Archaeology, Oxford, through the kind generosity of its director, E. T. Hall.

[27]See a critique such as J. A. Charles and E. A. Slater, "Archaeological Classification by Metal Analysis," *Antiquity* 44 (1970): 207–213; further arguments in *Antiquity* 47 (1973): 217–221; R. F. Tylecote, in *Antiquity*

44 (1970): 19–25, also outlines the problems of the method.

[28]W. T. Chase, "Comparative Analysis of Archaeological Bronzes," in C. W. Beck, ed., *Archaeological Chemistry* (Washington, D.C.: American Chemical Society, 1974), 148–185, shows the enormous variation achieved by different laboratories and different techniques on the same sample.

Analyses by Anne Millett, Research Laboratory for Archaeology, Oxford

Sample No.	Description	Results										Text Ref.
		Cu	Sn	Pb	As	Sb	Ni	Bi	Fe	Zn	Ag	
80	TumP 166D	90.9	6.3	0.98	0.55	0.27	0.087	nd	0.59	0.29	0.069	p. 77
81	MM 1 Att.	82.9	8.3	2.2	0.85	0.87	0.021	nd	3.0	1.9	0.11	p. 102
82	MM 1 Att.	75.2	10.0	6.0	1.7	2.3	0.029	nd	1.6	1.5	0.18	p. 102
83	MM 1 Rim	89.1	10.4	0.051	0.23	nd	<0.01	nd	0.070	nd	0.060	p. 102
84	MM 2 Att.	73.0	25.5	0.43	0.40	0.33	<0.01	nd	0.038	0.053	0.18	p. 104
85	MM 2 Rim	76.4	23.4	0.046	nd	nd	<0.01	nd	0.12	nd	0.043	p. 104
86	MM 3 Att.	90.6	8.1	0.43	0.38	0.17	0.018	nd	0.27	nd	0.083	p. 107
87	MM 3 Att.	91.2	7.7	0.42	0.39	0.16	0.019	nd	0.043	nd	0.087	p. 107
88	MM 3 Att.	89.7	9.3	0.48	0.40	0.17	0.013	nd	0.085	nd	0.099	p. 107
89	MM 3 Att.	91.3	7.9	0.35	0.21	0.14	0.012	nd	0.027	nd	0.072	p. 107
90	MM 3 Rim	82.2	17.6	0.13	nd	nd	0.012	<0.01	0.15	nd	0.061	p. 107
91	MM 5	75.7	24.2	0.074	nd	nd	nd	<0.01	0.023	nd	0.040	p. 110
92	MM 65 Lug	85.9	13.6	0.030	nd	nd	<0.01	<0.01	0.42	0.27	0.077	p. 129
93	MM 65 Rim	83.7	16.1	<0.02	nd	nd	<0.01	<0.01	0.19	nd	0.089	p. 129
94	MM 114	87.2	11.2	0.17	0.41	0.13	0.072	nd	0.26	0.58	0.41	p. 139
95	MM 126	90.1	9.3	0.092	0.23	0.10	0.028	nd	0.11	nd	0.072	p. 141
96	MM 226	ca.75.0	ca.10.0	ca.0.34	ca.0.47	nd	ca.0.012	nd	ca.3.7	>10.00	ca.0.054	p. 164
97	MM 254	ca.75.0	ca.15.6	ca.0.039	nd	nd	nd	nd	ca.0.081	>10.00	ca.0.013	p. 166
98	MM 335	ca.75.0	ca. 6.3	ca.0.094	nd	nd	ca.0.025	nd	ca.3.8	>10.00	ca.0.057	p. 171
99	TumW 2 Att.	84.2	9.2	5.8	nd	nd	0.036	nd	0.74	nd	0.070	p. 201
100	TumW 2 Rim	85.2	13.3	0.032	0.19	nd	0.067	nd	1.1	nd	0.056	p. 201
101	TumW 4	86.9	12.0	0.72	nd	nd	0.18	nd	0.073	nd	0.042	p. 201

cient metallurgists. Moreover, the beautiful finishing of these vessels by planishing and scraping and polishing is so fine that any trace of hammer marks has been removed.

With the mistaken logic of modern hindsight, I had looked at these cauldrons with their high tin contents, their thick everted rims, and their extraordinary smoothness and regularity and assumed that the cauldrons must have been cast because hammering them would have been too difficult.[29] (To build molds for such large, thin vessels is also no mean feat!) Ever since first studying these cauldrons, I have been looking for a sample that could be examined metallographically so as to solve this peculiar riddle. More recently I have had the opportunity to obtain a small fragment from a cauldron which was attached to a bull's-head handle attachment from Iran, related in general type to the Gordion handles.[30] Analysis by X-ray fluorescence showed the tin content of the cauldron to be about 18.3 percent. The photomicrograph (pl. 99A) shows very small grains with many heavily twinned boundaries and evidence of slip-bands in many of the grains indicating clearly that this cauldron was raised by continued hammering and annealing and that the final stage was hammering or polishing (evidenced by the slip-bands). Whether the forging was hot or cold is not clear from the microstructure, though I must repeat that the high tin content tends to point to hot-forging as the method of manufacture. By analogy I would also consider the Gordion cauldrons to have been made in this way, though it would be better corroborated by a metallographic examination of an actual cauldron fragment. Why a bronze of such high tin content was favored for these large cauldrons is not clear to me unless it had some malleable characteristics of which we are not aware. It should be added that not all the vessels had a tin content of over 18 percent, and in fact the bull cauldrons and omphalos bowls might have come from a different workshop favoring a less tin-rich alloy.

The other analyses of vessel parts are not especially noteworthy except for the fact that on cauldron MM 3 each of the four attachments was sampled, and they all show great consistency in trace element contents, but the tin (a major constituent) varies from 7.7 percent to 9.3 percent. This points up clearly the kind of problem these analyses present, for one would expect the four handle attachments to have been cast from a single charge, and that their compositions should therefore be virtually identical, but they vary over 20 percent in one of the major constituents. Whether this is a modern analytic or ancient foundry discrepancy we simply do not know.

The impurities of the two bull's-head attachments of MM 1 are interesting as they show considerable amounts of Pb, As, Sb, Fe, and even Zn (this appears rarely in such large quantities, as it is a highly volatile substance). The same pattern of trace elements in such large quantities appears on a stylistically homogeneous group of siren handle attachments from such disparate places as the *Circolo dei lebeti* in Vetulonia, and the sanctuaries at Olympia, Delphi, Mount Ptoön, and now here in these bulls' heads at Gordion. That is suggestive indeed, but what conclusions are we to draw?

Finally, the most interesting of all the Gordion analyses are those of MM 226, MM 254, and MM 335, three fibulae of Blinkenberg's types XII,7, 9, and 14, respectively. The analyses are not very precise because composition ranges fall so far outside the Research Laboratory's standards. But what is most interesting about them is their zinc content in excess of 10 percent. These are brasses rather than bronzes although they still contain appreciable amounts of tin. Since metallic zinc is very hard to reduce from its ore because it volatilizes at a relatively low temperature, we assume that the makers of these fibulae mixed some zinc oxide with their tin bronze to produce this unusual gold-colored alloy by diffusion of the zinc vapor rather than that they had metallic zinc available which they added to the casting charge.[31]

---

[29]Arthur Steinberg, *The Bronzes of the Bernardini Tomb*, Ph.D. dissertation, University of Pennsylvania, 1966 (Ann Arbor: University Microfilms, 1967), 186–192.

[30]Bull's-head handle attachment from Iran now in the Metropolitan Museum of Art. It was published in *MMJ* 1 (1968): 1 ff. by Oscar White Muscarella, who kindly

made the sample available to me.

[31]Forbes in *Technology* VIII (1964): 265–271 discusses brass production by melting zinc ores with copper and localizes its discovery somewhere in Asia Minor in the early first millennium B.C. We may well have chemical corroboration of this hypothesis in our Gordion data.

What is interesting is that three randomly chosen fibulae, all of different types, have such similar compositions, and all show the unusual zinc composition. That this alloy was the source of the myth of Midas' golden touch has been suggested before,[32] but here is a nice analytic corroboration of the myth!

A few bronzes analyzed from Altıntepe, on the western edge of the Urartian domain, have also been found to contain appreciable amounts of zinc, as have the handle attachments discussed previously. Whether these disparate finds are to be associated with the high-zinc fibula workshop of Gordion is unclear, but certainly open to conjecture.[33]

I would not venture to interpret these analyses any further without more metallographic examination of these bronzes. Suffice it to say that we have here a remarkable group of unusually finely hammered and cast pieces of complex shape.[34]

Cambridge, Massachusetts, 1978

D.   THREE ANALYSES BY X-RAY WAVELENGTH FLUORESCENCE

W. J. Young, Head of the Research Laboratory
The Museum of Fine Arts, Boston, Massachusetts

Three bronze objects from Gordion were submitted in 1959 to the Research Laboratory of the Museum of Fine Arts, Boston, for analysis by means of X-ray wavelength fluorescence using a bulk-type X-ray spectrograph.[35]

X-ray wavelength fluorescence is a nondestructive method of analysis giving quantitative and qualitative results. The X-ray spectrograph is a very important analytical tool for archaeological research, as analyses are made without the removal of a sample.

Primary radiation from the X-ray tube strikes the object being analyzed and emits characteristic X-ray spectra of elements in the specimen which may be in solid, liquid, or gaseous form. These primary rays will excite secondary X rays from the specimen, the frequencies of which are characteristic of the elements it contains. The fluorescent radiation is then collimated so that only a parallel beam of polychromatic radiation strikes the analyzing crystal of the Geiger counter spectrometer. The crystal separates the rays into their component wavelengths in the X-ray spectrum, representing the constituent elements in the same manner as a prism separates visual light into its various orders. These invisible X rays are detected by the Geiger-Müller tube, which can be made to travel automatically along a quadrant at the same rate of speed as the paper chart of the automatic recorder unrolls. As these rays are encountered by the Geiger tube, they furnish to the recorder electrical energy proportionate to the energy of the X-ray beam, and a series of peaks is recorded on the chart.

The objects were situated in a bulk-type X-ray spectrograph using a tungsten target X-ray tube at a tube voltage of 40-kv, 30-ma. A scale factor of 32 was used with a multiplier of 1 and a time factor of 4, at a scanning rate of one degree per minute 2θ, and charts were made.

From the above technique, the analyses indicated the following:

[32]Dorothy Kent Hill, "Bronze Working," in C. Roebuck, ed., *The Muses at Work* (Cambridge, Mass.: MIT Press, 1969), 61.

[33]When some Gordion bronzes were in Boston during the traveling exhibition *From the City of King Midas: Phrygian Art* (1958–59), W. F. Young, then director of the Research Laboratory at the Museum of Fine Arts, did X-ray fluorescence analyses of a fibula and two vessels and found them all to be rather rich in zinc (see pp. 289–290, app. II-D, Samples 102–104).

[34]A. Steinberg, "Technology and Culture: Technological Styles in the Bronzes of Shang China, Phrygia and Urnfield Central Europe," in *Material Culture*, 62–70.

[35]These analyses were made with the permission of the Turkish authorities while the traveling exhibition, *From the City of King Midas*, was in Boston in 1959.

Sample		Results					
No.[36]	Description	Cu	Zn	Sn	Pb	Fe	Text ref.
102	MM 114	82.0	2.0	11.0	5.0	0.25	p. 139
103	MM 169	81.0	12.0	4.0	2.0	0.30	p. 147
104	MM 325	86.0	8.5	3.0	3.5	0.30	p. 170

Boston, Massachusetts, 1959

III. IDENTIFICATION OF WOOD

A. SAMPLES OF WOOD FROM TUMULI P, MM, AND W

B. F. Kukachka, Forest Products Laboratory, Forest Service
U. S. Department of Agriculture, Madison, Wisconsin

Sample	Description	Results	Text ref.
1	Tumulus P. Wood from ceiling beam	Black pine *(Pinus nigra pallasiana)*	p. 4
2	TumP 5. Carrying stick with bark	Boxwood *(Buxus sempervirens)*	p. 12
3	Similar to TumP 115–119. Fragment of a wooden spoon	Boxwood *(Buxus sempervirens)*	p. 56
4	TumP 121–123. Small fragment of a wooden bowl or plate	Maple *(Acer pseudoplatanus)*	p. 57
5	Similar to TumP 121–123. Fragment of a shallow saucer/plate with perforated handle	Boxwood *(Buxus sempervirens)*	p. 57
6	TumP 141–144. A wooden bowl fragment	Black pine *(Pinus nigra pallasiana),* anatomically identical with our native red pine *(Pinus resinosa)*	p. 60
7	TumP 145. Fragment of deep wooden bowl with bronze ring handles	Pear *(Pyrus communis)*	p. 60
8	TumP 151C. Support at back of screen	Boxwood *(Buxus sempervirens)*	p. 65
9	TumP 151. Dark fragment from inlaid screen	Yew *(Taxus baccata)*	p. 62
10	TumP 151. Light fragment from inlaid screen	Boxwood *(Buxus sempervirens)*	p. 62
11	TumP 153. Tripod table fragment	Boxwood *(Buxus sempervirens)*	p. 67
12	TumP 154. Light fragment from top of inlaid table	Boxwood *(Buxus sempervirens)*	p. 68
13	TumP 154. Dark fragment from top of inlaid table	Yew *(Taxus baccata)*	p. 68

[36]The MFA examination numbers are: (for MM 114) #59.26; (for MM 169) #59.27; and (for MM 325) #59.31.

290

III.   IDENTIFICATION OF WOOD—*continued*

Sample	Description	Results	Text ref.
14	TumP 155. Fragment from bed/bier	Poplar (*Populus* sp.) similar to our native cottonwood	p. 70
15	TumP 159. Fragment from panel of footstool	Maple (*Acer* sp.) similar to our native red maple	p. 74
16	Tumulus MM. Wood from squared log of inner wall	Black pine *(Pinus nigra pallasiana)*[37]	p. 95
17	Tumulus MM. Wood from round log of outer wall	Juniper *(Juniperus drupacea)*[38]	p. 86
18	Similar to MM 380–387. Dark, powdery wood fragment from table top	Maple *(Acer pseudoplatanus)*	p. 181
19	Tumulus W. Tree bark?	Pine *(Pinus)* bark	no ref.

Madison, Wisconsin, 1957, 1958, 1960

B.   SAMPLE FROM WALL OF TUMULUS P

Cl. Jacquiot, Chef de la Division de Biologie
Centre Technique du Bois, 10, avenue de Saint-Mandé, Paris 75012

Sample	Description	Results	Text ref.
20	Tumulus P. Wall	Juniper *(Juniperus)* Ce bois pourrait provenir d'une des espèces de ce genre se trouvant au Moyen-Orient et d'assez grande taille pour fournir du bois d'oeuvre: *J. drupacea* Labill. *J. excelsa* Bieb. *J. macropoda* Boiss. *J. thurifera* L.	p. 6

Paris, September 14, 1956

---

[37]See p. 293, n. 46.

[38]See p. 293, n. 44.

C. BOIS DU TOMBEAU ROYAL DE GORDION[39]

H. Kayacık et B. Aytuğ, Chaire de Botanique forestière
Laboratoire de l'anatomie du bois, Université d'Istanbul, Turquie

Sample	Description	Results	Text ref.
21–22	Tumulus MM. Le plancher de la tombe.	If (*Taxus baccata* L.)	p. 95
23	Tumulus MM. Le plancher de la tombe.	Cèdre (*Cedrus libani* Loud.)	p. 95
24–28	Tumulus MM. Le mur de la tombe.	Pin sylvestre (*Pinus silvestris* L.)	p. 95
29	Tumulus MM. Le plafond de la tombe.	Pin sylvestre (*Pinus silvestris* L.)	p. 95
30–31	Tumulus MM. Les poutres de la tombe.	Pin sylvestre (*Pinus silvestris* L.)	p. 95
32–40	Tumulus MM. Les troncs de l'extérieur.	Genévrier (*Juniperus foetidissima* Willd.)	p. 86
41	Tumulus MM. Les troncs de l'extérieur.	If (*Taxus baccata* L.)	p. 86

Istanbul, 1968

D. SAMPLE FROM OUTER WALL OF TUMULUS MM[40]

Carl de Zeeuw, Curator, H. P. Brown Wood Collection
College of Environmental Science and Forestry, State University of New York, Syracuse, N.Y.

Sample	Description	Results	Text ref.
42	Tumulus MM. Wood from round log of outer wall = Ralph, Sample 1 (P-127).[41]	*Juniperus* sp.	p. 86

Syracuse, New York, 1975

---

[39]H. Kayacık and B. Aytuğ, "Recherches au point de vue forestier sur les matériaux en bois du tombeau royal de Gordion," *Orman Fakültesi Dergisi* (Istanbul: University of Istanbul), series A, 18, pt. 1 (1968): 48–52.

[40]This information was furnished in a letter dated May 28, 1975, from C. de Zeeuw to Peter I. Kuniholm. See Kuniholm, *Dendrochronology,* p. xlix.
[41]App. IV, p. 293.

IV. ¹⁴C

REVIEW OF ¹⁴C DATES FOR TUMULI MM AND W
BROUGHT UP TO DATE WITH THE MASCA CORRECTION FACTORS

Elizabeth K. Ralph, ¹⁴C Laboratory, Department of Physics, University of Pennsylvania

Sample	U. of P. Lab. No.	Provenience	*Christian Calendar Ages calculated with:*		
			Libby half life 5568	*New half life 5730*	*New half life plus MASCA corr. factor*[42]
1	P-127[43]	Tumulus MM Log from outer wall of tomb. Some shaping of log took place. *Juniperus drupacea* (Kukachka, 1958); *Juniperus* sp. (De Zeeuw, 1975)[44]	743 ± 90 B.C.	824 ± 94 B.C.	900 ± 90 B.C.
2	P-133[45]	Tumulus MM Squared log of inner wall. *Pinus nigra pallasiana* (Kukachka, 1958)[46]	981 ± 122	1069 ± 126	1220–1240 ± 130
3	P-275[47]	Tumulus MM Top of three-legged plain table collapsed on floor of tomb. *Acer pseudoplatanus* (Kukachka, 1958)	610 ± 52	687 ± 53	800 ± 50
4	P-128[48]	Tumulus MM Textiles from coverlet on bed.	673 ± 90	752 ± 94	820–840 ± 90
5	P-134[49]	Tumulus MM Greasy substance (food?) contained in bowl MM 56.	648 ± 117	726 ± 122	810 ± 120
6	P-363[50]	Tumulus W Roof beam fragments. Edges rotted. Beam was squared.	770 ± 45	852 ± 47	910–930 ± 50

Philadelphia, Pennsylvania, 1978

---

[42]After conversion to the 5730 half life, which is now considered to be the best estimate of the true value, the dates in the right-hand column have been corrected by the MASCA correction factors. These are based upon the ¹⁴C dating of tree-ring-dated samples, and are our best estimate of the real ages of the samples from Gordion. See E. K. Ralph, H. N. Michael, and M. C. Han, "Radiocarbon Dates and Reality," *MASCA Newsletter* 9, no. 1 (August 1973): 1–20.

[43]E. K. Ralph, "University of Pennsylvania Radiocarbon Dates III," *Radiocarbon* 1 (1959): 46–47.

[44]In 1958 a sample from P-127 was sent to B. Francis Kukachka for identification (see p. 291, app. III-A, Sample 17), and he advised that it was *Juniperus drupacea*. In 1975 another opinion was sought, from Carl de Zeeuw

(see p. 292, app. III-D, Sample 42). He believed that it was safer to leave this particular sample labeled as merely *Juniperus* sp.

[45]E. K. Ralph, *op. cit.*, 46–47.

[46]B. F. Kukachka in 1973 reported in a letter to P. I. Kuniholm that this specimen would better be designated as *Pinus nigra* without further classification.

[47]E. K. Ralph and R. Stuckenrath, Jr., "University of Pennsylvania Radiocarbon Dates V," *Radiocarbon* 4 (1962): 146–147.

[48]E. K. Ralph, *op. cit.*, 46–47.

[49]*Ibid.*

[50]Ralph and Stuckenrath, *op. cit.*, 146–147.

V. TEXTILES

THE TEXTILE REMAINS

Richard Ellis, Professor of Classical and Near Eastern Archaeology
Bryn Mawr College, Bryn Mawr, Pennsylvania

INTRODUCTION

This account of the textiles from Tumuli P, MM, and W at Gordion should be regarded as preliminary for two reasons. First, the textile remains from the other excavated parts of Phrygian Gordion have not yet been examined thoroughly, so that the samples treated here cannot be placed in the context of all the material available. It is intended to publish at a later time a supplementary volume dealing with all the Gordion textiles. Second, there are some types of examination—by scanning electron microscope and chemical analysis, for instance—that it has not yet been possible to apply to the samples included in this volume. The results of these types of examination will be included in the final publication of the textiles.

This appendix deals chiefly with the structure of the fabrics, in order to give an idea of the types of textiles discovered and some of the weaving and sewing techniques that they attest. I have not tried to distinguish locally made from imported fabrics or to do a comparative study of the techniques. Colored patterns are few and simple among these samples; they are described and illustrated here, but there would be little point in making a comparative study of the motifs until the publication of the much more elaborate designs found on textiles from the city mound.

It has been decided also to defer a complete catalog of the samples discovered until the general textile volume. Instead, a brief account is given of the finding places of the samples of each of the eleven fabrics that have been defined, and some guesses have been made about the uses to which the fabrics were put.

TERMINOLOGY

As far as possible, the terms used to describe the textile remains are those used by Irene Emery

in her book, *The Primary Structures of Fabrics.*[51] A few definitions may be given here:

Thread, yarn: These terms are used interchangeably.
End: A single thread of the warp.
Pick: A single thread of the weft.
System: One of the two sets of parallel threads that interweave to form a woven fabric; warp and weft, usually impossible to distinguish in these samples.
S-spun, Z-spun: See fig. 135.
Single: A yarn made by spinning together fibers in a single operation.
Plied yarn: A yarn made by twisting together two or more single yarns.
Doubled: Plied of two yarns. "Z2S" means "made of two Z-spun single yarns S-twisted together."
Set: The density of the arrangement of threads in one system of a fabric expressed in tpcm.
Tpcm.: "Threads per centimeter."
Balanced: Having about the same number of warp and weft threads per centimeter.
Shed: The space between two layers of warp threads, made by raising or lowering some of them, so that the weft can be passed across the entire warp in one action, instead of being darned over and under individual warp threads.
Heddle: A loop of cord used to raise a warp thread in making a shed.

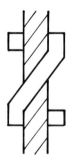

Figure 135. The meaning of the terms "S-twist" and "Z-twist."

---

[51](Washington, D.C.: The Textile Museum, 1966).

THE SAMPLES AND THEIR RECORDING

Each textile sample from Gordion was assigned a number such as "57-text-12," which designates the twelfth textile sample recorded in the 1957 season. The registrar's list gives sample number, name, volume, page, area, level, and date for each item. A brief description of the finding place is often found also on the box in which the specimen was placed, and many boxes also bear a reference, by volume and page numbers, to the passage in Young's notebook that describes the discovery of the sample. The sample numbers were not assigned at the excavation site, however, but in the expedition house, later on, and the diaries, therefore, never refer to a textile sample by its number. It is not always possible to make precise identifications of samples with textiles mentioned in the diaries.

THE CONDITION OF THE SAMPLES

The present condition of the textile samples varies greatly. In rare cases the cloth is still flexible and fairly strong, so that with reasonable care it can be handled and manipulated. The majority of specimens, however, are either soft and powdery, or extremely brittle. The powdery examples are mostly those that were pressed together in thick wads; their structure is usually very difficult to see. The brittle samples are usually those that owe their preservation to the proximity of copper. The structure of these pieces can usually be seen clearly, even when the fabric is broken into small fragments, as is normally the case.

Many of the samples appear to have been treated in the field with some kind of preservative, which has left small granules of a smooth whitish substance clinging to the yarns. No attempt has yet been made to remove this material. It does not obscure the structure of the fabric at all, but might impede later examination of the fibers. Except for some breaking of the brittler fragments, the samples do not appear to have deteriorated appreciably since they were discovered.

EARLIER STUDY OF THE SAMPLES

In 1962 Louisa Bellinger, then of the Textile Museum in Washington, D.C., published in the *Bulletin of the Needle and Bobbin Club* (New York)[52] a brief account of her examination of some of the textiles from Gordion, including samples from the three tumuli dealt with in this volume. Her observations have been of great use in my own study, though our conclusions differ in some instances. Since Bellinger did not refer to samples by number, it has often been impossible to identify the pieces that she discussed.

In the description that follows, I shall refer to Bellinger's article when her opinion differs from mine, or when she makes a statement that I am unable to confirm (such as her identification of some of the fibers).

METHODS OF EXAMINATION USED IN THE PRESENT STUDY

The following description of the textile samples from Tumuli P, MM, and W is based on visual examination carried out in the Near East Laboratory of the University Museum during 1977 and 1978. Besides the naked eye, I used a Bausch and Lomb binocular microscope that gives a magnification of from 10x to 70x; this instrument is well suited for examining the structure of fabrics and yarns. A more powerful microscope, giving a magnification of from 50x to 900x was used in an attempt to identify some of the fibers, but it has become clear that more sophisticated techniques and a greater number of comparative samples will be necessary to allow reliable fiber identifications to be made, if the condition of the fibers will permit it at all.

No chemical analyses of the fabrics were undertaken.

FIBERS

My own attempts to examine the fibers used in the Gordion textiles have shown that if positive identifications can be made, it will require more sophisticated techniques than I was able to use. Bellinger, in her 1962 article, identified several fibers: linen, hemp, wool, and mohair. I am unable to confirm these. In my list of fabrics I will call the fibers simply animal or vegetable and add Bellinger's identification if it is possible to find her reference to the sample in question. The

---

[52]Vol. 46 (1962): 4–33, hereafter cited as "Bellinger."

range of Bellinger's identifications is probably correct; certainly neither cotton nor silk is present in the samples from Tumuli P, MM, and W.

SPINNING

As far as I can determine all of the yarns in this group of textiles were spun in the Z-direction. A large proportion of the yarns are S-doubled; every yarn showing S-twist that I have seen appears, when observed under adequate magnification (40–50x), to consist of two smaller yarns plied together. Two-ply yarns of both animal and vegetable fibers were used for most fabrics. Single Z-spun animal-fiber yarns were used for both systems of a poorly preserved balanced cloth from Tumulus W (Fabric E), as one system of Fabrics F and G, in which the other system was of two-ply vegetable-fiber yarn, and as the face system of Fabric J, whose other system is hidden.

Some of the yarns are very fine. The doubled yarns of Fabric I, identified by Bellinger as mohair, are as fine as 0.1 mm. in diameter. The evenness of the spinning varies. In the finer fabrics (Fabric I) the diameter of the yarns in one system varies by no more than a factor of about 1.5; in other fabrics (such as Fabric A) the variation is as great as three or four times. Single yarns seem in general to have been loosely twisted: those that were used as singles show an angle of twist of 30° or less. While I have designated the doubled yarns used as "Z2S," it was in fact often impossible to see the twist of the individual plies. The angle of twist of the doubled yarns is usually about 45°.

DYES

Since no chemical analysis of the fabrics has been carried out, it is as yet impossible to say much about dyes that might have been used. Several different colors can be seen; most of them could be natural and probably are: yellowish-white to yellowish-brown to brown to grayish-brown. The only visually detectable color that is probably artificial is a dark red or purple. I have called the patterned bands designated Fabric G "red and white," but they are so faded and stained that they could equally well be called purple and yellow. Many kinds of stains can be seen on the fabrics; the most characteristic is the blue-

green color of copper salts, to which many of the fragments owe their preservation.

BASIC FABRIC STRUCTURE

Only two basic structures are certainly present in the fabric samples from Tumuli P, MM, and W: plain weave and felt. While weft wrapping ("Soumak") is definitely present in samples from the city mound at Gordion, it was not identified among the samples from these tumuli. The starting borders found on some of the samples of plain weave show a structure that is sometimes called "half-basket weave," since two "wefts"[53] were drawn simultaneously through each shed. This structure is in fact only a variety of "warp"-faced plain weave, and in any case was not used for entire pieces of cloth.

Some narrow strips of Fabric G from Tumulus P are basically plain weave fabrics with one system predominant, but employ yarns of a contrasting color, complementary to parts of the predominant system (the warp), in order to make patterns by weaving the yarns of one color while allowing those of the other color to float at the back. Again, this structure is only an elaborated form of plain weave.

The weave of the plain-woven samples is often approximately balanced, but ratios of the spacing of yarns in the two systems vary between 1:1 and 1:2. In Fabrics G and J, and in one sample of Fabric E, one system predominates. In some examples of Fabric J the ratio is as high as 1:6. In Fabric J the predominant system is probably the weft, but in most of the samples of other fabrics in which the warp and weft can be distinguished, the warp is more closely set than the weft. The actual number of yarns per centimeter varies widely: from about 13 to 40 in more-or-less balanced weaves, and from 8 in the hidden system of one sample of Fabric J to 60 in the predominant system of some strips of Fabric G.

In most samples the yarns of each system are fairly evenly spaced. Several samples of Fabric A, however, show crowding of some warp yarns together, with more open spaces between the groups. This effect was probably unintentional.

---

[53]The terms "warp" and "weft" are used in quotation marks when referring to the making of starting borders, since the "weft" becomes the warp of the main cloth.

The two systems of most fabrics are usually of nearly identical yarns. Exceptions are Fabrics F and G, in which the two systems can be of different fibers, colors, and twists, and Fabric J, where the fibers of the two systems are the same, but the predominant (weft?) yarns are singles, and the hidden (warp?) ones doubled.

Most of the felt samples incorporate layers of very loosely woven yarns, or crossed layers of parallel yarns that do not interlace.

EDGES

Most of the fabrics dealt with in this volume are torn or broken into small fragments. Nevertheless, it was possible to observe selvages, hems, and starting borders.

Plain Selvages

Selvages can be identified most clearly in our material on several examples of vegetable-fiber tapes (Fabric D). They are simple selvages in which the weft turns back across the fabric in every next shed, leaving a small loop at the edge of the tape. In some tapes the outermost warp end on each side was somewhat thicker than the others, and in one example this thicker end has been pulled out of the fabric for some distance, leaving unusually large selvage loops (fig. 136). The loops are always fairly large, however; there is no indication that they served any particular purpose.

Selvages can be seen also on a fragment of a narrow warp-faced band with red and white stripes (Fabric G), and on a warp-faced fragment matted together with several thicknesses of Fab-

Figure 136. Plain selvage of a Fabric D tape from Tumulus W.

ric E. The latter piece may be a special selvage treatment of Fabric E (a thin balanced cloth of single yarns), or a bit of Fabric G sandwiched in the wad. Both of these selvages appear to be plain selvages; neither can be seen very well.

Hems: Rolled

Two samples of Fabric A from Tumulus MM show neatly made rolled hems. One of the two hem fragments from the head of the bed was made on an edge with cut threads extending about 3 mm. beyond the cloth; this could be either a cut edge, or the fell of the cloth when weaving was finished. It is tempting to conclude that this edge represents the end of the weaving, since bits of starting borders for a fabric of the same type and about the same thread count were found at the other end of the bed. The edge was folded up and under, forming three thicknesses, about 5 mm. wide. The hem was secured by sewing with a strand consisting of paired Z-spun singles of the same fiber as the cloth (fig. 137; pl. 99D).

Another sample includes, besides some frag-

Figure 137. Rolled hem with straight stitches (Fabric A), from bed covers in Tumulus MM.

Figure 138. Rolled hem, overcast (Fabric A), from bed covers in Tumulus MM.

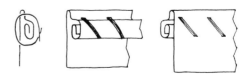

Figure 139. Rolled hem, overcast with ridge (Fabric A), from bed covers in Tumulus MM.

ments of hem like those just described, a more elaborate and decorative hem with a thicker, rounder roll. In some cases the roll was secured by whipping around the edge with a triple strand of Z-spun singles (fig. 138; pl. 99E). On a few fragments the roll is sewn down about 1 mm. away from the folded edge, forming an attractive ridge beside the roll (fig. 139; pl. 100A).

Hems: Stitched folds

In several examples of Fabric I, and one of Fabric A, two folded edges were placed together and stitched to one another with a running stitch (fig. 140A; pl. 101F). In one sample the two folds were inside each other, rather than side by side (fig. 140B); in another three folds were sewn together. The stitched folds of Fabric I were all found in proximity to fibulae, and apparently owe their preservation to that fact. In most cases the hole made by the fibula pin is still to be seen in the wadded fabric, and in several cases the stitched edge was still in contact with the multi-layered mass of the same fabric to which it had been pinned. All four layers of the folded fabric extend as far as the fragments were preserved. Since this distance is never more than 2-3 cm., it is possible that the stitched, folded layers are the remains of an elaborate hem treatment. It is more likely, however, that they are the edges of an entire piece of four-fold fabric, produced by folding one or two pieces of fine material and sewing the edges together.

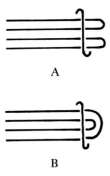

Figure 140. Stitched folds (Fabrics A and I) from samples caught in fibulae MM 352, 355, and 356 north of the skeleton, and MM 346 in mass of textile where right shoulder should have been. Tumulus MM bed.

Starting borders

Fragments of Fabrics A, C, and F show the type of edge that is recognizable as a separately woven band, whose "weft" was carried out in long loops on one side (fig. 141). The band was then attached to the loom with the "weft" loops forming the warp for the fabric proper. The chief characteristic of the starting border is the presence of two "weft picks" (that is, two warp ends of the finished fabric) in each shed. Each individual "pick" forms a loop at the edge of the border with a "pick" in the next shed; this structure results from drawing loops taken from a ball of yarn, rather than the ball itself, through each shed.[54] All our starting borders show this characteristic, with the exception that the border of the fine linen piece designated Fabric C has, at irregular intervals, a single yarn in a shed. Since this single "pick" occurs irregularly, it can hardly be an intentional part of the structure of the border. This anomaly is probably the result of using short lengths of "weft," the ends of which frequently had to be put into the shed singly.

None of these borders shows the use of more than one ball of "weft."

Starting borders of Fabric A have from 14 to 24 "warp ends." That of Fabric C has 16 or 17,

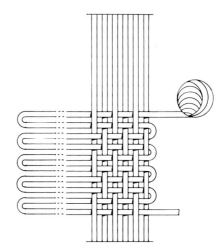

Figure 141. Weaving of a starting border (schematic, with only six "ends").

[54]See Marta Hoffmann, *The Warp-weighted Loom*, Studia Norvegica 14 (Oslo, Universitetsforlaget, 1964), 63–65 and 151–156 for the modern method of making and using such bands.

and the one tiny bit of starting border of Fabric F that preserves the transition to plain weave has about 18 "ends." Generally the "ends" of the border were taken singly to form the sheds, but in a few samples of Fabric A two adjacent "ends" have been taken together. This usually appears to have been simply a mistake. In a few cases a double "end" is found just before the transition to plain weave; this may have been intentional, though I cannot guess its purpose.

Many samples show the transition from the starting border to plain weave. The double "picks" of the border usually pass straight into the plain weave part (fig. 142), where they are separated by a pick of the main weft. In some cases, however, two "picks" of the border will cross each other before interweaving with the main weft (fig. 143). Crossings at this transition have been observed in fabrics from many other places.[55] The usual intention was probably to bring the two threads in each shed of the border into alternate positions, so that they will still be in the same shed when the plain weave is being woven. It would then not be necessary to cut the loops that were formed during warping; the loops could be made into a fringe, or even woven out to the end by darning.

This intention, however, cannot be the cause of the crossing of threads in the Gordion fabrics. For one thing, the crossing occurs at irregular intervals; while in one or two pieces it recurs at about every third pair of "picks," in another sample crosses are separated by seven or eight straight pairs at some points, while three crosses occur together at another. Moreover, it is almost always the two members of one pair of "wefts" that cross; the parts of the loop would still be in different sheds, and the loops would still have to be cut to permit an adequate shed to be made near the end of the warp. It is probable that the crossings are simply the result of mistakes, either in making the natural shed during warping, or in

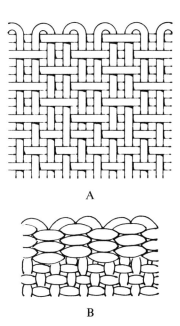

A

B

Figure 142. Transition from a starting border to plain weave. A. Schematic. B. Actual appearance.

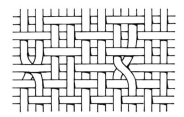

Figure 143. Transition from starting border to plain weave, with crossed warp threads.

knitting the heddles once the starting border was attached to the loom.[56]

While it would theoretically be possible to use such a starting border with any type of loom, in fact it is only known to have been used with the warp-weighted loom.[57] There is other evidence for the use of the warp-weighted loom in Phrygian Gordion,[58] and it is safe to assume that our bor-

[55]Hoffmann, *Warp-weighted Loom*, 160–163.

[56]A similar crossing of "wefts" was regularly carried out in a fabric from Qumran Cave I; see Grace M. Crowfoot, "The Linen Textiles," in D. Barthélemy and J. T. Milik, *Discoveries in the Judaean Desert* I: *Qumran Cave I* (Oxford: Clarendon Press, 1955), 31–32, fig. 8. The purpose of the crossing is unknown (cf. Hoffmann, *Warp-weighted Loom*, 353, n. 19).

[57]Hoffmann, *Warp-weighted Loom*, 151–153.

[58]R. Johnson (*Pottery Practices*, 221–238 and figs. 23–25) discusses the unbaked doughnut-shaped loom weights from the main room of TB-7 found in 1965, and Keith DeVries has told me that a further set of such loom weights was found in 1971 fallen in a line on the floor of the anteroom of TB-7 on the city mound.

ders were used for warping such looms. The fine linen fragment (Fabric C) shows signs of attachment to the loom: a triple strand of thread was whipped over the starting border of this piece, passing under about the tenth of the 16 or 18 "warp ends" and between every four to six double "picks." The whipping is not tight; it leaves enough space for a heavy cord or thin rod, which is now missing. The border has clearly been subjected to considerable strain; the ten "warp ends" enclosed by the whipping have been forced together much more closely than the rest. Probably the whipping attached the border to a cord, which was in turn lashed to the beam of a loom.

ACCESSORY STRUCTURES

Stitches

Simple stitches are found in several samples. The following types are attested.[59]

Running stitches were used for sewing together folded edges of Fabrics A and I, as described above under folded hems (see fig. 140).

Overcasting was used to secure rolled hems (fig. 138) and, apparently, to attach the starting border of Fabric C to a cord or thin rod that is now missing (pl. 100B).

Straight stitches were used to secure rolled hems (figs. 137, 139).

A more elaborate stitch was used to attach strips of red-and-white patterned Fabric G to other fabrics—Fabric B, in one case. It has not been possible to determine exactly how this stitch was made; it apparently functioned like a straight stitch, piercing the fabric on either side of the juncture of the two pieces, but its visible side has the appearance of a braid. It could be a plain straight stitch through which the thread was braided back, or it could be like Emery's "cross-knit loop stitch."[60]

All these stitches were made with a double or triple strand of Z-spun single yarn, of a fiber similar to that used in the cloth.

Fringe

No coherent fragments of fringe were found, but in a sample from the head of the bed in Tumulus MM (the sample that includes several hems of Fabric A) is a small, oval, knotlike structure about 1 cm. long and 5 mm. in diameter. It appears to be on the end of a three-fold strand about 2 mm. in diameter; the structure of the knot itself could not be discerned. There is nothing in the sample to show that this was part of a fringe, but a textile fragment from one of the Phrygian tumuli near Ankara has a fringe ending in little bobbles like this one.[61]

WEAVING ERRORS

Errors are fairly common among the samples studied here, particularly in Fabric A. It is common to find two yarns lying together in one shed. These are usually weft yarns, and must be due to the weaver's forgetting to change the shed. Sometimes, however, two "warp" yarns lie together in starting borders; there the feature must be either intentional, or be due to carelessness in knitting the heddles for weaving the border.

It is fairly common in Fabric A that a warp thread will occasionally fail to weave; in a few cases it fails repeatedly, with only enough intersections to keep it attached to the cloth. This error was probably due to a heddle of improper length.

In one sample of Fabric G a warp thread dropped out of the web, floated at the back for five picks, was brought back in in the wrong position, and finally crossed the adjacent warp thread to reach its proper position. This error was useful, since it showed which system was the warp; it is not likely that a weft thread would follow such a course.[62] Heddle failure was probably the cause of this error.

At one or two points in examples of Fabric G, the red and white warp threads were both woven together, instead of one or the other. The oppo-

---

[59]The terms used are taken from Emery, *Primary Structures,* 234–237.

[60]*Ibid.,* 243.

[61]Sevim Buluç, director of the Museum of the Middle East Technical University in Ankara, is publishing the

---

material from these tumuli. She very kindly showed me the textile fragments and gave me permission to cite them.

[62]The selvage on another sample of the same fabric was observed only later.

site error—the failure of *either* color to appear on the surface—is found in the piece of Fabric G with the fragmentary lozenge pattern (fig. 147). The fact that this error recurs in each preserved repeat of the pattern suggests that the pattern threads were controlled by individual groups of string heddles for each part of the pattern; at this point one heddle was accidentally omitted, or broke.

FABRICS

Many of the textile fragments from Gordion tumuli can be grouped into "fabrics," on the basis of similarity of fiber and technical peculiarities. To judge from circumstances in which they were found, some of these fabrics were used for specific purposes. It is also true, however, that the position of the fabric in the tomb—in contact with the body, or with copper, or exposed to water, and so on—has greatly affected the appearance of the remains and that samples that now appear distinct may once have been quite similar.

FABRIC A

Yarn

Fiber: vegetable in appearance (but Bellinger, p. 13: "golden-brown goat's wool, probably mohair").

Color: yellow-brown to orange-brown.

Spin: both systems the same; Z2S, 0.1–0.6 mm. diameter; usually moderately twisted, though some yarns are plied so hard as to be crinkly.

Weave

The basic structure is plain weave. The set of the yarns in most fragments varies between 16 and 24 per centimeter, and is approximately balanced. The ratio of the set of the two systems is usually no greater than 1:1.2. One bit from the cauldron MM 13 shows 13-14:20 tpcm. In pieces whose warp and weft can be distinguished, the warp is usually the more closely spaced system,

though the reverse does occur. The density of the fabric varies, with the following chief varieties:

1. Average loose: yarns 0.2–0.6 mm. diameter, 16–18 tpcm.
2. Average dense: yarns 0.2–0.6 mm. diameter, 20–24 tpcm.
3. Extra loose: yarns 0.2–0.5 mm. diameter, 13–14:14–15 tpcm.
4. Extra fine: yarns 0.1–0.15 mm. diameter, 30:35 tpcm.

In the "average loose" variety the yarns of one system are usually crowded together at intervals with more open stripes between (pl. 99B). The open stripes usually have one yarn in about 1 mm. One fragment from Tumulus MM has part of its starting border preserved and provides the following information about this spacing: (*a*) The crowded and spaced system is the warp. (*b*) The spacing begins immediately below the starting border but is not due to spacing in the border; the warp ends are pulled sideways from their positions in the border. (*c*) At intervals two warp ends cross each other between the border and the cloth, but this has nothing to do with the spacing. (*d*) The crowding and spacing occurs at irregular intervals, though it produces a fairly even striped effect on the whole. (*e*) The spacing tends to occur where there is a warp end of unusually small diameter, though this relationship is not consistent.

The striped effect produced by the crowding and spacing of the warp was probably not intentional. As I know from personal experience, it is a result that is hard to avoid when weaving a fairly loose fabric without a reed. The chief cause was probably uneven warp tension. The effect is not unattractive, however, and the weaver may not have tried very hard to avoid it.

There are weaving errors in several fragments of this fabric. Two yarns lying in the same shed occur often in some pieces; presumably these are weft yarns, and the weaver forgot to change the shed between picks. In one sample several fragments of a rolled hem show two yarns just at the point where the fabric was first folded; these may be two picks put in on purpose to mark the line of the hem.

Some samples show warp yarns that fail to weave at several intersections within one fragment. This error is presumably due either to warp threads that stick together, or to an incorrectly knit heddle.

Starting borders

Several fragments of starting borders for this fabric have been found; they are described above in the section on edge treatments (p. 298; see also pl. 99B, C). The number of "warp ends" in the border is 14 in one sample, 23 and 24 in others. There are always two "weft" yarns in each shed; there are no cases of single "wefts," as in Fabric C.

Hems

Most of the hems found on this fabric are of the rolled type; the varieties were described in the section on edges (p. 297). In the few fragments where the edge of the cloth can be seen, they show protruding yarns; the hems serve to protect either a cut edge, or the end of the woven fabric. Two samples of Fabric A include bits of rolled hems; one includes the starting borders also, and may be the remains of a piece of cloth folded end to end. The other, from the head of the bed in Tumulus MM, includes only hems; it is tempting to conclude that these hems were part of the same piece as the starting borders found at the foot of the bed. The thread counts of the fragments involved are similar enough to make this guess possible, but it cannot be proved.

One sample of Fabric A shows two folded edges stitched together, probably to produce a thicker material that could be handled as a single piece. This treatment is more common with Fabric I.

Location and Function

Fabric A was found only in Tumulus MM. The recorded loci are at the head and foot of the bed, and inside the small cauldron, MM 13. The bits from the bed may be the remains of sheets; the fabric in the cauldron appeared to have been a bag containing food.

FABRIC B

Yarn

Fiber: vegetable(?).
Color: yellowish-white to brown, in the same piece. Presumably the lighter color is original.
Spin: both systems the same; Z2S, strongly twisted; 0.2–0.3 mm. in diameter.

Weave

Plain cloth. Sample 56-text-4F is set 18:18 tpcm.; 56-text-1, 25:25 tpcm.

This fabric differs little from Fabric A and may belong within its range. The samples of Fabrics A and B differ in color and state of preservation, which may have obscured an original similarity. Fabric B is somewhat more carefully made than many of the samples of A; the yarns are more uniform in diameter, and the individual plies were more tightly spun, so that the doubling shows more distinctly. Fabric B probably had a crisper feel than did most pieces of A.

Location and Function

Fabric B was found only in Tumulus P. One sample of this fabric, referred to by Young as "cheesecloth," was taken from one of the pegs in the walls of the tomb chamber. The walls had apparently been hung with this material. One fragment, apparently belonging to the wall hangings, had a small strip of Fabric G sewn to it. The preserved part of the strip was red with a simple white stripe.

FABRIC C

Yarn

Fiber: vegetable (Bellinger, p. 14: "linen").
Color: light yellowish-tan.
Spin: both systems the same; Z2S, moderately twisted; 0.15–0.2 mm. in diameter.

Weave

Plain weave. Warp *ca.* 18 tpcm., weft *ca.* 22 tpcm. Warp and weft can be identified by the presence of a starting border on the only piece assigned to this fabric.

Starting border

The border was described above in the section on edges; it is 16 or 17 "ends" wide, and frequently has one "weft" thread in a shed instead of two as is always the case in Fabric A. This last feature is probably the result of using short pieces of "weft" when weaving the starting border.

This material is very thin and fine, rather like a modern handkerchief (see pl. 100B).

Location and Function

The identification of this single piece is uncertain. The box in which it was stored bore no textile sample number, but the note "Gordion '59, MMT. Interior of Tomb." Bellinger (p. 14) describes what is clearly this piece and states that it was found in 1959. However, there is no other record of textiles from Tumulus MM having been registered in 1959. One sample number, 57-text-3, is not otherwise accounted for, and the description matches this piece. Probably, therefore, it is the one fragment assigned to Fabric C, 57-text-3, remains of a cloth bag containing fibulae, found on the floor near the head of the bed in Tumulus MM (pp. 101, 156).

FABRIC D

Yarn

Fiber: vegetable (Bellinger, p. 15: "linen").
Color: yellowish-white, usually stained with copper salts.
Spin: both systems the same; Z2S, moderately twisted; 0.15–0.3 mm. in diameter.

Weave

Plain weave. This fabric is narrow tape (see pl. 100C). Both selvages of several examples are preserved. Most pieces have about 40 warp ends, set at 24 to 26 tpcm., that is, about 1.5 cm. wide. One fragment, of which only one selvage is preserved, is set at only 16–17 tpcm. The weft is more widely spaced, 10–12 tpcm. Some tapes have six or eight slightly thicker ends (0.25–0.3 mm. in diameter) at the selvage, with thinner threads (0.15–0.2 mm.) toward the middle. The weft usually resembles the thicker warp threads. In one fragment a still thicker yarn (0.5 mm. in diameter) of the same material passed through the selvage loops in one area, and lay against them in another; presumably this was a selvage cord that had been pulled out of the loops in one place. The selvage loops, as was described in the section on edges, are large and are often bent over against the face of the tape.

Location and Function

Samples of these tapes were found in all three major tumuli. They were apparently used to wrap objects, including bundles of other fabrics and bronze objects.

FABRIC E

Yarn

Fiber: animal(?).
Color: brown—all examples matted together and very much degraded.
Spin: both systems the same; Z singles, thin, but not easy to measure.

Weave

Plain weave. The characteristics of this fabric are hard to ascertain, since all the examples preserved consist of many layers matted together and are very much degraded. The weave is usually balanced, 18–22 tpcm. in each system. One fragment has, matted together with balanced weave, a warp-faced fabric next to a selvage. The warp of this fragment has about 35 tpcm., the weft 8–9 tpcm. Because of the condition of the sample it is impossible to tell whether or not this warp-faced fragment belongs to the same web as some of the balanced pieces.

Location and Function

All the samples of this fabric were found in Tumulus W. Two were found inside bronze bowl TumW 15 and a third adhering to the wall. One of the fragments in the bowl was accompanied by remains of tape (Fabric D) and of brown felt. The other two samples appeared to have been sandwiched with leather. The state of preservation is too poor to permit any guess as to the original form of the pieces or their purpose.

It is not impossible that this fabric is like that part of Fabric F that is woven entirely of singles, but that the similarity has been obscured by the different conditions of preservation. Fabric E has been identified only in Tumulus W; the one piece of Fabric F identified in Tumulus W is similar in appearance, and was assigned to Fabric F only because the yarns of the two systems were dissimilar; the same sample included fragments of Fabric E as well.

FABRIC F

The characteristic feature of this fabric is that it employs two dissimilar yarns.

Yarn A

Fiber: vegetable.
Color: usually yellowish-white; several examples of what appear to be the same fiber are black and look somewhat melted. This appearance is presumably the result of flameless heat.
Spin: Z2S, moderately twisted; 0.1–0.5 mm. in diameter.

Yarn B

Fiber: animal.
Color: sometimes yellowish-brown, probably a natural color; also dark red or purplish, presumably dyed.
Spin: Z single, loosely to moderately twisted; 0.15–0.25 mm. in diameter.

Weave

Plain weave. Webs have been found in which yarns A or B are used alone, and in which both are used together. One large fragment from Tumulus MM (pl. 100E) consists chiefly of a square about 9 cm. on each side, with yarn A as both systems, yellow-brown to brown in color. One system is set 15–16 tpcm., the other about 21 tpcm. On one side the yarn A in the more closely spaced system is replaced by red yarn B, at about the same number of tpcm., but averaging a little thinner than yarn A. The red area seems to have been at least 7 cm. wide.

The starting borders described below show that in this piece yarn A was the warp and yarn B the weft. Yarn A in this sample is blackened, while yarn B is yellowish-brown.

The two yarns of this fabric were certainly used to make stripes. Since fragments of all-A, all-B, and A-and-B fabrics were found together, it is possible that some kind of checks were made. There is no direct evidence for checks, however.

Starting border

Several tiny fragments of starting borders occur as parts of a fabric found adhering to the lion situla (MM 45). As is mentioned above, yarn B is the "warp" of the border, and yarn A the "weft"—that is, it is the warp of the cloth as a whole. These borders have two "weft" threads in each shed. One fragment has some double and some single "warp" threads, but most have single "warps" only. On one fragment the transition from the border to the plain weave is preserved; no crossed warp threads are visible (pl. 100D).

Location and Function

Four samples of this fabric were found in Tumulus MM. All four had been in contact with bronze objects: a small cauldron (MM 7), the lion and ram situlae (MM 45, 46) and a double-pinned fibula (MM 187). In the first three cases the multicolored cloth seems to have been used to wrap the vessels. The cloth from the fibula was "blanket-like" when found and includes bits of Fabric J and leather as well as Fabric F; it may have been a heavy cloak or series of garments. One sample from Tumulus W was identified as including Fabric F; a matted wad of what looked at first like Fabric E proved on examination to have two dissimilar systems.

FABRIC G

Yarn A

Fiber and spin like yarn A of Fabric F, always yellowish-white in color.

Yarn B

Fiber and spin like yarn B of Fabric F, always dark red or purple in color.

Weave

Warp-faced plain weave, sometimes with complementary warps. There is a selvage on one fragment, and it can be seen that the predominant system is the warp.

The warp includes both yarns A and B, set at 50–60 tpcm. These red and yellow-white yarns were arranged to produce warp-way stripes, end-and-end weft-way stripes, and more complex patterns in which two complementary warps alternate, one weaving on the surface, while the other floats at the back (fig. 144). The weft is of yarn B, at about 20 tpcm. It is probable that only narrow bands of this fabric were made; the widest seen in this group of textiles is about 2.5 cm. wide, as preserved, and was probably not much wider when it was made. Most of the other pieces are only 5–7 mm. wide.

The fabric seems to have been conceived as basically red, with patterns in white. The patterns seen on the fragments preserved are:

1. Simple warp stripes produced by setting up part of the warp with yarn A instead of yarn B. The weft is yarn B throughout, but is scarcely visible. A few fragments have only warp stripes on the parts that are preserved. Others have warp stripes as well as more complex patterns.

2. Short end-and-end weft-way stripes, offset against each other (fig. 145 and pl. 101A).

3. A meander pattern in white against a red background. In the pattern area there are two complementary warps, one red, and one white. Only one warp weaves at a time; the unused warp threads flat at the back of the fabric (fig. 146 and pl. 101B).

4. A pattern of white triangular shapes at the broken edge of the fabric (probably representing halves of compound lozenges) and a plain white warp stripe (see figs. 147A, B and pl. 101C). As the fabric is now, the inner lines of the triangular shapes do not quite join the outer lines; there is a missing thread at the surface at this point, however (fig. 147A), and if it is assumed that a white thread was intended to show there, the reconstruction in fig. 147B is probable. This type of pattern is seen in some of the tapestry fabrics from Megaron 3.

5. One wider band has a more elaborate pattern in white. The fragment is broken on all four sides of the pattern. The pattern may continue on the fourth side, in the warp direction, but it has been reconstructed as a closed rectangle (fig. 148 and pl. 101D, E). Very similar rectangular designs are seen on the tunic of King Warpalawas of Tabal, as seen on his rock carving at İvriz and his stele from Bor,[63] and on the inlaid wooden screens (MM 378 and 379) at Gordion.

One band of this fabric was sewn to a large piece of Fabric B. The sewn edge is the selvage. There is no indication of whether or not the band was attached at any other point. Only about 5 mm. of the width of the band is preserved and 4 mm. beyond the broken edge of the band but shows no traces of stitches. One other fragment of Fabric G shows stitches along one edge, though the cloth to which it was sewn is now missing.

Location and Function

All of the fragments of these decorated bands were found in Tumulus P, which is interesting in view of the fact that the similar Fabric F was identified only in Tumuli MM and W. Except for

---

[63]R. M. Boehmer, *AA* 88 (1973), figs. 3, 4. It is interesting to note that at İvriz and Bor the central, swastika-like part of the design is raised, while on this woven piece it is the white frame and the projecting hooks that

stand out in relief, because the white yarns are thicker than the red ones. It also appears that the weaver thought of the white areas as pattern, and the red as background, since the white strips are more consistent in width.

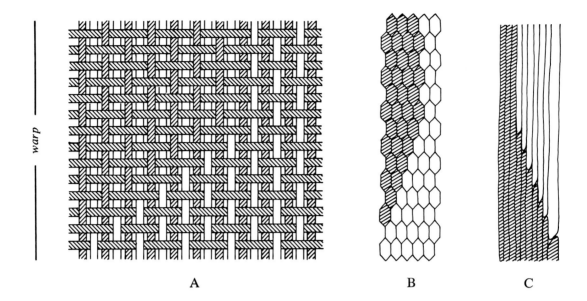

A   B   C

Figure 144.   Fabric G: the method of using complementary warps to make colored patterns. A. Schematic. B. Appearance with warp predominant (front). C. Appearance with warp predominant (back).

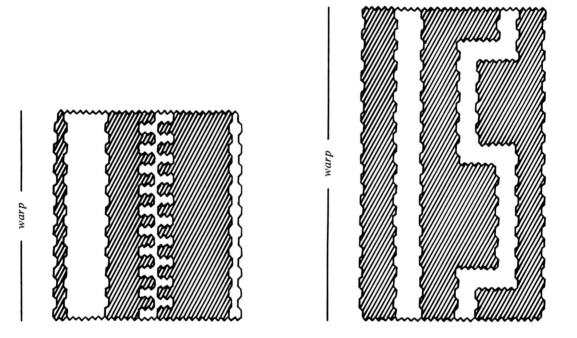

Figure 145.   Fabric G: pattern with warp stripe and offset, end-and-end stripes.

Figure 146.   Fabric G: pattern with warp stripe and meander.

306

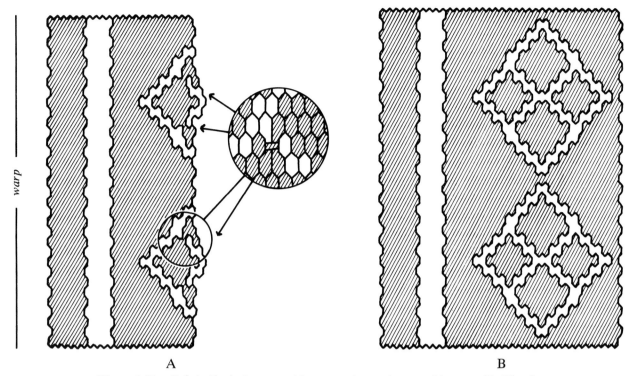

A   B

Figure 147.   Fabric G: A. Pattern with warp stripe and parts of lozenges(?). The detail shows the repeated error in the weave. B. Probable reconstruction of the fragment shown in A, if one assumes that the thread missing on the surface is light-colored.

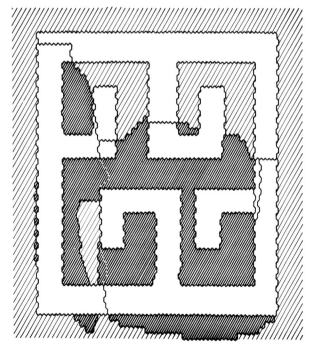

Figure 148.   Fabric G: probable reconstruction of rectangular pattern with meander hooks.

307

the piece mentioned above, which was sewn to a piece of Fabric B and presumably found on one of the wall pegs, there is no information about the precise location in the tomb of any of these bands. It is probable that their chief use was as decorations attached to other fabrics.

FABRIC H

Yarn

Fiber: animal(?).
Color: yellow, bluish gray, green metallicized.
Spin: Z-singles, moderately to tightly spun; 0.25–1 mm. in diameter.

Weave

Plain weave. Most of the samples show a balanced weave, with from 9–18 tpcm.

One group of fragments from Tumulus W is completely metallicized and has a thread count of 12 by 24 tpcm., with the two systems at a 45° angle to one another.

The fragments placed in this category share the feature of being made of fairly large, Z-spun single yarns. The bits preserved are too small, and too variously preserved, to allow more to be said of this fabric or even if it should be regarded as a single fabric.

Location and Function

Some fragments were found in Tumulus MM, together with remains of Fabric A, from the bed; some in Tumulus P under roof beam 8; and some in Tumulus W, adhering to the outer surface of the cauldron, TumW 2.

FABRIC I

Yarn

Fiber: animal (Bellinger, p. 14: "mohair").
Color: yellowish-brown or grayish-brown. One piece is yellowish-brown and reddish in different parts; this seems to be the result of staining rather than an intentional difference.
Spin: Z2S, moderately twisted; 0.1–0.2 mm. in diameter. The yarns in any one piece are rather more consistent in size than in most of the other fabrics.

Weave

Plain weave (pl. 101F). The weave is usually approximately balanced, from 28–46 tpcm. Some pieces have a less balanced ratio: 44:28 and 29:19 tpcm. The weave is always very even; threads are not crowded together, as in Fabric A.

No selvages, starting borders, or other edges were observed on this fabric, though they may be present; the samples are all wads of several thicknesses, which could not be unfolded fully. One fragment incorporates a narrow strip in which one system predominates. This strip is apparently in one piece with some balanced weave. There is only one thread in each shed, so that it is probably not a starting border. It is presumably just a part of the fabric in which the weft was beaten down to cover the warp for some reason.

The samples of this fabric that were found owe their preservation to the proximity of copper; in almost every case the wads of cloth were found near fibulae, and most of them are actually pierced by the pins. Several samples have hems consisting of two folded edges stitched together. If the predominant system in the part of the piece described above is the weft, then the folds and stitching of that piece run in the warp direction. In one case it was clear that two such hems had been pinned together by the fibula, and it is probable that this was so in all the samples. Unfortunately the number of preserved fragments of this fabric was too small to show whether they had been parts of a garment, shroud, or some other kind of cloth.

Location and Function

Eleven textile samples from Tumulus MM included fragments of Fabric I. All were in contact with the fibulae that lay beside the body, at shoulder, elbow, and hip level. They probably represented a single garment or shroud of several layers, stitched together at the edges and then fastened around the body by the fibulae.

FABRIC J

Yarn A

Fiber: animal (wool? Cf. Bellinger, p. 14).
Color: brown.
Spin: System A (warp?). Z2S, moderately
twisted; 0.3–0.7 mm. in diameter.

Yarn B

Fiber: as for A.
Color: as for A.
Spin: System B (weft?). Z-singles, lightly
twisted; 0.2–0.3 mm. in diameter.

Weave

Plain weave, with one system (the weft?) predominant. In the two fragments found, the hidden
system (the warp?) is set at 8–9 tpcm.; the other
system has in one case 26, in another 52 tpcm.
In the latter case, at least, the predominant system must be the weft; it would be hard to make a
warp of yarns each about 0.3 mm. in diameter lie
so closely packed.

Location and Function

One of the fragments was found together with
bits of Fabric F and leather, against a fibula in
Tumulus MM (see above under Fabric F). The
other was in an unknown location in Tumulus P.
The fragments are too small to allow a guess as
to what the original pieces may have been.

FABRIC K

Felt

Fragments of felt were found in all three major
tumuli; they were particularly numerous in Tumulus MM. Since all the samples are either
broken into tiny fragments or wadded into thick
masses, it is seldom possible to see the original
surface of a piece of felt, or to measure the original thickness.

Many of the felt samples have spun yarns lying
between layers of randomly arranged felted fibers.

Sometimes the yarns are grouped in strands of
from three to six or seven, lying together but not
plied. The strands usually lie parallel to one another at intervals of 5 mm. to 10 mm. Sometimes
parallel strands are crossed by others at more or
less right angles; sometimes the two sets seem to
interweave, but not consistently enough, or tightly
enough, to form an independent fabric. Because
of the difficulty in identifying the surface of any
individual piece of felt, it is not clear whether
these spun yarns were incorporated into the thickness to give it strength or whether they were on
the surface for decoration. In several cases the
yarns contrast in color with the surrounding felt,
but no intentional patterns have so far been
discerned.

Location and Function

One of the chief uses of felt was apparently as
bedding—traces were found beneath the bodies
in all three tumuli. In addition, purplish felt adhered to the seat of the stool (TumP 157) and
was found in several places suggesting a use as
pad, mat, or tablecloth. Felt may have been used
as hangings or clothing as well; several samples
were found together with layers of woven cloth
and leather.

CONCLUSIONS

Until some of the scientific tests mentioned
above have been carried out on the samples discussed here, and until the material from the city
mound has been examined in detail, any general
statements about textile technology at Phrygian
Gordion must be tentative. Nevertheless, some
fairly reliable observations can be made on the
basis of what is now known.

First, the phrase just used, "textile technology
at Phrygian Gordion," was chosen intentionally.
Though new data may alter this view, no features
of the material so far examined suggest that any
of the fabrics were imported from beyond the immediate vicinity of Gordion. The limited number
of decorative patterns represented in the tumulus
fabrics resemble designs found in other media at
Gordion, and on the sculptured garments of
Warpalawas at İvriz—a monument belonging to

the Phrygian cultural sphere.[64] Fibers and dye-stuffs could of course have been imported, even if the spinning and weaving were done locally. Further tests on the Gordion fabrics might give us information on the origin of raw materials, provided that comparative fabrics are found at other sites as well.

The starting borders found on bits of Fabrics A and F, together with rows of loom weights found in the burnt buildings on the city mound, show beyond reasonable doubt that the warp-weighted loom was used at Gordion. From the point of view of the Near East, this loom belongs to the North and West. It was characteristic of the Greek and Aegean world from the Bronze Age through classical times, and of central and northern Europe in the Iron Age.[65] By the Iron Age at least it was used in Palestine,[66] but was probably not part of the tradition of Egypt or Mesopotamia until Hellenistic times. In Anatolia its presence is attested at Neolithic Çatal Hüyük, and in the Early Bronze Age.[67] It is not certain whether it was used in the second millennium B.C. in Anatolia; its use at Gordion could represent either a continuation of local tradition or a reintroduction from the west. The warp-weighted loom was probably not the only type used at Gordion; the narrow bands of Fabrics D and G must have been made on some kind of smaller loom.

The technique of producing multicolored patterns by the use of complementary warps, employed in Fabric G, is otherwise attested in the ancient Near East, as far as I know, only in some

bands from the tomb of Tutankhamon.[68] A similar technique, but using complementary wefts, is found in fabrics from the city mound at Gordion. There the technique is found together in the same pieces with slit tapestry and weft wrapping ("soumak"), and was used freely when it was desired to make designs with lines running in the directions of the warp and weft, instead of diagonally, as is more practical with slit tapestry.[69] This technique of complementary threads may have been widely used in the ancient Near East; it could have produced many of the checker-like patterns seen on Mesopotamian and Greek representations.[70]

The only hint of clothing style from the tumuli is the multiple thicknesses of Fabric I pinned around the body in Tumulus MM. As used in the tumulus, this fabric is more likely to have been a blanket or shroud than a garment; but the technique of sewing the folded edges of this fine, thin fabric together to make a fourfold piece must have produced structures that were useful for cloaks or shawls. One may guess that the living as well as the dead used such light, warm pieces.

In general, the fabrics from the three great tumuli exhibit a high degree of technical skill. This is particularly noticeable in the fine, even spinning and close weave of Fabric I, and in the ingenious technique and fine workmanship of the Fabric G bands.

Bryn Mawr, Pennsylvania, 1979

[64]Boehmer, *AA* 88 (1973): 150–152.

[65]Hoffmann, *Warp-weighted Loom,* 17–22.

[66]Shalom Levy and Gershon Edelstein, "Cinq années de fouilles à Tel 'Amal (Nir David)," *Revue biblique* (1972): 57–58, pls. XX, XXVIII,11.

[67]Hoffmann, *Warp-weighted Loom,* 18, 392; Barbara Kadish, "Excavations of Prehistoric Remains at Aphro-

disias, 1968 and 1969," *AJA* 75 (1971): 136, ill. 11; pl. 29, fig. 32.

[68]G. M. Crowfoot and N. de G. Davies, "The Tunic of Tut'ankhamūn," *Journal of Egyptian Archaeology* 26 (1940): 117–125, pls. XV–XVII, XIX.

[69]Bellinger, 15–16, pls. 10a; 11a,c; 12; 13.

[70]See Boehmer, *AA* 88 (1973): 149–172.

PLATES

A.   Western part of Northeast Ridge Cemetery in winter, from the southwest. Tumulus K-II is in a line with the top of Tumulus MM (the largest). K-III lies at the foot of MM, and Tumulus P is at the right edge of the picture.

B.   Eastern part of the Northeast Ridge Cemetery, from the northeast edge of the city mound. Tumulus MM is at left, and Tumulus W is near the right edge.

PLATE 2

TUMULUS P

A. Tumulus P as it appeared before excavation, from the southwest. Tumulus MM is in
the background. The Yassıhüyük-Polatlı road passes between them.

B. Tumulus P. Drilling rig in action.

A.   Tumulus P. Cleaning of rubble from grave within circular opening in clay and through gap
left by fallen roof beams of upper roof.

B.   Tumulus P. Cover of grave chamber cleaned, from the south. At center is stump of mast.

PLATE 4   TUMULUS P

A. Tumulus P. South side of chamber, from the north. Fallen beams from lower cover lying over floor of chamber (center) and ends of broken beams of upper cover (at right).

B. Tumulus P. South wall of tomb chamber, with peg holes.

A.   Tumulus P. Crushed cauldron (TumP 1) on floor just east of center.

B.   Tumulus P. Finds in northwest quarter, from on and under bed.

PLATE 6   TUMULUS P

A.   Tumulus P. Finds in place on floor, northeast quarter, from the south.

B.   Tumulus P. Finds on floor, east end of chamber, including southeast quarter, from the west.

A.   Tumulus P. Grave chamber cleaned, from the north.

B.   TumP 2. Bronze cauldron.

SCALE   B 1:5

PLATE 8   *TUMULUS P*

A,B,C.   Bronze cauldron: front, side, detail of handle.

D.   TumP 5. Cauldron.   E,F.   TumP 6. Trefoil jug.

G.   TumP 7. Trefoil jug.   H.   TumP 8. Ladle.   I.   TumP 9. Ladle.

J,K.   TumP 10. Basin with lifting handles.

SCALE   A,B,D–K 1:5

A,B,C. TumP 11. Knobbed omphalos bowl.

D,E. TumP 12. Ribbed omphalos bowl.   F,G. TumP 14. Plain omphalos bowl.

SCALE   2:5

PLATE 10   TUMULUS P

A. TumP 16. Plain omphalos
        bowl.

D. TumP 21. Plain omphalos
        bowl.

B,C. TumP 20. Plain om-
            phalos bowl.

I. TumP 29. Plain bowl.

E,F. TumP 22. Plain ompha-
            los bowl.

G,H. TumP 25. Plain ompha-
            los bowl.

J. TumP 30. Plain bowl.

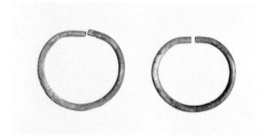

K. TumP 31 and 32. Ring handles for wooden
            bowls.

SCALE   1:4

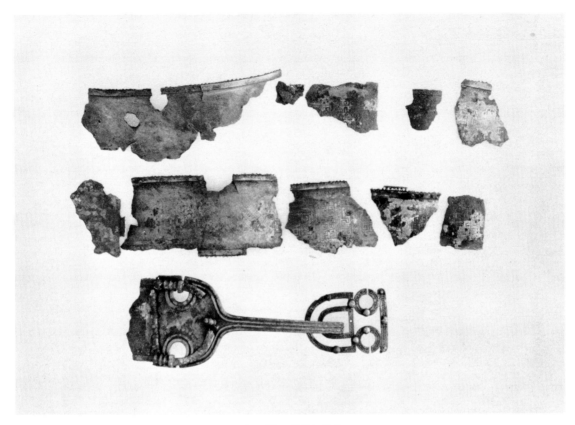

A.   TumP 34. Belt.

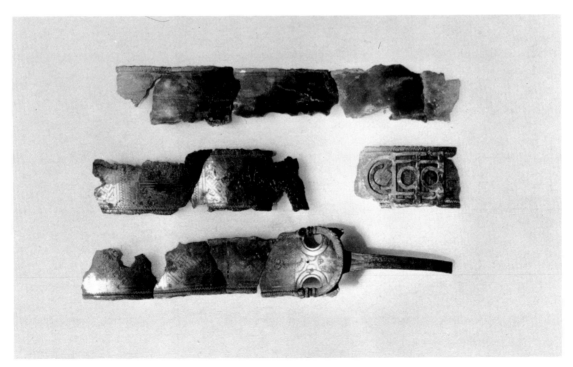

B.   TumP 35. Belt.

SCALE   1:3

PLATE 12

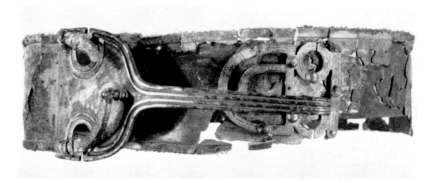

A.   TumP 34. Detail: closure of belt.

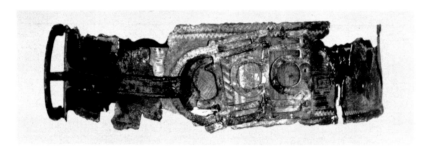

B.   TumP 35. Detail: closure of belt.

C.   TumP 36. Detail: belt hook.

D.   TumP 36. Detail: catch-plate of belt.

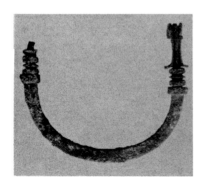

E.   TumP 37. Fibula (XII,3).

F.   TumP 38. Fibula (XII,3).

G.   TumP 39. Fibula (XII,3).

SCALE   1:2

A,B.   TumP 40. Miniature quadriga. Horses 1–4 and strips *A,B,* and *C.* Top and side views.

 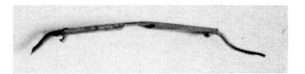

C,D.   TumP 40. Strip *D.* Top (if passed under strip *C*). Side (if passed over strip *C* back beyond the break).

E.   TumP 40. Strip *C.* Detail: fragment of support(?).   F.   TumP 40. Yoke, detail from rear.

G,H,I.   TumP 40. Wheels, inner faces and axle.

J.   TumP 40. Horse 2.

SCALES   A–D,G,H 1:2;   I,J 1:1

PLATE 14

TUMULUS P

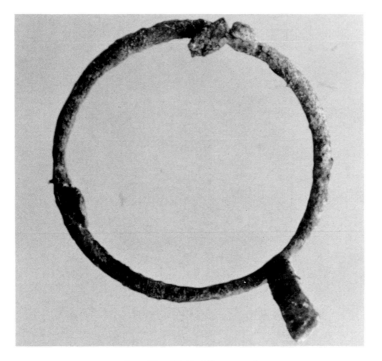

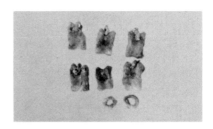

B. TumP 44. Astragals.

A. TumP 43. Ring stand.

C. TumP 45. Blue glazed juglet.

D,E. TumP 46. Egyptian blue juglet.

F,G,H. TumP 47. Egyptian blue two-handled dish.

SCALES   A,B 1:5;   C–H 1:2

A,B. TumP 48. Glass omphalos bowl, top and bottom.

C.   TumP 49. Brown-on-buff gander vase.

D,E.   TumP 49. Brown-on-buff gander vase.

SCALE   1:4

PLATE 16

TUMULUS P

A,B.   TumP 50. Brown-on-buff goose vase.

C.   TumP 52. Brown-on-buff askos. TumP 53. Black-on-red askos. TumP 51. Brown-on-buff askos.

D. TumP 54. Black-on-red round-
     mouthed jug.

E,F.   TumP 55. Brown-on-buff round-mouthed jug.

SCALE   A,B 1:4;   C–F 1:5

A,B.   TumP 55. Brown-on-buff round-mouthed jug.   C.   TumP 55. Detail.

D,E.   TumP 56. Brown-on-buff round-mouthed jug.   F.   TumP 57. Brown-on-buff round-mouthed jug.

I.   TumP 60. Brown-on-buff footed bowl.

G.   TumP 58. Black-on-red ram jug.   H. TumP 59. Black-on-red juglet.   J. TumP 61. Bichrome fruit stand.

SCALES   A,B,D–G,I,J 1:5;   H 1:2

PLATE 18

TUMULUS P

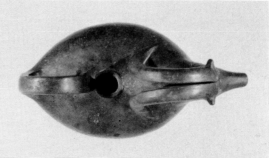

A,B.   TumP 62. Black polished goat jug.

E.   TumP 64. Black polished
      trefoil jug.

F.   TumP 65. Black polished
      trefoil jug.

C,D.   TumP 63. Black polished
        deer or bull jug.

G.   TumP 66. Black polished round-
      mouthed jug.

H.   TumP 67. Black
polished horn-shaped
      rhyton.

I,J.   TumP 68. Black polished ring
        vase with trefoil mouth.

SCALE   1:4

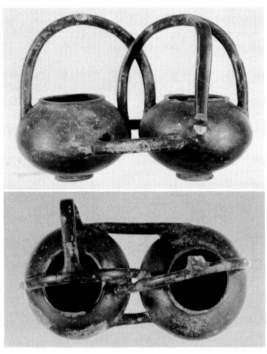

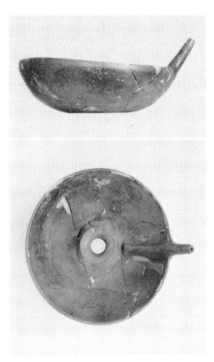

A,B. TumP 69. Black polished twin jars with linking basket handles.

C,D. TumP 70. Black polished socketed bowl with spout.

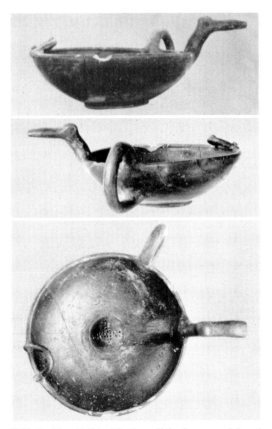

E,F,G. TumP 71. Black polished spouted bowl with two handles.

H,I. TumP 72. Black polished sieve-spouted jug with strainer top.

SCALE   1:4

PLATE 20

TUMULUS P

A,B.   TumP 73 and 74. Black polished sieve-spouted jugs.

C,D.   TumP 75. Black polished
sieve-spouted jug.

E.   TumP 77 (L); TumP 76 (R). Black polished sieve-spouted jugs
with relief decoration.

F.   TumP 79. Black polished dinos.

G,H. TumP 78. Black polished sieve-
spouted jug with relief decoration.

I.   TumP 80. Black polished dinos.

J.   TumP 81. Black polished dinos.

SCALES   A,E,G,H 1:4;   F,I,J 1:5

A. TumP 88. Black polished krater.

B. TumP 89. Black polished krater.

C. TumP 90. Black polished krater.

D. TumP 92. Black polished amphora.

E. TumP 95. Black polished amphora.

F. TumP 96. Black polished amphora.

G. TumP 98. Black polished amphora.

H. TumP 99. Black polished amphora.

I. TumP 105. Black polished storage jar.

SCALE   1:10

PLATE 22

TUMULUS P

A,B.   TumP 106. Horse.

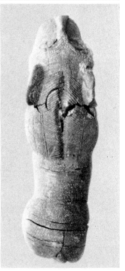

C,D,E,F.   TumP 107. Lion.

G,H,I.   TumP 108. Lion.

MINIATURE ANIMALS

SCALE   2:3

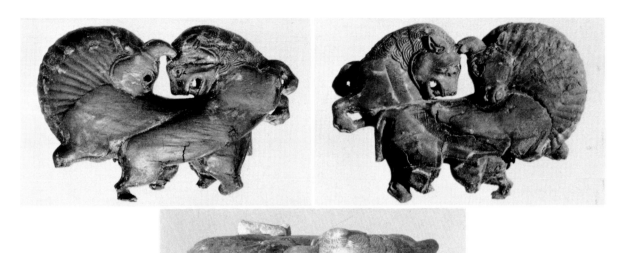

A,B,C.   TumP 109. Group: lion and bull.

D,E,F,G.   TumP 110. Yoked ox.

H.   TumP 111. Griffin eating fish.

MINIATURE ANIMALS

SCALE   2:3

PLATE 24   TUMULUS P

A,B.   TumP 111. Griffin eating fish.

C,D,E.   TumP 112. Deer (or bull?).

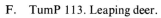

F.   TumP 113. Leaping deer.   G.   TumP 114. Fragmentary reclining stag.

MINIATURE ANIMALS.

SCALE   2:3

A.   TumP 115. Spoon.

B.   TumP 116. Bowl of spoon.

C.   TumP 118 (*L*). Handle of spoon. TumP 117 (*R*). Bowl of spoon.

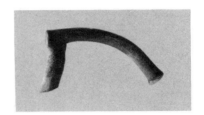

D.   TumP 119. Handle of spoon.

E.   TumP 120. Fragmentary ladle.

F.   TumP 121. Miniature saucer with bar
handles.

G,H.   TumP 122. Saucer with bar handles.

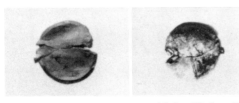

I. TumP 124. Small saucer with lug(?) handles.

J.   TumP 125. Fragmentary lug-
handled saucer.

K.   TumP 126. Saucer with
cross-looped handles.

L.   TumP 127. Saucer with loop handles.

SCALES   A–H 1:2;   I–L 1:3

PLATE 26   TUMULUS P

A. TumP 128. Saucer frag-
ment with T-shaped handle.

B.   TumP 129. Saucer with cut-away rim.

C. TumP 130. Saucer with
cut-away rim.

D.   TumP 131. Plate with
cut-away rim.

E. TumP 132. Plate with cut-away rim.

F.   TumP 133. Plate with cut-away rim.

G. TumP 134. Plate with cut-away rim.

H.   TumP 135. Plain saucer.

I.   TumP 137. Fragments: square bowl.

J.   TumP 138. Fragments: disk (lid?).

K.   TumP 139. Small rec-
tangular box.

SCALE   1:3

A. TumP 140. Conical pedestal,
     or funnel(?).

B. TumP 141. Fragmentary shallow
     bowl.

C. TumP 142. Fragment of a handled bowl.

D. TumP 143. Bar-handled bowl.

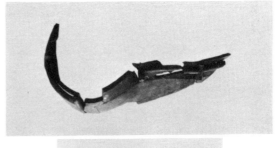

E,F. TumP 145. Bowl with
        bronze handles.

G,H. TumP 146. Bowl with
         bronze handles.

I. TumP 147. Fragments of a
     bowl.

SCALE   1:5

PLATE 28

TUMULUS P

A.   TumP 148 (*L*) and 149 (*R*). Pair of hawk attachments. Right sides.

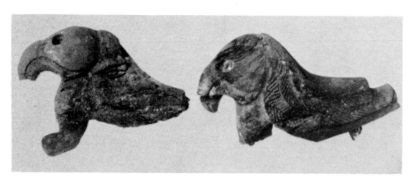

B.   TumP 149 (*L*) and 148 (*R*). Pair of hawk attachments. Left sides.

C. TumP 149. Hawk attachment, from top.

D,E.   TumP 150. Foot with frog's legs; front (*L*), back (*R*).

F,G,H.   Miscellaneous uncatalogued fragments.

SCALES   A–E, G 1:2;   F,H 1:4

A. TumP 151. Inlaid screen. Part *A*, upper portion of screen face.

D. TumP 151. Part *B*, top of top panel seen with holes receiving tongues from part *C*.

B. TumP 151. Part *A*, lower portion of screen face.

C. TumP 151. Part *A*, lower portion of screen, rear view.

E. TumP 151. Part *C*, back leg and support.

SCALE   1:10

PLATE 30   TUMULUS P

A.   TumP 152. Tripod tray table.

B.   TumP 153. Tripod(?) plain table.

C,D.   TumP 154. Mosaic table, top and leg.

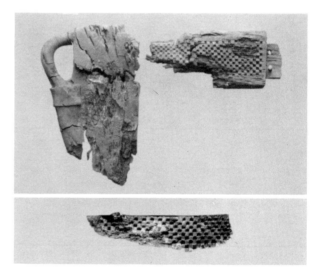

E,F.   TumP 155. Bed-bier. Fragments of headboard.

G.   TumP 155. Fragments of chamfered stretcher or
rail across head or foot of bed.

SCALES   A–D 1:10;   E,F 1:5

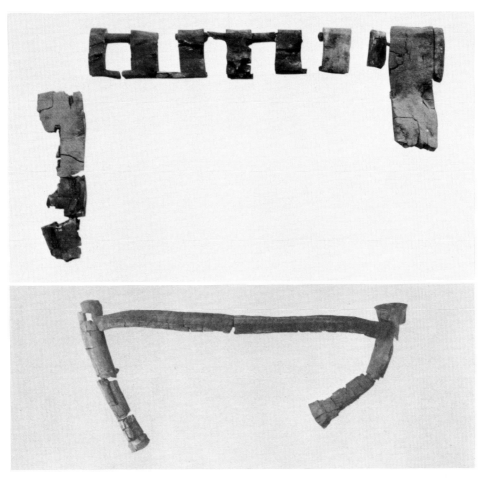

A,B.   TumP 155. Foot of bed-bier. Footboard (above), legs and frame (below).

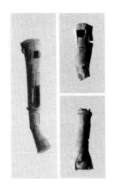

C.   TumP   156.
Pair of furniture
legs, *A*.

D.   TumP 156. Pair of furniture legs, *B*.

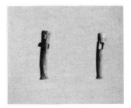

E.   TumP 156. Set of
small legs, *C* (2 out of
4).

G.   TumP 156. Square
legs, *E*.

F.   TumP 156. Set of
long legs, *D* (2 out of 4).

PLATE 32

TUMULUS P

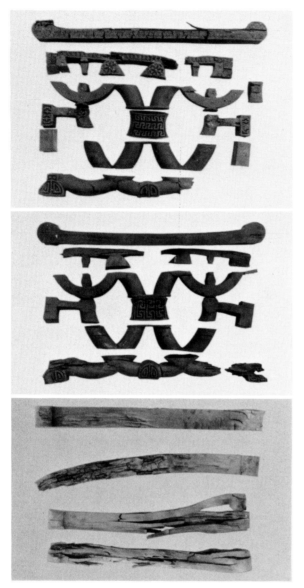

E. TumP 159. Stool panel with cut-out decoration.

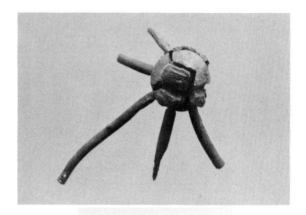

A,B,C. TumP 157. Inlaid stool panels *A*, *B* and top.

F,G. TumP 160. Fragments
of a parasol.

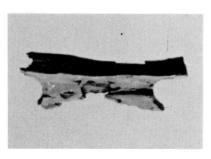

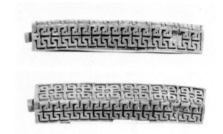

D. TumP 158. Stool panel with cut-
out decoration.

H. TumP 161. One of a
pair of finials.

I. TumP 162. Rung *A*. Two inlaid faces.

SCALES   A–C 1:8;   D,E,H 1:6;   F,G,I 1:4

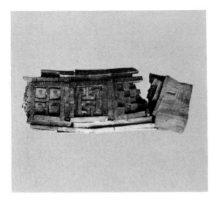

A.   TumP 163. Inlaid strip.

B.   TumP 164. Inlaid strips.

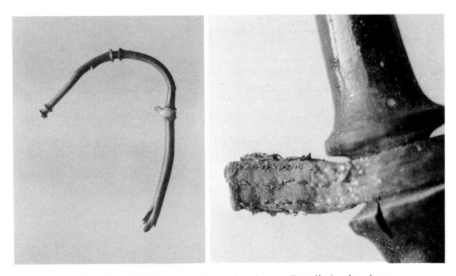

C,D.   TumP 165. Rod with leather loops. Detail: leather loop.

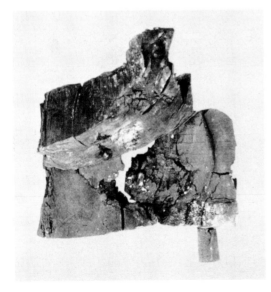

E.   TumP 166. Seat(?), fragment *A* and leg *D*.

F.   TumP 166. Detail: leg *D*.

G.   TumP 166. Seat(?), fragment *C*.

SCALES   A–C 1:4;   E,G 1:8;   F 1:2

PLATE 34

TUMULUS MM

A.   Tumulus MM. Surveying team at work, from the west–southwest.

B.   Tumulus MM. Drillers beginning at bottom, on the west side.

A.   Tumulus MM. Drillers at top, from the west.

B.   Tumulus MM. Opening trench and cross trench, from the southwest.

PLATE 36   *TUMULUS MM*

A.   Tumulus MM. Trench and cross trench, from the northeast. Tumulus K-III is directly across the road; K-I is at upper right. Photograph by James Whitmore, LIFE, © 1957, Time, Inc.

B.   Tumulus MM. Tunnel construction. From the west.

A.   Tumulus MM. Inner face of stone wall on west side.

B.   Tumulus MM. Rubble under clay dome.

A.   Tumulus MM. Log raft above roof, with modern propping.

B.   Tumulus MM. Outer face of outer log walls, northwest corner, showing overlap.

A.   Tumulus MM. Entrance door, outer and inner wooden walls, stone enclosure (upper right).

B.   Tumulus MM. Exterior south wall, with eaves of overhanging gable.

PLATE 40

TUMULUS MM

A. Tumulus MM. Interior of tomb chamber. Central cross beams and gable. South
face, from the southwest.

B. Tumulus MM. East wall of tomb with traces of nails for the suspension of gifts.

A.   Tumulus MM. Interior of tomb chamber. Bed (MM 389) before cleaning, from the
west. Plank at right is modern ramp for entering tomb.

B.   Tumulus MM. Skeleton, complete, partially cleaned, from the west.

PLATE 42   *TUMULUS MM*

A.   Tumulus MM. Interior of tomb chamber. The bed (MM 389), from the south.

B.   Tumulus MM. Area of bed cleared to floor, blocks and rails remaining, from
the south.

A. Tumulus MM. Interior of tomb chamber. Headboard of bed (MM 389), east end, with table (MM 387) and cloth bag; spilled fibulae are scattered on floor.

B. Tumulus MM. Table (MM 387) and debris of furniture in northeast corner after removal of fibulae and cloth bag.

PLATE 44   TUMULUS MM

A.   Tumulus MM. Interior of tomb chamber. Screens (MM 379 and 378) leaning against
the east wall. Omphalos bowl (MM 92) at lower right.

B.   Tumulus MM. Screen (MM 378).   C.   Tumulus MM. Lion situla (MM 45). Note textile.

A. Tumulus MM. Interior of tomb chamber. Screen (MM 378), table (MM 388) and bronzes in southeast corner. Table (MM 385) in right foreground and table (MM 386) at far right rear.

B. Tumulus MM. Table (MM 388) as found, from the south.

PLATE 46

TUMULUS MM

A.   Tumulus MM. Interior of tomb chamber. Cauldron (MM 3) against center of south wall.

B.   Tumulus MM. Cauldrons (MM 2 and MM 1) against south wall in southwest corner, from the north.

A. Tumulus MM. Interior of tomb chamber. Cauldron with bull's-head attachments (MM 1), interior showing remains of food and deteriorated pottery.

B. Tumulus MM. West side of chamber, from the north. Large bronze jugs with trefoil mouth (MM 19, 23, 25, 16, and 21 from front to rear).

C. Tumulus MM. South portion of group along west wall of chamber, from the east.

PLATE 48

TUMULUS MM

A.   Tumulus MM. Interior tomb chamber. West wall, center; globular jugs, disk-belts.

B.   Tumulus MM. Center floor, table (MM 380), from the west.

A. Tumulus MM. Interior of tomb chamber. Center floor, table (MM 380) left foreground; table (MM 383) left background; table (MM 381B) at right, from the west-southwest.

B. Tumulus MM. Center floor, south portion. Table (MM 381B) left foreground; table (MM 382) center foreground; table (MM 384) left center; cauldron (MM 3) against south wall, from the northwest.

PLATE 50

TUMULUS MM

A.   MM 1. Cauldron with bulls' heads.

B.   MM 1. Detail: bull's head *A*.

C.   MM 1. Detail: bull's head *B*.

SCALES   A 1:5;   B,C 2:3

A.   MM 2. Cauldron with four sirens.

B.   MM 2. Detail: siren *A*, rear view.

SCALES   A 1:5;   B 2:5

PLATE 52　　　　　　　　　　　　　　　　　　　　*TUMULUS MM*

A.　MM 2. Cauldron with four sirens. Detail: siren *B*, rear view.

B.　MM 2. Detail: siren *C*, rear view.

A.   MM 2. Cauldron with four sirens. Detail: siren *D*, rear view.

B.   MM 2. Detail: siren *A*, front.

C.   MM 2. Detail: siren *B*, front.

D.   MM 2. Detail: siren *C*, front.

E.   MM 2. Detail: siren *D*, front.

SCALES   A 2:5;   B–E 1:3

PLATE 54

TUMULUS MM

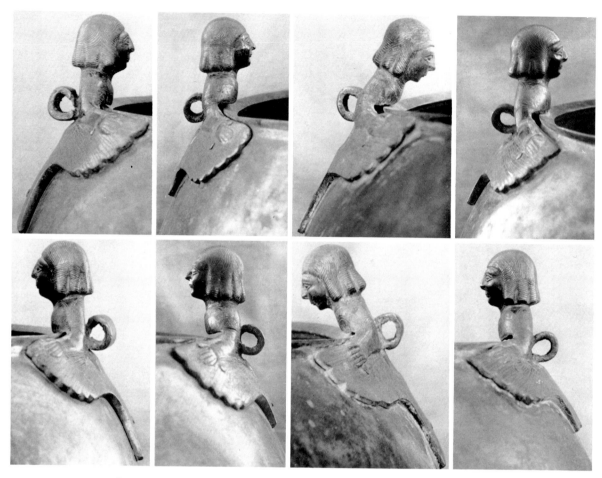

A.   MM 2. Cauldron with four sirens. Details: sirens *A–D*, profile views.

B.   MM 3. Cauldron with sirens and demons.

SCALES   A 1:4; B 1:8

A.   MM 3. Cauldron with sirens and demons. Detail: demon *A*, rear view.

B.   MM 3. Detail: siren *B*, rear view.

PLATE 56

TUMULUS MM

A.   MM 3. Cauldron with sirens and demons. Detail: demon *C,* rear view.

B.   MM 3. Detail: siren *D*, rear view.

SCALE   2:5

A. MM 3. Detail: demon *A*, front.

B. MM 3. Detail: siren *B*, front.

C. MM 3. Detail: demon *C*, front.

D. MM 3. Detail: siren *D*, front.

E. MM 3. Detail: demon *A*, profile.

F. MM 3. Detail: siren *B*, profile.

G. MM 3. Detail: demon *C*, profile.

H. MM 3. Detail: siren *D*, profile.

I. MM 3. Detail: siren *D*, profile.

MM 3.   CAULDRON WITH SIRENS AND DEMONS.

SCALES   A–H 1:2;   I 1:3

PLATE 58   *TUMULUS MM*

A. MM 4. Ring-handled small
     cauldron.

B. MM 5. Ring-handled small
     cauldron.

C. MM 4. Detail, T-shaped
     attachment.

D. MM 6. Ring-handled small
     cauldron.

E. MM 7. Ring-handled small
     cauldron.

F. MM 6. Detail, T-shaped
     attachment.

G. MM 8. Ring-handled small
     cauldron.

H. MM 9. Ring-handled small
     cauldron.

I. MM 9. Detail, T-shaped
     attachment.

J. MM 10. Small cauldron with bucket handles.

K. MM 11. Small cauldron. Detail: bucket handle.

SCALE   A,B,D,E,G,H,J 1:5

A,B. MM 12. Small cauldron with bucket handles and bull's-head attachments: *A (L)*, *B (R)*.

C. MM 13. Small cauldron with bucket handles and bull's-head attachments.

D. MM 14. Jug with side spout, sieved.

E. MM 14. Detail: spout.

F. MM 15. Jug with side spout, sieved.

SCALES   A–C 1:5;   D,F 1:3

PLATE 60
TUMULUS MM

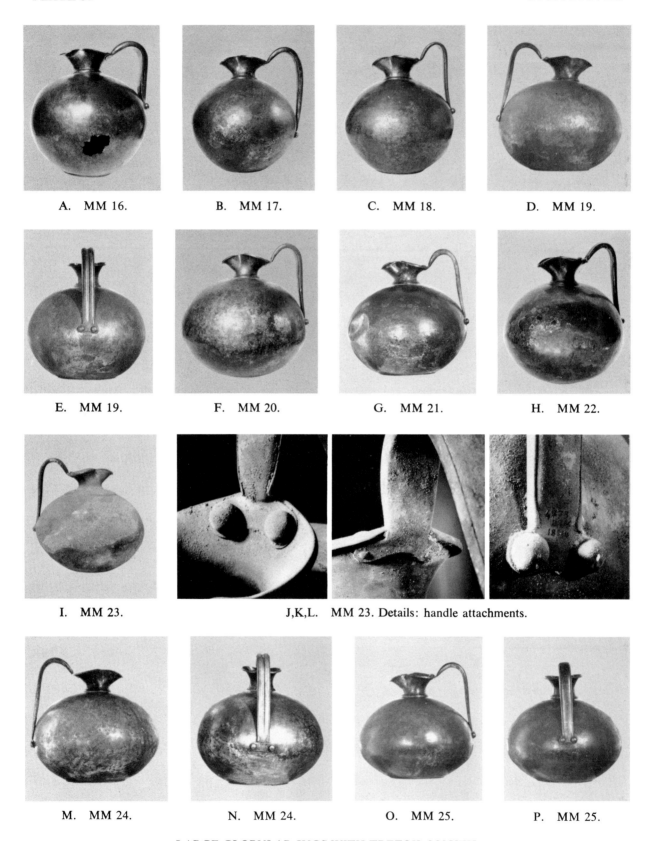

A.   MM 16.

B.   MM 17.

C.   MM 18.

D.   MM 19.

E.   MM 19.

F.   MM 20.

G.   MM 21.

H.   MM 22.

I.   MM 23.

J,K,L.   MM 23. Details: handle attachments.

M.   MM 24.

N.   MM 24.

O.   MM 25.

P.   MM 25.

LARGE GLOBULAR JUGS WITH TREFOIL MOUTH.

SCALE   A–I, M–P 1:10

A. MM 26.   B. MM 27.   C. MM 27.   D. MM 28.

E. MM 29.   F. MM 30.   G. MM 30.   H. MM 31.

I. MM 32.   J. MM 34.   K. MM 35.   L. MM 38.

M. MM 40.   N. MM 41.   O. MM 41.   P. MM 42.

SMALL JUGS WITH TREFOIL MOUTH.

SCALE   1:5

PLATE 62   TUMULUS MM

A. MM 44. Small jug with trefoil mouth.   B. MM 44. Detail: handle.

C. MM 45. Lion's-head situla, left side.   D. MM 45. Three-quarter view.

E. MM 45. Top view.   F. MM 45. Detail: face.

SCALES   A 1:4;   C–E 1:3

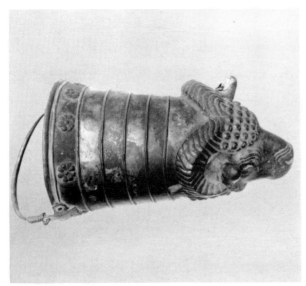

A.   MM 46. Ram's-head situla.

B.   MM 46. Detail: textile.

C.   MM 46. Left side.

D.   MM 46. Detail: face.

E.   MM 46. Top view.

SCALE   A,C,E 1:3

PLATE 64   TUMULUS MM

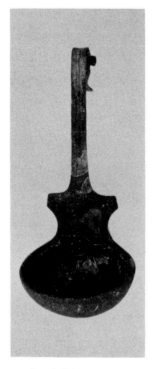

A.   MM 47. Ladle.   B.   MM 48. Ladle.

C.   MM 49. Spouted bowl with horizontal handle.

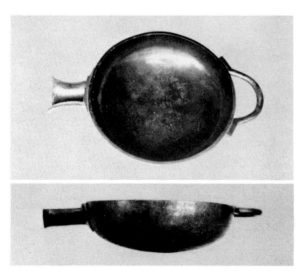

D.   MM 50. Spouted bowl with horizontal handle.

E.   MM 51. Bowl with lifting handles.

F.   MM 52. Bowl with lifting handles.

SCALES   A,B 1:3;   C–F 1:5

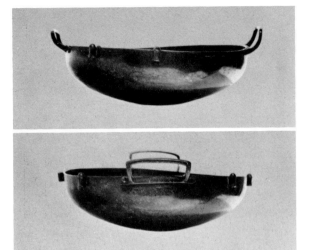

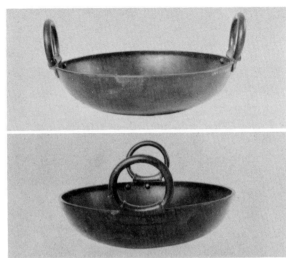

A.   MM 53. Bowl with lifting handles.

B.   MM 54. Bowl with lifting handles and fixed rings.

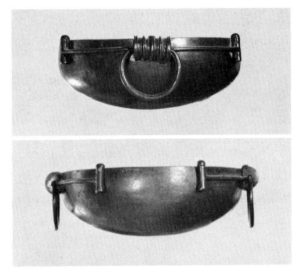

C.   MM 55. Bowl with swiveling ring handles.

D.   MM 56. Bowl with swiveling ring handles.

E.   MM 57. Bowl with swiveling ring handles.

F.   MM 58. Bowl with swiveling ring handles.

SCALE   1:5

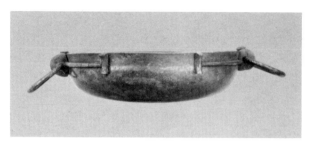

A.   MM 59.

B.   MM 60.

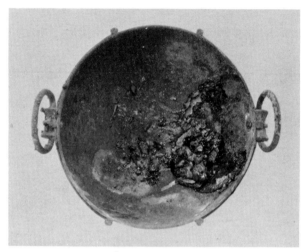

C.   MM 61. With contents.

D.   MM 60. Detail: handle.

E.   MM 61.

F.   MM 62.

G.   MM 63.

H.   MM 64.

BOWLS WITH SWIVELING RING HANDLES.

SCALE   A–C,E–H 1:5

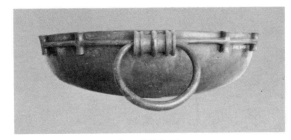

B.   MM 66.

A.   MM 65.

C.   MM 67.

D.   MM 68.

E.   MM 69.

F.   MM 68. Detail: handle.

G.   MM 69. Detail: handle.

BOWLS WITH SWIVELING RING HANDLES.

SCALE   A–E 1:5

PLATE 68

TUMULUS MM

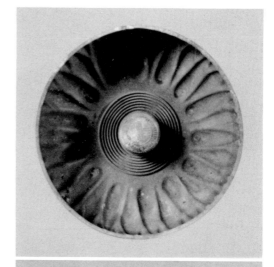

A. MM 70.

B. MM 71.

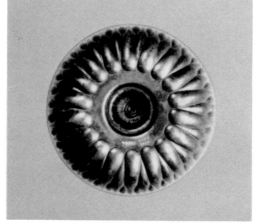

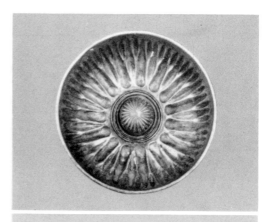

C. MM 72.

D. MM 73.

PETALED BOWLS WITH DECORATED OMPHALOS.

SCALE   1:4

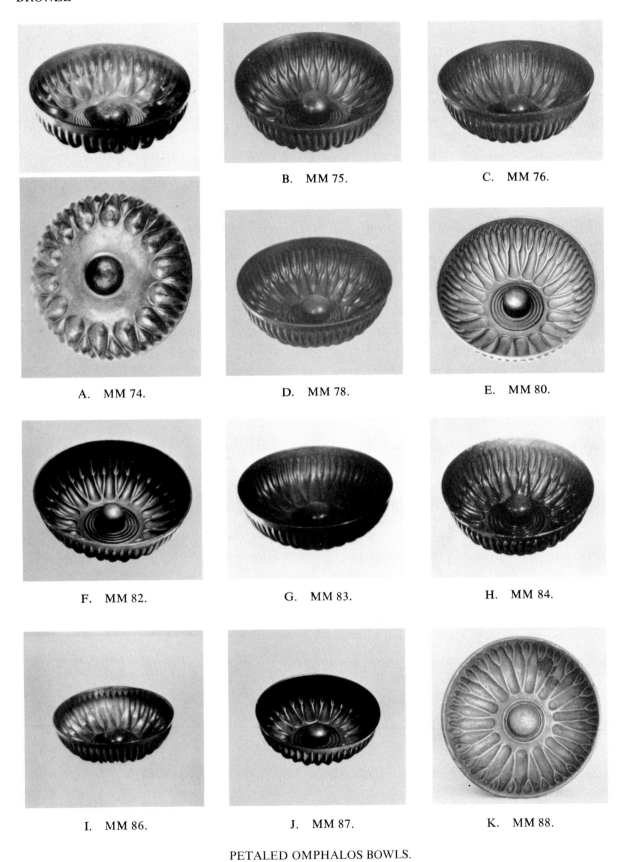

B. MM 75.

C. MM 76.

A. MM 74.

D. MM 78.

E. MM 80.

F. MM 82.

G. MM 83.

H. MM 84.

I. MM 86.

J. MM 87.

K. MM 88.

PETALED OMPHALOS BOWLS.

SCALE   1:5

PLATE 70

TUMULUS MM

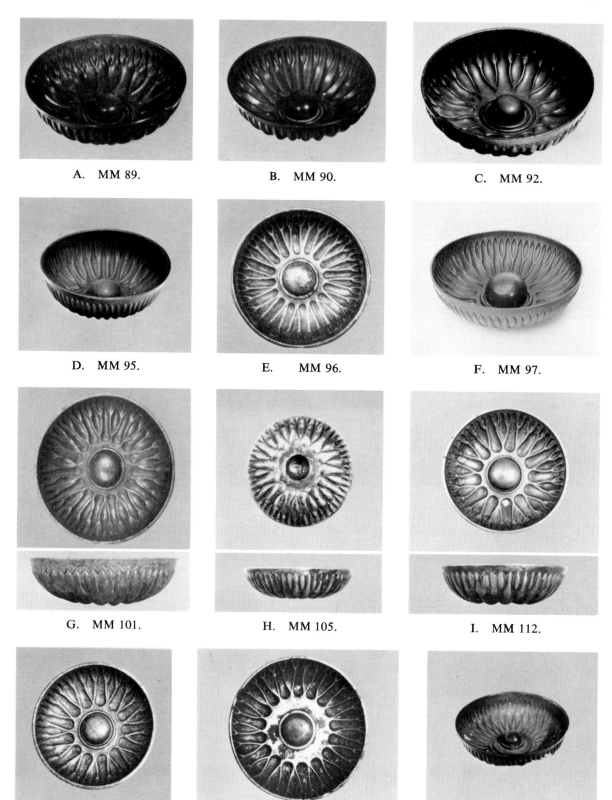

A.   MM 89.

B.   MM 90.

C.   MM 92.

D.   MM 95.

E.   MM 96.

F.   MM 97.

G.   MM 101.

H.   MM 105.

I.   MM 112.

J.   MM 115.

K.   MM 122.

L.   MM 123.

PETALED OMPHALOS BOWLS

SCALE   1:5

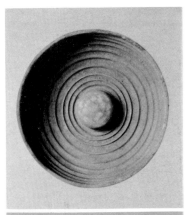

A.   MM 124. Grooved omphalos   B.   MM 125. Ribbed omphalos   C.   MM 126. Ribbed omphalos
         bowl.   bowl.   bowl.

D.   MM 127. Ribbed omphalos bowl.

E.   MM 128. Ribbed om-   F.   MM 129. Ribbed om-   G. MM 130. Ribbed omphalos
        phalos bowl.   phalos bowl.   bowl.

SCALE   1:5

PLATE 72

TUMULUS MM

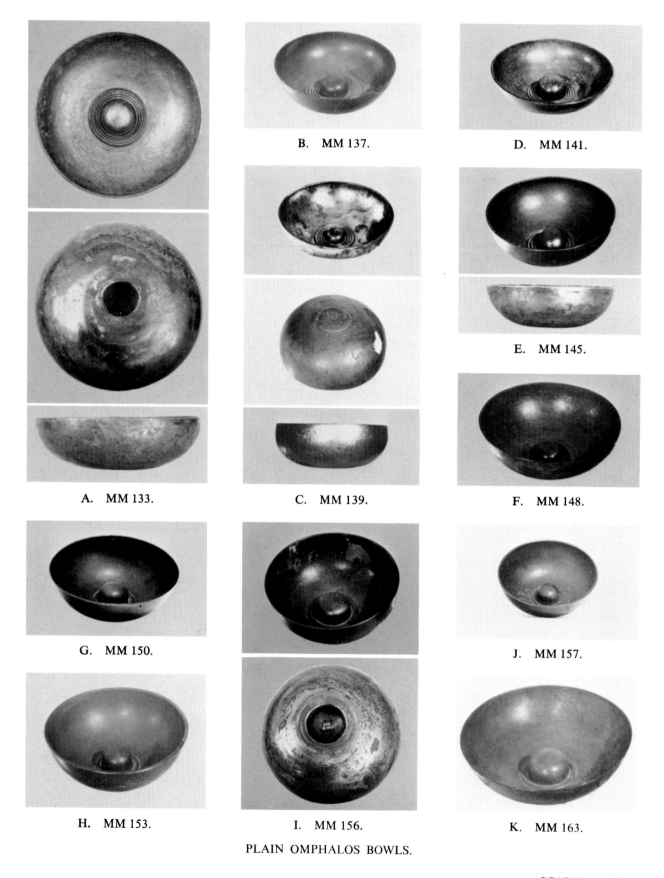

B. MM 137.

D. MM 141.

E. MM 145.

A. MM 133.

C. MM 139.

F. MM 148.

G. MM 150.

J. MM 157.

H. MM 153.

I. MM 156.

K. MM 163.

PLAIN OMPHALOS BOWLS.

SCALE   1:5

A.   MM 166. Plain omphalos bowl.

B.   MM 167. Plain omphalos bowl.

C.   MM 168. Plain deep bowl.

D.   MM 169. Plain deep bowl.

E.   MM 170*A*. Bronze and leather belt.

F.   MM 170*B*. Detail: disk-backer.

G.   MM   170*C*.
Detail: end-plaque.

H.   MM 171*A*. Bronze and
leather belt. Detail: disk.

I. MM 171*C*.
Detail: end-
plaque.

J.   MM 172*A*. Bronze and
leather belt. Detail: disk.

K.   MM 173*A*. Bronze and
leather belt. Detail: disk.

SCALE   1:5

PLATE 74   *TUMULUS MM*

A.   MM 174*A*. Detail: disk.

B.   MM 175*A*. Detail: disk.

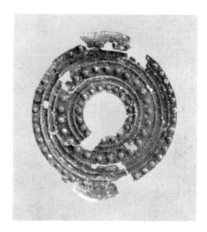

C.   MM 176*A*. Detail: disk.

D.   MM 177*A*. Detail: disk.

E.   MM 178*A*. Detail: disk front (*L*), back (*R*).

F-L.   Details: end-plaques (MM 177*C*, 178*C*, 179*A*, 179*B*, 179*C*, 179*D*, 179*E*).

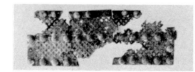

M.   MM 180*A,B,C*. Bronze belt. Details: plaques and buckle.

BRONZE AND LEATHER BELTS.

SCALE   1:5

A.   MM 181*A*. Beads.   B.   MM 181*B*. Beads.

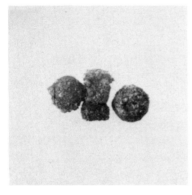

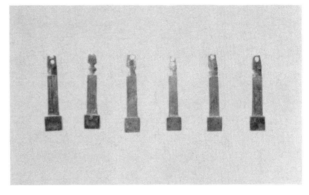

C.   MM 181*C*. Beads.   D.   MM 182. Pendants.

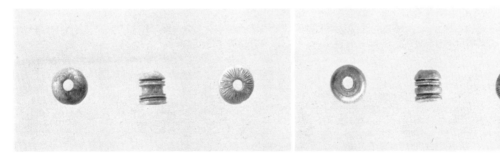

E.   MM 183. Sockets (6 of 7).

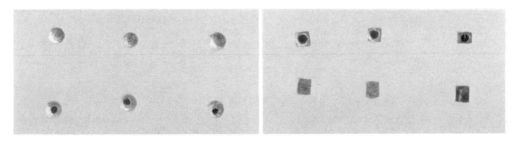

F.   MM 184. Socketed cubes and spheres (12 of 15).

SCALE   1:1

PLATE 76   *TUMULUS MM*

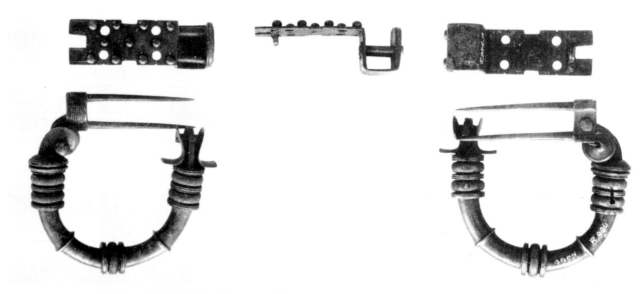

A,B,C.   MM 185. Double-pinned fibula with shield detached: front view, side view of shield, back view.

D.   MM 186. Double-pinned fibula (XII,14).

E.   MM 187. Fibula (XII,13).

F.   MM 187A. Fibula (XII,9).

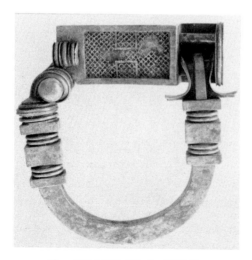

G.   MM 188. Fibula (XII,7).

H.   MM. 189. Fibula (XII,7).

I.   MM 190. Fibula (XII,7).

SCALE   3:4

A. MM 191. Double-pinned fibula
(XII,7).

B. MM 192. Fibula (XII,7).

C. MM 193. Fibula (XII,7).

D. MM 194. Fibula (XII,7).

E,F. MM 195 and 196. Pair of single-pinned fibulae (XII,7).

G,H. MM 207 and 208. Fibulae
(XII,7).

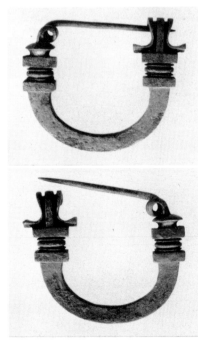

I,J. MM 213 and 214. Fibulae
(XII,7).

K,L. MM 233 and 234. Fibulae
(XII,7).

SCALE   3:4

PLATE 78

TUMULUS MM

A,B.   MM 243 and 244. Pair of single-pinned fibulae (XII,9).

C,D.   MM 251 and 252. Fibulae (XII,9).

E,F.   MM 261 and 262. Fibulae (XII,9).

G,H.   MM 267 and 268. Fibulae (XII,9).

I.   MM 281. Fibula (XII,9).

J.   MM 282. Fibula (XII,9).

K.   MM 283. Fibula (XII,9).

L.   MM 284. Fibula (XII,9).

SCALE   3:4

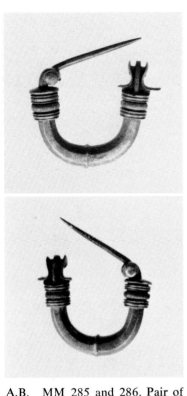

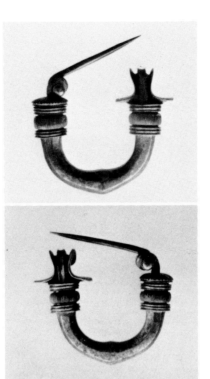

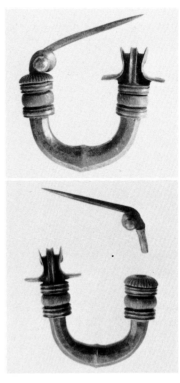

A,B.   MM 285 and 286. Pair of single-pinned fibulae (XII,11).

C,D.   MM 287 and 288. Fibulae (XII,11).

E,F.   MM 307 and 308. Fibulae (XII,11).

K.   MM 326. Fibula (XII,14).

G,H.   MM 318 and 319. Fibulae (XII,14).

I,J.   MM 322 and 323. Fibulae (XII,14).

L.   MM 327. Fibula (XII,14).

SCALE   3:4

PLATE 80

TUMULUS MM

A. MM 357. Tripod ring stand.

B. MM 358. Tripod ring stand.

C. MM 359. Tetrapod ring stand.

D. MM 360. Dinos.

E. MM 361. Dinos.

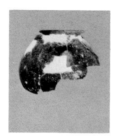

F. MM 362. Dinos.

G. MM 365. Dinos.

H. MM 366. Dinos.

I. MM 367. Dinos.

J. MM 370. Dinos.

K. MM 372.
Amphora.

L. MM 373.
Amphora.

M. MM 374.
Amphora.

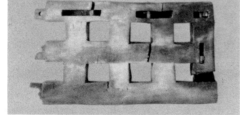

N,O. MM 378. Wooden screen. Details:
frame, B, side support, outside face, inside
face.

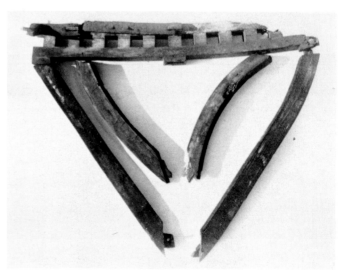

P. MM 378. Detail: rear of frame, B, and upper part of back
support, C.

SCALES   A–C 1:15;   D–M,P 1:10;   N,O 1:5

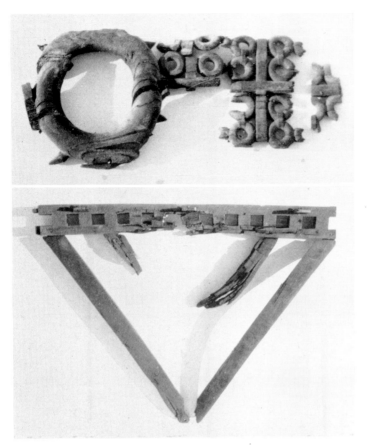

C.   MM 380. Plain table with three legs.

A,B.   MM 379. Screen. Details: top of back of frame, *B;* interior
of back of frame, *B*, and supports, *C*.

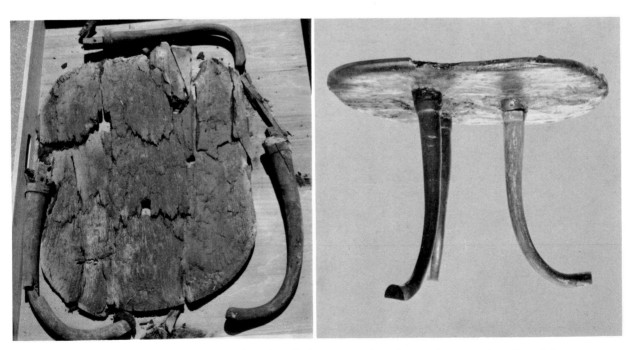

D,E.   MM 384. Plain table with three legs, before restoration. Composite restoration, from below.

SCALE   B–E 1:10

PLATE 82

TUMULUS MM

A.   MM 388. "Pagoda" table. Detail: four frame pieces.

B.   MM 388. Detail: front frame pieces with struts and handles.

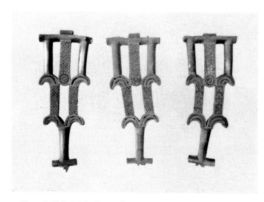

C.   MM 388. Detail: struts (Type 1), 3 of 8.

D.   MM 388. Detail: struts (Type 2), 2 of 6.

E.   MM 388. Detail: strut (Type 3), 1 of 4.

SCALE   1:6

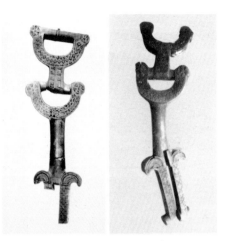

B,C. MM 388. Detail: rear leg props.

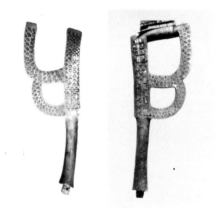

A. MM 388. "Pagoda" table. Details: single leg taking "rocker"
    (L), pair taking rear leg props (center and R).

D,E. MM 388. Detail: front leg props.

F. MM 388. Detail: front frame, props, and "rocker."

SCALE   1:6

A.   Tumulus MM (L) and Tumulus W (R) as seen from the hüyük (i.e., from the west-southwest).

B. Tumulus W. Entry trench and bulldozer, from northeast.

C.   Tumulus W. Cuts through clay to cavity over stone pile, from northeast.

D.   Tumulus W. Inner end of trench with cavity over stone pile, from northwest.

A.   Tumulus W. Cavity enlarged to expose stone pile. Wooden frame laid on surface.

B.   Tumulus W. Excavation of chamber viewed from surface left by bulldozer. Small frame inside larger frame; large stones are set over northeast corner to staunch flow of gravel. Broken roof beams being cleaned at bottom of trench; those at north half of west wall are still bent up protecting pottery. From southwest.

PLATE 86

TUMULUS W

A. Tumulus W. Clearing of floor of chamber after removal of roof beams, from south.

B. Tumulus W. Coarse pottery along west wall as found.

A.   TumW 1. Cauldron with bull's-head attachments.

B.   TumW 1. Detail: attachment *A*.

C.   TumW 1. Detail: attachment *B*. Back view
showing lead filler.

D.   TumW 1. Detail: attachment *B*, side view.

SCALES   A 1:4;   B–D 1:2

PLATE 88   TUMULUS W

A.   TumW 2. Cauldron with bull's-head attachments. Details: (*L*) attachment *A*; (*R*) attachment *B*.

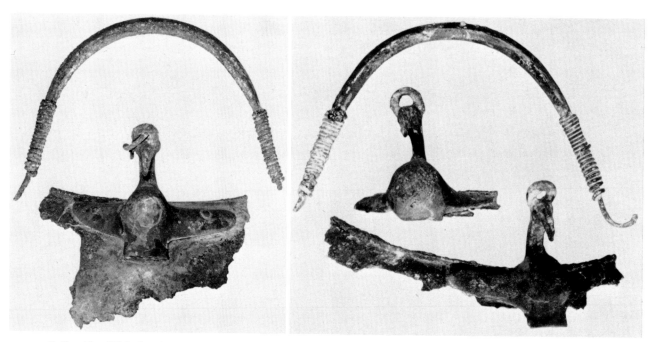

B,C.   TumW 3. Small cauldron with bird attachments and bucket handles. Details: handle and attachment.

D.   TumW 5. Sieve-spouted jug with round mouth.

E.   TumW 6. Footed jug with round mouth.

SCALES   A–C 1:2;   D,E 1:4

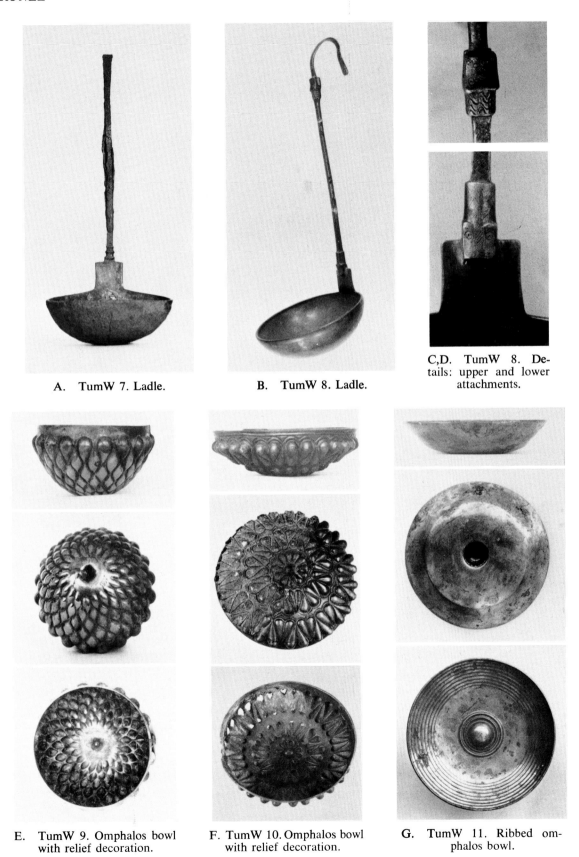

A.   TumW 7. Ladle.

B.   TumW 8. Ladle.

C,D.   TumW 8. Details: upper and lower attachments.

E.   TumW 9. Omphalos bowl with relief decoration.

F.   TumW 10. Omphalos bowl with relief decoration.

G.   TumW 11. Ribbed omphalos bowl.

SCALES   A,B 1:3;   E–G 1:4

PLATE 90

TUMULUS W

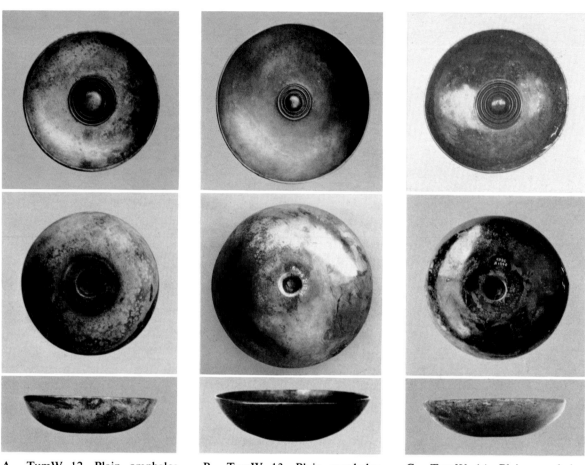

A. TumW 12. Plain omphalos bowl.

B. TumW 13. Plain omphalos bowl.

C. TumW 14. Plain omphalos bowl.

D. TumW 16. Plain omphalos bowl.

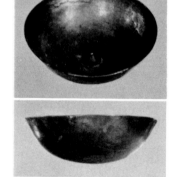

E. TumW 17. Hammered omphalos bowl without ridges.

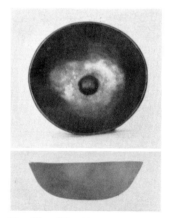

F. TumW 18. Hammered omphalos bowl without ridges.

G. TumW 19. Plain bowl.

H. TumW 20. Plain bowl.

I. TumW 23. Plain bowl.

SCALE   1:4

A.   TumW 25. Bronze and leather belt. Details: *C*, fragment (*L*); *A*, central disk (center); *B*, fragment (*R*).

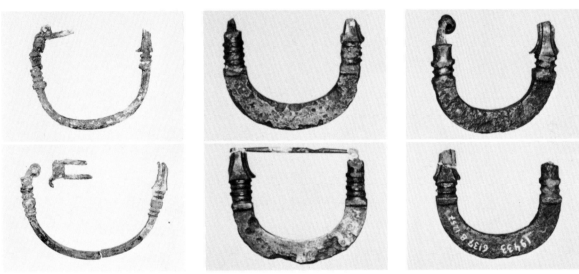

B,C.   TumW 27 and 28. Double-pinned fibulae (XII,3).

D,E.   TumW 29 and 30. Pair of single-pinned fibulae (XII,7A).

F,G.   TumW 31 and 32. Pair of single-pinned fibulae (XII,7A).

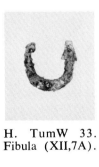

H.   TumW 33. Fibula (XII,7A).

N. TumW 43. Fibula (XII,7A).

I.   TumW 34. Fibula (XII,13).

J,K.   TumW 35 and 36. Pair of fibulae (XII,7A).

L,M.   TumW 37 and 38. Pair of fibulae (XII,7A).

O. TumW 48. Fibula (XII,7A).

SCALES   A 1:3;   B–O 1:2

PLATE 92   TUMULUS W

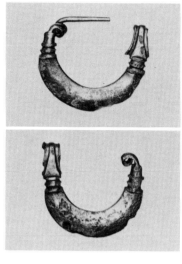

A,B.   TumW 52 and 53. Pair of   C,D.   TumW 56 and 57. Pair of   E,F.   TumW 59 and 60. Fibulae
       fibulae (XII,7A).   fibulae (XII,13).   (XII,13).

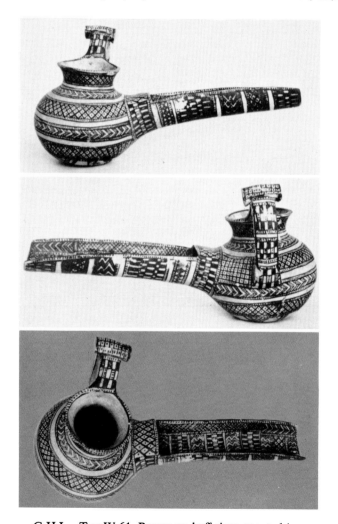

G,H,I.   TumW 61. Brown-on-buff sieve-spouted jug.   J,K.   TumW 62. Bichrome sieve-spouted jug.

SCALES   A–F 1:2;   G–K 1:3

A,B.   TumW 63. Black polished sieve-spouted jug.

C. TumW 64. Coarse black polished storage jar.

D. TumW 65. Coarse black polished amphora.

E. TumW 66. Coarse black polished amphora.

F. TumW 68. Rotted black polished amphora.

G. TumW 71. Black polished amphora, neck fragment.

H. TumW 72. Coarse red globular amphora with twisted handles.

SCALES   A,B 1:3;   C–H 1:10

PLATE 94

TUMULUS W: WOOD, IVORY

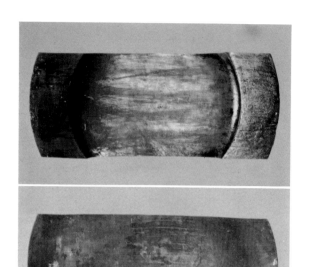

A,B.   TumW 75. Plate, top and bottom.

C,D.   TumW 76. Plate, top and bottom.

E.   TumW 77. Fragments of a plate, top.

F.   TumW 78. Fragments of a plate, top.

G.   TumW 80. Screen, lifted, but still folded as found.

H.   TumW 81. Ivory
globular pendant.

SCALES   A–F 1:5;   H 3:4

A. B 405. Fragments of a ring-handled bowl. Tumulus J.

B. B 1398. Pair of bull's-head attachments from cauldron. TB-1.

C. B 1431. Rim fragments from bronze cauldron. TB-1.

D. B 1445. Bronze bull's-head attachment. Front and back views. Megaron 4.

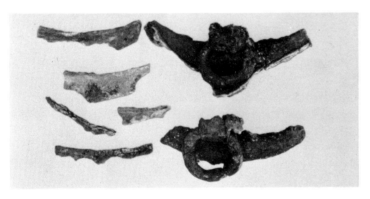

E. ILS 384. Pair of iron ring handles and bands attached to bronze cauldron. TB-1.

F. ILS 385. Iron tripod. TB-2.

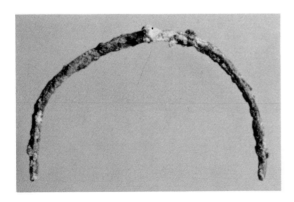

G. ILS 386. Iron band from a bronze cauldron(?). TB-2.

H. J 130. Gold fibula (XII,5). TB-2.

I. J 132. Silver fibula (XII,5). TB-2.

SCALES   A,C,E,G 1:5;   F 1:10;   H,I 3:2

PLATE 96   GORDION: COMPARANDA

A.   P 1190. Buff jug. CC-2.

B.   P 1270. Brown-on-buff jug with strainer
spout. CC-2.

C.   P 1312. Red/buff
jug. CC-1.

E.   P 1639. Black polished jug. Megaron 2.

F.   P 2359. Black mottled round-
mouthed jug. Megaron 3.

D.   P 1857. Brown-on-
buff footed jug. TB-4.

G.   P 2364. Painted
askos. TB-4.

H.   P 2602. Gray polished dinos. Megaron 3.

I.   P 2490. Painted
kothon-askos. TB-4
anteroom.

J.   W 84. Top of mosaic
table, in situ. Megaron 3.

SCALE   A–I 1:5

A.   MM 68. Inscription on wax (Young, No. 25).

B.   MM 67. Inscription on wax (Young, No. 32).

C.   MM 69. Inscription on wax (Young, No. 33).

PLATE 98

APPENDIX I

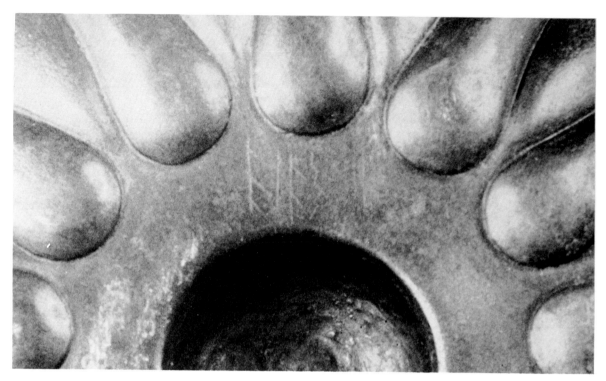

A.   MM 119. Inscription incised on bronze (Young, No. 30).

B.   MM 362. Inscription incised on pottery (Young, No. 31).

A. Photomicrograph of a cauldron fragment attached to a winged bull's-head handle attachment found in Iran, now in the Metropolitan Museum of Art. The very fine grain structure shows extensive twinned grain boundaries and heavy slip-bands in many of the grains indicating very heavy hammering, continual annealing, and a final working. Etched.

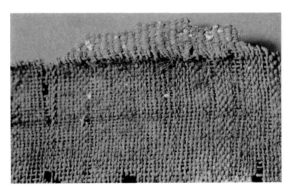

B. Large fragment of Fabric A, with starting border and crowded warp threads.

C. Starting border of Fabric A.

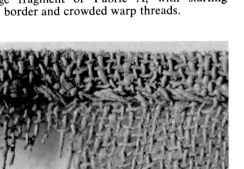

D. Flat rolled hem of Fabric A.

E. Round rolled hem of Fabric A.

SCALES   A 500:1;   B,E 2:1;   C,D 4:1

PLATE 100 APPENDIX V

A. Round rolled hem with ridge, Fabric A.

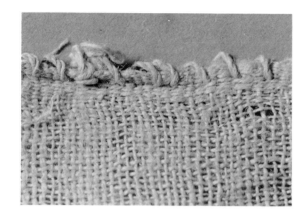

B. Starting border and cloth of Fabric C.

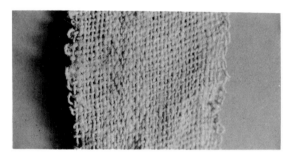

C. Tape, Fabric D.

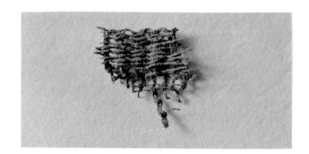

D. Starting border of Fabric F.

Yarn
A

Yarn
B

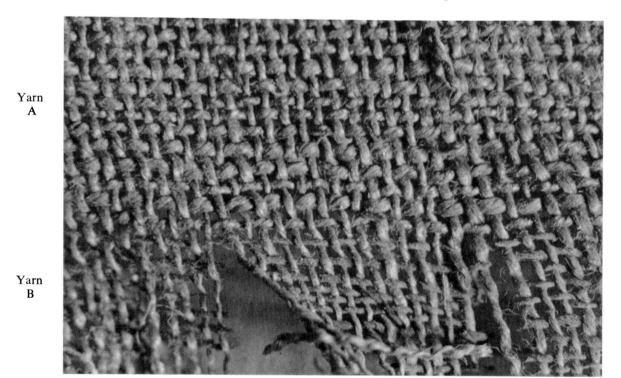

E. Fabric of Fabric F, with dissimilar yarns.

SCALES   A,D 4:1;   B,C 2:1;   E 8:1

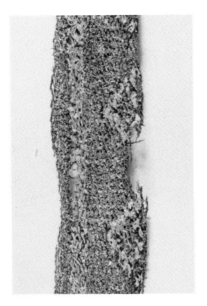

A. Fragment: warp stripe and off-set end-and-end stripes, Fabric G.

B. Fragment: warp stripe and meander, Fabric G.

C. Fragment: warp stripe and triangles, Fabric G.

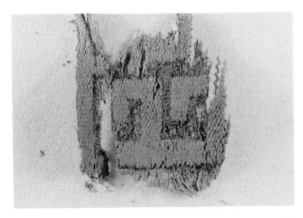

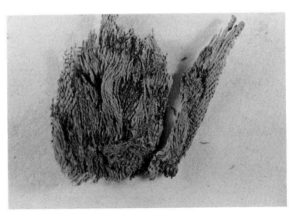

D. Fragment: rectangular pattern (front), Fabric G.

E. Fragment: rectangular pattern, Fabric G.

F. Edge of a fragment of Fabric I.

SCALES   A–C,F 4:1; D,E 2:1

INDEX

coarse ware, 213–215
dating, 215–216
decoration, 239 n.91
dinoi, absence of, 215–216
fine wares, 212–213
functions, 215, 216
jar, storage, 213, 216
jugs, sieve, 212–213, 215, 251–253, 266
　bichrome, 213
　black polished, 213
　brown–on–buff, 212–213
painted wares, 270
　bichrome, 213
　brown–on–buff, 212–213, 216
summary, 215–216
textiles, 265
　bedding, 309
　cloth, 197, 198, 199, 203
　clothing, 197
　Fabric D, 303
　Fabric E, 303–304
　Fabric F, 304
　Fabric H, 308
　Fabric K, 309
　wall hangings, 198
wood, 216–218
　bowls, 207
　disks, 216
　identification, 291
　plates, 216–217, 258
　screen, 217–218, 239 n.91, 261
　trays. See plates.
Tumulus X pottery
　amphora, 255–256
　dinoi, 254–255
　jug, sieve, 251
Tumulus Y pottery
　amphora, 255–256
　dinoi, 254–255
Tumulus Z
　dating, 255 n.152
　iron spike, 30
　pottery dinoi, 255 n.152
Turkey, Republic of
　Department of Antiquities and Museums, xxxi, 94
　Directorate General, 89 n.12, 95 n.13
　Ministry of Culture, xxxi
　Ministry of Education, xxxi
　Museum of Anatolian Civilizations, xxxi
　University of Istanbul, Faculty of Forestry, 95
Tutankhamon, fabric from tomb of, 310
Tyana. *See also* Warpalawas of Tyana.
　inscriptions, 271, 276

Uçankuş, H., 8 n.13
Urartu, 123
　bronze production, 221
　bronzes, 248 n.128
　cauldron attachments
　　bull's–head, 219–220, 221

siren and demon, 109, 109 n.39, 109–110 n.41
furniture legs with bronze sheathing, 77 n.148
stool, 72 n.142
Urballa/Warpalawas. See Warpalawas.
Urikki of Que, 220, 271

Van, cauldron attachments, 109, 110 n.41
Van Loon, M., 222

wall painting, 8, 8 n.13, 198
Warpalawas of Tyana, 110, 148, 244, 245, 265, 271
wax, 202
　inscriptions in, 129–130, 273–275
Williams, Charles K., II, 94
wood, 51–78, 176–190, 216–218
　animals, miniature, 51–56. *See also* Tumulus P.
　beds, 70, 187–190. *See also* Tumuli MM, P.
　bowls, 59–61, *See also* Tumulus P.
　box, 59
　commentary, 257–261
　curtain rod, 76 n.146. *See also* Tumulus P, rod
　　with leather loops.
　disks, 59, 216
　finials, 75
　funnel, 59–60
　furniture, 7–10, 61–77, 176–190, 217–218, 259–
　　260, 264–265. *See also* names of specific types,
　　and city mound, Tumuli MM, P, W.
　　attachments, 61–62
　　legs, 70, 72, 77
　　rungs, 75
　　strips, 76
　identification, 290–293
　parasol, 74–75, 76 n.146
　plates, 58–59, 258–259
　saucers, 57–58
　screens, 62–67, 176–181. *See also* city mound,
　　Tumuli MM, P, W.
　seat(?), 8 n.13, 77
　spoons, 56–57
　steam-bending, 24, 24 n.30, 179, 182, 258, 260
　stools, 72–74. *See also* Tumulus P.
　tables, 67–70, 181–188. *See also* city mound,
　　Tumuli MM, P.
　　Egyptian, XI Dynasty, 77 n.150
　　inlaid, 68–70, 183–187
　　long, 8
　　plain, 181–182
　　tripod, 67–68, 74, 181–182
　toys, 7, 10, 72. *See also* miniature animals.
　trays, 258–259
　vessels and lids, 57–61
　workers, Phrygian, 56

Xenophon, *Anabasis*, 251 n.141

Yariris and Kamanis, 237, 237 n.87
Yassıhüyük, xxxi, xxxvi
Yazılıkaya reliefs, 76 n.146
Young, Rodney Stuart, xxix, xxxv, xxxvi, 32, 51,

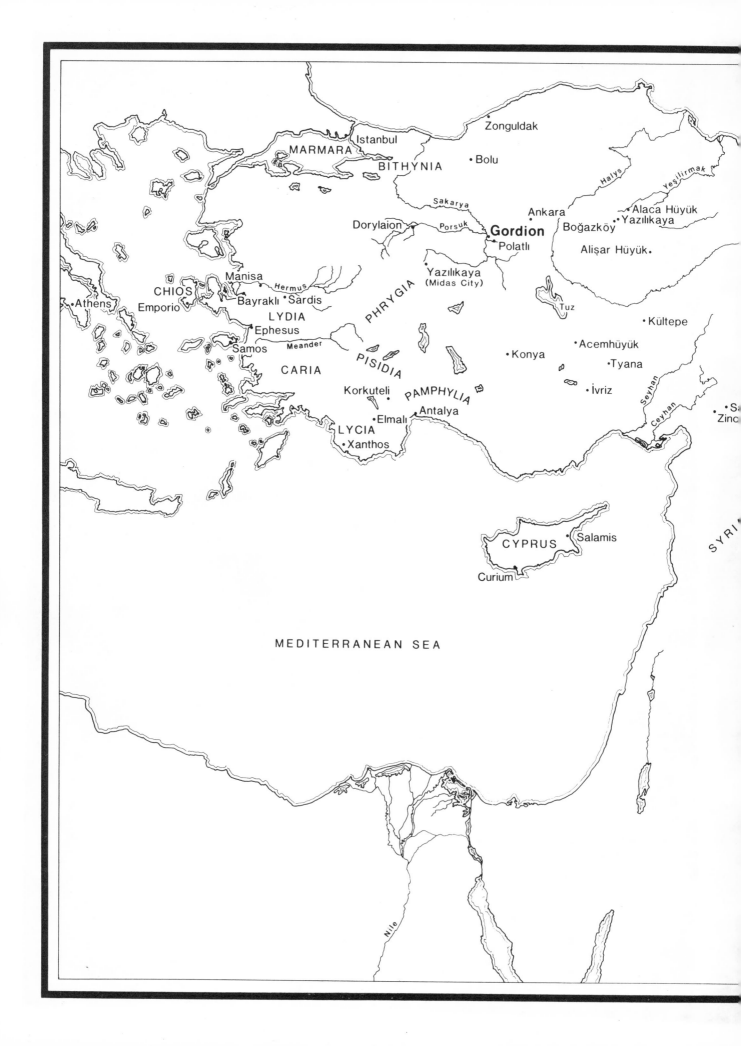